INTRODUCTION
TO PERSONALITY

INTRODUCTION

THIRD EDITION

NEW YORK   CHICAGO   SAN FRANCISCO   PHILADELPHIA   MONTREAL   TORONTO
LONDON   SYDNEY   TOKYO   MEXICO CITY   RIO DE JANEIRO   MADRID

TO PERSONALITY

WALTER MISCHEL
STANFORD UNIVERSITY

HOLT, RINEHART AND WINSTON

Grateful acknowledgment is made for photographs from the following sources:

Fred Weiss, pp. 17, 321, 368
Mimi Cotter, p. 39
L. Courteville—Agence TOP, p. 52
Rick Smolan, pp. 55, 79, 266, 346
Jack Simons, p. 85
Iris Kleinman, p. 91
American Red Cross, photo by Rudolph Vetter, p. 111
Authenticated News International, pp. 119, 531
Steve Hurwitz, pp. 134, 491
Bill Stanton, pp. 177, 428
Suzanne Szasz, p. 207
Arthur Singer, p. 266
Aureon Institute, p. 277
Rapho Guillimette, p. 339
A.T.&T. Photo Center, p. 380
Benedict J. Fernandez, p. 394
John King, p. 420
Magnum Photos, Inc., Gilles Peress, p. 448
Arthur Tress, p. 480
Six Flags Great Adventure, p. 504

(credits continued on page 623)

Library of Congress Cataloging in Publication Data

Mischel, W.
    Introduction to Personality

    Bibliography: p. 537
    Includes indexes
  1. Personality.   I. Title.
BF698.M555 1981   155.2   80-29201
ISBN: 0-03-056998-2

CBS COLLEGE PUBLISHING
Holt, Rinehart and Winston
The Dryden Press
Saunders College Publishing

PREFACE

The third edition of this book upholds the basic aims of its predecessors, but with significant changes in content and style, which are intended to increase the effectiveness and coherence of the presentation while retaining the basic structure. As before, this book is an introduction to major approaches, methods, and findings in the field of personality. It presents an overview of basic theories, strategies, issues, and conclusions in the psychological study of personality. Part I presents an overview of the theoretical conceptions provided by each of the major approaches to personality; Part II surveys the important applications associated with each theoretical approach. Part III (Personality Development and the Coping Process) continues to offer a systematic overview of major current research issues and findings.

The updating of developments in personality theory throughout the text includes the cognitivization of behavior theory, the revitalization of self-theories, the growth of the interactionist viewpoint, and the contemporary defense of personality traits as useful and necessary constructs. The separate chapter previously devoted to Dollard and Miller's psychodynamic behavior theory has been deleted in this edition, and that contribution is now incorporated as part of the heritage derived from psychodynamic theories (Chapter 3). In addition, a new summary overview of each major theoretical position is presented in tabular form to highlight its main features.

Traditionally, students have been introduced to personality psychology by reading about the ideas of major theorists. Theoretical orientations to personality study, in my view, are a necessary beginning but not an end in themselves. To offer a theoretical overview and historical perspective this book begins with a survey of the basic concepts and assumptions that major approaches share, and the fundamental differences between them.

But to go beyond an exposition of the alternative conceptions of personality proposed by different theorists, to move beyond views of people-in-general, also requires attention to tactics. The transition from abstractions concerning the possible nature of human beings to specific investigations of individuals is, after all, a chief difference between philosophy and psychology. Therefore this book surveys the distinctive tactics for personality study associated with each of the theoretical orientations discussed. A study of the methods that these orientations provide to assess people, and an overview of the results that come from these assessments, in turn should inform us about the strengths and weaknesses of the theories that guide the assessments. In this effort, the basic structure of Part II is retained. The case of "Gary W" continues to be used to illustrate updated versions of the applications of each theoretical approach to personality assessment and change.

It has long been fashionable to call personality psychology a young field and to profess how little we know about the mysteries of man. While no one

can quarrel with modesty, in fact the field continues to get older and, fortunately, apologies for its youth and ignorance are becoming less necessary. Indeed, studies that clarify the value and limits of our theories are accumulating
rapidly. In recent years empirical findings have been pouring in from many
sources as more researchers are studying socially relevant behaviors, gradually
illuminating the nature of personality processes and the causes of social behavior. It therefore is becoming possible now to introduce students of personality not only to the hypotheses of authorities but also to some of the findings
and conclusions (albeit tentative) that are emerging. This book therefore includes an integration of research on various core topics of the field (such as
identification, frustration-aggression, anxiety, defense, self-concepts—to name
but a few). These topics are presented not as a catalogue of facts but in the
hope of increasing students' understanding of complex human behavior so that
they may learn about its substantive nature and not merely about theoretical
speculations. Wherever possible research findings, in turn, are related to the
relevant theoretical orientations and methods, as well as to specific case examples, so that their implications for understanding basic issues become evident.

In this edition, Part III focuses explicitly on personality and the coping
process. Changes throughout this part reflect the vigorous growth of research
in the field, including new developments in such topics as genetic antecedents,
stress and illness, helplessness and mastery. Specific changes here include new
findings on biological bases of personality, social attachment, the roots of competence, the stability (continuity) of personality over time, and life-span development (Chapter 12). Chapter 13, which is new, centers on social learning
and cognition, and integrates material on basic social learning processes, identification and observational learning in personality development, and the cognitive social learning person variables (e.g., competencies, expectancies) that
result from these basic processes. In addition, new material is presented on
sex-typing, stable individual differences in aggression, the "Type A" pattern
and coronary proneness, helplessness and apathy, reactions to stress, predictability and control, avoidance and learned helplessness, and coping with tragedy (Chapters 14, 15, 16). The treatment of defense has also been updated,
with new material on "scripts," "subconscious information processing," selectivity in cognition, and individual differences in monitoring versus avoidance
as well as in the employment of attention during the coping process (Chapter
17). New material on metacognition in self-control, and on controls as traits,
including research on ego-control and ego-resiliency is incorporated in Chapter
18. Chapter 19, Social Cognition and the Self, is thoroughly reorganized, with
new sections on self-concepts, self-efficacy, and the self-perception of helplessness versus mastery, as well as new findings on self-focus, self-consciousness,
and self-monitoring, and on the attribution process as it relates to personality.
The final chapter presents a comprehensive updating of basic issues in the
field of personality, including the nature of personality coherence and continuity, the problem of appropriate units, the study of environments, and the nature and meaning of person-situation interaction.

The chapters of this book are presented in a sequence that I hope will provide a coherent, integrated survey of the field. At the same time, the presentation was deliberately designed to permit the instructor great flexibility in selecting material for the specific objectives of his or her course.

The sequence of chapters can be adapted readily to emphasize even more the specific links between each theoretical approach and the research most relevant to it. For example, the following chapter sequences group the conceptions and applications of each theoretical approach with research closely connected to it:

	Approaches			
	Trait	*Psychodynamic*	*Behavioral*	*Phenomenological*
Conceptions	2	3	4	5
Applications	6, 7	8	9, 10	11
Research	14, 15, 16, 19	13, 16, 17, 18, 19	12, 13, 15, 16, 18, 19	18, 19

The introduction (1) and the final chapter (20) cut across issues relevant to all the approaches. Of course, each of the research chapters also has some bearing on all the approaches, making conceptual overlap inevitable in Part III and permitting alternative groupings of that material. Finally, a comprehensive glossary has been added to define all major terms.

Readings in Personality (edited by Harriet N. and Walter Mischel, published by Holt, Rinehart and Winston) provides readings from original sources in a sequence that parallels the present text's organization.

Preparation of this edition was greatly helped by the thoughtful, detailed comments of many reviewers. Rhea Cabin prepared the index with care and thoughtfulness and was invaluable in the preparation of the manuscript throughout the many stages of the project. Phillip Peake diligently prepared the accompanying *Instructor's Manual*. I am grateful also to Elyce Misher for her important role in transforming the manuscript into a book.

Walter Mischel
Stanford, California

CONTENTS

CHAPTER 1

INTRODUCTION

Defining Personality

Most thoughtful people have asked the question, "What is personality?" but few agree on an answer. The term "personality" has many definitions, but no single meaning is accepted universally.

Many Definitions—Little Agreement

In popular usage, personality is often equated with social adroitness and effectiveness. In this usage, personality is the ability to elicit positive reactions from other people in one's typical dealings with them. For example, we may speak of someone as having "a lot of personality" or a "popular personality," and advertisements for glamour courses promise to give those who enroll "more personality."

    Less superficially, personality may be taken to be an individual's most striking or dominant characteristic. In that sense a person may be said to be a "shy personality" or a "neurotic personality," meaning that his or her dominant attribute appears to be shyness or neurosis.

More formal definitions of personality by psychologists also show little agreement. Influential personality theorists tell us that personality is:

> . . . the dynamic organization within the individual of those psycho-physical systems that determine his characteristic behavior and thought (Allport, 1961, p. 28).
> . . . a person's unique pattern of traits (Guilford, 1959, p. 5).
> . . . the most adequate conceptualization of a person's behavior in all its detail (McClelland, 1951, p. 69).

As these examples imply, there may be as many different meanings of the term personality as there are theorists who have tried to define it. Nevertheless, a common theme runs throughout most definitions of personality: "Personality" usually refers to the distinctive patterns of behavior (including thoughts and emotions) that characterize each individual's adaptation to the situations of his or her life. Each theorist uses the particular concepts and language of his theory to carve a particular formulation of personality. These different views of personality will become increasingly clear as we examine the concepts and findings of personality psychologists throughout this book.

The Field of Personality Psychology

Within the discipline of psychology, personality is a field of study rather than a particular aspect of the individual. In spite of the fact that there are many different approaches to personality, there is some general agreement about what the study of personality must include. Traditionally, "Personality is that branch of psychology which is concerned with providing a systematic account of the ways in which individuals differ from one another" (Wiggins, 1979, p. 395).

While individual differences are always a core part of the definition of this field, they are not necessarily the whole of it. Thus: ". . . the term 'personality psychology' does not need to be limited to the study of differences between individuals in their consistent attributes, as it has been traditionally. Personality psychology ultimately must also encompass the study of how people's [thoughts and actions] . . . interact with—and shape reciprocally—the conditions of their lives" (Mischel, 1980).

This expanded view recognizes that human *tendencies* are a crucial part of personality, but also asserts the need to study the basic *processes of adaptation* through which people interact with the conditions of their lives in their unique (distinctive) patterns of coping with, and transforming, the social–personal environment. This view of personality focuses both on personal tendencies (qualities) and on processes (such as learning and thinking) in the course of the individual's unique pattern of adaptation throughout the life cycle. No other area of psychology claims to cover as much territory as the field of personality does. Indeed personality study overlaps extensively with neighboring areas. The field of personality is at the crossroads of most areas of psychology: It is the point of convergence between the study of human development and change, of abnormality and deviance as well as of competence and fulfillment, of emotions and thought, of learning, and of social relations. The breadth of the field is not surprising because for many psychologists the object of personality study has been nothing less than the total person. Given such an ambitious goal, the student cannot expect to find simple definitions of personality study.

The potential scope and content of this field is broad indeed. Although the boundaries between personality psychology and other parts of psychology are far from rigid, personality theories do tend to share certain distinctive features; namely, they generally are attempts to "integrate many aspects of human behavior into a single theoretical framework. Not satisfied with an inventory of psychological facts, personality theorists derive and explain these facts from a central theme" (Bavelas, 1978, p. 1).

What should that central theme be? What should a good theory of personality contain and exclude? How should such a theory be built? How can one best analyze and study human behavior? The answers to all these questions are as complex as they are controversial. In dealing with them, different theorists throughout this book will compete for your attention, interest, and even loyalty.

Personality theorists not only tend to carve out large domains and seek broad integrations; they also tend to deal with questions of central personal, philosophical, and practical importance. It is personality theorists who typically have grappled with such vitally relevant questions as: What are the basic causes underlying everyday interpersonal behavior? What are the roots of, and best treatments for, psychological disorders? What is "healthy," adaptive, creative personal functioning and how can it be facilitated? What are the most fundamental, universal enduring psychological qualities of human nature and how do they arise, change, or maintain themselves throughout the life cycle? Given the scope and personal implications of these questions, it is no wonder that personality theories (and theorists!) tend to provoke heated controversies. Sometimes the arguments are so heated it becomes difficult to examine the questions objectively and to move beyond debate to research. Yet it is only through research that the psychological study of personality can make a distinctive scientific contribution.

Studying Personality

Studying the "total individual" or the "whole person" may be a worthy goal, but it is a practical impossibility. To progress beyond recognizing and admiring the complexity of human beings, researchers must select things about people that they can study. In practice, personality study deals with many aspects of the complex behavior of individuals. The term "behavior" is used broadly; it includes emotions and covert mental activities, such as thoughts or "cognitions," as well as overt actions.

Traditionally, personality study has been devoted to generating theories about human nature and individuality, and about the causes and meaning of important psychological differences among individuals. In this effort, many personality psychologists have tried to find the most enduring and stable human attributes. They also have attempted to measure complex human behavior as objectively as possible and to discover useful methods for studying individuals. In addition, personality psychologists study how people develop and change, as well as how they remain stable throughout the course of life.

An Example of Individual Differences

Consider these two cases: Charles and Susan both are college freshmen taking a large introductory course in economics. Their instructor returns the midterm examination in class, and both receive a D grade. Right after class, Charles goes up to the instructor. He seems distressed and upset: He perspires profusely as he talks, his hands tremble slightly, he speaks slowly and softly, almost whispering. His face is flushed and he appears to be on the verge of tears. He apologizes for his "poor performance" and seems to accuse himself bitterly. "I really have no good excuse—it was so stupid of me—I just don't know how I could have done such a sloppy job." He spends most of the rest of the day alone in his dormitory, cuts his classes, and writes a long entry in his diary.

Susan, on the other hand, rushes out of the lecture room at the end of class and quickly starts to joke loudly with her friend about the economics course. She makes fun of the course, comments acidly about the instructor's lecture and seems to pay little attention to her grade as she walks briskly to her next class. In that class (English composition) Susan participates more actively than usual and makes a few excellent comments that surprise her teacher.

This example illustrates what everyone knows: Different people "respond" differently to similar events. Both students received a D; yet each reacted differently to the experience. Why? How consistent are these differences? Would Charles and Susan show similar differences in their response to a D in physical education? Would each respond similarly if they were fired from their part-time jobs? Would Charles also be apologetic and self-effacing if he received a personal rebuff from a close friend? Will Susan treat a poor grade the same way when she is a senior? What do the observed differences in the reactions of the two students to their grade imply about their other characteristics? That is, on the basis of what we know about them already, can we predict accurately other differences between them? For example, do they also differ in their academic aspirations and in their past achievements and failures? Do they generally show different degrees of anxiety about tests? What might have caused such differences between them? How are such differences maintained, and how might they be changed? What else must we know about each to predict what he or she will do next? Personality psychologists ask questions of this sort.

To grasp the range and nature of the events encompassed by the field of personality, we must examine what psychologists of personality do professionally, and that is the purpose of this book. In this effort we will survey major *personality theories,* focusing on their basic *conceptions* in Part I and on their *applications* for assessment and change in Part II. Then we will examine research on *personality development and basic processes* (Part III) to present an overview of what is known about the determinants and nature of personality.

Personality Theories: Conceptions

Some personality psychologists are most concerned with theory and generate ideas about the causes and nature of "personality." Each theorist conceptualizes personality somewhat differently. Obviously, Sigmund Freud's view of personality, which emphasized unconscious motives, is very different from the formulations of an early behaviorist like John Watson, who stressed learned habits. Indeed the concepts employed by such widely differing theories may have almost nothing in common.

Some personality theorists believe that human behaviors have their roots in unconscious motives whose true nature is outside the individual's awareness and whose sources lie deeply buried in the distant past. Others focus on the current conditions of the individual's life and on present relationships and experiences. While some theorists search for signs of wishes, attitudes, and character traits that are not directly observable, others attend to the person's overt actions—the things the individual does—and seek to sample them as directly and precisely as possible.

A few of the many theoretical alternatives for conceptualizing the same behavior are shown in Figure 1-1. The same behavior—Jane's becoming tense

FIGURE 1-1
Examples of Alternative Conceptualizations about the Mechanisms (Reasons) Underlying the Same Behavior

SITUATION	CONCEPTIONS ABOUT POSSIBLE UNDERLYING MECHANISMS	RESPONSE
Jane is at her desk preparing for an exam tomorrow.	Jane is a generally fearful person with diffuse anxieties. Jane really fears "success" and unconsciously wants to fail. Jane has learned to fear exams and has poor study habits. Jane's upset reflects her identity crisis about herself as a person.	Jane becomes increasingly tense and cannot study effectively.

in response to an exam scheduled for tomorrow—is open to diverse interpretations about the reasons underlying her upset. Is Jane's reaction a sign of her more generalized fearfulness? Is it a symptom of an underlying problem provoked or symbolized in some complex way by the exam? Is it part of a learned pattern of exam fears and poor habits for studying? Is it related to more basic conflicts and insecurities about herself?

The conceptualizations one generates about the meaning of behavior are more than idle games: They guide the ways we think about ourselves and the solutions we seek in efforts to better our lives. For example, if Jane's tension reflects unconscious conflicts about academic success and a fear that success would undermine her "femininity" (Horner, 1972), it might help her to seek better insights into her own motives. In contrast, if Jane's behavior reflects poor study skills, it might be better for her to learn ways of reducing exam-related tensions (e.g., by learning to relax) while also mastering more effective ways of studying.

Students are easily puzzled by a field in which different theorists may fail to agree even about the meaning of the same behavior. It may help, however, to recognize that lack of agreement in this instance merely means that the same events can be construed in many different ways. The events are tangible and real enough: Nature goes on "minding its own business"; the events of life keep on happening no matter how people understand them. People behave and "do things" continuously, but the meaning of those actions and the reasons for them may be conceptualized from many vantage points and for many purposes.

In Part I of this book we will examine some of the major theoretical orientations to personality. We will survey some of the main ideas developed to describe and understand psychological differences among people, and we will consider the concepts that are central to diverse views of human nature. The range of these concepts is great. Included are ideas about our most basic human characteristics, about the motives and attitudes that may underlie actions, about the chief crises of life, about the conditions of experience that mold human values, beliefs, and choices, and about the processes and concepts through which people try to understand themselves and to make sense of the world.

When theorists develop their ideas, they often try to extend them as far as possible. They attempt to explore their ramifications and their implications about as many facets of life as possible. They test the limit of the ideas by probing their relevance for diverse areas. Such a stretching of concepts can be extremely fruitful for builders of theories because it helps them to generalize and to see how far their ideas may apply. Thus the theorist may try to make his or her ideas about the "unconscious" or the "self" or "early experience" or "conditioning" serve to explain a host of different human phenomena. One or two favorite concepts may be used to deal with everything from love to hate, from birth trauma to fears about death, from deep disturbance to great achievement. While such an extension of ideas may help the theorist, the perceptive student must always ask, "Does it fit?" and "How does the theorist know?" and "What would we have to do to discover whether he or she is right or wrong?" and "What are the consequences of thinking about it that way?"

Such an analytical, skeptical attitude is the essence of the scientific approach. It is a necessary attitude if we want to go beyond learning what different theorists say about human nature and personality to *testing ideas* so that we can discriminate between those that have no support and those that are worthy of further study, and so that we can develop better concepts whenever possible.

Personality Theories: Applications

To convert personality theories from speculations about people into ideas that can be studied scientifically, we must be able to put them into *testable* terms. It is basic to science that any position advanced, any conceptualization, must be potentially testable. This is what makes science different from the simple assertion of opinions or beliefs. Perhaps the most distinctive feature of modern personality psychology has been its concern with studying ideas about people empirically by actually putting them to the test.

Efforts to study personality scientifically are confronted by many problems. Attitudes toward the systematic and scientific study of personality often are ambivalent. On the one hand, it seems fascinating to try to gain insight into the causes of one's own behavior and the roots of one's own personality. But at the same time we may resist actually achieving such an understanding and seeing ourselves objectively. Many scholars feel that it does violence to a person's complexity and "humanness" to study and "objectify" him or her in the framework of science. Instead, they suggest that perhaps the most perceptive and provoking studies of personality are found in great literary creations, such as the characters of a Dickens or a Dostoyevsky novel.

People do not perceive themselves entirely objectively. Thus while it may be fashionable to say in public that human behavior, like that of other organisms, is "lawfully determined," privately the laws of nature may seem to be operating on everyone except oneself. Subjectively, while other people's behavior may be seen as controlled by "variables" or "conditions," one's own important thoughts, feelings, dreams, and actions may seem to defy such control and to resist objective assessment.

Even within the field of personality psychology, there is a certain amount of resistance to "objectifying" personality. For every personality psychologist who believes that people must be studied under carefully controlled experimental conditions, there is another who believes that individuals can be understood only by investigating them under "naturalistic," lifelike conditions. As one perceptive student of people noted, lives are "too human for science, too beautiful for numbers, too sad for diagnosis, and too immortal for bound journals" (Vaillant, 1977, p. 11).

While some personality psychologists commit themselves to quantitative, statistical techniques for gathering information from large groups, others rely on intuition and subjective judgments based on lengthy personal experience with a few persons. While some urge us to concentrate on "peak experiences"—moments of personal, spiritual, or religious climax and fulfillment—others prefer to systematically study simpler behaviors under conditions that permit a clearer analysis of causation—for example, the responses of a young child to specific instructions under the closely controlled conditions of a testing room at school.

Different experts favor different techniques of investigation, but all of them generally share a conviction that ultimately theoretical ideas about personality and human behavior must be tested and applied. To test theoretical ideas, it is necessary to turn from theories to methods and applications. Therefore in Part II we will consider methods of personality study and assessment. We will describe the main methods of assessing persons favored by each theoretical approach and examine their relevance for understanding the individual. It will become evident that personality assessment does not just supply assessments of persons: It also assesses the ideas and theory of the assessor. That is, efforts to measure and analyze behavior supply information not only about the people who are measured but also about the meaning of the tests and ideas used in the measurement process. What we learn about ten children from their answers to an intelligence test, for example, tells us something about the test and the concept of "intelligence," as well as something about the children.

Personality theories also may be applied to help improve the psychological qualities of our lives. Even people whose problems are not severe enough to seek help from professionals still search for ways to live their lives more fully and satisfyingly. But what constitutes a "fuller," "more satisfying" life? Given the diversity and complexity of human strengths and problems, it seems evident that simple notions of psychological adequacy in terms of "good adjustment" or "sound personality" are hopelessly naive. More adequate definitions of "adaptation" and "abnormality," of "mental health" and "deviance," hinge on the personality theory that guides one. The theoretical conceptions in Part I provide distinctive notions about the nature of psychological adequacy and deviance. Each also dictates the strategies chosen to try to change troublesome (problematic) behaviors and to encourage more adequate, constructive alternatives.

Many personality psychologists are concerned about practical questions regarding the prediction and modification of behavior. They tend to concentrate on a search for useful techniques to deal with human problems and to foster more advantageous patterns of growth. In addition to having enormous practical and social importance, attempts to understand and change behaviors provide one of the sharpest testing grounds for ideas about personality. Insights gained in this manner are being applied in further efforts to help people. These efforts include different forms of psychotherapy, various special learning programs, and changes in the psychological environment to permit people to develop their full potential. Research on these topics informs us about the usefulness and implications of different ideas about personality change. The concepts and methods relevant to adaptation, deviance, and personality change are discussed at many points in Part II.

Personality Development and the Coping Process

The field of personality is moving away from global theorizing about human nature. While still pursuing theory, most personality psychologists now try to cast their questions in a form that permits them to be studied empirically. By going beyond abstract speculation and studying people empirically, they hope to discover the conditions that determine complex behavior and important differences among individuals. Much contemporary personality research therefore focuses on the role of specific social experiences and events in personality development and in everyday adaptation. Part III considers personality development and discusses research on the basic coping processes through which people adapt to, and interact with, the conditions of their lives.

Research in personality has investigated an almost unlimited range of topics. For example, how does an individual gradually become a psychological "male" or "female"? That is, how does a person acquire a psychological sexual identity, a sense of being masculine or feminine, and the attitudes and behavioral patterns that differentiate him or her from the opposite sex? What are the effects of changing beliefs about male and female roles in society? What are the consequences of sexual identity?

"Aggression" is one pattern that regularly seems to characterize males more than females. But what determines aggression? Is it an instinctual, natural response to strong frustration, or a socially acquired pattern? If, for example, a man has an aggressive "killer instinct," would it help to provide socially acceptable "outlets" for aggression? Does watching aggression (for example, in ancient days in the Roman Colosseum or now on television and in movies and theaters) reduce the viewer's later tendency to be aggressive—or does it increase it? Given the pervasiveness of aggression and violence within individual lives and throughout society, the meaning of aggression and its potential control are topics of crucial social importance.

"Anxiety" is one of aggression's closest competitors for attention and study. Indeed it has become a truism that we live in an "age of anxiety" and that much of the time when people are not fighting they are worrying. How does anxiety develop, and what are its consequences for individuals who have it in different degrees? How do people cope with psychological pain and anxiety? In addition to fighting with others, individuals often seem to fight with themselves and to become conflicted and anxious in the process. Different researchers have conceptualized such internal conflicts in different ways, for example by suggesting "unconscious defenses." If so, against what do people "defend," and how do they do it?

How does the individual develop from the helplessness and dependency of the newborn to the competence and mastery of the adequate, mature adult who manages to control both self and environment to a considerable extent? In addition to engaging in all sorts of actions, people also generate concepts and theories about themselves. They evaluate their own actions, develop expectations about their own strengths and weaknesses, and, just like the scientist who studies them, try to understand and assess themselves. How do individuals develop concepts about themselves, and how do they come to regulate and assess their own behavior? Indeed, how may the individual become a theorist about the meaning of his or her own personality and life? And how do the qualities of the person interact with those of the environment in which he or she lives to determine behavior?

SUMMARY

1. To psychologists, personality is a field of study rather than a particular aspect of people. Personality psychology is a field of great breadth, overlapping the neighboring areas of human development, creativity and abnormality, emotions, cognition, learning, and social relations. This book is an introduction to the field of personality. It surveys personality theories and their applications, as well as personality development and basic coping processes.

2. Traditionally, much attention has been devoted to generating theories about human nature and individual differences. Personality theories differ in their degree of emphasis on the past and the present, the conscious and the unconscious, the directly observable and the relatively unobservable. The essence of a scientific approach to personality is to test various ideas, to evaluate the evidence supporting them, and to seek better ones. It is this potential testability of personality theory that differentiates a science of personality from the simple assertion of opinions or beliefs.

3. Major personality theories have important applications for assessment and personality change. They provide strategies for seeking information about people and for changing behavior in constructive ways. The widespread existence of psychological problems makes the search for effective strategies to improve the quality of life especially important. The successes achieved by these applications reflect on the value (and limitations) of the personality theories that guide them.

4. Contemporary personality research investigates the effects of experiences and events on personality and studies the nature and meaning

of important psychological differences among individuals. Examples of the topics investigated include sexual identity, the determinants of aggression, the nature and causes of anxiety, the development of competence and mastery, the concepts and theories that people develop about themselves, and the interaction of the individual with the environment.

Personality — learned or inherited

In Part I you will get an overview of major theoretical conceptions for the study of personality. The theoretical approach discussed in Chapter 2 emphasizes comparisons between persons with respect to their main psychological characteristics. A second approach to personality is most deeply rooted in the ideas of Freud (Chapter 3). It began in the psychiatric clinic with the intensive study of disturbed people. Quite different is the approach that grows out of the experimental tradition in psychology (Chapter 4). The experimentalist is most concerned with isolating important cause-and-effect relations in the objective analysis of behavior by experimental methods. Especially in recent years, the ideas and procedures used by the experimentalist have been applied to study people and to encourage necessary personality change. The final chapter of Part I (Chapter 5) discusses efforts to study the individual's ways of looking at the world. Here, the focus is on how people see or construe themselves and others, on how individuals come to know themselves and their world, rather than on their attributes and the causes of their actions.

PART I

PERSONALITY THEORIES: CONCEPTIONS

In Part I you will be introduced to the central conceptions associated with each of these major personality theories. Here you will get a broad overview of their central ideas as quickly and succinctly as possible. In later sections (Part II) we will return to these basic conceptions and will elaborate on each of them by examining their applications and consequences in greater detail and depth. Be alert to the fact that the presentation of theories in Part I thus provides only a first glimpse, outlining the basic concepts of major personality theories; their specific applications for personality assessment and for personality change are presented in Part II. Because the impact and value of personality theories to a large extent depend on their contributions to understanding and helping individuals, the richness—and limitations—of each position will not be entirely evident (and should not be judged with any finality) until you have studied its applications as well as its basic concepts.

CHAPTER 2

TRAIT THEORIES: CONCEPTIONS

[handwritten notes in green: statistical correlation · Allport · Cattell factor analysis · Eysenck · Common features to all 3 p25]

One of the most enduring approaches to personality seeks to label and classify people according to their psychological characteristics. Since the beginnings of language men have tried to describe each other by grouping the enormous differences among people into categories. This chapter discusses efforts to study personality by classifying individual differences into basic types and traits.

Types and Traits

In their early phases most sciences are concerned with *naming* things and *classifying* them into groups or categories in an orderly fashion. Such taxonomies are seen, for example, in the biological classification of living things into genera and species. In daily life people also categorize themselves on almost endless dimensions. Some of these involve overt attributes—for example, sex, race, nationality, occupation—while others require indirect inferences about hypothesized attributes—such as temperament, character, motives, attitudes.

Types

Some categorizations sort individuals into discrete categories or *types*. In the ancient theory of temperaments, for example, the Greek physician Hippocrates assigned persons to one of four types of temperament: *choleric* (irritable), *melancholic* (depressed), *sanguine* (optimistic), and *phlegmatic* (calm, listless). In accord with the biology of his time (about 400 B.C.), Hippocrates attributed each temperament to a predominance of one of the bodily humors; yellow bile, black bile, blood, and phlegm. A choleric temperament was caused by an excess of yellow bile; a depressive temperament reflected the predominance of black bile; the sanguine person had too much blood; and phlegmatic people suffered from an excess of phlegm.

Other typologies have searched for constitutional types, seeking associations between physique and indices of temperament. Such groupings in terms of body build have considerable popular appeal, as seen in the prevalence of stereotypes linking the body to the psyche: Fat people are "jolly" and "lazy," thin people are "morose" and "sensitive," and so on.

Formal classifications of the possible links between personality and somatic type were developed by the German psychiatrist Kretschmer and more recently by an American physician, William H. Sheldon. Sheldon's classification has received most attention. In 1942 he suggested three dimensions of physique and their corresponding temperaments. These are summarized in Figure 2-1.

As Figure 2-1 suggests, the endomorph is obese, the mesomorph has an athletic build, and the ectomorph is tall, thin, and stoop-shouldered. Rather than dividing people into three distinct types, Sheldon considered every individual's status on each dimension. He developed a seven-point rating system for meas-

FIGURE 2-1
Sheldon's Physique Dimensions and Their Associated Temperaments

PHYSIQUE	TEMPERAMENT
Endomorphic (soft and round, overdeveloped digestive viscera)	*Viscerotonic* (relaxed, loves to eat, sociable)
Mesomorphic (muscular, rectangular, strong)	*Somatotonic* (energetic, assertive, courageous)
Ectomorphic (long, fragile, large brain and sensitive nervous system)	*Cerebrotonic* (restrained, fearful, introvertive, artistic)

Are there links between physique and personality?

uring somatotypes. For example, a 7-3-1 would be high on endomorphy, moderate on mesomorphy, and low on ectomorphy, presumably with corresponding levels of the associated temperaments. Sheldon's typology thus was quite sophisticated, especially by comparison with earlier formulations.

Sheldon's ideas about the association between body build and temperament are supported to some extent when untrained people rate the personality characteristics of others. In part these findings may reflect the fact that stereotyped ideas about the characteristics of fat, athletic, and skinny people are shared by the raters. For example, if raters think most fat people are "jolly" and thin people are "sensitive," they may base their judgments of the individuals they rate on these stereotypes rather than on observed behavior. Thus they may rate a fat person as jolly, no matter how he or she behaves. Studies of behavior that avoid such stereotypes generally provide less evidence for the value of this system (e.g., Tyler, 1956).

Other typologies have grouped people into purely psychological categories. The Swiss psychiatrist Carl Jung, for example, considered all people either predominantly "introverts" or "extraverts." The introvert tends to withdraw into himself, especially when faced by emotional conflict and stress. He prefers to be alone, is shy, avoids people. In contrast, the extravert responds to stress by trying to lose himself among others. He tends to be in an occupation that lets him deal directly with many people—such as sales or promotional work—and he is likely to be conventional, outgoing, and sociable.

Jung's introversion-extraversion typology has continued to intrigue psychologists and has been extensively researched for many years. The results suggest that people differ in the degree to which they are introverted and extraverted rather than fitting into one or the other category exclusively. Most other hypothesized psychological typologies also turn out to involve a *continuum* of individual differences rather than discrete types.

Limitations of Typologies

Typologies are appealing because of their simplicity, but it is their simplicity that limits their value. Generally the behavior of individuals is so complex, diverse, and variable that they cannot be sorted usefully into a simplistic category or slot. While some human characteristics may be usefully typed (e.g., blood type, sex) and while human conditions sometimes may be typed (imprisoned or free, hospitalized or out-patient), it is hard to imagine a useful typology for pigeonholing the total individual into one of a few personality categories.

Traits versus Types

Typologies usually assume discrete, discontinuous categories (like male *or* female). Traits, however, are continuous dimensions on which individual differences may be arranged quantitatively in terms of *amount* of the characteristic the individual has (like degrees of intelligence). In fact, psychological measurements usually indicate a continuous dimension of individual differences in the

Typologies = discrete Categories

FIGURE 2-2 *Traits = Continuum dimensions*
Obtained Distribution for Individual Differences

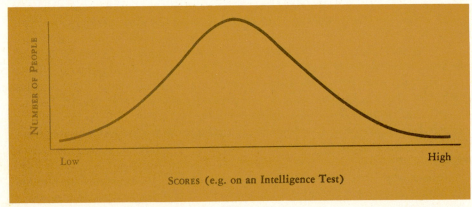

One continuous dimension (from low to high) is usually found.

degree of the measured attribute, with most people displaying an intermediate amount (Figure 2-2).

Many psychologists who use a trait approach investigate such personality dimensions as aggressiveness, dependency, and the striving to achieve high standards of excellence. Great differences have been found among people in the degree to which they show such dispositions.

The trait approach begins with the common-sense observation that individuals often differ greatly and consistently in their responses to the same psychological situation or stimulus. That is, when different people are confronted with the same event—the same social encounter, the same test question, the same frightening experience—each individual tends to react in a somewhat different way. The basic idea that no two people react identically to the same stimulus is shown schematically in Figure 2-3. Moreover, in everyday life most of us are impressed with the distinctive *consistency* of one individual's responses over a wide variety of stimulus situations: We expect an "aggressive" person to differ consistently from others in his or her responses to many stimuli.

In its simplest meaning, the term "trait" refers to consistent differences between the behavior or characteristics of two or more people. Thus, "a trait is any distinguishable, relatively enduring way in which one individual varies from another" (Guilford, 1959, p. 6.).

To understand the reasons for individual differences some early theorists also invoked the "trait" as an explanation: In their view the trait was the property within the person that accounted for his or her unique but relatively stable reactions to stimuli. Thus the trait became a construct to explain behavior—a hypothesized reason for enduring individual differences. Many spokesmen for the trait position have theorized extensively about these hypothesized dispositions. Before examining their formal views, however, we should consider how traits are used informally by people in daily life. Indeed we are all trait theorists in the sense that we generate ideas about our own dispositions and the characteristics of other people.

FIGURE 2-3
Individual Differences in Response to the Same Stimulus

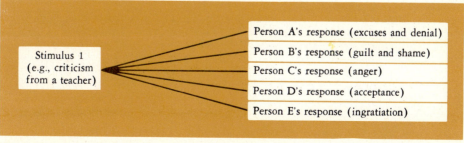

The trait approach emphasizes consistent differences among people in their response to the same stimulus.

Trait Attributions

When people describe each other psychologically in daily life, they spontaneously use dispositional or trait terms. We all characterize each other (and ourselves) with such terms as aggressive, dependent, fearful, introverted, anxious, submissive—the list is almost endless. We see a person behaving in a particular way—for example, sitting at a desk for an hour yawning—and we attribute a trait—"unmotivated" or "lazy" or "bored" or "dull."

These simple trait attributions are often adequate to "explain" events for many everyday purposes in common-sense psychology (Heider, 1958; Kelley, 1973). In these common-sense explanations, traits are invoked not just as descriptions of what people do but also as the causes of their behavior. Thus in everyday practice traits may be used first simply as adjectives describing behavior ("He behaves in a lazy way"), but the description is soon generalized from the behavior to the person ("He *is* lazy") and then abstracted to "He has a lazy disposition" or "He is unmotivated." These descriptions pose no problems as long as their basis is recalled—he is construed as behaving in a lazy way and no more. A hazard in trait attribution is that we easily forget that nothing is explained if the state *we* have attributed to the person from his behavior ("He has a trait of laziness") is now invoked as the *cause* of the behavior from which it was inferred. We then quickly emerge with the tautology, "He behaves in a lazy way because he has a lazy disposition," or because he is "unmotivated."

The trait approach to formal personality study begins with the common-sense conviction that personality can be described with trait terms, but it extends and refines those descriptions by arriving at them quantitatively and systematically. Efforts to explain individual differences by formal trait theories entail some of the same problems that arise when traits are offered as causes by the layman. However, numerous safeguards have been developed to try to control some of these difficulties (see Chapter 7).

Gordon Allport   *trait determines behavior*

One of the most outstanding trait psychologists was Gordon Allport, whose conceptions of traits have had an important influence for more than thirty years. In Allport's theory, traits have a very real and vital existence: They are the ultimate realities of psychological organization. Allport favored a biophysical conception that

> does not hold that every trait-name necessarily implies a trait; but rather that behind all confusion of terms, behind the disagreement of judges, and apart from errors and failures of empirical observation, there are none the less *bona fide* mental structures in each personality that account for the consistency of its behavior (1937, p. 289).

According to Allport, traits are determining tendencies or predispositions to respond. These dispositions serve to integrate what would otherwise be dissimilar stimuli and responses. In other words, a trait is

> a generalized and focalized neuropsychic system (peculiar to the individual) with the capacity to render many stimuli functionally equivalent, and to initiate and guide consistent (equivalent) forms of adaptive and expressive behavior (1937, p. 295).

Allport implied that traits are not linked to a small number of specific stimuli or responses, but are relatively *general* and enduring: By uniting responses to numerous stimuli, they produce fairly broad consistencies in behavior, as schematized in Figure 2-4.

Allport was convinced that some people have dispositions that pervade most aspects of their behavior. He called these highly generalized dispositions *cardinal* traits. For example, if a person's whole life seems to be organized around goal achievement and the attainment of excellence, then achievement might be his or her cardinal trait. Less pervasive but still quite generalized dispositions are *central* traits, and Allport thought that many people are broadly influenced by central traits. Finally, more specific, narrow traits are called *secondary* dispositions or "attitudes."

Allport believed that one's pattern of dispositions or "personality structure" determines one's behavior. This emphasis on structure rather than environment or stimulus conditions is seen in his colorful phrase, "The same fire that melts the butter hardens the egg" (1937, p. 102). Allport was an ardent spokesman for the importance of individual differences: No two people are completely alike, and hence no two people respond identically to the same event. Each person's behavior is determined by a particular trait structure.

According to Allport, traits never occur in any two people in exactly the same way: They operate in *unique* ways in each person. This conviction was consistent with his emphasis on the individuality and uniqueness of each personality. To the extent that any trait is unique within a person rather than

FIGURE 2-4
An Example of a Trait as the Unifier of Stimuli and Responses

STIMULI		RESPONSES
1. Meeting a stranger		outgoing, pleasant
2. Working with peers	Trait: Friendliness	helpful, encouraging
3. Visiting family		warm, interested
4. Dating a girlfriend		attentive, thoughtful

common among many people, it cannot be studied by making comparisons among people. Consequently Allport urged the thorough study of individuals through intensive and long-term case studies. He also believed, however, that because of shared experiences and common cultural influences, most persons tend to develop some *roughly* common kinds of traits: They can be compared on these common dispositions.

Many of Allport's theories were most relevant to the phenomenological approach (see Chapter 5) and to the in-depth study of lives rather than to the quantitative study of groups. He contributed to trait theory, but he was critical of many of the statistical methods and quantitative research strategies favored by other trait theorists.

R. B. Cattell   *clearly e group traits*

Raymond B. Cattell (e.g., 1950, 1965) has been another important proponent of trait theory. For Cattell the trait is also the basic unit of study; it is a "mental structure," inferred from behavior, and a fundamental construct that accounts for behavioral regularity or consistency. Like Allport, Cattell distinguished between *common traits,* which are possessed by all people, and *unique traits,* which occur only in a particular person and cannot be found in another in exactly the same form.

Cattell also distinguished *surface traits* from *source traits* (see Table 2-1 for selected examples). Surface traits are clusters of overt or manifest trait elements (responses) that seem to go together. Source traits are the underlying variables that are the causal entities determining the surface manifestations. In research, trait elements (in the form of test responses or scores) are inter-

---

TABLE 2-1
SURFACE TRAITS AND SOURCE TRAITS
STUDIED BY CATTELL

Examples of Surface Traits: (Cattell, 1950)	Integrity, altruism—dishonesty, undependability Disciplined thoughtfulness—foolishness Thrift, tidiness, obstinacy—lability, curiosity, intuition
Examples of Source Traits: (Cattell, 1965)	Ego strength—emotionality and neuroticism Dominance—submissiveness

NOTE: These are selected and abbreviated examples from much longer lists.

correlated statistically until collections of elements that correlate positively in all possible combinations are discovered. This procedure, according to Cattell, yields surface traits.

For Cattell source traits can be identified only by means of the mathematical technique of factor analysis (discussed further in Chapter 7). Using this technique, the investigator tries to estimate the factors or dimensions that appear to underlie surface variations in behavior. According to Cattell, the basic aim in research and assessment should be identification of source traits. In this view, these traits are divided between those that reflect environmental conditions (*environmental-mold traits*) and those that reflect constitutional factors (*constitutional traits*). Moreover, source traits may either be *general* (those affecting behavior in many different situations) or *specific*. Specific source traits are particularized sources of personality reaction that operate in one situation only, and Cattell pays little attention to them.

Cattell uses three kinds of data to discover general source traits: *life records,* in which everyday behavior situations are observed and rated; *self-ratings;* and *objective tests,* in which the person is observed in situations that are specifically designed to elicit responses from which behavior in other situations can be predicted. The data from all three sources are subjected to factor analysis. In his own work, Cattell shows a preference for factor analysis of life-record data based on many behavior ratings for large samples of persons. Some 14 or 15 clusters of intercorrelations or source traits have been reported from such investigations, but only six have been found repeatedly (Vernon, 1964).

In Cattell's system, traits may also be grouped into classes or modalities on the basis of how they are expressed. Those that are relevant to the individual's being "set into action" with respect to some goal are called *dynamic traits*, whereas those concerned with effectiveness in gaining the goal are *ability traits*. Traits concerned with energy or emotional reactivity are named *temperament traits*. Cattell has speculated extensively about the relationships between various traits and the development of personality (1965).

H. J. Eysenck

The extensive researches of the English psychologist Hans Eysenck have complemented the work of the American trait theorists, and supplemented it in many important ways. Eysenck (1961) has extended the search for personality dimensions to the area of abnormal behavior, studying such traits as *neuroticism.* He also has investigated *introversion-extraversion* as a dimensional trait (although Carl Jung originally proposed "introvert" and "extravert" as personality *types*). Eysenck and his associates have pursued an elaborate and sophisticated statistical methodology in their search for the dimensions needed for an adequate conceptualization of personality structure. In addition to providing a set of descriptive dimensions, Eysenck and his colleagues have studied the associations between people's status on these dimensions and their scores on a variety of other personality and intellectual measures.

Eysenck emphasized that his dimension of introversion-extraversion is based entirely on research and "must stand and fall by empirical confirmation" (Eysenck & Rachman, 1965, p. 19). In his words:

The typical extravert is sociable, likes parties, has many friends, needs to have people to talk to, and does not like reading or studying by himself. He craves excitement, takes chances, often sticks his neck out, acts on the spur of the moment, and is generally an impulsive individual. He is fond of practical jokes, always has a ready answer, and generally likes change; he is carefree, easygoing, optimistic, and "likes to laugh and be merry." He prefers to keep moving and doing things, tends to be aggressive and loses his temper quickly; altogether his feelings are not kept under tight control, and he is not always a reliable person.

The typical introvert is a quiet, retiring sort of person, introspective, fond of books rather than people; he is reserved and distant except to intimate friends. He tends to plan ahead, "looks before he leaps," and mistrusts the impulse of the moment. He does not like excitement, takes matters of everyday life with proper seriousness, and likes a well-ordered mode of life. He keeps his feelings under close control, seldom behaves in an aggressive manner, and does not lose his temper easily. He is reliable, somewhat pessimistic and places great value on ethical standards.

Eysenck and his colleagues recognized that these descriptions may sound almost like caricatures because they portray "perfect" extraverts and intro-

FIGURE 2-5
Dimensions of Personality

The inner ring shows the "four temperaments" of Hippocrates; the outer ring shows the results of modern factor analytic studies of the intercorrelations between traits by Eysenck and others (Eysenck & Rachman, 1965).

verts while in fact most people are mixtures who fall in the middle rather than at the extremes of the dimensions (see Figure 2-5). As Figure 2-5 shows, Eysenck suggested that the second major dimension of personality is *emotional stability* or *neuroticism*. This dimension describes at one end people who tend to be moody, touchy, anxious, restless, and so on. At the other extreme are people who are characterized by such terms as stable, calm, carefree, even-tempered, and reliable. As Eysenck stressed, the ultimate value of these dimensions will depend on the research support they receive.

Common Features of Trait Theories

Now consider the principal common characteristics of trait approaches.

Generality of Traits

Trait theorists often disagree about the specific content and structure of the basic traits needed to describe personality, but their general conceptions have much similarity. They all use the trait to account for consistencies in an individual's behavior and to explain why persons respond differently to the same stimulus. They view traits as dispositions that determine such behaviors. Each differentiates between relatively superficial traits (e.g., Cattell's suface traits) and more basic, underlying traits (e.g., Cattell's source traits). Each recognizes that traits vary in breadth or generality, Allport perhaps placing the strongest emphasis on the relative generality of traits across many situations. Each theorist also admits trait fluctuations, or changes in a person's position with respect to a disposition. At the same time, each is committed to a search for relatively broad, stable traits.

Search for Basic Traits

If it is assumed that behavior is mainly determined by broad traits that manifest themselves stably across many conditions, then it is understandable that personality psychologists should search for these dispositions and pay less attention to other variables. Guided by the assumption that highly generalized dispositions exist, a main objective of trait psychology has been to identify the individual's position on one or more dimensions (e.g., neuroticism, extraversion) through comparison with other persons tested under comparable, standardized conditions. If it is believed that positions on these dimensions are relatively stable across testing situations and over long time periods, then the main emphasis in the study of personality becomes the development of reliable instruments that can accurately tap the person's underlying traits. This has been the predominant concern of traditional trait approaches. Less attention has been paid to the effects of environmental conditions on traits and be-havior.

Inferring Traits from Behavioral Signs   *test results etc*

In the search for dispositions one always *infers* traits from the individual's behavior—for example, from what she says about herself on a questionnaire. The person's responses or behaviors are taken as *indicators* of underlying traits. The trait approach to personality is a "sign" approach in the sense that there is no interest in the test behavior itself. That is, test responses are of value not in their own right but only as *signs* of the traits that underlie them; test behavior is always used as a sign of nontest behavior (Loevinger, 1957). The trait psychologist is not interested in answers on an inventory or IBM score sheet for their own sake, but only in a subject's responses to a test as reliable cues or signs of her dispositions. It is therefore essential to demon-strate the relation between test behaviors and the traits they purportedly rep-resent. We will consider relevant efforts of this sort in detail later (Chapter 7).

Quantitative Methods

A main feature of the trait approach has been its quantitative methodology. This methodology is "psychometric" in the sense that it attempts to measure individual differences. The psychometric approach to individual differences tries to infer the underlying trait structure of individuals. Psychometricians study persons and groups on trait dimensions by comparing their quantitative scores on tests. To do this reliably the preferred research strategy is to sample many subjects, to compare large groups under uniform testing conditions, and to devise sophisticated statistical techniques in the search for basic traits (Chapters 6 and 7).

Trait Dimensions and Individual Differences

After many years of searching, trait theorists still disagree as to which trait dimensions are the basic units of personality. Some suggest as many as sixteen basic traits; others as few as two or three. Table 2-2 gives the five trait dimen-sions that were studied in one research program. For each dimension, it shows the adjectives describing the two ends of each rating scale it includes. In spite of disagreement about basic dimensions, there is usually some overlap in the findings of different trait theorists. Probably the two dimensions found most consistently involve extraversion-introversion and adjustment and integration as opposed to disorganization and anxiety (e.g., Vernon, 1964). Many contemporary trait researchers remain committed to identifying "the most important individual differences in mankind" (Goldberg, 1973, p. 1). Their effort rests on the assumption that the most significant individual dif-ferences—those that are most important in daily human relationships—

Somme *Surface*

TABLE 2-2	
SOME TRAIT DIMENSIONS AND THEIR COMPONENTS	

Trait Dimension	*Descriptive Components*[a]
I. Extraversion or Surgency	Talkative—Silent Frank, Open—Secretive Adventurous—Cautious Sociable—Reclusive
II. Agreeableness	Good-natured—Irritable Not Jealous—Jealous Mild, Gentle—Headstrong Cooperative—Negativistic
III. Conscientiousness	Fussy, Tidy—Careless Responsible—Undependable Scrupulous—Unscrupulous Persevering—Quitting, Fickle
IV. Emotional Stability	Poised—Nervous, Tense Calm—Anxious Composed—Excitable Not Hypochondriacal— Hypochondriacal
V. Culture	Artistically Sensitive— Artistically Insensitive Intellectual—Unreflective, Narrow Polished, Refined—Crude, Boorish Imaginative—Simple, Direct

SOURCE: Adapted from Norman (1963).
[a]Adjectives describing the two ends of the scales that comprise the dimension.

become encoded into the natural language of the culture as single-word trait terms. Using a variety of methods (discussed in Chapters 6 and 7) they try to identify basic trait terms in the language and to categorize them into comprehensive groupings. This classification task is an enormous one, given that thousands of trait terms (over 18,000 in one count) are found in English. The hope underlying this great effort is that the ultimate development of better theories of personality (and better methods of personality assessment) will be helped by having at hand an extensive, well-organized vocabulary for describing human attributes in trait terms.

Some highly sophisticated research is advancing this important but difficult goal. One of the most comprehensive efforts builds on the earlier work of Allport, Norman (shown in Table 2-2), and others. Eight scales of adjectives were developed for the domain of interpersonal behavior (Wiggins, 1979, 1980). The basic structure of this system is illustrated in Figure 2-6, which presents the eight dimensions. Note that each dimension is "bipolar," i.e., has two opposite ends or poles and that they are structured in a circular pattern like a pie. Each pole is made up of a set of adjectives so that *Ambitious* (*Dominant*), for example, is defined with such terms as persevering, persistent, industrious. The opposite pole, *Lazy* (*Submissive*), includes such terms as unproductive, unthorough, unindustrious. Wiggins reports that these eight dimensions fit well the results of earlier descriptions of the interpersonal domain (e.g., Leary, 1957), and that they are proving to be reasonably robust and useful when different samples of people are rated on them.

Research in the trait tradition does not only describe individual differences. It also examines the relationships between an individual's position on many

FIGURE 2-6
Wiggins' (1980) Taxonomy of the Interpersonal Domain

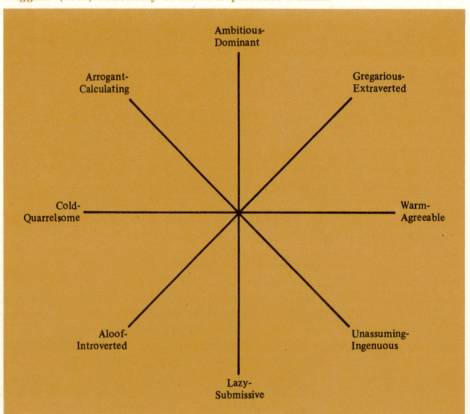

personality dimensions and his or her behavior in other situations. For example, a group of school children may be tested for their intellectual abilities and also given questionnaires concerning beliefs and attitudes. In addition they may be asked to rate their own attributes on several scales, and they may be rated on a set of characteristics by their teachers and their peers. The results are examined statistically to discover the associations or correlations among all of the obtained indications of behavior. When very many associations emerge from this procedure it often helps to simplify them by means of further statistical techniques. The findings of trait research help to illuminate the organization or structure of personality and indicate what kinds of behaviors are most likely to occur together. The results help us to answer questions like these: Do aggressive children become aggressive adults? Are adolescent boys who are aggressive at home likely to be aggressive at school?

New Directions and Overview

Prototypes: "Typical" People

members in a group still have own defining features

In a new direction that may allow a fresh approach to traits, psychologists have also begun to identify how we judge the "prototypicality" or "typicality" of different members of a category. Take, for example, the category "birds." To demonstrate the idea of "typicality" to yourself, think of the most typical, representative, or "birdlike" bird. You probably will think of a bird that is something like a robin or sparrow—not a chicken or an ostrich. The point is simply that some members of a category (in this case, birds) are better or more typical examples of a category: Some reds are "redder" than others, some chairs are more chairlike than others. This point has been elegantly documented for everyday categories of natural objects like furniture (Rosch et al., 1976). Thus natural categories may be organized around *prototypical* examples (the best examples of the concept), with less prototypical or less good members forming a continuum away from the central one (Rosch, 1975; Tversky, 1977).

The important point here is that trait categories, like other categories, may be best thought of *not* as well-defined, distinct, nonoverlapping categories in which each member of a category has all its defining features. (While many birds sing, not all do, and some nonbirds surely do.) Well-defined, nonoverlapping categories are built into artificial, logical systems used in laboratory studies of concept learning, but they are rare in the real world. If we turn from the abstract world of logic and formal, artificial systems to common, everyday categories—to furniture, birds, and clothing—the categories become "fuzzy." As the philosopher Wittgenstein (1953) first pointed out, the members of common, everyday categories do not all share all of a set of single, essential features critical for category membership. If you closely examine a set of natural objects all labeled by one general term (like "birds") you will not find a single set of features that all members of the category share: Rather, a *pattern* of overlapping similarities—a *family resemblance* structure—seems to emerge.

Might "typicality" and "family resemblance" and "fuzziness" also characterize everyday judgments about categories of people? The answer seems to be that they do (Cantor & Mischel, 1979; Wiggins, 1980). When making these judgments while forming our everyday impressions of people we seem able to agree about who is a more or less typical or even "ideal" kind of personality, just as we agree that a robin is a more birdlike bird than a chicken. For instance, such qualities as "sociable" and "outgoing" are the characteristics of a "typical extravert," and judges agree easily about the patterns of features that make for differences in the degree to which someone is a "typical extravert." It is to be hoped that the study of prototypicality rules and family resemblance principles in judgments of people will help show how consistency and coherence are perceived in spite of variations in behavior. To illustrate, someone who really knows Rembrandt's work, who has seen dozens of his paintings, can easily identify whether a previously unseen painting is a real Rembrandt, an imitation, or a fake. The same processes that permit us to make such judgments (to extract a central distinctive gist or unity from a wide range of variations) must surely underlie how we identify personality coherence in the face of behavioral variability, and agree that someone is or is not a "real" introvert, or an anxious neurotic, or a sincere friendly person. While this "prototypicality" approach to traits is still too young to evaluate firmly, it appears to be promising. One of its encouraging features is that it seems highly compatible with sophisticated attempts to quantify the structure of interpersonal behavior (e.g., Wiggins, 1979, 1980).

Interaction of Traits and Situations *influence action*

In recent years trait theorists have increasingly recognized that an adequate approach to the study of traits must also deal seriously with how the qualities of the person and the situation influence each other—that is, their "interaction" (e.g., Bowers, 1973; Endler, 1973; Mischel, 1973a). To study such interaction one must examine the ways in which the manifestations of a person's traits depend on his or her psychological situation at the moment. For example, rather than exhibit anxiety everywhere, an individual may be anxious only under some set of relatively narrow circumstances, such as test-taking in math, but not under many other conditions (e.g., Endler, 1973). Moreover, this anxiety may be expressed in some ways (such as subjective feelings of fear and upset) but not in others (for example, there may be no physical changes, such as increased perspiration or heart rate). The implications of these specific interactions for contemporary trait theory are profound, as will become evident when the applications of trait approaches are discussed in Part II, and when we consider the topic of interaction in detail (Chapter 20).

Overview of the Trait Approach

To complete our introduction of the trait approach, it is helpful to summarize some of its main points, features, and emphases. So much has been done within the framework of this approach that it becomes easy to lose its essential, core characteristics. Table 2-3 summarizes these characteristics. It reminds you that the main aim of the trait approach was to provide methods to infer and quantify people's social-personal traits. These traits were assumed to be stable and broadly consistent dispositions that underlie a wide range of behaviors across a number of related situations.

To infer traits one relies heavily on questionnaires, ratings, and other reports about the subject's dispositions. The subject's reports are taken as direct signs of the relevant dispositions. For example, the more often and intensely you rate yourself as aggressive, the more you are assumed to have an aggressive disposition. The focus of research is on measurement: to develop quantitative ways of describing important individual differences and their patternings. Traditionally, the trait approach has recognized that behavior varies with changes in the situation, but has focused on individual differences in response to the same situation. More recently, theorists and researchers have begun to try to take systematic account of the situation, as later chapters discuss.

Trait approach

TABLE 2-3
SUMMARY OVERVIEW OF TRAIT APPROACH

Basic units:	Inferred trait dispositions.
Causes of behavior:	Generalized (consistent, stable) dispositions.
Favored data:	Test responses (e.g., on questionnaires).
Observed responses used as:	Direct signs (indicators) of dispositions.
Research focus:	Measurement (test construction), description of individual differences and their patterning.
Approach to personality change:	Not much concerned with change: Search for consistent, stable characteristics.
Role of situation:	Acknowledged but of secondary interest until recently.

SUMMARY

1. Since earliest times people have labeled and classified each other according to their psychological characteristics. *Typologies* classify people into discrete categories. Among others, Hippocrates, Sheldon, and Jung have proposed typologies of personality, but the very simplicity that makes these typologies appealing also limits their value. An individual personality cannot be fitted neatly into one category or another.

2. *Traits* are continuous dimensions on which individual differences may be arranged quantitatively in accord with the amount of an attribute that the individual has.

3. In everyday life people habitually use trait terms. They employ these terms not just to describe what people do but also to explain their behavior. We have not really explained anything, however, if after attributing a trait to a person on the basis of behavior, we later invoke that trait as the cause of the very behavior from which we inferred it.

4. Trait theorists conceptualize traits as underlying properties, qualities, or processes that exist in persons. Traits also are constructs to account for observed behavioral consistencies within persons and for the enduring and stable behavioral differences among them in their responses to similar stimuli (situations).

5. For Allport, traits are the ultimate realities of psychological organization. They are the mental structures that account for consistency in behavior. In his view, traits are predispositions to respond, and they serve to integrate what would otherwise be dissimilar stimuli and responses. Traits are relatively general and enduring, although they may range in generality from highly generalized *cardinal* through *central* to *secondary* traits or more specific "attitudes." An individual's "personality structure" is his or her pattern of dispositions or traits. Allport emphasized this structure, rather than the environment or stimulus conditions, in his analysis of human behavior. He stressed individual differences and the uniqueness of each person. Although he recognized some roughly common traits on which individuals can be compared, he urged the intensive study of the individual. He disapproved of many of the statistical methods and quantitative research strategies favored by other trait theorists.

6. Cattell distinguished between *surface* traits and *source* traits. Surface traits are identified by statistical correlations; source traits, by factor analysis. Through factor analysis Cattell tried to estimate the basic dimensions or factors underlying surface variations in behavior.

Extensions of trait theory have been provided by Eysenck, who emphasizes the dimensions of introversion–extraversion and emotional stability (neuroticism).

7. In spite of their many differences, most trait theorists share the following theoretical assumptions and strategies:

   a. Traits are assumed to be general underlying dispositions that account for consistencies in behavior.
   b. Some traits are considered to be relatively superficial and specific; others that are more basic and widely generalized are assumed to produce consistencies across many situations.
   c. The predominant objective is the identification of underlying broad dispositions. Emphasis is on the measurement of an individual's position on one or more dimensions by means of objective instruments or tests administered under standard conditions.
   d. People's tested or sampled behaviors (including what they say about themselves) are viewed as signs of their underlying traits.
   e. To search for basic traits a psychometric strategy is used which samples and compares large groups of subjects quantitatively under uniform conditions.

8. In a new approach to traits, the focus is finding typical (prototypical or best) examples of particular categories about people. One tries to identify the pattern of overlapping similarities, "the family resemblance," shared by typical members of the category. For example, a typical extravert is sociable and outgoing.

9. There is still disagreement about which traits are the basic units of personality, but the search continues. There is also increasing recognition that the qualities of the person interact with those of the situation(s) in which he or she functions.

CHAPTER 3

PSYCHODYNAMIC THEORIES: CONCEPTIONS

Freud 35
Jung p 45
Fromm 52
Erikson 53
Donners miller 54
other Neo-Freuds p 56

Sampling many subjects, measuring their answers objectively, and quantifying the results, are the characteristics of the psychometric search for personality traits. Other psychologists (like Allport) have felt for many years that emphasis on the quantitative study of large groups of people slights the qualitative, intense study of the individual. Rather than relying on numbers and tests to describe people in terms of discrete traits, many personality psychologists, beginning in the early 1930s, hoped to achieve better insights by another route. Perhaps by studying the whole individual in depth, guided by clinical intuition and by informal techniques like the interview, one could achieve generally valid insights into human nature and could generate useful statements about individuals. There have been several different formulations in this general movement, but the most influential force has been Sigmund Freud's psychodynamic theory and its variations.

Most trait psychologists tried to map the structure of personality by discovering the stable psychological dimensions on which people could be compared. They emphasized the relatively enduring qualities of personality and the conscious content of the mind, as revealed by direct self-report and introspection. A completely different approach was developed almost single-handedly by the Viennese physician, Sigmund Freud. During his lifetime (1856–1939) Freud invented psychoanalysis, reshaped the field of psychology, and influenced many later developments in all the social sciences and in Western concepts of human nature.

Working as a physician treating disturbed persons in Vienna at the turn of the century, Freud startled the neo-Victorian world by formulating a theory that upset many prevalent assumptions about human nature. Before Freud, a person's behavior was believed to be under his or her conscious and rational control. Freud upset that conception drastically. Rather than seeing consciousness as the core of the mind, Freud compared personality to an iceberg: Only the surface tips show themselves overtly. Rather than viewing man as a supremely rational being, he construed him as driven by impulses and striving to satisfy deep and lasting sexual and aggressive urgings. Rather than relying on people's reports about themselves as accurate self-representations, he interpreted verbalizations and overt behavior as highly indirect, disguised, symbolic representations of unconscious underlying forces.

In the course of more than forty years of active writing and clinical research Freud developed a theory of personality, a method of treatment for personality disturbances, and an extensive body of clinical observations based on his therapeutic experiences and his analyses of himself. The following sections summarize some of the main points of Freud's theoretical position. It should be evident that what follows is a summary of a theory, not of a collection of facts. The evaluation of that theory is a separate task, and one that is undertaken in the many later parts of this book that assess relevant research evidence.

Freud developed both his theory and his psychoanalytic treatment on the basis of extensive clinical observation of neurotic persons. It was with the problems of *hysteria* that Freud began his observations of the neurotic process. He noted certain *sensory anesthesias* (losses of sensory ability, as in blindness, deafness, or loss of feeling in a body part) and motor paralyses that seemed to have no neurological origin. He proposed that these symptoms express a way of defending against unacceptable unconscious wishes. For example, a soldier who cannot admit his fear of facing battle develops a motor paralysis without a neurological basis. The fundamental feature of hysteria, according to Freud, is the presence of massive repression and the development of a symptom pattern that indirectly or symbolically expresses the repressed needs and wishes. On the basis of careful clinical observations Freud gradually generated his theory of personality, continuously modifying his ideas in the light of his growing clinical experiences and insights.

Psychic Structure

According to Freud (1933) personality has a three-part structure: id, ego, and superego. Although the three parts interact intimately, each has its own characteristics.

The Id

pleasure

The *id* is the mental agency that contains everything inherited, especially the instincts. It is the basis of personality, the energy source for the whole system, and the foundation from which the ego and superego later develop. The id, according to Freud, is the innermost core of personality, and it is closely linked to biological processes.

Increases in energy from internal or external stimulation produce tension and discomfort that the id cannot tolerate. The id seeks immediate tension reduction, regardless of the consequences. This tendency toward immediate tension reduction is called the *pleasure principle,* and the id obeys it, seeking immediate satisfaction of instinctual wishes and impulses, regardless of reason or logic.

Freud (1940) believed the impulses of the id to be chiefly sexual and aggressive instincts. He classified these impulses or instincts into the categories of "life" or sexual instincts and "death" or aggressive instincts. The psychological representations of these instincts are wishes, and they often are irrational and unconscious.

To discharge tension the id forms an internal image or hallucination of the desired object. The hungry infant, for example, may conjure up an internal representation of the mother's breast. The resulting image is considered a wish fulfillment, similar to the attempted wish fulfillment that Freud believed characterized normal dreams and the hallucinations of psychotics. "Primary process thinking" was Freud's term for such direct, reality-ignoring attempts to satisfy needs irrationally. Because mental images by themselves cannot reduce tension, the ego develops.

The Ego   *tries to control the id*

tests reality

The *ego* is a direct outgrowth of the id. Freud described its origin this way:

> Under the influence of the real external world around us, one portion of the id has undergone a special development. From what was originally a cortical layer, equipped with the organs for receiving stimuli and with arrangements for acting as a protective shield against stimuli, a special organization has arisen which henceforward acts as an intermediary between the id and the external world. To this region of our mind we have given the name of *ego* (Freud, 1933, p. 2).

The ego is in direct contact with the external world. It is governed by considerations of safety, and its task is preservation of the organism. The ego wages its battle for survival against both the external world and the internal instinctual demands of the id. In this task it has to continuously differentiate

Id – mental agent inherited contents

between the mental representations of wish-fulfilling images and the actual outer world of reality. In its search for food or sexual release, for example, it must find the appropriate tension-reducing objects in the environment so that tension reduction can actually occur. That is, it must go from image to object, and get satisfaction for id impulses while simultaneously preserving itself.

The ego's function is governed by the *reality principle,* which requires it to test reality and to delay discharge of tension until the appropriate object and environmental conditions are found. The ego operates by means of a "secondary process" that involves realistic, logical thinking and planning through the use of the higher or cognitive mental processes. That is, while the id seeks immediate tension reduction by such primary process means as wish-fulfilling imagery and direct gratification of sexual and aggressive impulses, the ego, like an executive, mediates between the id and the world, testing reality and making decisions about various courses of available action. For example, it delays impulses for immediate sexual gratification until the environmental conditions are appropriate.

The Superego

Here is a glimpse of Freud's view of the development of the third mental structure, the superego:

> The long period of childhood, during which the growing human being lives in dependence on his parents, leaves behind it as a precipitate the formation in his ego of a special agency in which this parental influence is prolonged. It has received the name of *superego.* In so far as this superego is differentiated from the ego or is opposed to it, it constitutes a third power which the ego must take into account (Freud, 1933, p. 2).

Thus the *superego* is the agency that internalizes the parental influence. It represents the morals and standards of society that have become part of the internal world of the individual in the course of the development of his personality. The superego is the conscience, the judge of right and wrong, of good and bad, in accord with the internalized standards of the parents and thus, indirectly, of society. It represents the ideal. Whereas the id seeks pleasure and the ego tests reality, the superego seeks perfection. The superego, for Freud, involved the internalization of parental control in the form of self-control. For example, the individual with a well developed superego refrains from "bad" or "evil" temptations, such as stealing when hungry or killing when angry, even when there are no external constraints (in the form of police or other people) to stop him. The hypothesized mechanisms in this process, and the research relevant to it, are crucial for understanding personality development; they will be discussed in detail in later chapters.

Personality Dynamics

According to Freud (1915), the three parts of the psychic structure—id, ego, and superego—are always in conflict. The dynamics of personality involve a continuous interaction and clash between id impulses seeking release and inhibitions or restraining forces against them—an interplay between driving forces or urgings and constraining forces that inhibit them. These urges or impulses and counterforces propel or motivate personality.

Conflict

The quest for immediate satisfaction of impulses reflects human beings' hedonistic nature: People are motivated to avoid pain and to achieve immediate tension reduction. This drive for immediate satisfaction of instinctual demands leads to an early and enduring clash between the individual and the environment. Conflict develops to the degree that the environment and its representatives in the form of other persons, notably the parents in childhood, exercise controlling functions that punish or impede immediate impulse expression.

The person in time comes to incorporate the societal code by which he or she is raised, largely through a process of internalizing parental characteristics and morals. Thus in Freud's view perpetual warfare and conflict exist between humans and environment. Insofar as societal values become "internalized" as part of the person, this warfare is waged internally between the components of personality and it produces anxiety.

Anxiety

Freud (1933) distinguished three kinds of anxiety. In *neurotic anxiety* the person fears that his instincts will get out of control and cause him to behave in ways that will be punished. In *moral anxiety* the person feels conscience-stricken or guilty about unacceptable things that she feels she has done or even contemplates. Both neurotic and moral anxiety are derivatives of *reality anxiety*, the fear of real dangers in the external world.

The sequence of events in reality anxiety (or "objective anxiety") is simple: A danger exists in the external world, the person perceives it, and this perception evokes anxiety. This sequence may be summarized as:

external danger → perception of danger → reality anxiety

Anxiety is a state of painful tension and, as with other tensions, the organism seeks to reduce it. When anxiety cannot be handled effectively by realis-

In *neurotic anxiety* the person fears that his instincts will cause him to behave in ways that will be punished.

tic methods, the organism may resort to unrealistic *defenses*. Elaborate defenses are developed to avoid anxiety and to come to terms with the instinctual impulses seeking release as they conflict with the barriers of the external world and with internalized inhibitions. These defenses serve as disguises through which people hide their motives and conflicts from themselves as well as from others.

Mechanisms of Defense

denial defense

Psychodynamic theorists emphasize that when a threat becomes especially serious it may lead to intense and widespread inhibitions. In the psychodynamic view, such defensive inhibition is desperate and primitive. It is a massive, generalized inhibitory reaction rather than a specific response to the particular danger. This *denial* defense is called forth when the person can neither escape nor attack the threat. If the panic is sufficient, the only possible alternative may be to deny it. Outright denial may be possible for the young child, who is not yet upset by violating the demands of reality testing. When the child becomes cognitively too mature to deny objective facts in the interests of defense, denial becomes a less plausible alternative and he or she may resort to repression.

repression

In psychodynamic theory *repression* usually refers to a particular type of denial: "the forgetting, or ejection from consciousness, of memories of threat, and especially the ejection from awareness of impulses in oneself that might have objectionable consequences" (White, 1964, p. 214).

Repression was one of the initial concepts in Freud's theory and became one of its cornerstones. Material in the unconscious that is relatively inaccessible to conscious awareness is said to be in a state of repression. The ego may become aware that the expression of a particular instinctual demand would be dangerous, and the demand must therefore be suppressed, removed, made powerless. Repression is thus a defense mechanism of the ego.

Freud (1920) believed that the mechanisms of denial and repression were the most fundamental or primitive defenses and played a part in other defenses. Indeed he thought that other defenses started with a massive inhibition of an impulse, which was followed by various elaborations.

In *projection* the person's own unacceptable impulses are inhibited and the source of the anxiety is attributed to another person. For example, one's own temptations toward homosexuality are attributed to a friend. Projection presumably gives relief because it reduces neurotic or moral anxiety. In this way, the unacceptable impulse to be homosexual, in this example, can be expressed indirectly, under the guise of the person's defending against "queer" friends, while avoiding the anxiety that would be generated by admitting homosexual wishes.

Replacement in consciousness of an anxiety-producing impulse by its opposite is another defense; it is termed *reaction formation*. For example, people frightened by their own sexual impulses may become actively involved in a "ban the filth" vigilante group that vigorously censors books and movies it construes to be obscene. Through projection and reaction formation the id impulse is expressed, but in a disguise that makes it acceptable to the ego.

Another defense mechanism is *intellectualization* or the tendency to transform emotional conflicts into abstract, quasi-intellectual terms. One example is the rationalization of feelings by making excuses. Thus, a man who has unconscious, deeply hostile impulses toward his wife might invent elaborate excuses that serve to disrupt and even terminate their relations without admitting his true feelings. He might create many spurious reasons to stay away from home and persistently disappoint and hurt his wife. He might invoke "pressures at the office," "a hectic schedule," "worrying about inflation and politics," and "fatigue" as excuses for ignoring, avoiding, and frustrating his wife.

Sublimation, according to Freud, is an ego defense that is particularly significant in the development of culture. It consists of a displacement or redirection of impulses from an object (or target) that is sexual to one that is social in character. For example, if in the course of normal development masturbation becomes too threatening to the young child, he or she may sublimate (or transform) these impulses into a socially acceptable form, such as horseback riding and other athletic endeavors.

Psychic Energy

Thus the essence of Freudian personality dynamics is the transformation of motives: The basic impulses persist and press for discharge, but the objects at which they are directed and the manner in which they are expressed are transformed (1917). Freud thought that these transformations involved a finite amount of energy that was contained in the person. This energy or *libido* is "cathected" (attached) onto aspects of the internal and external environment. The energy available to the organism may be continuously transformed and cathected, or focused, onto different objects, but the total amount of energy is conserved and stable. Freud's energy system thus was consistent with the hydraulic models of nineteenth-century physics. The id was seen as a kind of dynamo, and the total psyche was viewed as a closed system motivated to maintain equilibrium: Any forces that were built up required discharge. The discharge could be indirect. Cathexes (the investments of instinctual impulses in objects) could be *displaced* from one object to another, for instance from one's parents to other authority figures or more remotely, from the genitals, for example, to phallic symbols.

Some of these transformations or displacements are schematized in Figure 3-1. For example, if sadistic aggressive impulses are too threatening to self-acceptance, they might be transformed into a more socially sanctioned form, such as an interest in surgery. Likewise, sexual wishes toward the mother might be displaced into a career of painting madonnas, as some Freudians

FIGURE 3-1
The Psychodynamic Transformation of Motives: Examples of Displacement in the Form of Sublimation

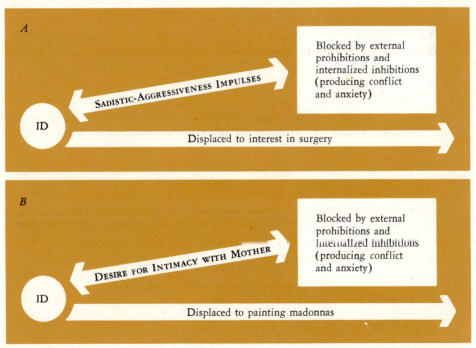

think happened among certain Renaissance painters. Freud (1909) himself suggested such dynamics in the case of Leonardo Da Vinci.

In sum, psychodynamics involve a continuous conflict between id impulses seeking discharge and defenses designed to transform these wishes into an acceptable form for the person. In the course of these transformations psychic energy is exchanged and cathected onto different objects.

Neurotic Anxiety and Signs of Conflict

Sometimes the defenses that disguise basic motives may become inadequate, as in pathological conditions, but even under the usual circumstances of everyday life the defenses are occasionally penetrated and the person betrays himself (Freud, 1960). Such betrayals of underlying motives are manifested most readily when defenses are relaxed, as in dream life during sleep or in jokes and slips of the tongue. The defense process involves distortion and displacement; private meanings develop as objects and events become symbols representing things quite different from themselves. It is believed that these meanings are partially revealed by behavioral "signs" or symptoms that may symbolize or indirectly represent disguised wishes and unconscious conflicts. For example, phobias such as the fear of snakes may reflect basic sexual conflicts; in this case, the feared snake has symbolic meaning.

It is now possible to consider the Freudian conception of how neurotic anxiety may develop. The sequence here (depicted in Figure 3-2) begins with the child's aggressive or sexual impulses that seek direct release. These expressions or efforts at discharge may be strongly punished and blocked by extreme external dangers or threats (e.g., intense parental punishment such as withdrawal of love) and hence lead to objective anxiety. The child may become especially afraid that these impulses will lead to loss of parental love, and in time, therefore, may come to fear his or her own impulses. Because this state is painful, the child tries to repress these impulses (or defend against them with other mechanisms). If the ego is weak, the repression is only partly successful and the instinctual impulses persist. Unless expressed in some accepta-

FIGURE 3-2
Sequence in Freudian Conception of Neurotic Anxiety

Internal Sexual and Aggressive Impulses	External Punishment and Danger	Objective Anxiety
Neurotic Anxiety	Emergence of Derivatives of Impulses	Partial Breakdown of Repression	Repression of Impulses

ble form, these impulses become increasingly "pent up," gradually building up to the point where they become hard to repress. Consequently there may be a partial breakdown of repression, and components or derivatives of the impulses may break through, producing some neurotic anxiety. Anxiety, in this view, functions as a danger signal warning the individual that repressed impulses are starting to break through the defenses. Rather than emerging directly, however, the person's unacceptable impulses or motives express themselves indirectly and symbolically in disguised or transformed ways.

Freud felt that the symbolic meaning of behavior was expressed most clearly in neurotic acts such as compulsions and obsessions. He cited the case of a girl who compulsively rinsed out her washbasin many times after washing. Freud thought that the significance of this ceremonial was expressed in the proverb, "Don't throw away dirty water until you have clean." He interpreted the girl's action as a warning to her sister, to whom she was very close, "not to separate from her unsatisfactory husband until she had established a relationship with a better man" (Freud, 1959, vol. 2, p. 28).

Another patient was able to sit only in a particular chair and could leave it only with much difficulty. In Freud's analysis of her problem, the chair symbolized the husband to whom she remained faithful. Freud saw the symbolic meaning of her compulsion in her sentence, "It is so hard to part from anything (chair or husband) in which one has once settled oneself" (Freud, 1959, vol. 2, p. 29). Thus the important object of conflict—the husband—was transformed into a trivial one—the chair. Freud cited these and many similar cases as evidence for the view that neurotic behaviors express unconscious motives

TABLE 3-1	
POSSIBLE MEANINGS OF SOME BEHAVIORAL SIGNS ACCORDING TO FREUDIAN THEORY	
Behavioral Sign	*Possible Underlying Meaning*
Fear of snakes	Sexual conflicts concerning genitals
Compulsive cleanliness	Reaction against anal impulses
Obsessive thought "My mother is drowning."	Imperfectly repressed hostility toward mother
Paranoid jealousy	Homosexual wishes
Preoccupation with money	Problems around toilet training
Crusading against obscenity	Reaction formation against own unacceptable wishes

and ideas symbolically and that the acts themselves have a defensive function in the dynamics of personality.

The clinician's task, then, is to decipher the unconscious meaning of the patient's behavior, and to discover the conflicts and dynamics that might underlie seemingly irrational behavior patterns. To illustrate, Table 3-1 shows some hypothesized equivalences between certain symptoms and psychodynamic states. Equivalences like these are hypothesized by skilled, psychoanalytically oriented clinicians, using methods like those discussed in Chapter 8.

The Origins of Neuroses   *Early Childhood*

In Freud's view, serious problems, such as the neuroses, and the roots of the symptoms that characterize them, begin in early childhood:

> . . . It seems that neuroses are acquired only in early childhood (up to the age of six), even though their symptoms may not make their appearance till much later. The childhood neurosis may become manifest for a short time or may even be overlooked. In every case the later neurotic illness links up with the prelude in childhood.
>
> . . . There is no difficulty in accounting for this aetiological preference for the first period of childhood. The neuroses are, as we know, disorders of the ego; and it is not to be wondered at if the ego, so long as it is feeble, immature and incapable of resistance, fails to deal with tasks which it could cope with later on with the utmost ease. In these circumstances instinctual demands from within, no less than excitations from the external world, operate as 'traumas', particularly if they are met halfway by certain innate dispositions (Freud, 1933, pp. 41–42).

Although, as these quotations indicate, neuroses were seen as the products of early childhood traumas plus innate dispositions, even the behavior of less disturbed persons was believed to reflect expressions of underlying unconscious motives and conflicts. These manifestations could be seen in the "psychopathology of everyday life"—the occurrence of meaningful but common unconscious expressions, as discussed next.

The Psychopathology of Everyday Life

Some of Freud's most fascinating—and controversial—ideas involved the elaboration of possible hidden meanings that might underlie such common occurrences as slips of the tongue, errors in writing, jokes, and dreams. In Freud's (1901, 1920) view, "mistakes" may be unconsciously motivated by impulses that the individual is reluctant to express directly or openly. To show that mistakes may really be motivated by underlying wishes, Freud pointed out many instances in which even the attempt to "correct" the error appears to betray a hidden, unacceptable meaning. In one case, for example, a dignitary introduced a general as "this battle-scared veteran" and tried to "correct" his

hidden meanings in everyday Talk

TABLE 3-2
EXAMPLES OF BEHAVIORAL MANIFESTATIONS
MOTIVATED BY UNCONSCIOUS WISHES

Manifestation	Latent (Unconscious) Wish	Transformation Involved
Slip of tongue: May I "insort" (instead of escort) you.	to insult	condensation: (insult + escort = "insort")
Slip of tongue: "Gentlemen, I declare a quorum present and herewith declare the session *closed*."	to close the meeting	association of opposites (open = closed)
Dream of disappointment in quality of theater tickets, as result of having gotten them too soon.	I married too soon; I could have gotten a better husband by waiting	symbolism (getting tickets too soon = marrying too soon)
Dream of breaking an arm	desire to break marriage vows	conversion into visual imagery (breaking vows = breaking an arm)

SOURCE: Freud (1920)

mistake by saying "bottle-scarred veteran." Examples of other seemingly innocuous manifestations, the latent (unconscious) wishes inferred to motivate them, and the underlying transformations, are summarized in Table 3-2.

Psychosexual Stages and Personality Development

Freud (1933) organized his theory of personality development around psychosexual stages. Body pleasure, Freud believed, is focused successively on different zones (mouth, anus, genitals) in the course of development. The oral, anal, and phallic stages unfold during the first five years of life. A quiet or repressive latency period of about five or six years follows these three stages. In adolescence the pregenital impulses are activated again at puberty. If they are successfully utilized, the individual reaches the mature or genital stage.

The pleasure derived from the oral, anal, and genital zones is related to one general source: the "libido" or energy of the sexual instincts. In each psychosexual stage the libido is focused on the pleasure-giving ("erogenous") zone that characterizes that stage and that provides unique potentialities for gratification or frustration. According to the theory, the person's experiences at each stage—oral, anal, phallic, and genital—leave a characteristic imprint that influences future development.

The special experiences (vicissitudes) encountered by sexual impulses at any of the early psychosexual stages, either in the form of overindulgence or deprivation, may produce "fixation." Fixation is an arrest in sexual impulses at an early stage of psychosexual development; it may lead to a character structure built around the unresolved difficulties of that period.

The Oral Stage

The dependent person is said to be fixated at the *oral stage,* which occurs at a time when the infant is totally dependent upon others for satisfaction of its needs. The oral stage characterizes the first year of life. According to Freud, it is divided into two periods: (1) sucking; (2) biting and chewing. Later character traits develop from these earliest modes of oral pleasure. More specifically, oral incorporation (as in sucking and taking in milk in the first oral period) becomes the prototype of such pleasures as those gained from the acquisition of knowledge or possessions. The gullible person (who is "easily taken in") is fixated at the oral, incorporative level of personality. The sarcastic, bitingly argumentative person is fixated at the second oral period—the sadistic level associated with biting and chewing.

The Anal Stage

During the *anal stage* (in the second year of life) toilet training is initiated, giving the child his or her first experience with imposed control of an instinctual impulse. The way in which this training is conducted affects later traits and values. Internal conflicts about withholding and retentiveness may arise in a person who has remained preoccupied with unresolved problems of the anal phase. The expressive character (cruel, destructive, tempestuous, and disorderly), according to the theory, results from fixation in the early anal phase, in which pleasure is localized in the expulsion of feces. This fixation may result from extreme repressive measures on the part of the mother (or other person) in toilet training. Pleasure is located in the retention of feces later in the anal phase. A person fixated at this level would show character traits of obstinacy and stinginess, precision and orderliness.

The Phallic Stage

Next the *phallic stage,* characterized by masturbatory stimulation and the observation of the anatomical distinction between the sexes, sets the scene for the "Oedipus complex." According to Freud, the Oedipus complex, though modified and repressed after the age of five, remains a vital force in later personality. Both boys and girls love their mother as the satisfier of their basic needs and resent their father as a rival for their mother's affections. In addition, the boy fears castration by the father as retribution for his incestuous desires for his mother and his death wish toward his father. Castration fear is reinforced by the child's conception of the female as a castrated male and often by direct threats of castration accompanying discouragement of the boy's masturbation. *Castration anxiety,* in the boy, results in the repression of his sexual desire for his mother and in hostility toward his father. Gradually, to reduce the anxiety of possible castration by the father, the boy tries to become like him or to "identify" with him.

Identification with the father in turn helps the boy gain some vicarious satisfaction of his sexual impulses toward his mother. In this last phase of the Oedipus complex of the male, the superego reaches its final development as the internalized standards of parents and society: The opposition to incest and aggression becomes part of the child's own value system.

In the female, penis envy, resulting from the discovery that she lacks the male organ, is the impetus for the exchange of her original love object—the mother—for a new object, the father. Unlike the boy's Oedipus complex, which is repressed through fear, the girl—having nothing to lose—persists in her sexual desire for her father. This desire does, naturally, undergo some modification because of realistic barriers.

A latency period, characterized by reduced overt sexuality, follows at the end of the phallic stage. Memories of infantile sexuality are repressed and socially forbidden sexual activity is forgotten.

The Genital Stage

The love objects of the pregenital period are essentially selfish or "narcissistic": That is, others are loved only because they provide additional forms of body pleasure to the child. Some of this narcissism eventually becomes channeled into genuine "object choices" or love relations, and the adolescent begins to love others for altruistic reasons. In the well-socialized adult the experiences of the oral, anal, and phallic stages have become fused and synthesized with genital impulses. This final phase of maturity is called the *genital stage,* and in it the individual is capable of genuine love and adult sexual satisfactions.

Fixation and Regression

The concepts of *fixation* and *regression* are closely connected with Freud's conceptualization of psychosexual stages of development. As previously noted, fixation means that a sexual impulse is arrested at an early stage. Regression is reversion to an earlier stage, the return of the libido to its former halting places in development. Fixation and regression are interdependent, for the stronger the fixations in the course of development, the more easily individuals regress to them when they meet later difficulties. Fixation is caused by too great an intensity of the inevitable conflict at each stage of psychosexual development. The excessive stress may be due to severe deprivation or to overindulgence of the libido at a particular stage, or to inconsistent alterations between indulgence and deprivation.

In sum, the psychodynamics of personality are intimately related to the individual's mode of coping with problems encountered at each stage of psychosexual development. The result is reflected in the nature of character formation symptoms, defense mechanisms, and relations with other people. When individuals' resolution of central problems at any stage of development is especially inadequate, later stress may cause them to regress to that earlier stage and to display behavior typical of that less mature period.

Freud's Theory of Identification

Many aspects of Freud's theory of psychosexual stages have been modified and even rejected in recent years. Some of his closely related concepts regarding identification, however, have continued to be influential.

Early personality development occurs in the setting of the family. In that context Freud strongly emphasized the child's attachment to the mother and the rivalry between son and father for her attentions (the *Oedipus situation*) as the early occasion for the expression, restraint, and conversion of impulses. But he also saw the relations between child and parent as the bases for identification with, or internalization of, the standards of the parent. This identification process Freud attributed to two mechanisms that operate during psychosexual development.

Anaclitic identification is based on the intense dependency of a child on his mother, beginning early in the course of the infant's development. Because of the helplessness of the infant, his dependency upon his caretaker is profound. Identification for girls is based mainly on this early love or dependency relation with the mother. In anaclitic identification the child must first have developed a dependent love relationship with his caretaker (usually the mother). Later, when the mother begins to withdraw some of her nurturant attention, the child tries to recapture her by imitating and reproducing her in actions and fantasy. The extensive research that has been devoted to this mechanism is discussed in later chapters.

For boys dependency or "anaclitic" identification with the mother is supplemented later by *identification with the aggressor*. The "aggressor" is the father during the Oedipal phase of development. Identification with the aggressor is motivated by fear of harm and castration by the punitive father in retribution for the son's fantasies and his libidinal wishes toward the mother. Freud described the situation vividly:

Carl Jung

. . . When a boy (from the age of two or three) has entered the phallic phase of his libidinal development, is feeling pleasurable sensations in his sexual organ and has learnt to procure these at will by manual stimulation, he becomes his mother's lover. He wishes to possess her physically in such ways as he has divined from his observations and intuitions about sexual life, and he tries to seduce her by showing her the male organ which he is proud to own. In a word, his early awakened masculinity seeks to take his father's place with her; his father has hitherto in any case been an envied model to the boy, owing to the physical strength he perceives in him and the authority with which he finds him clothed. His father now becomes a rival who stands in his way and whom he would like to get rid of (Freud, 1933, p. 46).

The hostile feelings that the boy experiences in the Oedipal situation engender great anxiety in him; he desires the mother but fears castration from the father. To defend against the resulting anxiety he resolves the Oedipal dilemma, repressing his aggressive wishes against his father and trying to become more like him. It is as though the boy believes that if he "is" the father he cannot be hurt by him. Identification with the aggressor requires that the boy have a strong (but ambivalent) relation with the father, in which his love for him is mixed with hostility because the father possesses the mother and interferes with the son's libidinal urges. Freud thought that, as a result of this additional process of identification with the aggressor, boys develop a stricter superego.

Neo-Freudian Psychoanalytic Developments

In the years since Freud, a number of psychoanalytic theorists have proposed modifications in Freud's original theory. Most of these positions rest on humanistic conceptions of people forged out of theorists' personal experiences with patients in psychotherapy and presenting their own conception of human nature. Many of these writings have helped to elaborate psychoanalytic concepts and to extend them in new directions.

Carl Jung   Carl Jung, an admirer and onetime associate of Freud, broke with his colleague and developed his own theory of psychoanalysis and his own method of psychotherapy. His approach became known as _analytical psychology_. Although it retains Freud's unconscious processes, it posits a _collective unconscious_—a transpersonal, inherited foundation of personality. The contents of the collective unconscious are _archetypes_ or "primordial images." Unlike the personal unconscious, whose contents were once conscious but have been forgotten or repressed, the contents of the collective unconscious have never been in consciousness and therefore are not individually acquired; they owe their existence exclusively to heredity. Examples of archetypes (primordial images) include God, the young potent hero, the wise old man, rebirth (resurrection), the Earth Mother, the Fairy Godmother, the hostile brethren, to list a few from a long collection found popularly in human legends and literature.

In Jung's view, the psyche included not only a conscious side but also a covert or *shadow* aspect that is unconscious. The process of personal growth involves an unfolding of this shadow and its gradual integration with the rest of the personality into a meaningful, coherent life pattern. The unconscious of every female includes a masculine, assertive element (the *animus*), the unconscious of every male includes a feminine, passive element (the *anima*). To be constructively masculine or feminine, individuals of each sex must recognize and integrate these opposite sex elements within themselves.

Jung described four basic ways of experiencing (contacting) the world: *sensing, intuition, feeling,* and *thinking,* summarized in Table 3-3. According to Jung, people differ consistently in the degree to which they emphasize each way of experiencing. One person, for example, might typically prefer intuitive leaps with little abstract thought, while another might know the world mostly through his or her senses with little use of either intuition or reason. In addition, recall that Jung was the one who had suggested a polarity of *extraversion-introversion* (as noted in the previous chapter). Like the four ways of experiencing, these two attitudes of extraversion-introversion are divided so that one is dominant in the conscious life while the other influences the unconscious side of the personality.

Jung broadened the concept of psychic energy. He did not exclude the sexual instinct of Freudian theory but thought it was only one among many instincts. Jung placed great emphasis on the directed aim or purposiveness of

---

TABLE 3-3
JUNG'S FOUR WAYS OF EXPERIENCING THE WORLD

Ways of Experiencing	Characteristics
Sensing	Knowing through sensory systems
Intuition	Quick guessing about what underlies sensory inputs
Feeling	Focus on the emotional aspects of experience—its beauty or ugliness, pleasantness or unpleasantness
Thinking	Abstract thought, reasoning

TABLE 3-4
**EXAMPLES OF UNCONSCIOUS SYMBOLIC MEANINGS BELIEVED
TO UNDERLIE ABNORMAL BEHAVIOR ("SYMPTOMS")
ACCORDING TO JUNG**

Behavior	Underlying Meaning
Asthma attack	"She can't breathe the atmosphere at home"
Vomiting	"He can't digest—(some unpleasant fact)"
Spasm and inability to swallow	"He can't swallow it"
Leg paralysis	"She can't go on any longer"

SOURCE: Jung (1964)

personality development. He believed that goal-directed behavior cannot be given an exclusively causal or historical explanation. For Jung the meaning of behavior may become fully intelligible only in terms of its end-products or final effects; we need to understand humans not only in terms of their past but also in the light of their purposes and goal strivings.

Jung, like Freud, emphasized symbolic meanings. He believed, for example, that "abnormal behaviors" are expressions of the unconscious mind; some examples of these expressions are shown in Table 3-4, and they reveal clear overlap with Freud's thinking. Also like Freud, Jung thought that abnormal behaviors were merely one way in which the contents of the unconscious may reveal themselves. More often, he felt, they are expressed in dreams.

Jung went beyond Freud, however, in his increasing fascination with dreams as unconscious expressions of great interest in their own right. (He believed that this contrasts with their use merely as starting points for saying whatever comes to mind, i.e., "free associations," discussed in Chapter 8.) As Jung put it: ". . . I came increasingly to disagree with free association as Freud first employed it; I wanted to keep as close as possible to the dream itself, and to exclude all the irrelevant ideas and associations that it might evoke" (Jung, 1964, p. 28).

In the same direction, Jung became intrigued by the unconscious for its own sake. He viewed the unconscious not just as the source of instincts but as a vital, rich part of everyone's life, more significant than the conscious world, full of symbols communicated through dreams. The focus of Jungian psychology became the study of people's relation to their unconscious; its method taught individuals to become increasingly receptive to their own dreams, and to let their unconscious serve as a guide for how to live.

@ Jung not only past but purpose & goal striving

FIGURE 3-3
A Mandala

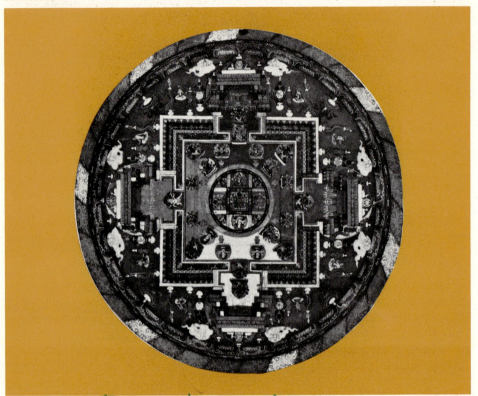

Jung = self striving for wholeness

Jung's conception of personality is complex, more a set of observations than a coherent theory. His observations often dwelled on the multiple, contradictory forces in life: "I see in all that happens the play of opposites" (1963, p. 235). Yet he also was one of the first to conceptualize a *self* that actively strives for oneness and unity. Jung saw the self (the striving for wholeness) as an archetype that is expressed in many ways. The expressions of the striving for wholeness include the *mandala* (a magic circle archetype shown in Figure 3-3), and various religious and transcendental experiences. He devoted much of his life to the study of these expressions in primitive societies, alchemy, mythology, dreams, and symbols. To achieve unity and wholeness the individual must become increasingly aware of the wisdom available in his or her personal and collective unconscious and must learn to live in harmony with it.

Erich Fromm

Fromm's (1941, 1947) psychology represents an expansion of fundamental Freudian concepts to the individual as a member of society. Freud saw person-

people understood in relation to others

ality development as a reaction to satisfactions and frustrations of physiological drives. In contrast, for Fromm people are primarily social beings to be understood in terms of their relations to others. According to Fromm, individual psychology is fundamentally social psychology. In addition to the biological factors, people have psychological qualities, such as tendencies to grow, develop, and realize potentialities, that result in a desire for freedom and a striving for justice and truth. Thus human nature has a force of its own that influences the evolution of the social processes.

Fromm criticizes Freud

The difference between Freud's biological orientation and Fromm's social orientation is illustrated by Fromm's explanation of character traits. Fromm criticized Freud's idea that fixation of libido at certain erogenous (pleasure-giving) zones is the cause of later character traits. According to Fromm, character traits develop from experiences with others. Psychosexual problems and attitudes are rooted in the whole of the character structure. They are expressions in the language of the body of an attitude toward the world that is essentially socially conditioned. According to Freud, cultural phenomena are the result of societal suppressions of instinctual drives. For Fromm, ideologies and culture in general are based on the social character, which is molded by the mode of existence of a given society. In turn, the dominant character traits become productive forces shaping the social process.

Another major point of departure from Freud is Fromm's belief that ideals like truth, justice, and freedom can be genuine strivings and not simply rationalizations of baser motives. Freud's psychology is a psychology of instinctual drives that defines pleasure in terms of tension reduction. Fromm's psychology tries to make a place for positive attributes, such as tenderness and the human ability to love, and implies that these human needs have a force of their own. He believes that character is not the result of passive adaptation to social conditions but of a dynamic adaptation on the basis of elements that are either biologically inherent in human nature or have become inherent as the result of historic evolution.

development life process

Erik Erikson

ego identity central — dev process thro-out life

[psychosocial stages]

The psychoanalyst Erik Erikson (1963) has proposed stages of development that call attention to problems of social adaptation (Table 3-5). As children grow up they face a wider range of human relationships. The solution of the specific problems at each of eight *psychosocial* stages (rather than psychosexual stages) determines how adequate they will become as adults. Erikson's focus on psychosocial development reflects the growing neo-Freudian emphasis on broad social and cultural forces, rather than instinctual drives alone.

At each stage of development Erikson hypothesizes a psychosocial "crisis" that arises from the person's efforts to solve the problems at that stage. For example, in the first stage of life (the "oral sensory" stage of the first year) the crisis involves "trust versus mistrust." Erikson hypothesizes that at this stage the child's relation to its mother forms basic attitudes about "getting" and

TABLE 3-5
ERIKSON'S STAGES OF PSYCHOSOCIAL DEVELOPMENT

Stage and Age	Psychosocial Crisis	Optimal Outcome
I. Oral-sensory (1st year of life)	Trust vs. Mistrust	Basic trust and optimism
II. Muscular-anal (2nd year)	Autonomy vs. Shame, doubt	Sense of control over oneself and the environment
III. Locomotor-genital (3rd through 5th year)	Initiative vs. Guilt	Goal-directedness and purpose
IV. Latency (6th year to start of puberty)	Industry vs. Inferiority	Competence
V. Puberty and Adolescence	Identity vs. Role Confusion	Reintegration of past with present and future goals, fidelity
VI. Early Adulthood	Intimacy vs. Isolation	Commitment, sharing, closeness and love
VII. Young and Middle Adult	Generativity vs. Self-absorption	Production and concern with the world and future generations
VIII. Mature Adult	Integrity vs. Despair	Perspective, satisfaction with one's past life, wisdom

SOURCE: Based on Erikson (1963) and modified from original.

"giving." If the crisis is properly resolved, the experiences at this stage lay the foundation for later trust, drive, and hope.

A notable innovation of Erikson's stages is that they extend beyond infancy to include crises of adolescence and adulthood. He sees development as a process that extends throughout life, rather than being entirely determined in the early years. In this developmental process, "ego identity" is the central point of organization.

The integration . . . of ego identity is . . . more than the sum of the childhood identifications. It is the accrued experience of the ego's ability to integrate all identifications with the vicissitudes of the libido, with the

Erikson's stages go much beyond childhood and include the psychosocial crises of the adult.

aptitudes developed out of endowment, and with the opportunities offered in social roles (Erikson, 1963, p. 261).

The underlying assumptions of his view of development are:

(1) that the human personality in principle develops according to steps predetermined in the growing person's readiness to be driven toward, to be aware of, and to interact with, a widening social radius; and (2) that society, in principle, tends to be so constituted as to meet and invite this succession of potentialities for interaction and attempts to safeguard and to encourage the proper rate and the proper sequence of their enfolding (Erikson, 1963, p. 270).

Erikson's ideas have become popular in many parts of our culture, and his thoughts concerning the "identity crisis" of adolescence are discussed widely. Indeed the phrase "identity crisis" has become a part of common parlance. Both provocative and literate, most of Erikson's ideas have had more impact on broad concepts of human nature and on the general intellectual culture than on specific scientific formulations. Erikson believes that all young people must generate for themselves some "central perspective and direction" that gives them a meaningful sense of unity and purpose, and that integrates the remnants of their childhood with the expectations and hopes of adulthood

(Erikson, 1968). This sense of identity involves a synthesis of how individuals have come to see themselves and their awareness of what the important other people in their lives expect them to be.

Other Neo-Freudian Analysts

In many ways the formulations of Fromm and Erikson are representative of the contributions of numerous other "neo-Freudians," such as Alfred Adler, Harry Stack Sullivan, Karen Horney, and David Rapaport. Generally these neo-Freudians advocate more concern with "ego-processes" and "reality testing" and less attention to the role of instincts, libidinal energy, and distinct psychosexual developmental stages.

For Freud the id and the instincts were the dominant aspects of the total personality. The ego was subservient to the id's instinctual wishes, even in healthy personalities. More recent theorists identified with the psychoanalytic tradition have put more emphasis on social variables shaping personality and have emphasized less the role of instincts and genetically determined maturation. These neo-Freudians or "ego psychologists" assert a "conflict-free sphere" of the ego (Hartmann, Kris, & Loewenstein, 1947; Rapaport, 1951). In their view, the ego has its own sources of energy and follows a course of development independent of the id and the instincts. That is, some portion of ego functioning is not determined by the attempt to avoid conflict between the id and the demands of society.

One of these neo-Freudians, Harry Stack Sullivan, most explicitly emphasizes the crucial importance of interpersonal processes and the human relations for the development of personality. He conceptualizes psychiatry as a form of *social* psychology. For Sullivan the individual can be understood only in his relations to the significant people in his life. A somewhat similar emphasis characterizes the writings of Alfred Adler, who focuses on the person's total "life style" and his "social interest," thus also viewing man as a social being. These theorists, just like Jung, Fromm, and Erikson, have influenced general views about man and personality and broad attitudes toward psychotherapy; they have not generated specific testable hypotheses for research. Most of them are or were practicing psychotherapists and humanistic writers rather than experimental researchers and scientists. Their contribution, therefore, may prove to have more impact on the history of ideas than on the field of psychology as a formal area of science.

The Behavioral Approach to Psychodynamics: Dollard and Miller

In another important direction, some American psychologists committed to the scientific, experimental study of behavior were also heavily influenced by Freud and developed his ideas in new ways. While they were intrigued by the insights of Freud and his followers, these behaviorally oriented psychologists were primarily dedicated to the scientific, rigorous study of psychology. They devoted themselves to the development of an experimental methodology through which precise and reliable research might be possible. Heavily influenced by strategies in other natural sciences, early workers in this field began with careful study of lower animals in highly controlled laboratory situations. While some were fascinated by Freud's bold speculations about the mind, most were skeptical about his informal clinical methods. Rather than probe the dreams and free associations of neurotic patients or theorize broadly about human nature and society, these researchers sought a system that would be objectively testable, preferably by laboratory techniques.

Psychologists in this tradition focused on the basic processes of learning through which an organism in interaction with its environment acquires and performs a repertoire of responses. They studied the learning mechanisms through which certain events—"stimuli"—become associated with particular behaviors or responses. Like all scientific theorists, their objective was to understand causes—in this case, learning or the ways in which stimuli become associated with responses.

In this section we will concentrate on the theory developed in the late 1940s by John Dollard and Neal Miller at Yale University. We will call their orientation "psychodynamic behavior theory" because it is the major effort to integrate some of the fundamental ideas of Freudian psychodynamic theory with the concepts, language, and methods of experimental laboratory research on behavior and learning.

Primary Needs and Learning

The newborn infant begins life with a set of *innate* or *primary* biological needs, such as the need for food and water, oxygen, and warmth. Satisfaction of these needs to some minimal degree is essential for the organism's survival. But although these needs are innate, the behaviors required to satisfy them involve learning.

For example, sucking is an innate response that is readily elicited in the newborn when a nipple stimulates its mouth. But although the sucking response itself may be innate, its efficiency increases with practice. Thus even the seemingly elementary response patterns required to satisfy primary needs depend on learning processes for their efficient execution. The most casual observation of other cultures quickly reveals that there are almost endless ways to fulfill even such primary needs as hunger and thirst. Through learning great variability develops in the ways in which needs are fulfilled. Consider, for example, food preferences: The gourmet dishes of one culture may be the causes of nausea in another. The same learned variability seen in food preferences is also found in standards of shelter, clothing, aesthetics, and values when one compares different cultures.

Most human behaviors involve goals and incentives whose relations to innate needs are extremely remote. People seem to strive for such exceedingly diverse goals as money, status, power, love, charity, competence, mastery, creativity, self-realization, and so on. These and many more strivings have been characterized and classified as human motives. Neal Miller and John Dollard have deeply explored the learning processes through which such motives may evolve from primary needs.

Starting with the basic assumption that behavior is learned, Dollard and Miller (1950) have constructed a learning theory to explain the wide range of behavior involved in normal personality, neurosis, and psychotherapy. In their view, the four important factors in the learning process are drive (motivation), cue (stimulus), response (act or thought), and reinforcement (reward). In its simplest form, their idea is that

in order to learn one must want something, notice something, do something, and get something (Miller & Dollard, 1941, p. 2).

These four events correspond respectively to "drive," "cue," "response," and "reward." Learning, in their view, is the process through which a particular response and a cue stimulus become connected.

Think of an animal in the psychologist's laboratory. Motivated by the *drive* of hunger, the animal engages in diffuse activity. At one point he happens to see a lever (*cue*). His *response*, at first accidental, is to press the lever, and this action releases food into his cup. The animal eats the food at once, thereby reducing the tension of his hunger drive (*reward or reinforcement*). Now in the future when he is hungry, he is more likely to press the lever again: The association between the cue stimulus (the lever) and the response (pressing it) has been strengthened. On subsequent trials the hungry animal will press the lever sooner. Let us consider each of the four components of learning separately.

Drive   *hunger sex etc*

According to Dollard and Miller (1950), any strong stimuli (internal or external) may impel action and thus serve as drives. The stronger the stimulus the greater its drive function. A mild stimulus (such as the faint sound of a distant horn) does not motivate behavior as much as a strong stimulus (the blare of the horn near one's ear). Examples of strong stimuli are hunger pangs and pain-inducing noise—they motivate behavior. While any stimulus may become strong enough to act as a drive, certain classes of stimuli (such as hunger, thirst, fatigue, pain, and sex) are the primary basis for most motivation. These stimuli are "primary" or innate drives. The strength of the primary drives varies with the conditions of deprivation: The greater the deprivation, the stronger the drive.

Often the operation of primary drives is not easy to observe directly. Society generally protects its members from the unpleasant force of strong primary drives by providing for their reduction before they become overwhelming. In instances when this is not true—for example, conditions of prolonged famine in India—psychologists usually are not present to study behavior systematically. Moreover, social inhibitions—for example, in the area of sex—may further prevent the direct or complete public expression of primary drives. Consequently, much visible behavior is motivated by already altered "secondary" or learned drives. It is these transformed motives that are most evident under conditions of modern society and that are important in civilized human behavior.

According to Dollard and Miller, these learned drives are acquired on the basis of the primary (unlearned, innate) drives and are elaborations of them. The acquisition of fear as a learned drive has been studied carefully. (Some of the specific mechanisms of such learning are discussed in detail in the next chapter.) A fear is learned if it occurs in response to previously neutral cues (e.g., a white room). A learned fear is also a drive in the sense that it motivates behavior (e.g., escape from the room) and its reduction is reinforcing.

In one study, rats were exposed to electric shock in a white compartment and were permitted to escape to a black compartment where there was no shock (Miller, 1948). Eventually the rats responded with fear to the white compartment alone (that is, without shock). Even when the shock (primary drive stimulus) was no longer present, the animals learned new responses, such as pressing a lever or turning a wheel, in order to escape from the harmless white compartment. In common sense terms, they behaved as if they were afraid of an objectively harmless stimulus. The motivation for this new learning lies, according to Miller and Dollard, in the reduction of the learned fear of the white compartment. Thus fear is conceptualized as both a learned response and a learned drive, and its reduction is considered to be a reinforcement.

Dollard and Miller's emphasis on drives, both "primary" and "secondary," is reminiscent of the Freudian emphasis on motives and impulses as the forces underlying behavior. While Freud's conceptualization stresses instinctual wishes, however, Dollard and Miller's makes room for many learned motives, whose roots are in primary drives.

Cue

"The drive impels a person to respond. Cues determine when he will respond, where he will respond and which response he will make" (Dollard & Miller, 1950, p. 32). The lunch bell, for example, functions as a cue for hungry schoolchildren to put away their books and get their lunchboxes. Cues may be auditory, visual, olfactory, and so on. They may vary in intensity, and various combinations of stimuli may function as cues. Changes, differences, and the direction and size of differences may be more distinctive cues than is an isolated stimulus. For example, a person may not know the absolute length of an unmarked line but yet be able to tell which of two lines is the longer.

In Dollard and Miller's formulation a very intense stimulus may become a drive. A stimulus thus may serve as both a drive and a cue, motivating behavior and directing it as well.

Response

Before a response to a cue can be rewarded and learned, it must of course occur. Dollard and Miller suggest ranking the organism's responses according to their probability of occurrence. They call this order the "initial hierarchy." Learning changes the order of responses in the hierarchy. An initially weak response, if properly rewarded, may come to occupy the dominant position. The new hierarchy produced by learning is termed the "resultant hierarchy." With learning and development, the hierarchy of responses becomes linked to language, and it is heavily influenced by the culture in which social learning has occurred.

Reinforcement

A reinforcement is a specific event that strengthens the tendency for a response to be repeated. A reduction in the strength of a drive reinforces any immediately preceding response. In other words, drive reduction serves as a reinforcement (or reward). This is true for both primary and secondary, or acquired, drives. The reduction or avoidance of painful stimulation, and of learned fears or anxieties associated with pain and punishment, also may function as a reinforcement. We saw earlier that rats seemed to work hard to escape from the white, fear-inducing compartment (Miller, 1948).

Miller and Dollard's concept of reinforcement as drive reducing or tension reducing has some similarity to Freud's "pleasure principle." Both concepts view need states as states of high tension and construe the reduction of tension, and the attainment of equilibrium, as the organism's goals.

Reinforcement is essential to the maintenance of a habit as well as to its learning. *Extinction* is the gradual elimination of a tendency to perform a response; it occurs when that response is repeated without reinforcement. The time required to extinguish a habit depends on the habit's initial strength and on the conditions of the extinction situation. Conditions of weak drive, effortful responses, short time between extinction trials, and strong alternative responses influence extinction.

According to Dollard and Miller, extinction merely inhibits the old habit; it does not destroy it. If new responses performed during extinction are rewarded, they may be strengthened to the point where they supersede the old habit. For example, if a child is praised and rewarded for independent, autonomous play but consistently nonrewarded (extinguished) when he or she dependently seeks help, the independent pattern will become predominant over the dependent one.

More recently Miller (1963) has speculated about possible alternatives to his drive-reduction concept of reinforcement learning. His hypothesis of an alternative to drive reduction includes the tentative assumption of "activating" or "go" mechanisms in the brain. These "go" mechanisms, Miller conjectured, could be activated in a variety of ways (such as by thinking), not merely by the reduction of drives or noxious stimulation.

Conflict

Individuals may experience conflict when they want to pursue two or more goals that are mutually exclusive. For example, a person may want to spend the evening with a friend but thinks he should prepare for an examination facing him the next morning; or she may want to express her anger at her parents but also does not want to hurt them. When an individual must choose among incompatible alternatives, he or she may undergo conflict.

Neal Miller's (1959) conceptualization of conflict, which is influenced by Lewin (1935), hypothesizes *approach* and *avoidance* tendencies. For example, in an "approach-approach" conflict the person is torn, at least momentarily, between two desirable goals. Conversely, people often face "avoidance-avoidance" conflicts between two undesirable alternatives: to study tediously for a dull subject or flunk the examination, for example. The individual may wish to avoid both of these aversive events, but each time he starts to move away from his desk he reminds himself how awful it would be to fail the test.

Some of the most difficult conflicts involve goals or incentives that are both positive and negative in valence. These are the goals toward which we have "mixed feelings" or ambivalent attitudes. For example, we may want the pleasure of a gourmet treat but not the calories, or we may desire the fun of a vacation spree but not the expense, or we may love certain aspects of a parent but hate others.

Recall that approach-avoidance conflicts had a predominant place in Freud's hypotheses regarding intrapsychic clashes—for example, between id impulses and inhibitory anxieties. Just as conflict is central to Freud's conception of personality dynamics, so it is the core of Dollard and Miller's theory. But whereas Freud developed his ideas about conflict from inferences regarding id-ego-superego clashes in his neurotic patients, Dollard and Miller tested their ideas in careful experiments with rats.

Miller's original theory of conflict was based on a number of animal experiments (e.g., Brown, 1942, 1948; Miller, 1959). In one study, for example, hungry rats learned how to run down an alley to get food at a distinctive point in the maze. To generate "ambivalence" (approach-avoidance tendencies), the rats were given a quick electric shock while they were eating. To test the resulting conflict, the rats were later placed again at the start of the alley. The hungry rat now started toward the food but halted and hesitated before reaching it. The distance from the food at which he stopped could be changed by manipulating either the amount of his hunger or the strength of the electric shock.

Dollard and Miller applied the concept of *goal gradients* to analyze conflict. Goal gradients are changes in response strength as a function of distance from the goal object. To assess the strength of approach and avoidance tend-

FIGURE 3-4
Approach and Avoidance Gradients

Adapted from Brown (1948).

encies at different points from the goal, a harness apparatus was devised to measure a rat's pull toward a positive reinforcement (food) or away from a negative reinforcement (shock).

The light harness enabled the experimenter to restrain the rat for a moment along the route to the goal and measure (in grams) the strength of the animal's pull on the harness at each test point (Brown, 1948). The rats pulled harder when they were restrained nearer the goal than when they were restrained farther away from it. This finding is evidenced by the slope of the approach gradient (shown in Figure 3-4) connecting the near test point and the far test point.

Similar procedures were used with rats who received an electric shock at the end of the alley. When these animals were later placed at the same point in the alley where they had been shocked before (but now with no shock), they ran away from the spot. Moreover, the nearer the rats were to that spot when tested in the restraining harness, the harder they generally pulled to get away (Figure 3-4). The steeper slope of the avoidance gradient (when compared to the approach gradient) is especially noteworthy.

On the basis of these and similar studies, Dollard and Miller conceptualized conflict in learning terms, according to the following principles:

1. The tendency to approach a goal (the gradient of approach) becomes stronger the nearer the individual is to the goal.
2. The tendency to avoid a negative stimulus (the gradient of avoidance) becomes stronger the nearer the individual is to the stimulus.
3. The gradient of avoidance is steeper than the gradient of approach. (That is, the strength of the avoidance tendency increases more quickly with nearness than does the tendency to approach.)

4. An increase in the drive associated with either approach or avoidance raises the general level of that gradient.

In sum, the drive-conflict model posits the simultaneous existence of drive-like forces (approach tendencies) and of inhibitory forces (avoidance tendencies). Predictions about behavior in an approach-avoidance conflict involve inferences about the strength of the approach tendencies and of the inhibiting forces, the resulting behavior being a function of their net effect. Within this general framework of drive-conflict theory, many formulations have been advanced that are similar to the intrapsychic conflicts between id impulses and ego defenses that are crucial in Freud's theory.

Neurotic Conflict

Conflict & Anxiety like for Freud

Like Freud, Dollard and Miller conceptualize conflict and anxiety as the core ingredients of neurotic behavior. In Freud's formulation, neurotic conflict involves a clash between id impulses seeking expression and internalized inhibitions that censor and restrain the expression of those impulses in accord with the culture's taboos. Dollard and Miller state the same basic ideas in the language of learning theory.

In Dollard and Miller's view of neurosis, strong fear (anxiety) is a learned drive that motivates a conflict concerning "goal responses" for other strong drives, such as sex or aggression. Specifically, when the neurotic person begins to approach goals that might reduce such drives as sex or aggression, strong fear is elicited in him or her. Such fear may be elicited by thoughts relevant to the drive goals, as well as by any overt approach attempts. For example, sexual wishes or hostile feelings toward a parent may be frightening; hence a conflict ensues between the wishes and the fear triggered by their expression. These inhibitory fearful responses further prevent drive reduction, so that the blocked drives (such as sex and aggression) continue to "build up" to a higher level. The person is thus trapped in an unbearable conflict between frustrated, pent-up drives and the fear connected with approach responses relevant to their release.

anxiety learned

The neurotic person in this dilemma may be stimulated simultaneously by the frustrated drives and by the fear that they evoke. The high drive state connected with this conflict produces "misery" and interferes with clear thinking, discrimination, and effective problem solving. The "symptoms" shown by the neurotic arise from the build up of the drives and of the fear that inhibits their release.

Like Freud unconscious factors

Anxiety and Repression

Like Freud, Dollard and Miller accept unconscious factors as critically important determinants of behavior, and, again like Freud, they give anxiety (or learned fear) a central place in dynamics. In their view, repression involves the learned response of *not-thinking* of something and it is motivated by the secondary drive of fear. That is, due to past experiences certain thoughts may have come to arouse fear as a result of their associations with pain or punishment. By not thinking these thoughts, the fear stimuli are reduced and the response (of not-thinking) is further reinforced. Eventually "not-thinking" (inhibiting, stopping, repressing) becomes anticipatory, in the sense that the individual avoids particular thoughts before they can lead to painful outcomes. This formulation is similar to Freud's idea that repression is the result of anxiety and functions to reduce the anxiety caused when unacceptable material starts to emerge from the unconscious to the conscious.

Dollard and Miller's account thus serves as a clear translation of the psychodynamic formulation of anxiety, repression, and defense into the terms of reinforcement learning theory. Defenses and symptoms (e.g., phobias, hysterical blindness) are reinforced by the immediate reduction of the fear drive. While the temporary effect of the symptom is drive reduction and momentary relief, its long-range effects may be debilitating. For example, a phobic symptom may prevent a person from working effectively and hence create new dilemmas, fear, guilt, and other conditions of high drive conflict.

Overview and Implications

It is not simple—and probably impossible—to capture the essence of the Freudian approach and its derivatives so that their main implications for current personality psychology can be understood. However, the risk of oversimplification should not deter us from seeking a broader perspective. The following sections dwell on some especially noteworthy points, without attempting to be complete.

Motivational Determinism

Freudian psychoanalytic theory offers a motivationally determined view of behavior. The causal chain can be complex and indirect, with the events in one area or system of the personality exerting their effects on another, but every behavior, no matter how subtle or trivial, has its ultimate motivational cause within the person's dynamics. Suppose, for example, a man fights with his wife about money, is personally immaculate and fussy about his appearance, and becomes very upset when he loses his umbrella. These seemingly different bits of behavior might actually be motivated by a common core: Unravel the dynamics and the causes will become apparent. Much of the process of psychoanalytic assessment and therapy is a search for such underlying causes. A psychodynamic explanation of behavior consists of a delineation of the motives that produced it. The focus is not on behavior but on the motivational roots that it presumably serves and reflects.

unconscious motives most important

Freudians tend to equate the deterministic nature of events with *motivational* determinism. They believe that all behavior, even the seemingly most absurd or trivial (like losing an umbrella), is motivated and functionally significant for the organism's adaptation. They may view any behavioral manifestation as a sign of basic, pervasive, and highly generalized but largely unconscious forces. This means that your most important motives are primarily unconscious. You may be victimized by these hidden motives, and perceive them only through the distortions of defensive maneuvers enacted in ways only dimly known to you. The basic psychodynamics are established early in life during the stages of psychosexual development and they shape your future possibilities and how you will deal with the world.

Image of The Person

Freud constructed a compelling image of what a person might be, erecting a sweeping and novel theoretical system of the individual's relationship to himself and to his world. Freud saw the person as struggling with himself and the world, blocked by anxieties, conflicted, and plagued by his own unacceptable wishes and unconscious secrets. This picture has captivated the imagination of many laymen as well as clinicians, and consequently has had an enormous impact on philosophical as well as psychological conceptions of human nature. In Freud's view humans are not the unemotional, rational beings that Victorian society thought they were. Instead, people are torn by unconscious conflicts and wishes whose vicissitudes push them in seemingly puzzling ways.

Freud's emphasis on unconscious impulses as the most basic determinants of behavior is seen in an analogy in which the relation of the id and the ego is likened to that between a horse and its rider:

> . . . The horse provides the locomotive energy, and the rider has the prerogative of determining the goal and of guiding the movements of his powerful mount towards it. But all too often in the relations between the ego and the id we find a picture of the less ideal situation in which the rider is obliged to guide his horse in the direction in which it itself wants to go (Freud, 1933, p. 108).

Thus in Freud's psychology the id is stubborn and strong and frequently the ego cannot really control it effectively. Freud believed that environmental sources of excitation were less important than inborn instincts in the dynamics of personality. He thought that external stimuli make fewer demands and, in any event, can always be avoided, whereas one's own impulses and needs cannot be escaped. Consequently he made instinctual impulses and their vicissitudes the core of personality functioning.

Such grand theoretical systems, whether in pre-Christian Greece or post-Victorian Vienna, have dramatic intellectual functions, regardless of their ultimate scientific standing. They supply us with a new language to describe ourselves and to bring some sense and structure to our often disordered experiences. Constructions like the "id" are ways of conceptualizing complex aspects of experience. It is essential to remember, however, that such constructions are just that: conceptualizations about experience and not revelations of fact. Their usefulness must be demonstrated: in their research harvest, in the fruitfulness of the predictions that can be derived from them, and in their convenience for psychotherapy. Later chapters will examine some of the relevant evidence.

The impact of Freud's theory on society and on philosophy, as well as on the social sciences, is almost universally hailed as profound; its significance is frequently compared with the contributions of Darwin. Freud's contributions have been widely acknowledged, and they need no new praises here. The evidence relevant to Freud's theory as a scientific psychological system, however, has been questioned persistently.

Although Freud attempted to create a general psychology of humans, his main systematic impressions were of thinking and feeling processes of conflict-ridden persons caught up in drastic personal crises. Moreover, Freud observed these tortured individuals only under extremely artificial conditions: lying on a couch during the psychotherapy hour in an environment deliberately made as asocial as possible. This drastically restricted observational base helped to foster a theory that is almost entirely a theory of anxiety and internal conflict and that pays little attention to the social environment and to the interpersonal context of behavior.

Furthermore, Freud tried to construct a theory of development at a time in history when few adequate concepts about learning were available in social science. Without having at hand a suitable set of learning concepts and terms for personality development, Freud relied on his own preference for a "body language": He preferred to say "oral" rather than "dependent," "anal" rather than "compulsive," "genital" rather than "mature." Freud's body language, while picturesque, unfortunately has made his theory difficult to integrate with scientific psychology. As we will see in the next chapter, some attempts have been made to translate Freud's ideas into different terms.

Testability of Freud's Ideas — *Theory hard to test*

One of the main criticisms is that Freud's theory is hard to test. That is true in part because his constructs are ambiguous and hard to quantify. The terms often are loose and metaphoric and convey different meanings in different contexts. He rarely gives clear, observable referents for them. Just what observations are required to conclude, for example, that an individual is fixated at the anal stage? Under what conditions may we conclude that he or she *is not* fixated at that stage? How can the extent or amount of fixation be assessed? Likewise, is the college student radical who commits himself to fight the "establishment" really "intellectualizing" his emotional conflicts with "authority figures" (like his father) and his "Oedipal problems," or is he truly motivated to undo political evils? What would he have to do to show that he is motivated by his professed idealism rather than by unconscious conflicts? Often the answers to questions like these depend on the clinical judgments of trained experts. It therefore becomes essential to study how closely experts really do agree with each other and how well they can support their opinions with evidence (Chapter 8).

According to many critics some aspects of Freud's theory consist of little more than labels or categories for grouping data. Such labels (for example, the "death wish") cannot be tested and cannot be assessed by any methodology. Bluntly, some of these concepts do not offer the possibility of ever being disconfirmed by research. One danger here is that the psychologist may be beguiled into believing that these labels increase her explanatory powers when, instead, they merely lead her to after-the-fact sweeping generalities. Sometimes it is easy to interpret truisms as if they were insights.

In spite of these problems, many attempts have been made to clarify Freudian constructs, especially those dealing with defense mechanisms and conflict, and to submit them to experimental study (e.g., Blum, 1953; Hilgard, 1952; Holmes & Schallow, 1969; Masserman, 1952; Sears, 1943, 1944; Silverman, 1976). Research has been plentiful and hundreds of investigators have produced a voluminous literature. Freud's followers have extended many of his concepts, emphasizing ego processes and social forces more than their mentor did and deemphasizing heredity and instincts. Some of the research that they have influenced is discussed in later chapters.

Psychodynamic Theory and Trait Theory

Finally, and surprisingly, the psychodynamic approach to personality shares some basic assumptions with trait theory. As we have seen, psychodynamic theories assume that people develop a stable, basic, core personality that exerts itself pervasively, albeit indirectly, and in disguised forms. Thus both trait theory and the psychodynamic approach assume the existence of enduring predispositions that determine behaviors across diverse situations. Again, like trait theory, these hypothesized underlying predispositions or psychodynamics are inferred from behavioral signs.

The psychodynamic strategy of this inferential process, however, is radically different from the procedure favored by most trait theorists. Most trait research has been guided by a measurement model in which trait indicators are *directly* and *additively* related to the inferred underlying trait (Loevinger, 1957). For example, the more submissive behavior the person displays, the stronger the underlying trait of submissiveness. In contrast, psychodynamic theory posits highly *indirect,* nonadditive relations between behavior and hypothesized underlying states. For example, submissive behavior may be interpreted as a sign of underlying aggression, or of passivity-hostility conflicts, or of resistance disguising some other, more threatening characterological problems. In other words, a person's "easy-going, friendly, eager-to-please behavior" actually may indicate underlying problems with anger; conversely, the aggressive individual may be concealing deeply passive, dependent tendencies. Far from being what they seem, actions according to psychoanalytic theory may be in the service of all sorts of motives.

If one accepts these psychodynamic beliefs, it follows that great attention should be paid to clinical inferences and tests designed to reveal the individual's "underlying personality" and dynamics from indirect behavioral signs. The methods and problems associated with these psychodynamically oriented clinical procedures are explored in later chapters.

Psychodynamic Behavior Theory

As was noted earlier, Freud constructed a theory of development without the benefit of learning concepts. He adopted a body language and invented new terms like "fixation" that made it difficult to coordinate his theory with experimental psychology. Dollard and Miller demonstrated that this coordination could be achieved. They drew on laboratory research with animals to devise a personality theory in learning terms that closely paralleled, and in many respects translated, Freudian theory. The psychodynamic emphasis on motives, on unconscious processes, on internal conflicts and defenses, such as repression, remained largely unchanged. Many psychologists found Freud's basic ideas more congenial and easier to adopt when they were put into the language of learning and experimental psychology. Consequently these concepts stimulated much research.

Many analyses of the individual's socialization into his culture have been guided by the motivational formulations of Miller and Dollard. In accord with their theory, inhibition training by socialization agents may produce conflicts between approach tendencies and avoidance tendencies, just as in Freud's view the child experiences conflict between his impulses and his anxiety regarding the consequences of expressing those impulses. Examples of this model are found in the analysis of motivational conflicts resulting from toilet training and from the socialization of sexual impulses (e.g., Mussen, Conger, & Kagan, 1974). In later years there have been many theoretical extensions (and criticisms, e.g., Maher, 1966) of conflict theory, with applications to diverse phenomena (e.g., Renner, 1964, 1967). Epstein (1962, 1967) has moved conceptually toward a more general theory of human conflict and anxiety.

Other psychologists have been troubled because the research by Miller and his colleagues is based mainly on animal studies. Indeed, this fact has earned it some of its greatest criticism. Careful investigation carried out with a lower species, such as the rat, whose behavior is far removed from human problems, may not hold up when extrapolations are made to people. Many critics have

TABLE 3-6 SUMMARY OVERVIEW OF PSYCHODYNAMIC APPROACHES	
Basic units:	Inferred motives and psychodynamics.
Causes of behavior:	Underlying stable motives and their unconscious transformations and conflicts.
Favored data:	Interpretations by expert judges (clinicians).
Observed responses used as:	Indirect signs.
Research focus:	Personality dynamics and psychopathology; unconscious processes; defense mechanisms.
Approach to personality change:	By insight into motives and conflicts underlying behavior.
Role of situation:	Deliberately minimized or ambiguous.

objected that human social behavior is of a fundamentally different nature than the behavior of animals in the laboratory and therefore requires a different methodology, as later chapters discuss.

Some critics found the rodent a philosophically and aesthetically unappealing model for humans and rejected animal analogies for human personality. They were repelled by the analogies between rat and person and believed that in the transition from the clinic to the laboratory some of the most exciting features of Freud's view of people were lost.

Of course the real test of a position is not its appeal to friends and critics, but the research and conceptual advances that it produces. Dollard and Miller's psychodynamic behavior theory cannot be evaluated in these respects until we have examined the relevant evidence, which is presented in later chapters.

This chapter has merely sketched the outline of psychodynamic conceptions. Some of the essentials are summarized in Table 3-6. The applications of these ideas for the assessment and treatment of persons probably have been more extensive than those of any other psychological theory. Consequently an adequate view of the meaning and implications of psychodynamic theory, and of its current status, cannot be achieved until these applications are examined in Part II.

SUMMARY

1. The most influential psychodynamic theory has been that of Sigmund Freud. Freud's theory and method of treating personality disturbances were based on extensive clinical observation of neurotic persons and on self-analysis.

2. In Freud's view, the id, ego, and superego form the tripartite structure of the personality. The *id* is the primary, instinctual core. It obeys the "pleasure principle," seeking immediate gratification of impulses. The *ego* mediates between the instinctual demands of the id and the outer world of reality. Its energy is derived from the id, and it operates by means of "secondary processes": logical thinking and rational planning. The ego functions to test reality, localizing the appropriate objects for gratification in the environment so that tension reduction can occur. The *superego* represents the internalized moral standards of the society, achieved through the internalization of parental control and characteristics in the course of socialization.

3. Personality dynamics involve a perpetual conflict between the id, ego, and superego. This conflict is accompanied by continuous transformations of the finite amount of energy or "libido" contained in the person. The basic conflict is between the person's instinctual impulses and learned inhibitions and anxieties regarding their expression. The major determinants of behavior are unconscious and irrational: Individuals are driven by persistent, illogical demands from within.

4. The desire for immediate gratification of sexual and aggressive instincts puts the person in conflict with the environment. The conflict becomes internal when the person has incorporated the prohibitions of the culture.

5. This struggle between impulse and inhibition produces anxiety. Defenses may be used by the ego when it is unable to handle anxiety effectively. Transformed by these defenses, the person's unacceptable impulses and unconscious motives express themselves indirectly or symbolically in disguised forms.

6. Freud's theory of personality development posits a series of psychosexual stages: oral, anal, phallic, and genital, so named for the erogenous zone which characterizes each. Later personality traits develop according to the individual's experience at each of these stages of maturation.

7. "Anaclitic identification" and "identification with the aggressor" are two Freudian identification mechanisms. The first is based on the

intense dependency of a child on the mother. The second, identification with the aggressor, is based on the boy's fear of potential castration by his father in retribution for his incestuous desires for his mother.

8. In general, the psychoanalytic followers of Freud have deemphasized the role of instincts and psychosexual stages and have concerned themselves more with the social milieu and the ego. Their conception of human nature has been less deterministic, less drive oriented, and more humanistic.

9. One especially striking departure from Freud is the psychology of Jung. Jung emphasized the unconscious and its symbolic and mystical expressions. He focused on dreams and on human beings' need to achieve unity through greater awareness of their collective and personal unconscious.

10. Freud's theory and image of the human being have had a profound impact, but it has proved difficult to test many of his ideas scientifically. Motivated by the desire for a scientific psychology compatible with Freud's basic ideas, Dollard and Miller attempted a fusion of psychoanalytic concepts with the more objective language and methods of laboratory studies of animal learning. Their theory emphasizes drive, cue, response, and reinforcement as the basic components of learning. *Drives* are strong stimuli that impel action. Primary or innate drives (such as hunger, pain, sex) are the basis of motivation. Many other drives or motives may be learned from their association with primary drive reduction. *Cues* direct behavior, determining when, where, and how the *response* (behavior) will occur. A *reinforcement* is any specific event that strengthens the likelihood of a response. Reinforcement is essential to the learning and to the maintenance of a response. Events that reduce a drive serve as reinforcements.

11. Dollard and Miller translate such Freudian dynamic concepts as internal conflict and repression into the terms of learning theory. They interpret conflict in terms of the simultaneous existence of approach and avoidance tendencies. Their theory suggests that the strength of these drive-like forces depends on the organism's distance from the goal object, and that behavior is a function of the net effect of approach and avoidance tendencies. Moreover, Dollard and Miller construed repression as a learned response of "not-thinking" that reduces the learned drive of fear.

12. Freud's theory has many implications for our view of the human being. The impact and value of this theory cannot be judged fully until we examine its applications.

CHAPTER 4

SOCIAL BEHAVIOR THEORIES: CONCEPTIONS

Skinner 73
Classic 75
Operate
Albert 76
Rotter 82

This chapter discusses more recent behavioral approaches for understanding behavior and personality. You will see that these conceptions share with Dollard and Miller's psychodynamic behavior theory a belief in the importance of learning for personality development. In many other respects, however, the positions discussed in this chapter depart sharply from the ideas that guided Dollard and Miller. Several varieties of behavior theory have been formulated in recent years, and many of them have developed in distinctly new directions. Among the most influential conceptions have been the ideas of B. F. Skinner, Julian B. Rotter, and Albert Bandura.

B. F. Skinner's Radical Behaviorism

Although he is also a learning theorist, B. F. Skinner's (1953, 1974) approach is radically different from Dollard and Miller's. Skinner differs fundamentally from these theorists in his concern with behavior rather than with dispositions and motives, and in his unwillingness to infer learned drives or any other internal motivational forces and traits.

Rejection of Inferred Motives and Dynamics

You saw in the last chapter that theorists have hypothesized many human motives but do not agree about the most basic ones. Theories concerning motivation have helped to reveal the variety and complexity of human strivings, and also have contributed to the development of research about their causes (Part III). Most investigators of motives were inspired by the model of experimental research on biological drives in animals. In animal studies of motivation, the hypothesized need of the animal (its hunger or sex drive, for example) has been linked clearly to observable conditions manipulated in the laboratory. For example, the strength of the hunger drive may be inferred in part from the amount of time that the animal has been deprived of food. When a dog has not been fed for two days, we may safely say that its hunger drive is high. In such cases, references to drives and motives are straight forward. Likewise, some careful investigations of hypothesized higher-order motives in people have specified clearly the objective conditions that define the motive (e.g., McClelland *et al.,* 1953).

Less rigorous applications of motivational theory to personality, however, may use motives loosely (for example as "wishes" and "desires"), and their value as explanations of behavior is open to serious question. The tendency to invoke motives as explanations of why people behave as they do is understandable, because that is how we "explain" behavior in common sense terms. To explain why a child spent an unusual amount of time cleaning and grooming himself neatly, we easily might say "because he had strong cleanliness needs" or "because he had a compulsive desire for order." Such hypotheses about motives may sound like explanations, but they tell us little unless the motive is defined objectively and unless the causes of the motive itself are established. What makes the child have "cleanliness needs"? What determines his "compulsive desires"? Why does he "wish" to be clean?

B. F. Skinner and his associates have criticized many concepts regarding human needs as being no more than motivational labels attached to human activities. Thus orderly behavior may be attributed to a motive for orderliness, submissive behavior to submissiveness needs, exploratory behavior to the need to explore, and so on. To avoid this circularity and to untangle explaining from naming, behaviorally oriented psychologists like Skinner prefer to analyze behaviors in terms of the observable events and conditions that seem to vary with them. Hence they refrain from positing specific motivations. Rather than hypothesize the needs that may propel a particular activity, they try to discover the events that strengthen its future likelihood and that maintain or change it. Thus they search for the conditions that regulate the behavior rather than hypothesize need states inside the person as motives that drive him. This approach leads to questions like: When does that child's cleaning activity increase, and when does it decrease in relation to observable changes in the environment (e.g., how the parents respond to the behavior).

For Skinner, psychology is the science of behavior: Inferences about unobservable states and motives are not adequate explanations, and they add nothing to a scientific account of the conditions controlling behavior. "Motivation" is simply the result of depriving or satiating an organism of some substance such as water or food for a given period of time. Thus a "drive" is just a convenient way of referring to the observable effects of such deprivation or satiation. Likewise, Skinner avoids any inferences about internal "conflicts" (e.g., among approach and avoidance tendencies), preferring an experimental analysis of the actual stimulus conditions that control the particular behavior.

Basic Strategy

Skinner's work is based on the premise that a genuine science of human behavior is not only possible but desirable. In his view, science should try to predict and determine experimentally (i.e., "control") the behavior of the individual organism. The cause-and-effect relationships in behavior become the laws of behavioral science (Skinner, 1974).

Skinner proposes a "functional analysis" of the organism as a behaving system. Such an analysis tries to link the organism's behavior to the precise conditions that control or determine it. Skinner's approach therefore concentrates on the observable covariations between "independent variables" (stimulus events) and "dependent variables" (response patterns). The variables in a functional analysis, according to Skinner, must be external, observable, and described in physical and quantitative terms. It will not do to say that a child becomes concerned with cleanliness when she "fears her father's disapproval": One must specify the exact ways that changes in the father's specific behavior (e.g., his praise) are related to specific changes in what the child does (e.g., how much she washes her hands per hour).

Insofar as relevant variables can be brought under the control of experimental manipulation, Skinner contends that the laboratory offers the best chance of obtaining a scientific analysis of behavior. Furthermore, the experimental study of behavior has much to gain from dealing with the behavior of animals below the complex human level. Science, Skinner points out, advances from the simple to the complex and is constantly concerned with whether the processes and laws discovered at one stage are adequate for the next.

Classical Conditioning and
Conditioned Reinforcers

Like most other experimental psychologists, Skinner recognized the importance of the type of "classical" or "respondent" conditioning initially discovered by Pavlov. To understand Skinner's own contributions, we must consider first the nature of classical conditioning. Classical conditioning (conditioned-response learning) is a type of learning (emphasized by Pavlov) in which a neutral stimulus (e.g., a bell) becomes conditioned by being paired or associated with an unconditioned stimulus (one that is naturally potent).

The essence of this phenomenon lies in the experiment in which a dish of food is presented often to a food-deprived (hungry) organism. In time, the empty dish alone will elicit a primary or unconditioned response—salivation. To some extent the empty dish thus becomes a conditioned reinforcer by virtue of its close association with the unconditioned reinforcing stimulus (food). Another example of a conditioned reinforcer is seen if a light is turned on each time food is given to a hungry animal. The light eventually becomes a conditioned reinforcer, and it may be used to some extent just as food is used to influence behavior.

Several rules govern the acquisition of conditioned reinforcers. The more often the conditioned stimulus (light in our last example) is paired with the unconditioned stimulus (food), the more reinforcing it becomes. There must not be too great a time interval between the two events (the light and the food). Finally the reinforcing power of the conditioned stimulus may be lost rapidly if it is never again associated with the unconditioned stimulus.

Conditioning principles have been extended to explain many complex social phenomena. Some studies of interpersonal attraction conceptualize the development of affections in conditioning terms (e.g., Byrne, 1969; Lott & Lott, 1968). These studies suggest that the evaluation of people and objects may be a function of the proportion of positive reinforcements associated with them (Griffitt & Guay, 1969). For example, your affection toward a friend may be related to the degree to which he or she has been associated with gratifications for you.

In addition to attractions and positive feelings, people often experience fears in personality development. Considering that the child's world is full of potential dangers, the prevalence of fears in childhood is not surprising, although their variety is sometimes startling. Even a casual inquiry into the fears of three-year-olds, for example, reveals how diverse their anxieties may be. Some of these, like fear of "robbers" and of "monsters," seem understandable. Others require more empathy for the different world of the small child: fear of being flushed down the toilet and drowning, or fear of being sucked into the vacuum cleaner. While such fears may seem amusing to the adult, they may be traumatic to the child.

Many stimuli are intrinsically dangerous to the developing child, and these painful stimuli (like hot stoves) are rapidly identified. But how do initially neutral stimuli acquire the power to evoke fearful and anxious emotional responses? According to learning theorists, laboratory research on aversive classical conditioning helps us to understand how anxiety develops in response to objectively nonthreatening events. Specifically, the individual may become afraid of intrinsically neutral things as a result of their close association with noxious or painful stimulation.

In *aversive classical conditioning*, the unconditioned stimulus is a pain-producing event. For example, if you see a light and experience an electric shock together for several trials, the light alone can come to evoke components of your emotional pain reaction to the shock. Neutral stimuli that are associated contiguously (close together in time) with an aversive uncondi-

FIGURE 4-1
Classical Conditioning (Aversive)

PHASE 1

Before   Potential conditioned   No special response
conditioning   stimulus (e.g., light) ──────▶ apart from brief
                                                attention

PHASE 2

During   Conditioned stimulus (light) and   ⎫   Unconditioned response
conditioning   unconditioned stimulus (e.g., pain- ⎬ ──▶ (e.g., fear, agitated
                producing shock), associated closely⎭   withdrawal, etc.)

PHASE 3

After   Conditioned stimulus   Elements of the
conditioning   alone (light)   ──────▶ unconditioned response
                                               (e.g., fear)

In classical conditioning, as a result of close association with an unconditioned stimulus (e.g., shock), a previously neutral event (e.g., light) may become a conditioned stimulus capable of eliciting an unconditioned response (e.g., fear).

tioned stimulus then become aversive conditioned stimuli capable of eliciting fear and avoidance responses. Thus through positive and aversive classical conditioning intense emotional reactions may be acquired to previously neutral stimuli. The classical conditioning design is shown in Figure 4-1.

The case of Albert illustrates classically conditioned responses and their generalization (Watson & Raynor, 1920). A severe rat phobia was induced in Albert, a young child, who had not been afraid of rats before, by simply pairing the presentation of a white rat with aversive stimulation. Just as Albert reached for the animal, a loud, fear-producing noise was made, and contiguous presentations of rat and aversive noise were repeated several times. Albert developed an intense fear reaction to the rat. His fear also generalized: When he was later presented with a wide range of new furry stimuli, including cotton, fur coats, human hair, wool, and other animals, he displayed a phobic reaction to them, although they themselves had not been paired with noise. This is a human example of the kind of learning manifested when rats who had been shocked in a white compartment responded fearfully to the compartment itself (Miller, 1948).

An especially dramatic demonstration of aversive (or "traumatic") conditioning was conducted with adult volunteers (Campbell, Sanderson, & Laverty, 1964). The unconditioned stimulus was extraordinarily traumatic: a temporary interruption of breathing, induced by the drug Scoline, which produces momentary motor paralysis without impairing consciousness. While producing no permanent harm, the drug temporarily generated in most volunteers a horrible terror and the feeling that they were dying. The conditioned stimulus was a neutral tone. On the basis of a single pairing (of tone with drug effects), a long-lasting, conditioned fear response to the neutral tone was generated in the subjects. This fear reaction was evidenced by marked changes in such emotional indicators as heart rate, muscle tension, and respiration. Moreover, this traumatic, conditioned emotional reaction was highly resistant to extinction; it persisted intensely despite many repeated extinction trials.

Results of this type have been interpreted as evidence that the neurotic emotional reactions found in phobias may reflect conditioning rather than unconscious wishes and intrapsychic conflicts (e.g., Bandura, 1969). The implications for both the theory and the treatment of disturbed behavior may be profound, as later chapters discuss.

Demonstrations like those reported in the foregoing studies are understandably rare because of the possible hazards to the volunteers. They serve, however, not just as academic demonstrations but provide a basis for the development of more effective therapeutic techniques. If the principles through which traumatic reactions are acquired can be understood, it should be possible to apply the same principles for therapeutic purposes.

Operant Conditioning and Response Consequences

Skinner incorporated into his position many concepts regarding classical conditioning, but he concentrated on another aspect of learning. According to Skinner (1953), most human social behaviors involve freely emitted response patterns or "operants." The term "operant" implies an active organism that "operates" upon its world, changing the environment and being changed by it. The outcomes of these operant response patterns modify the likelihood that similar responses will occur in the future. That is, operant behavior is determined by its consequences. If the outcomes or consequences of the response are favorable or reinforcing, then the operant will be more likely to be emitted again in future similar situations. Contrary to some widespread misconceptions, "reinforcers" or favorable outcomes are not restricted to such primitive rewards as food pellets or sexual satisfactions. Almost any events may serve as reinforcers, including such cognitive gratifications as information (Jones, 1966) or the achievement of competence.

On the other hand, if the consequences of the responses are not favorable (not reinforcing), then the operant is less likely to occur in the future. For example, if a father responds with attention and warm concern to his daughter's whining and clinging dependency, the chances increase that she will show similar dependency in the future. But if he systematically ignores the dependency and leaves it unrewarded, the behavior becomes less likely.

Most of Skinner's research on learning has concentrated on the role of rewards or reinforcement as determinants of behavior change. The usual meth-

FIGURE 4-2
Operant Conditioning

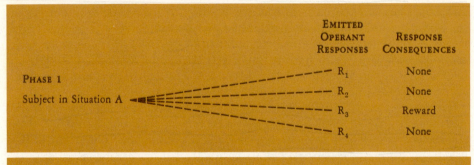

In any situation a subject emits many operant responses: If an operant is immediately followed by a reward (reinforcement) he will be more likely to emit it again in a similar situation.

ods in these studies has been to set up conditions in which an organism may freely perform or emit responses ("operants"). The experimenter preselects a particular response class (e.g., personal pronouns in interview talk, lever pressing in a study with rats). She then makes the delivery of a reinforcer contingent (dependent) on the subject's emitting the selected operant response. For example, she makes praiseful comments like "good" only when the interviewee uses such personal pronouns as "I" or "me." Or she may make food delivery to the animal contingent on the bar-pressing response. The process, called "operant conditioning," is shown graphically in Figure 4-2.

As will be discussed in later chapters, studies have shown repeatedly that alterations in response consequences (the outcomes to which the behavior leads) may change a wide range of behaviors, from psychotic talk, delinquency, and neurotic sexual aberrations to social interactions in nursery school. Most of these studies have tried to modify therapeutically such problematic behaviors as severe fears. They also have shown that individual behavior can be accurately predicted from knowledge of the environment in which the subject is to be observed. A child's dependent behavior at home, for example, may be predicted from knowledge of the parents' willingness to reinforce dependency (e.g., Bijou, 1965). Likewise, assessments of the adequacy of persons' adjustment may be most accurate when they are based on knowledge of the environmental conditions in their lives (Mischel, 1968).

Discrimination

The stimuli that signal the time or place when an operant will have favorable consequences are called *discriminative stimuli.* Changes in discriminative

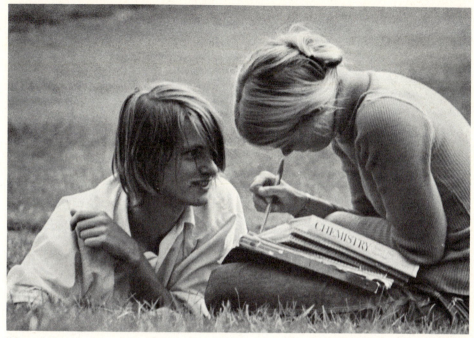

"Generalized reinforcers" often are subtle and involve complex human relationships.

stimuli lead to changes in behavior. Without discriminative stimuli we would not know the outcomes to which different behaviors would be likely to lead. We quickly learn to drive a car through green traffic lights but not through red ones, to talk to people who smile and not to those who seem uninviting, to shout exuberantly at football games but not during church sermons. Life without environmental cues regarding the probable consequence of behavior would be absurdly chaotic.

Conditioned Generalized Reinforcers

As noted before, neutral stimuli may acquire value and become conditioned reinforcers when they become associated with other stimuli that already have reinforcing powers and emotion-arousing properties. Conditioned reinforcers become *generalized* when they are paired with more than one primary reinforcer. A good example of a conditioned generalized reinforcer is money, because it can provide so many different primary gratifications (food, shelter, comfort, medical help, and alleviation of pain). Gradually generalized reinforcers may become quite potent even when the primary reinforcers upon which they were initially based do not accompany them any more. Some people, for example, seem to learn to love money for its own sake and work to amass "paper profits" that they never trade in for primary rewards.

Some generalized reinforcers are obvious—like money—but others are subtle and involve complex social relationships. Attention and social approval from people who are likely to supply reinforcement—such as parents, a loved one, or a teacher—often are especially strong generalized reinforcers. Such behaviors as showing off and pretending to be ill, for example, often may inadvertently be reinforced by people who attend to them and who react with interest, approval, or concern.

Because outcomes like attention and affection are not physical objects but features of other people's behavior, they tend to be difficult to define and to recognize clearly—both by the psychologist who tries to study them and by the person who is controlled by them. When we are not sure whether another significant person is being attentive or affectionate to us, our behavior will not be consistently reinforced by him. Under these conditions of inconsistent or intermittent reinforcement, behaviors may become highly perseverative, as seen in the frustrated lover's struggles for signs of affection or the insecure child's unremitting pursuit of attention.

Superstitions and Irrationality

The relationship between the occurrence of an operant response and the reinforcement that follows it is often causal. For example, turn the door knob and the door opens, the outcome reinforcing the action. Consequently in the future we are likely to turn door knobs to enter and leave rooms, and our behavior at the door seems rational. Often, however, the response-reinforcement relationship may be quite accidental, and then bizarre and seemingly superstitious behavior may be produced. For example, a primitive tribe may persist in offering human sacrifices to the gods to end severe droughts because occasionally a sacrifice has been followed by rain.

The genesis of superstition, according to Skinner, may be demonstrated by giving a pigeon a bit of food at regular intervals—say every 15 seconds—regardless of what he is doing. Skinner (1953, p. 85) describes the strange rituals that may be conditioned in this way:

When food is first given, the pigeon will be behaving in some way—if only standing still—and conditioning will take place. It is then more probable that the same behavior will be in progress when food is given again. If this proves to be the case, the "operant" will be further strengthened. If not, some other behavior will be strengthened. Eventually a given bit of behavior reaches a frequency at which it is often reinforced. It then becomes a permanent part of the repertoire of the bird, even though the food has been given by a clock which is unrelated to the bird's behavior. Conspicuous responses which have been established in this way include turning sharply to one side, hopping from one foot to the other and back, bowing and scraping, turning around, strutting, and raising the head. The topography of the behavior may continue to drift with further reinforcements, since slight modifications in the form of response may coincide with the receipt of food.

It may seem amusing to watch pigeons generate elaborate superstitious rituals and bizarre behaviors as a result of accidental reinforcement contingencies. It is tragic, however, if people inadvertently become bizarre and develop neurotic symptom syndromes in fundamentally similar ways. According to many Skinnerians, there is much overlap between the ways in which pigeons become victimized by the vicissitudes of reinforcement and the manner in which people may become twisted by the response-reinforcement arrangements in their lives. These ideas have been widely applied in both analyses and modifications of human problems (Chapters 9 and 10).

Summary

diff between Skinner & Miller

In sum, B. F. Skinner differs both from psychodynamic theorists and from Miller and Dollard by avoiding motivational and dispositional constructs. Instead of trying to infer motives and conflicts, Skinnerians devote themselves to the experimental analysis of the observable conditions controlling behavior.

The learning formulations of Skinner and other "neobehaviorists" have stimulated a great deal of systematic research on the effects of reinforcement, the patterning of reinforcement, and the phenomena of generalization and discrimination in learning. Many of these studies help to clarify the ways in which patterns of behavior develop and change; they will be discussed in later chapters that deal with socialization and behavior change.

Social Learning: Social Behavior Theory Becomes Cognitive

You know already that the behavior theories discussed so far emphasize the role of reinforcement or reward in learning. The importance given to reinforcement is understandable for at least two reasons. First, reinforcement and incentives have been shown repeatedly to be powerful influences in learning and in choice of behavior in many different settings. For example, as economists have long recognized, the pay-offs yielded by various alternatives are important determinants of choices in financial and business decisions. There also have been ample demonstrations that the consequences to which response patterns lead are critical determinants of psychological behaviors. Second, until recently most research on learning has studied animals rather than people, and with animals direct reinforcement was thought to be the main learning mechanism.

In more recent work with complex human and interpersonal behavior the possibility of *social* learning without any apparent direct reinforcement is being recognized. Now the concepts and principles of learning have been developed and extended to the interpersonal world, and have been taken out of the animal laboratory and applied to real life. These extensions include clinical psychology (e.g., Rotter, 1954; Rotter, Chance, & Phares, 1972; Ullmann & Krasner, 1969; Wolpe, 1958); personality development (e.g., Bandura & Walters, 1963); personality assessment and structure (e.g., Mischel, 1968, 1973a); and behavior change (Bandura, 1969; Eysenck & Rachman, 1965; Krasner & Ullmann, 1973). Moreover, many of the original learning concepts have been liberalized and integrated with ideas and findings from other areas (Chapter 5). Probably the most important aspect of this liberalization is the increasing attention to the person's cognitions—to what the person knows, thinks, believes, and expects. This trend may be called the growing "cognitivization" of behavior theory, and it takes many forms, as the following sections discuss.

Expectancies and Values

J. B. Rotter's (1954, 1972) social learning formulation introduces this more cognitive element to personality-oriented learning theories. He emphasizes the individual's subjective expectations about future outcomes and the subjective value of reinforcements in the person's psychological situation. In Rotter's theory, the probability that a particular pattern of behavior will occur depends on the individual's expectancies concerning the outcomes to which his or her behavior will lead and the perceived values of those outcomes. For example, whether a girl behaves dependently or self-assertively with her teacher depends on her expectations regarding the probable consequences (e.g., attention, disapproval, affection) of either behavior and the value to her of those consequences.

To predict behavior we must estimate the individual's relevant expectancies and values in the particular situation. The person's subjective expectancies regarding probable outcomes reflect past learning experiences in similar situations. That is, expectations are a function of the person's past reinforcement. Likewise, the subjective values of outcomes are a function of prior learning. Specific expectancies, in Rotter's formulation, are easily modifiable by even seemingly minor alterations in the individual's situation. "Generalized expectancies" are assumed to be more consistent and stable across situations. Thus generalized expectancies are more like traits, although they are construed as learned expectations.

Expectancies and values also have remained central concepts in more recent social learning formulations. For example, they are seen as important qualities of the person that help guide choices among available action alternatives in the situation (Mischel, 1973a). And a special type of expectancy, called efficacy (or "self-efficacy") has also been identified (Bandura, 1977). Self-efficacy refers to the individual's beliefs about his or her own effectiveness. It is the expectation that one can successfully conduct the action required.

learning = awareness

The Importance of Awareness in Learning

When you are aware of the contingencies and rules governing the consequences to which your responses will lead, you learn better (Bandura, 1969). Under many conditions private expectations and hypotheses about what is happening may affect actions much more than does the objective reality of the rules and reinforcements that actually govern the outcomes of behaviors. Thus awareness of the relevant rules and contingencies greatly facilitates learning.

Consider, for example, an operant conditioning situation in which the experimenter gave social reinforcement (saying "Mmm-hmm") to college sudents when they said human nouns (e.g., "girl") in a word-naming task. Not surprisingly, subjects who became aware of the contingency for reinforcement (i.e., guessed correctly that social reinforcement from the experimenter depended on their saying human nouns) greatly increased their output of human nouns

FIGURE 4-3
Awareness and Verbal Conditioning

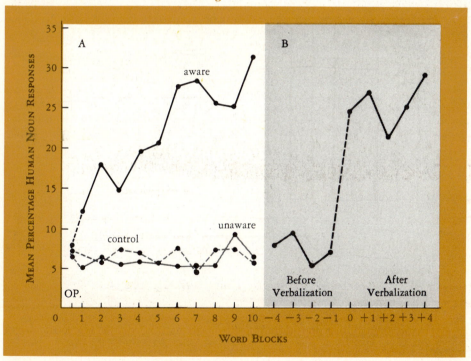

A, Mean percentage of human noun responses given by the aware, unaware, and control groups on each word block during the conditioning task. *B,* Mean percentage of human noun responses given by subjects in the aware group before and after they verbalized the reinforcement contingency correctly. (Adapted by Spielberger & De Nike, 1966, from De Nike, 1964.)

(De Nike, 1964). Those who remained unaware of the contingency did as poorly as subjects in a control group, who were reinforced randomly for 10 percent of their responses (see Figure 4-3, Part *A*). Most interesting, the students showed no appreciable improvement in their performance until they correctly discerned the contingency for reinforcement; as soon as they became aware of the contingency they gave dramatically more human noun responses (Figure 4-3, *B*).

Other research suggests, however, that some learning in humans can occur without awareness (Martin, Hawryluk, & Guse, 1974). This fact really should not be surprising considering that lower organisms with dubious capacities for cognitive symbolization and awareness—such as the cockroach and the earthworm—also manage to learn and can be conditioned.

Rules and Symbolic Processes

Instructions and rules also can improve learning greatly. Rules help us to link discrete bits of information and powerfully affect our ability to learn and remember those materials (e.g., Anderson & Bower, 1973). In socialization, if the rules governing reinforcement are verbalized, children can more readily learn the standards that they are supposed to adopt (e.g., Aronfreed, 1966). When children are informed that particular performance patterns are good and that others are unsatisfactory, they adopt the appropriate standards more easily than when there are no clear verbal rules (Liebert & Allen, 1967). Thus in child-rearing it helps not only to reward appropriate behavior but also to specify the relevant rule. In addition to praising kind behaviors, for example, the parent might describe what exactly is being rewarded, as, "That's good: I like it when you are nice and gentle with your baby sister."

Symbolic and cognitive processes also may be crucial in classical conditioning. Suppose, for example, that a person has been conditioned in an experiment to fear a light because it is repeatedly paired with electric shock. Now if the experimenter tells her that the light (the conditioned stimulus) will not be connected again with the electric shock, her emotional reactions to the conditioned stimulus can quickly extinguish (Bandura, 1969). On later trials she can see the light without becoming aroused.

Observational Learning   *cognitive learning*

modeling

Observational learning refers to learning without any direct rewards or reinforcement (e.g., Bandura, 1969, 1971). People learn by observing other persons and events and not merely from the direct consequences of what they themselves do. What you know and how you behave depends on what you see and hear and not just on what you get.

Sometimes learning without direct reinforcement is called "cognitive," sometimes "vicarious," and sometimes "observational" or "modeling." All

Children learn partly through observation and imitation.

these terms refer to an individual's acquisition of new knowledge and potential behavior through observation without receiving any direct external reinforcement for his or her own acts or without even making the observed response. Observational learning may occur when people watch what others ("models") do, or when they attend to the physical environment, to events, and to symbols such as words and pictures. Much human learning depends on perceptual-cognitive processes (like selective, focused attention) and on observation of the social and physical environment rather than on direct reinforcement for the individual's own actions. The acquisition of new behavior through observation is especially evident in the learning of language and of complex rules (e.g., Zimmerman & Rosenthal, 1974). We learn about "right" and "wrong," for example, by watching others as well as by acting ourselves.

models

examples

Acquisition versus Performance

No one does all the things he or she has learned and can do. Obviously there are discrepancies between what people have learned or know and can do, and what they actually do in particular situations. For example, most adolescent girls know how to throw stones, fight, and steal. But even among girls who have acquired these skills to the same extent, there are striking individual differences in the degree to which they choose to perform them. Likewise, although most people in our culture know how to rob or murder, only some actually commit such crimes. There are major discrepancies between what a person is able to do in any given situation and what he or she actually does. Therefore it is useful to distinguish between the learning or acquisition of behaviors and their performance.

Learning or the acquisition of novel responses is regulated by sensory and cognitive processes. It may be facilitated by incentives and reinforcements, but it is not dependent upon them (e.g., Bandura, 1971). That is, what people *can* do depends on what they *know* and on the skills, information, rules, and response patterns they have acquired or learned. These learned behaviors are acquired through observation and cognitive processes and not just through conditioning and direct reinforcement. Learning thus depends on the learner's attention to the task, and on how well he "codes" (organizes, represents) and rehearses the information from his senses (e.g., Bandura & Jeffery, 1973).

Incentives and reinforcement, however, influence response selection in *performance*. The choice of what to do in any given situation—of which response to select from among the enormous number of potential behaviors one is capable of enacting—depends on motivational variables and incentives. The behavior one selects depends on the outcomes one expects the different behavioral acts to yield.

A person may not perform a particular behavior because she never learned it initially. On the other hand, the response pattern may be potentially available to her, but it is not elicited by the particular stimulus and reward conditions. That is, her response may be inhibited; the incentive conditions in the situation may not be strong enough to elicit it. When a more potent incentive is introduced the response may be produced readily.

Effects of Observing Other People's Outcomes

Your expectations regarding the probable consequences of particular behaviors depend not only on the outcomes you have received for what you did in similar situations, but also on the consequences you have observed other people obtain. Watching the outcomes that other people receive may provide valuable information about the consequences that you probably will get for similar behavior.

When people observe that others ("models") obtain positive reinforcing consequences for a response pattern, they tend to act more readily in similar ways. For instance, if children see other children receive encouragement and praise for, let us say, aggressiveness at play, their own tendency to behave aggressively in similar situations will increase. Conversely, when social models are punished for their behavior, observers tend to become more inhibited about displaying similar behavior.

A study of imitation illustrates the effects of observing the consequences of other people's behavior. In this study, children watched a film of an adult who displayed novel aggressive responses, such as hitting and kicking a Bobo doll

TABLE 4-1	
EFFECTS OF MODELING AND OBSERVED CONSEQUENCES	
Observer Sees	*Probability That Observer Will Later Perform Model's Behavior*
No model	Lowest
Model's behavior punished	Low
Model's behavior without consequence	Higher
Model's behavior rewarded	Highest

(Bandura, 1965). The consequences produced by the adult's aggressive behavior were deliberately varied. In one condition the film sequence showed the adult's aggressive behavior punished; in a second it was rewarded; and in a third it had no consequences. When tested after the film, children who had observed aggressive behaviors punished imitated them less than those who had seen aggressiveness rewarded or ignored. Table 4-1 summarizes the general pattern obtained in research on this topic.

Did the differences in performance found by Bandura (1965) mirror differences in learning? Tests at the end revealed that when the children were offered attractive incentives to reproduce the model's responses, the differences between the conditions were erased. It seems that the children in all conditions had *learned* the model's behavior equally well; the observation of different consequences, however, had inhibited or facilitated their later *performance* of the behavior.

In sum, it is not necessary to enact particular behaviors in order to learn their consequences: Vicarious as well as direct consequences of performances affect subsequent behavior. For example, a bank clerk does not have to be arrested for stealing from the safe to learn some of the consequences of such behavior. Information that alters people's anticipations of the probable outcomes to which a behavior will lead should also change the probability that they will engage in the behavior—although it may not affect their ability to execute the behavior.

Vicarious experiences also may lead to strong conditioned emotional reactions (Berger, 1962). In one experiment, adults repeatedly observed the sounding of a buzzer paired with fear responses feigned by another adult. Gradually the observers themselves developed conditioned fear responses to the sound of the buzzer alone (Bandura & Rosenthal, 1966). Consider also the development of strong fears of dogs or snakes. Even someone who was never harmed by an animal may come to fear it intensely after observing the emotional upset of other people when they are faced with the animal.

Consistency and Discriminativeness in Personality

Social learning theory influences ideas about the nature of personality traits. Recall that trait theories hypothesize broad dispositions and cross-situational consistencies as the basic units of personality (Chapter 2). In contrast, social behavior theory suggests that a person will behave consistently across situations only to the extent that similar behavior leads, or is expected to lead, to similar consequences across those conditions (Mischel, 1968). According to the learning principles of stimulus generalization and discrimination, behaviors become widely generalized only when they are reinforced uniformly across many stimulus conditions. Most social behaviors are not uniformly rewarded across different settings or situations. For example, while physical aggression is encouraged among boys sparring in the gym, it is not supported when the boys aggress toward their fathers or their younger siblings. Consequently sharp discriminations develop, the individual becoming aggressive in one context and not in the other (Bandura, 1973).

Guided by the idea that behavior depends on its probable outcomes, many behavior theorists emphasize "behavioral specificity" rather than trait consistency across conditions that entail different discriminative stimuli. On the other hand, if responses are uniformly rewarded across diverse conditions, "generalization" occurs, and the person will show similar behaviors across many situations. For example, a boy whose father reinforces him for physical aggressiveness everywhere might become broadly aggressive and fight with his siblings as well as with his friends in many settings at home and at school. Thus, depending on stimulus conditions, the same person might show a trait like aggressiveness across several contexts or he might be highly discriminative and behave one way in some settings but quite differently in others.

Consider a woman who seems hostile and fiercely independent some of the time but passive and dependent on other occasions. What is she really like? Which one of these two patterns reflects the woman that she really is? Is one pattern in the service of the other, or might both be in the service of a third motive? Must she be a really aggressive person with a facade of passivity—or is she a warm, passive-dependent woman with a surface defense of aggressiveness? Social behavior theory suggests that it is possible for her to be *all* of these—a hostile, fiercely independent, passive, dependent, aggressive, warm person all in one (Mischel, 1969). Of course which of these she is at any particular moment would not be random and capricious; it would depend on discriminative stimuli—who she is with, when, how, and much, much more. But each of these aspects of her self may be a quite genuine and real aspect of her total being.

An Alternative to Motivational Vicissitudes

Psychodynamic theorizing assumes a set of basic personality motives and dispositions that endure, although their overt response forms may change. That is, basic motives persist although their behavioral manifestations are transformed defensively. In that view, for example, a child may develop severe fears as a way of reducing anxiety about rejection by the parents. A few years later the child may abandon the fears but display extreme and excessive obedience toward the parents. The obedience may simply be a substitute for the fears: The basic problem remains but its expression changes (Kagan, 1969). This model is analogous to the closed hydraulic system in physics in which a gallon of water is converted to steam and recondensed to liquid: The form of the water may be transformed, but its basic nature is conserved. Such a Freudian-derived personality model is widely shared by many personality psychologists.

Social learning theorists, however, believe that this model is inappropriate and has led to some tragic mistakes in clinical treatment and diagnosis for 50 years (e.g., Bandura, 1969; Mischel, 1968, 1969; Peterson, 1968). They suggest that seemingly diverse behaviors do not necessarily reflect a uniform underlying motivational pattern. Instead they view behaviors as relatively discrete and controlled by relatively independent causes and maintaining conditions.

In accord with the psychodynamic view, if a child shows attachment and dependency in some contexts but not in others, one would begin a search to separate the defensive facade from the basic motivation underlying it. But in the social behavior view, seeming inconsistencies, rather than serve one underlying motive, actually may be under the control of relatively separate causal variables. The two behavior patterns may not reflect a "symptom" or facade in the service of a motive but rather may reflect discrimination learning in the service of the total organism. Similarly, social learning theory suggests that while a child's fears sometimes may be in the service of an underlying motive, they are more likely to involve an organized but relatively independent response system that is evoked and maintained by its own set of regulating conditions.

This distinction between theoretical positions leads to quite different interpretations regarding the causes of personality problems. The case of "Pearson Brack," an American airman, offers one example (Grinker & Spiegel, 1945, pp. 197–207; Mischel, 1968).

Pearson Brack was a bombardier in the Tunisian theater of operations during World War II. During Brack's ninth mission his airplane was severely damaged by flak. It suddenly jolted and rolled, and then began to dive. The pilot regained control of the plane just in time to avoid crashing. During the plane's fall, however, Brack was hurled violently against the bombsight and was seriously injured. After his return from this mission he was hospitalized for a month and then, seemingly recovered, was returned to flight duty. On his next two missions, the tenth and eleventh, he fainted, and gradually his problem was brought to the attention of a psychodynamically oriented psychiatrist. Direct observation revealed that Brack's tendency to faint seemed specifically linked to being at an altitude of about 10,000 feet.

After intensive interviews, the psychiatrist concluded that Brack's fainting was connected to deep, underlying anxieties rooted in his childhood experiences. Brack was viewed as a basically immature person with long-standing insecurity who had inadequately identified with his father. The near-fatal plane incident was seen as essentially trivial, except in so far as it precipitated anxiety in an already insecure and immature individual.

In contrast, a social behavior analysis of the same case (Mischel, 1968) emphasized the severe emotional trauma that might have been conditioned to altitude cues during the mishap. That is, if Brack's injury occurred at about 10,000 feet, then any altitude cues present at that time might have become conditioned stimuli capable of eliciting a traumatic reaction (such as fainting). In that case, every time Brack later reexperienced cues connected with the accident (such as being in a plane at a comparable altitude), he would again become emotionally debilitated.

From the viewpoint of social behavior theory, the relevant causes of Brack's problem were the current conditions that seemed to control its occurrence, in this instance altitude cues that may have been associated with the trauma. But from the perspective of psychodynamic theory, the causes were Brack's inferred underlying anxiety and its antecedents in childhood. Consequently the psychiatrist searched for the hypothesized roots of the problem in the form of repressed underlying anxieties. After excluding organic damage, the psychiatrist hypothesized that the fainting reflected deep underlying anxiety, symptomatic of Brack's brittle personality structure. He interpreted Brack's fainting as a surface sign of basic fear and anxiety and of dynamics that could only be comprehended in the light of childhood traumas and identifications.

Who was right? Was Brack's fainting predisposed by an inadequate identification, or a conditioned traumatic reaction, or a little bit of both, or neither? At this juncture there is no way of answering these questions definitively. But be clear about this point: Regardless of who is correct, the psychodynamic and social learning views are fundamentally different. Evidence relevant to these two positions will be considered often in later pages.

Focus on Current Social Behavior

The social behavior view has many implications for the study of persons. Social behavior assessments do not describe people in generalized trait terms, sort them into type categories, or infer their conflicts and motives (Mischel, 1968). Instead they sample what the individual does now in relation to the conditions in which he or she does it. In this sense, behavioral assessment involves an exploration of the unique or "idiographic" aspects of the single person by analyzing how he or she changes in response to changes in stimulus conditions (Chapter 10). In the case of bombardier Brack, for example, behavioral assessments would entail studying changes in his emotional response to airplanes as a result of changing and rearranging altitude cues or other stimuli that seemed to affect his fainting problem most potently.

In sum, psychodynamic theories distinguish between overt or "sympto-

FIGURE 4-4
The Social Behavior Approach Emphasizes That the Same Person Behaves Differently in Response to Various Psychological Situations (Stimuli)

Stimulus 1 (criticism from teacher) ——— Response A (excuses and denial)

Stimulus 2 (criticism from mother) ——— Response B (anger)

Stimulus 3 (rejection from girlfriend) ——— Response C (remorse) ———

Stimulus 4 (hostility from peer) ——— Response D (aggression)   Person 1

Stimulus 5 (scolding from father) ——— Response E (apology)

matic" behaviors and their basic or underlying psychic causes. These causes are believed to be enduring motives and their defensive transformations established early in the course of the individual's psychosexual development. Consequently psychodynamic theories look for the motivational roots of personality in childhood. In contrast, social behavior analyses seek the current causes of the person's behavior. Social learning approaches to personality thus pay less attention to motivational and dispositional constructs and instead look more at behavior, and at the functional relations between what the person does and the psychological conditions of his or her life.

What people do, of course, includes much more than motor acts. Far more than rats and other lower organisms that have been favorite subjects in experiments, humans do exceedingly complex and varied things, and they do them in their heads and guts as well as with their hands and feet. But to understand these complex activities, social behavior theorists suggest that it might be wiser to spend more time looking at what people are doing rather than try to infer the global motives and traits propelling them.

Recall that trait theories emphasize differences *between* people in their response to the same stimulus. In contrast, social behavior theories emphasize differences in the behavior of the *same* peson as a result of even slight changes

Even the young child processes information actively and is not an empty organism.

in conditions. This emphasis on the role of the stimulus in the regulation of the individual's behavior is indicated in Figure 4-4. Social behavior analyses try to discover the impact or meaning of particular stimulus conditions in the person's life by observing how changes in those conditions alter what he or she thinks and does.

Cognition and Behavior

In recent years psychologists have become very much interested in "cognition." Cognition is a term with many meanings, but most simply it means processing of information (e.g., Neisser, 1967) as in thinking, and in the mental representation and manipulation of events. Cognition is involved in processes like selective attention, information gathering, and motivated or goal-directed thinking (problem solving), and in the expectations we develop.

Psychologists who are concerned with cognition emphasize that a comprehensive approach to personality and social behavior needs to consider the person's "representational" or "coding" processes. That is, they want to understand the *mediation* that occurs inside the person between the stimuli that impinge and the overt responses that follow (e.g., Baldwin, 1969). Cognitive orientations are discussed elsewhere in this book, but they overlap with contemporary social learning formulations to the extent that current social learning views include considerations of symbolic activities (as in observational learning, e.g., Bandura, 1977) and seek to study the individual's interpretation of events and experiences (e.g., Mischel, 1973a). Social learning theories thus take account of mediation; they do not view stimuli as impinging on an empty organism that automatically emits a set of specific fixed acts. Explicit recognition of the links between cognition and learning is found in a "cognitive social learning" approach to personality presented in Chapter 13.

What a stimulus does to an individual depends on many things. For example, unless the stimulus is noticed, obviously it will not influence the person. Likewise, the impact the stimulus has depends not just on its objective physical characteristics but also on how it is presented, including any instructions, labels, and contextual cues that serve to change its usual meaning. If you watch a murder scene knowing it is part of a rehearsal for a play, obviously you will react differently than if you think a real murder is being committed. A bottle of clear liquid labeled "poison" is very different from the same bottle without the label. It would be naive to restrict the definition of a stimulus sequence to its gross physical properties. In any given situation, behavior is influenced by the total stimulus complex rather than by any single, context-free stimulus acting in isolation.

Many psychologists strongly emphasize the importance of the individual's interpretation or "cognitive appraisal" of the situation. They call attention to the *meaning* of the stimulus. Behaviorally oriented psychologists recognize this point but usually go a step further, believing that their task must include isolating the exact variables that determine what a stimulus may mean in a particular context, so that they can identify the conditions that control meaning.

In recent years, most psychologists have recognized the importance of cognition and information for many aspects of complex behavior. Information and instructions may powerfully affect human learning processes and performance. For example, directions on how to reach one's destination in a new city obviously are more effective than trial-and-error gropings. Similarly, informational feedback about past performance and instructions about the present situation and about contingencies that will arise in the future critically affect the individual's behavior.

We already noted the effects that occur when people watch the behavior of live or filmed models directly. Important social and interpersonal behavior can also be modified by symbolic and cognitive processes that do not depend upon actual observation of a model's behavior. For example, individuals may alter their attitudes after either reading or hearing about the relevant behavior of others (e.g., Bandura & Mischel, 1965; Duncker, 1938). Often these symbolically produced effects are powerful, and may significantly alter such personality-relevant behaviors as self-control patterns, aggressiveness, and achievement strivings (Mischel, 1968). New information conveyed through language and symbols can dramatically change the meaning of stimuli and reinforcers.

The Active Organism   *self involved in behavior*

An emphasis on the role of stimulus conditions is easily misinterpreted as implying a passive view of people—an image of organisms that are empty except for some psychological glue that cements or bonds a bundle of responses automatically to impinging external stimuli. It is true that behavioral analyses attend to the exact covariations between changing conditions and the individual's changing behavior. But while alterations in conditions may come to regulate the individual's behavior, it is the person—not the stimulus or the situation—that is alive and that does the acting. Responses reside only in organisms, not in stimuli or conditions. Current behavior theories concentrate on stimuli in an attempt to understand and to change the person, hopefully for the better (Chapter 10).

Social learning approaches are recognizing that the individual is not a passive bundle of responses. We have long learning histories and long memories, and much of what has happened to us gets internalized and affects all our current responses and future expectations. We interpret ourselves and our behavior—we evaluate, judge, and regulate our own performance. In addition to being rewarded and punished by the external environment, people learn to monitor and evaluate their own behavior and to reward and punish themselves, thus modifying their own behavior and influencing their environment (Bandura, 1971; Mischel, 1973a, 1974). The principles that govern whether we reward or condemn our own behavior have been given much attention in recent theorizing on social learning. The conditions that control the choice of self-administered rewards and punishments, and their relevance for the maintenance and modification of behavior, will be discussed in later chapters.

Summary

In sum, according to social learning or social behavior theories, direct and vicarious learning experiences determine the potential behaviors available to the individual. The person's choice among these behavioral alternatives depends on the probable consequences (reinforcements) to which each alternative is most likely to lead in that particular situation (e.g., Rotter, 1954). Expectancies about these probable consequences depend on direct and vicarious past experiences in similar situations.

Even subtle changes in the situation may alter expectancies about the probable consequences of behavior. Therefore behavior is often specific for a situation, and individuals show great discrimination in what they do.

Social behavior theories seek to analyze the conditions that covary with changes in what people do. The focus therefore is on current behavior change in response to stimulus changes, rather than on inferences about global dispositions. But while the focus is on what the person is doing now, the behaviors studied include self-regulatory and self-control patterns, and the things the individual does privately and covertly. Similarly, while the emphasis is on the "stimulus" or situation, the stimulus often is exceedingly complex—including, for example, instructions and information about other people's behavior.

Overview and Implications

We have surveyed a great deal of information in this chapter. It is time to pause and seek some perspective on the main ideas and implications of the positions that have been discussed here and in the previous chapter.

The Varieties of Behavior Theories

Early efforts to apply concepts from learning theories to problems of personality relied heavily on "stimulus-response" formulations that had emerged from laboratory research on simple learning with lower animals. The most important concepts in these formulations were direct reinforcement (in the form of rewards and punishments for the animal's behaviors); primary and learned drives (the satisfaction of which was believed to have reinforcing effects); and conflict. More recent social learning formulations have focused on observational and cognitive processes in the learning of complex social and interpersonal behaviors. The term "learning theory" or "behavior theory" is often applied to all these positions, sometimes producing confusion because the positions have many fundamental dissimilarities. It is therefore important to distinguish between early "stimulus-response" models that focused on reinforcement and minimized cognitive processes, psychodynamic behavior theories that were based on Freud, and contemporary social learning theories that do not share those emphases.

Traditional Behavior Theories

Some of the earliest behavioristic formulations shared many of the basic assumptions of trait theory in the sense that they construed personality as a system of broad and relatively stable dispositions. Their term for these dispositions was "habits" rather than "traits," but they accepted some of the assumptions of trait theory. In particular, they believed that habits are generalized response dispositions with stable, consistent properties. Like most behavior theories, these early conceptualizations stressed that habits are learned (e.g., Watson, 1925). Extensions of these behavioral formulations have attempted to fuse the concepts of psychodynamic theory with principles and terms emerging from animal research in laboratory studies of learning. Indeed, Dollard and Miller have devised, as we saw in Chapter 3, a psychodynamic behavior theory that tries to integrate psychoanalytic ideas with the more objective language and methodology of experimental animal research.

Skinner's Radical Behaviorism

In an extremely different vein, other workers, stimulated most notably by B. F. Skinner, have focused on the empirical and experimental analysis of behavior. They avoid inferences about unobservable motives and states in the organism and dwell instead on the observable conditions that seem to control or cause behavior in clearly defined situations. These radically behavioristic views differ sharply from Dollard and Miller's focus on motives and psychic conflicts.

Social Learning and Social Behavior Theories

Most recently, a number of theorists have attempted to make learning and behavior theories more cognitive and "social" and less Freudian. They prefer to study complex social learning rather than simpler animal responding. Some inevitable confusion is introduced by the fact that the same term, "social learning theory," has been used by such diverse theorists as Dollard and Miller, Rotter, and Bandura. We are using the terms "social behavior" and "social learning" theories for approaches that focus on observed social behavior rather than on inferred motives (e.g., Bandura, 1969; Bandura & Walters, 1963; Mischel, 1968; Rotter, 1954). Social behavior theories actually draw on a wide range of phenomena and principles. Although they are committed to the understanding and analysis of behavior from the perspective of learning theory, they have tried to develop an adequately comprehensive, yet rigorous, approach to personality.

Influenced heavily by Skinner, most social behavior approaches emphasize what an organism *does* rather than make inferences about the attributes it *has* (Mischel, 1968). Social behavior analyses of human problems involve descriptions of the covariation between environmental conditions and what the person does, but they avoid inferences about the meaning of the behavior as a sign of some generalized trait or underlying motive. The focus is on what the organism is doing at the present moment rather than on the global dispositions, dynamics, or motives that it may possess or on the individual's inferred (but unobserved) history.

Most current social learning theories do not limit themselves to simple reinforcement principles. Although it is sometimes believed that contemporary social learning formulations neglect cognitive processes, in fact they rely heavily on them in their account of the development of all complex social behaviors.

Focus on Behavior versus Motives

Most modern behavioral approaches (beginning with Skinner's) try to handle the phenomena to which Freud and Miller and Dollard addressed themselves—but do so without invoking motivational constructs requiring inferences about hypothesized conflicts and needs.

Consider the problem of behavioral inconsistency. If one assumes that people have highly generalized traits and motives (as do trait and dynamic theories), then seemingly discrepant behaviors from one individual need special interpretations. Having judged a man to be basically hostile and impulsive, for example, how does one handle new evidence that he is also friendly and controlled? Both a Freudian and a Miller and Dollard analysis of such a person would search for underlying impulses and defenses or counter forces erected against them. The individual's discrepant behaviors might be signs of his underlying conflicts. His occasional "friendliness" and "controlled" behavior might be interpreted as a facade, or as a sign of unconscious efforts to defend against fundamental aggressive impulses, or as manifestations of an approach-avoidance conflict.

A contemporary social learning analysis (e.g., Mischel, 1968, 1969) approaches the same phenomenon quite differently. It focuses on subtle discrimination training throughout socialization. Rather than call upon special defensive mechanisms to mediate between hypothesized motives and supposedly discrepant surface behaviors, it views the diverse behaviors themselves as the predictable products of socialization processes, in which discrimination has a central role. If in the course of the individual's development "aggressiveness" and "impulsiveness" are modeled, expected, and rewarded in some situations but "friendliness" and "control" are learned and encouraged in other situations, then he will display both kinds of behavior, depending on just where he is and the particular conditions. Defense mechanisms, conflicts, displacement, or other underlying processes are not invoked to account for these seeming inconsistencies because the diverse behaviors are seen as the products of discrimination rather than as the signs of underlying conflict. The theoretical position you take on this issue has critical implications for your approach to most other phenomena of personality. Because of its importance, evidence relevant to this issue will be discussed often in later chapters.

The Complexity of Social Learning

Most contemporary social behavior theories recognize that people may generate patterns of behavior in complex ways; they do not simply and automatically emit discrete conditioned responses in relation to specific evoking stimuli. The complexity of the "rule systems" that may regulate how persons generate behavior may be seen best in language learning. Children's acquisition of the grammatical system of their language is an extraordinary accomplishment whose mechanisms still are not understood fully (e.g., Chomsky, 1965). It is also widely agreed that how people interpret and perceive internal and external stimuli influence how they ultimately react to them. While early "stimulus-response" theories often left a void between the stimulus and the response, more current learning approaches recognize that the organism is an alive, active processor and storehouse of information rather than a thoughtless, unfeeling automaton. Research and theorizing, however, investigate what people are *doing* (including what they are doing in their heads) rather than try to infer the global motives, dispositions, or traits that they *have*.

Although current behavior theories acknowledge the existence of internal states and processes, they emphasize that these internal events can only be studied through their behavioral referents and manifestations—such as self-reports or physiological measures of emotionality. Social learning approaches, like all other objective approaches, therefore have to rely on behavior as the basis of their observations.

The Limits of Learning: "Preparedness"

While behavior theories emphasize learning, they recognize that the structure and capacities of the organism limit what it can learn and do. Granted that learning is crucially important, within every species and every individual there are structurally imposed limits on potential behavior, as for example, in the limits of human memory (e.g., Miller, 1956). Behavioral learning theories have to recognize that response capacities are restricted by the capacities and characteristics of the organism.

These "built-in" restrictions may even affect the ease with which different types of associations can be learned. For example, people often develop severe fears of snakes and dogs, but rarely for electric outlets, in spite of their potential hazards. Why? Might some types of stimuli be more likely to become "conditioned" stimuli for different species? Research with animals suggests that species may be prepared innately to learn some associations but not others (e.g., Garcia, McGowan, & Green, 1972). Even people may be "prepared" to acquire fears of certain stimuli (e.g., snakes) more readily than they learn to fear other stimuli (e.g., houses, faces), after they have a negative experience with them (Öhman, Erixon, & Löfberg, 1975).

On the other hand, differences between species in what they learn easily are not necessarily due to biologically built-in preparedness. For example, such differences may reflect differences in their ability to discriminate particular stimuli and to associate paired events over time, rather than to an inborn preparedness to associate only certain types of stimuli (Krane & Wagner, 1975). The idea that people are prepared biologically to fear things that may have threatened human survival throughout evolution is provocative (Seligman, 1971), but as Bandura (1977, p. 75) has pointed out:

> It remains to be demonstrated whether the events people fear are better predicted from their threat to survival or from the degree to which they are correlated with direct, vicarious, and symbolic aversive experiences.

TABLE 4-2
SUMMARY OVERVIEW OF SOCIAL BEHAVIOR APPROACHES

Basic units:	Behavior-in-situation.
Causes of behavior:	Prior learning and specific expectations and cues in situation (including the behavior of others).
Favored data:	Direct observations of behavior in the target situation.
Observed responses used as:	Behavior samples.
Research focus:	Behavior change; analysis of conditions controlling behavior; self-control.
Approach to personality change:	By changing conditions; by experiences that modify expectations.
Role of situation:	Provides important information; interacts reciprocally with person.

Where Is the Person in Behavior Theory? Interactionism

Many critics appreciate the contributions of behavioral approaches for applied purposes (Part II) but fault them vehemently for excessive attention to the "stimulus" or "situation" (e.g., Adinolfi, 1971; Alker, 1972; Bowers, 1973). They view this overemphasis as part of a "situationism in psychology" that erroneously minimizes the importance of dispositional or intrapsychic determinants such as traits (Bowers, 1973). In this vein, Carlson (1971) wonders "where is the person?" in current behaviorally oriented psychology and implies that a focus on the momentary situational determinants of behavior may lead one to lose the person in personality psychology.

Recent versions of social behavior theory have explicitly rejected the idea that situations are the only (or even the main) determinants of all behavior. Indeed, they emphasize the reciprocal (mutual) interaction between the person and the situation, noting that people change situations actively and are not merely passively "shaped" by them (Bandura, 1977, 1978; Mischel, 1973a). They also insist that a full account of behavior must pay attention to the person's "self-system"; the standards and rules used in self-control, and the expectations about what one can and cannot do successfully.

Some of the main characteristics of social behavior approaches are summarized in Table 4-2. The table condenses points from both the more traditional (radical) and the newer, more cognitive versions of these approaches.

There tends to be agreement that an adequate approach to personality must deal both with the person and the situation, focusing on their interaction rather than on either one in isolation (e.g., Magnusson & Endler, 1977; Moos, 1974). It is much less clear how such interaction should be conceptualized and studied, as will become apparent in Parts II and III of this book. The controversies are complex, the implications are profound, and there is no final agreement on how to resolve the basic issues. An attempt to conceptualize some of the many problems of person-situation interaction is offered in the final chapter of this book.

SUMMARY

1. B. F. Skinner's approach differs from that of Dollard and Miller (and from psychodynamic views) in refusing to infer drives or other internal motivational forces or traits. In Skinner's position, empirical analysis of the stimulus conditions controlling behavior replaces inferences about internal conflicts and underlying motives. Skinner's conceptualization leads to the analysis of behavior in terms of conditioning processes.

2. In classical conditioning, a potent and a neutral stimulus event have been paired together so that eventually the previously neutral event alone evokes portions of the same response that the potent one did initially. Classical conditioning principles have been extended to explain some complex social phenomena and neurotic or abnormal behaviors such as irrational fears.

3. Operant conditioning refers to behavior changes produced by reinforcement or reward for responses. Information and attention, as well as food and sexual gratification, are among the many outcomes that can serve as reinforcers and increase the probability of a particular behavior in operant conditioning.

4. Contemporary social learning theories (also called "social behavior theories") recognize that the human being is a complex and active interpreter of the world. Nevertheless, they focus on what people are *doing* rather than on their underlying dispositions. They seek to understand the stimulus conditions influencing behavior.

5. J. B. Rotter introduced the notion of *expectancy* to personality-oriented learning theories. Expectancies about the consequences of behavior and the value to the person of those consequences determine choices. These expectancies and values are learned from past reinforcement.

6. Recent social learning theories emphasize observational learning. Complex and important potential behavior can be acquired without external reinforcement to the learner. Observational learning without direct reinforcement may account for the learning of many novel responses. Outcomes, incentives, and reinforcements are important, however, as determinants of what the person does in a particular situation, that is, which response one selects from the repertoire of alternatives available.

7. Social learning theory does not posit the existence of broad traits or dispositions. Instead, it views both consistency and discriminativeness in behavior as dependent on the conditions of learning and the cues in the situation.

8. Social behavior analyses study the covarying changes of conditions and behavior. Both the conditions and the behaviors may be exceedingly complex; they may involve much more than simple physical stimulus attributes. An especially important aspect of personality involves the person's self-reactions and self-regulation of outcomes that do not depend simply on the external environment.

9. Social behavior theory searches for causes in the current conditions that demonstrably control the person's present behaviors. This em-

phasis contrasts with traditional dynamic theories, which infer the person's motives, conflicts, and dispositions from behavioral "signs" and which construe behaviors as being in the service of underlying motives and their dynamic transformations.

10. Although behavior theories focus on learning, they recognize that an organism's inborn capacities limit what can be learned. There is some controversy about the degree to which people are innately "prepared" to learn certain associations (for example, specific fears) more easily than other associations.

11. The focus of social behavior theory is on what people are doing in the "here and now" rather than on reconstructions of their psychic history. There is a refusal to hypothesize drives, forces, motives, and other broad dispositions as explanations, and an emphasis on the individual's potential for change. Although often labeled "behavioristic," these features are not unique to a behavioral position. Surprisingly, they just as fully fit most of the existentially oriented and "phenomenological" positions, which will be discussed in the next chapter.

CHAPTER 5

PHENOMENOLOGICAL THEORIES: CONCEPTIONS

Jean Pisget
Carl Jung
Allport
Lewins
Maslow
Carl Rodgers
Kelly 113

This chapter presents an overview of several theories that deal with the "self" and with the person's subjective, internal experiences and personal concepts. There are many complexities and variations in the many versions of the orientation to personality presented in this chapter. In spite of these variations, however, a few fundamental themes emerge as its chief characteristics.

For purposes of abbreviation and simplicity, we will call the orientation in this chapter "phenomenological," although some of the positions here have been given other labels, such as "self" theories, "construct" theories, "humanistic" theories, "cognitive" theories, and "existential" theories. Most phenomenological theories are distinctive both in the concepts they reject and in the ones they emphasize. They tend to reject most of the dynamic and motivational concepts of psychoanalytic theories and motivational learning theories (Miller & Dollard) and also most of the assumptions of trait theories.

The rejection, or at least the minimization of motivational explanations, is accompanied by an emphasis on people's immediate experiences and on their current relationships, perceptions, and encounters. The person thus is viewed as an experiencing being, rather than as a "personality structure" or as a syndrome of "psychodynamics" and long-term dispositions. The focus of this orientation tends to be on the individual's subjective experience, personal view of the world and self, and private concepts. Most of the approaches discussed in this chapter also stress people's positive strivings and their tendencies toward growth and self-actualization.

Most of the theories presented here are concerned broadly with cognition—with how we come to know and understand the world and ourselves. An interest in cognition implies attention to the internal or mental processes through which individuals "code" and categorize information. Influenced by the Swiss psychologist Jean Piaget, cognitive theories call attention to people's "mental structures," and to the active ways in which the mind generates meaning and experience. Ulric Neisser, for example, puts it this way (1967, p. 3): "Whether beautiful or ugly or just conveniently at hand, the world of experience is produced by the man who experiences it." That statement, of course, does not imply that there is no "real" world of objects—houses, mountains, people, tables, books—and it does not suggest that the "environment" is a fiction that does not affect our private experience. The cognitive position stresses, however, that "we have no direct immediate access to the world, nor to any of its properties. . . . Whatever we know about reality has been *mediated,* not only by the organs of sense but by complex systems which interpret and reinterpret sensory information" (Neisser, 1967, p. 3).

Many studies on the mechanisms involved in cognition, and on the "stimulus as coded" (Lawrence, 1959), are being conducted in fields that bear only indirectly on personality, such as memory and perception (e.g., Anderson & Bower, 1973). Nevertheless, as a general orientation the cognitive approach has major importance for the study of persons.

Some personality psychologists concerned with cognition have tried to understand how the individual perceives, thinks, interprets, and experiences the world; that is, they have tried to grasp the individual's point of view. Their focus is on stimuli as they are interpreted, on events as they are represented cognitively inside the beholder, on persons and events of life as seen by the perceiver. In sum, they are most interested in the person's experience as *he or she* perceives and categorizes it—the person's phenomenology. Ideally, they would like to look at the world through the "subject's" eyes and to stand in her shoes, to *be* her long enough to experience a bit of what she experiences. This phenomenological stance is the main concern of the present chapter.

Sources of the Phenomenological Approach

The orientation presented in this chapter has numerous sources. For example, among the many early theorists who were fascinated with the self were William James, George H. Mead, and John Dewey. Another early theorist concerned with the self was Carl Jung. As early as the start of the century, Jung called attention to the organism's strivings for self-realization and integration, and the existence of creative processes that go beyond the basic instincts of

Freudian psychology. Also important were Gestalt psychology and existential philosophy. Given all these contributors, it becomes a bit arbitrary to select a few for detailed exposition. Hence, the ideas that are presented next should be considered merely representative and far from exhaustive.

Allport's Contribution

We saw in Chapter 2 that Gordon Allport recognized the existence of some common traits that all people might share in varying degrees. Some of his other ideas are most relevant to a phenomenological approach, however, and fit best in the present chapter. Allport emphasizes the *uniqueness* of the individual and of the integrated patterns that distinguish each person. He also notes the *lack of motivational continuity* during the individual's life and criticizes the Freudian emphasis on the enduring role of sexual and aggressive motives.

According to Allport, behavior is motivated originally by instincts, but later it may be capable of sustaining itself indefinitely without biological reinforcement. Allport sees most normal adult motives as no longer having a functional relation to their historical roots. "Motives are contemporary. . . . Whatever drives must drive now. . . . The character of motives alters so radically from infancy to maturity that we may speak of adult motives as *supplanting* the motives of infancy" (1940, p. 545). This idea has been called "functional autonomy" to indicate that a habit, say practicing the violin at a certain hour each day, need not be tied to any basic motive of infancy. The extent to which an individual's motives are autonomous is a measure of maturity, according to Allport.

Allport thus stresses the contemporaneity of motives (1961). In his view, the past is not important unless it can be shown to be dynamically active in the present. He believes that historical facts about a person's past, while helping to reveal the total course of the individual's life, do not adequately explain the person's conduct today. In his words, "Past motives explain nothing unless they are also present motives" (1961, p. 220).

While fully recognizing the unity of growth in personality development, Allport emphasizes that later motives do not necessarily depend on earlier ones. Although the life of a plant is continuous with that of its seed, the seed no longer feeds and sustains the mature plant. In human terms, while a musician may have been spurred to mastery of her instrument through the need to overcome inferiority feelings, her later love of music is functionally autonomous from its origins.

Allport was also one of the strongest advocates of the self as a key feature of personality. To avoid a homunculus or manikin-in-the-mind conception of self or ego, he has coined the term *proprium*. In his view, the propriate functions of the personality include bodily sense, self-identity, self-esteem, self-extension, rational thinking, self-image, propriate striving, and knowing. The proprium contains the root of the consistency that characterizes attitudes,

proprium

self develops in time

goals, and values. This proprium is not innate (a newborn does not have a self); it develops in time.

In addition to deemphasizing the person's early motivations and distant past, Allport focuses on the individual's currently perceived experiences, his or her phenomenological self and unique pattern of adaptation. He also favors a *wholistic* view of the individual as an integrated, biosocial organism, rather than as a bundle of traits and motives.

Lewin's Field Theory

what happens right now determines behavior

Still another important post-Freudian influence came from field theories (e.g., Lewin, 1936). These positions construed behavior as determined by the person's psychological life space—by the events that exist in the total psychological situation at the moment—rather than by past events or enduring, situation-free dispositions. The most elegant formulation of this position was Kurt Lewin's "field theory."

The field concept of physics culminating in Einstein's theory of relativity was the inspiration for Kurt Lewin's theory of personality. Einstein's concept of "fields of force" has an expression in the Gestalt movement of psychology, which asserts that each part of a whole is dependent upon every other part. The Gestaltists applied the notion of a field of interrelated components primarily to perception. They proposed that the way in which an object is perceived depends upon the total context or configuration of its surroundings. What is perceived depends on the *relationships* among components of a perceptual field, rather than on the fixed characteristics of the individual components.

Lewin proposed the application of field theory to all branches of psychology. Field theory for him was a set of concepts that facilitate the translation of phenomenological experience. In his view, such conceptualizing was the psychologist's primary task as a scientist.

$B = f(P, E)$

Lewin defined *life space* as the totality of facts that determine the behavior (*B*) of an individual at a certain moment. The life space includes the person (*P*) and the psychological environment (*E*), as depicted in Figure 5-1. Thus behavior is a function of the person and the environment, as expressed in the formula $B = f(P, E)$.

Lewin also discussed the question of the temporal relationship of an event and the conditions that produce it. Generally this question concerns whether past events only, or future events also, can cause change. Ordinary cause, based on the notion of causation in classical physics, assumes that something past is the cause of present events. Teleological theories assume that future events influence present events. Lewin's thesis is that neither past nor future, by definition, exists at the present moment and therefore neither can have an effect at the present. Past events have a position in the historical causal chains whose interweavings create the present situation, but only those events that are functioning in the present situation need to be taken into account.

FIGURE 5-1
Lewin's Life Space

The life space contains the person in his or her psychological environment, which is delineated by a boundary (the ellipse) from the nonpsychological world.

Such events are, by definition, current or momentary. In other words, only present facts can cause present behavior.

In representing the life space, Lewin therefore took into account only that which is contemporary. He termed this the principle of *contemporaneity* (Lewin, 1936). This does not mean the field theorists are not interested in historical problems or in the effects of previous experience. As Lewin (1951) pointed out, field theorists have enlarged the psychological experiment to include situations that contain a history that is systematically created throughout hours or weeks. For example, college students in an experiment might be given repeated failure experiences (on a series of achievement tasks) during several sessions. The effects of these experiences on the students' subsequent aspirations and expectancies for success might then be measured.

The boundaries between the person and the psychological environment and between the life space and the physical world are *permeable, that is, capable of mutual influence.* That makes prediction difficult because one cannot be sure beforehand when and what facts will permeate a boundary and influence a fact from another region. Lewin asserts that the psychologist might therefore concentrate on describing and explaining the concrete psychological situation in terms of field theory rather than attempt prediction.

Lewin (1935) rejected the notion of constant, entity-like personality characteristics such as unchanging traits. As a result of dynamic forces, psychological reality is always changing. The environment of the individual does not serve merely to facilitate tendencies that are permanently established in the person's nature (1936). Habits are not frozen associations, but rather the result of forces in the organism and its life space.

Lewin was similarly dissatisfied with the usual concept of needs. In descriptions of psychological reality, Lewin said, the needs that are producing effects in the momentary situation are the only ones that have to be represented. A need in Lewin's theory corresponds to a tension system of the inner-person region. Lewin was also interested in reward and punishment. Instead of the hedonistic formulations of early learning theorists, Lewin construed rewards as devices for controlling behavior in momentary situations by causing changes in the psychological environment and in the tension systems of the person.

For Lewin, behavior and development are functions of the same structural and dynamic factors. Both are a function of the person and the psychological environment. In general, with increasing maturity there is greater differentiation of the person and the psychological environment.

Lewin's field theory had a major impact on experimental social psychology. His students extended his ideas and pursued them through ingenious experiments designed to alter the subject's life space—by altering perceptions about the self, about other people, about events. The effects of these alterations on attitudes, aspirations, task persistence, and other indices were then examined carefully. Until recently Lewin's influence on personality psychology has been less extensive. There is now, however, an increasing recognition of the importance of the psychological situation in studies of traits and motives (e.g., Magnusson, 1980; Mischel, 1973a).

I like

Phenomenology and Existentialism

The writings of Snygg and Combs (1949) also stressed the phenomenological features of the field; they influenced psychologists interested in the subject's awareness and private experiences. More recently, Carl Rogers and George A. Kelly have developed positions in which private experiences, subjective perceptions, and the self all have an important part.

Somewhat similar themes emphasizing the role of higher-order "positive" motives—growth, fulfillment, and the self and its actualization—have been developed by Abraham Maslow and others. According to Maslow, for example, humans are innately good. Growth motivation moves the individual through hierarchically ordered degrees of health to ultimate self-actualization. "Every person is, in part, his own project, and makes himself" (Maslow, 1965, p. 308). Behavior is seen as goal directed, striving, purposeful, and motivated by higher actualization needs rather than by primary biological drives alone. (Some of Maslow's specific work is discussed in Chapter 11.)

The ideas of most of these theorists have much in common with the existential philosophical position developed by such European thinkers and writers as Kierkegaard, Sartre, and Camus and by the Swiss psychiatrists Binswanger and Boss. The key features of their orientation are expressed by Rollo May, an American proponent of existential psychology. Thinking about a patient of his in psychotherapy, May recognizes that he has available all sorts of information about her, such as hypotheses from her Rorschach and diagnoses from her neurologist. He then comments (1961, p. 26):

But if, as I sit here, I am chiefly thinking of these *whys* and *hows* of the way the problem came about, I will have grasped everything *except the most important thing of all, the existing person.* Indeed, I will have grasped everything except the only real source of data I have, namely, this experiencing human being, this person now emerging, becoming, "building world," as the existential psychologists put it, immediately in this room with me.

As May's remarks indicate, the emphasis of existentialists is on phenomeno-logical experience, on the "here and now" rather than on etiology or distant historical causes in the person's early childhood. Furthermore, the existential orientation sees the human being as capable of choice and responsibility rather than as the victim of unconscious forces or of habits. The Swiss existential psychiatrist Binswanger commented that Freudian theory pictured human beings not yet as people in the full sense, but only as creatures buffeted about by life. Binswanger believes that for a person to be fully himself—that is, to be truly realized or actualized as a human being—he must "look fate in the face." In his view, the fact that human life is deter-mined by forces and conditions is only one side of the truth. The other side is that we ourselves "determine these forces as our fate" (cited in May, 1961, p. 252). Thus in the phenomenological and existential orientation, humans are seen as beings whose actualization requires much more than the fulfillment of biological needs and of sexual and aggressive instincts.

The existentialists propose that we are inevitably the builders of our own lives and, more specifically, that each person is:

1. a *choosing* agent, unable to avoid choices throughout the course of life
2. a *free* agent, who freely sets life goals
3. a *responsible* agent, accountable personally for his or her life choices

Our existence in life is given but our essence is what we make of life, how meaningfully and responsibly we construct it. This is an often painful, iso-lated, agonizing enterprise. To find satisfying values, to guide our lives accord-ingly, to give life meaning—these goals are all part of the existential quest, and they require the "courage to be"—the courage to break from blind con-formity to the group and to strive instead for self-fulfillment by seeking greater self-definition and authenticity.

Finally, to grasp what it means to *be* also requires being in constant touch with the awareness of nonbeing, of alienation, of nothingness, and ultimately of the inevitability of death, everyone's unavoidable fate. The awareness of this inevitable fate and what that implies produces *existential anxiety*. The antidote for such anxiety is to face and live our lives responsibly, meaning-fully, and with courage and awareness of our potential for continuous choice and growth.

To understand some of the main features of the existential and phenomenological orientation more closely, we shall consider the ideas of one of its most articulate proponents, Carl Rogers, in the next section.

Carl Rogers' Self Theory

wholebetter approach

Unique Experience

Rogers' phenomenological theory of personality emphasizes the uniquely experienced reality of the person. Rogers regards behavior as the result of immediate perceptual events as they actually are experienced by the individual. Because no one else, no matter how hard he tries, can completely assume another person's "internal frame of reference," the person himself has the greatest potential for awareness of what reality is for him. In other words, each person potentially is the world's best expert on himself and has the best information about himself.

good

person knows self best

In Rogers' view, "behavior is basically the goal-directed attempt of the organism to satisfy its needs as experienced, in the field as perceived" (1951, p. 491). The emphasis is on the person's perceptions as the determinants of his or her actions: How one sees and interprets events determines how one reacts to them.

Self-Actualization

Like most phenomenologists, Rogers advocates abandoning specific motivational constructs and views the organism as functioning as an organized whole. He maintains that "there is one central source of energy in the human organism; that it is a function of the whole organism rather than some portion of it; and that it is perhaps best conceptualized as a tendency toward fulfillment, toward actualization, toward the maintenance and enhancement of the organism" (1963, p. 6). Thus the inherent tendency of the organism is to actualize itself. "Motivation" then becomes not a special construct but an overall characteristic of simply being alive.

In line with his essentially positive view of human nature, Rogers asserts that emotions are beneficial to adjustment. Instead of stressing the disruptive effects of anxiety, Rogers believes that "emotion accompanies and in general facilitates . . . goal-directed behavior, . . . the intensity of the emotion being related to the perceived significance of the behavior for the maintenance and enhancement of the organism" (1951, p. 493).

The organism in the course of actualizing itself engages in a valuing process. Experiences that are perceived as enhancing it are valued positively (and approached). Experiences that are perceived as negating enhancement or maintenance of the organism are valued negatively (and avoided). "The organism has one basic tendency and striving—to actualize, maintain, and enhance the experiencing organism" (Rogers, 1951, p. 487).

The Self

The self is a central concept for Rogers—indeed, his theory is often referred to as a self theory of personality. The self or self-concept (the two terms are equivalent for Rogers) is an "organized, consistent, conceptual gestalt composed of perceptions of the characteristics of the 'I' or 'me' and the perceptions of the relationships of the 'I' or 'me' to others and to various aspects of life, together with the values attached to these perceptions" (Rogers, 1959, p. 200). As a result of interaction with the environment, a portion of the perceptual field gradually becomes differentiated into the self. This perceived self (self-concept) influences perception and behavior. That is, the interpretation of the self—as strong or weak, for example—affects how one perceives the rest of one's world.

The experiences of the self become invested with values. These values are the result of direct experience with the environment, or they may be introjected or taken over from others. For example, a young child finds it organismically enjoyable to relieve himself whenever he experiences physiological tension in the bowel or bladder. However, he may sometimes also experience parental words and actions indicating that such behavior is bad, and that he is not lovable when he does this. A conflict then develops that may result in distortion and denial of experience. That is, the parental attitudes may be experienced as if they were based on the evidence of the child's own experience. In this example, the satisfaction of defecating may start to be experienced as bad even though a more accurate symbolization would be that it is often experienced as organismically satisfying. Rogers goes on to suggest that in bowel training, denial or distortion of experience may be avoided if the parent is able genuinely to accept the child's feelings and at the same time accepts his or her own feelings.

Consistency and Positive Regard

Rogers proposes two systems—the self (self-concept) and the organism—that may be in opposition or in harmony. When these systems are in opposition and incongruence, the result is maladjustment, for then the self becomes rigidly organized, losing contact with actual organismic experience and fraught with tensions. Perception is selective: We try to perceive experiences in ways consistent with the self-concept. The self-concept thus serves as a frame of reference for evaluating and monitoring the actual experiences of the organism. Unconscious denial of experience that is inconsistent with the concept of self is, Rogers believes, what the Freudians have tried to explain by the mechanism of repression. Experiences that are inconsistent with the self may be perceived as threats, and the more threat there is the more rigid and defensive the self structure becomes to maintain itself. At the same time, the self-concept becomes less congruent with organismic reality and loses contact with the actual experiences of the organism.

Rogers assumes a universal need for positive regard.

Rogers (1959) assumes a universal need for positive regard, which develops as the awareness of the self emerges. This need leads the person to desire acceptance and love from the important people in his life. Sometimes they may accept him conditionally (i.e. depending on his specific behavior), or may accept him in his own right and give him unconditional regard. The person needs positive regard not only from others but also from his self. The need for self-regard develops out of self-experiences associated with the satisfaction or frustration of the need for positive regard. If a person experiences only unconditional positive regard, his self-regard also would be unconditional. In that case the needs for positive regard and self-regard would never be at variance with "organismic evaluation." Such a state would represent genuine psychological adjustment and full functioning.

Most people do not achieve such ideal adjustment. Often a self-experience is avoided or sought only because it is less (or more) worthy of self-regard. For example, a child may experience anger toward her mother but avoids accepting that feeling because she wants to be a "good girl." When that happens, Rogers speaks of the individual's having acquired a "condition of worth." Experiences that are in accord with the individual's conditions of worth tend to be perceived accurately in awareness, but experiences that violate the conditions of worth may be denied to awareness and distorted grossly. When there is a significant amount of incongruence between the individual's self-concept and her evaluation of an experience, then defenses may become unable to work successfully. For example, if a young woman persistently experiences herself as painfully dissatisfied and "unhappy" in her efforts at schoolwork, but views herself as having to "succeed at college" in order to be an adequate person, she may experience great strain in her defensive efforts.

Rogers' theory, like Freud's, posits that accurate awareness of experiences may be threatening to the self and therefore may be prevented. Anxiety in Rogers' theory might be interpreted as the tension exhibited by the organized concept of the self when it senses (without full awareness, i.e., by "subceptions") that the recognition or symbolization of certain experiences would be destructive of its organization (1951). If a person's concept of the self has been built around his "masculinity," for example, experiences that might imply that he has some homosexual tendencies would threaten him severely. Anxiety thus involves a basic threat to the self, and defenses are erected to avoid it.

"Client-centered" (Rogerian) therapy seeks to bring about the harmonious interaction of the self and the organism and to facilitate a greater congruence between the conceptual structure of the self and the phenomenal field of experience. The warm and unconditionally accepting attitude of the counselor hopefully enables the client to perceive and examine experiences that are inconsistent with the current self-structure. The client can then revise this self-structure to permit it to assimilate these inconsistent experiences. According to Rogers, the client gradually reorganizes the self-concept to bring it into line with the reality of organismic experience: "He will *be,* in more unified fashion, what he organismically *is,* and this seems to be the essence of therapy" (1955, p. 269). In recent years Rogers has moved beyond individual client-centered therapy to form and lead many encounter groups intended to encourage psychological growth (see Chapter 11).

Rogers' Perspective on His Own Work

Looking back at the almost 50 years of his contributions to psychology, Rogers (1974) tried to pinpoint the essence of his approach. In his view, his most fundamental idea was that:

> . . . the individual has within himself vast resources for self-understanding, for altering his self-concept, his attitudes, and his self-directed behavior—and that these resources can be tapped if only a definable climate of facilitative psychological attitudes can be provided (Rogers, 1974, p. 116).

Such a climate for growth requires an atmosphere in which feelings can be confronted, expressed, and accepted fully and freely. His continued emphasis on the person's potential freedom, the hallmark of a humanistic orientation, remains unchanged:

> My experience in therapy and in groups makes it impossible for me to deny the reality and significance of human choice. To me it is not an illusion that man is to some degree the architect of himself . . . for me the humanistic approach is the only possible one. It is for each person, however, to follow the pathway—behavioristic or humanistic—that he finds most congenial (Rogers, 1974, p. 119).

In the same humanistic vein he decries modern technology and calls for autonomy and self-exploration:

> Our culture, increasingly based on the conquest of nature and the control of man, is in decline. Emerging through the ruins is the new person, highly aware, self-directing, an explorer of inner, perhaps more than outer, space, scornful of the conformity of institutions and the dogma of authority. He does not believe in being behaviorally shaped, or in shaping the behavior of others. He is most assuredly humanistic rather than technological. In my judgment he has a high probability of survival (Rogers, 1974, p. 119).

In sum, Rogers' theory highlights many of the chief points of the phenomenological and humanistic approach to personality. It emphasizes the person's perceived reality, subjective experiences, organismic striving for actualization, the potential for growth and freedom. It rejects or deemphasizes specific biological drives, and focuses on the experienced self rather than on historical causes or stable trait structures. A unique feature of Rogers' position is his emphasis on unconditional acceptance as a requisite for self-regard. Other theorists have emphasized different aspects of experience in their formulations. One of the most influential of these positions is George Kelly's theory, which is discussed in the next section.

George Kelly's Psychology of Personal Constructs

As students of general semantics often point out, "The map is not the terrain." Yet the two are often confused. Psychologically it is equally true that our constructs and abstractions about behavior are not the same as the behaviors that are being categorized. In addition to acting as motivated organisms, people also are perceivers and construers of behavior, and they generate abstractions about themselves and others. These hypotheses and constructions have long intrigued psychologists interested in subjective states, in phenomenology, and in the experience of the self.

The Subject's Constructs

In the psychodynamic approach, the motive is the chief unit, unconscious conflicts are the processes of greatest interest, and the clinical judge is the favored instrument. Kelly's (1955) personal construct theory, in contrast, seeks to illuminate the person's own categories rather than the hypotheses of the psychologist. Its main units are the person's constructs—the way we categorize our own experiences. Rather than seeing people as victimized by their impulses and defenses, this position views the human being as an active, ever-changing creator of hypotheses and a player of multiple roles.

According to Kelly, trait psychology tries to find the subject's place on the *theorist's* personality dimension. "Personal construct theory" instead tries to see how the subject aligns events on *his or her own* dimensions. It is Kelly's hope to discover the nature of the subject's construct dimensions rather than to locate his position on the dimensions of the psychologist's theory.

People as Scientists

The psychology of personal constructs explores the subjective maps that people generate in coping with the psychological terrain of their lives. Kelly emphasizes that, just like the scientist who studies them, human subjects also construe or abstract behavior, categorizing, interpreting, labeling, and judging themselves and their world. The individuals assessed by psychologists are themselves assessors who evaluate and construe their own behavior; they even assess the personality psychologists who try to assess them. Constructions and hypotheses about behavior are formulated by all persons regardless of their formal degrees and credentials as scientists. According to Kelly it is these constructions, and not merely simple physical responses, that must be studied in an adequate approach to personality. Categorizing behavior is equally evident when a psychotic patient describes his personal, private ideas in therapy and when a scientist discusses her favorite constructs and theories at a professional meeting. Both people represent the environment internally and express their representations and private experiences in their psychological constructions. Personal constructions, and not objective behavior descriptions on clear dimensions, confront the personality psychologist.

Kelly notes that most psychological scientists view themselves as motivated to achieve cognitive clarity and to understand phenomena, including their own lives. Yet the subjects of their theories, unlike the theorists themselves, are seen as unaware victims of psychic forces and traits that they can neither understand nor control. Kelly tries to remove this discrepancy between the theorist and the subject and to treat all people as if they were scientists.

Just like the scientist, subjects generate constructs and hypotheses with which they try to anticipate and control events in their lives. Therefore to understand the subject, one has to understand his or her constructs or private personality theory. To study an individual's constructs one has to find behavioral examples or "referents" for them. We cannot know what another person means when she says, "I have too much ego," or "I am not a friendly person," or "I may be falling in love," unless she gives us behavioral examples. Examples (referents) are required whether the construct is personal, for example the way a patient construes herself "as a woman," or theoretical, as when a psychologist talks about "introversion" or "ego defenses." Constructs can become known only through behavior.

Constructive Alternativism

The same events can be alternatively categorized. While people may not always be able to change events, they can always construe them differently. That is what Kelly meant by "constructive alternativism." To illustrate, consider this event: A boy drops his mother's favorite vase. What does it mean? The event is simply that the vase has been broken. Yet ask the child's psychoanalyst and he may point to the boy's unconscious hostility; ask the mother and she tells you how "mean" he is; his father says he is "spoiled"; the child's teacher may see the event as evidence of the child's "laziness" and chronic "clumsiness"; grandmother calls it just an "accident"; and the child himself may construe the event as reflecting his "stupidity." While the event cannot be undone—the vase is broken—its interpretation is open to alternative constructions, and these may lead to different courses of action.

Kelly's theory began with this fundamental postulate: "A person's processes are psychologically channelized by the ways in which he anticipates events" (Kelly, 1955, p. 46). Phrased differently, this postulate means that a person's activities are guided (stabilized, channelized) by the constructs (ways) he or she uses to predict (anticipate) events. This postulate shares with other phenomenological theories an emphasis on the person's subjective view, but it is more specific in its focus on how the individual predicts or anticipates events. The postulate is further elaborated by a set of formal corollaries. Although the details of the theory need not concern us here, several of the main ideas require comment.

Kelly is concerned with the *convenience* of constructs rather than with their absolute truth. Rather than try to assess whether a particular construct is true, Kelly attends to its convenience or utility for the construer. For example, rather than try to assess whether or not a client is "really a latent homosexual" or "really going crazy," he tries to discover the implications for the client's life of construing himself in that way. If the construction is not convenient, then the task is to find a better alternative—that is, one that predicts better and leads to better outcomes. Just as a psychologist may get stuck with an inadequate theory, so his subjects also may impale themselves on their constructions and construe themselves into a dilemma. Individuals may torture themselves into believing that "I am not worthy enough" or "I am not successful enough," as if these verdicts were matters of undisputable fact rather than constructions and hypotheses about behavior. The job of psychotherapy is to provide the conditions in which personal constructs can be elaborated, tested for their implications, and, if necessary, modified. Just like the scientist, the subject needs the chance to test personal constructs and to validate or invalidate them, progressively modifying them in the light of new experience.

Roles

Another idea that merits special attention is Kelly's emphasis on roles and role enactments. Rather than seeing humans as possessing fairly stable, broadly generalized traits, Kelly saw them as capable of enacting many different roles and of engaging in continuous change. A role, for Kelly, is an attempt to see another person through the other's glasses—that is, to look at a person through *his or her* constructs—and to structure one's actions in that light. To enact a role requires that behavior be guided by perception of the other person's viewpoint. Thus to "role play" your mother, for example, you would have to try to see things (including yourself) as she does, "through her eyes," and to act in light of those perceptions. You would try to behave as if you really were your mother. Kelly used the technique of role playing extensively as a therapeutic procedure designed to help persons gain new perspectives and to generate more convenient ways of living.

People Are What They Make of Themselves

Like other phenomenologists, Kelly rejects the idea of specific motives. His view of human nature focuses on how people construe themselves and on what they do in the light of those constructs. Kelly (like Rogers) believes that no special concepts are required to understand why people are motivated and active: Every person is motivated "for no other reason than that he is alive" (Kelly, 1958, p. 49). For Kelly, the concept of motivation "can appear only as a redundancy" (1958, p. 50).

He believes, like many existentialists, that the individual *is* what he *does* and comes to know his nature by seeing what he is doing. Starting from his clinical experiences with troubled college students in Fort Hays, Kansas, where he taught for many years, Kelly independently reached a position that overlaps remarkably with the views of such European existential philosophers as Sartre (1956). In Sartre's (1956) existentialist conception, "existence precedes essence": There is no human nature—man simply *is,* and he is nothing else but what he "makes of himself."

Feeling and Fulfillment

Kelly believes that his theory, though it focuses on the person's constructs, is not purely concerned with cognitive and intellectual functions. Constructs, he says, often are not verbal, and they may have highly emotional ingredients. Nevertheless some critics find that his view of the scientist neglects the person as an emotional being. Since Kelly's work, many phenomenologically oriented psychologists have become increasingly committed to the affective, nonverbal components of experience. This search for feeling is seen in numerous recent psychological movements, both within psychology as a formal discipline and in the larger social scene.

The concern with feelings, the sense of being "out of touch" and isolated from emotional experiences, is illustrated poignantly in these excerpts from a troubled college student's letter:

> Long ago I lost touch with my body—my brain became separated from my body, and started commanding it. My body turned into just a machine for transporting my brain around from place to place to talk unfeelingly and analytically with other detached brains. I was glad it was a big and efficient machine—but I thought it was the inferior part of me, and that my brain should be in charge and call the tune for my feelings, letting the "positive" ones out and keeping the "negative" ones safely tucked in. . . .
>
> But now I feel lost in that head, out of phase with people—and somehow I want to reach them and my own guts—to know what I really feel, and stop all these precious intellectual games—to really live and not just to exist—So what do I do now?

The idea expressed by this distressed student is shared by many others who want "to make contact" emotionally both with themselves and with other people.

Expanding Consciousness

Probably the most dramatic and controversial manifestation of this trend to achieve deeper feeling was the effort to expand consciousness and emotional experiences by means of psychedelic drugs. Initially drugs such as psilocybin and LSD were advocated most energetically by Timothy Leary and Richard Alpert when they were psychologists at Harvard in 1961 and 1962. In the 1960s the "mind-expanding" movement through drug-induced "trips" or psychic "voyages" gained many enthusiastic participants. Although drawing heavily on Freudian dynamic psychology for its interpretations, this movement had a different purpose from that espoused by most neo-analytic followers of Freud. The neo-analysts emphasized "ego psychology" and the impulse-free (or "conflict-free") spheres of the ego and of rational control processes. Many advocates of consciousness expansion, instead, seemed to seek a return of the "primacy of the id"—a focus on feeling and fantasy, on "primary processes" rather than on logic and rational thought. This effort to capture pure feeling, to experience more closely one's bodily states, to escape from "ego" and "superego" and societal constraints, and to live fully in the "here and now," was seen most vividly in the "hippie" movement and the "drug culture" of the 1960s. We shall consider these experiences again in later sections (Chapter 11).

Such drugs as LSD undoubtedly produce major alterations in subjective experience, including the intensification of feelings (e.g., Leary, Litwin & Metzner, 1963), but enthusiasm for them was soon tempered by the recognition that they entail serious risks. While the much less controversial drug, marijuana, has received increasing acceptance, there also has been a trend to search for greater awareness without the aid of any drugs.

Away from Alienation

Several routes to increasing awareness have relied on psychological experiences rather than on drugs. These efforts include meditation (Ornstein, 1972), encounter groups, and "marathons" of the type developed at the Esalen Institute in Big Sur, California (Schutz, 1967). While meditative techniques have been based mainly on Oriental religious sources (Ornstein & Naranjo, 1971), the encounter or "sensitivity training" movement has drawn on various role-play and psychodrama techniques, on existential philosophy, and on Freudian dynamic psychology. The resulting syntheses are seen in the ideas of the "Gestalt therapy" of Fritz Perls (1969), in the efforts to expand human awareness and to achieve "joy" and true communication (e.g., Schutz, 1967), and in the pursuit of "peak experiences" and "self-actualization" (e.g., Maslow, 1971). Because the implications of these positions are most relevant for psychotherapy and personality change they will be discussed in that context in later sections (Chapter 11).

Toward Fulfillment: Maslow's
Self-Actualizing Person

One of the most influential spokespersons for the importance of becoming "in touch" with one's true feelings and fulfilling oneself totally was Abraham Maslow (1968, 1971). Maslow's theory overlaps considerably with that of Rogers. He also emphasized human beings' vast positive potential for growth and fulfillment. The striving toward actualization of this potential is a basic quality of being human:

> Man demonstrates *in his own nature* a pressure toward fuller and fuller Being, more and more perfect actualization of his humanness in exactly the same naturalistic, scientific sense that an acorn may be said to be "pressing toward" being an oak tree, or that a tiger can be observed to "push toward" being tigerish, or a horse toward being equine. . . . (Maslow, 1968, p. 160).

Maslow's commitment was to study "optimal man" and to discover the qualities of those people who seemed to be closest to realizing all their poten-

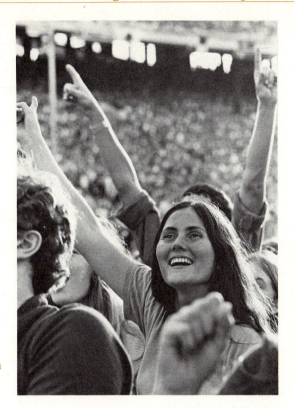

In a "peak experience" the person may achieve a moment of fulfillment and joy.

tialities. In his view, one has higher "growth needs"—needs for self-actualization fulfillment—that emerge when more primitive needs (physiological needs, safety needs, needs for belongingness and self-esteem) are satisfied. Maslow wanted to focus on the qualities of feeling and experience that seem to distinguish self-actualizing, fully functioning people. Therefore, he searched for the attributes that seemed to mark such people as Beethoven, Einstein, Jefferson, Lincoln, Walt Whitman, as well as some of the individuals he knew personally and admired most. These positive qualities are elaborated as part of the humanistic view of the "healthy personality" in Chapter 11.

Self-actualization may be seen not only as a human need and as a quality of certain people, but also as a subjective experience that many of us may have, even if only momentarily, at some points in life. Maslow called this special state a "peak experience"; a temporary experience of fulfillment and joy in which the person loses self-centeredness and (in varying degrees of intensity) feels a nonstriving happiness, a moment of perfection. Words that may be used to describe this state include "aliveness," "beauty," "ecstasy," "effortlessness," "uniqueness," and "wholeness." Such peak experiences have been reported in many contexts, including the esthetic appreciation of nature and beauty, worship, intimate relationships with others, and creative activities.

Overview and Implications

Many personality psychologists welcome the emphasis on the person's cognitions, feelings, and personal interpretations of experience stressed by the theories discussed in this chapter. Indeed this concern with how individuals construe events and see themselves and the world has been a most influential force, and it has generated a great deal of research. The resulting contributions are widely acknowledged. Some of the main features of the phenomenological approach are summarized in Table 5-1.

Table 5-1 distills some shared characteristics. But do not forget that the approaches surveyed in this chapter are quite diverse and far more complex

---

TABLE 5-1
SUMMARY OVERVIEW OF PHENOMENOLOGICAL APPROACHES

Basic units:	The experienced self; personal constructs and self-concepts; subjective feeling and perceptions.
Causes of behavior:	Self-concepts and underlying feelings and conflicts.
	Free (not mechanistic or predetermined) choices; what one "makes of oneself."
Favored data:	Self-disclosure and personal constructs (about self and others).
Observed responses used as:	Signs (of the person's inner states).
Research focus:	Self-concepts; self-awareness and expression; human potential and self-actualization.
Approach to personality change:	By increased awareness, personal honesty, internal consistency and self-acceptance.
Role of situation:	As the context for experience and choice; focus on the situation-as-perceived.

than this summary suggests. In spite of their diversity, these approaches share a focus on the self-as-experienced, on personal constructs, on feelings, and on the possibility of freedom. They search for data and methods that explore how people can disclose and reveal themselves more fully and honestly. They also see greater self-awareness, consistency, and self-acceptance as crucial aspects of personal growth and actualization.

The existential belief that "man is what he makes of himself" and what he conceives himself to be is extremely appealing to many people. It also raises some key issues. First, psychologists committed to a deterministic view of science have to ask what are the *causes* that govern what individuals make of themselves and conceive themselves to be—how do individuals come to make themselves and conceive themselves in particular ways? While philosophers may put the springs of action and cognition into the will (as Sartre does), the scientifically oriented psychologist seeks the variables that account for the phenomena of being and will itself. While able to accept in part the idea that individuals are what they make of themselves, the psychologist as a scientist has to go further and search for the conditions that make them, including those conditions that influence (or make) their self-conceptions.

The existential idea that the person is "in possession of herself," rather than possessed by a human nature, and that she is what she makes of herself, has profound implications for the study of personality. Instead of a search for where the individual stands with regard to the assessor's dimensions, the assessor's task becomes the elaboration of what the individual is making of herself. To the extent that the assessor seeks a full account, however, she also must search for the causes of that existence. This last step is where most psychologists concerned with observable causes part company with the existentialist. It is also the point at which many psychologists have chosen for themselves a humanistic existentialism rather than a deterministic psychology.

Are Cognitions the Causes of Behavior? No

In spite of the obvious importance of personal constructs and other cognitions, one cannot assume that they are the main causes of the person's behavior. Verbal constructs and cognitions do not always cause or even influence nonverbal behavior and the things we do. The relations between personal concepts and other behaviors often are quite indirect and remote. Currently there is relatively little evidence that changes in personal constructs—or in opinions, beliefs, or values—must always produce important behavior changes (Festinger, 1964). Often cognitive and value changes may *follow* as a function of particular behavioral performances, rather than serve as the causes for these performances (e.g., Bem, 1972; Festinger, 1957). That is, constructs and cognitions may be realigned to make them consistent with behavior and may be used to justify that behavior. The issues and evidence on this topic are discussed in later chapters.

Incomplete Explanations

Perhaps the most fundamental criticism of cognitive and phenomenological explanations is that they are incomplete and do not provide a sufficiently detailed and comprehensive analysis of the causes controlling behavior. In Kelly's theory, for example, personal constructs are viewed as key determinants of behavior, but what determines the constructs that a person has? Offering the construct as a cause of the observed behavior may be an example of an unfinished causal explanation. According to Skinner, such unfinished analyses are found whenever mental states, perceptions, cognitions, feelings, motives, or similar constructs are offered as explanations of behavior while the determinants of the mental states themselves are ignored. Skinner (1964, p. 93) has called this the use of "mental way stations" for unfinished causal sequences and says:

> A disturbance in behavior is not explained by relating it to felt anxiety until the anxiety has in turn been explained. An action is not explained by attributing it to expectations until the expectations have in turn been accounted for.

In his view, a comprehensive analysis must include the conditions or *variables* that control the behavior of interest and not merely the hypothetical intervening mental steps.

Phenomenological positions have been criticized for removing the perceiver or "construer" from the causal chain—and hence removing him from scientific study. This feature—problematic for researchers interested in discovering the causes of human behavior—may also be one of its attractions for humanistically oriented psychologists.

Some phenomenological theorists have accused their behaviorally oriented critics of treating people as "empty organisms," machine-like automatons devoid of thought and feeling, merely reflexive creatures. But the issue is not the existence of mental activity and its importance, but rather the most useful and interesting strategies for discovering more about how the brain works and generates observable "outputs." Few psychologists really suggest that people's internal processes and mental activities should be ignored or excluded in psychological studies. As Skinner has noted, even advocates of a rigorous behavioral position believe that:

> No entity or process which has any useful explanatory force is to be rejected on the ground that it is subjective or mental. The data which have made it important must, however, be studied and formulated in effective ways (Skinner, 1964, p. 96).

But what are the "effective ways"? For humanists they are not the ways of behaviorism. Indeed, they insist that Skinner and his followers are dedicated to an unfruitful model of science, to trivial measurement strategies, and to a muddled view of causation. They argue, for example, that a proper understanding of people requires attention to the future purposes that guide them, rather than to their possible historical roots (Rychlak, 1976). Skinner, of course, would want to know what are the variables that in turn control those purposes. The issues continue to be hotly debated (Wandersman, Poppen, & Ricks, 1976).

Is the Self a "Doer"?

Phenomenological accounts of the self in personality have been criticized most strongly for being descriptive rather than explanatory (see Brewster Smith's 1950 discussion). In his analysis, Smith has noted the importance of distinguishing between two different meanings of the self. One meaning of the self is as the *doer* of behavior. That meaning refers to the diverse processes that comprise the individual's personality. The self as doer is simply a summary term for these processes. The second meaning is the *self-as-object*. This definition refers to the person's concepts and attitudes about himself.

Smith argues that this distinction between the self-as-doer or process, and the phenomenal construct of the self—that is, the self-as-object perceived by the individual—has been confused by phenomenologists. He notes that Rogers, for example, talks about the self this way:

> When the self is free from any threat of attack or likelihood of attack, then it is possible for the self to consider these hitherto rejected perceptions, to make new differentiations, and to reintegrate the self in such a way as to include them (Rogers, 1947, p. 365).

Smith questions these feats of the self, commenting on the confusion between the self as a causal agent and the self as an experienced phenomenon:

> Can a phenomenal self consider perceptions and reintegrate itself . . . , or is this rather double-talk resulting from the attempt to make one good concept do the work of two? (Smith, 1950, p. 520)

Thus Smith faulted self theorists for endowing the self-as-object (which is a concept that the individual has about himself) with all sorts of causal powers, such as the ability to evaluate itself, guard itself, and change itself.

The Self as a Basic Schema (Category)

There certainly have been many problems with the definition of "self" and its place in personality theory. But these difficulties should not obscure the enduring and central importance of the self as an integrative personality construct. The challenge will be to avoid endowing the self with mysterious powers without losing its subjective reality. Subjectively, there is little doubt of the "I," "me," or "self" as a basic reference point around which experiences and the sense of personal identity itself seem to be organized. Recently, there have been some promising efforts to treat the self not as a "thing" but as a schema, cognitive category, or map that serves as a vital frame of reference for processing and evaluating experiences. This cognitive approach to the self promises to be researchable as well as theoretically appealing (e.g., Markus, 1977), as discussed in Chapter 19.

Social Behavior Theory, Existentialism, and Phenomenology

Psychological theories sometimes have unexpected similarities. In the last chapter we saw that social behavior theory involves a focus on what the person is doing in the here and now, rather than on reconstructions of personal history, and a reluctance to hypothesize drives, forces, motives, and other psychic dispositions as explanations. This chapter has shown that all these features, surprisingly, are not unique to a behavioral position. They just as fully seem to describe the platform of some existentially oriented and phenomenological psychologists. This conceptual union may be unexpected. Yet the behavioral focus on what the person is doing, rather than on attributes or motives, fits the existential doctrine exquisitely. As Sartre put it, "existence precedes essence." He meant by that phase that

> man first of all exists, encounters himself, surges up in the world—and defines himself afterwards. If man as the existentialist sees him is not definable, it is because to begin with he is nothing. He will not be anything until later, and then he will be what he makes of himself. Thus, there is no human nature. . . . Man simply is (Sartre, 1965, p. 28).

Thus a renunciation of preconceptions about motives, traits, and the content of human nature is hardly unique to Skinnerians and other contemporary behaviorists. George Kelly meant something similar when he said, "I am what I do," and urged that to know what one is one must look at what one does. Substantive constructs about universal human "essences," about specific dynamics, agencies of the mind, fundamental complexes and conflicts, sexual and aggressive drives or other basic motives as foundations of later development—all these and similar constructs about the nature of personality are as rejected by existentialism as they are by current social behavior theories. Similarly, both positions insist that it is impossible to conceptualize people apart from the context or environment in which they exist.

The possible conceptual compatibility between modern social behavior theory and the existential-phenomenological orientation seems to hinge on several common qualities. Both share a focus on the here and now, a reluctance to posit specific motivational and trait constructs, an emphasis on what the person is doing—on "where he is at"—rather than on the constructs of the psychologist who studies him, a disinterest in distant historical reconstruction, and a concern with new action possibilities for the individual. These commonalities are impressive.

While the overlap between the behavioral and existential-phenomenological orientation seems intriguing, the magnitude of their union should not be exaggerated. First, is attention to the subject's *phenomenology* really compatible with a behavior approach? Skinner's focus on observable behavior has emphasized the simplest sort of physical responses, such as movements, in order to obtain the most precise possible response measures. It would be difficult to see how subjective experience can be studied in such terms. In more recent extensions, however, social learning theorists stress that it would be absurd to try to define out of existence the concepts, perceptions, and experiences of the people we are studying (Mischel, 1973a). Indeed these phenomena can be studied like any other complex behaviors—if appropriate observable events are found as referents for them. There have been many suggestions for doing that, for example in the work of George Kelly and others (reviewed in Mischel, 1968).

The social behavior and existentialist positions do suffer from one critical incompatibility. The existentialist takes the philosophical position that the individual is responsible, and attributes to him or her the ultimate causes of behavior. In Sartre's phrase, a person "is what he wills to be" (1956, p. 291).
Though the behaviorist may share Sartre's desire to put "every man in possession of himself," rather than allow him to be possessed by psychic forces, a behavioral analysis of causation cannot begin with the person's will as the fundamental cause of what he does, nor can it end with his constructs as a final explanation of his behavior.

George Kelly (personal communication, 1965) once emphasized his belief that personal constructs are the basic units and that it is personal constructs, rather than stimuli, that determine behavior. He recalled vividly from his Navy experience during World War II how very differently he related to the same officer on different occasions depending on how, at the time, he construed that officer. He remembered that the captain seemed different to him in an informal role, chatting with his jacket off, from the way he seemed when he wore his officer's coat. You see, Kelly said, it is not the stimulus—the captain—but how I construed him that channelized my reactions to him.

But a social behavior theorist would find this story an excellent example, not of "construct control," but of "stimulus control": With his four stripes on, you see the captain one way; without his four stripes, you see him differently. To understand the construct change, in the behavioral view, you have to include in your understanding how those four stripes came to control it.

The phenomenological and behavioral positions differ in their focus of attention: The former seeks to know and understand the subject's experience; the behaviorally oriented psychologist wants to clarify the conditions that control the subject's ultimate behavior, including the events that control her constructs, cognitions, and feelings.

A behavioral approach insists on specific causal analyses that precisely link what the individual does and construes to the conditions in which he or she does it. Without becoming embroiled here in philosophical complexities, we can say that existential positions seem to stop sooner in their causal analyses, making humans the ultimate cause of what they do. Similarly phenomenological positions put the causes of behavior in the perceptions and constructs of the individual. In behavioral analyses, as Skinner has emphasized, one needs to consider not only how people's perceptions and concepts affect their behavior, but also what are the observable causes and the controlling conditions governing the perceptions and concepts themselves. The humanistically oriented existentialist may want to remove the individual from the causal chain and to make the person the prime cause of his or her own behaviors; the behaviorally oriented psychologist seeks to put people in nature's causal chain and to delineate the conditions that determine what they do and therefore what they are.

Is a reasonable synthesis of phenomenological psychology and social learning theory possible? Perhaps. Such a synthesis would require the ability to view people both as active construers who perceive, interpret, and influence the environment and themselves and as creatures in nature, continuously responsive to the conditions of their lives (as discussed in Chapter 20).

SUMMARY

1. The diverse theories discussed in this chapter all reject specific motivational and dynamic concepts. Instead they focus on the immediate perceived experience and concepts of individuals, and on their strivings toward growth and self-actualization.

2. Allport's theory of personality stresses the functional autonomy of motives and argues that motives that are functioning currently in the mature individual may be independent of their historical roots. He gives central importance to the phenomenological or perceived self.

3. Lewin's field theory introduces the notion of life space and the importance of the psychological environment. His theory stresses the immediate relationships between person and environment and elements in the environment, rather than dealing with these as absolute entities. Contemporaneity is an important feature of this viewpoint. Lewin was dissatisfied with the usual concepts of traits and needs and saw behavior and development as functions of dynamic changes in the psychological environment and in the tension systems of the person.

4. Many of the positions discussed in this chapter have in common an interest in subjective experience and a positive view of human na-

ture. The human being is seen as purposeful and striving toward self-fulfillment, not simply as driven by unconscious forces and motivated by the necessity to satisfy biological needs.

5. The existentialists focus on the "here and now." They emphasize that we build our own lives, and that each person is a choosing, free, responsible agent.

6. Carl Rogers' theory is illustrative of the central characteristics of the phenomenological approach to personality. The emphasis is on the person's unique experienced reality. In this theory the *self* (self-concept) is a conscious perception of self-as-object. This self-concept develops as the result of direct experience with the environment and may also incorporate the perceptions of others. The experienced self in turn influences perception and behavior. Maladjustment occurs when the sense of self and a person's perceptions and experiences are in opposition and disharmony.

7. George Kelly's theory stresses the necessity of understanding the individual's own dimensions, categories, and hypotheses rather than viewing him or her in terms of the psychologist's constructs. It also emphasizes the convenience of the person's hypotheses and constructs for dealing with experience. Role play may help the person to select and practice more satisfactory, convenient modes of construing his world in alternative ways.

8. Psychedelic drugs, meditation, and encounter groups have been favored by recent movements that emphasize nonverbal, emotional components of experience and existence. Some of these approaches seek to explore and expand consciousness and awareness through a variety of techniques aimed at escape from the "reality-oriented ego" into the realm of pure feeling and enhanced sensitivity. Others search for fulfillment through self-actualization and "peak experiences," as Maslow emphasized.

9. The phenomenological emphasis has made many contributions. Nevertheless, it also has been criticized. A focus on people's subjective perceptions and cognitions does not necessarily uncover the causes of their behavior. Indeed the relations between cognition and behavior may be highly complex. Moreover, sometimes self theorists seem to confuse the self as an experienced phenomenon and as an agent determining behavior. Finally, explanations that do not look beyond the individual to the stimulus conditions causing the phenomenal experiences may be criticized as incomplete accounts.

10. Current behavior theories share some common features with phenomenological approaches. In the phenomenological approach of Kelly, for example, we know a woman by what we see her doing. Curiously,

a similar statement could come from contemporary behavior theorists. Another often unexpected similarity between the social behavior approach and the phenomenological orientation is that both favor concentrating on the "here and now" situation rather than on inferences about the person's past.

11. Lest the reader erroneously exaggerate the closeness between the empiricism of such behaviorists as Skinner and the phenomenology of the existentially oriented, it should be stressed that there are fundamental differences between them. A chief difference between current social behavior views and the views discussed in this chapter has to do with the heavy emphasis that cognitive formulations place on the *causal role* of cognitions and self-concepts as pervasive determinants of the behaviors comprising personality. The question is not the existence of such cognitions and self-concepts, but, rather, their adequacy as explanations of the complex phenomena of personality.

In this part of the book we will examine some of the main applications for assessment and personality change associated with each of the orientations discussed in the preceding pages. Each of the theoretical conceptions surveyed in Part I has led to distinctive methods for studying persons and for attempting to produce constructive personality change. These applications have been quite diverse, and the reader will be introduced to assessment techniques ranging from questionnaires to projective tests and behavior sampling, and to therapeutic approaches that extend from psychodynamic psychotherapy to behavior modification and encounter groups.

Each of the main applications will be discussed in the context of the orientation and assumptions most relevant to it. The findings, issues, and problems from these applications in turn can shed light on the relevant theoretical conceptions.

The theories adopted by personality psychologists are not rigid entities but broad guidelines that change as knowledge and concepts change. Therefore orientations often overlap, and methods may merge and borrow from theoretical and technical neighbors. Nevertheless there also are real differences. To highlight some of the critical differences among approaches in concrete terms, each will be applied to an analysis of the same person—"Gary W." As psychologists, how should we construe Gary? What is he "really" like? How can we get to know and understand him better?

PART II

PERSONALITY THEORIES: APPLICATIONS

Each orientation supplies its own answers to these questions. It will be seen that the concepts and methods of each orientation add distinctive information about Gary. Sometimes the new information may seem consistent with the old; sometimes it may seem to conflict with it; sometimes it may reflect the complexity of Gary's personality; and sometimes it may illuminate the strengths and weaknesses of current psychological ideas and techniques.

Each theoretical approach also has influenced conceptions of the meaning of personality "adaptation" (adjustment) and "deviance." Definitions of adaptation depend on the personality theory to which one adheres. Each of the main theoretical approaches to personality discussed in Part I has its own view of what constitutes "ideal adjustment" and "maladjustment." Recall, for example, the Freudian emphasis on recognition of unconscious impulses, and Rogers' concern with self-actualization and congruity. Clearly, each theorist would interpret adequacy and deviance in terms of his guiding constructs about personality. The theoretical orientation you adopt thus guides how you evaluate people and how you assess the adequacy or inappropriateness of their behavior, as Part II will show.

Theories of personality can be evaluated at least partly according to their relevance and efficacy for the modification of human behavior. Personality changes occur throughout life, but usually it is impossible to study them systematically. Hence their exact nature remains unclear. In most research situations the conditions that can be studied tend to be of momentary duration and little strength. Ethical concerns as well as practical limitations prevent psychologists from generating really powerful and enduring changes in the laboratory. Instead, the major changes of life unfold under the chaotic, uncontrolled conditions of the real world, and we glimpse only fragments of this process. An important exception is the therapeutic setting in which individuals seek help for problems that plague them. In the context of research on therapy and personality change, therefore, psychological principles for the modification of human behavior can receive their definitive test. The results should inform us not merely about the efficacy of particular techniques but also more broadly about the nature of personality and the conditions under which it may change—for good or for ill.

While some approaches (particularly trait theories) have had a great deal of impact on personality assessment, they have had little influence on strategies for personality change. Conversely, other positions (especially behavioral approaches) have had the greatest impact on procedures for generating change, and still others (psychodynamic and phenomenological approaches) have influenced both personality assessment and personality change to a large degree.

The next two chapters, 6 and 7, consider applications most relevant to trait theories. Specifically, Chapter 6 gives a brief history of trait measurement, describes some trait instruments and strategies, and gives examples of their applications. Chapter 7 provides a more general discussion and evaluation of basic issues relevant to the uses of the trait approach. Chapter 8 deals with applications guided mainly by psychodynamic theories. Chapters 9 and 10 consider the chief methods of behavioral theories for personality assessment and behavior modification respectively; and Chapter 11 explores the applications of the phenomenological orientation.

As you progress through Part II, you will increasingly see that an adequate understanding and appraisal of personality theories depend on knowing more than what each theorist asserted; it requires the closest attention to the applications that his conceptions have generated and to the problems, issues, failures, and successes that those applications reveal.

CHAPTER 6

TRAIT THEORIES: APPLICATIONS (I)

Galton
Cattell
Bolton
Binet
Wechsler
Guilford
Gary W Case
MMPI
F Scale
Terman Miles

This chapter examines some of the major applications of trait theories. It begins by looking at the history of the trait approach to measurement and then illustrates some of the main methods and tactics that have grown from those roots. It also considers some of the problems that have arisen in those applications and some of the new research directions designed to clarify the nature of personality.

Probably the most important impact of the trait approach has been its methodology: It has provided basic concepts and measures to assess individual differences and to test hypotheses about personality. The most appealing feature of this methodology is that it permits a quantitative, orderly study of individual differences in an area that always before had defied measurement.

Late in the nineteenth century trait psychologists recognized the hazards of basing impressions of people on informal, subjective judgments about them. Consequently they tried to go beyond casual impressions by devising more formal tests. In this way they hoped to develop objective procedures for measuring important individual differences. For these trait theorists any attempt to study personality without tests would be as naive as a biological science without microscopes. Since the end of the nineteenth century there have been continuous systematic efforts to study personality traits quantitatively by means of tests. This movement, often called the *psychometric trait approach*, has been one of the main forces in the study of personality; its roots extend far into the past and its implications for an understanding of personality are profound.

Roots of the Psychometric Approach

Psychometric testing started in the psychological laboratories during the last decades of the nineteenth century. Sir Francis Galton was administering tests in his London laboratory as early as 1882, in an effort to establish an inventory of human abilities. In his studies of human inheritance, he included measures of sensory acuity, reaction time, and strength of movement. His aim was to measure the resemblance between large numbers of related and unrelated persons. Galton also devised a questionnaire that was an important forerunner of those developed in later years.

James McKeen Cattell was an American psychologist who had a major role in the development of psychological testing. In 1890 Cattell suggested a standard series of tests for the study of mental processes. These tests were typical of the kind appearing at that time. They included measures of strength of grip, rate of arm movement, amount of pressure needed to produce pain on the forehead, reaction time for sound, and speed of color naming.

Tests of reading, judgment, and memory were also being used with some schoolchildren toward the end of the last century. A first attempt to evaluate test scores systematically is found in a study by T. L. Bolton that appeared in 1892. Bolton analyzed data from about 1500 schoolchildren, comparing their memory spans with their teachers' estimates of their "intellectual acuteness," and found little correspondence. A 1901 monograph likewise reported disappointing results: The relationships found between Cattell's various tests at

Intelligence testing grew out of efforts to separate retarded children into special programs.

Columbia College and students' academic standing were negligible (Wissler, 1901).

The simple, specific, sensorimotor measures popular in the laboratories at the end of the nineteenth century were important forerunners of later tests. But the tests favored during this period were primarily laboratory-bound techniques for comparing individual differences on single measures rather than on organized scales. It was the development of intelligence testing in the early twentieth century that made "psychometrics" a special and prominent field in its own right (Watson, 1959).

Intelligence Testing

Intelligence testing evolved in response to practical demands, primarily the need to separate the "uneducable" or severely retarded children into special schools that could provide a simplified curriculum. In the 1890s, Alfred Binet, a Frenchman and a physician by training, began to try to measure intelligence. He wanted to discover how "bright" and "dull" children differ and began empirically, without any clear preconceptions about the nature of their difference. Binet and his associates believed that available tests lacked measures of complex processes and overemphasized sensory tasks. It was their hope that individual differences in ability would be reflected better in more complex tasks. Accordingly they proposed a series of tests including measures of aesthetic appreciation, attention, comprehension, imagination, memory, mental imagery, moral feelings, muscular force, force of will, motor ability, suggestibility, and visual discrimination.

Ultimately, Binet's scales successfully differentiated children with respect to scholastic standing. Reactions to the Binet scales were enthusiastic because they seemed to fill the urgent need for a practical way to study mental processes without depending on an individual's introspective reports. The test supplied a single overall score that offered a general and simple summary of mental status. This summary score permitted ready comparisons between individuals in terms of their level of mental development. The Binet scales were revised and extended several times, most notably by Lewis M. Terman of Stanford University in 1916. Terman's revision produced the now classic Stanford-Binet, which became a popular standard for all later work on mental ability testing.

Virtually all of the developments in mental and personality testing have been influenced more or less directly by Binet's original work. Following the pioneering work of Binet, an extremely influential series of intelligence scales that are still very popular was developed by David Wechsler. These scales assess the individual's standing in relation to large numbers of other people of the same age, and thus have considerable practical value. The person's general intelligence quotient or "IQ" score summarizes his "full-scale" or total test achievement. His standing on the main subcomponents of the test also is com-

FIGURE 6-1
Items Similar to Those on Standard Intelligence Tests (such as the Wechsler Intelligence Scale)

puted. Items similar to those found on such IQ scales are presented in Figure 6-1.

Early Personality Measurement *Psychoneurotic Inventory*

Early questionnaires and inventories to measure individual differences in personality arose in the wake of the successful measurement of intelligence and flourished especially during the 1920s and 1930s. Interest in self-description or self-report as a method of personality assessment was stimulated by an inventory devised during World War I (Watson, 1959). This was Woodworth's *Personal Data Sheet,* later known as the *Psychoneurotic Inventory,* and it was aimed at detecting soldiers who would be likely to break down under wartime stress. Because it was highly impractical to give individual psychiatric interviews to recruits, Woodworth listed the kinds of symptoms psychiatrists would probably ask about in interviews and condensed them into a paper-and-pencil questionnaire of more than one hundred items. Examples are: "Do you wet your bed at night?" "Do you daydream frequently?" The respondent must answer "yes" or "no" to each question, and the tally of his answers is his final score. Soldiers who gave many affirmative responses were followed up with individual interviews. This method was valuable as a grossly condensed, simplified, and economic alternative to interviewing all subjects individually. Often questionnaires are still employed as substitutes for interviews.

The Woodworth questionnaire was not used widely, but it was a forerunner of the many other self-report devices that flourished in the next two decades. These self-report devices compared people usually with respect to a single summary score, which served as an index of their "overall level of adjustment," just as single scores or mental quotients were developed to describe the level of "general intelligence." In addition to efforts to assess adjustment and psychiatric status, attempts to measure individuals on various personality dimensions soon became extremely popular.

The Nature of Trait Tests

The psychometric approach to the study of personality relies on tests intended to tap personality traits. These traits or dispositions are assumed to be quantifiable and scalable. As J. P. Guilford, a leading spokesman for the psychometric trait position, said:

> By [scalability] we mean that a trait is a certain quality or attribute, and different individuals have different degrees of it. . . . If individuals differ in a trait by having higher or lower degrees of it, we can represent the trait by means of a single straight line. . . . Individual trait positions may be represented by points on the line (Guilford, 1959, pp. 64–65).

Scoring Traits

Thus traits like aggressiveness or introversion, or submissiveness or masculinity, for example, may be conceived as quantifiable attributes similar to physical dimensions. It is assumed that individuals differ from each other more or less enduringly in the degree (or amount) to which they possess each of these attributes. It is also assumed that at least some traits are *common* in the population. Measurement usually proceeds with respect to one trait at a time. On the basis of his test results, each individual is assigned a point position on a single trait scale. It is generally assumed that most traits are scalable in some way and can be described quantitatively. Given these assumptions, the challenge for psychometricians is to find the appropriate measurement operations for important personality traits (Guilford, 1959).

To illustrate, Figure 6-2 depicts a hypothetical profile of test scores for one person on eight trait scales. The profile suggests that this man's scores were highest on the "submissiveness" test, lowest on the "aggressiveness" test, and intermediate on the other measures.

But what do these scores mean? Just how high or low is this person on each of these attributes? The scores have little meaning unless they can be

FIGURE 6-2
One Person's Hypothetical Test Profile on Eight Trait Scales

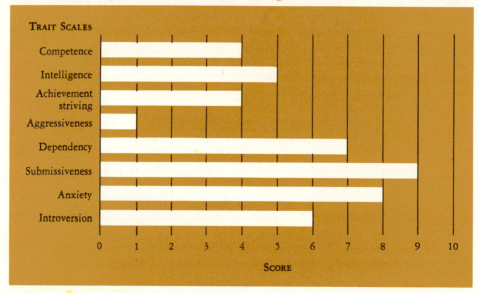

compared with norms or with the scores of other people who took the same tests. Trait psychologists compare the scores of different people on one measure at a time, as Figure 6-3 illustrates. The figure shows a hypothetical distribution of scores for 230 people on a dependency scale.

A comparison of the dependency score from Figure 6-2 with the data in Figure 6-3 suggests that on this measure the subject's score (7) was the same as that of 40 of the 230 tested people, that only 60 people scored higher, and that 130 scored lower than he did.

FIGURE 6-3
Number of People at Each Score Level on a Dependency Test

The meaning of these comparisons depends, of course, on many considerations, such as the appropriateness of the comparison sample. For example, how many of the 230 people were much older or younger than the subject, or came from utterly different backgrounds, or were of the opposite sex? Most important, the meaning of the scores depends on the nature and quality of the test.

Structured Self-Reports and Ratings

Data about persons can be obtained from three sources: people may report or rate (judge) aspects of themselves; other people may judge the person; or performance may be elicited and observed directly.

Psychometric inferences about traits usually have been based on self-reports. The term "self-report" refers to any statements a person makes about

FIGURE 6-4
Examples of Different Types of Structured Test Items

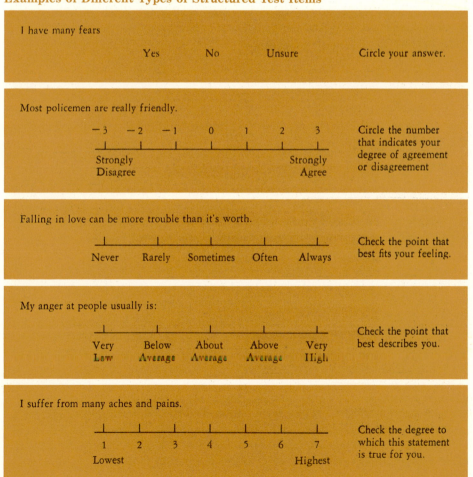

herself; "structured" self-reports are statements in the form of restricted reactions to items. On structured self-report tests the respondent must react to sets of questions or items with one of a limited number of prescribed choices (e.g., "yes," "no," "strongly agree," "frequently," "don't know"). Examples are shown in Figure 6-4. These items contrast with open-ended or unstructured tests (like the projective devices in Chapter 8), on which the subject may supply her own reactions freely. The distinction between "structured" and "unstructured" or "open-ended" tests is a matter of degree only. The extent to which a test is structured depends on the items and the instructions to the subject: Less structured techniques allow greater variation in response.

Many formats have been devised for eliciting trait ratings (see Figure 6-4). On some scales, for example, the subject may be told that "7" indicates that the item is completely applicable to himself and "1" indicates complete non-applicability, and that he should check the point on the continuum that describes his own reaction. On scales like this, subjects are asked to express the extent of their aggreement or disagreement with the particular item or to rate themselves with respect to the particular descriptions supplied. They may also be asked to judge the attributes of other people they know, for example, their peers at work or in school, or members of their family.

Objectivity of Measurement

In their approach to testing, trait-oriented psychologists (as well as those of many other theoretical persuasions) emphasize "objectivity." "Objectivity" in the study of personality is the condition that exists when every observer (or "judge") who sees a particular sample of behavior (e.g., a test answer sheet) draws the same conclusions from it. Objectivity depends on the entire testing procedure, including the interaction between the examiner and the subject, the instructions and test items, the available response choices, and the scoring and interpretation procedures. Anything that enhances the uniformity of the testing conditions to which different subjects are exposed increases the objectivity of a test. Objectivity is also furthered by standardized (uniform) test materials, instructions, answer sheets, and scoring procedures. Effective standardization requires uniformity in other conditions that could affect test performance. Depending on what is being measured, these conditions may include the time of administration, the physical conditions under which measurement occurs, the sex of the examiner, and so on. The psychometrician thus attempts to make the stimulus material as uniform as possible by giving every subject the same standardized test and directions.

A lack of objectivity increases the risk of bias and unfairness, as when a test is given to some people by a "friendly" examiner in a comfortable, relaxed setting but to others by a "cold" examiner in a noisy, crowded room. Likewise, objectivity is reduced, and fair comparisons among people are prevented, if the test questions are changed on different occasions or scored differently depending on the prejudices of the tester or other momentary whims.

No matter how careful the attempt to maintain objectivity may be, it is beset with problems. In practice it has become increasingly evident that scores on any personality trait test are affected by all sorts of variables that are irrelevant to the trait the test is trying to measure. For example, even such gross examiner and subject characteristics as sex, as well as such subtler attributes as friendliness, may affect scores (Masling, 1960; Mischel, 1968). Other irrelevant characteristics of the respondent, such as his or her manner, may significantly affect the examiner's evaluation of the test results. There are many possible sources for bias. More attractive or appealing persons, for example, may be scored more liberally, even when scoring is relatively objective and standardized, as it is on intelligence tests (Masling, 1959).

In spite of some early hopes to the contrary, no psychological test provides anything remotely analogous to a mental X-ray. A test merely yields a sample of behavior under particular eliciting conditions. The observed behavior is always elicited in a context—in a psychological situation. No matter how carefully standardized, the test is never able to eliminate or "control out" all determinants other than the trait of interest. The consistency and meaning of what is being sampled therefore must be demonstrated and cannot be assumed no matter how uniform the eliciting conditions may be for all subjects.

Correlations

The specific techniques for assessing the consistency and meaning of test behavior are considered later (Chapter 7). At this point it suffices to note that most applications of trait psychology involve a search for *correlations* among tests. Such correlations simply examine the degree of association (relation) between the scores achieved by a group of individuals on one set of measures with their scores on another set. For example, do people who score high on Test 1 also tend to score higher on Test 2, and do those who score low on Test 1 also score low on Test 2? To the degree that the relative position of individuals remains consistent across the measures, high correlations are obtained; conversely, when relative positions change easily, correlations decrease, indicating that responses to the two tests are not as closely related. When correlations among tests are high, responses on one test can be used to predict responses on the other; e.g., if you succeed on 1 you are likely to succeed on 2. When correlations are low, one cannot predict performance (relative position) on one test from knowing scores on the other test.

The Case of Gary W.

So far we have been considering tests in general, ignoring the individual person. A focus on methods can seem barren unless we pause periodically to apply those methods to the individual. Therefore we now turn to "Gary W."

Gary W. is not an unusual person, except in the sense that every individual is unique. He is presented here as a "case" example of an essentially normal human being whose characteristics and history are neither dramatically bizarre nor especially exciting. Often case histories serve to illustrate rare and even esoteric qualities—the strange sex criminal, the twisted neurotic, the "split personality." Our purpose in considering Gary, however, is not to display odd and curious bits of abnormality, not to shock and titillate, but rather to concretize and make more real the methods and ideas created to deal with personality. Lest our concepts and techniques become excessively abstract, we must apply them to the data of daily life and examine their relevance—and occasionally their irrelevance—for understanding the particular individual (and not just people in general). For this reason we have selected "Gary" as an "ordinary" person, one among hundreds of millions, but still, like all individuals, unique enough to surprise us occasionally, complex enough to defy pat explanations, troubled enough to encounter problems, and human enough to be confused about himself, at least some of the time, and to confuse even more often those who try to understand him.

As we proceed, new information regarding Gary W. will be made available so that the contributions of different kinds of personality data can be evaluated more competently. In addition, as the applications of different theoretical approaches to personality are discussed, Gary will be conceptualized from the perspective of each of them. Thus in later chapters Gary will be construed from the perspectives of the major frameworks available for studying personality.

At this point the information about Gary will be limited to a few demographic facts that introduce him and his background, impressions of his personality obtained from a friend, and some psychometric data about him guided by the methods and concepts of the trait approach.

Gary W.: Demographic Facts

Gary W. was born in Boston 25 years ago. He comes from an old New England family of moderate means. His father is a businessman. Both parents are alive, and currently in the midst of divorcing. Gary has an older and now married brother who is a successful physician.

After attending a private boarding school as an adolescent, Gary went to Hilson college. His record was good but not outstanding. On tests of intellectual ability (the Wechsler Adult Intelligence Scale) Gary's scores indicated he was of superior intelligence. Upon graduation he entered the Navy and received an officer's commission. He served for three years, part of the time stationed around Southeast Asia, and then returned to seek a Master's Degree in business. Currently he is in graduate school and still unmarried. Here is what one of his friends says about him.

Impressions of Gary W. by a Fellow Graduate Student:

From the moment I first met Gary, one year ago, he seemed likable enough, but he always seemed preoccupied. His personality had a forced quality, as though he were trying to be something he wasn't. Central to his personality is his overconcern with himself. It's not conceit, but rather continual self-observation and self-criticism. In personal relationships he seems always to be trying to figure out what the other person expects of him and seems to have no personality of his own. He can be friendly and outgoing with a shy, self-conscious person. He often displays a cynical humor and arbitrary bossiness bordering on personal insult, which seems to be his only method of feeling at ease. Feeling at ease seems to mean dominating the relationship as completely as possible. If he encounters someone more capable than he is, Gary tends to draw back within himself, too afraid of being shown up by the other person to develop any kind of close relationship. Gary is something of a "loner." He has few close friends, since his relationships are based on domination (or fear of being dominated) rather than companionship. Gary is very conscious of social standards, grades, any measure of superiority. If he doesn't reach the mark, he feels he is a failure, but even if he does he seems not to be satisfied. An ironic feature of his personality is that though he seems to seek attention, he is uncomfortable once he gets it. When speaking to a group of people, he becomes extremely nervous, and, at times, so confused that he cannot continue, and starts falling apart. He wants to succeed. He is ambitious and able, and very persistent. He seems really driven to do well.

So far we know relatively little about Gary. The impression his friend gives us, while interesting, may be of dubious value: We know neither its accuracy nor its meaning. Then how can we proceed further and find out more about Gary? From the viewpoint of trait theory, we want quantitative information that reliably reveals Gary's status on important dispositions. One major step in that direction is provided by Gary's scores on psychometric tests. So that these data can be properly understood, they will be introduced in the context of our discussion of some major trait measures. Examples of these measures, and issues generated by them, are given next.

Psychometric Scales: Examples and Problems

Most trait-oriented research has tried to study important attributes through questionnaires. Psychometric trait assessment usually is based on lengthy scales that require many responses. Typically these scales require the individual to report his or her *general* reaction to broad and hypothetical situations, rather than specific responses to a few concrete real choices. The most thoroughly studied questionnaire is the Minnesota Multiphasic Personality Inventory (MMPI), and it has become the basis for investigating many personality traits and types.

The MMPI

*3 control scales
13 base scales*

The MMPI best exemplifies most features of the psychometric approach. This widely used, influential test contains a set of self-report scales that initially were devised to classify mental patients into types on many psychiatric dimensions (Hathaway & McKinley, 1942, 1943). In format, the MMPI comprises 550 printed statements to which one may answer "true," "false," or "cannot say" (undecided). The items range over diverse topics and differ widely in style. They inquire into attitudes, emotional reactions, psychiatric symptoms, the subject's past, and other content, with items similar to these:

Sometimes I think I may kill myself.
My greatest troubles are inside myself.
I certainly have little self-assurance.
I wish I were not so awkward.
I am shy.

Psychometric self-report tests such as the MMPI are called "psychometric," "objective," and "standardized." All these adjectives correctly describe the printed stimulus material, the scoring procedure, and the administration. The stimulus materials are objective and standardized or reproducible in the sense that they usually are presented as printed items on questionnaires, inventories, or rating scales. Likewise, the scoring procedure is objective because the respondent has to react to each question or item with one of a limited number of prescribed or "structured" choices by selecting, for example, from printed answers like "yes," "no," "strongly agree," "frequently," "don't know."

Both the questions and the instructions on psychometric tests, however, usually require the respondent to extrapolate extensively from behavior; to go far beyond direct behavior observation; and to supply subjective inferences about the psychological meaning of behavior. While the stimulus questions are standardized, that is, printed and therefore always the same on each occasion, their exact referents often are unclear. For example, the test asks questions like "Are you shy?" or "Do you worry a lot?" or "Is it really wise to trust other people?" Such ambiguous items require respondents to interpret behavior and to provide inferences about psychological attributes. Hence, they must construe and evaluate behavior, and generalize about it, rather than describe particular behaviors in particular contexts on clear dimensions.

One really cannot expect that people would be either willing or able to reveal themselves accurately in response to such items. Such an expectation would be especially unreasonable when the respondents are emotionally upset, disturbed, or aware that their answers may be used to make important decisions about them and their future. Recognizing these problems (e.g., Meehl, 1945), researchers have tried to establish the meaning of particular answer patterns on the test empirically by research.

The investigator starts with a pool of items and administers them to a group known to differ on an external criterion or measure (for example, males versus females, or hospitalized versus nonhospitalized people). Ideally, the test scales are constructed so that ultimately only those items are retained that best discriminate among people who differ on the selected external criteria. For example, if an item such as "I cry easily" tends to be answered affirmatively by people who have been hospitalized for psychiatric problems, but not by those who have no history of psychiatric hospitalization, the item would be retained on a "maladjustment" scale. Gradually the meaning of the scales becomes defined by their associations with other measures or information. The procedures have to be repeated or replicated, to assure that only the relatively stable associations between configurations of test behavior and criterion information are retained.

For example, the MMPI scales are administered to many groups of subjects, such as college students, medical personnel, and nonpsychiatric patients, as well as psychiatric patients who have been independently diagnosed as having symptoms of some type of schizophrenia. The items then are examined to determine the ones on which there are significant differences between the answers of particular diagnostic groups as compared to "normals." In this manner it becomes possible gradually to devise scales that discriminate among different groups of people.

MMPI items have been sorted into ten basic scales named Hypochondriasis (Hs), Depression (D), Hysteria (Hy), Psychopathic deviate (Pd), Masculinity-femininity (Mf), Paranoia (Pa), Psychasthenia (Pt), Schizophrenia (Sc), Hypomania (Ma), and Social introversion (Si). It would be incorrect, however, to think that these scales tap the entities whose names they bear. Instead, these labels serve as abbreviations for scales whose meanings are defined by their extensive correlations (associations) with other indices (e.g., psychiatrist's ratings of adjustment, scores on other personality questionnaires). These correlations have been amassed during several decades of vigorous research with the MMPI scales.

In addition to the ten basic scales, three "control" scales have been devised. The L or Lie scale was intended to measure the tendency to falsify about oneself by "faking good." High scores on this scale indicate that the individual has endorsed many items that suggest he does unlikely things such as daily reading all the newspaper editorials or never telling a lie. The K scale, the second control, was intended to indicate defensiveness in the form of a tendency to present oneself in a more socially desirable way. The F scale, the third control, sought to tap the intrusive effects of answering the items carelessly and confusedly, as indicated by describing oneself as having rare and improbable characteristics.

The results of an individual's MMPI answers (or the summary of a group's average responses) may be recorded in the form of a "profile." Such a profile for our case, Gary W., is illustrated in Figure 6-5. Gary's position on each scale is summarized in terms of converted or T scores. These scores readily provide quantitative comparisons against norms, a T score of 50 being the average score for the particular normative reference group. In recent years sophisticated procedures have been developed to discriminate people with extreme scores for many different diagnostic and selection purposes. Collections of MMPI profiles have been "coded" in different ways and catalogued in "handbooks" or "atlases" which may be conveniently used to compare a single individual's profile to similar profiles and information collected in many cases (Marks & Seeman, 1963; Gilberstadt & Duker, 1965).

Gary's MMPI profile fits most closely a 2-8/8-2 code in the atlas developed by Marks and Seeman (1963, p. 137). We can see what types of information the atlas provides for individuals whose average MMPI profiles are most similar to Gary's. The atlas tells us that people with this type of profile are most often described with characteristics like these:

> Keeps his distance and avoids close relations with people; tends to fear emotional involvement with others; manifests his psychic conflicts with somatic symptoms, tends to be resentful, shows obsessive thinking, feels tense, jumpy, and high-strung.

The atlas also provides much other normative or "average" information found previously for people with Gary's profile. These data are a helpful first approximation. How well they really fit Gary and how closely they match other data about him is still an open question. On first impression, some of the atlas statements seem at least somewhat consistent with the impressions given by Gary's fellow graduate student, who also judged him to be "shy" and a "loner." On the other hand, the same student rated Gary as high in ambition, aspiration level, and "drive." These ratings seem to contradict parts of the atlas information. Specifically, the 2-8/8-2 atlas code lists high aspirations and ambitiousness as characteristics that are *least* descriptive of people with his profile. Who is right? Is Gary's friend inaccurate, or does this part of the atlas simply not fit Gary? To achieve further understanding of Gary, we would need much more information about him.

Research on the MMPI continues at the rate of about a hundred studies a year. In addition, the MMPI has become the model for dozens of other personality questionnaires. Many investigators drew on the large pool of MMPI items to create special personality scales (e.g., dealing with anxiety), whose meaning they studied empirically. Popular descendants of the MMPI include the California Psychological Inventory (CPI), the Taylor Manifest Anxiety Scale (MAS), and the Jackson Personality Inventory (1976).

FIGURE 6-5
Gary's MMPI Profile

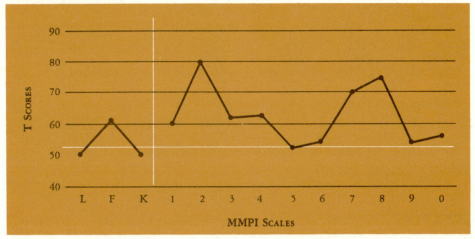

Similar to Atlas Code Type 2-8/8-2, Marks and Seeman (1963).

The California *F* Scale

MMPI scales and atlases have some practical value in personality assessment and clinical work. Many psychologists, however, are most interested in the search for theoretically important personality traits, and have tried to use a variety of personality questionnaires for that purpose. One of the most popular and extensively researched of these self-report measures is the California *F* Scale (Adorno et al., 1950). This measure was intended to assess authoritarian attitudes. It contains a set of items like these:

> The most important thing to teach children is absolute obedience to their parents.
> Any good leader should be strict with people under him in order to gain their respect.
> Prison is too good for sex criminals. The should be publicly whipped or worse.
> There are two kinds of people in the world: the weak and the strong.
> No decent man can respect a woman who has had sex relations before marriage.

Strong agreement with items like these results in a high *F* Scale, or "authoritarianism," score.

Gary's score on the *F* Scale was slightly below average when compared to other college students. What does that imply about him? As with all scales, the meaning of high or low scores on this measure depends on the network of associations that have been found for the test in research.

An enormous set of correlations has emerged from more than a hundred studies that have related F Scale scores to other variables. Correlations have been found with such diverse variables as intelligence, family ideology, prejudice, anxiety, voting behavior, military reenlistment intent, and cooperation in psychological experiments (Titus & Hollander, 1957), and even reactions to the U.S.-Soviet space race (Mischel & Schopler, 1959).

For example, in one study among college students with high scores on the California F Scale (suggesting strong ideological conservatism), 76 percent stated they preferred the Republican Party, whereas 65 percent of those low on the F Scale preferred the Democratic Party (Leventhal, Jacobs, & Kurdirka, 1964). The relationships between F Scale scores and stated voting behavior indicated that students with high F Scale scores tended to choose the more conservative political candidate.

The F Scale is most strongly correlated with other paper-and-pencil measures, but not as closely associated with nonquestionnaire measures of interpersonal behaviors (Titus & Hollander, 1957). Correlations between the F Scale and other questionnaires sampling attitudes (e.g., toward minority groups) sometimes reach impressive magnitude. The relationships obtained between the F Scale and non-questionnaire measures, on the other hand, tend to be much lower in magnitude. Scores on the F Scale also tend to be highly correlated with education, more highly educated people tending to respond in a much less authoritarian fashion.

Masculinity-Femininity

Another trait dimension that has received much attention psychometrically is "masculinity-femininity." Inferences about masculinity or femininity in research have relied mainly on people's verbal reports about their sex-role attributes, attitudes, interests, values, and preferences, or on ratings made by their parents or peers. On the paper-and-pencil Terman-Miles masculinity-femininity (M-F) test, for example, adolescents and adults are asked to report their interests, emotional attitudes, and so on (Terman & Miles, 1936). The Gough Femininity Scale likewise is a paper-and-pencil inventory that asks for self-descriptions in a two-choice format (Gough, 1952).

Other tests have avoided asking subjects to characterize their own traits and instead require them to indicate the kinds of toys, games, and activities they would prefer. All of these measures ask subjects to indicate their preferences for stereotypically masculine or feminine objects or activities. On the IT Scale, for example, the child is presented with a drawing of "IT," an ambiguous child-figure, and asked to choose what IT would like in a series of objects or picture cards associated with either masculine or feminine sex roles (for example, cowboy guns or dress-up dolls). The resulting scores are intended to reflect the child's degree of masculinity-femininity in his or her sex-role preferences (Brown, 1957).

Masculinity-femininity measures traditionally have been constructed empirically so that on each item the response scored "masculine" is the one that is endorsed by most males while the one scored "feminine" is the one favored verbally by the majority of females. Individuals' masculinity-femininity scores therefore serve as an index of how closely their self-reports, self-descriptions, and preferences correspond with those of the majority in their sex. Similarly, when an observer rates the attributes of others on a masculinity-femininity dimension, the score is intended to reflect that rater's judgment of how closely the ratee matches the attributes supposedly displayed by most males or females. (More recent approaches and issues in the study of sex roles are discussed in Chapter 14.) Gary's scores on a traditional masculinity-femininity self-report inventory placed him within the average range for male college students.

The Problem of Response Sets

The interpretation of psychometric self-report scales like the foregoing may be complicated by "response sets." Response sets are certain special response tendencies in people's answers to test questions. Such "sets" have to be understood in order to interpret self-reports and ratings properly. One of the most studied response sets is the tendency to endorse socially undesirable items.

Differences among people in their willingness to express complaints and to describe themselves openly in socially undesirable terms may substantially influence their answers to self-report inventories (e.g., Edwards, 1957, 1959, 1961). On psychiatric scales like the MMPI, scores indicating maladjustment and negative traits (like depression, paranoia, hypochondirasis) depend on the respondent's willingness to endorse socially undesirable statements. His scores on these scales will be high if he confesses such things as irregular bowel habits and bodily ills and eccentric or bizarre and socially taboo thoughts and acts. His profile may therefore reflect the degree to which he endorses socially undesirable items rather than other traits.

It is difficult to evaluate the social desirability interpretation of self-report scores on psychiatric inventories. Even a true self-report of real problematic or idiosyncratic behavior would require endorsing socially undesirable items (Block, 1965). For example, Gary's scores on an anxiety questionnaire might be elevated because he tends to describe himself in socially undesirable terms, or because he is accurately describing some of his real troubles and fears.

Apart from its problems as a response set, social desirability has also been researched extensively as a personality characteristic or motive. Crowne and Marlowe (1964) conducted some thorough studies of the motive to seek social approval. As part of their studies they constructed a measure of social desirability (SD) and assessed how groups of persons who differed in SD behaved in a number of experimental situations. In general, results suggested that people who were high on the Marlowe-Crowne SD scale, when compared to those with low scores, tended to be more cautious, conventional, and persuasible. Thus the same variable that complicates test interpretations may also be a meaningful dimension for substantive personality research.

Another response set is agreement or "acquiescence," which is the tendency to agree with statements, especially ambiguous attitude statements, irrespective of their specific content. On self-report questionnaires like the California *F* Scale, or the MMPI, the total scores are a direct function of how often the respondent agrees with, or says "yes" to, the items. This is because questions are worded so that agreement increases the trait score. The more often the person answers "yes" on the California *F* Scale, for example, the higher his "authoritarian" score will be. Therefore it is difficult to distinguish the role of scale content from the effect of a tendency for subjects to say "yes" to items regardless of their content.

Yes-saying or acquiescence to *any* opinionated or doctrinaire generalizations about social issues, regardless of specific content, according to some interpretations may greatly influence answers on the California *F* Scale (Bass, 1955). Messick and Jackson (1961) likewise believe that acquiescence response sets have critical effects on inventories of the true-false or agree-disagree type such as the MMPI. They believe that the factors found on such tests may primarily reflect response style rather than specific item content (Jackson & Messick, 1958).

To correct for the role of agreement response sets, some investigators have tried to rephrase the items to reverse their meaning and to have both favorable and unfavorable versions for each item. The wording of many inventory items, however, is difficult to reverse. Chapman and Campbell (1957) discuss the problems of trying to reverse an *F* Scale item like "the wild sex life of the old Greeks and Romans was tame compared to some of the goings-on in this country, even in places where people might least expect it." As they put it:

> How is this item to be reversed? One could say "the sex life that goes on even in places where one least today expects it is nothing compared to the wild sex life of the Greeks and Romans." Thus reversed, the item would still seem to appeal to the prurient moralizing that the initial item sought to tap (Chapman & Campbell, 1957, p. 129).

Several analyses have questioned the importance of agreement response sets on self-report devices (e.g., Block, 1965; Norman, 1966; Rorer, 1965). They argue that tendencies to agree with items regardless of their content may play a fairly trivial role. Block (1965), for example, showed that the basic factor structure of the MMPI did not change even when only scales balanced to eliminate the role of agreement response sets were employed. Nevertheless, it has now become a standard practice to try to avoid response sets in scale construction by attempting to balance the number of items keyed true and false (Wiggins, 1973).

As was illustrated in the Crowne and Marlowe studies of SD, there also have been some efforts to view individual differences in response sets as reflecting stable, trait-like "stylistic" consistencies, rather than as measurement errors that require correction. These response styles, in turn, have been conceptualized as traits and their correlations with other personality indices have been sought. Thus one researcher's methodological troubles may be another's personality dimension.

Do the Measures Overlap?

In addition to response sets, self-report trait tests often share another problem. High correlations among paper-and-pencil inventories may partly reflect the fact that inventory constructors often borrow items from earlier inventories. Different tests actually may contain similar items presented in similar formats. For example, Eysenck's (1952) measure for inferring neuroticism and extraversion-introversion contains such questions as: Are your feelings easily hurt? Are you rather shy? Do you find it difficult to get into conversation with strangers? Are you troubled with feelings of inferiority? Very similar items occur on such tests as the MMPI. Even within the subscales of a single test, items may overlap considerably. Shure and Rogers (1965) noted that the basic scales of the MMPI consist of items that overlap 69 percent, on the average, with items on one or more other scales of the test.

Campbell and Fiske (1959) analyzed many of the correlations among personality measures reported in the literature. They found that much commonality was attributable to similarity or overlap between the methods employed to elicit responses. In other words, correlations among measures intended to tap different traits often are largely due to similarities between sampling methods (Campbell, 1960; Campbell & Fiske, 1959). If, for example, three questionnaires are used to measure "dependency," the correlations obtained among them may be more attributable to similarity in the questionnaires than to the trait consistency they intend to elicit. If different methods were employed (e.g., a questionnaire, a peer rating, and a behavior observation), the correlations would be substantially lower. On the basis of a review of relevant studies, Campbell and Fiske (1959) concluded that the effect of method is usually greater than the effect of the trait measured. Applied to our case, this means that we have to be sure that the patterns of traits attributed to Gary do not merely reflect overlap among the questionnaires he has answered.

Moreover, we would want to know if Gary's trait would test out identically if it were measured by a technique that is not a questionnaire. To be most confident of his level of authoritarianism, for example, we would want to see what he *does* with authority figures behaviorally as well as what he *says* about authority on questionnaires. To have faith that he is a "loner," fears emotional involvement, and is anxious, we would want to measure each of these attributes in several ways, not just by questionnaires. Otherwise, how could we be sure that the impression we get of him reflects more than his manner of talking about himself on inventories?

Is It More Than Intelligence?

It is also important to examine the correlations found between personality tests and measures of intelligence. Consider, for example, the relations among measures of personality and performance in a small group. Mann (1959) reviewed and surveyed the voluminous research on this topic in the years from 1900 to 1957. The personality variables in his survey included adjustment, extraversion-introversion, dominance, masculinity-femininity, and interpersonal sensitivity. He also measured intelligence. The behavior of the people in groups served as the performance criteria. These behaviors were scored on leadership, popularity, activity rate, conformity, and other dimensions. From the hundreds of correlations obtained it was concluded that "the best predictor of an individual's performance in groups is intelligence" (p. 264).

Mann's results are not atypical. Many personality measures are substantially correlated with tests of intelligence. Intelligence has been found to correlate negatively with authoritarianism and prejudice, and positively with certain measures of honesty and indices of impulse control, creativity, and so on. The magnitude of these correlations is quite variable, but not infrequently it is as large as the associations between the personality test and the other external referents that serve to define it (e.g., Getzels & Jackson, 1962). The correlations obtained among personality indices therefore may depend partly on relations between the personality measures and intelligence. Intelligence may play an especially important role in self-report inventories and other paper-and-pencil personality questionnaires that intend to assess maladaptive behavior (Mischel, 1968).

In light of these facts, Campbell and Fiske (1959) have rightly urged that investigations of all traits should include correlations between the ostensible trait and measures of intelligence. If a personality trait covaries (correlates) largely with intelligence, to invoke it as a new disposition is of little value.

SUMMARY

1. Mental testing at the turn of the century was the forerunner of later developments in the psychometric approach to personality. The intelligence test developed by Binet early in the twentieth century profoundly influenced the history of psychometric mental and personality testing.

2. In the psychometric approach to personality, the aim is to measure an individual with respect to one or more single traits, such as aggressiveness or introversion. In order to measure objectively, the psychometrician attempts to create *standardized* self-report questionnaires and rating scales that will yield results that can be *reproduced* easily by independent observers.

3. Gary W. is introduced to elucidate the applications of the trait approach. His case will also be subjected to the methods of other theoretical approaches in subsequent chapters.

4. The MMPI is one of the most widely used personality tests. It contains a set of self-report scales whose meanings are defined empirically by their correlations with other test indices and with behaviors displayed by the person in other situations. MMPI "atlases" provide descriptive information for various average test profiles or code types.

5. The California *F* Scale and the various masculinity-femininity scales are typical of the pencil-and-paper questionnaires used to study important attributes in the psychometric trait approach.

6. Attention has been called to response "sets," which may affect the meaning of self-reports and ratings. Among these sets are the willingness to endorse socially undesirable statements, and the tendency to agree (or disagree) with ambiguous statements regardless of their content. Many researchers consider response sets as interferences that may cause errors in psychometric tests. Others see them as indicative of personality traits, such as the disposition to behave in socially desirable ways.

7. Similarity and overlap of measurement methods often contribute to the correlations found among traits. To demonstrate that a distinctive trait is being tapped, it is helpful to study it by at least two different methods.

8. It is also necessary to demonstrate that a new trait test measures a trait that is not already measured by another test. Intelligence measures are frequently substantially correlated with personality tests. Therefore it is important to demonstrate that any new personality test is not mainly redundant with IQ tests.

TRAIT THEORIES: APPLICATIONS (II)

Test 7-11

M.M.P.I
Factor Analysis 155
—Allport
—Odbert 156

D'Andrade

traits Testing

Reliability 160, Validity 161

E. Rosch 174   *Eysenck p 180*

Cantor & Mischel 174   *D, Andrade p 157*

Wallach 174

Zigler & Phillips 178   *Kraepelin 178*

Applications of the trait approach to personality are discussed further in this chapter. We move now beyond specific tests and strategies generated by the trait approach to consider more general issues that must be understood in order to achieve a perspective on trait theories, their applications, their problems, and their value.

From Test Responses to Basic Traits

How can one go from test responses to the traits that they reflect? As noted before (Chapter 2), trait theorists are interested mainly in discovering basic traits, not just in comparing people's test scores. In their search for "underlying traits" they begin with test responses, usually in the form of self-ratings or ratings by others. But the range of possible trait ratings is as large as the number of trait names available in the language. A casual glance at any dictionary makes it plain that when people try to describe personality in trait terms, an almost endless set of names is available to them. A systematic

search for all "trait names" in a standard English dictionary produced some 18,000 terms (Allport & Odbert, 1936). In a later effort Cattell (1947, 1957) selected from this list 4504 terms that Allport (1937, p. 366) had characterized as real traits of personality.

Simplifying Test Responses

Trait terms that number in the thousands—even the 550 responses of the MMPI—are unmanageable as descriptive units, especially in attempts to evaluate many people and to characterize the patternings of their behavior. Consider, for example, the mass of data yielded by the 550 MMPI responses from each of a hundred persons.

To extract order parsimoniously from such a stack of facts, investigators searching for underlying traits try to group responses into more basic clusters of units that are correlated with each other but independent of the other responses. For this purpose many trait psychologists (e.g., Cattell, 1965) have turned to factor analysis, a mathematical procedure that helps to sort test responses into relatively homogeneous clusters.

Does Factor Analysis Discover Basic Traits?

Factor analysis does not necessarily reveal the basic traits of persons. The results depend on the tests and the subjects selected by the researcher, and on the details of his or her procedures and decisions. Factor analysis is a very useful tool for reducing a large set of correlated measures to fewer unrelated dimensions. As such, it can be a powerful aid to psychological research by clarifying which response patterns go together. Suppose, for example, that 50 students have answered 10 personality questionnaires, each of which contains 100 questions. A factor analysis of this mass of information can show which parts of the test performances go together (i.e., are closely correlated with each other yet uncorrelated with other parts).

But as Overall (1964) has noted, factor analysis cannot establish which characteristics of persons or things being measured are "real" or "primary." The factors obtained are simply names given to the correlations found among the particular measures. In other words, factor analysis yields a greatly simplified patterning of the test data put into it; but it cannot go beyond the limitations of the original tests and it depends on many decisions by the investigator (e.g., in the type of factor analysis he or she conducts). Consequently, while the factor analytic search for underlying "source traits" (Chapter 2) favored by such trait theorists as Cattell (1965) may yield mathematically pure factors, their psychological meaningfulness and relevance for the person's actual behavior cannot be assumed or taken for granted; they must be demonstrated.

Both the approach and the problems of trying to discover traits through factor analysis of ratings are illustrated in a series of extensive and sophisti-

factor studies

cated factor-analytic studies (Norman, 1961, 1963; Tupes & Christal, 1958, 1961). These studies investigated the factors obtained for diverse samples of subjects rated by their peers on rating scales. The scales themselves originated from a condensed version of the thousands of trait names originally identified by Allport and Odbert's search for trait names in the dictionary. After much research, 20 scales were selected and many judges were asked to rate other people on them. The results were carefully factor-analyzed.

The same set of five relatively independent factors appeared consistently across several studies. This exciting finding led to the conclusion that a "highly stable structure of personal characteristics has been identified" (Norman, 1963, p. 581). The five factors (summarized in Table 2-2) were extraversion, agreeableness, conscientiousness, emotional stability, and culture.

It seemed reasonable to conclude from these results that a stable, five-factor structure of personality exists. The findings came from many different samples of subjects and raters; the data included ratings based on interpersonal observations up to three years in length; and, most important, the agreement found between factors across samples was excellent (Norman, 1963). The conclusion that these data revealed a consistent, stable, generalized, five-factor personality structure rested on the basic assumption that the "obtained structure reflected the organization of these attributes in the ratees" (Passini & Norman, 1966, p. 44).

In fact, this assumption was not justified. Surprisingly, the factor structure that emerged when total strangers were rated was very similar to the five-factor structure obtained from ratings of people the raters knew well (Passini & Norman, 1966). In this study judges rated fellow college students whom they did not know. The judges' contacts with the ratees in the rating situation were made by being in the same room with them for less than 15 minutes, and there was no opportunity for verbal communication. The rating task was made credible by asking the raters to judge the subjects as "you would imagine" them to be. The authors pointed out that the raters could not possibly have known the ratee's attributes on dimensions like "sociable-reclusive," "cooperative-negativistic," or "responsible-undependable." The results nevertheless yielded factors extremely similar to the five factors found from ratings by close acquaintances in the earlier studies. As the authors noted, the main information available to the raters "was whatever they carried in their heads"!

Trait Structures: In the Perceiver or in the Perceived?

Thus the factors identified by trait ratings may reflect the social stereotypes and concepts of the judges rather than the trait organization of the rated persons. Mulaik (1964), for example, conducted three separate factor-analytic studies, using many trait-rating scales, to determine the degree to which the method reveals the subject's personality factors as opposed to the rater's conceptual factors. The judges in one study rated real persons on the scales, including family members, close acquaintances, and themselves. In a second study they rated stereotypes like "Suburban Housewife," "Mental Patient," and "Air Force General." The raters in the third study rated the "meaning" of 20 trait words. An index of factor similarity revealed much similarity between the factors found for ratings of real persons and those found for ratings of stereotypes and words. On the basis of these and many similar results the investigator concluded that personality factors that emerge from ratings may reflect the raters' conceptual categories rather than the traits of the subjects being judged.

In a closely related vein, a debate has been raging about how to interpret the meaning of all personality ratings. Beginning in 1965, a logical and empirical analysis of personality ratings and questionnaires led D'Andrade to conclude that the associations (correlations) found among such measures "are primarily an artifact of the rater's or the questionnaire taker's cognitive structure, and not a reflection of the real world" (1974, p. 181). He claims that personality ratings tell us about "what is like what" in the heads of the judge, not "what goes with what" in the behavior of the judged. His basic argument is that when rating or judging personality, judges unwittingly believe that items that "go together" semantically (i.e., in the language because they seem similar or related), like "sincere" and "kind" or "aggressive" and "masculine," are also "inferred to be behaviorally characteristic of the same person even when, as is typically the case, conceptual relationships among items do not correspond to the actual behavioral relationships among items. . ." (Shweder, 1975, p. 455).

You will not be surprised to learn that such a sweeping attack on personality measurement did not go unanswered for long. In a careful reply, Block, Weiss, and Thorne (1979) point out methodological flaws in the argument—and just as unsurprisingly Shweder and D'Andrade (1979) counterattack, pointing at basic flaws in the criticisms made against them.

Some of the many issues raised by these debates will be explored further in later chapters. It should be clear, however, that in spite of many problems of interpretation, the descriptions of people obtained from different raters in different contexts often do agree with each other. For example, ratings of a student by peers may match to a considerable degree independent behavior ratings by other observers. Thus, agreement was found between peer nominations on clearly described dimensions of aggressive and dependent behavior and separate behavior ratings of actual aggressive and dependent behavior (Winder & Wiggins, 1964). Subjects were first classified into high, intermediate, and low groups on aggression and dependency on the basis of their peer reputations. Separate behavior ratings made later indicated that the three groups differed from each other significantly in the amount of aggression and dependency they displayed overtly in an experimental situation. Similarly, college students who were preselected as extremely high or low in aggressiveness (on the basis of ratings by their peers) also tended to be rated in similar ways by independent judges who observed their interaction (Gormly & Edelberg, 1974).

In sum, people obviously do not perceive an empty world. There are congruences between a rater's trait constructs and the traits of people he or she rates (e.g., Norman, 1966, 1969; Lay & Jackson, 1969), but these relationships tend to be much more complex than a naive trait psychology of "common sense" would suggest (Mischel, 1968, 1979).

In light of all these problems it becomes understandable that different investigators may arrive at somewhat different schemas of trait organization. Nevertheless, a few basic trait dimensions seem to be found over and over again. Introversion-extraversion, adjustment, and some variation of potency ("strong-weak") and adequacy ("good-bad") are often included. And within the domain of interpersonal behavior reasonably similar dimensions continue to be found in a variety of samples, providing evidence for structures that "are among the clearest reported in the personality literature to date" (Wiggins, 1979, p. 407). It is difficult to know the extent to which these structures reflect the conceptual dimensions shared by observers or the attributes of subjects. Probably they reflect both to some extent, and perhaps the two are almost impossible to separate clearly. What perceivers know certainly influences their judgments: We expect certain qualities to go together and therefore may be primed to see them as co-occurring. But it seems unlikely that our expectations are pure fictions, unrelated to actual regularities in the real world. Structure exists neither "all in the head" of the perceiver nor "all in the person" perceived; it reflects instead an interaction between the beliefs of observers and the characteristics of the observed. Instead of debating about the existence or reality of these co-occurrences, we need to study them with increasing precision.

Evaluating Trait Tests

To evaluate trait approaches and their applications requires that we evaluate the trait tests on which they rely. In recent years there has been a loud public outcry against the widespread use of trait tests in schools, business, and government. Critics both inside and outside the psychological profession have raised grave questions about the ethics, as well as the value, of many personality assessment practices that are most central to the trait approach. Neither the questions nor the answers are simple.

Ethical Concerns

There have been strong objections to judging people's personalities with tests. Much of the public outrage has centered on the fear that tests are invasions of privacy, that they force people to answer questions that may be used to discriminate against them. Understandably people are reluctant to have testers pry into their lives and extract information that may contribute to negative decisions about them. The problem is even more keen if the tests are of dubious validity.

Proper evaluation of the ethics of personality assessment and rational assessment of the testing procedures are matters of great social importance. The public and its legal representatives (in Congress, for example) have been handicapped by widespread ignorance of the tests and the techniques underlying their development. The ethical and social problems involved in the multimillion dollar personality-testing business are formidable indeed. The scope of the problem is indicated by the publication of literally thousands of personality tests, many of which are widely used throughout our society. Given the magnitude of the problem and the public's confusion about personality testing, it is especially important to consider in some depth the main problems that arise in attempts to interpret what personality tests really do and really don't permit us to say about individuals. We now have a considerable amount of data about Gary W., for example, but we are still very uncertain about how to evaluate it. How sure can we be of the impressions we have? How wise or hazardous would it be to base important decisions on this information?

The rest of this chapter will consider only problems relevant to the interpretation of objective personality trait tests. In later chapters, the discussion will be extended to many other techniques for evaluating personality. As we have seen, trait-oriented research usually has assessed differences between people on paper-and-pencil inventories and questionnaires. Many problems arise in efforts to clarify the meaning of the answers. Notice that almost all the psychometric information we have about Gary is based on what he *says* about himself. His MMPI profile, his California *F* Scale, his masculinity-femininity score, all rest on self-reports on questionnaires. Since we want to know more about Gary than how he answers questionnaires, it is crucial to establish what his scores do and do not imply about him.

Tests Can Deceive

In daily life people function like trait psychologists to the extent that they infer personality dispositions from behavioral cues. Often these impressions are formed quickly and are based on minimal information. The taxi driver who claims he can spot the main qualities of his rider's personality in 10 minutes is a common example. Usually such snap diagnoses are not taken seriously and are dismissed easily as clichés. When a personality description is offered by a more creditable diagnostician it tends to be accepted much more readily even if it is equally wrong. College students in one study were administered personality tests and then were all given written personality interpretations (Ulrich, Stachnik, & Stainton, 1963). Although the interpretations were supposedly based on their psychological test results, in fact each of the 57 students obtained the same report, illustrated by the following excerpts (p. 832):

You have a strong need for other people to like you and for them to admire you. . . . Your sexual adjustment has presented some problems for you. . . . Disciplined and controlled on the outside, you tend to be worrisome and insecure inside. . . . Some of your aspirations tend to be pretty unrealistic.

The vast majority of the students indicated the reports captured their personalities excellently. Of the 57 students, 53 rated the report either excellent or good, only three giving it an average rating, one calling it poor, and none very poor. Their overall enthusiasm was also reflected in spontaneous comments of great praise. For example, "I agree with almost all of your statements and think they answer the problems I may have." Or, "On the nose! Very good. I wish you had said more, but what you did mention was all true without a doubt. I wish you could go further into this personality sometime." Other students indicated they felt they had been helped substantially by the interpretations.

The ease with which these students were duped about their own personality is not at all atypical; it reflects less their gullibility than the intrinsic hazards of personality impressions and everyday trait descriptions. When personality impressions are stated in broad terms they are difficult to disconfirm. The individual may readily add extra meaning to clichés and adopt them with great confidence even when they turn out to be untrue (or untestable). Thus the naive person may attribute profound significance to the vague comments provided by palmists and newspaper astrologers and may accept as personal revelations "insights" that could fit almost anyone.

It is therefore extremely important for psychologists to provide real support and evidence for their statements about personality and to make their statements in a form that is testable. You should approach the matters of "reliability" and "validity" in personality study (defined and discussed next) not as mere textbook terms to be memorized and not used: Instead, try to see these concepts as guides for establishing the value of psychologists' claims about the nature of personality.

Reliability

A number of techniques are available for estimating the consistency or "reliability" of personality observations or measures. When the same test is given to the same group of people on two occasions, a retest correlation or "coefficient of stability" is obtained. This measure provides an index of *temporal reliability.* Generally, the longer the time interval, the lower the coefficient of stability. If there is only a short interval between test and retest, the two occasions are not entirely independent. For example, if subjects remember some of their initial responses, the correlation is strengthened.

Other reliability estimates are more concerned with the consistency with which different parts or alternate forms of a test measure behavior. The correlation between parts of a single form gives an index of *internal consistency.* Consistency may also be measured by the intercorrelation of scores on *alternate forms* of a test administered to the same set of subjects. The alternate-form method is especially valuable for assessing the effects of an intervening procedure, such as psychotherapy or special training, on test performance, because it avoids the contaminating effects of administering the same form twice.

If subjective judgment enters into scoring decisions, a special kind of reliability check is needed. This check is called *interscorer agreement* or consistency, and it is the degree to which different scorers or judges arrive at the same statements about the same test data. For example, if three judges try to infer personality traits from subjects' interview behavior and dream reports, it would be necessary to establish the degree to which the three assessors reach the same conclusions. As noted before, interscorer agreement is easiest to achieve when scoring is objective, as on highly structured tests (for example, when all answers are given as either "yes" or "no").

The reliability of a test increases when the number of items in the test is increased. Measures that consist of single items ("Are you happy?") tend to have very low reliability and therefore do not allow any meaningful conclusions. While this point is obvious and has been made often before in psychology, personality psychologists sometimes seem to forget it. Therefore, demonstrations and reminders that reliability requires combining many items into a measure are important and worth making (Epstein, 1979).

Validity

A woman's self-report on a 10-item questionnaire provides her *stated* reactions to the items under the specific testing conditions. Thus if a person reports that she is "very friendly," that is what she *says* about herself on the test. To know more than that, one needs validity research to establish the meaning and implications of the test answers. The various types of validity research are summarized in Table 7-1.

Content or face validity is the demonstration that the items on a test adequately represent a defined broader *class* of behavior. For example, judges would have to agree that the different items on a "friendliness" questionnaire all in fact seem to deal with the class or topic of friendliness. In practice, content validity often is assumed rather than demonstrated. Even if the content validity of the items is shown acceptably, it cannot be assumed that the answers provide an index of the individual's "true" trait position. We do not know whether or not the person who says she is friendly, for example, is really friendly. A self-description is a self-description, a description by another person is another person's description, and the relationships between such data and other nontest events have to be demonstrated.

TABLE 7-1 STRATEGIES AND PURPOSES IN PSYCHOMETRIC PERSONALITY TEST CONSTRUCTION		
Type of Validation	*General Procedure*	*Use of Test Responses*
1. Content	Demonstration that test content is representative of a broader class	Self-description
2. Criterion a. concurrent	Correlation between test scores and other presently available data	Substitute for less convenient sample with known correlation to criterion
b. predictive	Correlation between test scores and later status on a criterion	Selection, placement, and other diagnostic and classificatory decisions; discrimination between groups
3. Construct	Invention of theory regarding what accounts for obtained test scores; empirical demonstration of theory, using diverse strategies	Inference about personality attributes; personality description in terms of psychological constructs; refinement of theory

To go beyond description of the sampled behavior, one has to determine the relationship between it and scores on other measures that serve as referents or standards, thus providing *criterion validity*. For example, psychiatrists' ratings about progress in therapy, teachers' ratings of school performance, the subject's behavior on another test, her self-report on another occasion, may be selected as criteria. In our discussion of the MMPI in the last chapter we noted several examples of "criterion validity research," although we did not call it by that name. Recall, for instance, the correlations between score patterns and such external information about the respondents as their history of psychiatric hospitalization. Criterion validity may be established by a correlation among concurrently available data (such as current test score and present psychiatric diagnosis). Criterion validity also can be predictive if it comes from correlations between a measure and data collected at a later time, for example, pretherapy diagnosis and adjustment ratings after a year of psychotherapy. Correlations may be looked for between data that seem to have a strong surface similarity in content, such as a child's arithmetic performance on an IQ test and his future success in an arithmetic course. Or they may be sought between measures whose contents appear quite dissimilar, such as a patient's drawings and a psychiatric diagnosis.

Tests based on criterion validity may be used for various practical purposes, depending on their specific validation procedures. Obviously a test may have concurrent validity and still be unable to predict future behavior. Likewise, a test may have predictive validity without concurrent validity if, for example, it can predict suicide five years before a patient kills himself but relates to no other measure at the time of administration.

Personality psychologists guided by trait theory usually want to infer and describe a person's dispositions from his or her test responses. *Construct or trait validation* is the effort to elaborate the inferred traits determining test behavior (Campbell, 1960). The concept of "construct validity" was introduced by trait psychologists for problems in which the assessor accepts

no existing measure as a definitive criterion of the quality with which he is concerned. Here the traits or qualities underlying test performance are of central importance (American Psychological Association, 1966, pp. 13–14).

The chief characteristic of construct validation is the simultaneous validation of the test and of the trait construct. The investigator interested in the traits supposedly accounting for personality test responses must generate a concept or theory about the underlying dispositions or traits that she believes determine responses on her test. She then can employ a variety of methods to establish a network of relationships intended to illuminate what is related to her concept about the underlying disposition and what is not.

Traditionally, construct validity involves the following steps. The investigator begins with a hunch about a dimension on which individual differences can be compared, for example, "submissiveness." She might regard submissiveness as a "tendency to yield to the will and suggestions of others" (Sarason, 1966, p. 127). To study this tendency she devises a measure of submissiveness. She has no one definite criterion, however, and instead may use diverse behavioral samples as indices of the subject's underlying trait of submissiveness. She then proceeds to formulate and test hypotheses about how submissiveness, as displayed on her tests, does and does not relate to other behaviors in particular situations. On the basis of her findings she progressively revises and refines her construct. Thus construct validation involves testing and revising hypotheses about relations by examining the empirical associations among responses evoked in different situations.

Construct validation is distinguished from other strategies on the grounds that in construct validity the investigator's construct is not fully *equivalent* to any *one* behavioral measure or criterion. The investigator may not be at all sure about the particular criteria that are most appropriate for the construct. Construct validation thus is simply hypothesis testing and theory building with imperfect and incomplete operations and with many referents for the investigator's emerging concept.

Construct Validity: An Example

Textbook accounts of trait methodology generally describe it distantly, with abstractions, discussing such concepts as reliability and validity, as in the preceding pages. In actual practice most researchers begin much more concretely, with a hunch or a direct observation, and try to follow their lead within a broad methodological framework. This much more tangible, step-by-step discovery process may be illustrated by studies of delay of gratification as a personality construct.

It is commonly believed that people differ in their preference or tolerance for delayed gratification. It has often been noted that young children find it hard to wait for delayed rewards. Clinically, the inability to postpone gratification for the sake of delayed rewards is generally considered an important factor in immaturity, maladjustment, and "psychopathy." Mowrer and Ullmann (1945), for example, thought the inability to tolerate delay of reinforcement was a critical factor in the development of criminal behavior. Surprisingly, in spite of the important role of delay of reward in many personality theories, little systematic research had been devoted to the topic before the series of studies described next.

Devise a Measure

As a first step, the actual reward preferences of children in a Trinidadian village were assessed (Mischel, 1958). Additional information was also collected about each child in an effort to establish relationships between reward preferences and other characteristics. The subjects of the first study were boys and girls between the ages of 7 and 9, in the elementary section of a rural Trinidad school. In preexperimental sessions, two rewards or "reinforcements" of use for the experimental situation had to be selected. For this purpose, in a pre-test a smaller sample of boys and girls from the same age group, but taken from another rural Trinidadian school, were seen in individual sessions. In these meetings their preferences for various specific reinforcements were elicited. As a result, two reinforcements (both candy, but varying markedly in size, price, and packaging,—i.e., a 1-cent and a 10-cent candy) were chosen.

In the main study, at the village school itself, the children's task was to fill out a simple questionnaire. All the youngsters were sufficiently literate for this, as the questionnaire simply asked each child to indicate his ethnic group, age, socioeconomic status, and presence or absence of the father within the household. After the subjects completed the questionnaire, the experimenter displayed the two kinds of reinforcements and said: "I would like to give each of you a piece of candy, but I don't have enough of these (indicating the larger, more preferred reinforcement) with me today. So you can either get this one (indicating the smaller, less preferred reinforcement) right now, today, or, if you want to, you can wait for this one (indicating), which I will bring back next Wednesday [one week later]." The fact that getting the smaller candy immediately precluded getting the larger one the following week, and vice versa, was stressed. The children were asked to indicate their choice on their questionnaires.

Explore the Network of Correlations

The data were analyzed statistically to assess any relations between preference for either of the reinforcements and other measures. For example, is a child's tendency to delay gratification also a sign of his maturity? The relationship between age and reward preference is found in Table 7-2, which shows the percentage of children in each age group choosing immediate versus delayed rewards (Mischel, 1958). A larger proportion of children chose to delay gratification at the older age levels. This finding fits the common view that increasing maturity brings an increasing ability to delay gratification. Since the finding has now been replicated several times, one may feel more confident about its accuracy (e.g., Melikian, 1959; Mischel & Metzner, 1962).

It is also widely believed that lower-class youngsters tend to be more impulsive than those from higher socioeconomic backgrounds. Comparison of the "high" versus "low" socioeconomic groups on reward preferences, however, did not yield a significant difference. The lack of relationship here could not be considered definitive, however, because the measure of socioeconomic level employed was extremely crude (type of housing). A failure to find an association among variables in this instance leaves one unsure whether the measures were inadequate or whether the relationship really did not exist.

To further develop the construct validity of preference for immediate,

	Age		
TABLE 7-2			
PERCENT CHOOSING IMMEDIATE OR			
DELAYED REWARD AT EACH AGE			

Choice	7	8	9
Immediate reward	81%	48%	20%
Delayed reward	19%	52%	80%

SOURCE: Adapted from Mischel (1958).

smaller rewards, as opposed to delayed, larger rewards, its relations to other variables, such as social responsibility, were explored next (Mischel, 1961b). It was hypothesized that youngsters who prefer immediate, smaller rewards would show less social responsibility than those who tend to choose larger, delayed rewards. This prediction was based on the belief that in a choice situation people select to wait for delayed more valuable rewards to the degree that they expect the more attractive reward actually to materialize. Such expectations require subjects to have faith that the promise-maker will keep his promise. The children, in other words, must trust that the agent who promises delayed gratifications will really supply them. Such trust or willingness to postpone immediate smaller gratification probably is also a basic ingredient of social responsibility; therefore ability to delay gratification should be positively related to social responsibility scores and negatively related to delinquent or criminal behavior.

Social responsibility was measured by answers to a carefully constructed and independently validated self-report questionnaire—the Social Responsibility Scale—as well as by the behavioral criterion of known delinquency. The Social Responsibility Scale has been found to correlate substantially with other measures of personal and social adjustment; it was designed to "discriminate children who have, with their peers, a reputation for responsibility as contrasted with children who have little reputation for responsibility" (Harris, 1957, p. 326). Harris' theory of responsibility, to which the items in the scale are related, conceptualizes responsibility "as a composite of attitude elements reflecting behavior classifiable as reliable, accountable, loyal, or doing an effective job" (Harris, 1957, p. 322).

The subjects were Trinidadian children. Some came from a large elementary government school on the outskirts of the capital city. Another sample came from a boys' "industrial school" that, in reality, is a reform school for committed juvenile delinquents; it also is on the outskirts of the capital. Just as in the initial study, an actual behavior choice that elicited preference for either immediate, smaller rewards or delayed, larger rewards was used at each school, and the Social Responsibility Scale was administered to each group. In addition, at the industrial school two items were added to obtain a preliminary test of the consistency with which subjects prefer immediate or delayed rewards. They were: "I would rather get ten dollars right now than have to wait a whole month and get thirty dollars then," and "I would rather wait to get a much larger gift much later rather than get a smaller one now."

The results showed, as was predicted, that a significantly larger proportion of delinquents chose immediate, smaller rewards. Moreover, and also as expected, among the delinquent children, those who preferred the delayed, larger reward had significantly higher social responsibility scores. Where three measures of reward preference had been used, the reliability or consistency of such preferences (Table 7-3) could be examined. The results showed a significant, but far from perfect, association among the responses on the three measures. Because these measures had much in common in their phrasing and were all

TABLE 7-3
CONSISTENCY OF PREFERENCE FOR IMMEDIATE
OR DELAYED REWARDS: RELATION OF CHILDREN'S
ACTUAL CHOICE TO THEIR QUESTIONNAIRE PREFERENCES

	Questionnaire Preferences		
Actual Choice	*Consistently Immediate*	*Consistently Delayed*	*Inconsistent*
Immediate, smaller candy	12	4	15
Delayed, larger candy	4	19	16

NOTE: Each number represents a child: e.g., 12 children who consistently said they preferred immediate reward on the questionnaire also chose an immediate, smaller (rather than a delayed, larger) candy.
SOURCE: Adapted from Mischel (1961b).

obtained within the same testing situation, the data provided only a limited first step in the appraisal of the consistency of such reinforcement preferences within people.

Extend and Modify the Construct

In light of the overall encouraging results obtained in these studies with a simple index or delay-of-reward, later studies pursued the topic further and more systematically. More items were added to the measure of reward preferences, and the extended procedure was administered in various cultural settings in different parts of the world to further explore the meaning of the results obtained by discovering their correlates. Simultaneously the test items themselves were progressively revised, and the internal consistency and reliability features of the test were examined more systematically.

Gradually the program of research obtained significant correlations between preference for delayed, larger reinforcement or immediate, smaller gratifications and many other theoretically relevant behaviors, so that it provided an extensive network of construct validity. For example, children who chose to wait for rewards tended to have higher social responsibility, to cheat less, and to yield to temptation more slowly (Mischel & Gilligan, 1964). They also tended to be more concerned about achievement (Mischel, 1961b) and to be somewhat brighter (Mischel & Metzner, 1962) than children who chose immediate gratifications, although these relationships were not very strong. Children who delay are also rated differently by parents and teachers on a number of personal characteristics. Although these ratings may be somewhat different when there are even slight variations in the delay situation (Bem & Funder, 1978), on the whole they seem to provide a consistent picture when enough children are tested (Mischel & Peake, 1981).

Moreover, preference for delayed rewards not only increases with age and differs radically across cultures, but also varies predictably as a function of certain rearing conditions in the home (Mischel, 1966b). Preferences for delayed rewards in choice situations are unrelated, however, to the standards children set for rewarding their own behavior (Mischel & Masters, 1966), and to their choice between immediate and delayed unavoidable punishments of different magnitudes (Mischel & Grusec, 1967). Other studies have investigated delay behavior experimentally and have systematically explored many of the conditions that control it. In this fashion a continuously expanding network of construct validity may be gradually established and progressively revised (e.g., Klineberg, 1968; Shybut, 1968; Gallimore, Weiss, & Finney, 1974; Mischel, 1974). A fundamentally similar strategy has guided explorations of the construct validity of numerous traits.

Traits, Situations, and Their Interactions

A main goal of trait psychology has been to discover the individual's position on one or more personality dimensions by comparing him or her with other persons tested under similar conditions. It was assumed that an individual's position on these dimensions would be relatively stable across testing situations and over lengthy time periods, if the test was sufficiently reliable. Therefore the main focus in trait psychology was on the development of reliable instruments administered under standard conditions. Such instruments were thought to tap accurately the person's presumably stable, highly generalized traits across a relatively large number of situations or settings.

The early psychometricians tended to follow the example of simple physical measurement, hoping that the measurement of traits would be basically similar to such measurements as table length with rulers, or temperature with thermometers. They unquestioningly assumed that broad trait structures exist and lead people to behave consistently. Consequently, they did not pay much attention to the role of environmental variables as determinants of behavior. Instead, they concentrated on standardization of measurement conditions in the hope that broad traits would emerge.

How Broad or Specific Are Traits?

Will a person who is "conscientious" about homework also be conscientious about keeping social appointments and honoring obligations and responsibilities to other people? Will an individual who is anxious about school also be anxious about meeting strangers or taking on a new job? How broad (general) or specific (narrow) are traits like conscientiousness and anxiety? Do people have dispositions that reveal themselves consistently in a wide range of behaviors and over many situations? These questions have been asked for years, and the answers remain the subject of intense debate. Perhaps no topic in personality psychology is more controversial—and more important—than the question of the relative specificity versus generality of traits.

To the surprise of early trait theorists, a great deal of research has shown that performances on trait measures are affected by a variety of stimulus conditions, and can be modified by numerous environmental changes (Masling, 1960; Mischel, 1974; Peterson, 1968; Vernon, 1964). Most important, it has been found that normal people tend to show considerable variability in their behavior even across seemingly similar conditions. A person may be dependent with his wife, for example, but not with his boss, and even his dependency at home may be highly specific, varying as a result of slight situational alterations, such as subtle changes in his wife's reactions to him, or the presence of other family members. Thus behavior may be much more situation-specific and discriminative than early trait theorists had thought.

Studies of individual differences on common trait dimensions have produced many networks of correlations. These associations tend to be large and enduring when people rate themselves or others with broad trait terms (e.g., Block, 1971). For example, on questionnaires, people may describe their traits consistently (e.g., E. L. Kelly, 1955). When ongoing behavior in specific situations is sampled objectively by different, independent measures, however, the association generally tends to be quite modest. Thus while people often show consistency on questionnaires and ratings, these data tend to have limited value for predicting their actual behavior in specific situations.

The correlational research on delay of gratification discussed in the last section is fairly representative of correlational research done on other personality dimensions. As we saw, some supporting validity data were easily obtained. The networks of relationships from such research extend far and wide and provide ample evidence that people's behavior has some consistency, that it is not totally situation-specific. What a person does in one setting is not independent of what he does in other settings, and it is, of course, related to what he did before and to what he will probably do again. In general, however, correlational work on voluntary delay of reward and on other personality dispositions suggests that the strength of the associations generally tends to be too low for confident predictions about behavior in the individual case.

Therefore we have to be most cautious about generalizing from an individual's test behavior to his or her personality and behavior outside the test. For example, we cannot safely conclude that Gary's lack of authoritarianism on the California *F* Scale precludes his behaving in highly arbitrary, "authoritarian" ways under certain life conditions. Perhaps, then, his friend was right when he noted that Gary could be "arbitrary" and "bossy," with an insulting, cynical humor. The same friend also described Gary as "friendly and out-going"—but only when he is "with a shy, self-conscious person." As these examples indicate, Gary's authoritarianism, his friendliness or hostility, and other key features of his behavior are not situation-free attributes: They depend on many modifying conditions and hence are relatively specific. Likewise, the fact that Gary's self-reported sex-role interests and attitudes gave him an "average" score on the masculinity-femininity dimension in no way precludes his having diverse sexual problems that are not "average." For example, while his interests may be stereotypically masculine to an average degree, he still may be plagued by idiosyncratic sexual conflicts and may be suffering from relatively unique behavioral problems in his actual sexual relations.

"Behavioral specificity," or the dependence of behavior on specific situational conditions, has been discovered regularly on character traits like rigidity, or social conformity, or honesty, or aggression, or on most other non-intellective personality dimensions (Mischel, 1968; Peterson, 1968; Vernon, 1964). Specificity tends to be high, for example, among the components of traits like dependency, or self-control, or attitudes toward authority—although trait theorists originally believed these to be highly generalized dispositions. Results of this kind present a basic problem for approaches to personality that assume the existence of relatively situation-free, broad dispositions.

The phrase "personality coefficient" has been coined to describe the modest correlation (usually between .20 and .30) typically found in personality research linking responses on questionnaires to other behavior (Mischel, 1968). Such correlations are too small to have value for most individual assessment purposes other than gross screening decisions. For example, Gary's MMPI profile might be useful as a preliminary screening device to help decide whether or not he might need further testing before being selected for a "sensitive" government job. It would be of more limited value, however, in predicting specific important things about his behavior as an individual.

The evaluation of all data on trait consistency depends of course on the standards selected to evaluate them. A modest consistency coefficient (of about .30, for example) can be taken as evidence either of the relative specificity of the particular behaviors or of the presence of some cross-situational generality (Burton, 1963). Furthermore, one has to infer dispositions from imperfect behavioral measurements that involve errors. Nevertheless, it is gradually being recognized that behavioral fluctuations reflect more than imperfections in measuring instruments (Loevinger, 1957). All individuals may be consistent in their own behavior on some traits (e.g., Bem & Allen, 1974). But on many traits most of us show only limited consistency across situations (Mischel, 1973a). The utility of describing everyone in broad trait terms (e.g., "impulsive," "dependent") is therefore being questioned deeply. Indeed, it has to be challenged (Peterson, 1968), and it raises many complex issues (discussed again in Chapter 20).

Stable over Time,
but Discriminative across Situations

The specificity of behavior *across situations* should not be confused with its *stability over time* in similar situations. In fact, there is continuity over long periods of time, especially when people rate themselves or when observers rate them (Mischel, 1968, 1979). And these two types of ratings often are significantly related to each other and to relevant behavior. Consistency over time, and agreement among judges in personality ratings is not disputed. Indeed there is more and more evidence showing impressive coherences in behavior patterns even when measured over many years (Block & Block, 1979). Lives do have coherence, and we tend to view ourselves and others as relatively stable people, without questioning our basic identity and continuity over time.

What *is* in dispute is the consistency of behavior not over time but across situations, especially when one infers personality dimensions from ongoing behavior sampled by methods that go beyond trait ratings, such as direct observations. Studies with objective measures of behavior as it occurs naturally have indicated that a given individual's actions are often rather specific to the particular situation and tend to be patterned uniquely (e.g., Mischel, 1968; Peterson, 1968; Shweder, 1975; Shweder & D'Andrade, 1979). Objective, specific measures of ongoing behavior tend to yield erratic evidence of consistency across situations. While the patterns are often coherent and meaningful (i.e., nonrandom), they also tend to be complex and unevenly related to personality ratings (Block, 1977).

In Defense of Traits

Although they acknowledge that the specific situation is important, many psychologists are convinced that past research has underestimated the personal constancies in behavior. They point out that if we want to test how well a disposition (trait) can be used to predict behavior we have to sample adequately not only the disposition but also the behavior that we want to predict (Ajzen & Fishbein, 1977; Block, 1977; Epstein, 1979; Jaccard, 1974; Weigel & Newman, 1976). Yet in the past, researchers often attempted to predict single acts (for example, physical aggression when insulted) from a dispositional measure (e.g., self-rated aggression). Generally such attempts did not succeed. But while measures of traits may not be able to predict such single acts they may do much better if one uses a "multiple act criterion": a pooled combination of many behaviors that are relevant to the trait.

The methods and results of this new line of research are illustrated in a study in which undergraduate women were given the "dominance scale" from two personality inventories (Jaccard, 1974). The women also were asked whether or not they had performed a set of 40 dominance-related behaviors (e.g., have initiated a discussion in class, have argued with a teacher, have asked a male out on a date). As is so often the case, the dominance scales from the personality inventories did not predict the individual behaviors well. But the researcher found that when the 40 behavioral items were summed into one pooled measure they related substantially to the personality scores. Namely, women high on the dominance scales also tended to report performing more dominant behaviors, and the reverse was also true. Thus a longer, aggregated and therefore more reliable behavioral measure revealed associations to other measures (the self-reports on the personality tests) that would not otherwise have been seen.

This study provided a useful demonstration. But the results were limited by the fact that both the dispositional (personality) and the behavioral measures were based on the subjects' own self-reports. It is possible that the women might have been biased to describe themselves in consistent ways regardless of what they actually did. However, essentially similar results are starting to be found when the behaviors are measured directly by observation (e.g., Weigel & Newman, 1976), but final conclusions cannot be reached until there are further compelling demonstrations.

In much the same vein, there have been a number of demonstrations to show that reliability will increase when the number of items in a test sample are increased and combined. It is important to remember that "There is nothing magical about a correlation coefficient, and its interpretation depends on many considerations. The accuracy of reliability of measurement increases with the length of the test. Since no single item is a perfect measure, adding items increases the chance that the test will elicit a more accurate sample and yield a better estimate of the person's behavior" (Mischel, 1968, p. 37). Making this point empirically, Epstein (1979) demonstrated that temporal stability (of, for example, self-reported emotions and experiences recorded daily, and observer judgments) becomes much larger when it is based on averages over many days than when it is based on only single items on single days. Such demonstrations help by reminding psychologists again that reliability is essential before one can hope to have validity. However, most of the evidence so far again is relevant to the temporal stability of traits, not to broad cross-situational consistency of behavior in social or personal domains.

Uses and Misuses of Traits

Certainly behavior is not completely situation-specific. We do not have to start with a blank mind in every new situation; we have memories, we generalize from past to future, and our earlier experiences influence our present behavior. Overall "average" differences between individuals can be construed easily and used to discriminate among them for many purposes. Knowing how your friend behaved before can help you predict how he or she probably will act again in similar situations. The impact of any situation or stimulus depends on the person who experiences it, and different people differ greatly in how they cope with most stimulus conditions. It is a truism that one person's favorite "stimulus" may be the stuff of another's nightmares and that in the same "stimulus situation" one individual may react with aggression, another with love, a third with indifference. The evidence does not imply that different people will not act differently with some consistency in particular classes of situations; it does suggest that the particular classes of conditions tend to be much narrower than traditional trait theories have assumed, and for purposes of important individual decision-making require highly individualized assessments of what the specific situations mean to the person.

To apply these abstract points more concretely, it might help to think again about Gary. It is certainly possible to form some generalizations about his seemingly major qualities, strengths, and problems. Such generalizations help us to differentiate Gary from other people, and to compare him with them. We learned, for example, that the MMPI indicated Gary tended to be interpersonally distant, to avoid close relations with people, and to fear emotional involvement. Such characterizations may help one to gain a quick overall impression of Gary. But in order to predict what Gary will do in specific situations, or to make decisions about him (as in therapy or vocational counseling), it would be necessary to conduct a much more individually oriented study that considers the specific qualities of Gary as they relate to the specific situations of interest in his life. Just when does Gary become more—or less— "interpersonally distant"? Under what conditions does he *not* avoid close relations with people? When does his tendency to "fear emotional involvement" increase? When does it decrease? The analysis and prediction of specific behavior requires that we ask specific questions like these to link behavior to conditions rather than to paint personality portraits with more general characterizations.

The utility of inferring broad traits depends on the particular purpose for which the inference is made. Although inferences about global traits may have limited value for the practical prediction of a person's specific future behavior in specific situations, or for the design of specific treatment programs to help him, sometimes they have value for the person himself—for example, when he must abstract attributes to answer such everyday questions as: "Is your friend reliable?"; "What kind of person is my sister?"; "Might this person be a good roommate?"; or "What are *you* like?" Inferences about broad traits also may have value for such purposes as gross initial screening decisions (as in personnel selection), studying average differences between groups of individuals in personality research (Block, 1971), or the layman's everyday perception of persons (e.g., Mischel, Jeffery, & Patterson, 1974; Schneider, 1973). Finally, while comparisons *between* people in large, unselected groups on most common traits suggest that discriminativeness tends to be the rule, for some people a considerable degree of consistency can be demonstrated, at least on some dimensions some of the time (Chapter 20).

Basic "Natural" Trait Categories?

Recognizing the complexity of the links between traits and behavior, some theorists and researchers, working in still another direction, have become interested in how trait categories are used by the lay person. They want to understand the nature and function of the categories that people use to classify each other naturally in everyday life. These natural categories may include an impure mix of trait terms with other everyday "knowledge packages" about types of people found in common speech. These packages are the stereotypes (or the "schemas") we use when we refer to people as typical absent-minded professors, or "jocks," or male chauvinist pigs or "laid back" southern California types or crashing-bores-to-be-avoided-at-all-costs. Popular person schemas are also illustrated by Jung's archetypes: the earth mother, the wise old man, the prodigal son.

New interest in everyday natural person categories was created by some important studies of common object taxonomies conducted by Eleanor Rosch and her colleagues (1976). They asked people to describe the attributes (physical appearance, shape, function, movements) common to the objects included under different category labels (such as furniture, or birds) in three-level taxonomies (e.g., furniture, chair, kitchen chair). They found that certain levels of abstraction in these taxonomies maximized such desirable qualities as the richness (number) of attributes commonly associated with most category members. Rosch and her colleagues concluded that the optimal level of abstraction in the three-level object taxonomies was the middle level; at that level broad, inclusive, but still rich and distinctive categories are formed. These categories (called "basic level") are inclusive enough to cover many different kinds of objects within one category, but detailed and vivid enough to allow one to describe in great detail the typical appearance, shape, and function of a typical category member. Categorizing at this middle level of abstraction maximizes both parsimony—a few broad categories are formed—and richness—there are many features common to members of each particular category—making for an ideal system of communication.

Cantor and Mischel (1977, 1979) have been trying to extend this general approach to learning about the uses and limits of *person* categories at different levels of abstraction to help clarify the enduring and perplexing problem of selecting the most appropriate units for the study of social behavior. As a first step, to construct some representative person taxonomies, they began at the most abstract or "superordinate" level with the major common factors from peer-rating studies of personality (e.g., Norman, 1963). "Emotionally unstable person," for example, was one superordinate category; extravert was another. The middle levels were constructed to have person categories at lower, less inclusive levels of abstraction (such as "phobic" in the unstable person hierarchy or "P. R. type" and "comic joker" in the extravert hierarchy). The lowest or subordinate level included such subtypes as "claustrophobic" and "hydrophobic" (in the emotionally unstable hierarchy) or "door-to-door salesman" and "press agent" (in the extravert hierarchy). After the hierarchical nature of these structures was confirmed, subjects were asked to generate lists of common attributes. The degree of agreement for these person classifications was then assessed to determine the number and type of shared attributes at each level of inclusiveness in each hierarchy.

The results seemed highly encouraging. Specifically, the effort to pursue the analogy between the categorizations of common everyday objects (pants and chairs and cars) and that of people (like extraverts and P. R. types) so far has yielded considerable convergence. The person types at the middle level in these taxonomies were found to be richer in the sense that they had more shared attributes than those judged to be true of members of the superordinate categories. There also was less overlap between the attribute lists for neighboring categories at this middle level of abstraction than at the more finely tuned and detailed level of subordinate categorizations. The subordinate categories yielded the greatest richness and vivid imageability. But categories at this lower level were not ideal for highlighting the differences between the types of persons in neighboring categories. The middle level in the taxonomies seems to allow one to use just a few basic categories to capture the gist of another person in a rich and vivid way, while still being able to contrast that person with other discriminable general types. This middle level may be best when one wants to describe "what X is like in general," distinguish how "X and Y differ from each other," and apply one's knowledge about types of people in general in order to enrich the description of a particular individual. In contrast, to predict what specific molecular behaviors X will perform when observed under particular, well-defined circumstances, the more finely tuned specific, narrow categories of the subordinate level may be more helpful. But to reduce the whole person domain to two or three major categories or dimensions, as in a grand theory of personality (cf. Jung, 1923; Eysenck, 1967), one may want to use the highest, most inclusive or superordinate level (the level of extraverts, for example). While consistent, coherent descriptions, capturing the gist of another's behavior are achieved by moving to more abstract levels of person categorization, more vivid, salient person images require less inclusive slots. The choice of level must surely depend on one's purpose.

Dispositions and Conditions Interact

Some studies have tried to analyze the role of situations and of conditions as well as the role of dispositions. Sophisticated trait research has started to take situations and "stimulus conditions" into account seriously (e.g., Argyle & Little, 1972; Endler, 1973; Moos, 1974). Knowledge of individual differences alone often tells us little unless it is combined with information about the conditions and situational variables that influence the behavior of interest. Conversely, the effects of conditions depend on the individuals in them. Research results consistently suggest that the interaction of individual differences and particular conditions tends to be most important.

Consider, for example, Moos's (1968) studies of self-reported reactions by staff and psychiatric patients to various settings in the hospital. The findings were based on ratings in nine settings with regard to a dimension of "sociable, friendly, peaceful" versus "unsociable, hostile, angry" behavior. These results revealed, first, that different individuals reacted differently to the settings. Second, a given person might be high on the dimension in the morning but not at lunch, high with another patient but not when with a nurse, low in small group therapy, moderate in industrial therapy, but high in individual therapy, etc. An entirely different pattern might characterize the next person.

We might be able to predict many of the things Gary will do simply by knowing something about the situation in which he will be: At school in an economics course Gary is likely to behave very differently than he does on a date with his girlfriend at a football game. On the other hand, our predictions in each case probably would be best if we considered Gary's relevant qualities as an individual—his academic interests and skills, his attitudes toward girls, his past behavior on dates at football games—as well as the situation when we try to predict his behavior in each setting. In other words, we may predict best if we know what each situation means to the individual, and consider the unique interaction of the person and the setting, rather than concentrating either on the situation itself or on the individual in an environmental and social vacuum.

Moderator Variables

Wallach (1962) and Kogan and Wallach (1964) have noted that many "moderator variables" may influence the correlations found in trait research. That is, the relations between any two variables often depend on several other variables. For instance, correlations between measures of risk-taking and impulsivity may be found for males but not for females; they may even be negative for one sex but positive for the other. Similarly, relations between two measures might be positive for children with low IQ but negative for highly intelligent children, or they might occur under "relaxed" testing conditions but not under "anxious" conditions. The concept of moderator variables was introduced to trait theory to refer to the fact that the effects of any particular disposition generally are "moderated" by or dependent upon many other conditions and variables. Such variables as the person's age, sex, IQ, the experimenter's sex, and the characteristics of the situation all are common moderators of test behavior.

The Assessment of Settings

One trend in recent studies has been to describe settings or "ecological" variables rather than dispositions. This approach is seen best in the work of Barker and his associates, which emphasizes detailed description of the environments in which children behave (e.g., Barker & Wright, 1951; Barker, 1968). In a basically similar vein, other researchers have made an effort to sample carefully

Some researchers have tried to analyze the nature of situations, such as mental hospital wards.

some of the specific characteristics of different social settings and to systematically analyze the nature of situations (e.g., Ittelson et al., 1974; Moos & Insel, 1974; Price, 1974). These and other workers have been analyzing the characteristics of the environment, rather than searching only for the traits of the subject, and have been exploring the specific interactions of the person and the environment in ways discussed in Chapter 20.

Adaptation, Deviance, and Change

By now it should be plain that the major applications of the trait approach have been tests and measurement procedures for studying individual differences. Trait theories emphasize the stability of human qualities, not their change and potential modification. It should not be surprising that trait-oriented approaches to human adaptation and to "abnormal" behavior also have searched for a taxonomy for classifying troubled persons according to their stable, enduring traits. Examples are the vigorous efforts to characterize individuals on dimensions such as "emotional stability versus neuroticism"

(Eysenck & Rachman, 1965). Likewise, the classical typologies of "mental illness" are based on the assumption that problematic behaviors reflect underlying, consistent dispositions and that people with psychological problems can be classified reliably into different types. The most influential of these classifications remains the psychiatric diagnostic system originally devised more than 50 years ago by Emil Kraepelin, but frequently revised since then (e.g., Davison & Neale, 1974).

In sum, the trait approach has led to a long search for a taxonomy of deviance that would classify people into different categories on the basis of the abnormal "signs" (trait indicators) displayed in their behavior.

Taxonomies of Deviance

With taxonomies of deviance, as with all classification schemes, a crucial question is how well experts can reach agreement. Clinicians (e.g., psychiatrists) can achieve fair and even good agreement when they classify people into a few major psychiatric categories like "neurotic" versus "psychotic." They agree much less, however, when they attempt more subtle classifications into specific subcategories such as type of neurosis or psychosis (e.g., Ash, 1949; Schmidt & Fonda, 1956; Sandifer et al., 1964).

Zigler and Phillips (1961) studied the frequency of 35 psychiatric symptoms among hundreds of mental hospital patients who had been diagnosed into four major categories (psychoneurotic, schizophrenic, manic-depressive, and character disorder; see Table 7-4). The 35 symptoms (such as depressed, withdrawn,

TABLE 7-4
PERCENTAGE OF INDIVIDUALS IN TOTAL SAMPLE AND IN EACH DIAGNOSTIC CATEGORY MANIFESTING EACH SYMPTOM

Symptom[a]	Total Hospital (N = 793)	Manic-Depressive (N = 75)	Psycho-Neurotic (N = 152)	Character Disorder (N = 279)	Schizophrenic (N = 287)
Depressed	38	64	58	31	28
Hallucinations	19	11	4	12	35
Emotional outburst	14	17	12	18	9
Self-depreciation	12	16	16	8	13
Bizarre ideas	9	11	1	2	20
Headaches	6	7	10	4	5
Mood swings	5	9	5	4	4
Lying	3	0	1	7	0
Depersonalization	3	4	1	0	6

[a]Every fourth symptom is shown from a total list of 35. Adapted from Zigler and Phillips (1961).

irresponsible behavior, lying) are drawn from descriptions of patients by the doctor at admission (Phillips & Rabinovitch, 1958). Of the 35 symptoms, 30 or more were found in the diagnosed manic-depressives, in the character disorder group, and in both the neurotic and schizophrenic groups. Thus persons who are given different psychiatric disease labels actually may display highly overlapping behaviors.

Zigler and Phillips' (1961, p. 73) overall results indicated that "membership in a particular diagnostic group conveys only minimal information" about the individual's behavior. Their findings probably also reflect the fact that the behavior of troubled individuals, just like the behavior of those who function more effectively, changes across situations and over time. It is as difficult to pigeonhole people into psychiatric diagnoses as it is to categorize them according to normal types and traits.

More recent studies, using the revised version of the standard psychiatric diagnostic system for schizophrenia, also conclude that it is an inadequate classification and does not provide a satisfactory nomenclature (Blashfield, 1973). Partly in response to such criticisms, and recognizing the inadequacies of the standard psychiatric classification system, the American Psychiatric Association has recently revised its official Diagnostic and Statistical Manual of Mental Disorders (DSM III) extensively. Rather than classifying someone on the basis of symptoms alone, the revised system takes account of current physical disorders (e.g., diabetes, hypertension) which may or may not play a role in the psychiatric disorder, considers the severity of stressful events (e.g., business failure, death of spouse) happening in the past year, and estimates the highest level of adaptive behavior (e.g., job performance, family relationships) demonstrated in the previous year. Adding these considerations to the diagnostic system hopefully may make it easier to plan treatment and predict outcomes effectively. However, critics of the new system already point out that in spite of the revision's greater comprehensiveness, mental disorders are still defined as a subset of medical disorders (Schacht & Nathan, 1977).

The weaknesses of the diagnostic system have been illustrated dramatically by studies in which normal persons sought admission to psychiatric hospitals (Rosenhan, 1973). They found that perfectly "sane" individuals (including professionals and graduate students in the "mental health" fields) are consistently treated by the hospital staff as if they were insane as soon as they are admitted and placed in the role of "mental patients." Having been labeled "psychotic," the pseudopatients continued to be treated as insane even when their behavior was totally rational and "normal." The results demonstrated vividly the perils of "being sane in insane places": the "patients" were judged by where they were rather than by their own behavior.

Recognizing the many problems, but challenged by them, trait-oriented psychologists continue to search for better typologies of adaptation and deviance based mainly on factor analyses of a variety of rating scales (e.g., Lorr et al., 1965; Wiggins, 1973). Other researchers focus on differences in the adjustment history and prognosis (probable recovery) of different subgroups of psychiatric patients (e.g., Farina, 1972; Phillips, 1953).

The search for taxonomies of deviance from a trait perspective also has been encouraged by recent evidence from studies of other cultures. Anthropologists suggest that at least some severe forms of deviance (for example, the sort called "schizophrenia" in Western societies) may be virtually universal (Murphy, 1976). This finding bolsters the belief that underneath all the complexities some trait-like "mental illnesses" may exist more or less across societies: A universal taxonomy of deviant dispositions therefore may be required for at least some types of disturbances. Some forms of psychological problems may still prove to be disease-like (e.g. Kety, 1979).

The Genetic and Biochemical Approach

Trait theories tend to imply that at least some basic personality traits are likely to have both a genetic and a biochemical source. The search for a genetic component in personality traits is seen in Eysenck's (1967) work on introversion-extraversion, and in research on schizophrenia and other patterns of severe disorder (e.g., Gottesman, 1963, 1966; Gottesman & Shields, 1969; Rosenthal, 1971; Snyder, et al., 1974). At present, there are some important, highly suggestive leads about genetic bases of certain psychological individual differences (some of which are discussed in Chapter 12). Conclusions, however, still seem a long way from being either exact or final. Similarly, the search for biochemical (organic) conditions associated with particular personality patterns (especially patterns that are severely deviant) continues actively. But for most forms of social and interpersonal deviance no organic causes have been found and the majority of these problems are considered nonorganic or "functional" in origin. While recognizing the potential importance of genetic and biochemical research for complex human behavior, other psychologists search for ways in which the psychological environment can be harnessed effectively to improve the quality of human adaptation now (e.g., Chapter 10).

SUMMARY

1. Factor analysis is a mathematical procedure that sorts test responses into homogeneous clusters. It is a useful procedure for simplifying data but it does not automatically reveal basic traits. For example, the personality factors identified from ratings of personalities may partly reflect the rater's conceptual categories.

2. Trait research tends to focus on correlations among what people say on paper-and-pencil inventories and questionnaires. The interpretation of these questionnaire findings poses some special problems, because what a person says about his attributes does not necessarily reflect accurately either his traits or the things that he does outside the test. Self-reports thus may or may not be closely related to other indices of the person's nontest behavior.

3. No matter how carefully the psychometrician designs and standardizes his procedures, the psychological situation affects responses on personality tests. Therefore the consistency (*reliability*) and meaning (*validity*) of a personality test has to be demonstrated by research.

4. According to trait theory, an individual's test behaviors are signs from which his or her underlying dispositions may be inferred. *Criterion validation* assesses the relationship between the obtained sample and other criterion data, either concurrently or predictively. *Construct validation* tries to elaborate the inferred traits determining test behavior. The researcher guided by the construct "anxiety," for example, must demonstrate through studies how his measures and results illuminate the meaning of his construct.

5. Studies on delay of gratification as a personality dimension illustrate the way in which construct validity research proceeds from direct observation and hunches, through standardization of a measure and demonstrations of reliability and validity on a step-by-step basis.

6. Although early trait theorists assumed the existence of relatively broad traits, research suggests that what people do depends on numerous moderating conditions. Evidence for the existence of broad traits has been questioned severely—and defended vigorously. On the other hand, although specific behavior changes across situations, there is evidence for the stability and coherence of lives even over long periods of time.

7. While measures of traits are often not able to predict single acts, they may be able to predict a pooled combination of many behaviors relevant to one trait.

8. Complex interactions among dispositional and situational variables influence behavior. The relationship between any two variables—a child's dependency and his school achievements, for example—may be moderated by many other variables, such as his age, IQ, anxiety, the type of task, and the conditions of testing.

9. Recent studies of dispositions have tried to analyze the role of situations and of conditions as well as of individual differences. Other researchers are focusing on settings and the environment, rather than on the dispositions of the individual.

10. The trait approach has been applied to a search for a taxonomy of deviance. Such a taxonomy classifies people into various types, as in psychiatric diagnosis, on the basis of their abnormal behaviors. Taxonomies of deviance tend to have limited reliability because of the variability of the behaviors displayed by individuals within most categories. The trait approach also continues to stimulate research into the possible genetic and biochemical bases of both normal and abnormal personality traits.

CHAPTER 8

Oedipal = 184— (handwritten)

PSYCHODYNAMIC THEORIES: APPLICATIONS

(handwritten margin notes:)
Freud 187, 202
dreams 187
McClelland 193
Crow 199
murray 199
white 194 Book
clinical Judgement
Techniques 187
—projective
—Rorschach 188
—Holtzman
—TAT
interscorer Consistency
reliability p 193
Eysenck p 204
Golden 201

Global Psychodynamic Orientation

Freudian psychology was especially exciting because it promised a methodology for at last studying personality in proper depth and for treating complex human problems with the sophistication they deserved. Chapter 3 conveyed some of the main concepts that guide the psychodynamic study of personality. Guided by these concepts, psychodynamically oriented psychologists try to induce the person to reveal unconscious processes, conflicts, and dynamics. In this approach, the objective is to unravel disguises and defenses, to decipher the symbolic meanings of behaviors, to uncover unconscious motives, and to identify the "underlying causes" of the person's behavior.

Psychodynamic theorists clearly recognized the inconsistencies among a person's overt behaviors across seemingly similar situations. Thus the "behavioral specificity" found in trait measures and discussed in the last chapter was no surprise to many of them. They felt, however, that the observed inconsistencies in behavior could be understood as merely superficial diversities that masked the fundamentally consistent, underlying motives that actually drove the person enduringly. Recall in this regard Freud's focus on the vicissitudes of impulses. According to psychodynamic theory, the basic motives persist and press for discharge across diverse settings, but their overt manifestations or "symptoms" are transformed defensively. Hence the task is to find the person's fundamental motives and enduring dynamics behind the defensive facade and surface distortions of the overt behavior.

Minimizing the Situation

To achieve these aims the psychodynamically oriented psychologist tries to eliminate situational interferences so that external determinants of behavior can be minimized and defenses bypassed. It was hoped that generalized dynamic patterns would, under ambiguous conditions, penetrate the person's defenses and reveal themselves. Therefore techniques were developed in which cues in the situation are kept deliberately vague and unclear. These beliefs about the importance of stimulus ambiguity guide the conduct of the assessment interview and of all other information-gathering. Instead of asking detailed and structured questions, psychodynamic inquiries tend to be "open-ended" probes that leave the respondent's task unclear so that underlying motives and dynamics can emerge.

Psychodynamic assessment tends to emphasize global personality descriptions and reconstructions of the person's history. These historical reconstructions deal with the ways in which the person handled sexual and aggressive impulses during childhood struggles with problems characteristic of each psychosexual stage. Clues are also sought about traumatic experiences, central defenses, and basic character traits. The following excerpts are taken from a psychodynamic report written about our "Gary W." and based on interviews and special test situations that will be discussed later in this chapter. The report not only provides new information about Gary, but also illustrates some of the features of a clinical psychodynamic case conceptualization guided by Freudian theory.

An Example: Excerpts from Freudian Conceptualization of Gary W.

Oedipal themes abound in the case of Gary W., although he has grown a long way toward resolving them. W. emotionally describes his feeling that his father was his "severest critic" and that he is his mother's favorite. He says that he no longer sees adults as all-knowing, and he refers to his father as mellowed and "out of it." He reports warmth and affection for his mother, although these feelings are mixed.

In his own sibling relationships, Gary seems to have displaced much of his rivalry with his father onto his older brother. W. describes great outbursts of anger vented on Charles with obvious intent to injure. He compares Charles with their father and says that the two are alike in many respects. He is on better terms with Charles since the latter was in a car crash in which he got pretty smashed up. (This in some respects parallels his present hostile condescension, rather than competitive hostility, toward the father since the latter has proved himself a failure in business.)

A recent revival of the Oedipal situation occurred when Gary's girl friend left him for his roommate. She may well have symbolized his mother to him more than is usual: She is older, was married before, and has a child from the previous marriage. After he confessed his love to his girl, she told him that she had been seeing his roommate. W. felt humiliated and "wounded in my vanity" because these events went on "behind my back." His feelings are reminiscent of the chagrin felt by the little boy when he realizes his father's role vis-a-vis his mother. W. attempted to resolve his anger by recognizing that he was not in a position financially to marry her whereas his roommate was. His apparent satisfaction that his roommate after all has not married her, and that they may have broken up, also is consistent with the conceptualization that this relationship was filled with Oedipal themes.

The incomplete resolution of the Oedipal conflict is further evident in W.'s fear of injury and physical illness, in the depression which has followed a motorcycle accident (castration anxiety)—and in the distinction he makes between girl friends ("good girls") and sex objects ("fast girls"). Incomplete identification with his father, whether a cause or a result of this unresolved situation, is apparent. His search for a strong male figure is evident in his reactions to the headmaster and teacher at boarding school, described respectively as "a very definite, determined sort of person" and "not the sort of man you could push around." He is quite openly disparaging of his father, albeit on intellectual grounds. (This tends to be W.'s typical style.)

According to Gary, his mother sees sex as something bad and nasty. This report, as well as his suggestion that his mother's frigidity has undermined his father's masculinity, may represent wishes that his mother may not be responsive to his father. He himself may regard sexuality ambivalently—his sexual experiences seem to involve much parental rebellion and he keeps his sex objects separate from his affections. When he speaks about sex he talks crudely of "making it."

Gary's anxiety in social situations in general, and his fear of public speaking in particular, are further indices of his basic insecurity and his brittle defenses. He is concerned that he will be found lacking. The underlying castration anxiety is expressed symbolically in his comment that when he stands up to speak in public, he is afraid "the audience is ready to chop my head off," and when there is a possibility of debate, that he will be "caught with my pants down."

Gary shows some concern about homosexuality. He mentions it spontaneously when talking about friendship, and his descriptions of living in close proximity with other males include tension, friction, and annoyance. This anxiety is illustrated in his uncomfortable relationship to his present roommate. His first two responses to cards on the Rorschach are also interesting in this connection. Laughter accompanies the statement that two figures are "grinding their bottoms." The perception of animals rather than human figures further serves as a defense to reduce his anxiety. Paranoid tendencies appear in both the fantasy and interview material (e.g., seeing "eyes" on the Rorschach) and suggest some projection of the homosexual conflict.

The battle being waged between impulses, reality, and conscience are evidenced by Gary's concern with control and his obsessive-compulsive traits. W. makes a tenuous distinction between passion and reason, rejecting the former and clinging to the latter. He extends this distinction to interpersonal relations, drawing a line between "companionship" and "love." He reports an inability to empathize and form good object-relations. An example of repression of affect is W.'s difficulty in expressing anger. In this area, as in others, he tends to intellectualize as a way to systematize and control anxiety. His problems in expressing anger may also be reflected in his speech difficulties and in his verbal blocks, especially in public and social situations.

Instinctual elements arise to disturb the tenuous control gained by secondary processes. He complains that he sometimes gets drunk when he should be accomplishing things. He says he admires people with enough self-discipline not to drink, smoke, and sleep late. He speaks of trying to force himself not to do the things he knows are bad for him and interfere with his long-range objectives.

The need to control is also apparent in his performance and behavior on many of the psychological tests, where his approach is analytic rather than imaginative, and his expressive movements tight and controlled. (His attention to detail and his constant intellectualization of real feeling on the Rorschach, his hobby of insect study, and his admission that often "trivialities" bother him for a long time add up to a picture of restriction and repression in the service of anxiety reduction.) There is an anal retentive aspect of this need to control, which comes out rather clearly in his interaction with the assessor when he says testily, "Didn't you show that to me already—are you trying to squeeze .... " A further compulsive trait in W. is represented in his rigid, compulsive counting, and the way he rigidly breaks his ability self-ratings down into component parts, and strives to ensure complete accuracy and coverage of whatever he is discussing about himself.

The need for control may circle back to castration anxiety. The two themes come together in W.'s fear of physical injury and in his fear of losing his brain capacity. The culmination of these two fears occurred when W.'s motorcycle failed him, and he is still preoccupied with this incident. He relates these fears more directly to the Oedipal conflict when, in the phrase association test, he links anger at his brother with fear of losing his "marbles."

Note that the focus in this report is on hypothesized underlying dynamics. It is implicitly assumed that sexual and aggressive motives and unconscious conflicts widely affect many behaviors. Statements about behavior tend to be relatively global and undifferentiated. The emphasis is on unacceptable impulses and defenses for coping with the anxiety they arouse. There is also an attempt to link current sexual and aggressive problems to relations with the parents and to Oedipal problems in early childhood.

If this report is valid it offers a whole new perspective on Gary, and provides a way of seeing meaning and unity throughout his diverse behaviors. For example, his relations with his brother and with women became part of his larger efforts to cope with Oedipal problems. Indeed, a main attraction of psychodynamic theory is that it offers a systematic, unified view of the individual. Rather than seeing the person as a bundle of discrete traits, it views him as an integrated, dynamic creature. When his underlying core personality is revealed, his seemingly diverse, discrepant behaviors become meaningful, and all fit into the total whole. It becomes easy to see why such an elegant conceptual system is attractive. But the key question that has to be answered by scientifically oriented students is: Does the system have validity? Do psychodynamic reports of the kind made about Gary provide accurate and useful insights?

Relying on the Clinician

Psychodynamic assessors rely mostly on their own intuitions. While the interpretation of responses on psychometric tests is objective and straightforward, the interpretation of clinical data is usually highly subjective and dependent more on the clinician than on the tests. The rules for relating behavioral signs to unconscious meanings and dynamics are largely implicit, and the constructs themselves tend to be difficult to specify. Consequently, the psychoanalytically oriented assessor has to depend mainly on clinical judgments.

The merit of such clinical assessments depends on two things. First, it depends on the evidence supporting the techniques upon which the personality psychologist relies in generating his inferences. Second, it depends on the value of clinical judgment itself. Because psychodynamic theories rest on the belief that the core of personality is revealed by highly indirect behavioral signs, evidence for the value of these indirect signs of personality is most important. This chapter reviews some of the main clinical methods that have been studied in the search for valuable signs of personality. Probably the most important of these methods are the projective techniques.

Projective Techniques

dream association
Free association

Free association and the analysis of dreams are the methods of personality study that come most directly from Freud's work. In free association, you are instructed to give your thoughts complete freedom and to report daydreams, feelings, and images no matter how incoherent, illogical, or meaningless they might seem. This technique may be employed either with minimum of prompting or by offering brief phrases ("my mother . . ."; "I often . . .") as a stimulus to encourage associations.

Freud believed that dreams were similar to the patients' free associations. He thought the dream was an expression of the most primitive workings and contents of the mind, the "primary process." Dreams were interpreted as fulfilling a wish or discharging tension by inducing an image of the desired goal. Through the interpretation of dreams, Freud felt that he was penetrating into the unconscious.

Integrating Psychodynamic Concepts
and Psychometric Methods

Free association and dream analysis, while remaining the basic tools of ortho-dox psychoanalytic therapy, have had only indirect impacts for the personality assessments conducted by psychologists. Both techniques have been used for research purposes and as parts of larger projects for the intensive assessment of individuals. They have not, however, been widely adopted in personality study, probably because they are considered too time consuming and are believed to require extensive contact with the subject to establish a comfortable atmosphere free of initial inhibitions before they can be used profitably. Most personality psychologists currently believe it is uneconomical to devote much time to gathering dream data and free-association material.

In the principal techniques of classical psychoanalysis, the depth interview and free association, the assessment conditions are the opposite of standardization and objectivity. Clinical intuition and personal experience are used to secure interpretations that the clinician believes fit the particular person. In these "depth" studies, psychodynamics are inferred in accord with the general principles of psychoanalytic theory. These clinical studies by psychoanalysts typically are based on relatively informal direct clinical observations of individual clients during psychoanalysis. Unfortunately these analyses often tend to be reported so loosely that their research value is dubious (Janis, 1958).

While intrigued by psychodynamic theory, many clinically oriented personality psychologists also have been influenced in their approach by psychometric testing, with its long tradition of concern with reliability and objective measurement. As we have seen, psychometric testing must be formal enough to permit standardized administration and to allow research about the reliability and validity of the quantitative results. Through projective tests, many psychologists wished to combine at least some of the quantitative features of psychometric testing with the insights they hoped to achieve from clinical judgments about psychodynamics. Probably the two most influential projective techniques have been the Rorschach and the Thematic Apperception Test.

The Rorschach

The Rorschach is one of the most popular projective tests. Developed by the psychiatrist Herman Rorschach in 1921, the Rorschach test consists of a series of complex, bilaterally symmetrical inkblots on 10 separate cards (Figure 8-1). Some of the blots are black and white, and some colored. The subject is instructed to look at the inkblots one at a time and to say everything that the inkblot could resemble or look like. The examiner then generally conducts an inquiry into the details of the subject's interpretation of the blot, and the stimulus characteristics that led to it.

Responses may be scored for location (the place on the card that the response refers to) and such determinants as the physical aspects of the blot (e.g., shape, color, shading, or an expression of movement) that suggested the

FIGURE 8-1
Inkblot Similar to Those
in the Rorschach Test

FIGURE 8-2
Picture Similar to Those
on the TAT

Gary's Reactions to Two of the Rorschach Inkblot Cards:

Response:

This looks like two dogs, head-to-foot (laughs), licking each other.
That's about it, that's all.

Inquiry answers (to the question "What about the inkblot made you think of two dogs?):

They're sort of fuzzy . . . kinda shapeless. It was the dark skin and the furry effect that made me think of it.

Response:

Didn't we have this one already?
This could be an ogre laughing—his head thrown back and he's laughing, his eyes and mouth wide open.
These over here look like insects, tsetse flies in fact, with tiny, tiny legs, and small, delicate and rather beautiful wings.
That's it, that's enough.

Inquiry answers:

It's the shaggyness and the hugeness, the massiveness of the shape.
The wings over here, head here.

---

response. The originality of the responses, the content, and other characteristics also may be coded. The frequency of various responses may be counted and then used in interpretation. The interpreter may seek to relate these scores to aspects of personality, such as creative capacity, maturity, contact with reality, emotional control, and anxiety. A more recent inkblot test, similar to the Rorschach but with a more objective, standardized procedure, is the Holtzman inkblot technique (1961).

The Thematic Apperception Test (TAT)

The Thematic Apperception Test or TAT was developed by Morgan and Murray in the Harvard Psychological Clinic research program during the 1930s.

The test consists of a series of pictures and one blank card (see Figure 8-2). Somewhat different sets of pictures are available for young males (under 14), young females, adult males and adult females. The cards are presented one at a time.

Subjects usually are told that it is a story-telling test and that they are to make up as dramatic or interesting a story as they can for each picture. They are instructed to tell what has led up to the event shown in the picture, to describe what is happening at the moment, what the characters are feeling and thinking, and then to give the outcome. They are encouraged to give free reign to their imagination and to say whatever comes to mind. Typically, the length of time that elapses before the subject begins telling the story and the total time for each story are recorded.

As suggested by the name of the test, it is expected that subjects will interpret an ambiguous stimulus according to their individual readiness to perceive in a certain way ("apperception"). Furthermore, the themes that recur in these imaginative productions are thought to have basic significance. Special scoring keys have been designed for use with the TAT (e.g., McClelland et al., 1953; Mussen & Naylor, 1954), or the stories may be used "clinically," the clinician interpreting the themes intuitively in accord with his or her personality theory.

Two of Gary's Stories from the TAT

Card depicting two men: Two men have gone on a hunting trip. It is dawn now and the younger one is still sound asleep. The older one is watching over him. Thinking how much he reminds him of when he was young and could sleep no-matter-what. Also, seeing the boy sleeping there makes him long for the son he never had. He's raising his hand about to stroke him on the forehead. I think he'll be too embarrassed to go ahead with it. He'll start a fire and put on some coffee and wait for the younger man to wake up.

Card depicting young man and older woman: This depicts a mother-son relationship. The mother is a strong, stalwart person. Her son is hesitating at the doorway. He wants to ask her advice about something but isn't sure whether it's the right thing to do. Maybe he should make up his own mind. I think he'll just come in and have a chat with her. He won't ask her advice but will work things out for himself. Maybe it's a career choice, a girl friend . . . I don't know what, but whatever it is, he'll decide himself. He'll make his own plans, figure out what the consequences will be, and work it out from there.

Characteristics of Projective Techniques

The main characteristic of projective techniques like the Rorschach and the TAT is the way in which the testing situation is usually structured so that the task is *ambiguous*. Typically, there are also attempts to *disguise the purpose* of the test (e.g., Bell, 1948), and the person is given *freedom to respond* in any way that he or she likes.

In projective testing assessors confront you with ambiguous stimuli and ask ambiguous questions. For example, they ask, "What might this be?" "What could this remind you of?" [while showing an inkblot] or say, "Create the most imaginative story that you can [showing a picture], including what the people are thinking and feeling, what led up to this situation, and how it all comes out." Or they read words and ask you to "say the first thing that comes to mind."

The same stimulus materials with different instructions could be used non-projectively by asking you to trace the blots, count the pictures, or spell the words in the association list. Similarly, almost any test item can be used projectively with appropriate instructions. Some stimuli, of course, lend themselves more readily than others to projective use, primarily because they more

FIGURE 8-3
Some Differences between an Objective Performance Test and a Projective Test

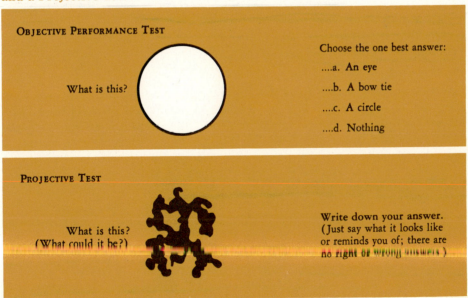

OBJECTIVE PERFORMANCE TEST

What is this?

Choose the one best answer:

....a. An eye

....b. A bow tie

....c. A circle

....d. Nothing

PROJECTIVE TEST

What is this?
(What could it be?)

Write down your answer.
(Just say what it looks like or reminds you of; there are no right or wrong answers.)

In objective performance tests the subject must choose between definite right or wrong answers. In projective tests the stimulus and instructions are ambiguous and the subject has greater freedom to respond in accord with his or her interpretation of the stimulus.

Psychoanalytically like projection

easily evoke a wide range of responses. Therefore, fairly vague stimuli such as inkblots, unclear pictures, barely audible sounds, clay, plastic materials, and paint have been favorites. Some differences between projective techniques and more objective, structured performance tests (such as tests of achievement and ability) are shown in Figure 8-3.

Projective techniques have been favored by psychoanalytically oriented assessors because they assumed that the "unconscious inner life" is at least partially revealed in responses to the projective test situation. The assumptions underlying projective tests reflect the influences of psychoanalytic theory: the emphasis on the unconsciously motivated nature of behavior, the importance of unconscious material, and the conception that the person has a central, enduring "core" or basic personality organization. This core personality is reflected more or less pervasively in the person's behavior, according to psychodynamic theory. And this core is most readily revealed through free responses in an ambiguous, nonthreatening situation of the kind created by projective tests (MacFarlane & Tuddenham, 1951).

Traditionally, projective techniques are presented to the subject with special pains to disguise their purposes. This practice reflects the belief that projective data reveal unacceptable unconscious aspects of the person. Presumably the person has erected defensive maneuvers and censorship operations that prevent the expression of these impulses unless the defenses are relaxed. But although the general characteristics and purposes of projective tests are widely agreed upon, there is much uncertainty about the actual nature of the "projection" that occurs in response to these tests.

Scoring and Interpretation

For many years the field was full of workers eagerly trying to invent projective devices. This search for stimulus materials that would elicit rich data about personality resulted in a proliferation of techniques, many of them lacking serious research support. Summaries of these tests are widely available, and reviews have been numerous (e.g., Wiggins, 1973; Zubin, Eron, & Schumer, 1965).

difficult to measure

While it has been relatively simple to invent projective devices, it has been extremely difficult to establish what they measure. The initial aim and hope of projectivists was to create a "situationless" situation in which only the core or central aspects of personality would emerge (Frank, 1939). The data elicited by these techniques, however, instead of providing a royal road to the unconscious, seem to include a mixture of verbal responses, momentary states, bits of autobiography, and so on. Projective response, like most other behavior, is "subject to conscious control and distortion and therefore is not necessarily a reliable or valid reflection of personality" (Holmes, 1974, p. 328).

not always valid

Just what is projected in response to the stimuli employed by projective devices is unclear and controversial (e.g., Murstein, 1963; Zubin, Eron, & Schumer, 1965). Thus the meaning of the person's answers is open to diverse clinical interpretations, depending heavily on the theoretical preferences and subjective judgments of the interpreter.

Scores on projective techniques usually depend extensively on the clinician's judgments about the meaning of the responses as signs of traits or dynamic states in the subject. *Interscorer consistency*, or *interscorer reliability*, must be demonstrated whenever scoring involves subjective judgments, as often occurs with projective data. Interscorer reliability decreases to the extent that highly subjective interpretations are required by the judge. That is, reliability is likely to be low when judgments depend upon the intuitions of the interpreter. For example, "old man strangling boy on couch" in a TAT story might be categorized as reflecting underlying "psychopathic trends," "defense against repressed homosexuality," or "hostile acting-out," depending on the interpreter's subjective judgments. Many critics have recognized that such interpretation may be markedly influenced by projection on the part of the interpreter. Manuals with explicit instructions for scoring help to increase agreement among judges. Agreement is also increased when judges are trained with examples and sample scoring decisions so that they can learn to make similar judgments.

Scoring TAT Themes: Need for Achievement

One especially important research application of projective techniques has been developed by David C. McClelland and his colleagues (1953), who scored various fantasy indices on the TAT. Specifically, these researchers studied motives as expressed through TAT stories. The motive of greatest interest to them was the need to achieve ("*n* Ach"), defined as competition with a standard of excellence.

The need to achieve has been studied extensively by scoring achievement imagery in stories to TAT cards. If, for example, the person creates stories in which the hero is studying hard for a profession and strives to improve himself, to compete against standards of excellence, and to advance far in his career, the story gets high *n* Ach scores. This technique has become an important way of measuring the motive to achieve. It is notable in part because it is a rare example of a fairly objective use of projective data. While this technique is not employed widely with individual clients in clinical assessment, it has been used often in research. Manuals that are sufficiently detailed and objective to permit good scoring reliability have been developed for scoring achievement needs (Atkinson, 1958).

Although TAT and other projective themes and fantasies are interesting in their own right, their relations to other behaviors tend to be complex and indirect. Thoughts and fantasies as measured through projective and story-telling techniques usually are correlated only marginally with measures of relevant overt behavior. For example, achievement concerns and ideation measured from TAT stories relate only in limited ways to other measures of achievement (such as grades or vocational achievements). The same is true for other content areas, such as the associations between aggression imagery and aggression-relevant overt behavior. These conclusions emerge from an enormously extensive tabulation of the correlations obtained between many kinds of motivational imagery (TAT themes) and behavior ratings reported by Skolnick (1966). Sometimes measures of fantasy and thought were found to be positively related to relevant actions, less often negatively, and most frequently not at all. McClelland (1966), reviewing this survey, noted that while the overall number of significant associations implied some degree of relationship, "the relationship is not close." About 25 percent of the predicted relationships were supported, generally at low magnitudes. Although the correlations tend to be small, many associations have been found between n Ach and other measures, sometimes over long periods of time.

Applied to the individual case, this means we cannot assume that fantasy themes revealed on projective tests are reflected directly in aspects of the person's nontest behavior. For example, Gary might show relatively little achievement striving on the stories he tells to the TAT; nevertheless, he might feel driven to achieve outstandingly in financial and business activities. Moreover, his achievement orientation in business might not be generalized to other areas. For example, he might show much less concern with achievement in intellectual pursuits and social relations. Although limited in their value for understanding the single case, TAT themes may be used fruitfully to study group differences and broad trends. The results often are provocative and theoretically valuable. McClelland (1961), for example, has found intriguing relations between TAT achievement themes and many economic and social measures of achievement orientation in different cultures.

Validity of Projective Tests

For more than three decades psychologists have searched for important information about personality by means of projective tests. Hundreds of studies have been conducted on the validity of these projective techniques. The volume of research has become too great for a complete review even in books devoted to that purpose.

The overall results on the major projective techniques suggest that some significant validity correlations are often found. In clinical applications, however, these associations tend to be difficult to interpret firmly because of many methodological problems (e.g., Cronbach, 1949; Zubin, Eron, & Schumer, 1965).

Even when obvious identifying data are removed from the protocols, for example, people's comments may provide test-irrelevant clues about their occupation, education, ideational bizarreness, interests, achievements, etc. Knowing that the subject is a doctor, for instance, affects interpretations by giving judges many extra cues about the person, but the interpretations in this case reveal nothing about the specific value of the test as a personality measure. Similarly, the degree of variation among people in the sample affects how easily judges can discriminate among them. For instance, judges might reliably discriminate the Rorschach protocols of a dozen graduate students from those of twelve acutely disorganized and hospitalized schizophrenics, but they might find it much harder to differentiate among the students.

Apart from the fact that correlations may be inflated by methodological inadequacies, they are still generally so low that they limit the utility of projective tests for making good decisions about individuals. That is, when the correlations tend to be very low (for example in the .20 to .40 range or lower), they permit one to say little about the person tested. According to critical reviews, predictions based on personality inferences from projective data generally tend to be less accurate than those more easily available from cheaper and simpler data (Mischel, 1968; Peterson, 1968).

Other researchers, while recognizing the practical limitations of projective testing, continue to be fascinated by the projective situation as a method for studying important personality processes. They construe such tests as the Rorschach as providing a kind of perceptual test or an interview setting. In these situations they seek to study persons clinically or to conduct research on the mechanisms of projection (e.g., Zubin, Eron, & Schumer, 1965). While it is not clear just how most psychologists now use projective tests, it is a sobering fact that regardless of the evidence that undermines them, their popularity in everyday clinical practice has persisted as strong as ever (Wade & Baker, 1977).

Some clinical psychologists have noted that clinical assessments, in accord with psychodynamic theory, require individualized judgments of the meaning of the person's total pattern of behavior. Therefore they argue, properly, that the total personality configuration must be evaluated. This kind of global personality assessment involves intuitive judgments about the meaning of behavior patterns and their relations. Global assessment requires experienced clinicians guided by theory, as well as by intuition, and draws on many data sources rather than on just one or two tests.

Clinical Judgment

While trait theorists rely on tests to infer personality, dynamic theorists rely on the clinician. Most of Freudian theory depends on the hypotheses and inferences generated by experienced clinicians. Consequently while the methodology of trait theory involves research on tests and dimensions, the methodology of dynamic psychology to a large degree involves research into the efficacy of clinicians and their judgments. Some of the most sophisticated clinical studies were conducted by the "Harvard personologists," as discussed next.

The Harvard Personologists and Global Assessment

Henry A. Murray, Robert W. White, and their many colleagues at the Harvard Psychological Clinic provided a rare model for the intensive clinical study of individual lives. Throughout the 1940s and early in the 1950s this group vigorously devoted itself to the portrayal of persons in depth. The Harvard "personologists" (as these students of personality called themselves) were influenced strongly by the dynamic motivational psychology of Freud, by "biosocial" organismic views that emphasized the wholeness, integration, and adaptiveness of personality, and by Gordon Allport's stress on the uniqueness and individuality of every person. They synthesized these influences into a distinct assessment style that became widely respected although only rarely adopted by other psychologists.

The Harvard group focused on intensive studies of small samples of subjects. In one project (Murray, 1938) Harvard college undergraduates were studied over a period of many years and data were gathered on their personality development and maturation at many points in their lives. The techniques in this general "longitudinal" strategy included administering projective and objective tests of many kinds at different times, gathering extensive biographical data on each person, obtaining their own autobiographical sketches, observing their behavior directly, and conducting elaborate interviews with them. These methods probed ingeniously and thoroughly into many topics and most facets of their lives (see Table 8-1). The results often provided rich narrative accounts of life histories, as in Robert White's *Lives in Progress* (1952), which traced several lives over many years.

The assessors in the Harvard clinical studies were experienced psychologists who interpreted their data clinically. Usually a group of several assessors

---

TABLE 8-1
EXAMPLES OF TOPICS INCLUDED IN THE
STUDY OF LIVES BY THE HARVARD PERSONOLOGISTS

Personal history (early development, school and college, major experiences)

Family relations and childhood memories (including school relations, reactions to authority)

Sexual development (earliest recollections, first experiences, masturbation)

Present dilemmas (discussion of current problems)

Abilities and interests (physical, mechanical, social, economic, erotic)

Aesthetic preferences (judgments, attitudes, tastes regarding art)

Level of aspiration (goal setting, reactions to success and failure)

Ethical standards (cheating to succeed, resistance to temptation)

Imaginal productivity (reactions to inkblots)

Musical reveries (report of images evoked by phonograph music)

Dramatic productions (constructing a dramatic scene with toys)

SOURCE: Based on Murray (1938).

diagnostic council

studied each subject, and to share their insights they pooled their overall impressions at a staff conference or "diagnostic council." These councils became a model for clinical practice. In them a case conference was conducted in detail and in depth about each individual. On the basis of the council's discussions, inferences were generated about each subject's personality. They inferred basic needs, motives, conflicts, and dynamics; central dispositions, attitudes, and values; main character strengths and liabilities. Each piece of assessment information thus served as a sign of the individual's personality as it was interpreted by the council of assessors.

This clinical strategy is illustrated in one of the important applied projects of the personologists—their effort to select officers for the supersensitive Office of Strategic Services (OSS) during World War II. OSS officers in World War II had to perform critical and difficult secret intelligence assignments, often behind enemy lines and under great stress. The personologists obviously could not devote the same lengthy time to studying OSS candidates that they had given to Harvard undergraduates in the relaxed prewar days in Cambridge. Nevertheless, they attempted to use the same general strategy of global clinical assessment. For this purpose, teams of assessors studied small groups of OSS candidates intensively, usually for a few days or a weekend, in special secret retreats or "stations" located in various parts of the country. Many different measures were obtained on each candidate.

One of the most interesting innovations was the situational test. In this procedure subjects were required to perform stressful, life-like tasks under extremely difficult conditions. For example, "The Bridge" task required building a wooden bridge under simulated dangerous field conditions and under high stress and anxiety. But such situational tests were not used to obtain a sample of the subjects' bridge-building skills. Instead, the clinicians made deep inferences, based on the behavior observed during the task, about each subject's underlying personality. It was these inferences of unobserved attributes or dispositions, rather than the behavior actually observed in the sampled situation, that entered into the assessment report and that became the bases for clinical predictions. In this fashion, behavior samples and situational tests were transformed into inferences about underlying dispositions.

To illustrate, in the *Assessment of Men* by the OSS staff (1948), the bridge-building situation was used to generate answers to questions like these (p. 326):

Who took the lead in finally crossing the chasm? And why did he do it? Was it to show his superiority? Why did each of the others fall back from the trip? Did they fear failure? It is obvious that the chief value of this situation was to raise questions about personality dynamics which required an explanation on the basis of the personality trends already explored. If these could not supply a reasonable explanation, then new information had to be sought, new deductions made.

FIGURE 8-4
Global Psychodynamic Assessment

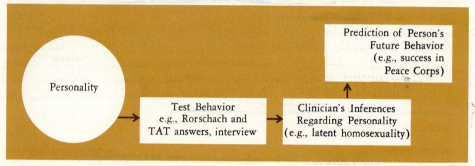

The clinician infers the subject's personality from his test behavior and predicts his future behavior by judging how a person with that personality would probably react to specific future situations.

In the situational test, just as on the projective test, behavior thus was clinically interpreted as a clue revealing personality. Although behavior is sampled and observed, the observations serve mainly as signs from which to infer the motives that prompted the behaviors.

In the global clinical assessment strategy the assessors form their impressions of the person on the basis of many data sources: performance on various projective and objective tests, the autobiography and total personal history, and reactions to thorough interviews. Several assessors study the same person and each generates his or her own clinical impressions. Later, at a conference, the assessors discuss and share their interpretations and pool their judgments. Gradually they synthesize their impressions and achieve consensus, jointly arriving at a conceptualization of each subject's overall personality structure and dynamics (like the psychodynamic conceptualization of Gary given earlier in this chapter). To predict the person's behavior in a new situation (for example under attack behind enemy lines), they try to infer, from the personality they have hypothesized, how such an individual would probably react to the demands and stresses of that situation. This global assessment model is schematized in Figure 8-4.

Assessing the Clinician

The explorations of the Harvard personologists made it plain that research on the clinical use of test data actually is inseparable from research on clinical judgment. That is because interpretations about the meaning of test responses as signs of underlying dynamics usually depend on the clinician's subjective inferences. In recent years, therefore, much attention has been devoted to investigations of clinical judgment.

Global judging ability has been evaluated by many different methods (Cline, 1964; Taft, 1955; Wiggins, 1973). Perception of emotional expression in photographs, pictures, and movies has sometimes been used in clinical skill research. Clinical judging skills also have been assessed by having judges rate and rank traits, write personality descriptions, match persons with data about them, and predict behavior. Predictions may be about specific behavior, like answers on a personality inventory, or about behavior as general as the person's future occupational success and personality adjustment. Judges have been asked to predict the subject's own responses (e.g., self-ratings, test scores), as well as data about the subject obtained from observers (e.g., peers, experts). Some of the main results are reviewed next—and they have surprised many people.

Effects of Clinical Training

To study clinical ability researchers have compared the relative accuracy of judges who had varying degrees of clinical training with those who were untrained. Studies of this kind compare the judgmental accuracy of psychologists, psychiatrists, psychiatric social workers, or other trained clinicians with the judgments of clinically inexperienced groups (e.g., nurses, secretaries, college students). Some studies also investigate the effects of amount of training, usually by comparing the accuracy of judges who have different degrees of clinical experience. The effect of special training programs on subsequent judgmental skill has also been measured.

Crow (1957) studied the effects of clinical training upon global judgmental skill. He placed senior medical students in either an experimental group that received extensive instruction on physician-patient relationships and obtained experience in such relationships through prolonged contacts with patients, or in a control group that remained unexposed to intensive interpersonal training. All students were given tests of interpersonal perception at the beginning, during, and at the conclusion of the training year. On each occasion these tests measured how accurately the judges predicted the self-ratings and actual MMPI test responses of patients whose interview behavior they observed on films.

Unexpectedly, the clinically trained students tended to be *less* accurate than those in the control group. Training led these judges to become much more variable in their estimates (paying more attention to individual differences) than those in the control group. In addition, the trained judges expected less agreement than there was between the patients' self-ratings and their actual test responses. The more the judges tried to take account of individual differences between patients, the less accurate they became. In other words, because of their clinical training, judges became more sensitive and responsive to what they perceived to be individual differences. Consequently they also became less accurate than those who based their predictions on their stereotypes.

On the whole, studies show no clear advantage for trained judges. Psychologists do not score consistently better or worse than nonpsychologists (e.g., secretaries, college students, nurses), and clinical training and experience do not usually improve the accuracy of global judgments (e.g., Danet, 1965; Goldberg, 1959; Kremers, 1960; Luft, 1951). Clinical training and experience may even be somewhat detrimental and may reduce judgmental accuracy, or at least introduce systematic biases, such as a greater emphasis on pathology and less favorable prognoses (e.g., Soskin, 1954, 1959; Taft, 1955). Surprisingly, giving judges accurate feedback information about their predictions does not seem to facilitate their predictive accuracy (Sechrest, Gallimore, & Hersch, 1967).

It is possible to criticize much of the laboratory research on accuracy of interpersonal perception and global judgment because it uses artificial situations that do not represent the actual diagnostic problems confronting the practitioner. It may be argued that in practice clinicians are free to base their inferences on their favorite diagnostic technique and are not constricted by the experimenter's techniques. Recognizing these objections, a number of investigators have studied the effects of training on accuracy in common diagnostic tasks typical of those used in the clinic (e.g., Goldberg, 1959). Again, the results tend to be negative and thus consistent with those found from the more artificial laboratory studies (Mischel, 1968).

Combining Clinical Judges and Tests

In their clinical practice, many judges tend to rely on a fairly standard battery of personality tests and techniques for the assessment of most problems. Perhaps to obtain good results the clinician has to draw on all these diagnostic aids. This set of procedures usually includes the Rorschach inkblots and often also the TAT and the MMPI. Many clinicians also ask the client to complete a series of unfinished sentences, to draw some pictures, and to participate in a short interview. Responses to all these tests then are interpreted clinically. Researchers have tried to analyze the relative contributions of the different parts of the total procedure as it is used in the clinic.

For example, Kostlan (1954) studied which of the most common data sources and data combinations allow the clinician to make the best personality inferences. He selected four popular sources of clinical information: the social case history, the MMPI, the Rorschach, and an incomplete sentence test (on which the person must finish such sentence stems as "I feel . . ."). Twenty experienced clinical psychologists were the judges, and each was assigned data for five outpatients at a Veterans Administration Psychiatric Clinic. The clinicians worked under each of five conditions. In four conditions *one* of the data sources was missing. For example, the clinician obtained the Rorschach, the sentence completions, and the social history, but not the MMPI. In a fifth condition the clinician saw only a face sheet stating minimal identifying information (age, marital status, occupation, education, and referral source). The judges studied and used the diagnostic data as they would normally, and then indicated their inferences about the patient on a 283-item checklist. To assess the accuracy of these inferences they were compared with those made by a panel of judges who used all four sources of clinical information, and with progress reports from the patients' therapists.

The minimal identifying facts on the fact sheet (age, marital status, etc.) provided inferences that were not surpassed in accuracy by judgments based on any other data source or combination, unless the clinician also had the social case history. Thus only inferences from data that included the social history were more accurate than those from the identifying data alone.

Golden (1964) studied the incremental effects when experienced clinicians combine the Rorschach, TAT, and MMPI tests as opposed to using them singly. He found that neither the reliability nor the validity of clinical inferences increased as a function of the number of tests used, nor were there any differences between tests or pairs of tests. In another study, information from none of the tests used improved predictions beyond the level attained from biographical data alone, and student nurses predicted as well as clinicians when both had only the basic biographical information (Soskin, 1959).

To evaluate clinical inferences properly you also must know their reliability. How well do experienced clinicians reach agreement with each other in the inferences that they derive from standard data sources? A classic study of the reliability of clinical judgments examined the inferences made by expert clinicians from each of five sources (Little & Schneidman, 1959). The sources included the Rorschach, TAT, MMPI, and case histories. Agreement among judges about personality dynamics was only slight. On the whole, the investigators found their results "distressing" (p. 26). No matter how fascinating inferences about personality dynamics may seem intuitively, they cannot be useful when expert judges cannot agree about them.

In a sophisticated study of judgment reliability (Goldberg & Werts, 1966), experienced clinical psychologists independently ranked each of four sets of ten neuropsychiatric patients on one of four traits. The traits were adjustment, ego strength, intelligence, and dependency. These rankings were based on one of four data sources (the MMPI, Rorschach, Wechsler Intelligence Test, or a vocational history). The overall results revealed that "the judgments of one experienced clinician working from one data source bear no relationship to the judgments of another clinician working from another data source" (p. 204), even when the different clinicians are all experienced and are diagnosing the same patient on what is supposed to be the same trait. Essentially similar results have come from numerous other investigations. For example, the average clinical interjudge agreement was negligible for inferences from the Rorschach, TAT, and sentence completion protocols (Howard, 1962).

Are There Good Judges of Personality?

There are large individual differences in accuracy among judges for any judgment task. Is judgmental accuracy strongly consistent across diverse situations so that we can generalize confidently about relatively good or poor judges? One group of studies (Cline, 1964) found some generality in judgmental accuracy. Other studies, however, provided no support for any consistency in the accuracy of clinical judgments (e.g., Crow & Hammond, 1957; Krech, Crutchfield, & Ballachey, 1962).

In spite of the overall negative research findings on judgmental accuracy, many clinicians have subjective faith in the utility of their judgments. Is confidence about the validity of inferences related to their empirical accuracy? Oskamp (1965) found that judges became more confident of their judgments as they received more information about a case. However, although self-confidence increased with information, accuracy did not. Moreover, clinicians may confidently agree with each other about the meaning of cues, even when the cues are not valid indicators (e.g., Chapman & Chapman, 1969; Goldberg, 1968; Mirels, 1976). On the other hand, some careful research does suggest that personality judgments are not mere illusions (Jackson, 1980). For example, judgments about how different personality attributes "go together" are related to independent information about the judged people, such as their own self-reports (Jackson, Chan, & Stricker, 1979).

In sum, studies of clinical inference generally have led to negative conclusions about its predictive validity (e.g., Goldberg, 1959; Holtzman & Sells, 1954; Kelly & Fiske, 1951). Experienced clinicians tend to be no more accurate than inexperienced nonprofessionals like secretaries (Goldberg, 1959; Crow, 1957; Soskin, 1959). The accuracy of trait inferences is not improved by clinical training; when the judge departs from common stereotypes he or she may become less accurate (e.g., Crow, 1957; Stelmachers & McHugh, 1964). Moreover, these conclusions generally obtain regardless of the test data on which judges base their interpretations (e.g., Stelmachers & McHugh, 1964). Thus while clinical judgments are often better than random guesses, they usually provide poorer predictions than those available from cheaper and simpler sources like biographical and social case history information, or from the combination of facts by statistical rules (called "actuarial prediction"; see Meehl, 1954; Wiggins, 1973). But clinical judgments cannot be dismissed as merely illusory, since they sometimes are linked to such independent information as the person's own self-reports (Jackson, Chan, & Stricker, 1979).

Adaptation, Deviance, and Change

Psychodynamic theories have not only had a profound effect on personality assessment, but they have also shaped ideas about adaptation, deviance, and personality change to a degree probably unsurpassed by any other psychological approach.

The Healthy Personality

For Freud, a "healthy personality" showed itself in the ability to love and work and required a harmony among id, ego, and superego. Referring to the goal of psychotherapy, Freud used the phrase "Where id was, there shall ego be." He meant that for the healthy personality rational choice and control replace irrational, impulse-driven compulsion. A healthy personality also required "mature" (genital) psychosexual development. In the healthy person, for Freud, genital sexuality replaces earlier forms of psychosexuality. That is, the healthy individual is one who achieves psychosexual maturity, having progressed through the psychosexual stages of development (Chapter 3) without becoming fixated at (or without regressing back to) any early, pregenital stages.

From the psychodynamic perspective, adequate adaptation requires that the individual achieves and accepts sufficient insight into her own unconscious motives. The person who can cope adequately is the one who can face her impulses and conflicts without having to resort to massive unconscious defenses that sap her psychic energy in the service of distorting either her own wishes or reality itself. "Symptoms" represent the return of unsuccessfully repressed materials, reemerging to torture the person in disguised forms; breakdowns represent the inadequacy of defenses to deal with unconscious conflicts and the failure of the ego to achieve sufficient strength to cope with the demands of external reality and the internal pressures of id and superego as they wage their warfare.

In Freud's words (1940, pp. 62–63):

> . . . The ego has been weakened by the internal conflict; we must come to its aid. The position is like a civil war which can only be decided by the help of an ally from without. The analytical physician and the weakened ego of the patient, basing themselves upon the real external world, are to combine against the enemies, the instinctual demands of the id, and the moral demands of the superego. We form a pact with each other. The patient's sick ego promises us the most candor, promises, that is, to put at our disposal all of the material which his self-perception provides; we, on the other hand, assure him of the strictest discretion and put at his service our experience in interpreting material that has been influenced by the unconscious. Our knowledge shall compensate for his ignorance and shall give his ego once more mastery over the lost provinces of his mental life. This pact constitutes the analytic situation.

Behavior as a Symptom of Psychodynamics

Consistent with psychoanalytic theory, the psychodynamic approach views an individual's problematic behavior as symptomatic (rather than of main interest in its own right) and searches for the possible causes of these symptoms by making inferences about the underlying personality dynamics. For example, an individual who has a bad stutter might be viewed as repressing hostility, one with asthma as suffering from dependency conflicts, and one with snake fears as victimized by unconscious sexual problems. This focus on the meaning of behavior as a symptom (sign) guides the psychodynamic strategy for understanding both normal and abnormal behavior. Thus the psychodynamically oriented clinician seeks to infer unconscious conflicts, defense structure, problems in psychosexual development, and the symbolic meaning and functions of behavior.

Many features of the traditional psychodynamic approach to adaptation and deviance are illustrated in the Freudian conceptualization of Gary (pp. 183–186). The report refers to Gary's fear of injury, his anxiety in social situations and fear of public speaking, and his problems in forming close relations. Rather than conceptualizing these behaviors as problems in their own right, they are viewed as signs (symptoms) that reflect (often very indirectly) such hypothetical, inferred problems as his "castration anxiety," "need for control," "unresolved Oedipal themes," "brittle defenses," and "basic insecurity."

Psychoanalytic Psychotherapies

Most forms of psychotherapy that view problematic behavior as a symptom have tried to achieve change by helping the individual to gain insight, awareness, and self-acceptance. Traditionally, this type of therapy is pursued in the context of a relationship between the client and the clinician that evolves over a lengthy period of time during regular interview meetings. Generally the meetings involve a verbal exchange of about an hour's duration several times weekly in the clinician's office. The major influence on such psychotherapy has been Freud's psychoanalytic therapy. The objective of psychoanalytic therapy is to give the person insight into the unconscious motives and conflicts believed to determine his behavior. Freud maintained that the major aim of psychoanalytic treatment should be to make the person's unconscious become conscious. In the ideally psychoanalyzed person, unconscious motives purportedly become largely recognized and conscious. Therefore psychoanalytically oriented treatment tries to increase the person's capacity for insight so that he can recognize his unconscious impulses and their expressions. In addition to getting insight, the person hopefully learns to "accept" his impulses. Such insight, and the conversion of the unconscious to the conscious by removal of repressions and other defenses, is believed to reduce symptoms and to be a prerequisite for durable behavior change.

The focus is on the inferred personality dynamics and unconscious motives rather than on the observed symptoms because of the belief that changes in the overt behavior (or symptoms) will lead to new (and perhaps even worse) behavioral manifestations unless the underlying conflicts and psychic problems are treated (Chapter 3). That is, "symptom change" or behavioral alterations, are believed to be followed by new symptoms, or "symptom substitution," unless the psychic roots are uncovered. For example, in this view, removal of a snake phobia might produce new symptoms unless the unconscious and symbolic meanings of the fear are explored and their dynamic bases changed. Similarly, frigidity in a woman might be seen as a symptom of her basic sexual conflicts. If that is true, then efforts to teach her to enjoy sexual relations would only mask her underlying problems without solving them. In Gary's case, efforts to directly reduce his fear of public speaking, for example, might result in even more severe unconscious blocks such as facial ticks or speech impairment. The psychodynamic conceptualization suggests that help for Gary's fears, or for his interpersonal problems, requires working with him to achieve and accept insights into their emotional origins and unconscious meanings.

From the psychoanalytic viewpoint, insight means more than intellectual or rational recognition of one's unconscious impulses. Psychoanalysts often distinguish intellectual from emotional insight, the latter being considered vital for therapeutic progress and for fully adequate functioning. Emotional insight implies that the person "works through" her problems and comes to understand and accept her impulses fully, not merely in an abstract, detached, rational way.

According to psychoanalytic theory, the greatest barrier to insight is the person's own defensiveness. The potential eruption of unconscious materials generates anxiety, which the individual avoids by developing *resistance* to facing her conflicts and true motives. For example, she may try unconsciously to steer the therapeutic interview away from the issues and feelings that are most problematic for her. In psychoanalysis these resistances are slowly overcome, with the aid of interpretation by the therapist. The person's free associations (saying whatever comes to mind) and the analysis of her dreams are important vehicles for facilitating the release of repressed material and overcoming defensive resistance.

This process of working through and achieving insights is believed to grow out of the intense transference relationship that the client develops with respect to the therapist. Psychodynamic theory suggests that feelings and problems that were experienced initially in relations with the parents or siblings during childhood now are transferred to the relationship with the therapist. Gradually, according to the theory, unconscious resistances and defenses against threatening ideas and feelings are overcome: The client slowly faces, works through, and accepts her unconscious impulses and conflicts. She thus achieves insight and basic change in her personality.

While Freud's ideas have been most influential, many treatment variations and innovations have been introduced by Freudians and other contemporary psychotherapists. The specific style and conduct of the psychotherapeutic interview thus has gone through many changes, and the exact procedures and interpretations that are used depend on the theoretical viewpoint of the particular clinician (e.g., Alexander & French, 1946). To the extent that different psychotherapists adhere to somewhat different concepts about the nature of basic personality dynamics, they are likely to emphasize different interpretations and techniques and to focus on different aspects of the client's behavior.

Limitations and New Directions in Psychotherapies

Criticisms

Traditional psychodynamic psychotherapies in general have been criticized in recent years on at least three counts.

1. First, the validity and meaning of the client's insights into his unconscious motives and "real underlying feelings" has been questioned. If experienced clinicians cannot reach agreement about the psychodynamic meaning of the client's behavior, and if they adhere to different conceptions of human motivation and personality dynamics, depending on their particular theory, then what do the client's "insights" and "awareness" really mean? The question is particularly troublesome in light of the limited support found for the role of unconscious processes in research on defense mechanisms (Chapter 17). Given these facts, skeptics suggest that the patient's "cure" may largely consist of his conversion to the clinician's belief system (e.g., Bandura, 1969). Thus clients whose therapists are Freudians may acquire Freudian insights; those treated by Jungians gain Jungian insights; those treated by disciples of Fromm achieve insights consistent with his view; and so on. In other words, in treatment the client may learn to conceptualize himself in terms of his clinician's favored theoretical constructs.

This criticism is cogent, but it does not necessarily imply that these reconceptualizations have no value. Consider, for example, a man who has construed himself as "a failure, a queer, stupid and weak." It is plausible that he may benefit from reconceptualizing himself, in part, for example, as "neurotic, conflicted, victimized by a castrating mother, and driven by unconscious guilt." Regardless of their absolute truth value, such reinterpretations may provide the individual with a less aversive and more convenient set of constructs about himself. It would be most important, however, to show that these reconceptualizations also help the person to deal more effectively with his life problems and with the troubles that led him to seek help in the first place.

2. Second, the value of traditional therapeutic activities is seriously questioned by studies on the outcomes that they yield. In 1952 Eysenck's review of treatment outcomes noted that the improvement rate was about 64 percent for patients who received intensive and prolonged psychotherapy. This rate did not exceed the improvement rate (72 percent) for similar patients who were treated only custodially (by confinement in mental hospitals) or by general practitioners. In a follow-up almost 10 years later, Eysenck (1961) found nothing to change the picture. On the contrary, more data indicated that untreated patients did not differ from those who received intensive psychotherapy, both groups showing some improvement.

Eysenck's conclusions are themselves open to severe criticism and are not widely accepted (e.g., Bergin, 1971; Kiesler, 1966; Rosenzweig, 1954). The methodological limitations of most research on treatment outcomes are great, and therefore firm conclusions have been hard to reach; the literature on the

Psychotherapy research must discover "*what* treatment by *whom,* is most effective for *this* individual with *that* specific problem . . ."

outcomes of psychotherapy is extremely difficult to interpret. Nevertheless, while not as dismal as Eysenck implied, most of the results (e.g., Bandura, 1969; Bergin, 1966, 1971; Kazden & Wilson, 1978) do not provide strong evidence in favor of traditional psychotherapy. The research evidence supporting psychoanalytic therapy leads even highly sympathetic reviewers to conclude, "Quantitative research on psychoanalytic therapy presents itself, so far, as an unreliable support for clinical practice" (Luborsky & Spence, 1971, p. 430). Yet many experienced clinicians remain convinced that much of value exists in psychodynamically oriented therapy and believe that future research should be devoted to identifying its most promising components. Regardless of theoretical orientation, there is wide agreement that research must be more specific than it has been, and must be aimed at discovering "*what* treatment, by *whom,* is most effective for *this* individual with *that* specific problem, and under *which* set of circumstances" (Paul, 1967b, p. 111). While traditional psychotherapy taken as a whole may not produce strong overall effects, some people may be significantly helped by it while others may be actively hurt by it. The potential gain or loss would depend on the particular person, problem, and therapist.

   3. Finally, assuming that traditional psychotherapies surely do help some people, they still would have only limited value for meeting the enormous psychological problems that our society faces. Indeed only a small percentage of people would qualify for traditional psychotherapy. In regard to psychoanalysis, for example, Freud believed that the good prospective patient should possess a reasonable degree of education and be fairly young; she should be sufficiently distressed by her problems to want to change, but not too distressed because psychoanalytic therapy cannot be conducted with severely confused,

depressed, or debilitated persons (Freud, 1959, Vol. 1). Similarly, people with severe fears or obsessions were thought to be poor risks because they had given in to their symptoms completely, thus reducing anxiety and motivation for therapy (Freud, 1959, Vol. 2). Given these limitations and the costs and time required for psychoanalytic treatment, the method would be either inappropriate or unavailable for most troubled people even if it were proved valuable for some. As early as 1918 Freud said:

> You know that the therapeutic effects we can achieve are very inconsiderable in number. We are but a handful of people, and even by working hard each one of us can deal in a year with only a small number of persons. Against the vast amount of neurotic misery which is in the world, and perhaps need not be, the quantity we can do away with is almost negligible. Besides this, the necessities of our own existence limit our work to the well-to-do classes. . . . At present we can do nothing in the crowded ranks of the people, who suffer exceedingly from neuroses (1959, Vol. 2, p. 401).

Many clinicians have recognized the need for new forms of therapy and behavior change; numerous promising strategies have been developed to meet practical challenges in helping people. These efforts cover such diverse approaches as community mental health programs and preventive counseling in the schools (e.g., Cowen, Gardner, & Zax, 1967), therapy conducted conjointly with the whole family rather than with the individual alone (Satir, 1967), and innovations stimulated by the concepts of existential psychology (e.g., Laing, 1965). Perhaps the most popular new developments are therapeutic groups (discussed in Chapter 11) and behavior therapies (Chapter 10). There also are attempts to integrate the best elements of psychodynamic therapy with the best features of behavior therapy (Wachtel, 1977).

Implications

Confronted with results of the kind reviewed in this chapter, psychologists have reacted in many ways. Some have construed the negative research data on psychodynamically oriented clinical applications as reflecting mainly on specific techniques, judges, or clinicians, or on the limitations of the research strategies (e.g., Wachtel, 1973), but not on the basic assumptions of the psychodynamic approach that guided them. As a result many still use, and rely on, techniques like the Rorschach and the TAT, often employing them more like an interview than a standardized test. They point out that these devices simply provide a set of ambiguous stimuli to which the person reacts; the clinician then bases his assessments in part on his interpretations of the dynamic meanings revealed by the test behavior. Likewise, they continue to practice psychodynamically oriented therapy, noting: "We dare not make changes so we stay with the old model, not because it is necessarily the best, but because we have poor rules for testing it" (Luborsky & Spence, 1971, p. 432). Critics contend, however, that the justifiability of this practice depends upon the evidence supporting the value of clinical inferences and judgments about dispositions and the efficacy of psychodynamic therapy.

Alternative Strategies

Regardless of what the ultimate conclusion may prove to be, many psychologists are beginning to pursue a variety of directions vigorously. In one direction, the clinical judgment process itself is being analyzed (e.g., Bieri et al., 1966; Jackson, 1979; Wiggins, 1973). Rather than studying the accuracy of the judge, researchers are examining *how* she judges personality and the mechanisms of her inferences. Other investigators have been studying a closely related area: "person perception" and the processes through which people form impressions of each other and of themselves (e.g., Anderson, 1965, 1972). Attention is thus turning to the "information processing" of the human judge and to the cognitive activity of the clinician. Investigations in this vein reveal some of the complexities of the information processing that underlies social judgments in general, and clinical inferences in particular. Computers also may help to simulate human judgment processes and even serve as analogs for personality structure and dynamics. For example, Dr. Kenneth Colby has been designing computer programs that behave like psychoanalysts and is studying how they work. This strategy has made the high-speed computer its ally (e.g., Colby, 1965; Colby & Hilf, 1973; Loehlin, 1968).

Some researchers also have tried to analyze the processes that occur in various types of person-clinician interactions such as the interview in psychotherapy and to discover the essential skills of effective therapists (e.g., Truax & Mitchell, 1971). They suggest that the limitations of the clinician may reflect more on his lack of interpersonal skills than on the personality theory that guides him. Consequently they emphasize the therapist's personality more than his personality theory.

In still another direction, some psychodynamically oriented investigators have turned to research on cognitive processes, emotions, and "ego functions." Their interest has tended to shift away from unconscious motives and impulses to the person's modes of dealing with information, to cognitive styles for handling problems. "Cognitive styles" refer to self-consistent ways of approaching and transforming information, especially through perception, memory, and thought. Influenced by the "ego psychologists," psychodynamic researchers have looked for consistent cognitive and emotional styles that people might habitually employ in coping with the problems of their lives.

These researchers are influenced by psychodynamic concepts, but they follow a methodology that does not depend on the clinician and that takes full account of current developments in the study of cognition and information processing (e.g., Singer & Antrobus, 1972). For example, they rely on objective tests of perceptual and cognitive problem-solving (e.g., the speed with which the subject can find a hidden figure embedded in a picture), as in the work of Witkin (1965).

Need for New Assumptions?

A final reaction to negative data of the sort discussed in this chapter has questioned not merely psychodynamic methods but also the theoretical assumptions that guide them (e.g., Bandura, 1977; Krasner & Ullmann, 1973; Peterson, 1968). Thus not only the methods are being challenged but also the psychodynamic constructs that led to them and govern their use. These critics have started to pursue completely different routes. Rather than inferring unconscious motives, searching for insights, or seeking generalized dispositions, they are trying to discover the specific conditions that cause important *change* in behavior (for example, as discussed in Chapter 10). They also have urged an approach to persons that focuses on the experimental analysis of their behavior, described in the next chapter.

SUMMARY

1. Psychodynamically oriented psychologists attempt to study personality in depth and try to eliminate situational interferences in the hope of circumventing defenses and reaching basic dynamics and motives. Guided by psychoanalytic theory, the traditional focus has been on reconstructions of early history, particularly the early handling of sexual and aggressive impulses, and inferences regarding personality in global, dynamic terms.

2. In the psychodynamic approach, the Rorschach and the TAT (Thematic Apperception Test) are projective tests that have been especially popular. The Rorschach consists of a series of complex inkblots. The subject says what the inkblots resemble or look like to him or her. The TAT consists of a series of ambiguous pictures for which subjects are asked to make up a story.

3. The main characteristics of projective techniques are that they are presented as ambiguous tasks for the subject; the purpose of the test is disguised, and the person is free to respond as he or she wishes. Clinicians than may interpret the meaning of the answers in accord

with their theories, experiences, and intuitions, trying to infer the person's psychodynamics and personality from his or her responses.

4. Several procedures have been devised to handle the complex questions of reliability and validity of interpretations made from projective test responses. It is especially important to demonstrate interscorer consistency—the degree to which different judges arrive at the same interpretive statements from the same test data. Manuals with explicit instructions and practice training help increase agreement among judges.

5. The study of achievement motives as expressed through TAT stories has been carefully standardized by means of objective scoring procedures. Research on the need for achievement as expressed in TAT themes has yielded an extensive network of correlations.

6. Research on the clinical uses of projective tests indicates that many methodological problems make it difficult to interpret the results clearly. Most important, the correlations that are found tend to be too low to permit more accurate predictions about individuals than could be made from simpler data.

7. The clinician is a central instrument in psychodynamic assessment. Harvard personologists have provided a model for the intensive clinical study of individuals. Trained assessors collected diverse data on each subject and, in council, made inferences about the individual's personality dynamics.

8. The validity of clinical judgment must be evaluated empirically. Surprisingly but consistently, studies on the effect of clinical training do not show a clear advantage for trained judges in making global judgments. Research also indicates that the information from various clinical tests does not enable the experienced clinician to make more accurate predictions than he or she could have made from biographical data. Experienced judges may not agree with each other in their inferences about personality dynamics even when they are using the same test data from the same individual.

9. The psychodynamic approach to adaptation and deviance distinguishes between symptom and underlying disorder and seeks such hypothetical causes as internal conflicts, dynamics, and unconscious motives.

10. Influenced by Freud's theory, most traditional approaches to personality change have emphasized insight and awareness and acceptance of unconscious motives and feelings, although there have been many variations in specific techniques and theory. The efficacy of these

approaches to personality change has been questioned on both practical and theoretical grounds and there now is a search for useful innovations such as encounter groups.

11. Reactions to criticisms regarding psychodynamic assessment and psychotherapy have been divided. On the one hand, the problems have been judged to reflect inadequacies in specific techniques and research methods. Consequently further attention is being focused on clinical processes and on clarifying person-clinician interactions. Influenced by the "ego psychologists" and new orientations in psychodynamic theory, other researchers have turned to the study of personality and "cognitive styles." Another reaction has been more radical: It has questioned the basic theoretical assumptions that guide psychodynamic applications and has found other ways of conceptualizing, assessing, and modifying behavior.

CHAPTER 9

BEHAVIORAL THEORIES: APPLICATIONS (I)

Lucass Class
Presentation
S2452 237
Disease model D34
Melcalfe's p214

Because there have been several distinctly different behavioral approaches to personality, it should not be surprising that each of these has led to somewhat different applications. The psychodynamic behavior theory of Miller and Dollard drew mainly on the experimental methods of general psychology, testing its hypotheses in carefully conducted experiments. Psychologists influenced by B. F. Skinner's formulations often began by studying pigeons and other animals in the laboratory. More recently they have applied their ideas to clinical settings and devised assessments and behavior change programs for a wide range of human problems. The assessment and modification of complex behavior in diverse clinical and experimental settings also has been guided by various other social learning theories. This chapter considers the applications of behavioral theories to assessment; the next chapter examines their applications to behavior change.

telemetry p224

Characteristics of Social
Behavior Applications

Applications of current social behavior theory focus on selected, carefully defined behaviors and the observable stimulus conditions that seem to covary with them. One tries to observe what the person does, rather than to infer what he or she has or is. The search is for the stimulus conditions controlling or causing particular behavior patterns; one does not try to interpret the behaviors as indirect signs of the person's underlying motives and dispositions. For this purpose behavioral assessments seek to specify objectively the response patterns of interest, and to identify relevant stimulus conditions.

The common denominator of all behavioral methods is their emphasis on the careful measurement of specific behavior in relation to systematic changes in stimulus conditions. This focus on the covariation between changes in events (the stimulus conditions) and changes in responses (the person's behavior) is a fundamental feature of "stimulus-response" approaches. The emphasis on how changes in stimulus conditions lead to alterations in responses is also a chief characteristic of the experimental method that has been an important model for behavioral approaches.

Behavior as Sign or Sample?

The trait and dynamic approaches discussed in previous chapters searched for tests from which to infer dispositions, or depended on clinical judges to interpret people's dynamics from their behavior. Investigators who were guided by the assumption that personality traits and dynamics would be very broadly pervasive studied behavior in highly generalized or "typical" contexts, rather than in well-specified situations. Their preference for items dealing with reactions to general rather than specific situations is related to their belief in broad dispositions that cause general and enduring behavioral consistencies across many different situations. In accord with that belief, they have selected items that refer to relatively general, vague, or typical situations, trying to minimize the role of specific stimuli or conditions. The most extreme forms of this preference for ambiguous stimuli are the blurred pictures of the TAT or the inkblots of the Rorschach.

In contrast, behavioral assessments have been guided by a greater emphasis on the role of stimulus conditions as moderators and regulators of behavior. Rather than seeking behavioral signs of the individual's general traits and motives, behavioral approaches have focused on the specific conditions and processes—both "inside" and "outside" the person—that might govern his or her behavior. For this purpose behaviorally oriented psychologists have followed an experimental strategy in which stimulus conditions are varied so that one can observe systematically any changes in the behavior of interest in relation to the changing conditions.

In one sense, all psychological approaches are based on behavioral observation: Check marks on MMPI answer sheets and stories in response to inkblots obviously are behaviors just as much as crying or running or fighting. Moreover, we saw that the dynamic approach also samples such life-like behaviors as bridge-building under stress in the OSS research. The difference between approaches depends on how these behaviors are used. As we saw, in the dynamic orientation the observed behaviors serve as highly indirect *signs* (symptoms) of the dispositions and motives that might underlie them. In contrast, in behavior assessments the observed behavior is treated as a *sample*, and interest is focused on how the specific sampled behavior is affected by alterations in conditions. Behavioral approaches thus seek to directly assess stimulus-response covariations.

Case Example: Conditions
Controlling Gary's Anxiety

The general strategy of behavior assessment can be illustrated by once again considering the case of Gary W. An assessment of Gary in the framework of a behavioral orientation obviously would focus on his behavior in relation to stimulus conditions. But that behaviors, and in relation to which conditions? Rather than seeking a portrait of Gary's personality and behavior "in general," or an estimate of his "average" or dominant propensities and attributes, a behavioral perspective dictates a much more specific focus. The particular behavior patterns selected for study depend on the particular problem that requires investigation. In clinical situations, priorities are indicated by the client; in research contexts, they are selected by the investigator.

During his first term of graduate school Gary found himself troubled enough to seek help at the school's counseling center. As part of the behavioral assessment that followed, Gary was asked to list and rank in order of importance the three problems that he found most distressing in himself and that he wanted to change if possible. He listed "feeling anxious and losing my grip" as his greatest problem. To assess the behavioral referents for his felt "anxiety," Gary was asked to specify in more detail just what changes in himself indicated to him that he was or was not anxious and "losing his grip."

He indicated that when he became anxious he felt changes in his heart rate, became tense, perspired, and found it most difficult to speak coherently. Next, to explore the covariation between increases and decreases in this state and changes in stimulus conditions, Gary was asked to keep an hour-by-hour diary sampling most of the waking hours during the daytime for a period of two weeks and indicating the type of activity that occurred during each hour. Discussion with him of this record suggested that anxiety tended to occur primarily in connection with public speaking occasions—specifically, in classroom situations in which he was required to speak before a group. As indicated by the summary shown in Table 9-1, only on one occasion that was not close in time to public speaking did Gary find himself highly anxious. That occasion turned out to be one in which he was brooding in his room, thinking about his public speaking failures in the classroom.

Having established a seemingly reliable covariation between the occurrence of anxiety and public speaking in the social-evaluative conditions of the classroom, his assessors identified the specific components of the public speaking situation that led to relatively more and less anxiety. The purpose here was to establish a hierarchy of anxiety-evoking stimuli ranging from the mild to the

TABLE 9-1 OCCURRENCE OF GARY'S SELF-REPORTED ANXIETY ATTACKS IN RELATION TO PUBLIC SPEAKING		
Occurrence of Anxiety	*Hours with Anxiety* (10)	*Hours without Anxiety* (80)
Within 1 hour of public speaking	9 (90%)	0 (0%)
No public speaking within 1 hour	1 (10%)	80 (100%)

exceedingly severe. This hierarchy then was used in a treatment designed to gradually desensitize Gary to these fear stimuli by "systematic desensitization" (described in the next chapter).

Note that this behavioral assessment of Gary is quite specific: It is not an effort to characterize his whole personality, to describe "what he is like," or to infer his motives and dynamics. Instead, the assessment restricts itself to some clearly described problems and tries to analyze them in objective terms without going beyond the observed relations. Moreover, the analysis focuses on the *conditions* in which Gary's behavior occurs and on the covariation between those conditions and his problem. Behavior assessment tends to be focused assessment, usually concentrating on those aspects of behavior that can be changed and that require change. Indeed, as will be seen often in this chapter, behavior assessment and behavior change (treatment) are closely connected.

The foregoing assessment of Gary illustrates one rather crude way to study stimulus-response covariations. Of course there are many different ways in which these covariations can be sampled. This chapter illustrates some of the main tactics developed for the direct measurement of human behavior within the framework of the social behavior orientation.

Direct Behavior Measurement

For many purposes in personality study it is important to sample and observe behavior in carefully structured, life-like or *in vivo* situations. In clinical applications, direct observation may give both client and assessor an opportunity to assess life problems and to select treatment objectives. Direct observation of behavior samples also may be used to assess the relative efficacy of various treatment procedures. Finally, behavior sampling has an important part in experimental research on personality.

The types of data collected in the behavioral approach include situational samples of both nonverbal and verbal behavior, as well as physiological measurements of emotional reactions. In addition, a comprehensive assessment often includes an analysis of effective rewards or reinforcing stimuli in the person's life. Examples of all of these measures are given in the following sections.

Situational Behavior Sampling *Life Situation*

Many informal attempts have been made to record people's behavior in ongoing life-like situations. For example, a concealed observer may try to write or dictate an account of the naturalistic behavior that he is watching. This procedure has the disadvantage of requiring the observer to devote part of his attention to the actual recording and thus restricts the attention he can pay to the subject's ongoing behavior. Informal observations often also suffer from lack of precision. Lovaas and his associates (1965b) wanted a comprehensive description that would contain not only the behaviors the subject performed but also the duration and the specific time of onset of each type of behavior. Such detailed information is needed if one wants to determine the covariations among an individual's specific behaviors, or their alterations in relation to various changes in the environment and in the behavior of other people.

Lovaas and his collaborators (1965b) devised an apparatus that consists of a panel of buttons that are depressed by the observer. Each button represents a category of behavior (for example, "talking," "running," "sitting alone") and is attached to an automatic pen-recorder. Whenever a button is depressed, the corresponding pen on the recorder is activated. A continuous record is thus provided.

The observer depresses the button when the subject starts the specific behavior designated by that button and does not release the button until the particular behavior is discontinued. The observer after a little practice can devote his whole attention to watching what the subject is doing and yet record up to twelve different categories of behavior without looking at the button panel. The apparatus permits a record that is precise enough to include duration and the specific time of onset of each behavior. The method can then be applied to discover covariations among the individual's different behaviors and between his behavior and that of other people in the situation.

Even without the aid of such sophisticated apparatus, there have been many attempts to measure important interpersonal and emotional behaviors precisely. Some impressive examples come from assessments of the intensity or magnitude of such emotional behaviors as seemingly irrational fears (phobias).

The strength of diverse avoidance behaviors has been assessed reliably in clinical situations by exposing fearful individuals to series of real or symbolic fear-inducing stimuli. For example, fear of heights was assessed by measuring the distance that the phobic person could climb on a metal fire escape (Lazarus, 1961). The same people were assessed again after receiving therapy to reduce their fears. In this phase, the subjects were invited to ascend eight stories by elevator to a roof garden and to count the passing cars below for two minutes. Claustrophobic behavior—fear of closed spaces—was measured by asking each person to sit in a cubicle containing large French windows opening onto a balcony. The assessor shut the windows and slowly moved a large screen nearer and nearer to the subject, thus gradually constricting her space. Of course each subject was free to open the windows, and thereby to terminate the procedure, whenever she wished, although she was instructed to persevere as long as possible. The measure of claustrophobia was the least distance at which the person could tolerate the screen.

To measure fear and avoidance responses to snakes, fearful volunteer subjects were exposed to snakes in a laboratory (Lang & Lazovik, 1963; Lang, Lazovik, & Reynolds, 1965). At first each volunteer was asked simply to look down into a topless glass case, 15 feet from the entrance to the room, that contained a nonpoisonous, five-foot black snake. Subjects were assured that the snake was harmless and were invited to come as close as they could. If they could come all the way to the case, the experimenter touched the snake and asked the subjects to try to do so also. If the subjects succeeded, the assessor picked up the snake barehanded and asked the subjects to hold it. Each of the increasingly bold approach steps was scored. In addition to measuring approach behavior directly, some studies also asked people to rate their subjective reactions after trying the actual approach behavior (Lang, Lazovik, & Reynolds, 1965).

Another study assessed nursery-school children's fear of dogs (Bandura, Grusec, & Menlove, 1966). Each child was led into a room containing, in the far corner, a playpen in which a dog was enclosed. The children's approach behavior was scaled objectively according to how near they ventured toward the animal. To get the highest scores the child had to climb into the playpen and sit in it while playing with the dog.

Direct behavior sampling has also been tried extensively in the analysis of psychotic behavior. One study, for instance, employed a time-sampling technique. At regular 30-minute intervals, psychiatric nurses sought out and observed each hospitalized patient for periods of one to three minutes, without directly interacting with him (Ayllon & Haughton, 1964). The behavior observed in each sample was classified for the occurrence of three previously defined behaviors (for example, psychotic talk), and the time-check recordings were used to compute the relative frequency of the various behaviors. This time-sampling technique was supplemented by recordings of all the interactions between patient and nurses (such as each time the patient entered the nursing office). The resulting data served as a basis for designing and evaluating a treatment program.

Verbal Behavior

What people say—their "verbal behavior"—may be just as important as what they do nonverbally. Most personality assessors, guided by trait and psychodynamic theories, have focused on verbalizations as signs of personality, rather than as descriptions of reactions to stimulus conditions. In social behavior assessment, on the other hand, what the person says is intended to help define the relevant stimuli and the response patterns that they have come to evoke and to specify the covariations between them. For example, a number of self-report techniques have been used to sample specific self-reported fears (Geer, 1965; Lang & Lazovik, 1963; Wolpe & Lang, 1964). These schedules list many items that were found to elicit frequent anxiety in patients. The respondent indicates on scales the degree of disturbance provoked by such items as strangers, bats, ugly people, mice, making mistakes, and looking foolish.

As was illustrated in the assessment of Gary's public speaking anxieties, a daily record may provide another valuable first step in the identification of problem-producing stimuli. Many behaviorally oriented clinicians routinely ask their clients to keep specific records listing the exact conditions under which their anxieties and problems seem to increase or decrease (Wolpe & Lazarus, 1966). The person may be asked to prepare by himself lists of all the stimulus conditions or events that create discomfort, distress, or other painful emotional reactions.

Metcalfe (1956) conducted an analysis of stimulus conditions controlling bronchial asthmatic seizures in a young female patient. The young woman kept a detailed diary during an 85-day period in which she was hospitalized but free to visit outside. She was instructed to record all symptoms related to respiration, particularly "real asthmatic attacks" (involving tightness of the chest, wheezing, and severe respiratory distress). She also was asked to record physical symptoms not related to respiration and all her activities such as games, dancing, occupational therapy, shopping, meetings, and visits.

In this time period asthmatic attacks occurred on 15 of the 85 days. An examination of the temporal relations between her self-reported activities and asthmatic attacks indicated that contacts with her mother appeared to be a main eliciting condition for asthma: 9 of her 15 attacks followed recent contact with her mother. Moreover, 80 percent of her asthma-free days occurred when she had no contact with her mother. No strong relations were found between the occurrence of attacks and other possible sources of stress, such as interviews. Further assessments confirmed that contact with the mother in the home appeared to be the main stimulus for asthmatic episodes. As Metcalfe's case study suggests, verbal reports (in the form of written records) may be helpful in behavior assessment, especially when it is inconvenient and unfeasible to observe the person's daily life patterns directly.

Although often helpful, verbal descriptions are not completely adequate substitutes for direct sampling of life behaviors in vivo. Many people (for example, children, disorganized adults, people with language deficiencies) cannot supply accurate descriptions. Moreover, even with articulate individuals, verbal self-reports may not be accurate.

Metcalfe also showed his client words associated with the mother and mother-relevant pictorial stimuli on the TAT and Rorschach. Neither these stimuli nor interview discussions about her mother elicited asthmatic attacks.

Not adequate

TABLE 9-2
MEASURING SELF-EFFICACY EXPECTANCIES

Listed below are situations that can arouse anxiety, annoyance, and anger. Imagine the feelings you might have in each situation, such as your heart beats faster and your muscles tense. Indicate whether you could tolerate now the emotional strain caused by each of the situations.

Under the column marked *Can Do,* check (✔) the tasks or activities you expect you could do *now*.

For the tasks you check under *Can Do,* indicate in the column marked *Confidence* how confident you are that you could do the task. Rate your degree of confidence using a number from 10 to 100 on the scale below:

10	20	30	40	50	60	70	80	90	100

Quite Uncertain	*Moderately Certain*	*Certain*

	Can Do	Confidence
Attend a social gathering at which there is no one you know.	_____	_____
At a social gathering, approach a group of strangers, introduce yourself, and join in the conversation.	_____	_____
At a social gathering, discuss a controversial topic (politics, religion, philosophy of life, etc.) with people whose views differ greatly from yours.	_____	_____
Be served by a salesperson, receptionist, or waiter whose behavior you find irritating.	_____	_____
Complain about poor service to an unsympathetic or sales or repair person.	_____	_____
When complaining about bad service, insist on seeing the manager if you are not satisfied.	_____	_____
In a public place, ask a stranger to stop doing something that annoys you, such as cutting in line, talking in a movie, or smoking in a no-smoking area.	_____	_____
Ask neighbors to correct a problem for which they are responsible, such as making noise at night, not controlling children or pets.	_____	_____
At work, reprimand an uncooperative subordinate.	_____	_____

SOURCE: Examples selected from Bandura & Reese, 1981.

These results show that responses to verbal or symbolic presentations of stimuli (in interviews and tests) may not be adequate substitutes for assessment of direct reactions to the real events supposedly represented by the symbolic stimuli.

Measuring Expectancies

As part of their increasing use of cognitive constructs, behavior theorists have paid more attention to the measurement of people's cognitive (mental) activities, especially their expectancies (Bandura, 1978; Merluzzi and associates, 1981). This new focus reflects the belief that the impact of the environment depends on what the individual knows, expects, and values (Mischel, 1973). Self-efficacy expectations, defined as the person's conviction that he or she can execute the behavior required by a particular situation, have been shown to be especially important predictors of behavior (Bandura, 1978). Therefore there have been many attempts to measure such expectations.

Self-efficacy is assessed by asking the person to indicate the degree of confidence that he or she can do a particular task. For example, Bandura and Reese (1981) wanted to assess the recovery of patients who had suffered heart attacks. A large number of tasks were described to the patients. These included such potentially stressful things as driving a few blocks in the neighborhood, driving on a freeway, driving on a narrow mountain road. They also included situations that would induce other kinds of emotional strain, as illustrated in Table 9-2. For each item the respondent indicates the confidence level for being able to do the task.

Measurement of Bodily Changes

Measures of bodily changes in response to stimulation also provide important information, especially when the stimuli are stressful or arousing. Various indirect measures of bodily reactions during emotional activity have been developed. One of the most convenient methods is the polygraph recording of some of the critical effects produced by the bodily activity involved in the reactions of the autonomic nervous system. The polygraph apparatus contains a series of devices that translate indices of body changes into a visual record by deflecting a pen across a moving paper chart.

One popular component of polygraphic measurement is the *electrocardiogram* (EKG). As the heart beats its muscular contractions produce patterns of electrical activity that may be detected by electrodes placed near the heart on the body surface. Figure 9-1 shows a record of heartbeats monitored by the polygraph, the area from one peak to another on the record representing one beat of the heart. An especially useful index of heart activity is based on the *rate* at which the person's heart is beating: It is measured in terms of the time between each beat on the electrocardiogram.

FIGURE 9-1
Heart Rhythm in an Elderly Subject

A, Normal heart rhythm (control level, rate 80). B and C, Initial beats show an abnormally irregular heartbeat during extreme emotional arousal. Last two beats show the heart rate has increased to 115. D, Following the end of arousal, heart rate returns to control level; abnormal beating is no longer present. (Courtesy of George Prozan, M.D.)

In a basically similar manner, changes in blood volume may be recorded by means of a *plethysmograph*. Other examples of valuable indices include changes in the electrical activity of the skin due to sweating (recorded by a galvanometer and called the *galvanic skin response* or GSR), changes in blood pressure, and changes in muscular activity.

Intense emotional arousal is generally accompanied by high levels of "activation" (e.g., Malmo, 1959), shown by increases in the activity of the cerebral cortex, increases in muscle tension and, at the behavioral level, increasingly vigorous activity and excitement. The degree of activation in the cerebral cortex may be inferred from "brain waves" recorded by the electroencephalograph (EEG), as illustrated in the records shown in Figure 9-2. As the EEG

FIGURE 9-2
Various Human EEG Patterns under Several Arousal States

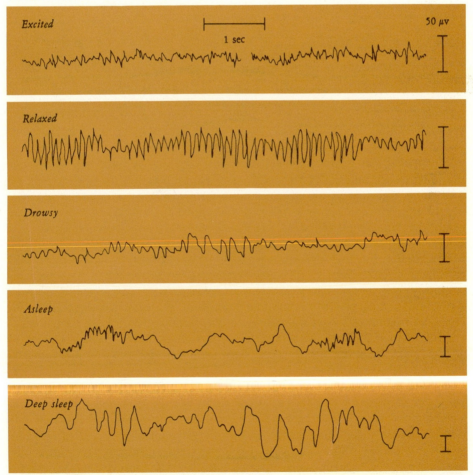

From H. Jasper, in Penfield and Erickson, *Epilepsy and Cerebral Localization,* 1941. Courtesy of Charles C Thomas, Publisher, Springfield, Ill.

patterns in this figure indicate, the frequency, amplitude, and other character-istics of brain waves vary according to the subject's degree of behavioral arousal and excitement.

It is obviously difficult to study bodily changes in life-like situations if one has to keep the subject in a fixed position and hooked up with elaborate wir-ing to a big machine. While these conditions permit laboratory studies they hinder attempts to sample physiological changes under *in vivo* conditions. A radio link between the electrode and the main apparatus makes it possible to eliminate the usual wires and provides many advantages, permitting the re-searcher to move the subject outside the confines of the laboratory. This pro-cedure is called *telemetry*. The subject wears a simple miniature radio trans-mitter, which relays the signals from biological events picked up by electrodes. The transmission is picked up by the distant recording apparatus, which con-verts it into the usual pen-and-paper record. Such a system is used routinely to monitor the physiological status of astronauts, for example.

Relations among Measures → The ways people respond

The foregoing examples of behavioral measures illustrate the multiplicity of human response systems. People respond verbally, through overt social and interpersonal actions, and covertly through thoughts and feelings, as well as physiologically through changes in bodily activity. The relationships among a person's various reactions, both across response systems and among sub-measures within a system, tend to be extremely complex.

Sometimes significant correlations across response systems are found. For example, Geer (1965) administered a fear survey schedule to undergraduates to select a high fear and a low fear group for spider phobia. An equal number of high and low fear subjects were then assigned to experimental and control conditions. In the experimental condition subjects were shown pictures of a spider; in the control condition they saw pictures of a snake. For all subjects measures of autonomic arousal were taken physiologically in the form of GSR responses through finger electrodes. When they were presented with pictures of spiders, people who had reported high spider fear on the inventory showed significantly greater GSRs than did the other subjects. Moreover, this in-creased autonomic arousal was found only in response to directly relevant fear stimuli. When subjects with high fear of spiders were shown pictures of snakes, their GSR did not increase. The verbal report and the physiological measures were concordant in this case.

On the other hand, behavioral specificity is often found. When one com-pares across response systems, for example by obtaining verbal self-reports as well as overt behavior samples in the same domain, the different response sys-tems turn out to be only partly similar, or even unrelated, and often inde-pendent (Mischel, 1968). In other words, we cannot assume that particular response measures will be closely correlated with other aspects of the person's behavior. For example, in one study the subjects were recruited by a newspaper advertisement inviting them to participate in procedures to help eliminate fear of snakes. In fact, "38 percent of the subjects who had defined themselves as snake phobic proved, much to their surprise, relatively fearless" on a behavioral test that required them to approach and handle a live snake (Bandura, Blanchard, & Ritter, 1969, p. 178). The same problems of behavioral specificity (lack of extensive correlations among different aspects of an individual's behavior) discussed in regard to trait and psychodynamic approaches apply equally in the context of behavior assessment. Consequently, whenever possible it is preferable to use diverse tests—for example, overt behavior, self-reports, and direct autonomic measures—both to assess behaviors and to determine the effects of treatments on altering them. An encouraging feature of self-efficacy measures is that they do seem to predict the relevant behaviors at high levels of accuracy. For example, a consistently strong association was found between rated self-efficacy and the degree to which people showed increased approach behavior toward previously feared objects after they had received treatment for their fears (Bandura, Adams, & Beyer, 1977).

Note again that behavior assessments sample behaviors but usually do not interpret them as possible signs of traits and motives. That is, behavior assessments do not assume that a person's test behavior will be a sign of his or her nontest behavior. They do not assume, for example, that how you respond to incomplete sentences on a test will relate to your interpersonal behavior at home. Instead, behavior assessments seek to sample the relevant behavior directly—for example, to observe the individual's specific interpersonal behaviors with his or her family at home. If inferences beyond the sampled behaviors were to be made, all the problems of reliability and validity discussed in earlier chapters would, of course, apply here just as well. In other words, to the extent that one does not directly sample the behaviors of interest, and wants to extrapolate, for example, from what the person does in a laboratory test situation to what he or she does in real life (or from brain waves to social behavior), one must show the reliability and validity of the measurements just as much as when one wants to generalize from scores on a trait questionnaire to actual behavior.

Measuring Rewards or Reinforcing Stimuli

So far we have considered the direct measurement of various responses. Behavior assessments, however, analyze not just what people do (and say and feel), but also the conditions that regulate or determine what they do. For that reason, behavior assessments have to find the rewards or reinforcers that may be influencing a person's behavior. If discovered, these reinforcers also can serve as incentives in therapy programs to help modify behavior in more positive or advantageous directions as discussed in the next chapter. Psychologists who emphasize the role of reinforcement in human behavior have devoted much attention to discovering and measuring effective reinforcers. People's actual choices in life-like situations, as well as their verbal preferences or ratings, reveal some of the potent reinforcers that influence them. The reinforcement value of particular stimuli also may be assessed directly by observing their effects on the individual's performance (e.g., Weir, 1965).

Primary reinforcers like food, and generalized conditioned reinforcers such as praise, social approval, and money, are effective for most people. Sometimes, however, it is difficult to find potent reinforcers that it would be feasible to manipulate. In some learning situations with children and with chronic behavior problems it has been especially difficult to find realistic and effective reinforcers. For example, in one programmed instruction project, the investigators tried to use social approval and information feedback about test results as reinforcers for their pupils (Birnbrauer, Bijou, Wolf, & Kidder, 1965). The investigators soon discovered that right and wrong answers seemed to be one and the same to the children. Indeed, often the children did not even look at the answers the teaching programs supplied. Learning academic subjects was of little value to these children, and the researchers had to find better reinforcers. In other situations it has been discovered that such social rewards as praise may have little value with disturbed or delinquent patients (e.g., Atkinson, 1957; Cairns, 1959). Sometimes smiles and praise from the clinician may even lead to anxiety and hostility rather than to the intended beneficial effects.

A main problem in finding reinforcers with disturbed groups (such as hospitalized schizophrenic patients) has been that many of the usual reinforcers prove to be ineffective, especially with people who have spent many years living in the back wards of a mental hospital. Ayllon and Azrin (1965) have shown how effective reinforcers can be discovered for seemingly unmotivated psychotic patients. These reinforcers then can serve to motivate the patients to engage in more adaptive behavior. The assessments in these investigations were guided by the principle that any behavior with a high natural frequency of occurrence can serve as a reinforcer for other less likely behaviors (Premack, 1965).

As a first step the patients were observed directly in the ward to discover their most frequent behaviors in situations that permitted them freedom to do what they wished. Throughout the day observers carefully recorded the things the patients did, or tried to do, without pressures from the staff. The frequency of these activities provided an index of their potential values as reinforcers.

Six categories of reinforcers were established on the basis of extensive observation. These categories were: privacy, leave from the ward, social interactions with the staff, devotional opportunities, recreational opportunities, and items from the hospital canteen. "Privacy," for example, included such freedoms as choice of bedroom or of eating group, and getting a personal cabinet, a room-divider screen, or other means of preserving autonomy. "Recreational opportunities" included exclusive use of a radio or television set, attending movies and dances, and similar entertainments.

TABLE 9-3
MEAN TOKENS EXCHANGED FOR VARIOUS AVAILABLE
REINFORCERS (BY 8 PATIENTS DURING 42 DAYS)

Reinforcers	Mean Tokens Paid	Number of Patients Paying Any Tokens
Privacy	1352.25	8
Commissary items	969.62	8
Leave from ward	616.37	8
Social interaction with staff	3.75	3
Recreational opportunities	2.37	5
Devotional opportunities	.62	3

SOURCE: Based on Ayllon and Azrin (1965).

The patients could obtain each of the reinforcers with a specific number of tokens, and they earned these tokens by participating in such rehabilitative functions as self-care and job training. A sensitive index of the subjective reinforcement value of the available activities is obtained by considering the outcomes for which the patients later chose to exchange most of their tokens. Over 42 days the mean tokens exchanged by eight patients for the available reinforcers are shown in Table 9-3. Note that chances to interact socially with the staff and opportunity for recreation and spiritual devotion are most unpopular. These data on reinforcement value suggest that, with chronic hospitalized patients such as these, therapy programs that rely primarily on social motivations would not fare well, and that such reinforcers as privacy, autonomy, and freedom might be the most effective incentives.

Reinforcement, Rewards, or Incentives?

Students sometimes wonder if "reinforcement" is just jargon for terms like "reward" or "incentive." The terms do overlap in meaning, but some behavior theorists prefer "reinforcement" to "reward" for an important reason. Many events that look as if they should be "rewards" in common sense terms may turn out to have little effect on the behavior of a particular person. Thus such "rewards" as praise and verbal approval may mean nothing to a delinquent teen-ager, just as monetary rewards may have little impact on the behavior of a young child and rewards like "attention from others" may actually be aversive to a schizophrenic patient. Moreover, in some cultures and under some conditions people work hard to be allowed to eat insects, or to whip themselves until they bleed, and have to be restrained physically not to cut and torture themselves. Such painful activities hardly seem to be "rewarding." Consequently, some psychologists prefer the term "reinforcement" for the particular events—whatever they happen to be—that come to strengthen behavior under particular conditions. "Reinforcement" is defined empirically by its effects rather than by its intrinsic qualities. This empirical approach to reinforcement avoids invoking motives and thus deliberately prevents psychologists from confusing their desires with those of the people they are studying. However, the empirical definition of reinforcement leaves many theoretical questions unanswered.

Moreover, a large number of conditions may influence what events will and will not be effective reinforcers for a particular individual at any given time. These moderating conditions include the person's age, sex, culture, reference group, prior experience—in short, the total developmental and learning history and the details of the particular situation at the moment. The meaning of any incentive or potential reinforcing stimulus, and hence its impact on the individual, depends on many moderating conditions—such as its context. For example, the value of a reinforcer depends on its *relation* to other stimuli. Suppose, for example, that while you are admiring the attractive treats on display in the window of a food store, a poor old man stumbles by and becomes sick in front of the store window. This sight would at least momentarily affect the subjective value for you of the food on display.

The incentive value or potential reinforcement value of an event (the food in this example) depends on the total context and not just on the item by itself. Ice cream with a cockroach crawling nearby on the table does not have the same value as ice cream in a pleasant setting. It is arbitrary to separate a single stimulus from other important features of the situation, and research supports the idea that the relations and contrasts among potential reinforcers influence the impact they have on behavior (e.g., Reynolds, 1961). In practice we never can know a person's total experiences relevant to any stimulus. Hence it becomes difficult to predict the acquired meaning of specific stimuli for an individual unless we actually sample and observe her behavior directly. Unless we know the meaning of a stimulus for the particular individual her behavior may seem mysterious.

Assessing the Conditions
Controlling Behavior

To assess behavior fully, behavior theorists believe that we have to identify the conditions that control it. But how do we know whether or not a response pattern is really controlled or caused by a particular set of conditions? Behaviorally oriented psychologists test the conditions by introducing a change and observing whether or not it produces the expected modification in behavior.

They ask: Does a systematic change in stimulus conditions (a "treatment") in fact change the particular response pattern that it supposedly controls? If we hypothesize that a child's reading problem is caused by poor vision, we would expect appropriate treatment (such as corrective eye glasses or corrective surgery) to be followed by a change in the behavior (that is, an improvement in reading). The same should be true for psychological causes. For example, if we believe that the child's reading difficulty is caused by an emotional problem in her relation to her mother, we should try to show that the appropriate change in that relationship will yield the expected improvement in reading. That is, to understand behavior fully we need to know the conditions that cause it. We can be most confident that we understand those conditions when we can show that a change in them yields the predicted change in the response pattern.

A rigid distinction between behavior assessment and treatment (i.e., behavior change) thus is neither meaningful nor possible. Indeed, some of the most important innovations in behavior assessment have grown out of therapeutic efforts to modify problematic behavior (discussed in the next chapter). A main characteristic of these assessment methods is that they are linked closely to behavior change and cannot really be separated from it.

Functional Analyses

The close connection between behavior assessment and behavior change is most evident in "functional analyses"—that is, analyses of the precise covariations between changes in stimulus conditions and changes in a selected behavior pattern. Such functional analyses are the foundations of behavior assessments, and they are illustrated most clearly in studies that try to change behavior systematically. The basic steps may be seen in a study that was designed to help a girl in nursery school (Allen et al., 1964).

Ann was a bright four-year-old from an upper-middle-class background who increasingly isolated herself from children in her nursery school. At the same time she developed various ingenious techniques to gain prolonged attention from the adults around her. She successfully coerced attention from her teachers, who found her many mental and physical skills highly attractive. Gradually, however, her efforts to maintain adult attention led her to become extremely isolated from other children.

Soon Ann was isolating herself most of the time from other youngsters. This seemed to be happening because most of the attention that adults were giving her was contingent, quite unintentionally, upon behaviors that were incompatible with Ann's relating to other children. Precisely those activities that led Ann away from play with her own peers were being unwittingly reinforced by the attention that her teachers showered on her. The more distressing and problematic Ann's behavior became, the more it elicited interest and close attention from her deeply concerned teachers.

Obviously Ann was slipping into a vicious cycle that had to be interrupted. Consequently a therapeutic plan was formed according to which Ann would no longer receive adult attention for her isolate behavior and her attempts at solitary interactions with adults. At the same time the adults gave her attention only when she played with other children. That is, attention from adults became contingent on her playing with her peers.

As part of the assessment, two observers continuously sampled and recorded Ann's proximity to and interactions with adults and children in school at regular 10-second intervals. The therapeutic plan was instituted after five days of base-line data had been recorded. Now whenever Ann started to interact with children an adult quickly attended to her, rewarding her participation in the group's play activities. Even approximations to social play, such as standing or playing near another child, were followed promptly by attention from a teacher. This attention was designed to further encourage Ann's interactions with other children. For example: "You three girls have a cozy house. Here are some more cups, Ann, for your tea party." Whenever Ann began to leave the group or attempted to make solitary contacts with adults, the teachers stopped attending to her.

Figure 9-3 summarizes the effects of the change in the consequences to Ann for isolate behavior with her peers. Notice that in the base-line period before the new response-reinforcement contingencies were instituted Ann was spending only about 10 percent of her school time interacting with other children and 40 percent with adults. For about half the time she was altogether solitary. As soon as the contingencies were changed and adults attended to Ann only when she was near children, her behavior changed quickly in accord with the new contingencies. When adult-child interactions were no longer followed by attention, they quickly diminished to less than 20 percent. On the first day of this new arrangement (day 6), Ann spent almost 60 percent of her time with peers.

To assess the effects of reinforcement more precisely, the procedures were reversed on days 12 to 16. Adults again rewarded Ann with their attention for interacting with them and disregarded her interactions with children. Under these conditions (the "reversal" days in Figure 9-3), Ann's previous behavior reappeared immediately. In a final shift (beginning on day 17), in which attention from adults again became contingent upon Ann's interacting with children, her contact with peers increased to about 60 percent. After the end of the special reinforcement procedures (day 25), periodic postchecks indicated that Ann's increased play behavior with peers tended to remain fairly stable.

A similar type of functional analysis was conducted by Bijou (1965). In this case, a mother had many problems with her six-year-old son, whom she described as extremely overdemanding. The mother first was oriented to the procedures and data collection techniques of the researchers, and the general assessment strategy was formulated and discussed. The mother and son next were asked to play in a playroom as they normally would at home. After receiving the family's consent, observers monitored and recorded these interactions from an adjacent observation room.

FIGURE 9-3
Percentages of Time Spent by Ann in Social Interaction during Approximately Two Hours of Each Morning Session

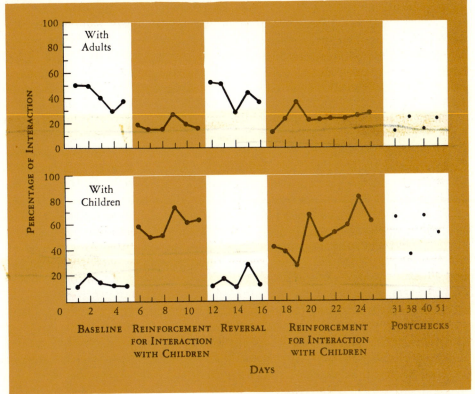

From E. K. Allen, B. Hart, J. S. Buell, F. R. Harris and M. M. Wolf. Effects of social reinforcement on isolate behavior of a nursery school child. *Child Development,* copyright 1964 by the Society for Research in Child Development, Inc., *35,* No. 2, 310.

The mother's verbal and nonverbal immediate reactions to each of her child's behaviors were recorded with great care. For example, "excessive demandingness" was defined, in part, as verbal demands by the child to the mother, like "You go there and I'll stay here!" or "No, that's wrong! Do it this way." These behaviors were observed directly in the interaction between mother and child in the play room. After each instance of demanding behavior from the child, the mother's immediate reactions were scored. These data provided information about the maternal behaviors that might be reinforcing and maintaining the child's demandingness with her.

The assessors then tested experimentally whether or not the mother's observed responses to the child's demands were really maintaining his behavior.

In this period the mother was counseled to try different reactions to the child's inappropriate behaviors, such as ignoring them totally. She was simultaneously helped to explore experimentally some new reactions to the child's more adaptive, prosocial behaviors (like cooperative play) that would help to strengthen these new behaviors. The subsequent interactions were again observed, assessed, and progressively modified as necessary to increasingly achieve the selected therapeutic goals. Thus personality assessment and behavior change become inextricably fused: The assessments guide the therapeutic program, and the efficacy of the treatment program is in turn continuously assessed.

The same basic designs and concepts have been extended to assess and modify important interpersonal behaviors within the home. In these studies, at the parents' request, the problematic parent-child relationship is observed directly in the home. When distressing interpersonal dilemmas are found, the parent is helped to change his behavior toward the child. These changes are designed, practiced, and assessed in everyday home situations in ways that ultimately lead to a more satisfying relationship (e.g., Hawkins and his colleagues, 1966; Rekers & Lovaas, 1974; Wahler and his collaborators, 1965).

A final example of functional analysis comes from a series of studies (Lovaas, Freitag, Gold, & Kassorla, 1965a) assessing the conditions controlling self-destructive behavior in a psychotic nine-year-old girl. This child was extensively and severely self-destructive, tormenting herself violently. Her tragic repertoire included banging her head and arms and pinching and slapping herself repeatedly. Her intensely maladaptive behaviors dated back at least to her third year of life, and currently she engaged in almost no appropriate social activities. Her self-destructive tortures included sticking her head in an electric wall heater, thus setting her hair on fire. She spent much time in repetitive and stereotyped physical self-stimulation, and her interactions with others were minimal.

To explore the possible conditions controlling the child's self-destructiveness, the investigators studied how changes in selected variables affected the child's objectively measured self-destructive behavior. These assessments were made over a period of many sessions. One of the most important parts of the study investigated systematically any changes in the girl's self-destructive behavior following withdrawal of reinforcement (in the form of attention) for previously rewarded behavior.

The assessments revealed that her self-destructiveness seemed to increase most when attention was withdrawn from response patterns for which she previously had been reinforced. Thus the withdrawal of attention (reinforcement) from a previously reinforced response appeared to be the critical stimulus for the girl's self-destructive behavior. In accord with learning theory, the assessors interpreted their results as indicating that in the child's past her self-destructive behavior had led to the reinstatement of attention whenever people had started to withdraw attention from a response pattern they had previously reinforced. Put most simply, this means that whenever her previously reinforced responses began to be unattended by others (extinguished), the girl could consistently reinstate the reinforcement (attention) by hurting herself.

The pain connected with being burned (or the anxiety connected with warnings about the dangers of fire) serves to deter most children from burning themselves, playing with matches, and injuring themselves. But that is not the whole picture. While hurting oneself is painful, it sometimes may be the only way to obtain such valued outcomes as parental attention. Experimenting with matches and stoves may be dangerous and potentially painful, but it also attracts mother's interest quickly. Thus the same stimulus that supplies pain can also lead to positive consequences and hence may serve to support seemingly bizarre behaviors—such as self-destructive acts. A complete analysis must deal with all the acquired meanings of a stimulus for the individual—not just the normative ones.

A complete analysis also must consider the total relations among stimulus conditions rather than focus on single aspects of reinforcement in isolation. These assessments showed, for example, that this child was highly discriminating in the very particular times and circumstances during which she became self-destructive. For example, massive withdrawal of attention—as when the experimenter withheld attention from an entire session—did not affect her self-destructive behavior. In contrast, the removal of smiles and attention only for previously reinforced responses led to radical changes in her behavior.

The same principles and methods illustrated in this section have been applied to assess a large variety of normal and deviant behaviors in settings that include the home, the school, and the hospital (Goldfried & Sprafkin, 1974).

Experimental Treatments with Groups

The preceding section gave examples of the experimental analysis of behavior in the single case. Such analyses are especially valuable in clinical applications. For most research purposes, however, the majority of personality psychologists prefer to study many people rather than isolated individuals, hoping to obtain more general results. A basic experimental procedure is followed for that purpose. First, the behaviorally oriented personality psychologist selects a problem, choosing the variables whose effects she wants to understand.

In clinical settings the person's difficulties dictate what has to be assessed. In research, however, the problem, and hence the behaviors to be studied, may be dictated by the experimenter's theory and interests. If one is interested in the effects of success and failure on cheating, for example, she might want to devise a very competitive achievement situation in which children would be led to think either that they are doing well or that they are failing. She could later observe how these manipulations influenced how much each child cheated in a standardized "temptation" situation in which attainment of a valuable prize required the subject to violate the rules.

Usually the investigator studies the effects of one variable at a time. The essence of the procedure is to select groups of subjects who are comparable in all respects and who receive the same treatments with the critical exception of the one variable the investigator wants to test. For example, in one method adopted in personality research with children, the youngster bowls in a realistic miniature "electronic" bowling alley in which his bowling scores are illuminated automatically on a display panel after each trial. The apparatus is designed so that his "scores" can be programmed by the experimenter in a way that seems realistic though it is actually independent of the child's performance. The scores the child actually receives depend, of course, upon the condition to which he is assigned, so that variables like "success" and "failure" can be systematically manipulated over many trials.

In addition to manipulating performance through feedback, such a method also permits one to study in other, separate experiments, many different social and interpersonal conditions. Examples are the effect of achievements ostensibly obtained by peer or adult models, and the social evaluation processes by which the subject compares his performance with that of others. These and many other variables can be selected, one at a time, and their effects can be assessed.

An Illustrative Experiment

To illustrate more concretely, in one study with the bowling game children were randomly assigned into one of three conditions: "success," "failure," and a "control" condition in which they neither succeeded nor failed. Success and failure were manipulated by supplying the children with different norms for interpreting the relative quality of their bowling achievements, while the actual scores they received were identical (Mischel, Coates, & Raskoff, 1968). In the *success* condition, the child was told at the outset, "From our previous testing we've found that boys [girls] of your age should be able to score about 10 on this game; any score above 10 is a very good score, and any score below 10 is a poor score." These children later received "good scores" often during 60 turns on the bowling task. In the *failure* condition, each subject was told that "boys [girls] of your age should be able to score about 30 on this game; any score above 30 is a very good score, and any score below 30 is a poor score." Thus, these youngsters were led to expect that an average of at least 30 was needed to do well, but they actually averaged only 20 and they received "good scores" very rarely during their 60 bowling trials.

In the *control* condition the children did not receive scores for their bowling performance. The score lights never went on, and the game was left unplugged. Subjects were told, "We haven't set up the scoring part of the game yet; we're still just working on the runway and the ball return mechanism." It was emphasized that no skill was involved, and that the child was bowling only to provide information about how adequately the machine functioned. These children were exposed to the same apparatus and procedures as the others, but without experiencing either success or failure.

Thus children in all groups presumably received comparable treatment except for the success-failure manipulation. The effects of manipulating this one variable on their behavior during and after the game could then be assessed systematically by comparing children in the three groups. For example, one class of subsequent behavior might be the children's estimates of their probable future performance on similar tasks. Or one might see how the children later rewarded their own performance (for example, by helping themselves to freely available candy treats in any amounts they wished to take). Various statistical procedures can then be used to determine whether observed differences between groups are reliable and meaningful. The actual findings from studies of this sort are discussed later (Chapter 18).

Of course, the experimental method is basic to all science and is in no sense restricted to research within the framework of behavioral psychology. Although behaviorally oriented researchers have tended to favor experimental methodology, experimental techniques also are employed extensively in psychodynamic and trait-oriented research and are valuable parts of the methodology of all psychological approaches, as later chapters will show. The experimental method is included in the present chapter, however, because it is the very essence of the social behavior approach to assessment.

Adaptation and Deviance

Behavioral theories also influence how one thinks about adaptation and deviance, as this section shows.

Evaluating the Consequences of Behavior, Not the Person

In the behavioral approach one avoids evaluating the health, adequacy, or abnormality of the person or personality as a whole. Instead, when judgments must be made, they focus on evaluation of the individual's specific behaviors. Behaviors are evaluated on the basis of the kinds of consequences that they produce for the person who generates them and for other people who are affected by them. "Advantageous" (adaptive, constructive) behaviors are those whose consequences are judged to be favorable; conversely, "disadvantageous" (problematic, maladaptive, destructive) behaviors are those that yield negative effects.

Evaluations about the positive or negative consequences of behavior are social and ethical judgments that depend on the values and standards of the community that makes them. Advantageous behaviors are those judged to have positive personal and interpersonal consequences (e.g., helping people "feel good," or increasing constructive, creative outcomes) without any aversive impact on others. Behaviors that have negative, life-threatening, destruc-

Judgments about behavior depend on the values and standards of the community.

tive consequences, or those that endanger the full potentialities of the person or other people (e.g., debilitating fears, homicidal attempts), would be considered maladaptive.

The behavioral approach also implies a high value for the development of the individual's total competencies and skills so that he or she can maximize opportunities and options. Similarly, the person must be able to discern the important contingencies and rules of reinforcement in his or her life in order to maximize satisfactions and minimize aversive, disadvantageous outcomes. To be able to overcome unfavorable environments and life conditions, a high premium is also put on the development of effective strategies for self-control and for modifying the impact of the environment itself to make it more favorable.

Beyond these generalizations, the behavioral approach to deviance has sharply attacked the traditional "disease" models that view problematic (deviant, disadvantageous) behaviors as symptoms of an underlying mental illness, as discussed next.

Bases of "Disease Models"

Historically, with the growth of modern biology and medicine, disease explanations of abnormal behavior became especially favored. At the turn of this century the discovery and cure of a psychotic disorder stemming from syphilis ("general paresis") greatly reinforced the belief that deviant behavior might be a sign of organic disease. Similarly, more recent findings concerning biochemical and genetic antecedents in certain forms of mental deficiency bolstered the biological approach to psychological problems.

In the biological view, deviant behaviors are construed as symptoms of underlying organic pathology. Different types or patterns of deviant behavior (e.g., delusions, depression) presumably might be linked to different types of pathology (e.g., brain infections, tumors), just as different symptoms of physical disease may be attributed to particular underlying organic causes. As noted previously (Chapter 7), research continues in the search for organic causes of psychological problems, but at present most difficulties in social behavior appear to be "functional" (nonorganic). Nevertheless, the disease view is still widely used as an *analogy* for conceptualizing psychological problems even when no physical disease has been implicated. In this quasi-disease approach the person is seen as a "patient" whose deviant behaviors are considered "symptoms" of underlying *mental* or emotional pathology comparable to a physical disease like influenza or cancer. The patient's disturbed behavior is not the focus of interest because it is seen as merely symptomatic of underlying pathology, as was illustrated in the psychodynamic approach to problematic behaviors.

Criticism of the Disease Model

Behaviorally oriented critics argue that while the disease model may be appropriate for the analysis and treatment of physical illness in medicine, it is not useful for conceptualizing psychological problems (e.g., Bandura, 1969; Krasner & Ullmann, 1973). When there are no identified discrete organic causes (like germs) that can be tied clearly to social behavior, speculations about hypothesized pathology cannot help the troubled person. On the contrary, conceptualizing behavior in terms of diseases whose properties and physiological bases are not established can divert the assessor from the psychological and life conditions that influence the maladaptive behavior. The disease model may also lead to an unfortunate emphasis on psychiatric hospitalization, rather than on new learning experiences in life settings and on social education (e.g., Hobbs, 1966).

Szasz (1960) has been a foremost critic of the "disease approach" to psychological problems. He believes that to speak of "mental illness" as if it were a disease-like sickness is to subscribe to a myth. He contends that the so-called sick person has problems of living and is not a victim of "demons, witches, fate, or mental illness" (Szasz, 1960, p. 118). The term "mental illness" may have had some value initially in that it permitted troubled and unusual individuals to be considered "sick" rather than morally reprehensible. But while shielding the individual from social criticism, the concept of mental illness also divests him of the privileges and human rights that are part of responsibility. Szasz maintains that the hospitalized, legally committed mental patient in fact loses his basic freedoms and is victimized by society rather than by a disease.

Moreover, the widespread practice of construing the whole person as either "sick" or "healthy" is often unjust, because a person may function perfectly well in many aspects of her life and be incompetent or deficient only in some domains. In fact, most "mentally ill" individuals are capable of much adequate and responsible behavior and show impairments that are relatively specific rather than generalized (Fairweather, Sanders, Cressler, & Maynard, 1969). Therefore many therapists bemoan the "common tendency to classify people as either sick or well, even though a person's social status *should* primarily be determined by her ability to assume particular rights and duties" (Fairweather et al., 1969, p. 18).

These criticisms of the disease model do not deny the possibility that future research may reveal distinctive pathology, genetic patterns, or brain or hormonal problems correlated with at least some patterns of deviant behavior that now are considered to be of psychological origin. In spite of these reservations, however, the limitations of the disease model for understanding and treating most behavior problems are being increasingly recognized. As Peterson (1968, p. 5), for example put it: "A child who strangles kittens or spits at his mother does not have a disease although he does have something that somebody judges to be a problem." Beyond these theoretical criticisms, the utility of the psychiatric disease approach depends in part on how well expert judges can agree about the type of mental disease that an individual may have and, as we have seen (Chapter 7), there is little agreement about specific diagnostic classifications.

In Defense of the Disease Model

Anthropologists often have noted that what seems normal in one culture may seem strange or abnormal in another. However, a close analysis of deviance in other cultures yields some surprising results. For example, the Eskimos on an Alaskan island and Yoruba group in Nigeria both have a word which translates as "insanity" (Murphy, 1976): They use this word for a pattern of conduct such as hearing voices, talking to oneself, and having outbreaks of violence—a pattern very close to the Western definition of schizophrenia. People who consistently show such a pattern are considered ill in both cultures. As the anthropologist who studied them noted, both the Eskimos and the Yorubas use the labels for insanity to:

> . . . refer to beliefs, feelings, and actions that are thought to emanate from the mind or inner state of an individual and to be essentially beyond his control; the afflicted persons seek the aid of healers; the afflictions bear strong resemblance to what we call schizophrenia. Of signal importance is the fact that the labels of insanity refer not to single specific attributes but to a pattern of several interlinked phenomena. Al-

most everywhere a pattern composed of hallucinations, delusions, disorientations, and behavioral aberrations appears to identify the idea of "losing one's mind," even though the content of these manifestations is colored by cultural beliefs (Murphy, 1976, p. 1027).

Results like these, plus evidence for the role of genes in these types of behavior (e.g., Kety et al., 1975) suggest that at least some forms of behavior involve more than specific violations of particular disturbance. Such results imply that at least some problematic patterns of behavior may turn out to have a "disease-like" aspect.

Deviance as Problematic Behavior

Even severe critics of the disease model generally recognize that at least some patterns of behavior may exist in many cultures or even everywhere. But they still insist that the vast bulk of human problems reflect unfortunate social learning environmental supports. They therefore focus their attention on the disadvantageous behaviors themselves. Rather than viewing maladaptive patterns as merely symptoms or signs of underlying diseases or dynamics, this view rejects the symptom-disease distinction and concentrates on the individual's problematic behaviors. For example, rather than interpreting an individual's fear of snakes as possibly symbolic of unconscious sexual conflicts, the behavior therapist deals with the snake phobia itself and attempts to treat it in its own right. Thus in the behavioral approach the focus shifts from hypothesized but unobservable physical or mental disorders in the person to problematic behaviors. The focus on behavior was illustrated in the assessment of Gary in this chapter. Rather than infer Gary's traits and motives, or try to reconstruct his history, the troublesome behaviors (e.g., anxiety related to public speaking) were identified so that they could be modified directly.

The social behavior orientation to deviance usually assumes a fundamental *continuity between normal and abnormal behavior* (e.g., Bandura 1977; Kanfer & Phillips, 1970; Ullmann & Krasner, 1969). This orientation, rather than attributing deviance to distinct pathology or basically different conditions, sees it as governed by the same laws that might (under other specific circumstances) lead to adequate or even creative behavior. That is, normal and abnormal behavior are not viewed as distinctly separate entities; instead, all behavior—regardless of its social value—is analyzed in the same terms. For example, observational learning processes are basically the same regardless of whether a child's parental models are criminals or pillars of social virtue. The behaviors the child learns will be different in these two cases but the learning principles will be the same. Similarly, reinforcement principles presumably are the same regardless of whether incompetent behaviors or creative ones are reinforced. Thus disadvantageous interpersonal behaviors and deviance may result from inadequate or inappropriate social learning in regard to any (or all) aspects of personality development (Part III of this book). Examples of disadvantageous behaviors include antisocial reactions to frustration, excessive avoidance patterns in the face of stress and threat, unduly severe self-evaluations, and negative self-concepts. Belief in the continuity of normal and abnormal behavior also implies that the same basic strategies may be used to understand and study disadvantageous behaviors and more normative behaviors, as was evident in the last chapter.

Moreover, the emphasis of the behavioral orientation on the specificity of behavior implies that an individual may engage in deviant or disadvantageous behaviors only under some conditions and not under others. A boy may be hyperaggressive at school but not at home, failing in schoolwork but excelling in sports, popular with boys but terrified of girls. Gary may be anxious about public speaking but quite calm when facing sports competitions and even when climbing hazardous mountain peaks. In the behavioral orientation, therefore, one refrains from characterizing the person as normal or deviant, and concentrates instead on a delineation of specific problematic behaviors and the situations in which they occur.

Finally, in the social behavior orientation attention is devoted to the *current,* immediate causes of behaviors rather than to their historical development in early childhood. This focus on current causes implies a belief that behavior change techniques can be used to modify problems regardless of their historical beginnings in the individual's past. Regardless of *why* Gary developed public speaking anxiety, behavior therapists want to modify the fears that trouble him now.

SUMMARY

1. Although there are various behavioral approaches to personality, their methods have in common the careful measurement of behavior in relation to specific stimulus conditions. Behavioral observation is common to all psychological approaches: It is the use that is made of the data obtained that distinguishes between approaches. In the psychodynamic orientation behaviors serve as indirect *signs* of hypothesized underlying dispositions and motives. Behavioral approaches treat observed behavior as a *sample,* and the focus is on how the specific sample is affected by variations in the stimulus conditions.

2. Analysis of the case of Gary W. illustrates the behavioral assessment of anxiety: Rather than attempting to make statements concerning underlying motives and conflicts, the search is for how changes in stimulus conditions produce changes in the response patterns of interest.

3. Ways in which behavior may be measured directly include situational behavior sampling, both verbal and nonverbal, and the physiological measurement of emotional reactions. In behavior sampling, the emphasis is on detailed information concerning the onset, magnitude, and duration of the behaviors of interest and the circumstances of their occurrence. The subject may supply this information through various self-report techniques such as daily records, lists of problematic situations, or responses on preset survey scales (schedules). Polygraphic measurement of bodily changes includes indices of heart rate, changes in blood volume and blood pressure, changes in muscular activity and in sweat gland activity. Brain waves also provide clues about changes in activity level. Telemetry makes possible the sampling of bodily changes outside the laboratory under real-life conditions.

4. The correlations found among these different response measures often are not very high and tend to be complex. A notable exception is the strong link between self-efficacy expectations and relevant behavior.

5. The assessment of the reinforcing value of stimuli may be made from an individual's choices in life-like situations, verbal preferences and ratings, or the observed effects of various stimuli on actual behavior. In clinical work it may be especially important to discover rewards that are effective for the individual concerned. Sometimes the usual reinforcers are not effective and new ones must be sought to facilitate therapeutic progress.

6. Functional analyses, the foundations of behavior assessments, are illustrated by studies of single cases. Careful observation of the behavior in question as it naturally occurs suggests what specific conditions maintain this behavior. Then systematic changes are made in those conditions until the problem behavior no longer occurs and more satisfying behaviors are substituted.

7. In research using experimental groups the researcher selects and manipulates a variable. To assess the effects of this variable, he or she compares groups that receive identical treatments except for the one variable that the experimenter manipulates. Statistical techniques help to determine whether the differences found between the groups as a result of the experimental treatment are reliable and meaningful.

8. Behaviorally oriented approaches to adaptation and deviance propose an alternative to both psychiatric diseases and inferred psychodynamics. They suggest, instead, a focus directly on the behaviors themselves and on what the person does rather than his or her hypothesized underlying mental diseases or dynamics.

CHAPTER 10

Cognitive Restriction p 269
Albert Ellis = Rational Emotive therapy

Densitization 248
Observational learning 249
Conditioned Aversion 249
Contingency Contracting 256
Therapeutic Communities 256

BEHAVIORAL THEORIES: APPLICATIONS (II)

Banduras p 261 self efficacy
Jourard p 265

Wolpe p 243
Hawkins p 253
Logass p 254
Fairweather p 258

Drug Induced -259
Medication -301

Behavioral theories 3 of Reasons

The most important applications of behavioral approaches have been their innovations for producing change. Traditional approaches to personality change, as noted in Chapter 8 emphasized insight, awareness, and the acceptance of feelings. In recent years social behavior theories (Chapter 4) have been leading to new methods of behavior change based on specific learning experiences. These learning forms of therapy have three main common features. First, they attempt to modify the problematic behavior itself; therefore they are called "behavior therapies." Second, like the social behavior theories and assessments that guide them, behavior therapies emphasize the individual's current behaviors rather than the historical origins of his or her problems. Third, most behavior therapists assume that disadvantageous or "deviant" behavior can be understood and changed by the same learning principles that govern normal behavior.

Traditionally it has been customary to sharply distinguish normal personality psychology from the study of abnormal personality and to consider these two topics separately. Recently this distinction is becoming blurred. Behavior therapists are trying to show that they can use the same psychological principles to modify all sorts of human problems, regardless of the specific type of problem or its severity. Indeed they prefer to treat severely disturbed human behaviors—such as longstanding, bizarre difficulties that have been highly resistant to other forms of treatment—to demonstrate the potency of their methods and of the principles that guide them.

Behavior therapies are having an increasingly important impact not only on techniques for treating disturbed people but also on theories about the basic nature of personality and its modification. The methods and findings of behavior therapy are posing major challenges to traditional concepts about normal and abnormal personality and the conditions necessary for personality change in highly disturbed, as well as in more adaptive, people.

Behavior Therapy: Basic Strategies

In this section we will consider some of the main techniques and findings of behavior therapy based on the concepts of learning theories. Thereafter we shall examine some of the implications for theorizing about personality.

Desensitization

Learning principles for therapeutic behavior change have been available for more than 50 years, but until recently they were only rarely applied because most therapists were afraid that "symptom substitution" would occur. It was widely believed that the removal of problematic behaviors would be followed by other symptoms that might be even more severely debilitating than the original ones. Joseph Wolpe, a psychiatrist who became skeptical about psychoanalytic theory, took the risk of attempting direct behavior modification with many of his patients. In 1958 he published a book describing a method of "systematic desensitization" based on the principle of classical conditioning.

Wolpe was impressed by the work of such early learning theorists as Pavlov and believed that neurosis involves maladaptive learned habits, especially anxiety (fear) responses. In neurotic behavior, he hypothesized, anxiety has become the conditioned response to stimuli that are not anxiety-provoking for other people. He reasoned that therapy might help the neurotic individual to inhibit anxiety by *counterconditioning* him to make a competing (antagonistic) response to anxiety-eliciting stimuli. In his words, "If a response antagonistic to anxiety can be made to occur in the presence of anxiety-evoking stimuli so that it is accompanied by a complete or partial suppression of the anxiety responses, the bond between these stimuli and the anxiety response will be weakened" (Wolpe, 1958, p. 71). His attempt to desensitize the individual to anxiety-evoking stimuli includes three steps.

1. *Establishing the anxiety stimulus hierarchy.* First the situations that evoke distressing emotional arousal and avoidance are identified by means of a detailed assessment usually conducted through interviews. Sometimes a person has many areas of anxiety, such as fear of failure, self-doubts, dating, guilt about sex, and so on. Regardless of how many areas or "themes" there are,

TABLE 10-1 ITEMS OF DIFFERENT SEVERITY FROM FOUR ANXIETY HIERARCHIES*				
Severity *(Degree of* *Anxiety)*	*Anxiety Hierarchies (Themes)*			
	1 *Interpersonal* *Rejection*	2 *Guilt about* *Work*	3 *Test-Taking*	4 *Expressing* *Anger*
Low	Thinking about calling Mary (a new girlfriend) tonight	Thinking "I still haven't answered all my mail"	Getting the reading list for the course	Watching strangers quarrel in street
Intermediate	Asking for a date on the telephone	Taking off an hour for lunch	Studying at my desk the night before the final	My brother shouts at his best friend
High	Trying a first kiss	Going to a movie instead of working	Sitting in the examination room waiting for the test to be handed out	Saying "No! I don't want to!" to mother

* These items are examples from much longer hierarchies.

each is treated separately. For each theme the person grades or ranks the component stimuli on a hierarchy of severity ranging from the most to the least intensely anxiety-provoking events (see Table 10-1). For example, a person who is terrified of public speaking might consider "reading about speeches while alone in my room" a mildly anxiety-provoking stimulus while "walking up before the audience to present the speech" might create severe anxiety in him (e.g., Paul, 1966). In Gary's case, "the minute before starting a formal speech" was the most anxiety provoking, while "watching a friend practice a speech" and "taking notes in the library for a speech" were only moderately disturbing. As another example, a woman who sought treatment for sexual frigidity indicated that "being kissed on cheeks and forehead" evoked merely mild anxiety but thinking about items like "having intercourse in the nude while sitting on husband's lap" produced the most intense anxiety in her (Lazarus, 1963).

2. *Training the incompatible response (relaxation)*. After identifying and grading the stimuli that evoke anxiety it is necessary to provide the person with responses that can be used later to inhibit anxiety. Many responses (such

as eating and assertive sexual activity) are incompatible with anxiety. Wolpe therefore prefers to use relaxation responses because they can be taught easily and are always inherently incompatible with anxiety: No one can be relaxed and anxious simultaneously. The therapist helps the client to learn to relax by elaborate instructions that teach first to tense and then to relax parts of the body (arms, shoulders, neck, head) until gradually an almost hypnotic state of total calm and deep muscle relaxation is achieved. Most people can learn how to relax within a few sessions. The critical problem is to learn to relax to anxiety-evoking stimuli, and that task is attempted in the next phase.

3. *Associating anxiety stimuli and incompatible responses.* In the critical phase, counterconditioning, the client is helped to relax deeply while presented with the *least* anxiety-arousing stimulus from the previously established hierarchy. The stimulus event usually is described verbally or presented symbolically (in a picture) while the client is deeply relaxed and calm. As the therapist says the words for the item the client tries to generate the most vivid image of it that his or her imagination can form. As soon as the client can concentrate on this item while remaining calm, the next, more severe item from the hierarchy is introduced until, step by step, the entire heirarchy is mastered.

If at any point in the procedure the client experiences a decrease in the relaxed state (becoming anxious) while presented with an anxiety stimulus, he or she signals the therapist. The client is promptly instructed to discontinue the image of the stimulus until he or she regains calmness. After the client is fully relaxed again, a somewhat less severe item from the hierarchy is presented so that he or she can concentrate on it without anxiety. When that has been done successfully the client is ready to advance to the next item in the anxiety hierarchy and the step-by-step progress up the list can be resumed.

In sum, the desensitization (counterconditioning) procedure attempts to make responses strongly antagonistic to anxiety (such as relaxation) occur in the presence of mildly anxiety-evoking stimuli, so that the incompatible response will at least partially prevent the anxiety response. Thus the association between the aversive stimulus and anxiety becomes reduced, while the association of the stimulus with the relaxation reaction becomes strengthened (e.g., Guthrie, 1935; Wolpe, 1958).

Desensitization has been used to modify diverse avoidance patterns and "neurotic" behaviors as well as specific fears. Wolpe (1963), for example, treated an adolescent boy who had a severe hand-washing compulsion. This boy often spent up to three-quarters of an hour in an elaborate ritual of cleaning his genitals after urination and then devoted up to two hours to washing his hands. Wolpe noted that the youngster's washing rituals were always precipitated by urination. Consequently, the boy was desensitized to stimulus hierarchies that dealt with urine and urination. Wolpe reported excellent and rapid progress under this regime. When urination no longer provoked anxiety, the boy abandoned his cleanliness ritual.

Clinical reports of successful desensitization may be encouraging, but they do not provide definitive proof that the clinical procedure, rather than other factors in the client's life, was responsible for the observed improvement. More conclusive evidence has come from controlled experiments. The findings from these studies generally indicate that desensitization is a valuable method for modifying phobias and reducing anxiety (Kazdin & Wilson, 1980; Wilson & O'Leary, 1980).

One careful experiment, for example, studied the efficacy of desensitization for treating intense public-speaking anxieties (Paul, 1966). Students who had severe anxieties about speaking in public were assigned to one of four conditions. In one group they received Wolpe's desensitization treatment, learning to relax to progressively more threatening imagined situations connected with public speaking. Students in a second condition received brief traditional, insight-oriented psychotherapy from an expert clinician. In a third condition the students served as control subjects, obtaining only placebo "tranquilizers" and bogus training allegedly designed to help them "handle stress." Thus these subjects were given attention but received no specific treatment. In each of the above conditions the students had five contact hours over a six-week period for their treatments, so that all were given the same amount of time. A fourth group was used as a no-treatment control, taking a pre- and post-treatment assessment battery of tests but receiving no special treatment.

Before and after treatment all students were assessed by tests, ratings, and observations of their behavior. Public-speaking anxiety was measured through self-report, physiologically and behaviorally (by observations of actual public-speaking behavior under stress). As Figure 10-1 indicates, systematic desensitization was consistently the best treatment. Brief insight-oriented psychotherapy did not differ from attention-placebo, although people in both these conditions obtained greater anxiety reduction (on some measures) than did the untreated controls. On the physiological measures, only the desensitization group showed a significant reduction in anxiety when compared to the no-treatment controls. A follow-up on the test battery six weeks later, and another one two years later, found that improvement was maintained (Paul, 1966, 1967). There were no indications of "symptom substitution." On the contrary, students who had received the counterconditioning treatment in addition to becoming desensitized to public-speaking anxiety, also improved in overall college grades when compared to students in the other conditions (Paul & Shannon, 1966).

Observational Learning

Fears and other strong emotional reactions may be modified through observational learning. In one study, groups of preschool children who were intensely afraid of dogs observed a fearless peer model playing with one. The brave model displayed progressively bolder approach behavior to the dog while the fearful children watched from a safe distance (Bandura, Grusec, & Menlove, 1967). Over a series of eight brief sessions the model progressed from briefly

FIGURE 10-1
Mean Reduction in Anxiety (from Pretest to Posttest) in Each of Three Measures

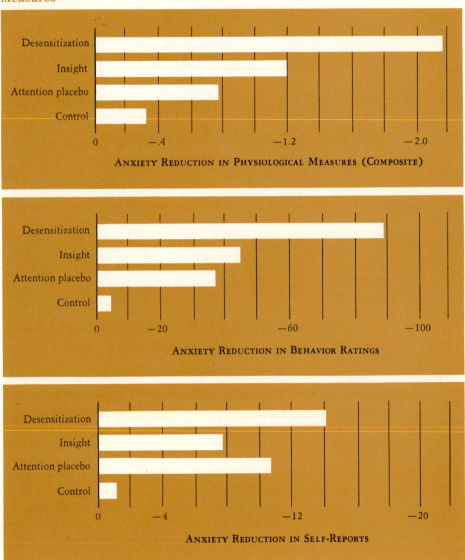

Adapted from Paul (1966).

petting the animal through the bars while the dog was locked in a playpen to ultimately joining him inside the playpen. In this last phase the child model played joyfully with the dog, hugging and feeding the animal wieners and milk from a baby bottle. Children who had watched the model showed much greater approach behavior to dogs when compared later to their peers in control groups.

FIGURE 10-2
Photographs of Children and Adults Modeling Progressively Bolder Interactions with a King Snake

From Bandura, Blanchard, and Ritter (1969).

In behavior therapy, snake fears have received much attention because of the symbolic sexual significance attributed to them by psychoanalytic theory (Brill, 1949). If such phobias are symbolic of an underlying psychodynamic problem (as is postulated by psychoanalytic theory), then a genuine cure of the phobia cannot be achieved without first modifying the unconscious conflicts supposedly symbolized by the phobic symptom. Many behavior therapists have tried to eliminate these phobias directly without any exploration of their possible unconscious meanings and historical etiology to see whether or not they can obtain enduring improvement (e.g., Lang & Lazovick, 1963). The success of such direct methods would contradict predictions of psychoanalytic theorists and would be of considerable theoretical and practical significance.

In a comprehensive experiment Bandura, Blanchard, and Ritter (1969) studied how various treatment combinations affect severe fear of snakes in adult volunteers. These intensely phobic subjects were assigned randomly to groups that received either systematic desensitization, symbolic modeling in the form of a film, or live modeling with guided participation. In addition, some were assigned to a nontreated control group. The systematic desensitization treatment was the standard Wolpe procedure. In the symbolic modeling treatment, subjects observed a film of children, adolescents, and adults engaging in progressively more threatening contact with a snake. This film began by showing the fearless models handling plastic snakes and progressed through scenes in which the models touched and held a large king snake and let it crawl freely over them (Figure 10-2). Subjects in this treatment were also taught to relax throughout the period of exposure. Moreover, they were able to regulate the film presentation so that if they became anxious they could stop the film and reverse it back to an earlier, less threatening point until they were able to reinduce relaxation and gradually master the next scene.

Finally, in the "live modeling with guided participation group" the fearful subjects first safely observed live models interacting boldly with the snake behind an observation window. Then the model handled the snake fearlessly in front of the subject and gradually led the subject into touching, stroking, and then holding the snake's midsection, first with gloved and then bare hands, as he continued to hold the snake firmly by the head and tail. Progress throughout was paced according to the individual subject's apprehensiveness and proceeded step by step, calmly, until each one was able to perform all the tasks with the snake.

Before and after completion of their respective treatments, the volunteers in all groups were tested for the strength of their fear and avoidance of snakes. They also completed an extensive fear inventory. Some of the main results are shown in Figures 10-3 and 10-4. Of the three methods, modeling with guided participation was most powerful; it produced virtually complete removal of phobic behavior in every subject.

Conditioned Aversion

So far we have discussed how stimuli that evoke negative emotional reactions (such as anxiety) can be neutralized. While some people suffer because they have learned to react negatively to certain stimuli, others are plagued because they become pleasurably aroused by stimuli that most people in the culture find neutral or even aversive. One example of this problem is homosexual attraction; another is fetishistic behavior, in which the person may become sexually excited by such objects as undergarments. In these cases, things that are neutral or even disgusting for most people have acquired the power to produce pleasurable emotional arousal. While such reactions may provide the person with some immediate pleasure, they often are severely disadvantageous in their long-term consequences for him. They may, for example, provoke severe guilt and negative self-reactions, as well as scorn and punishment from others, and therefore treatment is needed if the person desires change.

A positively valued stimulus may be neutralized by counterconditioning if it is presented contiguously with stimuli that evoke extremely unpleasant reactions. Gradually, as a result of repeated pairings, the previously positive stimulus acquires some of the aversive emotional properties evoked by the noxious events with which it has been associated.

FIGURE 10-3

Effects of Modeling and Desensitizations on the Development of Approach Responses to Previously Feared Stimuli

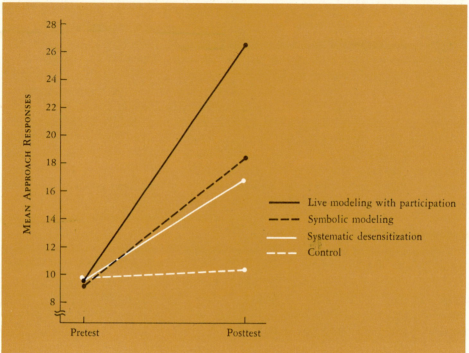

Mean number of approach responses performed by subjects before and after receiving their respective treatments. (From Bandura, Blanchard, & Ritter, 1969.)

Consider, for example, helping a man who wants to rid himself of homosexual feelings. In conditioned aversion treatment he might be exposed repeatedly to mildly pleasurable homoerotic stimuli (such as photos of attractive men) paired with intensely negative reactions such as drug-induced nausea or pain from self-administered electric shock. Gradually the homoerotic stimuli should become neutralized or even aversive (e.g., Feldman & Werry, 1966).

One young man developed an intense attraction to girdles and became anxious unless he wore one throughout the day (Clark, 1963). His unusual fetish had many debilitating effects on other aspects of his life. For example, his relations with his wife suffered severely because he compulsively wore her undergarments; he also was unable to work without his fetishes. A careful assessment revealed that some of the main fetishistic objects that aroused him included stockings and girdles as well as photos of girdle wearers. To obtain help, the client voluntarily hospitalized himself. During a period of one week, drug-induced nausea was repeatedly paired with presentations of the fetishistic objects. He was encouraged to wear the undergarments and to contemplate

FIGURE 10-4
Reduction in Fear Levels after Modeling and Desensitization Treatments

Mean level of fear arousal associated with approach responses that subjects performed before treatment and the fear levels reported in the post treatment period for the same subset of approach responses. (*Pre* refers to the intensity of fear subjects experienced when each snake approach response was described to them, and *Dur* signifies the fear level they reported while actually performing the corresponding behavior. From Bandura, Blanchard, & Ritter, 1969.)

fetishistic pictures while he became increasingly sick from the medication. As his nausea developed, he also listened to a recording that he had made earlier on which he had described his fetishistic pleasures in elaborate detail. These treatments occurred about twice daily. Follow-up tests administered three weeks later, and again three months after therapy, indicated that the client was back at work "enjoying a normal sex life and symptom free" (Clark, 1963, p. 405). Similar techniques have been used to treat other fetishes (Raymond, 1956) and homosexuality (e.g., Freund, 1960).

Might such counterconditioning produce excessive generalization? For example, might counterconditioning a man who has a fetishistic attraction to women's undergarments cause him to lose not only his interest in the fetish but also in women? In one study (Gelder & Marks, 1969; Marks & Gelder, 1969), many fetishists and transvestites received electric shock while they engaged in their deviant acts either overtly or in imagination. For example, one transvestite was aversively counterconditioned to a series of items including panties, pajamas, and a slip—one item at a time. His excitement (measured by erectile responses) diminished only to the specifically counterconditioned items and did not generalize to untreated ones. Thus, after completion of the aversion therapy the client remained responsive to appropriate heterosexual stimuli (such as female nude photos), but his sexual arousal to the specific

FIGURE 10-5

Relation of Alcohol Abstinence to Number of Supplementary Conditioning Sessions

Based on Voegtlin et al. (1942).

deviant fetish was eliminated. Human learning often is highly discriminative: The effects of conditioning depend on the specific stimuli conditioned and do not necessarily entail massively generalized changes.

Systematic counterconditioning has also been attempted with other unfortunate addictions such as alcoholism. Bandura (1969) surveyed the findings of 15 studies reporting aversion therapy for alcoholics. The studies contained from 15 to more than 4000 people and used different types of aversive stimuli. After follow-up, which ranged from a few months to 10 years, the percentage of complete alcohol abstinence found ranged from 23 to 96 percent. The largest study (Lemere & Voegtlin, 1950) followed 4096 cases from 1 to 10 years and found 51 percent complete abstinence. The data from these studies suggest that the long-term efficacy of aversion therapy depends on many considerations, such as the options available to the client after removal of his addiction and his persistence in the treatment.

Given that an alcoholic individual has received aversion therapy for alcohol, will he or she soon revert to drinking again? Figure 10-5 suggests that the answer partly depends on whether or not the person seeks and obtains supplementary conditioning sessions. Note that those who returned for four or more supplementary conditioning trials achieved 100 percent abstinence in this study. Generally, voluntary participation and strong motivation to change seem to increase the success rate of aversion therapy. For example, aversion therapy helped self-referred homosexuals to achieve heterosexual orientations much more frequently than it did homosexuals who were reluctant to change but were coerced into therapy by relatives or legal authorities (Freund, 1960).

Psychologists often are reluctant to use treatments that inflict pain on a troubled person. However, it must be remembered that aversion therapies usually are attempted after other forms of help (such as interview therapies) have been tried unsuccessfully. In some cases aversion treatments have come as a last resort in lieu of more drastic treatments, such as long imprisonment or irreversible brain surgery (Raymond, 1956).

Aversion therapies usually are not imposed on the client: They are voluntary and the person submits to it with full knowledge and consent, except when legal authorities have charge of the case. Indeed it is this very dependence on the client's cooperation that limits the efficacy of the treatment. That is, after the initial counterconditioning trials the client often may revert to his or her fetish or to other deviant attractions without submitting voluntarily to further treatment. Since it becomes impractical to hospitalize him continuously or remove him from exposure to the problematic stimuli, he must learn to administer aversive stimulation to himself whenever necessary. For example, he may be taught to administer electric shock to himself from a small, portable, battery-operated apparatus concealed in his clothing, or to induce aversive thoughts or imagery whenever he experiences the mildest homosexual urges (or the slightest temptation to drink, in the case of alcoholics). Thus, counterconditioning procedures ultimately provide the individual with a form of *self*-control. Whether or not he continues to practice and seek this self-control is up to him. And whether or not he practices self-control determines how effectively his new behavior will be maintained.

Changing the Consequences of Behavior

Many psychologists have tried to modify maladaptive behaviors by changing the consequences to which those behaviors lead. Guided to a large extent by B. F. Skinner's ideas about learning (Chapter 4), they try to withdraw reinforcement for undesired behavior and to make attention, approval, or other reinforcement contingent on the occurrence of more appropriate, advantageous behavior. Their basic procedure (discussed in the previous chapter as it bears on assessment) is well illustrated in the work of Hawkins and his colleagues (1966).

Hawkins' case was Peter, a young child of low intelligence. Peter was brought to a clinic by his mother because he was "hyperactive" and "unmanageable." Because the problems seemed to involve the relations between Peter and his mother, he was assessed and treated directly in his home. His mother served as a therapist under the guidance of the professional workers.

A first task was to specify the problematic behaviors. Direct observations of Peter in the home revealed the following problems to be among the most common and disturbing ones:

1. biting his shirt or arm
2. sticking his tongue out
3. hitting and kicking himself, other people, or objects
4. using derogatory names
5. removing his clothing and threatening to remove it.

The frequency of these and similar behaviors was carefully recorded at 10-second intervals during one-hour observation sessions in the home. After the first assessments were completed, the mother was helped to recognize the occurrence of Peter's nine most objectionable behaviors. Whenever these occurred during subsequent one-hour sessions at home she was taught to respond to them with definite steps. These steps involved signaling to Peter when his behavior became disruptive and, if a verbal warning failed, isolating him briefly in a separate, locked "time out" room devoid of toys and other attractions. Release from the room (and reinstatement of play, attention, and nurturance) was contingent on Peter's terminating the tantrum and showing more reasonable, less destructive behavior. This arrangement was opposite to the one the mother may have inadvertently used in the past, when she became increasingly solicitous, concerned, and attentive (even if distressed) as Peter became increasingly wild. Subsequent assessment revealed that the new regime was effective in minimizing Peter's outbursts. While apparently helpful to Peter's development, however, the modification of his tantrums may have been just one step toward the more extensive help he needed.

In another case, a three-year-old girl developed "regressive" behaviors and reverted to crawling rather than walking. Naturally this regression resulted in serious problems for her and brought great concern from worried relatives. An analysis of her behavior suggested that her regressive, babyish actions were being fostered inadvertently and maintained by the attention they produced. Consequently the therapy tried to rearrange the response-reinforcement contingencies so that crawling and infantile acts were not rewarded by the attention of concerned adults. Attention and other reinforcers were made contingent on more adaptive and age-appropriate behaviors, such as jumping, running, and walking (Harris et al., 1964).

We saw this same general strategy in the case of the isolated nursery-school-child, Ann, discussed in the last chapter in the context of assessment. Recall that this strategy generally contains a series of clear stages (e.g., Bijou, 1965). Categories of problem behaviors are selected and the frequency with which they occur in a naturalistic context is recorded. Next, the assessor observes and records the reinforcing consequences that seem to maintain the behavior. Guided by this analysis, the therapist arranges for new and more advantageous response-reinforcement relations to substitute for the naturally occurring observed ones. He then repeatedly assesses the resulting changes.

For example, Lovaas (1967; Lovaas et al., 1965a) attempted to modify the speech of psychotic children. These children made bizarre word combinations and often simply echoed the words they heard. In the treatment sessions Lovaas reinforced appropriate verbal behavior (with verbal approval and sweets) and ignored psychotic talk. Figure 10-6 shows the frequency of a child's psychotic verbal and nonpsychotic verbal behavior at selected points during a series of sessions. In each session the child's speech was recorded as "psychotic" when it was senseless or odd ("spaghetti Irene," "helicopter pillow") but was scored "appropriate" when it was contextually meaningful ("I

FIGURE 10-6
Effect of Reinforcing Appropriate Verbal Responses on the Frequency of Appropriate and Psychotic Verbal Behavior in a Child

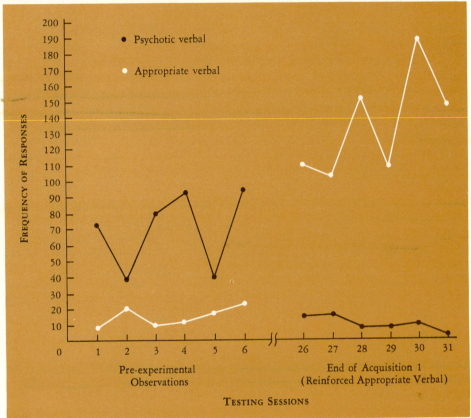

Adapted from Lovaas (1967).

want a cookie," or "Let's clean up" at the end of the session). Figure 10-6 shows frequency of the two types of verbal behavior in the first six pretherapeutic, observational sessions and in the last six sessions of an acquisition (learning) series in which reinforcement was contingent on appropriate verbal behavior.

Using a combination of modeling and reinforcement procedures, Lovaas and his co-workers (1966) also modified the deficient speech and social behaviors of severely disturbed ("autistic") children who were unable to talk. First the therapist modeled the sounds himself. He rewarded the child only for vocalizing the modeled sounds within a specified time interval. As the child's proficiency increased the therapist proceeded to utter more complicated verbal units so that gradually training progressed from sounds to words and phrases. As the training continued, rewards from the therapist became contingent on the child's reproducing increasingly more elaborate verbalizations more skill-fully (i.e., more quickly and accurately). The combination of modeling and re-inforcement procedures gradually helped the child to learn more complex meanings and complicated speech.

People often are deemed maladjusted mainly because they have not learned how to perform the behavior patterns necessary to effectively meet the social or vocational demands they encounter. They cannot behave appropriately because they lack the skills required for successful functioning. For example, the socially deprived, economically underprivileged person may suffer because he or she never has acquired the response patterns and competencies needed to obtain success and avoid failure in school and in vocational and interper-sonal situations. Similarly, the high school dropout in our culture does indeed carry an enduring handicap. Behavioral inadequacies, if widespread, may lead to many other problems, including severe emotional distress and avoidance patterns to escape the unhappy consequences of failure and incompetence. Using reinforcement principles, many special learning programs have been de-signed to teach people a variety of problem-solving strategies and cognitive skills (e.g., Bijou, 1965), to improve classroom learning (Birnbrauer et al., 1965), to help rehabilitate psychotic children (Ferster & DeMyer, 1961), to as-sist families to cope with serious conduct disorders displayed by their children (Patterson, 1974), and to help achieve many other changes in behavior (Karoly, 1980).

Contingency Contracting

A move to enroll the person actively in his or her own behavior change pro-gram whenever possible is reflected in the increasing use of "contingency con-tracting" (e.g., Rimm & Masters, 1974; Thoresen & Mahoney, 1974). An exam-ple was the treatment of "Miss X" for drug abuse as described by Boudin (1972). Miss X, a heavy user of amphetamines, made a contingency contract with her therapist. She gave him $500 (all of her money) in ten signed checks of $50 each and committed him to send a check to the Ku Klux Klan (her least favorite organization) whenever she violated any step in a series of mutu-ally agreed upon specific actions for curbing her drug use. After applying the contract for 3 months, a follow-up for a 2-year period indicated that Miss X did not return to amphetamine use. The principle of contingency contracting can be extended to a wide variety of commitments in which the client explic-itly authorizes the therapist to use rewards and punishments to encourage more advantageous behaviors in ways formally agreed upon in advance.

Therapeutic Communities (Motivating Environments)

There also have been efforts to modify the behavior problems of groups of peo-ple by altering the reinforcement they get in their environment. Much of this work has been conducted with hospitalized adult patients diagnosed as chronic schizophrenics (e.g., Atthowe & Krasner, 1968; Ayllon & Azrin, 1965; Fairweather, 1964, 1967). Many of the patients treated in these studies were hospitalized in the first place because of severe behavioral inadequacies. Moreover, their initial inadequacy and dependency problems usually became much worse as a result of the mental hospital regime in which they lived. The hospital routine tends to "institutionalize" the patient, discouraging individuality and fostering dependency by removal of privacy, fixed daily routines for eating, medication, and cleaning, and reinforcement (by privileges and praise) for passive, docile conformity. After being institutionalized for many years under such a regime, patients tend to become progressively more deficient in interpersonal and vocational skills, and increasingly dependent upon the hospital. With passing years they lose whatever contacts with family and relatives they may have had in the "outside world," and their prospects of ever achieving a life beyond the institutional shelter approach zero. Here is one comment on the typical plight of the long-term mental hospital patient:

> The great majority of patients still remain untreated. Recent statistics indicate that the median age of state mental hospital patients is approximately 65 years. This means that half of all patients in state mental hospitals are at such an advanced age that vocational opportunities are almost totally lacking and family ties have usually been broken. Even if there were nothing wrong with them, it would be difficult to discharge them into the outside world, since the outside world has no place for them. The longer these patients remain in the mental hospital, the more severe their behavioral problems seem to grow. One currently hears the phrases "hospitalism" and "institutionalization," which describe a state of apathy and lack of motivation that is acquired by a stay at a mental hospital. The hospital community is usually geared to providing the biological necessities of life, and perhaps some minimal level of recreational opportunities, but the overall relationship is a parasitic dependency in which the patient need not function in order to obtain most, if not all, of the activities or privileges that might still be of interest to him (Ayllon & Azrin, 1968, p. 3).

To help overcome this grim situation, new programs with these patients are attempting to increase their independence and to help them achieve more adequate self-care and autonomy by creating a more appropriately motivating environment. Reinforcement is made contingent on their becoming more independent, first in the simplest functions, such as grooming and self-feeding and then, gradually, in more complex and interpersonal domains such as work and social relations.

In one hospital ward long-term psychotic patients received tokens similar to money when they participated in therapeutic activities (Ayllon & Azrin, 1965). For engaging in such functions as self-care, productive work, and rehabilitative jobs, both on and off the ward, the patients received tokens that

FIGURE 10-7

Total Number of Hours of On-Ward Rehabilitative Performance by a Group of 44 Patients

From Ayllon and Azrin (1965). For related research see T. Ayllon and N. Azrin, *The Token Economy.* New York: Appleton-Century-Crofts, 1968.

they could exchange for what they desired from a large array of alternatives (Chapter 9). It was found that the patients worked successfully at their rehabilitation jobs when the attainment of tokens depended on it. If receipt of the desired tokens was not made contingent upon adaptive behaviors, the patients quickly resumed their more usual, psychotic hospital behavior. The dependence of the patient's prosocial behavior upon contingent reinforcement is illustrated in Figure 10-7.

Some recent behavior change programs minimize the role of the professional therapeutic agent as a controller of the client's behaviors and, instead, try to transfer responsibility to the client and his or her peer group as rapidly as feasible. An outstanding example is the therapeutic community designed by Fairweather to rehabilitate chronic psychotics who had been hospitalized for years. This program tried to move long-term schizophrenics out of the hospital and into a specially designed patient lodge located in the larger community as rapidly as possible. Fairweather recognized that many psychotic patients who have undergone more than two years of hospitalization become "marginal men" who continue to remain in the hospital and, if discharged, are returned to the hospital within a few months (Fairweather, 1964). Therefore he tried to develop small social systems that could function in the community itself and provide these chronic psychotics with a greater measure of autonomy. He tried to organize this social system so that the members would regulate and discipline each other and share all responsibility for the step-by-step progress of their community.

To start, a group of patients were organized in the hospital and lived and worked together in a special ward. The patients were given the greatest autonomy possible over their own behavior throughout the program. They had to make increasingly complex and difficult decisions about their collective behavior, beginning with the simplest functions (e.g., self-care, dressing). The entire group was held responsible for the behavior of all its members at each stage of the program and advanced through a carefully graded series of steps; each new step required new responsibilities but also provided more privileges (e.g., weekend passes). Reinforcement (progress to the next step) was always contingent upon success at the earlier, prerequisite step.

Soon the group moved from the hospital to the lodge, and after a month there they began to function as a basically independent, self-sufficient organization. For example, they organized and maintained a commercial and residential janitorial and yard service employing their own members, took care of their own records, arranged their transportation, and assumed responsibility for their own living, working, and health arrangements. Consultants to the lodge were gradually replaced by nonprofessional volunteers and then slowly were withdrawn completely. In time the patients themselves fully assumed such responsible roles as nurse and work manager. Within three years all external help was withdrawn, and the ex-patients then remained together freely as an autonomous, self-sufficient group in the community (Fairweather 1967; Fairweather et al., 1969).

It would be naive to think that the lodge program quickly transformed these schizophrenics who had been hospitalized for years into totally new individuals. It did, however, provide a degree of competent and self-sufficient functioning to a group that previously had been considered virtually hopeless and had been utterly dependent on caretakers in a hospital, and it did so at a cost in professional time and money that was vastly cheaper than confining the patients to the custodial care of the hospital. Ex-patients living in the lodge remained in the community much longer, and were employed much more steadily, than matched patients in control groups, who were simply released from the hospital (Fairweather et al., 1969). The average cost of the community lodge was less than $5 daily, while the daily cost of hospitalizing these individuals tends to be from about three to ten times as great. The value in terms of improvement in the quality of the patients' lives outside the hospital obviously is incalculable.

Behavior Therapy: Complications

So far we have discussed examples of some of the main behavior change strategies. In clinical practice, their applications often become more complicated.

Converting the Global to the Specific

Broad Motives

Behavior therapists usually have treated specific, clearly definable behaviors, such as concrete fears, fetishes, speech problems, sexual handicaps, and motivational deficits. Many people, however, suffer from much more diffuse problems that are not as easily delineated. A person may complain, for example, of an "identity crisis," "feeling miserable," "wasting my life," or may even say "I hate my personality" or "I am lost—I just don't know what's wrong." People tend to conceptualize themselves in broad trait terms rather than in behavioral descriptions. When a person begins to describe herself she may say "I am too timid" or "I am an introvert"; she probably will not say "My heart rate seems to increase sharply and I feel dizzy and start to stutter when I have to address a group of strangers in a new situation, especially in a social setting." Thus while in some cases the treatment objectives are self-evident (as when a person is terrified of birds), in most cases it is not so easy to specify just what requires treatment and the particular behaviors that should be the goals of treatment.

In these cases the client describes her problems and objectives in vague terms with broad, global labels. The clinician's task then must be to help her elaborate and examine what she means in behavioral terms (e.g., Mischel, 1968). This may be done by written reports such as diary records, by direct discussion, or by asking the person to perform in specially structured situations in which the stimulus conditions are deliberately and systematically varied, as in an experiment.

If a person describes himself as, for example, "depressed," the clinician can explore with him just when he feels depression and when he does not. To specify examples or behavioral referents for depression, the clinician inquires into just what happens when the client feels more depressed and less depressed and the changes that occur in him and in his behavior when he experiences the depression. For example, the clinician might ask, "How do you know when you are depressed?" The purpose of these probes is to obtain behavioral examples for subjective experiences, not to validate or invalidate the truth or falsity of the client's phenomenology. The goal here is the discovery of the behaviors that are problematic for him and the conditions governing them.

Similarly, role-play situations may be used in which the meaning of the complaint is explored thoroughly. Suppose a client complains of not being sufficiently "aggressive and assertive." To understand what she means by that construct the assessor could ask her to indicate when she feels insufficiently "aggressive and assertive." Suppose she mentions "when I first meet a new person." The assessor then might suggest a role play and take the part of a person who is just being introduced to the client. In this role situation the client then has to respond as she would in real life. Afterward the roles may be reversed and explored further. These procedures should help to clarify the construct "aggressive-assertive" and to see its relations to the client's behavior. The role plays can be quite specific—for example, first meeting with a potential employer, asking an attractive man for a date, or having to criticize a "subordinate" at work.

An adequate assessment should make it possible to convert global problems into behavioral terms. On closer analysis, one young man's "existential neurosis," for example, translated in part to such tangibles as his current academic failures at school, his inadequate acceptance by peers in social relations, his frustrations due to the recent breakup of his engagement, and his indecision about vocational objectives. Each of these problems was treatable, and their improvement increased his sense of well-being.

Combining Learning Principles

In contemporary applications, behavior therapists generally combine diverse learning methods, rather than favoring only one. For example, to train highly passive persons to become more assertive there have been ingenious combinations of behavioral rehearsal, modeling, and coaching (e.g., McFall & Twentyman, 1973). Innovative treatment strategies also have been developed for social action programs and educational problems in the classroom (e.g., O'Leary & Kent, 1973), and combinations of modeling and direct reinforcement tactics have been devised for the treatment of severely disturbed (autistic) children (Lovaas et al., 1967) and for reducing cross-sex behavior (Rekers & Lovaas, 1974). In a similar vein, a number of learning-based methods have been synthesized in a step-by-step program of arousing experiences designed to increase sexual responsivity in nonorgasmic women (LoPicolo & Lobitz, 1972). The use of learning principles is also evident in the well-publicized program of Masters and Johnson (1970) for the treatment of sexual inadequacy in both sexes. The hallmark of all these programs is that they search for the most effective combinations of treatments possible and do not confine themselves to a single method, while still adhering to the general orientation of the behavioral approach.

Self-Efficacy

Although many different techniques may all produce changes in behavior, might they all work through the same basic mechanism? Bandura (1978) has proposed that there is such a common mechanism: people's expectations of personal *efficacy* or *"self-efficacy."* Self-efficacy is the belief that one can personally master a particular behavior (i.e., that one can undertake and perform a necessary action). Behavior therapy works, according to Bandura, by increasing efficacy expectations and thus leading people to believe that they can cope with the difficult situations that previously threatened them. In this view, individuals will try to overcome a particular fear to the extent that they expect they can do so successfully. Any methods that strengthen expectancies of personal efficacy (mastery) will therefore help the person. The best methods will be the ones that give the person the most direct, compelling success experiences, thereby increasing efficacy expectancies most. For example, actually climbing a fire escape successfully is a better way to overcome a fear of heights than just thinking about it because it provides a more complete success experience and a stronger expectation for future mastery.

A Caution

Behavior therapies have been criticized on many grounds, often justly, often foolishly. It has been noted, for example, that some therapies that are at best loosely connected with learning theory claim to be derived from it, that the actual practice of behavior therapy may include many uncontrolled and unreported factors, and that learning theory itself often may be inadequate to deal with complex life phenomena (Breger & McGaugh, 1965). Moreover, the efficacy—and limitations—of particular forms of behavior modification for particular types of problems needs much more research (e.g., Eysenck & Beech, 1971). At present too many claims for the value of behavior change strategies still rest on case studies rather than on large scale comparisons among different methods. In addition to asking "does it work?" about each type of change strategy, one must ask "does it work better than other available alternatives?"

Critics of behavior therapies rightly note that the history of therapeutic efforts to achieve personality change is full of promising false starts and of movements whose claims and enthusiasms greatly exceeded their ultimate results. Even ardent proponents of behavior therapy now are starting to recognize that its adoption is not without danger:

There are hazards in the rapid growth of behavior therapies: that a premature orthodoxy may develop, that claims to scientific roots will not be translated into scientific appraisal and renovation, that a new generation of practitioners may be created whose lack of awareness of unresolved basic theoretical and empirical questions would create undeserved longevity for still another generation of ineffective techniques, that safeguards by society in the use of clinical behavior-control methods will not be sufficient to protect individual rights or to avoid premature social experimentation with unforeseen negative effects. However, the potential benefits, given sufficient critical evaluation and constructive research, are at least equally great (Phillips & Kanfer, 1969, p. 122).

Will a behaviorally oriented approach to the modification of complex behavior turn out to be just another false promise? Perhaps. But a behavioral orientation to personality change has one great advantage: It advances or stumbles as the science that nurtures it does. Thus its promise and its hazards are those of the science of social behavior rather than of any one person's convictions about what personality has to be or about what human nature really is.

Behavior Change and Personality Change

Critics recognize that behavior therapy may produce alterations in the individual's specific behavior, but they question the genuineness and "depth" of such behavior modification. Their doubts seem to center on several points.

Is There Transfer?

Will beneficial effects achieved in behavior therapy *transfer* or generalize to the life situations in which the person must actually function on his own? Will a timid person who has practiced more assertive behaviors in the safety of his therapist's office really become more masterful on his job? Will he become more confident with the headwaiter who snubs him? Will a person who has learned to think calmly about taking tests during desensitization in the therapist's office also become calm when he must actually take examinations?

Generalization is enhanced to the degree that the stimulus conditions sampled in treatment are similar to those in the life situation in which the new behaviors will be used. Therefore behavior therapists try to introduce into treatment situations that closely approximate the life situations in which behavior change is desired. For example, if a person can think calmly about public speaking but becomes debilitated when he tries it, treatment might teach him to speak calmly in public rather than to think about it in private. Similarly, if a person is able to take examinations effectively but devalues and derogates her own achievements, an appropriate treatment might help her to reevaluate her performance rather than to change her test-taking skills. In other words, treatment should be directed as closely and specifically as possible to the intended terminal behaviors or objectives.

Just like the social behavior theories that guide them, behavior therapies emphasize that a person's behavior tends to be specific to particular stimulus conditions. Therefore they try to obtain close congruity between what is practiced in therapy and the behavioral objectives desired in the person's life. Consider, for example, a client who wants to improve his relations with his wife. The behavior therapist probably would focus on movement toward specific objectives in the marriage, such as improvements in sexual techniques and better forms of communication and toward specific changes in the assignment of roles and responsibilities with regard to financial decisions, recreational choices, household chores. Much lower priority would be given to more global aspects of the client's attitudes toward women in general (e.g., his feelings toward his mother). In treatment those behaviors would be encouraged and practiced that would be most similar to the ones the client wants to achieve in his daily life.

The emphasis on specificity also dictates that treatment should sample as extensively as possible the relevant stimuli or situations in which improvement is desired. Effective desensitization for snake phobia, for example, would include exposing the client to many types of snakes in many contexts; practice in assertiveness would sample many types of relationships in which assertiveness is required; training for nonpsychotic speech in autistic children would sample many aspects of language in many speaking contexts.

To facilitate generalization many therapists also believe it is best if the treatment occurs in the relevant life setting rather than in an artificial one like a laboratory or a clinic. Therefore they are bringing their treatment services into the community rather than waiting for people to be brought to mental hospitals or other institutions. For example, just as academic learning programs for children are conducted in schools so may social learning programs for youngsters with interpersonal problems be located in the school system itself. Similarly, if parent-child relations are problematic, it may be better to have consultants observe and help to modify the problems where they occur—in the home—rather than transport the family to a clinic. Moreover, in these *in vivo* settings, teachers, the parents, friends, and other nonprofessionals may be enrolled to help in the treatment process (e.g., Patterson, 1974). To help a married couple, it may be more appropriate to work with their relationship directly, treating the couple together rather than each mate in isolation. There is a trend now to engage in the treatment process the people with whom the client has important daily relations, rather than rely on repeated contacts with clinics, hospitals, special agencies, and professional personnel (Hawkins et al., 1966). Similarly, group situations often are better than treating the individual alone, especially if improving relations with other people is one of the treatment objectives. For example, Paul and Shannon (1966) found that the group provided a setting in which anxious students could spontaneously and naturally extinguish many of their social fears through their own mutually supportive interactions.

Community centers, settlement houses and clubs, civic organizations, school systems, all provide opportunities for bringing behavior change programs to the community. Considering the magnitude of the need for help, the traditional model, in which one client speaks with one expert therapist in an office several times weekly, cannot be enough.

A concern with community-oriented action programs and with "preventive health" of course has not been limited to advocates of behavior modification. In recent years an increasing number of psychologists, guided by many different theoretical orientations, have noted that effective programs to deal with the enormous problems of people in our society will have to go beyond the "patching and healing" of psychologically wrecked individuals. Just as the individual's biological health, indeed survival, depends on the conditions around her, so does her psychological adaptation hinge on the living conditions of her personal environment. There is a psychological as well as a biological ecology, an intimate, continuous interplay of people and environment. A destructive psychological environment that submits people to excessive stress, insufficient gratification, confusing and conflicting demands, brutally chronic aggression, frustrating routines, can create havoc in human lives more quickly than any therapy can repair them. A satisfying life requires a satisfying environment. An adequate approach to psychological welfare will have to be concerned with prevention of problems before they become too difficult to handle, and with the construction of a psychological environment in which people can live without debilitatingly twisting themselves and each other.

Fear of Behavior Modification

It is often said that behavioral theories and their applications to behavior modification tend to dehumanize the person. In the popular media images abound of white-coated behaviorists trying to create a society of human robots who will be controlled like puppets by conditioning and other forms of "mind control." Such fears are shared even within the profession of psychology. As the humanistic psychologist, Sidney Jourard (1974, p. 20–21) put it:

> I have always been uneasy about the behavioristic approach to man, because it appeals to the power motive in the behavior scientist. Moreover, research in behaviorism is frequently funded by agencies interested in controlling the behavior and experience of others, not necessarily with their knowledge or consent nor always with the best interest of the controllees at heart.

In part these images and accusations may be encouraged by the jargon of overzealous "behavior modifiers" who sometimes seem eager to apply the language and methods of the animal laboratory to the human condition with little sensitivity to the differences and implications. The better applications of behavior theory, however, seem increasingly alert to ethical issues and committed to actively enrolling the "subject" of behavior changes both in the choice of objectives and in the voluntary implementation of the methods for achieving them. This movement seems especially apparent in the growing emphasis on *self*-control, rather than on external control, in the modification of disadvantageous behavior (e.g., Meichenbaum, 1977; Thoresen & Mahoney, 1974).

Toward Self-Management

Ideally, behavior change programs are designed to increase individuals' independence and competence as rapidly as possible so that external control of their behavior by the therapeutic regime can be reduced quickly and ultimately terminated. Many techniques can help to achieve that objective (e.g., Bandura, 1969; Kanfer, 1980). For example, although carefully dispensed external reinforcement (like tokens or praise) may be necessary at first to help a disturbed child learn to speak, read, and write, the satisfactions deriving from these new activities, once they begin to be mastered, should help him or her to maintain and develop them further, even when the therapist's help is gradually withdrawn. Similarly, while hospitalized psychiatric patients may require tokens to initiate more adaptive new behavior, such as rehabilitative work, ultimately the new behaviors themselves, if properly selected, should provide them with enough gratifying consequences so that they can maintain their new gains on their own. In other words, the new, more advantageous behaviors, which the person first practices to get "external" reinforcement, should be chosen to have reinforcing properties that gradually make them rewarding in their own right.

The foregoing examples entail the same phenomena we see in the gradual shift from external to internal control in the acquisition of new but difficult skills outside the therapeutic situation under the conditions of daily life. The young child who is learning to play the piano may at first be highly dependent on praise, attention, treats, and parental guidance to induce him or her to practice. However, to the extent that his learning program is structured effectively (by design or accident), his piano practice will be increasingly supported by the pleasure of the activity (e.g., the sounds he produces, and the satisfactions and "sense of competence" he starts to derive from playing). If the learning experience is successful, then in time the child "wants to play" and "loves

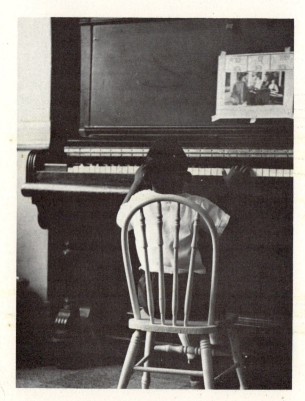

Gradually there may be a shift from performing for external rewards to performing for its own sake.

the piano." This transition, subjectively, seems to involve a shift from performing to please others to performing to please oneself, a transition from behavior for the sake of the "extrinsic" rewards it yields to behavior for "its own sake"—that is, for "intrinsic rewards." Depending on social learning conditions, the behavior that offers the intrinsic rewards for which people strive may range from painting miniatures to racing sports cars, from playing the flute to wrestling, from climbing rocks to yoga exercises, from lifting weights to gourmet cooking. Thus whether or not an activity becomes intrinsically rewarding may have less to do with the activity than with the manner in which it was learned and the conditions influencing its performance. Often in the course of socialization the conditions of learning inadvertently are poorly arranged. We see that fact in the frequency with which activities like piano practice or schoolwork become occasions for aversive family quarrels rather than for pleasure.

To achieve relatively durable change, one needs to carefully consider the steps in the transition from control of the new behavior by external agents to self-control:

After participants adopt new patterns of behavior on the basis of their utilitarian value, the next phase in the program may require direct training in self-reinforcement. This is achieved by gradually transferring evaluative and reinforcing functions from change agents to the individual himself. Rewards are now made contingent not only upon occurrence of desired behavior, but also accurate evaluation of one's own performances. Although at this stage the person judges when his behavior warrants reward according to the prevailing contingency structures, others still serve as the reinforcing agents. After accurate self-evaluative behavior is well established, the reinforcing function is likewise transferred so that the individual both evaluates his own behavior and reinforces himself accordingly. In addition, the artificial material rewards are gradually reduced as the person's behavior is brought increasingly under the control of self-administered and symbolic consequences. The ultimate aim of the training in self-reinforcement is to produce a level of functioning at which participants can control their own behavior with minimum external constraints and artificial inducements (Bandura, 1969, p. 620).

The transition summarized in the above paragraph may, in practice, take a long time to achieve successfully; often it remains incomplete. It would be wishful thinking to believe that we can attain major transformations in interpersonal behavior more rapidly than we can achieve competence in a musical instrument or in a sport. Moreover, just as skill at the piano depends on practice, so do new gains in social behavior depend upon the maintenance of appropriate environmental supports when the person tries out new repsonses. Favorable schedules of feedback and reinforcement from others for one's

TABLE 10-2
EXAMPLES OF COPING SELF-STATEMENTS

Preparing for a Stressor
  What is it I have to do?
  I can develop a plan to deal with it.
  Just think about what I can do about it. That's better than getting anxious.
  No negative self-statements, just think rationally.
  Don't worry. Worry won't help anything.
  Maybe what I think is anxiety is eagerness to confront it.

Confronting and Handling a Stressor
  I can meet this challenge.
  One step at a time; I can handle the situation.
  Don't think about fear—just about what I have to do. Stay relevant.
  This anxiety is what the doctor said I would feel. It's a reminder to use my coping
    exercises.
  This tenseness can be an ally, a cue to cope.
  Relax; I'm in control. Take a slow, deep breath. Ah, good.

Coping with the Feeling of Being Overwhelmed
  When fear comes, just pause.
  Keep focus on the present; what is it I have to do?
  Let me label my fear from 0 to 10 and watch it change.
  I was supposed to expect my fear to rise.
  Don't try to eliminate fear totally; just keep it manageable.
  I can convince myself to do it. I can reason my fear away.
  It will be over shortly.
  It's not the worst thing that can happen.
  Just think about something else.
  Do something that will prevent me from thinking about fear.
  Just describe what is around me. That way I won't think about worrying.

Reinforcing Self-Statements
  It worked; I was able to do it.
  Wait until I tell my therapist about this.
  It wasn't as bad as I expected.
  I made more out of the fear than it was worth.
  My damn ideas—that's the problem. When I control them, I control my fear.
  It's getting better each time I use the procedures.
  I'm really pleased with the progress I'm making.
  I did it!

SOURCE: From Meichenbaum and Cameron (1974).

newly acquired, more advantageous behaviors are essential to avoid extinction. If patients newly discharged from a mental hospital, or treated drug addicts, return to the same environment of stress and dissatisfaction that debilitated them in the first place, there is little hope that they will maintain any therapeutic gains for a long time. Treatments specifically designed to encourage self-management are starting to be developed (e.g., Homme, 1965; Kanfer, 1980; Thoresen & Mahoney, 1974); and they draw on the same basic concepts and methods discussed under "Self-control" in the context of normal personality development (Chapter 18).

Efforts to improve self-management and self-regulation directly, especially in excessively impulsive individuals, are providing many different promising methods. These techniques, based mainly on learning concepts, make it possible for people to achieve much more self-directed behavior. Some good results have been found in areas that range from studying to the control of weight, smoking, and crippling fears (Watson & Tharp, 1972). A favorite technique provides subjects with "controlling responses" that help them to resist the pressures of the situation and to pursue, instead, their more difficult but desired objectives. Controlling responses include various self-instructions designed to sustain the individual's continued work and effort even under difficult conditions (e.g., Kanfer & Zich, 1974; Meichenbaum & Goodman, 1971). For example, young children are helped to resist transgression if they are first given a verbalization (such as "I must not turn around and look at the toy") to repeat to themselves later when they are alone and faced by the temptation (Hartig & Kanfer, 1973). In the same vein, anxious college students may be helped to cope by learning and practicing calming, problem-solving self-instructions which they can verbalize to themselves when faced with stressful situations (e.g., Meichenbaum & Cameron, 1974). Examples of the kinds of coping statements clients are taught to make to themselves (first overtly, then silently) to handle stress and anxiety are shown in Table 10-2.

Cognitive Behavior Modification and Restructuring

Especially when dealing with problems of self-control, behavior therapists increasingly draw on cognitive methods. These cognitive methods include helping clients to talk to themselves differently (Meichenbaum, 1977), as in the examples just given, and other forms of mental problem solving (Goldfried & Goldfried, 1980). An important example is *cognitive restructuring*: ways to view problems differently by thinking about them more constructively and less irrationally. The most influential form of cognitive restructuring is Albert Ellis's (1962, 1977) Rational Emotive Therapy. This approach is based on the idea that irrational beliefs produce irrational behaviors. It follows that if people are taught to think more rationally their behavior will become less irrational and their emotional problems will be reduced.

Some very common irrational beliefs, according to Ellis, are the ones summarized in Table 10-3. These beliefs are irrational in the sense that they do

---

TABLE 10-3
WIDESPREAD IRRATIONAL BELIEFS

1. An adult human must be loved or approved by almost everyone.
2. In order to feel worthwhile, a person must be competent in all possible respects.
3. People who are bad, wicked, or villainous should be blamed and punished severely.
4. When things are not the way you want them to be it is a catastrophe.
5. People have little or no control over the external causes of the bad things that happen to them.
6. The best way to handle a dangerous or fear-producing event is to worry about it and dwell on it.
7. It is easier to avoid certain life difficulties and responsibilities than it is to face them.
8. One needs to depend on others and to rely on someone stronger than oneself.
9. One's present behavior is determined primarily by one's past history.
10. One should be upset by the problems of others.
11. There is always a perfect solution to a human problem, and it is essential to find it.

SOURCE: Based on Ellis, 1962.

---

not accurately represent the individual's real world. Reacting to situations on the basis of such irrational beliefs will produce ineffective behavior and such maladaptive emotions as anxiety and depression. Irrational beliefs may be revised by rational restructuring, as when a person who believes she must be loved by everybody rethinks this potentially debilitating attitude and realizes its impossibility.

Some evidence supports the value of rational emotive therapy. For instance, self-verbalizations (how one talks to oneself) can affect emotional arousal (e.g., Russell & Brandsma, 1974). Irrational self-statements do seem to be associated with maladaptive emotional reactions (e.g., Goldfried & Sobocinski, 1975) and many problem behaviors may be reduced by teaching clients to restructure (revise) their irrational self-statements. Some of Ellis's techniques and concepts are therefore now being used by many behavior therapists. While the approach seems promising, the relations between attitudes and actions are more complex than Ellis's theory suggests, and his position tends to oversimplify the complex and multiple determinants of behavior. Rational restructuring may help some people with some problems, but it is only one technique among many potentially fruitful alternatives. Its value still has to be tested, and the evidence to favor it so far is not yet convincing (Rachman & Wilson, 1980; Wilson & O'Leary, 1980).

Symptom Substitution?

It is sometimes suggested that behavior therapies neglect the causes of the person's problematic behavior and thus leave the "roots" unchanged while modifying only the "superficial" or "symptomatic" behaviors. This criticism implies that behavior therapists ignore the basic or underlying causes of problems. Advocates of behavior therapy insist that they do seek causes but that they search for *observable* causes controlling the current problem, not its historically distant antecedents nor its hypothesized but unobservable psychodynamic mechanisms. This search for observable variables and conditions controlling the behavior of interest was demonstrated most clearly in the functional analyses discussed in Chapter 9. Traditional, insight-oriented approaches have looked, instead, for historical roots in the person's past and for theoretical mechanisms in the form of psychodynamics. The difference between these two approaches thus is not that one looks for causes whereas the other does not: Both approaches search for causes but they disagree about what those causes really are.

> All analyses of behavior seek causes; the difference between social behavior and [psychodynamic] analyses is in whether current controlling causes or historically distant antecedents are invoked. Behavioral analyses seek the current variables and conditions controlling the behavior of interest. Traditional [psychodynamic] theories have looked, instead, for historical roots and developmental etiology (Mischel, 1968, p. 264).

Traditional approaches ask about their patient, "Why did she become this kind of person?" Behavioral approaches ask, "What is now causing her to behave as she does and what would have to be modified to change her behavior?" Does a neglect in treatment of the psychodynamics hypothesized by traditional therapies produce symptom substitution? In spite of many initial fears about possible symptom substitution, behavior change programs of the kind discussed in the preceding sections tend to be the most effective methods presently available; the changed behaviors are not automatically replaced by other problematic ones (e.g., Davison, 1968; Lang & Lazovik, 1963; Paul, 1966; Rachman, 1967). On the contrary, when people are liberated from debilitating emotional reactions and defensive avoidance patterns, they become able to function more effectively in other areas as well. After reviewing the relevant literature on symptom substitution, Grossberg (1964) notes that the overwhelming evidence is that therapy directed at elimination of maladaptive behavior is successful and the results are stable. In addition:

> Unfortunately, psychotherapists seem to have stressed the hypothetical dangers of only curing the symptoms, while ignoring the very real dangers of the harm that is done by not curing them (Grossberg, 1964, p. 83).

While fear of symptom substitution is no longer the deterrent to direct behavior modification it once appeared to be, many thorny theoretical and practical issues still remain. For example, the exact meaning of "symptom" often is not defined in theoretical discussions of symptom substitution, so that one is unsure about what might constitute a substituted symptom. How many weeks, months, or years might have to elapse before the substituted symptom can be expected to emerge? If the symptom is disguised in another form just how would we distinguish it from a problem that is wholly new? If a person whose snake phobia was removed develops problems at work or with his wife three years later, is he showing symptom substitution or new problems? In its extreme form the idea of symptom substitution may be untestable, because one cannot know what is a substituted symptom and what is a new problem.

On the other hand, some enthusiastic proponents of behavior modification overlook the complexity of the client's problems and may oversimplify the difficulties into one or two discrete phobias when in fact the client may have many other difficulties. In that case, it would not be surprising to find that even after removal of the initial problem the individual still is beset with such other psychological troubles as self-doubts, feelings of worthlessness, and so on. Such a condition of course would imply that the person had an incomplete treatment rather than that symptom substitution had occurred. It would be extremely naive to think that reducing Gary's public speaking anxiety, for example, would make his life free of all other problems. Whatever other difficulties he might have would still require attention in their own right.

People are especially likely to display additional disadvantageous behaviors if their treatment has consisted mainly of removing problematic behaviors without strengthening alternative adaptive patterns. Consider a former alcoholic who used to drink partly to reduce the aversiveness and frustrations that she continuously faced at work. She is likely either to drink again or to engage in other maladaptive avoidance efforts unless she also learns to cope more effectively with the stresses of her job. Or consider a child whose bizarre behaviors (hurting herself, aggressing against siblings) were maintained by the parental attention they provoked. Efforts to extinguish these maladaptive behaviors by withdrawing attention from them are unlikely to succeed in the long run unless the parents also give their child some attention when she engages in more desirable behaviors.

In sum, to avoid the emergence of disadvantageous behaviors, a comprehensive program must provide the person with more adaptive ways of achieving reinforcement; such a program may have to go beyond merely reducing the most obvious problems.

The previously noted specificity of behavior, and its dependence on the particular stimulus variables at work in each situation, also occurs in therapeutically induced behavioral changes. Behavior modification does not automatically produce generalized positive effects that remove all the person's troubles. But there is more evidence for positive generalization than there is for symptom substitution. For example, people whose phobias for snakes were removed by behavior change techniques also reported a reduction in the number and intensity of fears of other animals (Bandura, Blanchard, & Ritter, 1969). They showed more positive attitudes toward other animals and became less concerned about the possibility of being harmed physically.

Behavior Change and Self-Concept Change

Often we may expect that improvements in competence will be accompanied by appropriate changes in self-reactions. Self-concepts generally reflect the individual's actual competencies: Self-perceptions to a large extent reflect the information that we get about the adequacy of our own behaviors (Chapter 19). Thus the individual who learns to perform more competently and thereby achieves more gratification is also likely to develop more positive attitudes toward himself or herself. As a result of being able to overcome fears and anxieties one should also become more confident. Reducing Gary's fears of public speaking would not be a cure-all, but it might certainly help him to feel more positively about himself and would open alternatives (e.g., in his career opportunities) otherwise closed to him. But while this is often true, it does not always happen. Indeed critics of behavior therapy note that people may suffer not because their behavior is inadequate but because they evaluate it improperly. That is, some people have problems with distorted self-concepts more than with performance.

Behavior theorists consider such self-concept problems to be just as much behavior problems as any other difficulties; in these cases, the behaviors are self-evaluation and self-labeling. Often a person labels himself and reacts to his own behaviors very differently than do the people around him and the rest of society. A successful Mafia leader, for example, may experience few immediate aversive personal consequences although his activities lead to severe distress for others. On the other hand, an esteemed financier may receive the rewards and praise of society while he is privately unhappy enough to contemplate suicide. Or a popular college student who is the prom queen of her school might have secret doubts about her sexual adequacy and femininity and might be torturing herself with these fears.

Thus many human problems entail inappropriate self-evaluations and self-reactions. In these cases the difficulty often may be the person's appraisal of his or her performances and attributes rather than their actual quality and competence level. For example, a student may react self-punitively to his scholastic achievements even when their objective quality is high. The student who is badly upset with himself for an occasional "low A" may need help with self-assessment rather than with school work. From the viewpoint of behavior theory such problems should be amenable to modification by the same learning principles used to change any other type of behavior. In practice, however, behavior therapies still have paid relatively little attention to self-assessments; the mechanisms involved in both the growth and treatment of self-evaluative problems require much more research (Bandura, 1977).

Am I What I Do?

What happens when the conditions of reinforcement change stably in a person's life? What happens, for example, to the mother-dependent little boy when he finds that his school peers begin to have less tolerance for his "babyish" attention-getting bids and instead esteem assertiveness and self-confident independence? Usually the child's behavior will change in accord with the new contingencies. If the contingencies remain stable, so does the child's new pattern; if the contingencies shift, so does the behavior. Then what has happened to the child's dependency trait?

Many theorists, as we saw throughout Part I, would argue that the basic personality structure remains and that merely its overt manifestation has altered. But is this just a "symptom" change that does not really affect the personality structure that generated it and the psychological life space in which it occurs? Advocates of social behavior theory contend that to treat the person as truly active and dynamic, we must recognize that she changes as her behaviors do. A behavioral view sees behavior change in an individual not as a merely superficial overlay. Consistent with the existentialist view of human nature, behavior theory insists that to find out what a person *is* we need to know what she *does*; and if her actions change then so does she.

Behavior theorists emphasize that discontinuities—real ones and not merely superficial or trivial surface changes—are part of the genuine phenomena of personality (Mischel, 1973a). They believe that an adequate conceptualization of personality has to recognize that people change as the conditions of their lives change. In that view an adequate account of human personality must have as much room for human discrimination as for generalization, as much place for personality change as for stability, and as much concern for people's self-regulation as for their victimization by either enduring intrapsychic forces or by momentary environmental constraints.

SUMMARY

1. Behavior therapies attempt to modify disadvantageous behavior directly by planned relearning experiences and by rearranging stimulus conditions.

2. Systematic desensitization is used to help people overcome fears or anxieties. In this procedure, the individual is exposed cognitively (i.e., in imagination) to increasingly severe samples of aversive or fear-arousing stimuli; simultaneously she is helped to make responses incompatible with anxiety, such as muscle relaxation. Gradually the anxiety evoked by the aversive stimulus is reduced and the stimulus is neutralized.

3. Just as strong emotional reactions may be acquired by observing the reactions of models, so may they be modified by observing models who display more appropriate reactions. In addition to modeling fearless behavior, the model also may guide the phobic person directly to behave more bravely when faced with the anxiety-producing stimulus.

4. Inappropriate, disadvantageous positive emotional reactions to stimuli may be seen in fetishism and homosexuality. In these behaviors counterconditioning treatments may help the individual to overcome his deviant attractions. It is possible to neutralize a positive arousing stimulus (e.g., a fetishistic object) by repeatedly pairing it with one that is very aversive (e.g., shock). Periodic follow-up treatments help to sustain the new emotional reactions.

5. Maladaptive behaviors also may be modified by changing the consequences to which they lead. The basic procedure is to withdraw attention, approval, or other positive consequences from the maladaptive behavior and to make rewards contingent instead on the occurrence of more advantageous behavior. First the naturally occurring response-reinforcement contingencies are identified; then new and more advantageous response-reinforcement relations are instituted.

6. In some of the newest behavior change programs, responsibility is transferred as quickly as possible from the therapist to the client and his peer group. In one therapeutic community, chronic psychotics who had been hospitalized for many years were organized on a special ward. Their autonomy was gradually increased, and their rewards were made contingent on their increasingly responsible self-management as a group.

7. People often describe their problems and their objectives in broad terms so that it is difficult to specify the particular behaviors that need to be changed. In these cases a first step may be to help the client to elaborate his or her difficulties as precisely as possible in behavioral terms.

8. In everyday life, as well as in psychotherapy, several different forms of behavior therapy may occur simultaneously. Current behavior therapies often combine several learning strategies, such as modeling, desensitization, direct reward, rather than confining themselves to one.

9. There is much controversy with regard to the depth and endurance of behavior change. Some of the most important questions concern transfer of gains to life situations, the capacity of the individual for

self-control independent of the therapeutic regime, the possibility of symptom substitution, and the adequacy of behavior change techniques to deal with a person's self-concepts. Basically, these questions ask, does behavior change entail genuine, durable change—that is, basic personality change—or is it restricted to relatively minor, specific behaviors that have limited applicability to major life problems?

10. To facilitate transfer from treatment to life, one introduces into treatment stimulus conditions that are as similar as possible to the life situations in which the new behaviors will be used. In treatment one samples as extensively as possible the relevant stimuli or situations and tries to conduct the treatment in the same life setting in which improvement is desired.

11. By achieving greater competence and gratifications from his or her new, more adequate behaviors, the individual should become able to function increasingly without external reinforcement and support. New behavior change methods are being developed to encourage self-management so that the individual may gain relative independence and control of his or her own behavior as rapidly as possible.

12. Many learning programs directed at the elimination of maladaptive behaviors have shown promising results. The modified behaviors are not automatically replaced by other problematic ones, and there is more evidence for positive generalization than for symptom substitution, although the theoretical issues are complex.

13. Often people suffer because they evaluate their behavior improperly. Behavior theorists believe they can modify problems stemming from inappropriate self-assessments by the same learning principles used to change other types of maladaptive behavior.

14. Social behavior theories contend that people are what they do. Therefore behavior change is the prerequisite for any alteration in personality. In that view, there is no personality change apart from behavior change, although the behaviors involved often may be covert and subtle, as in thoughts and self-evaluations, and therefore difficult to measure.

CHAPTER 11

PHENOMENOLOGICAL THEORIES: APPLICATIONS

Semantic Differential

Maslow 293

Gestalt p 296

Kelly 275, 287

Assessing self 299

Q technique

Q sort 282

Rodgers 284, 294

Schutz 296

Aronson 297

The phenomenological orientation discussed in Chapter 5 has many significant applications for both personality assessment and change. As we saw, the main feature of the phenomenological orientation is its emphasis on the person's experience as he or she perceives it. In Kelly's phrase, if a man's private domain is ignored "it becomes necessary to explain him as an inert object wafted about in a public domain by external forces, or as a solitary datum sitting on its own continuum" (1955, p. 39). On the other hand, if different individuals are to be construed within the same general system of laws, then common denominators and higher levels of abstraction also must be discovered. To study the individual's experiences within the framework of scientific rules, methods have to be found to reach those private experiences and to bring them into the public domain.

People as Their Own Experts

Phenomenologists like Rogers and Kelly seek to go beyond introspection and to anchor their theories to objective and scientific methods. In Rogers' view, for example, the therapist enters the internal world of the client's perceptions not by introspection but by observation and inference (1947). A concern with objectivity is reflected in Rogers' extensive efforts to study persons empirically, and these efforts are what place his work in the domain of psychology rather than philosophy. The same concern with objective measurement of subjective experience has characterized Kelly's approach to assessment. This chapter considers some of the main efforts that have been made by phenomenologically oriented psychologists to study experience objectively and to provide strategies to facilitate personal growth and awareness.

Gary W.'s Self-Conceptualization

The starting point of phenomenological study begins with the person's own viewpoint. To approach that viewpoint one may begin with the individual's self-presentation, as expressed in the way he depicts and describes himself. Some of the raw data of phenomenology are illustrated in the following self-description recorded by Gary W. when he was asked to describe himself as a person.

Excerpts from Gary's Self-Description:

I'm twenty-five years old, and a college graduate. I'm in business school working toward an MBA.

I'm an introspective sort of person—not very outgoing. Not particularly good in social situations. Though I'm not a good leader and I wouldn't be a good politician, I'm shrewd enough that I'll be a good businessman. Right now I'm being considered for an important job that means a lot to me and I'm sweating it. I know the powers at the office have their doubts about me but I'm sure I could make it—I'm positive. I can think ahead and no one will take advantage of me. I know how to work toward a goal and stick with whatever I start to the end—bitter or not.

The only thing that really gets me is speaking in a large group. Talking in front of a lot of people. I don't know what it is, but sometimes I get so nervous and confused I literally can't talk! I feel my heart is going to thump itself to death. I guess I'm afraid that they're all criticizing me. Like they're almost *hoping* I'll get caught with my pants down. Maybe I shouldn't care so much what other people think of me—but it does get to me, and it hurts—and I wind up sweating buckets and with my foot in my mouth.

I'm pretty good with women, but I've never found one that I want to spend the rest of my life with. Meanwhile I'm enjoying the freewheelin' life. I hope someday to find a girl who is both attractive and level-headed. A girl who is warm and good but not dominating and who'll be faithful but still lead a life of her own. Not depend on me for every little thing.

My childhood was fairly typical middle-class, uptight. I have an older brother. We used to fight with each other a lot, you know, the way kids do. Now we're not so competitive. We've grown up and made peace with each other—maybe it's just an armistice, but I think it may be a real peace—if peace ever really exists. I guess it was his accident that was the turning point. He got pretty smashed up in a car crash and I guess I thought, "There but for the grace of God . . . ." I count a lot on being physically up to par.

Dad wasn't around much when we were growing up. He was having business troubles and worried a lot. He and mother seemed to get along in a low-key sort of way. But I guess there must have been some friction because they're splitting now—getting divorced. I guess it doesn't matter now—I mean my brother and I have been on our own for some time. Still, I feel sorry for my Dad—his life looks like a waste and he is a wreck. A walking tragedy.

My strengths are my persistence and my stamina and guts—you need them in this world. Shrewdness. My weaknesses are my feeling that when it comes to the crunch you can't really trust anybody or anything. You never know who's going to put you down or what accident of fate lies around the corner. You try and try—and in the end it's probably all in the cards.

Well, I guess that's about it. I mean, is there anything else you want to know?

Can People Assess Themselves Accurately?

How can we begin to interpret Gary's self-portrait? It is possible to proceed in terms of one's favorite theory, construing Gary's statements as reflections of his traits, or as signs of his dynamics, or as indicative of his social learning history, or as clues to the social forces that are molding him. But can one also make Gary's comments a bridge for understanding his private viewpoint, for glimpsing his own personality theory and for seeing his self-conceptions? Because each of us is intimately familiar with his own conscious, perceived reality, it may seem deceptively simple to reach out and see another person's subjective world. In fact, we of course cannot "crawl into another person's skin and peer out at the world through his eyes," but we can "start by making inferences based primarily upon what we see him doing rather than upon what we have seen other people doing" (Kelly, 1955, p. 42). That is, we can try to attend to him rather than to our stereotypes and theoretical constructs.

A most direct way to inquire about another person's experience is to ask him, just as Gary was asked, to depict himself. Virtually all approaches to personality have asked people for self-reports. In most orientations these reports have served primarily as cues from which to infer the individual's underlying personality structure and dynamics. Perhaps because of the assumption that people engage in extensive unconscious distortion, the subject's own reports generally have been used as a basis for the clinician (or the test) to generate inferences and predictions about him, rather than as a means of conveying the subject's view of himself.

Can people be "experts" about themselves? Can they assess themselves? Can their reports serve as reliable and valid indices of their behavior? For example, in his self-appraisal Gary predicts that he can succeed in the job for which he is being considered. Is this self-assessment accurate, or is it a defensive hope, or an opportunistic ploy, or a belated effort at self-persuasion?

Some studies have tried to examine whether people can assess and predict their own behavior adequately. If they cannot, then the value of phenomenological inquiries would be limited severely; if they can, then it may be not only interesting but also useful to listen to their self-assessments most seriously. To establish the utility of a person's direct report about himself, you must compare it with the predictions about him that can be made from other data sources. For example, you must compare the individual's self-reports with the statements drawn from sophisticated psychometric tests or from well-trained clinical judges who use such techniques as the interview and the projective test to infer the subject's attributes.

It has been a surprise for many psychologists to learn that simple self-reports may be as valid as, and sometimes better predictors than, more sophisticated, complex, and indirect tests designed to disclose underlying personality. Thus, Marks, Stauffacher, and Lyle (1963) tried to predict future adjustment for schizophrenic patients. They found that simple self-reports on attitude scales (like the California F Scale, discussed in Chapter 6) may yield better predictions than did psychometrically more sophisticated scales. Simple attitude statements (on the California F Scale) have also been one of the best predictors of success in the Peace Corps; they have been more accurate than far more costly personality inferences. Interviews and pooled global ratings from experts did not prove nearly as accurate as self-reports were (Mischel, 1965). Another study found that two extremely simple self-ratings (one on "adjustment" and one on "introversion-extraversion") may be as stable and useful as are inferences from factor scores based on sophisticated personality-rating schedules (Peterson, 1965). Three studies designed to test the same personality characteristics both by direct and indirect measures generally found the direct measures to be better (Scott & Johnson, 1972).

In another study the TAT stories of college students were scored for 10 "signs" of aggression (Lindzey & Tejessy, 1956). These signs were correlated with diverse criteria of aggression, including diagnostic council ratings based on observation and interview, scores on a projective picture frustration test, and self-ratings of aggressiveness. The self-ratings were associated with significantly more signs of aggression than were any of the other predictors. Similarly, students' self-rankings of achievement needs predicted their actual long-term achievements (grades) better than did experts who inferred the students' achievement motivation from the TAT (Holmes & Tyler, 1968).

Hostility, somatic concerns, achievement concerns, and religious concerns were studied by several methods in a sophisticated investigation (Wallace & Sechrest, 1963). The methods for measuring these traits included self-reports (in the form of self-descriptions), reputation rating by peers, projective techniques (incomplete sentences, Rorschach, and TAT), and behavioral indices such as scholastic average and number of visits to health services. The self-descriptions were as valid as any other source. Self-descriptions and peer ratings consistently gave better correlations than any other combination of methods.

Another study showed that individuals' self-ratings were the best predictors of peers' ratings of them (Hase & Goldberg, 1967). The self-ratings were better than the predictions based on *any* of several scales, including the best statistical equations based on the best scale combinations.

In still another study, the self-reports (on the MMPI) of psychiatric patients experiencing different crises (such as depression, anxiety, severe marital problems) were compared to other sources of information about them (Koss & Butcher, 1973). What the patients said about themselves (the item content) was analyzed carefully. The results indicated that generally they were "both willing and able to reveal truthful information about themselves" (p. 234) and to correctly identify significant aspects of their crisis situation. In a striking number of cases, what the individuals directly revealed was corroborated by other sources of information about them. These and related findings (e.g., Payne & Wiggins, 1972) further document the ability of people to volunteer correct self-statements. For example, endorsing statements such as "Most of the time I feel blue," or "I don't care what happens to me" or "Most of the time I wish I were dead" tends to accurately reflect the individual's depressive and suicidal condition. Similarly, assaultive individuals tended to be quite candid about reporting that they were said to be hotheads and sometimes had to smash things or behave in shocking or harmful ways.

At first glance evidence for the value of direct self-reports might seem more relevant to the trait approaches discussed in Chapters 6 and 7 (since many trait measures rely on self-reports) than to phenomenology. In fact, the evidence in this section does not speak to the question of the existence and nature of generalized personality traits; it merely shows that people can report directly about their own behavior with as much or better accuracy than we can get from other more indirect inferences and information about them (Mischel, 1972).

In sum, useful information about people may be obtained most directly by simply asking them. The predictions made in simple, direct self-ratings and self-reports generally have not been exceeded by those obtained from more psychometrically sophisticated personality tests, from combined test batteries, from indirect measures and clinical judges, and from complex statistical analyses (Mischel, 1968, 1972). These conclusions seem to hold for such diverse content areas as college achievement, job and professional success, treatment outcomes in psychotherapy, rehospitalization for psychiatric patients, and parole violations for delinquent children.

Techniques for Studying Subjective Experience

Thus it seems under some conditions people may be able to report and predict their own behavior at least as accurately as experts can make inferences about them through less direct techniques. Consequently, it often is reasonable to ask the person directly how she will behave, and in many instances the self-statements obtained may be as accurate as, or better than, any other data sources. These conclusions do not imply that people can always predict their own behavior accurately. There may be many circumstances in which the individual lacks either the information or the motivation to foretell his own behavior. Even if a criminal plans to steal again we cannot expect him to say so to the examining prosecutor at his trial. Moreover, many future behaviors may be determined by variables not in the person's control (e.g., other people, accidents). The obtained findings do suggest that techniques designed to obtain direct self-estimates and self-predictions merit serious attention. Some of these techniques will be reviewed in this chapter. One especially useful technique for obtaining reports about the self is the Q-technique or Q-sort.

The Q-Sort Technique

The Q-sort consists of a large number of cards, each containing a printed statement (e.g., Block, 1961). The cards may contain such statements as "I am a submissive person," "I am likable," and "I am an impulsive person." Or the items might be "is a thoughtful person," "gets anxious easily," "works efficiently."

The Q-sort may be used for self-description, for describing the ideal self, or even to describe a relationship. For a self-sort, the client would be instructed to sort the cards to describe herself as she sees herself currently, placing cards in separate piles according to their applicability, ranging from those attributes which are least like her to those which are most like her. For example, the terms that Gary W. had indicated as most self-descriptive were: "haughty, determined, ambitious, critical, logical, moody, uncertain."

For an ideal sort, the subject would be instructed to use the cards to describe the person she would most like to be—her ideal person. To describe a relationship, she would sort the cards into piles ranging from those that are most characteristic of the relationship to those least characteristic. Research-

FIGURE 11-1
A Forced Q-Sort Distribution of Descriptive Statements

oriented Rogerians have made especially extensive use of the Q-sort to study changes in the perceived self in the course of therapy.

As these examples indicate, a chief feature of the method is that the subject is instructed to sort the cards into a prearranged or "forced" distribution along a continuum from items that are least characteristic (or descriptive) to those that are most characteristic of what she is describing. The forced distribution is usually approximately normal (see Figure 11-1). To achieve a normal distribution the subject must place relatively few items in the "most characteristic" and "least characteristic" piles, and must sort most of the statements into categories near the center of the distribution. The forced distribution makes it easier to deal with the results statistically in research. It also may control response sets, such as the tendencies to stick to the "average" ratings or to give extreme ratings. On the other hand, the forced distribution has been criticized for forcing subjects into molds that they feel do not accurately reflect their perceptions. A person might feel that most of the statements do not belong in the middle category, yet she is forced by the instructions to sort them into it. For example, in a self-sort one individual might feel that the majority of the statements are highly characteristic, while another person might believe that most of the statements do not apply to her at all.

The items for a Q-sort may come from a variety of sources. They may stem from a particular theory of personality (Stephenson, 1953), from therapeutic protocols (Butler & Haigh, 1954), or from personality inventories (Block, 1961). To establish empirically the validity of Q-sort reports, one has to proceed exactly as was discussed in the context of trait measurement. That is, one has to examine the correlations between the Q-sorts and other data of interest. It is also possible to use the Q-sort to describe the characteristics associated with successful performance in a given task. For example, one can find the profile of qualities "most characteristic" of people who successfully delay gratification in a particular situation. One can then search for those individuals who best match that profile when trying to predict who will or will not do well in that type of situation (Bem and Funder, 1978).

For many phenomenologically oriented psychologists, the self-statements also may be of central interest in themselves, and their value as predictors or as valid indices of anything else may be irrelevant. In that case, people's self-reports are of intrinsic interest, apart from their possible relations to other information about them. One simply wants to see the person's self-characterization for its own sake.

Interviews

Most modern phenomenologists have recognized that self-reports may not reveal everything important about behavior and may not give a complete picture of personality. Persons may be conscious of the reasons for their behavior but be unable or unwilling to report them. Or they may not be conscious of all their experiences, in which case they cannot communicate them no matter how hard they try. In spite of these limitations, such phenomenologists as Rogers prefer the client's frame of reference as the vantage point for understanding. The psychologist's task, in Rogers' view, is to provide conditions that are conducive to growth and that facilitate free exploration of feelings and self.

One cannot expect people to be honest about themselves when they fear that their statements may incriminate them or lead to negative decisions about their future. In order for a person to reveal private feelings, he or she needs a nonthreatening atmosphere that allays anxieties, reduces inhibitions, and fosters self-disclosure (Jourard, 1967). Phenomenologically oriented psychologists therefore pay much attention to creating conditions of acceptance, warmth, and empathy in which the individual may feel more at ease for open self-exploration. These conditions of acceptance are illustrated vividly in "client-centered" (Rogerian) therapy, discussed later in this chapter. Rogerians have not only tried to create conditions conducive to personal growth; they also have studied those conditions in the interview.

In their earliest efforts the approach was informal. They selected excerpts from recorded interviews in client-centered therapy mainly to document how the clients' verbalizations reflect their self-pictures, and how these pictures change in the course of therapy (e.g., Rogers, 1942; Rogers & Dymond, 1954). Since these early beginnings, the content analysis of interview protocols has become a systematic research method. Going far beyond the mere tape recording of interviews, researchers have devised theory-relevent categories for reliably scoring the client's expressions. For example, many investigators have scored changes in self-references on various dimensions during therapy. They have grouped these self-references into such categories as positive or approving

FIGURE 11-2
General Hostility Conflict and Sex Conflict Statements

General hostility conflict statements about husband, and sex conflict statements about husband, in six random selected therapy hours with one client. (From Murray, Auld, & White, 1954.)

self-references, negative or disapproving self-references, ambivalent self-references, and ambiguous self-references. The scores obtained could then be correlated with other aspects of the therapy, such as the point in the relationship at which they occurred, or the association among diverse types of changes as therapy progressed. For example, it has been possible to try to test propositions such as the idea that increasing acceptance of self leads to increasing acceptance of others. Research in this vein has been vigorous and extensive (e.g., Chordokoff, 1954; Marsden, 1971; Truax & Mitchell, 1971).

Rogerians have not been the only ones to attempt content analysis of verbal behavior in interviews. The technique of scoring content has been favored in descriptive studies of all sorts of psychotherapy and not just in phenomenological approaches. A typical question in psychodynamically oriented therapy, for example, might trace changes in types of conflict expressed in various phases in psychotherapy. To illustrate, Figure 11-2 depicts the percentage of total statements judged to deal with general hostility conflict as opposed to sex conflict in the course of the first 15 psychotherapy hours (Murray, Auld, & White, 1954). As the figure suggests, sexual conflicts began to be expressed increasingly in later sessions, whereas more general conflicts were readily verbalized in earlier phases of the relationship. These content analyses, of course, depend on the clinician's inferences about the underlying meaning of the client's statements; they do not reflect the subject's phenomenology directly.

As these studies indicate, phenomenological data from the interview have been objectified and investigated with diverse research strategies guided by many different theoretical viewpoints. Thus while the interview is a favorite tool for the phenomenologist, the data from the interview can be analyzed in many different ways. In general, the interview continues to be, for most of the major theoretical orientations, a source of data for personality assessments. Its popularity probably reflects its great flexibility and the vast range of topics that it can cover rapidly.

The validity of the interview is the subject of extensive research. When it is used to infer personality dynamics and to predict behavior from those inferences, its validity is usually not impressive (e.g., Fisher, Epstein, & Harris, 1967). On the other hand, many phenomenologically oriented psychologists use the interview to observe how the individual interprets himself and describes his experiences. They employ the interview as a direct sample of the person's self-description (the ways he sees and presents himself) regardless of the validity of the data he provides as "signs" of his nontest behaviors or of his psychodynamics. They seek to create an atmosphere conducive to honest self-disclosure, an atmosphere in which self-revelation is actively encouraged (e.g., Jourard, 1974).

The Semantic Differential

Another route for phenomenologically oriented assessment has been developed to study meanings. This technique, the "semantic differential," yields ratings of the meaning of the persons, events, or concepts the investigator wants to study.

On the semantic differential test the meanings of diverse words, phrases, and concepts are rated on many scales (Osgood, Suci, & Tannenbaum, 1957). The rater (or subject) is supplied with a stimulus word like "feather," or "me," or "my father," or with a phrase like "my ideal self," and is asked to rate each stimulus on a graphic, 7-point, bipolar scale. Polar adjectives like "rough-smooth" or "fair-unfair" are the extremes of each scale. The rater is instructed to mark the point that most nearly indicates the meaning of the stimulus concept for her. For example, she must rate "my ideal self" on scales like those shown in Table 11-1. The technique is both objective and flexible, and it permits investigation of the meanings of words and concepts of all sorts, as well as of changes in these meanings as a result of special experiences or procedures (for example, psychotherapy).

A great deal of factor-analytic research has repeatedly indicated three main, dichotomous, semantic factors. A primary *evaluative* (good-bad) factor seems to be most important. Two other major factors are *potency*, represented by scale items like hard-soft, masculine-feminine, strong-weak, and *activity*, tapped by scales like active-passive, excitable-calm, and hot-cold. Mulaik

TABLE 11-1
EXAMPLES OF CONCEPTS AND RATING SCALES FROM THE SEMANTIC DIFFERENTIAL

Concepts whose meanings the subject is asked to rate

    MY ACTUAL SELF

    MY IDEAL SELF

    MASCULINITY

    FOREIGNER

    MOTHER

Scales for rating the meaning of concepts

strong	:	:	:	:	:	:	weak
pleasant	:	:	:	:	:	:	unpleasant
hard	:	:	:	:	:	:	soft
safe	:	:	:	:	:	:	dangerous
fair	:	:	:	:	:	:	unfair
active	:	:	:	:	:	:	passive

SOURCE: Based on Osgood, Suci, and Tannenbaum (1957).

(1964) and Vernon (1964) have pointed out that these three semantic factors from studies of concept meanings are similar to the factors found in trait ratings. Thus trait factors from ratings of persons are often close to the meaning factors found in semantic differential studies of words and concepts.

Constructs

The Rep Test and the Elaboration of Personal Constructs

Recall that George Kelly (1955) emphasized that different people may construe the same event differently and that every event can be construed in alternative ways. Suppose, for example, that you see a person quietly letting himself be abused by someone else. You might conclude that the person is "submissive." Yet the same behavior might be construed by other observers as sensitive, cautious, intelligent, tactful, or polite.

The personal construct is the central unit of George Kelly's theory. Kelly's (1955) definition of a construct is the way in which two things are seen as alike and as different from a third. A construct is a category that contains at least two events and excludes at least one other. Kelly's operation for measuring a construct is best seen in his Role Con-

---

TABLE 11-2
ELABORATION OF PERSONAL CONSTRUCTS:
EXAMPLES FROM GARY W.

1. List the three most important people in your life:
   me   my brother   my father
   How are any two of these alike and different from the third?
   My brother and I both know how to be tough and succeed, no matter what—my father is soft, knocked out, defeated by life.
2. Think of yourself now, five years ago, and five years from now. How are any two of these alike and different from the third?
   Five years ago I was warmer, more open and responsive to others than I am now. Now I'm mostly a scheming brain. Five years from now I hope to have recaptured some of that feeling and to be more like I was five years ago.

---

struct Repertory Test or "Rep" test. On the Rep test the subject may list many people or things that are important to her (e.g., self, mother, brother). After she lists these items (or the assessor lists them for her), she considers them in groups of three. In each triad she has to indicate how two items are similar to each other and different from the third. In this way the subjective dimensions of similarity among events, and the subjective opposites of those dimensions, may be evoked systematically (Table 11-2). It is also possible to study the characteristics of the person's construct system—for example, the number of different constructs she has in her construct repertory.

Like the semantic differential, the Rep test is a flexible instrument that can be adapted for many different purposes, and it provides a convenient and fairly simple way to begin the exploration of personal constructs. Some examples, taken from the study of Gary W., are shown in Table 11-2 (which illustrates the general type of procedure that may be used to elaborate personal constructs).

Research on the temporal stability of personal constructs evoked by Kelly's Rep test indicates a good deal of consistency over time (Bonarius, 1965). For example, a high retest correlation (.79) was found for constructs after a two-week interval (Landfield, Stern, & Fjeld, 1961), and factor analyses of the Rep test suggest that its main factor is stable (Pedersen, 1958), and thus that an individual's main constructs may be relatively permanent.

According to Kelly, the individual's personal constructs gradually become elaborated through her answers on the Rep test, and through her behaviors in the interview and on other tests (such as the TAT). To illustrate some features of the assessment of personal constructs, here is an analysis of our case based on how Gary spontaneously elaborates and contrasts the constructs with which he views the world. What follows are excerpts from an attempt by an assessor to summarize some of Gary's main conceptions.

A Personal Construct Conceptualization of Gary W.

Rationality-Emotionality is a construct dimension that seems to be of considerable importance for Gary. This construct is elaborated most clearly when he is discussing his interpersonal relationships. A sexual relationship with a woman is described in such terms as "spiritual," "instinctive," "sublime," and "beyond rationality." It is characterized by intense feeling and the primacy of emotions, and it is based on physical attraction. Real friendships, in contrast, are based upon verbalizable grounds—rational bases such as interests and ways of thinking that are common to both parties.

The distinction between the rational and the emotional is echoed when Gary describes his worries in terms of those that are "rational" versus those that are "immediate and threatening." In discussing anger, he says that he has learned to cover up his feelings, but that his emotions sometimes "surface." He no longer gets violently angry, as he did when he was a child, but is "controlled," "stony," and "devious." He gives the most positive evaluation to reason, and contrasts what is reasonable with what is "worthless."

Transposed onto a time line, his distinction between reason and emotion forms part of the contrast between adults and children. After he was about 12 years old, Gary "psyched out" his father, so the latter was no longer his "enemy" but instead became his "friendly, rational adviser." He also describes shifts in his relations with his mother and with his brother which apparently involve handling his feelings toward them in a less explosive way.

Power and control versus dependence and weakness seems to be a major dimension on which adults and children differ. Adults are the enemies of children. In several of his TAT stories, as well as in his interview descriptions of his childhood experiences, what parental figures require of a child is typically the opposite of what the child wants. Gary describes life as a child as involving "denial, helplessness, nothing and nobody on my side." It was a time when he "couldn't control events," when he was being "manipulated" and "shamed." Gary contrasts foresight, and events that he can plan and control, with accidents, terror, and the unpredictable.

Defeat-Success is a closely related dimension around which a number of constructs are clustered. Defeat is defined in terms of lack of money, passivity, compliance, dependence, frustration, undermined masculinity, and physical pain. Success means money, activity, freedom, independence, control, and being a "real" man.

Security-Liberty is another major dimension for Gary. In describing jobs, acquaintances, and life styles, he talks in terms of "the ordinary 9 to 5 job complete with wife, kids, and mortgage," versus the "free and easy life." "Blind obedience" is contrasted to "judging the issues for oneself." Gary describes himself as being "uncertain," and contrasts being free-wheeling with plodding determination. He sees himself as being currently without "acceptance" and "success" and he feels "cut off." His own "procrastination" hinders his "drive," but he hopes his "ambition will win out" and gain him both security and liberty.

As far as *role conceptions* are concerned, Gary now sees his father as "emasculated" and "knocked out," although once he saw him as "a giant" and as his "enemy." The father seems to have moved along the conceptual continuum from "power and control" to a point where he is seen as inadequate and as being competition no longer. He dislikes his father for the middle-class values that he feels he represents and for his passivity. There is also the implication that he resents his father for not comparing favorably with his mother. The turning point in Gary's feelings for his brother, whom he disliked for sharing many of their father's qualities, came when his brother was smashed up in a car crash. He now sees him as less conventional, more humorous and self-examining.

Gary sees his mother, and ideal women in general, as "independent partners" rather than "devouring" sources of affection. Instead of making their families central in importance, they achieve success and recognition in work outside their home. They keep the male "alive" by providing stimulation through their competence, which extends even to athletics, rather than being dependent and "clinging." Gary sees himself as similar to his mother and says he loves her best, next to himself. On the more negative side, he sees his mother as frigid and incapable of expressing affection. However, in view of his own evaluation of emotionality, this criticism is a highly qualified one. He sees his mother as having in many ways been the cause of his father's defeat, but constantly adds that she did not intend this result and feels bad about it, that it was a by-product of other admirable qualities she possesses.

His relationship with his mother is characterized by control of expression of both anger and love. He sees her dominating tendencies as dangerous, as evidenced by his childhood conception of her as omniscient and omnipotent. This fear seems to have generalized to his grandmother and to other women, as evidenced by his TAT stories.

In his relationships with women there seems to be a general distinction between sex objects and companions. In describing a sexual relationship that he felt had no potentialities for friendship, Gary says, "If we hadn't been able to 'make it' we would have stopped seeing each other." He generally prefers women who are stimulating and challenging, though he fears all forms of domination, through either authority or emotional ties.

In his relationships with men outside his family, Gary prefers distance and respect and finds that closeness leads to friction, as with his present room-mate. At school he found two older men whom he could look up to: a teacher to whom he was grateful for not being "wishy-washy" and another person whom he describes as being a "real man."

Behavioral Referents for Personal Constructs

The foregoing descriptions indicate some of Gary's main constructs and role conceptions. These emerged from his self-descriptions and verbalizations. When a person starts to express his constructs, he usually begins with very diffuse, oversimplified, global terms. For example, Gary called himself "shrewd," "too shy," "too sharp." He also said he wanted to "feel more real," to "adjust better," and to "be happier."

What can the construct assessor do with these trait verbalizations? As we have seen in earlier chapters, psychodynamically oriented clinicians rely chiefly on their intuitive inferences about the symbolic and dynamic meanings of verbal behavior. Trait-oriented psychometric assessments either investigate the accuracy of the persons' statements as indices of their nontest behavior, or treat their verbalizations as signs of their position on a personality dimension. A personal construct analysis of language, on the other hand, is completely different. The main aim of such an analysis is to decipher the content of what is being conveyed and to discover its behavioral referents and consequences; its aim is not to translate what is said into signs of underlying motives, of unconscious processes, or of personality dimensions.

Often it is hard to find appropriate words for deeply subjective states. Talk about private experiences, including thoughts and feelings, tends to be ambiguous. For example, statements of the kind commonly presented in clinical contexts, like "I feel so lost," generally are not clear. Instead of inquiring into *why* the person feels "lost," personal construct assessments try to discover referents for just *what* the statement means. An adequate personal construct assessment of what people say involves the analysis of what they mean. For this purpose the assessor's initial task is like the one faced whenever behavioral referents and operational definitions are sought for unclear theoretical constructs. Just as the psychologist interested in such concepts as extraversion, identity, or anxiety must find public referents to help specify what he or she means, so must the client find public referents for his or her private concepts, difficulties, and aspirations.

In sum, Kelly urges a specific and elaborate inquiry into personal constructs by obtaining numerous behavioral examples as referents for them. Kelly has described in detail many techniques to explore the conditions under which the individual's particular constructions about emotional reactions may change (1955).

Nonverbal Communication

Techniques like the semantic differential and the Rep test sample what the people *say*—that is, their verbal behavior. But significant communication among people is often nonverbal—it can involve facial expressions, movements, and gestures. Nonverbal expressions have intrigued psychologists of many theoretical orientations who are interested in the subject's perceptions and inner states. Research has begun to explore the possible meanings and effects of such nonverbal expressions as eye contact and the stare.

It has been found, for example, that when an interviewer evaluates subjects positively they increase eye contact with him; when he evaluates them negatively, they decrease eye contact with him (Exline & Winters, 1965). The effects of eye contact seem to interact with the verbal content conveyed in the relationship. One study varied whether an interviewer looked at the subject frequently or hardly at all, and whether the conversation was positive or threatening (Ellsworth & Carlsmith, 1968). When the verbal content was positive, more frequent eye contact produced more positive evaluations of the interviewer. In contrast, when the verbal content was negative more frequent eye contact produced more negative evaluation.

Although much is still unknown about nonverbal communication, many results have been encouraging. It has been shown, for instance, that "when people look at the faces of other people, they can obtain information about happiness, surprise, fear, anger, disgust/contempt, interest, and sadness . . . Such information can be interpreted, without any special training, by those who see the face . . ." (Ekman, Friesen, & Ellsworth, 1972, pp. 176–177).

Adaptation, Deviance, and Change

The phenomenological orientation also has had profound influences on applied approaches to psychological "health," to problematic behavior, and to personality change.

Humanistic View

The Healthy Personality

The phenomenological orientation implies a "humanistic" view of adaptation and deviance. There are many variations, but in general personal genuineness, honesty about one's own feelings, self-awareness, and self-acceptance are posi-

TABLE 11-3
SOME QUALITIES OF MASLOW'S "SELF-ACTUALIZING" PEOPLE

1. Able to perceive reality accurately and efficiently.
2. Accepting of self, of others, and of the world.
3. Spontaneous and natural, particularly in thought and emotion.
4. Problem-centered: concerned with problems outside themselves and capable of retaining a broad perspective.
5. Need and desire solitude and privacy; can rely on their own potentialities and resources.
6. Autonomous: relatively independent of extrinsic satisfactions, for example, acceptance or popularity.
7. Capable of a continued freshness of appreciation of even the simplest, most commonplace experiences (for example, a sunset, a flower, or another person).
8. Experience "mystic" or "oceanic" feelings in which they feel out of time and place and at one with nature.
9. Have a sense of identification with humankind as a whole.
10. Form their deepest ties with relatively few others.
11. Truly democratic; unprejudiced and respectful of all others.
12. Ethical, able to discriminate between means and ends.
13. Thoughtful, philosophical, unhostile sense of humor; laugh at the human condition, not at a particular individual.
14. Creative and inventive, not necessarily possessing great talents, but a naive and unspoiled freshness of approach.
15. Capable of some detachment from the culture in which they live, recognizing the necessity for change and improvement.

SOURCE: Based on Maslow (1968).

tively valued; "self-realization," the ultimate in fulfillment, involves a continuous quest to know oneself and to actualize one's potentialities for full awareness and growth as a human being. Denouncing "adjustment" to society and to other people's values as the road to dehumanization, the quest is to know oneself deeply and to be true to one's own feelings without disguise, to be oneself in the "here and now." Conversely, human problems are seen as rooted in distortions of one's own perceptions and experiences in the service of furthering the expectations of society, including the dictates of one's own self-concept with its needs for "positive regard" (Chapter 5).

One especially articulate description of the "healthy" personality from a humanistic viewpoint is provided by Maslow (1968). His characterization of the qualities of "self-actualizing" people is summarized in Table 11-3. Slightly different, but overlapping, perspectives come from other humanistic spokes-men (e.g., Jourard, 1974).

In sum, in spite of its many different versions, the phenomenological-humanistic orientation tends to view the "healthy person" as one who:

health person

1. becomes aware of herself, her feelings, and her limits; accepts herself, her life, and what she makes of her life as her own responsibility; has "the courage to be."
2. experiences the "here-and-now;" is not trapped to live in the past or to dwell in the future through anxious expectations and distorted defenses.
3. realizes her potentialities; has autonomy and is not trapped by her own self-concept or the expectations of others and society.

To help achieve these ideals, several avenues for constructive personality change have been favored by advocates of the phenomenological approach, as discussed next.

Client-Centered Psychotherapy

One of the most influential applications of the phenomenological approach was the "client-centered" therapy developed by Carl Rogers (Chapter 5). Rogers rejected most of Freud's concepts regarding the nature of psychodynamics and psychosexual development. He also avoided all diagnostic terms, refusing to put his labels on the client. He maintained, however, the interview format for psychotherapy (using a face-to-face arrangement rather than the orthodox psychoanalyst's couch for the client). Rogers and his students focused on the client-clinician relationship. Usually they required many fewer sessions than did psychoanalytic therapy, and they dealt more with current than with historical concerns in the client's life.

For Rogers (1959) the therapist's main task is to provide an atmosphere in which the client can be more fully open to his own "organismic" experience. To achieve a growth-conducive atmosphere, the clinician must view the client as intrinsically good and capable of self-development. The clinician's function is to be nonevaluative and to convey a sense of unconditional acceptance and regard for the client. To reach the client effectively the clinician must be "genuine" and "congruent"—an open, trustworthy, warm person without a facade. The congruent therapist, according to Rogers, feels free to "be himself" and to accept himself and the client fully and immediately in the therapeutic encounter, and he conveys this openness to the client by simply being himself. When a genuinely accepting, unconditional relationship is established, the client will become less afraid to face and accept his own feelings and experiences. Becoming open to the experience of himself as he is, he can reorganize his self-structure. Now, hopefully, he will accept experiences that he had previously denied or distorted (because they did not fit his self-concept) and thus achieve greater internal congruity and self-actualization.

Rogers thus advocated an empathetic, interview-based relationship therapy. He renounced the Freudian focus on psychodynamics and transference. Instead, he wanted to provide the client an unconditionally accepting relationship—an atmosphere conducive to "growth" (self-actualization). In this relationship the focus is on emphatic understanding and acceptance of feelings rather than interpretation, although the latter is not excluded. The clinician is relatively "nondirective"; the objective is to let the client direct the interview while the clinician attempts to accurately reflect and clarify the feelings that emerge.

In client-centered therapy, permissiveness and unqualified acceptance on the part of the therapist provide an atmosphere favorable to personal honesty. Psychologists are urged to abandon their "objective" measurement orientation and their concern with tests. Instead, they should try to learn from the client how he or she thinks, understands, and feels. "The best vantage point for understanding behavior is from the internal frame of reference of the individual himself" (Rogers, 1951, p. 494). Although their focus is on empathy, the Rogerians have not neglected objective research into the relationship, as was noted earlier in this chapter in the context of interview research. As a result, Rogerians have helped to illuminate some of the processes that occur during client-centered therapy and also have provided considerable evidence concerning its effectiveness (e.g., Truax & Mitchell, 1971).

Client-centered psychotherapy has been shown to produce some significant alterations. An extensive review of outcome research indicated that some clients may improve significantly (on measures of self-concept change), while others deteriorate significantly during treatment (Bergin, 1966). Bergin's review concluded that some forms of Rogerian psychotherapy may cause clients to become either significantly better or worse than untreated controls. For example, Gendlin (1962) reported detrimental effects from client-centered relationship therapy for some people, especially those diagnosed schizophrenic. Consequently, some current therapy research is trying to identify the characteristics of clients, clinicians, and client-clinician combinations that might predispose particular forms of therapy to success or failure (e.g., Bergin, 1971). If these attributes can be isolated it might be possible to offer particular forms of client-centered therapy only to those who can benefit from them. Research in the same vein is also aimed at trying to isolate the conditions under which certain interpersonal skills of the therapist, such as "empathy, warmth and genuineness" may be especially helpful (Truax & Mitchell, 1971).

Similarities and Differences among Approaches

It is evident that Rogers' client-centered psychotherapy differs in many ways from Freudian psychotherapy. Indeed, when Rogers first proposed his techniques they were considered revolutionary. Sometimes his approach to psychotherapy is even described as the polar opposite of Freud's. While there are major differences between Freudian and Rogerian approaches to psychother-

Similarities
Rogers
& Freud

differences

apy, on closer inspection there also are some fundamental similarities. Both approaches retain a verbal, interview format for psychotherapy; both focus on the client-clinician relationship; both are primarily concerned with feelings; both emphasize the importance of unconscious processes (defense, repression); both consider increased awareness and acceptance of unconscious feelings to be major goals of psychotherapy. To be sure, the two approaches differ in the specific content that they believe is repressed (e.g., id impulses versus organismic experiences), in the motives they consider most important (e.g., sex and aggression versus self-realization), and in the specific insights they hope will be achieved by the client who has been successful in psychotherapy (the unconscious becomes conscious and conflict is resolved versus organismic experience is accepted and the self becomes congruent with it). But these differences should not obscure the fact that both approaches are forms of relationship treatment that emphasize awareness of hypothesized unconscious feelings and the need for the client to accept those feelings. As such, both approaches differ from the direct focus on behavior in assessment and treatment which is the fundamental feature of the behavioral approaches discussed in the preceding two chapters.

Yet there also is some commonality (often unexpected) between certain qualities of the behavioral approach and that of Rogers and other phenomenologists. Specifically, diagnostic labels and psychiatric analogies in dealing with human problems are avoided by Rogerians (and many other phenomenologists) as much as by behaviorally oriented psychologists. Rogerians have consistently rejected trait tests and many of the constructs that guided them.

Phenomenologically Oriented Groups

As part of the search for growth and expanded awareness, in recent years a variety of group treatments have become popular. These group experiences go beyond the verbal exchange of the traditional client-clinician interview and seek to achieve better communication and contact among a group of people as well as to increase each individual's insight and self-awareness. This trend toward group experiences is found in diverse forms, especially in encounter groups and marathons like those developed at the Esalen Institute in California (Schutz, 1967) and in the "Gestalt therapy" of Fritz Perls (1969).

Encounter groups have many different labels, such as human-relations training group (T-group), sensitivity training group, personal growth group, and include many varieties of experiences, but in this discussion the focus is on their common qualities.

diff. kinds of groups

Schutz (1967) in his book *Joy* notes that encounter group methods involve *doing* something, not just talking. The aim is to help people to experience, to feel, to make life more vital. In this quest he advocates a host of group methods that include body exercises, wordless meetings, group fantasy, and physical "games." These games range from gentle face and body explorations by

Proponents of encounter groups emphasize their value for enhancing contact and communication among many people, not just those with severe problems.

mutual touching and holding to physically aggressive encounters involving shoving, pushing, and hitting. In many activities the group leaders and group members interpret the meaning of the members' behaviors as their encounters occur.

Elliot Aronson (1972, p. 238) describes what is learned in group experiences this way: ". . . in a psychology course I learn how people behave; in a T-group I learn how I behave. But I learn much more than that: I also learn how others see me, how my behavior affects them, and how I am affected by other people." Referring to the process through which such learning occurs, Aronson (p. 239) emphasizes learning-by-doing; ". . . people learn by trying things out, by getting in touch with their feelings and by expressing those feelings to other people, either verbally or nonverbally." Such a process requires an atmosphere of trust so that members learn not how they are "supposed" to behave but rather what they really feel and how others view them.

At a theoretical level, the encounter group movement seems to involve a complex synthesis of both Freudian and Rogerian concepts with a focus on nonverbal experiences and self-discovery. The psychodynamic motivational

framework is largely retained and is used in many of the interpretations, but it is implemented by direct "acting-out" procedures for expressing feelings through action in the group, by body contact designed to increase awareness of body feelings, and by games to encourage the expression of affection and aggression. Thus many of Freud's and Rogers' ideas have been transferred from the consulting room to the group encounter, and from verbal expression to body awareness and physical expression. Indeed in recent years Carl Rogers (1970) has extended many of his theoretical concepts to the encounter experience and has become one of its leading advocates. Rather than talking about impulses, feelings, and fantasies, the individual is encouraged to act them out in the group. For example rather than talk about repressed feelings of anger toward his father the individual enacts his feelings, pummelling a pillow while screaming "I hate you Dad, I hate you."

Many of these therapies are phenomenologically oriented and seem to emphasize the achievement of greater consciousness and personal integration. The aim is to help individuals to gain awareness, self-acceptance, and spontaneity and ultimately to achieve fulfillment and joy. The objective seems to include a feeling of wholeness and of independence and autonomy. Such a concern with "doing your own thing" and achieving self-acceptance characterizes the "Gestalt therapy" advocated by Fritz Perls (1969). The philosophy of that position is summarized in the "prayer" of Gestalt therapy (Perls, 1969, p. 4):

> I do my thing, and you do your thing
> I am not in this world to live up
> to your expectations
> And you are not in this world to
> live up to mine.
> You are you and I am I
> And if by chance we find each
> other, it's beautiful.
> If not, it can't be helped.

Effects of Encounter Groups

Subjective reports of positive changes as a result of group experiences abound, as illustrated in this testimonial cited by Rogers (1970, p. 129):

> I still can't believe the experience that I had during the workshop. I have come to see myself in a completely new perspective. Before I was "the handsome" but cold person insofar as personal relationships go. People wanted to approach me but I was afraid to let them come close as it might endanger me and I would have to give a little of myself. Since the institute I have not been afraid to be *human*. I express myself quite well and also am likeable and also can love. I go out now and use these emotions as part of me.

While such reports are encouraging they of course are not firm evidence, and they are offset in part by reports of negative experiences and "bad trips" (e.g., Lieberman et al., 1973). Some behavior changes do seem to emerge, but their interpretation is beset by many methodological difficulties (Campbell & Dunnette, 1968). When careful control groups are used some doubt is raised if the gains from encounter experience reflect more than the enthusiastic expectancies of the group members. For example, people in weekend encounter groups showed more rated improvement than did those who remained in an at-home control group: but improvement in the encounter groups did not differ from that found in an on-site control group whose participants believed they were in an encounter group although they only had recreational activities (McCardel & Murray, 1974).

Nevertheless, a number of experimental studies indicate specific changes that may occur in some types of groups. These changes include a decrease in ethnic prejudice (Rubin, 1967), an increase in empathy (Dunnette, 1969) and in susceptibility to being hypnotized (Tart, 1970), and an increased belief by subjects that their behavior is under their own control (Diamond & Shapiro, 1973). This evidence is accompanied by a greater awareness on the part of encounter group enthusiasts that not all groups are for all people, that bad as well as good experiences may occur, and that coerciveness in groups is a real hazard that needs to be avoided (Aronson, 1972).

Huxley,
Leary, & Alpert

Drug-Induced Changes in Experiences

As another route to greater awareness, some psychologists have hoped to explore the effects of drug-induced changes in mental states. The most notable examples were the efforts to "expand consciousness" and explore subjective states by means of "psychedelic" or consciousness-altering drugs such as LSD-25 (e.g., London, 1969; Solomon, 1967).

As noted previously (Chapter 5), efforts to expand consciousness and emotional experiences by means of psychedelic drugs provide the most controversial examples of the search for deeper feelings and awareness. Psychedelic drugs, first advocated by Aldous Huxley and then by Timothy Leary and Richard Alpert, became widely used in the 1960s. According to some participants these drug experiences are profoundly meaningful. For example, according to one testimonial (Leary, Litwin, & Metzner, 1963, p. 570), a female graduate student, after ingesting psilocybin in the company of a supportive group of close friends reported that she:

> . . . was delighted to see that my skin was dissolving in tiny particles and floating away. I felt as though my outer shell was disintegrating, and the 'essence' of me being liberated to join the 'essence' of everything else about me. . . . All of this time I was drifting about in a wonderously beautiful heaven of visual imagery and music.

Another student wrote:

> Then, I began a series of growth or learning experiences. I felt that understanding about oneself and about all human beings was part of the secret. The ability to communicate (on a deep level) was very important, as was the growth of competence and control over oneself and one's world. . . . One of the most disturbing insights was the fact that science was just a small game with its own set of rules. . . . It was even more circumscribed than the game of life in the Euro-American tradition. . . . Part of my successive growth and learning experience included the sensation of trying to incorporate everybody within myself. This I saw very strongly as one of the main causes of human suffering—how alone we all were. . . . Another part was that of accepting one's own defects, the parts of oneself one usually keeps hidden—physical desires, areas of incompetency, antisocial desires (Leary, Litwin, & Metzner, 1963, p. 570).

Skeptics may question how novel these insights really are, and wonder about their meaning. There also have been reports of intense terror and distress reactions during drug-induced experiences. According to these reports, such "unsuccessful trips" sometimes have resulted in severe personality disorganization and psychotic episodes. As often happens when topics become explosive social controversies, it is difficult to arrive at a comprehensive and sober evaluation of the phenomenon that produced the agitation. Understandably, widespread drug use and abuse has created great public concern. As was noted in Chapter 5 the amount of research on the therapeutic effects of drugs like LSD is limited (e.g., Leary, Litwin, & Metzner, 1963; Savage and his associates, 1964), and the dangers from such drugs are considerable, as is now widely recognized.

Much of the research on the effects of psychedelic drugs has been informal and based mainly on personal testimonials from people who have taken LSD-25 or other consciousness-altering drugs. There also have been some more formal efforts both to study such drugs and to use them as a method for observing cognitive changes. A study by Honigfeld (1965) provides a simple example of how drug-induced cognitive changes may be assessed objectively in an experimental framework. A small group of male adult volunteers were studied individually following injections with either LSD-25 or epinephrine. The investigators were interested in the temporal effects of these drugs on language. For this reason they asked each subject to describe his drug experience verbally, as introspectively as possible, by tape recording his reactions at fixed intervals while alone. The resulting recordings were later scored objectively to assess the intelligibility of the spontaneous speech. The results are depicted in Figure 11-3, which shows the mean intelligibility scores obtained by subjects in each of the two drug conditions at various times after receiving the drugs.

Concern with the possible dangers of some of the exceedingly potent drugs used in the explorations of drug-induced changes in experience has restricted

FIGURE 11-3
Changes in the Intelligibility of Speech after Drugs

From Honigfeld (1965).

Meditation & Consciousness-Raising

much of the experimental research on the psychological effects of these chemi-
cals. On the other hand, some ingenious efforts have been successfully conducted to explore the interaction of emotionally arousing drugs and cognitive
states (e.g., Schachter & Singer, 1962, see Chapter 19). In another direction,
there are growing efforts to explore and expand the nature of human awareness by use of meditation and other "consciousness-raising" methods without
recourse to drugs (e.g., Ornstein, 1972; Ornstein & Naranjo, 1971).

The Person's Experience and the Unconscious

For many years most psychologists slighted people's perceptions and constructs and did not consider them as phenomena of interest in their own right.
They preferred, instead, to infer what dispositions and motives might underlie
the person's phenomenology and behavior.

The historical neglect of the subject's viewpoint probably has many reasons. One was the belief that because of unconscious distortions and defenses,
people's self-appraisals were biased and inaccurate. Some psychologists thus
refrained from studying the perceptions, concepts, and reasons of the individual because they felt these data were not really scientific. But it is entirely
legitimate philosophically and logically to take account of individuals' reported subjective perceptions—the rules they use and the reasons they give to

explain their own actions (T. Mischel, 1964). It is not legitimate, however, to assume that these rules and reasons are useful bases for predicting what individuals will do—their behavior—in other situations. The links between persons' reported feelings and beliefs and their other behaviors must be demonstrated empirically.

Another reason for neglecting the subject's viewpoint in personality study was the difficulty of finding objective methods of studying private experiences. But while such experiences are obviously difficult to study, they demand attention. Indeed it has become evident in recent years that the person's conceptual dimensions and perceptions play a key part in most of the phenomena of personality psychology. The importance of the individual's concepts and categories has been shown in areas that range from the perception of persons on through the phenomena of learning itself, as later chapters discuss.

Objecting to the neglect of the "subject's" private experience in psychology, the phenomenological orientation in the last few decades has sought to explore the individual's perceptions and personal constructs. This movement, under the leadership of such theorists as Rogers and Kelly, has had a major impact on the study of personality.

Although the phenomenological orientation focuses on the subject's viewpoint, in some of its variations it also seeks to infer his or her unconscious characteristics and conflicts. For example, Carl Rogers in some of his formulations (e.g., 1963), has emphasized integration, unity, and people's achieving congruence with their "inner organismic processes." Rogers thought that these organismic processes were often unconscious. As a result of unfortunate socialization procedures in our culture persons often become dissociated, "consciously behaving in terms of static constructs and abstractions and unconsciously behaving in terms of the actualizing tendency" (Rogers, 1963, p. 20).

Encounter groups (Schutz, 1967) also pay considerable attention to unconscious processes. In this sense they also depend, just as psychodynamic theorists do, on clinical inferences about the person's behaviors as signs whose meaning individuals themselves do not know consciously. The emphasis on interpretation of underlying meanings is evident in this excerpt from a typical introduction to an encounter session provided by the "trainer" (leader):

. . . you, not me, decide what to do in here, such as the topic you want to talk about or the activities you try . . . but I can be counted on to ask, "What's going on?" The idea is to try to understand not only what we do or say—the content level—but also the feelings underneath, the processes going on (Lakin, 1972, p. 20).

Except for the fact that the setting is a group in which the members will be active and participate in the interpretation, this orientation may not be very different from the type supplied in more traditional psychotherapy. As such, the problems of reliability and validity found in connection with clinical judgment (Chapter 8) apply here just as strongly. It of course may be argued that group members are always entirely free to reject any interpretations they feel do not fit them. But given the susceptibility of humans even to subtle group pressures, such "resistance" may require more independence than can be expected realistically. To try to guard against poor group practices, many advocates of encounter experiences note the importance of the leader's competence and experience and urge that prospective members choose their groups with the greatest care, cautioning "Let the buyer beware!"

To the extent that the psychologist accepts the idea that unconscious processes are key determinants, and relies on clinical judgment to infer them, she faces all the dilemmas previously discussed in the context of clinical judgment. That is true whether one intends to infer unconscious processes in the service of the actualizing tendency and personal growth, or in the service of id impulses of sex and aggression, or in the service of underlying source traits. Regardless of the hypothesized nature of the unconscious mechanisms, it is incumbent upon psychologists to demonstrate their ability to make such inferences validly, reliably, and usefully. But no methodological difficulties should deter psychologists from listening more closely to what their "subjects" can tell them.

SUMMARY

1. The assessment techniques discussed in this chapter represent attempts to study the person's subjective experience within the framework of scientific rules. Most phenomenologically oriented personality psychologists try to bring the individual's private experiences into the public domain by studying subjective experiences with objective techniques. This chapter has shown that the phenomenological orientation to personality has available a variety of methods for studying personal meanings and experiences objectively. The phenomenological approach hence is not merely a point of view about personality; it also offers distinctive techniques for studying persons.

2. Gary W.'s self-conceptualization serves as an example of the raw data of phenomenology. In the phenomenological view, the person may be his or her own best assessor. Research indicates that self-assessment has yielded predictions as accurate as those from more sophisticated personality tests, from combinations of tests, from clinical judgments, and from complex statistical analyses. Thus the person may be a good predictor of his or her own behavior for such diverse outcomes as success in college, in jobs, and in psychotherapy.

3. One especially useful technique for obtaining a person's self-appraisal is the Q-sort. In this measure the person takes a large number of cards, each containing a descriptive statement, and sorts them into categories in a forced distribution. These Q-sorts may be used for self-description, to describe the ideal self, or to describe a relationship. The information yielded by a Q-sort may be of intrinsic interest, or it may yield correlations with other data of interest.

4. The interview has been favored by phenomenologically oriented psychologists. Through empathy the interviewer tries to explore the person's feelings and self-concepts and to see the world from his or her framework and viewpoint. Content analysis has been used by Carl Rogers and others in research on processes in the interview.

5. The "semantic differential" is a rating technique that permits the objective assessment of the meaning of the rater's words and concepts. Research with these scales reveals an evaluative, a potency, and an activity factor. These three factors are similar to those found often in trait ratings of persons.

6. The Role Construct Repertory (Rep) Test was devised by George Kelly to systematically study personal constructs. The test tries to explore the subjective dimensions of similarity among events (people or things) and the subjective opposites of those dimensions as the individual construes them. Interviews and other techniques (such as the TAT) also may be used to elaborate personal constructs more fully. A personal construct conceptualization of Gary W. illustrates some of the main features of the personal construct approach to phenomenology.

7. Recently attention has been given to the importance of nonverbal expressions, movements, and gestures.

8. The phenomenological orientation also has influenced views of what constitutes healthy personality and it has significant practical applications for personality change. Most influential have been Rogers' client-centered therapy and a variety of encounter group experiences. These methods offer potential gains for some people but may be hazardous under certain conditions.

9. In other directions, efforts have been made to explore the use of psychedelic drugs and of meditation to change consciousness and to increase personal awareness.

10. Although phenomenological analyses tend to focus on experience and perceptions, sometimes extensive inferences are made about hypothesized unconscious problems and conflicts beyond the individual's awareness. In those cases the psychologist faces all the problems encountered in psychodynamic efforts to make clinical inferences. It is necessary to demonstrate the reliability and validity of the clinician's inferences, regardless of his or her particular theoretical orientation.

The previous sections provided broad overviews of major approaches to personality and of the main ideas and applications associated with each. In this section the focus will shift from frameworks and strategies for conceptualizing individuals and changing behavior to the basic processes involved in personality. Our central concerns here will be the development and causes of the overt and covert behavior patterns that have been studied by personality psychologists. Therefore we will consider some of the main findings that have come from personality research.

Investigators of personality have been guided by each of the major theoretical orientations and, most often, by a theoretical mixture that draws on some ideas from many conceptualizations. Hence in practice it becomes difficult to separate the contributions of various theories. Nevertheless, wherever possible, we shall point out major controversial issues so that some of the most important differences between orientations will become more evident. We also will be alert

PART III

PERSONALITY DEVELOPMENT AND THE COPING PROCESS

to the implications of the research evidence for the status of central theoretical constructs.

The first chapter of this part introduces the topic of socialization and personality development. Later chapters will focus on the findings of research on diverse topics relevant to basic personality processes, focusing on how the individual copes with the stresses and challenges of life. These topics include the nature and formation of sexual identity, the development of psychological differences between the sexes, and how people deal with frustration, aggression, conflict, and anxiety. Subsequent chapters in this part will examine the nature of psychological defense and the ways in which people can learn to achieve self-control. Then we will examine how individuals form concepts about themselves and become their own assessors. Finally, we will return to one of the most enduring and central issues in psychology: How can we conceptualize the interaction of the person and the conditions of his or her life?

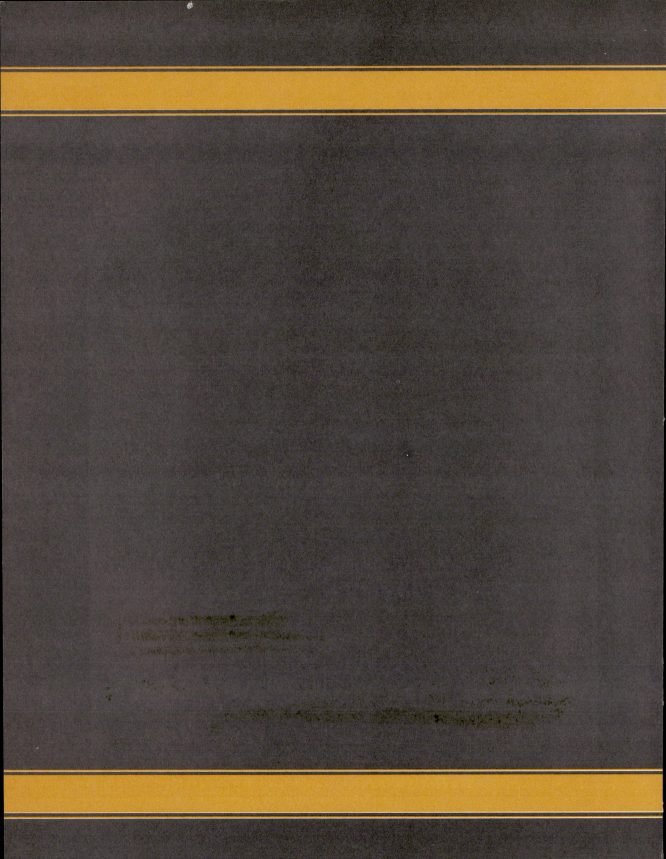

CHAPTER 12

EARLY PERSONALITY DEVELOPMENT

Stage theories

Patterns of Development

Personality development is such a vast topic that one has to find ways to simplify it and slice it into more manageable, smaller units. One way to do that is to focus on the major events or milestones in personality development at various points in the life cycle. Many conditions and events throughout development provide special challenges and seem to be dominant concerns or themes for most people at different points in their lives. For example, young children may be especially concerned with discovering their competencies and gaining a sense of their own "mastery"; adolescents may seem particularly prone to "identity crises" about their goals and purposes in life; and the middle and later years have their own distinctive challenges. At least in our own culture many life events tend to be roughly sequential, reflecting a patterning dictated both by biological maturation and by social practice.

Maturation and Learning

The orderly development of the person begins in the mother's womb long before the baby's birth. The development of the fetus progresses according to a relatively fixed time schedule, dictated largely by genetic determinants but also dependent upon the biological environment. Embryological development proceeds in accord with the organism's genetic nature and unfolds relatively independently of experience as long as a proper environment is provided.

After birth, maturation of structure and of some functions continues in an orderly pattern similar to what we see in prenatal growth. Maturation has a part in such development patterns as standing and crawling, walking, progressively skillful use of hands and fingers, and talking. In all of these, maturation and learning collaborate. The close interaction of maturation and learning is seen most clearly in the acquisition of language. Readiness to learn language depends on age and biological development, yet the language one acquires and ultimately speaks depends on what one hears and on learning experiences.

Biological Bases of Personality

It is fruitless to debate the importance of maturation versus learning and to argue about which one is more important. Humans are both biological and social organisms, and the effects of heredity, maturation, learning, and environment are impressive and interact in their impact on the total organism. The role of genetic and maturational processes is seen most clearly when one examines embryological development and the structural features of human growth.

Beyond physical development, inheritance certainly contributes to intelligence. Research with twins raised in various environments (either together or apart) suggests that when environments are similar, measured intelligence tends to be increasingly similar to the degree that the individuals have an increasing proportion of genes in common (e.g., Cartwright, 1974; Vandenberg, 1971). Consistent with these results, it is often suggested that a person's genetic endowment sets an upper limit or ceiling on the degree to which his or her intelligence can be developed (e.g., Royce, 1973); the environment may help or hinder achievement of that ceiling. Even some personality characteristics, such as emotional expressiveness (including sociability and extraversion measured on personality questionnaires like the MMPI) may involve a genetic component (e.g., Dworkin et al., 1977; Gottesman, 1963, 1966; Wilson, 1977). Anxiety is another example of the kinds of personal qualities in which genes may play a part (Dworkin, 1981). Some psychological disorders, most notably schizophrenia, also may involve at least a small degree of heritability (e.g., Gottesman & Shields, 1969; Kety, 1979; Rosenthal, 1971), and certain kinds of mental deficiency reflect a specific genetic influence (Vandenberg, 1971). People are physical creatures, and biology provides their basic foundations. Although at present neither the magnitude nor the mechanisms of the genetic and hormonal contribution to personality and social development are clear, they are receiving increasing attention in research. Biochemistry and genetics will surely help our future understanding of behavior, but currently most psychologists still focus on psychological rather than biological conditions in their research on personality.

Genes and glands are obviously important, but social learning also has a dramatic role. Imagine the enormous differences that would be found in the personalities of twins with identical genetic endowments if they were raised apart in two different families—or, even more striking, in two totally different cultures. Through social learning, vast differences develop among people in their reactions to most of the stimuli they face in daily life. As a result of social learning processes, stimuli that terrify one person may delight the next and leave a third indifferent. We see, for example, an adolescent who seems angered or bored by the same goals his parents pursue avidly, and parents, in turn, who are horrified by the activities and values their daughter seems to treasure.

The massive effects of learning experiences on personality throughout life in no way denies the role of genetic and constitutional factors. Indeed some individual differences in behavior seem to characterize even the young infant. Thus young babies appear to differ from each other in such patterns as the vigor of their activity, their irritability and how easily they cry, the rate at which they become satiated by stimuli, and their threshold for shifting attention (e.g., Korner, 1971). These initial patterns are quickly acted upon by parents and other important persons in the baby's environment and affect the attitudes and behaviors of these caretakers in their relations with the child in a continuous interaction (e.g., Bell, 1968).

Stages in Psychological Development

Some theories hypothesize definite, distinct sequences in personality and cognitive development. A search for critical or central happenings at different times in life is most characteristic of *stage theories*. We saw such a theory in Freud's conception of psychosexual development from the oral to the anal, phallic, and genital stages. Freud emphasized the importance of biological events (changes in erogenous zones) as foci for conflict in personality development. Others have stressed key themes in psychosocial development, as we saw, for example, in Erikson's (1950) view of phases and crises in interpersonal development (Chapter 3). Still other theorists have hypothesized stages in cognitive development (Piaget, 1960) and in moral development (Kohlberg, 1969).

Stage theories suggest that there are distinct qualitative differences in personality and cognitive processes at different ages. For example, the "cognitive-developmental" stage theory hypothesizes that people have "cognitive structures" or "rules" for processing information (as in thinking), and that these structures are fundamentally different at different points in development. Kohlberg (1969) believes that these cognitive structures serve to change "stimulus inputs" (information from the environment) and that, in turn, the structures are changed by the inputs. The hypothesis that makes this stage theory is that such structures undergo basic transformations during development and thus become qualitatively different. The *sequence* of transformations, according to a stage theory, is definite and fixed, but the *rate* of development may be changed by experience.

Are there definite stages? There is disagreement about the validity of stage theories. Some psychologists see personality and cognitive development as a continuous process in which learning experiences may accumulate in a variety of sequences, depending on the specific learning opportunities the child happens to be exposed to. Others emphasize that certain functions and skills—such as walking or talking, for example—develop most rapidly and dramatically at certain "critical periods." They suggest that some psychological functions develop best only at particular phases of development. Many are convinced that at least cognitive development entails distinct levels or stages of organization.

While there is controversy about the need to construe discrete stages in psychological development, it is widely recognized that socialization is not a haphazard accumulation of bits of behavior but entails, instead, some orderly development. That is true at least to the degree that some complex social behavior patterns are sequential. They require the preexistence of other earlier learning and structures. Some things usually are learned much more readily after other things have been acquired. Likewise, the absence of certain behaviors and skills makes the development of behaviors that depend on them less likely and more difficult.

It also is generally recognized that the content and organization of personality may be radically different at different points in development. Obviously the ideas, beliefs, values, skills, and interests of the three-year-old are not those of the same person at 40. The child is father to the man, but what a person does and is changes with development. Hence it is often intriguing to examine lives at different points in time, when different events and crises are salient, and to assess the nature of the stability and of the change found over the years (e.g., Block, 1971; Block & Block, 1980).

Early Childhood

The Infant's Dependency

The most universally recognized condition of human beings may be their helplessness and passive dependency in early infancy. The infant emerges from the uterus as a highly perishable creature whose survival depends on prolonged care from others. Babies can do almost nothing to fulfill their own needs, and depend on others to provide gratifications and to reduce discomforts. Although

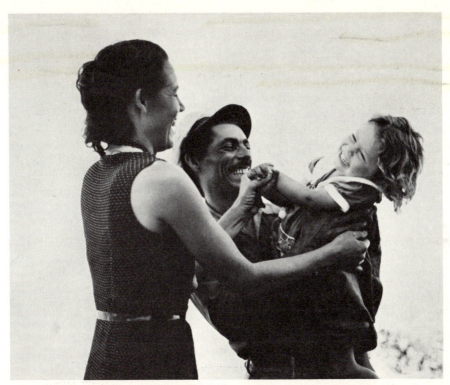

The relationship between the child and his or her caretakers is a transaction, not a one-way affair.

infants cannot take care of their needs, a set of responses are available to them: They scan the environment, cry, suck, smile, thrash about, and vocalize. Some of these responses can exert considerable effects on the environment, as seen in the control over their mothers that some babies rapidly achieve by active crying. Thus while babies cannot satisfy needs directly, they can and do learn to summon and influence caretakers, and the relationship is a transaction rather than a one-way affair from the start.

The Feeding Situation

Throughout life the human organism engages perpetually in transactions with the environment, and in this exchange each continuously alters the other. The remarkable plasticity of behavior, and the organism's magnificent sensitivity to crucial environmental changes, can be seen even in the baby's feeding activities if they are analyzed closely.

Usually the mother is the person who provides the child with fulfillment of his or her biological needs during infancy. She feeds him, comforts him, rocks and cuddles him, diapers him, and talks to him. Some theorists consider the relationship that develops between mother and child during this period as the prototype for the child's sense of "basic trust" (Erikson, 1950) and the foundation for later development. As we saw in Freud's "oral stage," psychoanalytic theory attributes the greatest importance to the role of the lips, tongue, and mouth as erogenous zones and to the secondary pleasure of sucking and swallowing in connection with feeding. There is disagreement about the nature and consequences of these pleasures, but there is no question that feeding and the experiences around it are major events of early infancy.

The mouth and the activity of feeding figure prominently in many personality theories, yet until recently such activities as sucking have been objects for speculation rather than for direct observation. As happens often in science, conjecture precedes experimental research, and experimental research awaits a methodology for studying the phenomena of interest.

 A good example of harnessing a vital phenomenon so that it can be studied thoroughly is reported by Bruner (1967). To study sucking in the infant, an apparatus was devised that records changes in sucking pressure. The apparatus consists of an ordinary baby's nursing bottle except that the bottle is connected electrically to a polygraph.

The baby's sucking is not only registered on the polygraph, it is also monitored by a programming device that can be adjusted to activate milk delivery to the baby through a milk-pulsing system. The program of milk delivery can be set so that it occurs only when the baby sucks in a specified way, or at fixed intervals after each suck, or after every other suck, and so on. Thus it becomes possible to examine the precise relationships between changes in reinforcement (milk delivery) and changes in particular characteristics of the sucking response.

Results from research of this type reveal the surprising flexibility even of nutritional sucking. Using changes in sucking activity as the dependent variable and manipulating a variety of stimulus changes experimentally, investigators have found many indications of highly sensitive learning during the first few months of life. Bruner (1967, p. 16) reports, for example, that during a 15-minute session "suctioning will virtually drop out if mouthing alone produces milk." Thus even babies show subtle discrimination and responsiveness to changes in the outcomes they receive.

Beyond Orality

Although the feeding situation is a critical phase of early development, it is only one component of the total relationship between the growing organism and the world, and contributes only one important part of the experience and stimulation available to him or her. Thus the baby is more than an "oral" creature. She responds to stimulation of the mouth, lips, and tongue, but in addition, she sees, hears, and feels, obtaining stimulation visually, aurally, and from being handled.

One project that was devoted to the ideal of cultivating optimal develop-

FIGURE 12-1
The Development of the Tendency To Explore the Surround (Control Group)

Adapted from B. L. White and R. Held, Plasticity of sensorimotor development in the human infant, in J. F. Rosenblith and Allinsmith, eds., *The Causes of Behavior II,* pp. 60–70; copyright 1966 by Allyn and Bacon, Inc., Boston.

ment studied physically normal but institutionalized infants. Convinced that in spite of an abundance of theories developmental psychology has much too little real data, Professor Burton L. White of Harvard University began by carefully observing infants as they lay in their cribs in the wardrooms of the institution. He and his colleagues recorded the quantity and quality of visual-motor activity to study the babies' attention. On the basis of these observations they plotted the development of the infants' tendency to explore the visual surroundings, as depicted in Figure 12-1. Some of the findings surprised the investigators.

One important revelation for me which resulted from these weekly observations was that, contrary to my academically bred expectations, infants weren't really very oral during the first months of life. In fact, between two and six months, a far more appropriate description would be that they are visual-prehensory creatures. We observed subject after subject spend dozens of hours watching first his fists, then his fingers, and then the interactions between hands and fingers. Thumb-sucking and mouthing were rarely observed except for brief periods when the infant was either noticeably upset or unusually hungry (White, 1967, p. 207).

These observations point up how much more we need to know about the details of the infant's activities before we can reach conclusions about what events characterize early development. It may be, as this investigator's comments imply, that the "oral" infant will turn out to be much more attentive and active, and less oral and passive, than was believed in early formulations. Indeed, close observation of young children suggests a dramatic increase in the infant's competence by the second or third month. More wakefulness and alertness, greater receptivity to stimulation, more directed attention and less fussing begin to characterize the baby (Sroufe, 1977). Stimulation becomes less unsettling and may be sought out actively as the baby becomes more and more attentive, even to its own movements.

Early Stimulation

In recent years there has been a growing recognition in our society that an alarmingly large number of people fall tragically short of their human potential. In most parts of the world, including the United States, major segments of the population live in underprivileged and deprived environments that stifle their potential development. In spite of the magnitude of this problem, we are just beginning to study and understand how a child's world may be structured so that experience can have the best effects on his or her growth and development.

Some intriguing experimental work with animals has suggested that post-natal handling and other forms of early stimulation may have major effects on subsequent development (e.g., Dennenberg, 1964; Levine, 1957, 1962). Animals like mice, cats, and dogs grow up to be superior on many tests if they are handled or stimulated with relative frequency early in development. For example, some rats were raised in a dimly lit, quiet room with no opportunity to contact or see other animals. "Enriched" rats, in contrast, were raised in groups of 10 animals, had "toys" in their cages, and received special learning and "play opportunities." The stimulated, "educated" rats were shown to differ from the deprived ones even in the brain chemistry of their cortexes and in the weight of their brains (Bennett and his associates, 1964; Rosenzweig and collaborators, 1960). Early handling and stimulation may also be important for human development (e.g., Casler, 1961; Yarrow, 1961). Conversely, growing up in a stimulus-impoverished environment may have negative effects on development.

To study the consequences of depriving an infant of social stimulation would require exposing him to prolonged total isolation. Such experiments with humans are out of the question for obvious ethical reasons, and under natural conditions babies fortunately are not submitted to total social deprivation. In experimental research, however, monkeys have been raised in isolation (without any social contacts); they have been kept alone in a cage for the first six months of life (Harlow & Harlow, 1966). When later removed from isolation these monkeys showed extreme social abnormalities. The typical animal crouched and seemed fearful, avoiding all social contact. If the isolation period was less than 6 months, the animal generally recovered and showed normal behavior; if it extended from 6 to 12 months the consequences tended to be grave and irreversible—the animal tended to become extremely fearful, and his social and sexual behavior remained abnormal.

Taken collectively, the studies in this and preceding sections suggest that early stimulation is an important condition for proper development, and that a severe, prolonged absence of minimal stimulation may have pronounced negative consequences. Later studies also show that stimulation is important for many aspects of development (Sroufe, 1977). For example, visual stimulation with colorful objects and crib ornaments such as mobiles may speed up the baby's development of visually directed reaching in the first few months of life (White, 1971). For such stimulation to help, however, the infant must be maturationally ready for it. Stimulation before the infant is mature enough, or excessive stimulation, may be ineffective or even harmful.

Social Attachment

Around the middle of the first year of life the home-reared infant normally begins to show signs of specific attachment to the mother and to other people, especially the father. Although there are individual differences in this development, most children start to manifest attachment in about the seventh month. Human attachment takes many forms. Seeking contact and proximity, clinging, following, calling, and crying are examples (Ainsworth et al., 1971; Bowlby, 1969). When the people the child is attached to are present, unfamiliar situations and strangers evoke less distress. In contrast, when the child is separated from the people he is attached to, he may become anxious and distressed, especially in new situations.

The strength of this attachment may be inferred from the amount of the child's protest when separated momentarily from a person with whom he was comfortable and close. Usually approximately a month after the first signs of attachment begin, the child also starts to show fear when confronted by strangers (Shaffer & Emerson, 1964). Thus it is during the second part of the first year that children form clear discriminations between familiar and strange people. In contrast, during the first six months of life (especially from 2 to 6 months), the infant seems to seek stimulation more diffusely, and to smile at strange faces as well as familiar ones.

Social attachment, according to some theorists, may have its roots in the close association between the caretaker (usually the mother) and reduction of the infant's bodily tensions through feeding. Because of her close association with the biological tension-reduction produced by food, the mother thus becomes a satisfying and sought-after object for the child. In turn, other people also become objects for the child's attachments on the basis of generalization as well as for the reinforcement they supply in their own right (Dollard & Miller, 1950).

To test this idea of the link between feeding and attachment, one would have to separate the mother's feeding function from her other maternal attributes. This separation, practically impossible in the human situation, was achieved simply and ingeniously in experiments with monkeys (Harlow & Zimmerman, 1959). In these studies young monkeys were reared in isolation from their true mothers and were supplied with two artificial and inanimate "laboratory mothers." Neither laboratory mother really looked like a monkey. One was composed of wire mesh and, although she was hardly "soft and cuddly," could be clung to by the young monkey. The other "mother" was a similar shape but was covered with a towel-like terry cloth and hence was much more "cuddly."

Monkey test

The main question studied was: Would the young monkeys always cling to the mother-figure that supplied food? Accordingly food was made available from a bottle attached to the chest of one or the other mother during each monkey's development. In test trials the monkeys then were free to go to either mother. Regardless of which mother was the source of food, the young monkeys generally chose the cuddly terry-cloth mother and spent more time clinging to her. Moreover, contact with the cuddly mother seemed to be a source of security for the infant: He explored strange objects more freely when holding on to her hand, and he seemed less fearful in new environments if he could make contact with the cloth mother. The behavior of the monkeys who had been fed by the wire-mesh mother was highly discriminative. They ran to her for food when hungry but then returned to the soft-contact mother for clinging and spent most of the day with her.

The results suggest that attachment behaviors may arise independent of the food source and hunger reduction. This is perhaps most evident in animal species such as ducklings, which feed themselves from birth on but nevertheless exhibit close attachment to their mother, following her around much of the time. Association with feeding and the comfort of tension reduction often do enhance attachment, but they may not be either its main or only cause (Sroufe, 1978). Indeed, attachment is so universal in young children that ". . . it seems almost pointless to ask why it occurs. Surely it is simply something natural—something built into human nature" (Maccoby, 1980, p. 62–63).

Later Development

Development involves a gradual transition from helplessness and dependency to active mastery, independence, competence, and autonomy. As children mature biologically and achieve better motor and cognitive skills they gain many new possibilities for self-assertion and active mastery. For example, with crawling and walking comes a new mobility that permits youngsters to manipulate the environment more actively and to explore the world more fully. Many of these exploratory behaviors delight the parents, but others may be extremely upsetting, as when the child explores the medicine cabinet or the electrical outlets rather than the toy box.

Sex and Aggression

Two patterns of behavior that are especially problem-producing in our culture are *aggression* and *sex*. "Aggression" is behavior aimed at inflicting injury or harm on others; it always has a victim. When the child bangs a pegboard with a hammer the parents approve, but when he or she bangs siblings and playmates the social environment quickly reacts against these actions and the battles start.

Sex is the second behavior pattern about which socializing agents are likely to become disturbed. The child's investigations of the environment include exploration of his or of her own body. They notice genitals and especially the fact that some people have a penis and others do not. Children express interest in these biological facts and in their own bodies, and may enjoy touching themselves and others.

Under some unfortunate conditions, the child's experiences regarding aggression and sex can become a basis for anxiety and extreme inhibition. Alternatively, these experiences, like other aspects of one's developing personality, may be managed without undue trauma. Threats and feelings that sexual and aggressive activities are bad can easily be conveyed through both the attitudes displayed by socializing agents and the things they say and do directly to the child when he or she engages in sexual or aggressive behaviors or tries them out tentatively. Conversely, a failure to learn to control aggression and sex in socially approved ways may be as detrimental to development as are excessive anxiety and inhibition. The diffusely aggressive youngster who has not learned when and what he or she *cannot* hit and hurt is likely to have as many problems as the youngster who is distressed at any expression of aggressiveness. These comments about aggression apply equally to the socialization of sex.

Curiosity and Information Seeking

While early psychological theorists stressed biological drives and simple rewards and punishments in their analyses of human motivation, more recent formulations have recognized the role of information and cognitive variables. These formulations emphasize that the informational qualities of stimuli affect their impact (e.g., Berlyne, 1966). Such attributes as novelty, complexity, and surprise, for example, influence the child's attention.

Children as well as adults seem to seek moderate amounts of uncertainty or predictable change. The desire for some surprise is seen, for example, in many types of play and recreational activity, such as the "fun houses" and grotesque distorting mirrors of amusement parks. When the environment is utterly unchanging for prolonged time periods, people become unbearably bored and perceptual and intellectual functions may be hampered. Yet extreme surprise and novelty may provoke anxiety and distress. For example, when chimpanzees are exposed to harmless but surprising sights (such as a model of a chimpanzee's head without the body) they may become terrified. Strong fear has also been reported in children in response to strange or novel sights and sounds. Similarly, while adults enjoy things that are unexpected, the borderline between pleasant surprise and unpleasant shock is often thin.

In general, novel and complex stimuli attract more attention than do completely familiar and simple events. For example, such features of the environment as irregularity of arrangement, and incongruity all enhance the observer's alertness and general arousal (Berlyne, 1966; Nunnally & Lemond, 1973). On the other extreme, an ever-changing, totally unpredictable environment is chaotic and anxiety-producing; it leaves the individual overwhelmed rather than alert. The specific ways in which the structure of the child's world best encourages curiosity without causing distress deserve extensive research.

Competence Motivation

Robert White (1959) has suggested that many human motives, such as play, curiosity, and adventure seeking, may be subsumed under a more fundamental desire for competence or effective functioning and mastery. White further suggests that such a competence or "effectance" motive may be intrinsic, and that many activities (like play) may be enjoyed for their own sake, whether or not they reduce or satisfy primary drives like hunger or thirst. White has discussed the nature of effective or competent coping with the environment as seen in such common activities as walking, exploring and crawling, and language. He comments that the behavior that is effective in all these efforts "is directed, selective, and consistent, and it is continued not only because it serves primary drives, which indeed it cannot serve until it is almost perfected, but because it satisfies an intrinsic need to deal with the environment" (White, 1959, p. 319).

Competence or "effectance" motivation thus implies a desire to achieve mastery of a task simply for its own sake. The particular tasks to be mastered may be virtally infinite—any response pattern is potentially perfectable, whether it is tightrope walking, building towers with toy blocks, flower arranging, or scientific theory building. The actual origins of hypothesized higher-order motives like competence are hard (if not impossible) to trace definitively. Regardless of their roots, it has become clear, however, that many different types of gratification can serve as goals and incentives that people may pursue passionately in their own right.

Cognitive Development and Competence

Psychodynamic theorists originally emphasized instincts of sex and aggression and the importance of resolving conflicts with oral, anal, and Oedipal problems in development. More recently psychologists have recognized that the acquisition of competence is also a vital component of adequate adaptation (White, 1959). In every society, but especially in those that stress achievement, a failure to develop at least minimal skills and areas of adequacy dooms the individual to a life filled with dissatisfactions.

Personality development thus is not rigidly separated from cognitive and intellectual development and from the growth of competence and skills (Kohlberg, 1969; Mischel, 1973a). Adequate functioning in our society, and individu-

Competence motivation refers to the desire to achieve mastery.

als' conceptions of their own worth, depend on their ability to cope with problems and on their self-evaluation of achievements. As later chapters will emphasize, concepts about oneself, and the manner in which one assesses his or her own accomplishments and failures, are critical aspects of personality development. Experiences and self-assessments connected with competence and mastery probably begin in earliest childhood, but they do not stop there. Throughout life competencies develop and self-evaluations are made in areas that range from one's work to one's sexuality and one's total self. Indeed, excessively harsh self-evaluations may lead to painful self-torture, just as excessively lenient self-appraisals, especially when accompanied by grossly inadequate performances, may lead to their own problems.

The exploratory behaviors, the curiosity- and mastery-oriented activities

FIGURE 12-2
Cognitive Development Is Reflected in These Drawings by a Girl at Three Points in Childhood. Each Time the Child Was Asked To "Draw a Picture of a Girl."

Age 4   Age 5½   Age 7½

displayed by the young child, are boosted incalculably by cognitive development (Figure 12-2) and by the acquisition of language. As children become verbal they begin to label things, including themselves, and to form increasingly complex discriminations. These discriminations are based not only on physical attributes but also on semantic features—on what things are called. Gradually the individual's increasingly explicit self-awareness as an entity differentiated from the rest of the world comes to include a more delineated concept of self as a distinct person construed to have stable attributes (Chapter 19).

The Roots of Competence

The child's developing competence may be firmly rooted by the age of three years (White et al., 1976). Certain experiences are especially critical for the growth of linguistic, intellectual, and social skills. Especially important is the amount of "live" language the child gets: the more the better (White et al., 1976). Live language comes not from overheard speech or exposure to language on television and radio but from adults talking directly to the child. White notes that parents who seem to rear exceptionally competent children seem to design and organize their child's environment especially well. They also are firm disciplinarians who show great affection for their child. They are responsive to the child, ready to serve as "personal consultants" when the child needs them, but they let the child initiate social interactions.

Achievement

Closely related to the desire for competence is the individual's tendency to strive for achievement. The desire to "do well" and the achievement of competence in intellectual and social behavior have received much attention in current approaches to personality. For example, research on achievement-related motives and behaviors shows that they have some generality across situations. Even by nursery school age, children display some consistency in their achievement strivings. Children who seek approval from their mothers for achievement tend to behave similarly toward their nursery school teachers (Crandall, Preston, & Rabson, 1960). Children who often initiate achievement efforts at home display similar behaviors during free play in nursery school. Consistency in achievement striving is greatest across similar activities. For example, the intellectual striving of elementary school children was substantially correlated with their striving on mechanical tasks; however, strivings for intellectual and mechanical achievement were not related to achievement striving in athletics. (Moss & Kagan, 1961).

Achievement behavior, especially in the form of intellectual striving, may be one of the more stable aspects of personality, showing some consistency over long periods of time. The preschool child who strives to master cognitive and intellectual skills tends to maintain this motivation during high school and early adulthood (Moss & Kagan, 1961). Boys and girls who start school with strong motivation to do well and to achieve recognition thus may tend to develop into young adults who are concerned with intellectual accomplishments and achievement, although there are many exceptions.

The individual's degree of achievement striving tends to be related to the degree of intelligence and level of general ability. For example, ratings of how much children strive for achievement and recognition are related positively to the children's scores on intelligence tests. That is, brighter children are more oriented toward achievement. Moreover, these positive relationships between achievement strivings and intelligence seem to be maintained throughout childhood and in early adulthood (Kagan & Moss, 1962). The positive relationship between ability and achievement striving is not surprising. The more intelligent, competent, skillful children can more readily achieve satisfaction for their achievement efforts because they are more likely to do well. Hence their motivation to strive for excellence becomes strengthened by the reinforcement of success.

Other people's reactions also influence the child's degree of achievement striving. For example, children who often displayed strong achievement efforts outside the home tended to be those whose mothers frequently and spontaneously rewarded their efforts to achieve, even when the youngsters were not seeking approval (Crandall, 1963). The mothers of children who became high in achievement strivings seemed to foster independence early in their children's development. They generally ignored their children's requests for help and, instead, encouraged their tentative efforts to gain mastery and achieve solutions by themselves (Winterbottom, 1958). Mothers who rewarded early accomplishments in their children seemed to facilitate their children's intellectual strivings and their desire to do well in school and to learn new skills. Likewise, the encouragement of mastery of basic skills—such as walking and talking—early in childhood, tends to facilitate subsequent school achievement (Mussen, Conger, & Kagan, 1979).

Conversely, the child who grows up in a home or subculture in which adequate stimulation is absent and intellectual achievement is not recognized is much less likely to develop the achievement orientation, skills, and academic striving necessary for success in school work. An environment that provides the young child with good opportunities to observe and practice verbal and intellectual skills may enhance substantially the chances for high intellectual achievements and competence (Wolf, 1966). Thus the child's intellectual abilities (as measured by IQ tests) and the stimulation, encouragement, and support that the environment provides for achievements jointly influence actual accomplishments.

Agents of Socialization and Sources of Learning

Beginning in infancy, the child's commerce with the world involves relations with significant social agents who, deliberately or inadvertently, transmit the culture to which they belong. Just as one approach to socialization focuses on critical events in development, another popular approach concentrates on the *agents* of socialization who are most salient at different points in the child's life, and on the influences that they exert on him or her during development. One may analyze, for example, the different types of social behaviors modeled and encouraged by the mother, the father, siblings, school peers, teachers, and so on in the many settings of the child's life at each age period. Obviously, each of these models and settings is responsible for much of what the child learns and becomes, and each may contribute to the development of different content in the total personality.

The parents, for example, play the greatest role in the development of attitudes about the home and family. Peers, in contrast, become the sources of many of the child's attitudes and interpersonal behaviors at school and at play, influencing the youngster's concepts about his or her interpersonal competencies and deficits. The type of roles and attitudes encouraged or disapproved by each of these sources depends on such variables as the child's age, sex, and socioeconomic position within the particular culture.

In addition to individual socialization agents, one must also consider the role of social institutions as an influence on personality development. In the broadest sense the culture into which the child happens to be born dictates many of the social forms and behavioral possibilities available to him or her. The rules, values, prohibitions, and sanctions of the culture, as well as its accumulated knowledge, are transmitted actively by the schools and by the many other social organizations in which the individual participates. The mass media in technically sophisticated societies permit and influence the rapid transmission of changing norms and values.

Do the Beginnings Predict the Future?

As you know from earlier sections, the degree of stability in each person's qualities is a major question of interest both to the layperson and the professional psychologist. Do early characteristics predict later qualities? When parents say "Charlie was always so friendly, even as a little baby," are their comments justified? Can we predict the six-year-old's behavior from responses in the first year of life? Is there much continuity in the qualities and behaviors of the child throughout childhood?

A number of important connections have been found. For example, babies who make certain responses with lower intensity at birth tend to show some positive qualities later in life (see Figure 12-3). Such newborn behaviors as lower sensitivity to touch on the skin, for example, in the newborn predicted more mature communication and coping at age two and one-half and at age seven and one-half. High touch sensitivity and high respiration rates at birth were related to low interest, low participation, lower assertiveness and gregariousness, and less communicativeness in later years (Bell et al., 1971; Halverson, 1971a, 1971b). But these links between newborn and later behaviors were exceptions.

Most of the relations that were examined turned out to be nonexistent, and the associations that were found generally were not strong. So there are some connections between a newborn's qualities and characteristics later in life, but in the individual case one could not predict confidently from responses at birth to later characteristics:

> To use an analogy, newborn behavior is more like a preface to a book than a table of its contents yet to be unfolded. Further, the preface is itself merely a rough draft undergoing rapid revision. There are some clues to the nature of the book in the preface, but these are in code form and taking them as literally prophetic is likely to lead to disappointment (Bell et al., 1971, p. 132).

But as one progresses beyond the "preface of the book" to the first few chapters (to the early years of life) continuities in development do become increasingly more evident (e.g., Block & Block, 1980, in press). Children who are seen as more active, assertive, aggressive, competitive, outgoing and so on at age three years are also more likely to be described as having more of those qualities later in development, for example. In sum, the specific links between qualities of the child say in the fourth year and in the eighth year may be complex and indirect, but a thorough analysis of the patterns indicates that threads of continuity do emerge over time. Thus childhood characteristics may be connected coherently to later behavior and attributes at least to some

FIGURE 12-3
Examples of Relationships between Children's Behavior at Different Ages.
The Relationship Holds for Both Sexes Unless Otherwise Indicated in the
Chart.

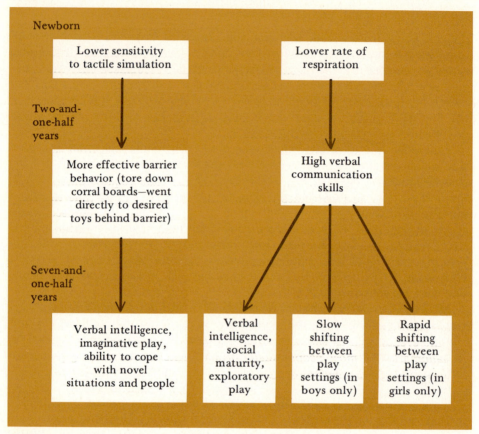

(Based on data from Bell, et al., 1971; Halverson, 1971a, 1971b; Halverson &
Waldrop, 1974)

degree (Arend, Gove, & Sroufe, 1979; Block, 1971). Experiences in the early
pages of the book do affect what happens in the later pages of life, although
these early experiences do not prevent the possibility of genuine changes in
later life. The amount of stability or change over time probably varies for different types of characteristics and different types of experiences at different
points in the developmental progression.

Life-Span Development

Although it has been fashionable in psychology to focus on the events of early
childhood, socialization does not stop at age five. Children's early school expe-

riences, their increasing involvements with activities and relationships beyond their family, their sexual urges at puberty, their cognitive growth and intellectual successes and failures at school, their interpersonal adventures—all these events contribute to shape the people that they continue to become, and each of these milestones can be construed as an especially intriguing phase of total development.

Early psychoanalytic theories of development focused attention on the first few years of life, but more recent formulations have recognized that the challenges and crises of adaptation extend throughout life. One sign of the popular recognition of this fact is the widespread concern with the "identity crises" of puberty and adolescence that may leave individuals confused about what adult life roles to make their own (Erikson, 1950, 1968).

Socialization does not end with individuals' ultimate exodus from their parental home. Now their adoption of various new adult roles—social, marital, economic—all involve them in new relationships that require different resources and yield new outcomes that in turn change them. In time the children become parents, and they who were the object of socialization become its agents, transmitting to their children the values and behavior patterns that have become their own. The responsibilities, challenges, and crises of middle life gradually shift into those of advanced age, and with that shift again come new dilemmas, crises, and experiences that alter the person further. And so it goes, a continuous interaction between person and events that mutually modify each other until the very end of life, with continuous changes throughout the life span (Baltes, 1979).

While events such as the ones discussed in this chapter tend to be normative landmarks for most people, many other events can be turning points in the lives of particular individuals. A serious illness, a tragic accident, a chance meeting, a religious conversion, a new political commitment in college—any of these can become extremely significant. The impact of such events depends on what has happened to individuals throughout their previous history; in turn, the consequences of these events may permeate far into their future.

We are saying that a multiplicity of events throughout development may exert critical influences on people and hence partly determine what they become and do at any later point in their lives. That is, behavior is multiply determined by many happenings. All these conditions influence the person and, in turn, interact with variables in the current situation as determinants of behavior.

SUMMARY

1. Maturation and learning *both* are important in the development of the human organism. Genetic and maturational processes predominate in embryological development and structural features of human

growth. The importance of learning for personality development does not preclude the possibility that genetic and constitutional factors may influence social behavior in many complex ways. Language acquisition is an example of the close interaction of maturation and learning.

2. Freud's psychosexual theory, Erickson's theory of interpersonal phases and crises, and Piaget's stages of cognitive development are examples of stage theories of development. It is uncertain whether or not it is necessary to construe development as occurring in discrete stages. It is widely agreed, however, that some patterns—such as language development—are sequential.

3. Feeding, and the child's experience around it—generally with the mother—is a major event in early infancy. In spite of the dependency and relative helplessness of the infant, research has shown that even babies are sensitive to environmental changes and may by their responses in turn affect the environment. For example, by crying the child may quickly come to exert some influence on his or her caretakers. Thus the social transactions between the human organism and its environment begin at birth.

4. Even very early in life, stimulation from many sources affects the child. Early formulations that characterized the infant as mainly passive, dependent, and oral thus have to be modified to take account of the greater activity and attentiveness found in recent studies that have closely observed how young babies actually spend their time. The baby sees, hears, and feels as well as feeds, and all these experiences affect his or her relationship to the world.

5. Children normally begin to show signs of emotional attachment to their primary caretaker around the middle of the first year. Some research with animals indicates that these attachment behaviors may develop quite independent of feeding.

6. Sex and aggression are two patterns of behavior especially likely to produce problems in our culture because they generate anxiety and conflict for many people. The child's experiences in these areas may become a basis for later problems. Proper development is enhanced if the child learns to successfully discriminate the appropriate occasions for the expression of these behaviors and for their inhibition.

7. Although early psychodynamic theories stressed the role of sex and aggression, more recently psychologists have recognized that the development of curiosity, of competence, and of adequate achievement is necessary for self-esteem and effective coping. Cognitive and intellectual development and the experiences and self-assessments con-

nected with these functions are integral parts of personality development.

8. Achievement strivings and behaviors are among the more consistent aspects of personality. Even young children show some consistency across situations in their strivings for intellectual achievement and recognition. These strivings also may show considerable stability over time. Achievement behaviors tend to be related to children's ability and to the stimulation and encouragement for achievement available in their environment.

9. The child learns from many sources. The various agents of socialization (e.g., parents, siblings, schoolmates, and teachers) may exert their influence at different age periods and in different situations. Personality development and change do not end in early childhood but continue throughout life. The events of young adulthood, middle life, and advanced age bring their own responsibilities, challenges, and crises.

10. Some early personal qualities may persist over time, although their specific forms may change. There are threads of continuity in development, at least for some characteristics shown as early as age three years, although the process of adaptation and change continues throughout the life span.

CHAPTER 13

SOCIAL LEARNING AND COGNITION

Descriptions of what is learned, and from whom, where, and when it is learned, throughout development are often informative and intriguing. To understand personality development adequately, however, one must go beyond such descriptions to analyze how personality is acquired—that is, the mechanisms of personality development. An emphasis on *process,* on the variables that regulate social learning and cognitive and emotional development, should help us to understand the general rules of personality development regardless of the particular models or settings that are most influential at specific points in the person's life. We have already considered the role of early stimulation and experience. Now we will review the principles of social learning in personality development.

Basic Processes

Direct Rewards

We discussed some of the basic processes involved in social learning in Chapters 4 and 9. Recall that the valence or value of neutral stimuli may be changed through contiguous association with emotion-evoking stimuli, as seen in *classical conditioning*. This happens throughout personality development. For example, the child's attitudes toward defecation and body functions are affected by the emotional events closely connected with them. If toilet functions and fear-producing experiences (such as harsh punishment) become regularly associated, anxiety may become linked with various components of the eliminative functions. So the untrained child who is made to feel a failure for soiling himself may become anxious about going to the toilet and refuse to go. Likewise, because of the closeness of the urethra, anus, and external genitals, it may be especially easy for the child to generalize his reactions from toilet functions to sexual activity. Conversely, positive attitudes may be developed by an appropriate association among neutral and positive stimuli. As a result of their close association with highly affective stimuli, other stimuli thus may become either aversive or positively valued in their own right. The effects of such conditioning may be seen clearly when previously neutral stimuli start to elicit fears (phobias) because of their association with fear-provoking events.

Remember also that even seemingly deeply ingrained behavior patterns, including many severe social deviations, may be changed when new response-reinforcement relations are established, as is demonstrated in *operant conditioning*. The outcomes that children obtain when they try behaviors influence their future readiness to try similar behaviors. For example, if whining and a temper tantrum attract the attention of a busy mother, the outburst is more likely to be repeated than if it were left unattended. Likewise if the baby easily gets help from father even for the most trivial problems as soon as she gets into difficulty, she is more likely to develop strong dependency habits involving him.

Opportunities to practice new behavior and to experience its positive consequences facilitate the future occurrence of similar behavior, but it is also easy to use "rewards" unwisely in socialization. A major purpose of socialization is to wean the individual from external controls and rewards so that behavior will become increasingly guided and supported by "intrinsic" gratifications, i.e., it will be done for its own sake. Therefore it is essential to use incentives wisely and only to the extent necessary to initiate and sustain desired behavior. External incentives may be important in order to encourage a person to try activities that have not yet become attractive for him or her. For example, approval and praise from parents for trying to play a violin may be helpful first steps in encouraging the child's earliest musical interests. But when the youngster begins to experience activity-generated satisfactions (e.g., from playing the music itself) it becomes important to avoid excessive external rewards. The latter would be unnecessary and possibly detrimental, leading the child to play for the "wrong reasons" and to easily extinguish his or her interests when external rewards become sparse or are removed altogether. The same considerations would apply in the socialization of such activities as concern for fairness, empathy, helpfulness, and attention to the longterm consequences of behavior. While such sensitivities would initially be encouraged by external response consequences (rewards), ultimately they should become sustained by the gratifications generated by the activities themselves.

Thus it should be clear that "overjustification" of an activity by excessive external reward may interfere with the satisfactions (intrinsic interests) that would otherwise be generated by the activity itself (e.g., Lepper, Greene & Nisbett, 1973). Excessive external rewards may even have boomerang effects and lead the recipient to devalue and resist the rewarded activity. For example, a child who enjoys books may lose interest in them if bribed with money to keep on reading. Such resistance is especially likely in a culture whose members value a sense of autonomy and freedom. Under such conditions, any seemingly undue or exaggerated external rewards may be interpreted as pressures and coercions, which may lead to intense resistance either overtly or covertly (e.g., Brehm, 1966), as in the "rebelliousness" of adolescents.

Generalization and Discrimination

Considerable *generalization* occurs if a response pattern is uniformly rewarded under many conditions or in many settings. If, for example, the child is encouraged to behave aggressively with older people as well as with peers, and when visiting other families as well as at home, he or she is likely to develop some generalized aggressive patterns.

Similarity among stimulus situations increases generalization effects. Generalization occurs not only to physically similar stimuli, but also to those that are related in terms of meaning (Lang, Geer & Hnatiow, 1963). For example, when subjects receive an electric shock during exposure to rural words like "barn" or "cow," they may later show emotional reactions to other words connected with farming like "hay" or "horse" (Diven, 1937; Lacey & Smith, 1954). The mechanisms of higher-order generalization are complex and incompletely understood (e.g., Braine, 1963; Feather, 1965). The effects depend on the exact circumstances of the individual's history with the particular stimuli and on the details of the eliciting situation, but the processes still are not completely clear.

Discrimination occurs when a response pattern is reinforced in the presence of one stimulus attribute and nonreinforced, or extinguished, in the presence of other stimulus properties. This happens, for example, when physical aggression is encouraged toward peers at school but not when the principal is watching. When behavior is reinforced in the presence of some stimuli but not of others, discrimination results and the individual displays the behavior in some situations (those in which it will probably be reinforced) but not in others.

We already have seen examples of the sharpness of human discrimination in many contexts. Recall the fact that Gary W.'s anxieties were confined mainly to public speaking in evaluative group situations; the psychotic and self-destructive girl (described in Chapter 10) hurt herself consistently only when people withdrew attention from behaviors that they had previously reinforced; and the babies in Bruner's sucking research quickly learned to change their sucking and mouth movements in accord with the particular reinforcement schedule employed by the milk-dispensing program as noted in Chapter 12.

Discrimination training is a major part of the socialization process. In almost all cultures, for example, children learn within the first few years to control their bowel and bladder functions. They learn to regulate themselves so that they defecate and urinate only under some conditions and in some places and not under other circumstances. Similarly the toddler soon learns that while active exploration in the sandbox is permitted and encouraged, similar play near the stove or in the living room leads to quite different outcomes. As a result, children quickly learn extremely subtle discriminations, and their behavior begins to depend on the exact conditions. As these examples suggest, consistencies in behavior from one situation to another can only be expected when behavior yields similar consequences across the situations. The concepts of discrimination and generalization suggest that broad consistency in behavior patterns may be found only to the degree that the patterns are uniformly reinforced across many stimulus conditions. Throughout development children learn a seemingly endless variety of roles and thus become increasingly discriminating in what they do.

The Patterning of Outcomes

The patterning or sequencing ("scheduling") of reinforcement affects the future occurrence and strength of the reinforced behavior (e.g., Ferster & Skinner, 1957). Sometimes the scheduling of reinforcement may be even more important than the nature of the reinforcer (Morse & Kelleher, 1966). Continuous reinforcement usually increases the speed with which responses are learned. Intermittent reinforcement tends to produce more stable behavior that is more persistently maintained when reinforcement stops. For example, rewarding temper tantrums intermittently (by occasionally attending to them in an irregular pattern) may make them very durable. Since many potentially maladaptive behaviors, such as physical aggression and immature dependency, are rewarded intermittently, they can become very hard to eliminate.

Anxiety and Punishment in Socialization

Some learning theorists focus on the role of rewards, but punishment or "aversive stimulation" is also important in socialization. In laboratory studies of anxiety the unconditioned stimulus is usually a painful electric shock and the stimulus to be conditioned is a discrete event such as a distinctive neutral tone or a buzzer. Generally human life is not that simple and neat. Often "aversive stimuli" involve punishments that are administered in less obvious and less controlled ways. These punishments may be conveyed subtly, by facial expressions and words rather than by brute force, and in extremely complicated patterns, by the same individuals who also nurture the child, giving love and other positive reinforcement. Moreover, the events that are punished

often involve more than specific responses; they sometimes entail long sequences of overt and covert behavior.

The effects of punishment are especially complicated because the punitive
parents not only punish the child but, in so doing, model aggression (Bandura,
1973; Gelfand et al., 1974). The resulting effects can seem quite paradoxical.
Consider, for example, the father who tries to suppress aggression in his son by
punishing him physically. Later, in the father's absence, the boy may imitate
the very aggressiveness that the father modeled while punishing him.

The behaviors that are considered inappropriate and punishable depend on
such variables as the child's age and sex as well as the situation. Obviously the
helplessness and passivity that are acceptable in a young child may be maladaptive in an older one, and the traits valued in a girl may not be valued in a
boy. While the mother may deliberately encourage her son's dependency and
discourage his aggressiveness, his school peers may do the reverse, ridiculing
dependency at school and modeling and rewarding aggression and self-assertion. Given this multiplicity of variables, the influence of punishment on personality development is, not surprisingly, both important and complex (e.g.,
Aronfreed, 1968; Walters & Grusec, 1977).

A careful review of research on the effects of punishment upon children's
behavior concludes, in part, that:

> aversive stimulation, if well timed, consistent, and sufficiently intense,
> may create conditions that accelerate the socialization process, provided
> that the socialization agents also provide information concerning alterna-
> tive prosocial behavior and positively reinforce any such behavior that
> occurs (Walters & Parke, 1967, p. 218).

The important point to remember here is that when punishment is speedy
and specific it may suppress undesirable behavior, but it cannot teach the
child desirable alternatives. Therefore, parents should use positive techniques
to model and reinforce appropriate behavior that the child can employ in
place of the unacceptable response that has to be suppressed (e.g., Walters &
Parke, 1967). In that way the learner will develop a new response that *can* be
made without getting punished. Without such a positive alternative, the child
faces a dilemma in which total avoidance may seem the only possible route.
Punishment may have very unfortunate effects when the child believes there
is no way in which he or she can prevent further punishment and cope. If you
become convinced that no potentially successful actions are open to you, that
you can do nothing right, depression and hopelessness may follow (Seligman,
1975). In sum, learning to fear potentially dangerous stimuli and to inhibit a
host of behaviors, such as extreme antisocial aggression, is an integral part of
personality development. Punishment may have negative effects, however,
when it is administered in ways that, intentionally or unwittingly, lead to
massive behavioral inhibition or to debilitating anxieties and depression
(Chapters 16 and 17).

Child-Rearing Practices and Reinforcement

Laboratory demonstrations of learning are impressive, but they do not illuminate the socialization patterns and reinforcement practices that occur naturally in everyday life. Results relevant to socialization practices obtained from field studies of families tend to be much more complex and more difficult to interpret. There are many reasons for these complexities.

Under naturalistic conditions any particular behavior pattern may be subjected to extremely complex outcomes. It is often rewarded on some occasions by some people (but not by others) in highly irregular ways. For example, peers may reinforce a child for behaviors that teachers and parents react to with disapproval. Even the same person—say a teacher—may praise a child for a behavior in one setting but not in another, rewarding aggression, for example, at play but not in the classroom. Finally, the child may see others rewarded for behavior that is not condoned for him or her. The slum-dwelling child sees the neighborhood gangster with cars, nice clothes, and girl friends, and even the middle-class child sees televised heroes getting gratifying pay-offs for violence and aggression.

Such vicarious reinforcement may counteract and undermine the effects of direct reinforcement. This conflict happens, for example, when parents, in full view of their children, enact, enjoy, and receive ample rewards for the very practices that they deny their children and even punish them for.

The effects of reinforcement under naturalistic conditions are especially complicated because socializing agents such as the mother and father always have a multiple role. These agents of the culture not only encourage and discourage or "shape" the child's behavior through direct tuition, but they also model relevant behavior. The information conveyed to the child through these diverse modes is often inconsistent.

Many puzzles in the relationships between child-training practices and the child's subsequent behavior may reflect lack of attention to the discrepancies between the behaviors the child observes used by powerful and successful models and those that he is taught directly. One should expect, for example, that if a father tries to train his child to become "open and sincere" while he himself behaves deceitfully, he may well rear a child who develops conflicts about honest self-expression. To understand socialization properly it is thus important to take account of both modeling and direct training influences (e.g., Mischel & Liebert, 1966).

Identification

Some of the most striking features of personality often seem to develop independently of direct reinforcement. For example:

A pervasive quality such as masculinity (or femininity) receives at least some intentional reinforcement by parents and peers, of course, but the training task required for creating this kind of role conformity seems too great to permit an explanation in terms of the direct reinforcement of each of the behavioral components that compose the roles (Sears, Rau, & Alpert, 1965, p. 2).

To understand the development of personality with concepts other than direct reinforcement, many researchers have invoked the process of "identification." In their view, the developing child acquires a broadly integrated pattern of basic attitudes and values that encompass his or her sense of sexual identity as well as conscience and standards of moral judgment and conduct. This set of basic dispositions, they believe, may be facilitated by some of the processes discussed in the last section, but these theorists stress that additional concepts are required. The present section deals with those concepts.

Defining Identification

Identification has been the favorite theoretical mechanism to explain how children develop broad attributes and generalized behavior patterns similar to those of their parents and of the other significant social models in their lives. The theorizing of Sigmund Freud has had an enduring impact on formulations about identification, but the concept of identification has had at least three distinct meanings in Freudian thinking and in the extensions provided by most of his followers.

First (according to Bronfenbrenner's 1960 analysis), identification refers to *behavior,* as when one person acts or feels like another person (called the "model"). Behavioral similarity between two people, however, does not necessarily mean that one person has identified with the other. It may be caused by different variables that independently produced the same effects in both persons. A father and son may both, for example, be unhappy at the same time, but each independently and for completely different reasons.

Second, identification also refers to a *motive,* in the form of a generalized disposition to act or to be like another. This motive usually refers to the tendency to emulate the idealized standards and behaviors of the parent. Many definitions of identification stress that the child must have a motive to be like the model and to want to possess some of his or her attributes (Mussen, Conger, & Kagan, 1979). It is quite likely that most children subjectively experience a strong motive or wish to become more like their parents. Such a wish is illustrated in the following dialogue between a 6½-year-old girl and her father:

DAUGHTER: I love you. . . . I want to be just like you.
FATHER: In what ways?
DAUGHTER: In all ways.
FATHER: Why?
DAUGHTER: Because I love you.
FATHER: And why do you want to be just like me?
DAUGHTER: 'Cause then I could do all the things you do—

FATHER: And?
DAUGHTER: And that would be fun.

This young girl certainly seems to be expressing a motive to become like her father. A scientifically satisfying account of what causes her to take on some of the parental characteristics, however, would be incomplete if it simply noted her motive to be like the parent. A more complete analysis has to consider the causes of the motive itself. We are back again with the need to consider the conditions that control or regulate experiences as well as the subjective or perceived features of the experience itself. A closer examination of the child's expressed wish hints at some of the reasons for it. The girl is saying she wants to be like her father because she loves him and because if she were more like him she could do all the "fun" things he does. A great deal of research has been devoted to understanding the processes implied by this girl's comments, as later sections discuss.

Finally, a third meaning of the term identification refers to the *process* or mechanisms through which the child comes to emulate a model and to be like him or her. Concepts regarding such mechanisms have been posited by different theorists, beginning with Freud (Chapter 3). These concepts have been created to understand how children "internalize" parental and societal standards for appropriate sex-role behavior and moral conduct, and how they "incorporate" (or make part of themselves) many of the attributes and characteristics of their parents, especially the same-sex parent.

The Role of the Parent and Father-Absence

Most studies of identification have emphasized the child's immediate family, and especially the parents, as models. Identification theories have focused on the father as the main model for the development of appropriate sex typing in boys. In the Freudian view, for example, if the father is absent the boy tends to remain mother-identified and is more likely to develop latent or even overt homosexual tendencies and feminine attributes (e.g., Fenichel, 1945). Guided by psychodynamic theory, much research has been devoted to the effects of father-absence on personality development. Studies on this question indicate that father-absent boys generally tend to show less appropriate sex-typing (e.g., Bach, 1946; Lynn & Sawrey, 1959).

Children whose fathers are absent may be less adequately socialized than comparable father-present children, not just in sex-linked attributes but also in non-sex-typed behaviors. For example, there is a significant relation between father-absence and preference for immediate gratification for children aged 8 to 9 years (Mischel, 1958, 1961c). The father-absent youngsters were less willing to wait for delayed rewards than were children from father-present homes. This relationship held *regardless of the child's sex,* and it was replicated consistently. It suggests that father-absence may be a sign of an inadequate home environment that is not conducive to trust, to voluntary delay of reward, or to other characteristics of appropriate socialization for children of both sexes.

The relationship between father-absence and preference for immediate gratification was found for young children but not for older ones (Mischel, 1961c). It may be that as children gain more experiences outside the limits of their immediate families they become increasingly influenced by extrafamilial sources. They then become less dependent upon the expectations and response patterns modeled and supported in the home, and their behaviors become more influenced by social reinforcement from peers (e.g., Patterson & Anderson, 1964) and by sociological variables.

It is sometimes assumed that the development of sex-appropriate social behaviors in the boy depends on his adopting the characteristics of his father. For the girl, normative sex-typing and socialization supposedly hinges on her adopting behaviors modeled by her mother. These assumptions seem plausible only for sex-role stereotypes, according to which fathers embody masculinity and mothers are the personification of femininity. If we transcend these stereotypes and examine individual lives more closely, some greater complexities become apparent.

Obviously enormous individual differences exist among fathers in their "masculinity" (no matter how it is defined), just as among millions of mothers vast differences exist in "femininity." Consequently, a boy who closely emulates his father actually may through this identification acquire "feminine" characteristics, to the degree that his father displays feminine attributes. Similarly, the girl who identifies closely with a "masculine" and dominating mother would herself become correspondingly masculine. Given these considerations, one cannot assume that the extent to which a child shows socially normative behaviors—such as appropriate conformity to social standards of honesty and self-control—serves as a reliable index of identification.

For example, would the son of a hardened criminal show more identification if, unlike his father, he became a pillar of society, or would he be more strongly identified if he followed closely in his father's path? The belief that the amount of normative behavior (in sex roles, conscience, self-control, or other hypothesized products of identification) shown by the child is an index of the degree to which he has identified with the parents seems to be rooted in the idea that the parents are the sources of the superego and the transmitters of social rules, norms, and restrictions. When the parents themselves violate social norms, however, their ability to fulfill roles as superego models transmitting societal standards becomes highly questionable.

Observational Learning in Personality Development

In the past, identification has been singled out as a special process that required concepts different from those needed to account for other forms of social learning. According to some more recent formulations, however, the development of the diverse components of personality may be described by the basic principles of social learning, and specifically by observational learning.

Social Learning through Identification or Observation?

Bandura and Walters (1963) first pointed out that although numerous distinctions have been proposed between observational learning and identification, the same phenomena are encompassed by both terms. Both imitation and identification refer to the tendency for a person to produce the actions, attitudes, or emotional responses exhibited by real-life or symbolized models. Consequently, Bandura argues that, for the sake of clarity and parsimony, the terms "identification," "imitation," and "observational learning" may be used interchangeably to refer to behavioral modifications produced by exposure to modeling stimuli (1969).

Unlike some earlier behavior theories, current social learning theories no longer depend on the concept of specific reinforcement for discrete acts, and on the tedious "shaping" or "training" of each minuscule role component by

Complex behaviors may be learned rapidly through observation without having to be reinforced.

external reinforcements administered by the parent or other socialization agents. Indeed, it now has been shown often that children may rapidly learn large and complex sequences through cognitive-perceptual processes that require their observing events rather than being reinforced for performing acts (Zimmerman & Rosenthal, 1974).

Observational Learning and Cognition

While learning studies with animals have emphasized direct reward or reinforcement, people learn through observation and symbolic processes, as well as by more direct methods. In this regard, a distinction has been made between *acquisition,* or learning, and *performance* (Chapter 4). We noted that what a person knows and can do depends in part on cognitive and observational processes. Indeed as was discussed earlier, even young babies under normal conditions soon become visually attentive and responsive to what they observe in the environment. On the basis of observational and cognitive processes, children gradually learn a vast repertoire of potential response patterns—of things they *can* do.

Information about the probable consequences of particular behavior patterns can be acquired vicariously, by observing other people and the outcomes they receive. Observing the outcomes other people get for aggressiveness, for example, influences the observer's tendency to perform similar behavior (e.g., Bandura, 1977). Performance thus often may be determined by vicarious and inferred response consequences rather than by direct "trial and error" learning. For example, a young adolescent does not have to be laughed at by his peers in order to learn the consequences of trying "sissyish" behavior. Observing positive consequences, such as attention or praise, for a response pattern tends to increase the probability that he will engage in similar activities. Conversely, when social models are punished severely for their actions, people who watch them will later tend to show greater inhibition of similar behavior (Bandura, 1965).

Any information that changes the person's anticipations about the probable outcomes of a behavior should modify the likelihood that he or she will perform similar behavior. For example, a boy learns about the things his parents are likely to reward and those they will probably punish not just from what the parents do to him but also from what he sees them do to his siblings. He also learns about adult roles by observing his parents and the outcomes or "payoffs" they get for various behavior patterns. Through observation children may learn a variety of complex general rules (Zimmerman & Rosenthal, 1974) that can apply to everything from conduct to language and problem-solving.

What Does Observational Learning Require?

It is necessary now to consider briefly the basic processes that occur in observational learning. These processes have four components: attention, retention, reproduction, and motivation (Bandura, 1977).

To learn from observation it is obviously essential to *attend* to the distinctive features of the modeled behavior. Models would have little longterm impact if we did not *remember* (retain) their behavior after watching it. Consequently, organizing and rehearsing what was observed are important ingredients of learning from models. Especially when the behavior involves complex motor activities (as in swimming, driving, or tennis), the observer also must be able to put together physically the components of the action. Such *motor reproduction* requires accurate self-observation and feedback during rehearsal. For example, it is essential to observe the consequences of particular movements on the steering wheel, and on the gas and brake pedals of the car, when learning to park. Finally, to go from knowledge to performance the observer must have the *motivation* (reinforcement) to enact the behaviors that he or she has learned.

Exposure to Diverse Models: Effects of Model Characteristics

The developing child synthesizes and adopts components from many models. She observes diverse models play many roles and thus starts to learn some of the behaviors relevant to the roles that she herself will assume at different points in her life. For example, by watching her parents she begins to learn about how to be a parent; by observing her teachers she learns how to be a teacher; by observing her playmates she learns various role relationships with peers. The potential roles acquired in this fashion may then be utilized at the appropriate times in her own life, when she has to face situations that require them. Thus when the child becomes a parent she may find herself, to her own surprise (and sometimes chagrin), acting remarkably as her parents did twenty years earlier.

Thus under normal life conditions, children are exposed to many models, and they adopt in varying degrees the behavior of many of these models rather than simply copying one. The child's behavior reflects a synthesis and a creative, novel recombination and integration of elements; it is not a mechanical replica of a single model (Bandura, Ross, & Ross, 1963a). For example, all the models in a family, including the siblings, and the sex constellation of the entire family, affect the sex-role learning of all its members (Rosenberg & Sutton-Smith, 1968). Children's social behavior patterns and preferences therefore are not just a child-sized version of those exhibited by the same-sex parent.

Parents are the most potent models in the child's life for several reasons. First, the parents usually are the earliest models in the child's development; second, they are the most enduring models, usually being present longer than any other social agents; third, the child's parents are by far the most powerful people in his or her life. They provide nurturance and control his resources, and in his early life, his very survival depends on them. Consequently the parents become prime models for the child, much of whose observational learning is based on watching mother and father.

Although parents are the earliest and most important models, the child is exposed to many other models—for example, siblings, grandparents, televised heros. Yet obviously children do not emulate the behaviors of everyone they see, and they do not imitate in equal degrees all the people they know. Therefore it is important to understand the variables that determine the extent to which children take on for themselves the attributes and behaviors displayed by the different models they observe throughout development.

Many recent studies have tried to clarify how the characteristics of models influence the extent to which observers imitate them. The results are directly relevant to theories of identification because in these theories several different hypotheses have been advanced about the conditions that enhance modeling. The results also help us to understand how children may acquire the behavioral repertoires that gradually make up their personalities.

The young girl who wished to be like her parent (cited at the start of this chapter) hinted at two of the main variables that determine the likelihood that an observer will emulate a model. She mentioned wanting to be like her father because she loved him and, second, because then she could do all the fun things that he does. As the following research indicates, her intuitive reasons seem to be largely correct. Many studies have analyzed what characteristics of the model influence observers to adopt aspects of the modeled behavior. The most important of these characteristics include the model's (1) nurturance or rewardingness; (2) power; and (3) similarity to the observer. It has been found that such attributes as the model's noncontingent rewardingness or nurturance, her power and control over resources, and her perceived similarity to the observer all facilitate the observer's tendency to emulate her (Bandura, 1977). But while these model attributes often increase imitation, they are not essential for observational learning, at least in the older children usually studied. That is, children are more willing and likely to adopt the characteristics and actions of models who are rewarding, powerful, and seem similar to them. But they are capable of learning the behaviors even of models who do not have those qualities.

Effects of the Observer's Characteristics

So far we focused on the characteristics of the models, but the observer's (or "subject's") characteristics also influence which models he will attend to and the ways in which he may be affected by them (Akamatsu & Thelen, 1974).

Sex is one of the person's many important attributes that moderate observational learning. For example, boys tend to imitate physically aggressive models more than do girls. In one experiment, adult models displayed aggressive behavior toward a Bobo doll, pummeling and kicking the doll vigorously, while nursery school children observed (Bandura, Ross, & Ross, 1961). After a short delay the child was put in a new setting in which toys and another Bobo doll were available. The child was left to play freely, and the frequency of his physical and verbal aggressiveness, as observed through a one-way mirror, was recorded. Children who had observed an aggressive model showed more aggressiveness than did those exposed to a nonaggressive model, but boys imitated the model's physical aggressiveness more than did girls.

Apart from sex differences in susceptibility to social models, various personality characteristics and situational factors may predispose individuals to be influenced more by particular modeling stimuli. For example, more dependent children may show more imitative behavior (D. Ross, 1966). Imitation is also enhanced by a history of failure, especially punishment for independence (Gelfand, 1962), and by social deprivation experiences (Rosenblith, 1961). The characteristics of the observer may be especially important when the cues about appropriate behavior in the situation remain ambiguous (e.g., Akamatsu & Thelen, 1974).

Products of Identification: What Is Acquired?

So far we have considered some of the conditions that may enhance identification and observational learning. According to some theorists, a vital feature of identification is that it leads the child to acquire or "internalize" a broad pattern or syndrome of personality traits. According to Sears and other theorists, the product of the identification process is a pattern of closely interrelated traits, somewhat similar to the components of the superego in Freudian theory. Specifically, Sears and his associates hypothesized that this pattern includes "adult role formation, self-control, self-recrimination, prosocial forms of aggression, guilt feelings, and other expressions of conscience" (Sears, Rau, & Alpert, 1965, p. 1).

They thus assumed that many broad personality traits—such as conscience, and adult-role-taking in the child—are the closely intercorrelated products of the child's identification with parents, especially the parent of the same sex. In fact, they found some consistency in the hypothesized products of identification, but the empirical results generally do not strongly support identification as a unitary process that leads to widely generalized behavioral products (Sears, Rau, & Alpert, 1965), as will be discussed further in the next chapter. Rather than comprising broadly generalized traits that are interrelated closely, many of the hypothesized products of identification seem to be relatively specific patterns that may be independent of each other. These findings lead some researchers to prefer to construe identification not as a special, unitary process but, instead, as part of observational learning or modeling.

The specificity (discriminativeness) found across situations for most social behaviors is *not* so great that we cannot recognize continuity in people. It is also not so great that we have to treat each new behavior from a person as if we never saw anything like it from him or her before. But the obtained specificity does suggest that the degree and subtlety of discrimination shown in human behavior appear to be as impressive as the variety and extensiveness of generalization. What people do in any situation may be altered radically even by seemingly minor variations in their prior experiences or in the specific contexts of their current lives (e.g., Kagan, 1980).

This state of affairs—namely, the enormously subtle discriminations that people continuously make and, consequently, the flexibility of behavior—is congruent with the findings on discrimination training throughout socialization. The relative specificity of behavior and its dependence on environmental conditions is an understandable result of complex discrimination learning and subtle cognitive differentiation. When the evoking and maintaining conditions for behavior change—as they generally do across settings—then behavior changes also. When maintaining conditions remain stable—as they often do for the same behavior pattern in the same setting at different times—then behavioral stability may be expected and found (Mischel, 1973a).

Summary

Conceptions of the identification process that were influenced most by Freud's ideas have regarded it as a special phenomenon requiring special concepts. Some more recent formulations consider identification as basically similar to any interpersonal modeling through which observers learn and adopt the attributes, attitudes, and actions of other people. Viewed in this perspective, the study of identification becomes part of the investigation of observational learning. Extensive research has explored many of the conditions that enhance observational learning. We all adopt components from the behaviors of many models and synthesize these components into unique new patterns. Indeed, identificatory processes are not confined to the child's imitation of parents, but involve observational learning from many sources and models throughout life. While observational processes affect what the individual knows and can do, reinforcement and motivational conditions regulate his performance of the behaviors available to him.

Cognitive Social Learning Person Variables

When people respond to the environment they are confronted with a potential flood of stimuli; how are these stimuli selected, perceived, processed, interpreted, and used by the individual?

To answer these questions requires the development of more adequate conceptualizations of individual differences or "person variables." In recent years a great deal of personality research has focused on the processes through which social behaviors are acquired, evoked, maintained, and modified. Throughout this chapter you have seen examples of these processes (such as observational learning). Much less attention has been given to the psychological *products* within the individual of cognitive development and social learning experiences. A focus on processes—on the psychological conditions that influence behavior—is an important advance in a field that traditionally has dwelt on the stable attributes of persons with little attention to how conditions affect what people think and feel and do. But a comprehensive psychology of personality also must attend to person variables that are the products of each individual's total history and that, in turn, regulate how new experiences affect him or her.

The person variables to be discussed in this section were proposed to provide a synthesis of seemingly promising constructs about persons developed in the areas of cognition and social learning (Mischel, 1973a); hence they are called "*cognitive social learning* person variables." The selections should be seen as only suggestive and always open to progressive revision. These variables were not expected to provide ways to accurately predict broadly cross-situational behavioral differences between persons; the discriminativeness of behavior and its unique organization within each person are facts of nature, not limitations unique to particular theories. But these variables should suggest useful ways of conceptualizing and studying specifically how the qualities of the person influence the impact of stimuli ("environments," "situations," "treatments") and how each person generates distinctive complex behavior patterns in interaction with the conditions of his or her life.

First, one must deal with the individual's *competencies* to construct (generate) diverse behaviors under appropriate conditions. Next, one must consider the individual's *encoding* and categorization of situations. A comprehensive analysis of the behaviors a person performs in particular situations also requires attention to his or her *expectancies* about outcomes, the *subjective values* of such outcomes, and his or her *self-regulatory systems and plans*. The following five sections discuss each of these person variables. While these variables obviously overlap and interact, each may provide distinctive information about the individual and each may be measured objectively and studied systematically.

Competencies: What CAN You Do?

Through direct and observational learning each individual acquires information about the world and his or her relationship to it. As a result of learning and cognitive development each of us develops competencies to construct (create, generate) many cognitions and behaviors. Our competencies include such knowledge as the rules that guide conduct (Chapter 18), the concepts generated about self and others (Chapter 19), and a host of interpersonal and physical skills.

The concept of "competencies" refers to the individual's abilities to transform and use information actively and to create thoughts and actions (as in problem-solving), rather than to a store of static cognitions and responses that one "has" in some mechanical storehouse. Each individual acquires the capacity to actively construct a multitude of potential behaviors with the knowledge and skills available to him or her. Great differences between persons exist in the range and quality of the cognitive and behavioral patterns that they can generate, as becomes obvious from even casual comparison of the different

Different individuals may encode even the same situation in different ways.

competencies, for example, of a professional weight lifter, a chemist, a retardate, an opera star, or a convicted forger.

Encoding Strategies and Personal Constructs: How Do You See It?

Personality psychology also must consider the ways we encode (represent, symbolize) and group information from stimulus inputs. The same "hot weather" that upsets one person may be a joy for another who views it as a chance to go to the beach. A stimulus perceived as "dangerous" or "threatening" by one person may be seen as "challenging" or "thrilling" by the one next to her. The "environment," the "situation," the "stimulus" perceived, coded, and categorized by each person, and these cognitive operations influence the impact that they have.

People can readily perform *cognitive transformations* on stimuli, focusing on selected aspects of the objective stimulus (e.g., the taste versus the shape of a food object); such selective attention, interpretation, and categorization change the impact the stimulus exerts on behavior (Geer, Davison & Gatchel, 1970; Holmes & Houston, 1974; Schachter, 1964). How we encode and selectively attend to observed behavioral sequences also greatly influences what we learn and subsequently can do. Clearly, different persons may group and encode the same events and behaviors in different ways (e.g., Argyle & Little, 1972) and selectively attend to different kinds of information.

Even if we focus on "behavior" we canot avoid the fact that the definition and selection of a behavior unit for study requires grouping and categorizing. In personality research, it is psychologists who do the categorizing; they include and exclude events in the units they study, depending on their interests and objectives. They choose a category—such as "anxiety," or "masculinity-femininity," for example—and study its behavioral referents. In the study of individuals, however, it soon becomes evident that the "subject" (like the psychologist) also groups events into categories and organizes them actively into meaningful units. The layman usually does not describe experience objectively; as the phenomenologists emphasize (Chapters 5 and 11), each person groups events in terms of his or her own categories and perceptions (G. Kelly, 1955) and these may or may not overlap with those of the psychologist or of others. For example, what is "conscientiousness" for one person may have an entirely different meaning for another (Bem & Allen, 1974); a trait dimension that fits me may be quite irrelevant for you.

People abstract and infer traits and other dispositions to describe and explain their experience and themselves, just as professional psychologists do, and it would be strange if personality psychologists ignored the concepts, perceptions, and experiences of those whom they are studying. We noted before that people categorize their own personal qualities in relatively stable trait terms (e.g., on self-ratings and self-report questionnaires). These self-categorizations, while often only complexly related to nonverbal behavior, may be relatively durable and generalized (Chapter 19) and an adequate psychology of personality must take them into account.

Expectancies: What Will Happen?

So far the person variables considered deal with what the individual *can* do and how one categorizes (codes) events. But we also must move from what we know and how we perceive (categorize) events to what we *do,* from potential behaviors to actual performance in specific situations. This move requires attention to the determinants of *performance.* For this purpose, the person variables of greatest interest are the individual's expectancies. If you cheat on the final exam and are caught, what do you expect will be the consequences? If you tell your friend what you really think of him, what will happen to your relationship? If you switch to another career plan, what will be the probable effects?

To predict specific behavior in a particular situation it is essential to consider the individual's specific expectancies about the consequences of different behavioral possibilities in that situation. These expectancies guide the person's selection (choice) of behaviors from among the many which he or she is capable of constructing within any situation. We generate behavior in light of our expectancies even when they are not in line with the objective conditions in the situation. If you expect to be attacked you become vigilant even if your fears later turn out to have been unjustified.

One type of expectancy concerns *behavior-outcome relations*. These *behavior-outcome expectancies* (hypotheses, contingency rules) represent the "if____, then____" relations between behavioral alternatives and expected probable outcomes in particular situations. In any given situation, we generate the response pattern which we expect is most likely to lead to the most subjectively valuable outcomes (consequences) in that situation (e.g., Mischel, 1973a; Rotter, 1954). In the absence of new information about the behavior-outcome expectancies in any situation, one's performance will depend on one's previous behavior-outcome expectancies in similar situations. That is, if you do not know exactly what to expect in a new situation (a first job interview, for example) you are guided by your previous expectancies based on experiences in similar past situations. This point is illustrated in a study which showed that the expectancies people brought to a situation influenced their behavior in the situation when no other relevant information was available (Mischel & Staub, 1965). But the same study also showed that new information about probable outcomes in the particular situation may quickly overcome the original expectancies. The new information produces highly specific situational expectancies that influence performance most significantly.

Adaptive performance requires the recognition and appreciation of new contingencies. To cope with the environment effectively, we must identify new contingencies as quickly as possible and reorganize behavior in the light of the new expectancies. Strongly established behavior-outcome expectancies may handicap our ability to adapt to changes in contingencies. Indeed, "defensive reactions" may be seen in part as a failure to adapt to new contingencies because one is still behaving in response to old contingencies that are no longer valid (Chapter 17). For example, if on the basis of past experiences a man overgeneralizes and becomes convinced that people will take advantage of him unless he is hostile toward everyone, his own suspicious, aggressive behavior may prevent him from ever being able to disconfirm his belief, even when people are trying to be considerate. The "maladaptive" individual is behaving in accord with expectancies that do not adequately represent the actual behavior-outcome rules in his current life situation.

A closely related second type of expectancy concerns *stimulus-outcome relations*. The outcomes we expect depend on a multitude of stimulus conditions. These stimuli ("signs") essentially "predict" for us other events that are likely to occur. More precisely, each of us learns that certain events (cues, stimuli) predict certain other events. Outside the artificial restrictions of the laboratory, in the human interactions of life, the "stimuli" that predict outcomes often are the social behaviors of others in particular contexts. The meanings attributed to those stimuli hinge on learned associations between behavioral signs and outcomes.

For example, through learning, "shifty eyes," "tight lips," "lean and hungry looks," obese body build, age, sex, eye contact, posture, gestures, and many even subtler behavioral cues (e.g., regarding the status and power of others) come to predict for us other behaviors correlated with them. If your friend nods "understandingly" when you start to talk frankly about a personal problem you will proceed differently than if she taps her foot "impatiently," gets up abruptly, or yawns. Each of these "signs" implies a very different outcome in the particular situation. Some expected stimulus-outcome associations presumably reflect the perceiver's idiosyncratic (unique) learning history, and his or her own evolving personal rules about stimulus meanings. Many of these associations, however, are likely to be widely shared by members of the same culture who have a common language for verbal and nonverbal communication.

Finally, a third type of expectancy consists of *self-efficacy expectations:* the person's confidence that he or she *can* perform a particular behavior, like handling a snake or making a public speech. As discussed before (Chapter 9), measures of these expectations predict with considerable accuracy the person's actual ability to perform the relevant acts. And therapeutic improvement of efficacy expectancies in turn allows the person to function more effectively (Bandura, 1978).

Subjective Values: What Is It Worth?

Two individuals who have similar expectancies nevertheless may act differently because the outcomes they expect have different *values* for them (e.g., Rotter, 1954, 1972). For example, if everyone in a group expects that approval from a teacher depends on saying certain things, there may be differences in how often they are said due to differences in the perceived value of obtaining the teacher's approval. Praise from the teacher may be important for one person (e.g., a youngster striving for grades), but not for another (e.g., a rebellious adolescent who rejects school). Such differences reflect the degree to which different individuals value the same expected outcome. What delights one person may repel his or her neighbor. Therefore it is necessary to consider still another variable: the subjective (perceived) value for individuals of particular classes of events, that is, their stimulus preferences and aversions, their likes and dislikes, their positive and negative values.

Self-Regulatory Systems and Plans: How Can You Achieve It?

While behavior depends to a considerable extent on externally administered consequences for actions, people regulate their own behavior by self-imposed goals (standards) and self-produced consequences (Chapter 18). Even in the absence of external constraints and social monitors, we set performance goals for ourselves and react with self-criticism or self-satisfaction to our behavior depending on how well it matches our expectations and standards. The expert sprinter who falls below his past record may condemn himself bitterly, while the same performance by a less experienced runner who has lower standards may produce self-congratulation and joy.

Another feature of self-regulatory systems is the person's adoption of *contingency rules* and *plans* that guide his or her behavior in the absence of, and sometimes in spite of, immediate external situational pressures. Such rules specify the kinds of behavior appropriate (expected) under particular conditions, the performance levels (standards, goals) which the behavior must achieve, and the consequences (positive and negative) of attaining or failing to reach those standards. Plans also specify the sequence and organization of behavior patterns (e.g., Miller, Galanter, & Pribram, 1960; Schank & Abelson, 1977). Individuals differ with respect to each of the components of self-regulation depending on their unique earlier histories or on more recently varied instructions or other information.

Self-regulation provides a route through which we can influence our environment substantially, overcoming "stimulus control" (the power of the situation). We can actively *select* the situations to which we expose ourselves, in a sense creating our own environment, entering some settings but not others, making decisions about what to do and what not to do. Such active choice, rather than automatic responding, may be facilitated by thinking and planning and by rearranging the environment itself to make it more favorable for one's objectives. If one cannot study well in the midst of noise one may try to find a quiet place for work or attempt to soundproof one's room as much as possible. Even when the environment cannot be changed physically (by rearranging it or by leaving it altogether and entering another setting), it may be possible to *transform* it psychologically by self-instructions and ideation (Chapter 18), as in mental self-distractions or, conversely, concentrated attention.

Summary of Person Variables

To summarize, individual differences in behavior may be due to differences in each of the discussed person variables (summarized in Table 13-1) and in their interactions. First, individuals differ in their *competencies,* i.e., in their ability to generate cognitions and actions. For example, because of differences in skill and earlier learning, individual differences may arise in cognitive-intellective achievements. Differences in behavior also may reflect differences in how individuals *categorize* (encode) a particular situation. That is, people differ in how

---

TABLE 13-1
**SUMMARY OF COGNITIVE SOCIAL LEARNING
PERSON VARIABLES**

1. COMPETENCIES: ability to construct (generate) particular cognitions and behaviors. Related to measures of IQ, social and cognitive (mental) maturity and competence, ego development, social-intellectual achievements and skills. Refers to what the person knows and *can* do.
2. ENCODING STRATEGIES AND PERSONAL CONSTRUCTS: units for categorizing events, people, and the self.
3. EXPECTANCIES: behavior-outcome and stimulus-outcome relations in particular situations; self-efficacy or confidence that one can perform the necessary behavior.
4. SUBJECTIVE VALUES: motivating and arousing stimuli, incentives, and aversions.
5. SELF-REGULATORY SYSTEMS AND PLANS: rules and self-reactions for performance and for the organization of complex behavior sequences.

SOURCE: Adapted from Mischel (1973a).

they encode, group, and label events and in how they construe themselves and others. Performance differences in any situation depend on differences in *expectancies* and specifically on differences in the expected outcomes associated with particular response patterns and stimuli. Differences in performance also may be due to differences in the subjective *values* of the expected outcomes in the situation. Finally, individual differences may reflect differences in the *self-regulatory systems and plans* that each individual brings to the situation. Obviously these person variables should be seen as just one way to view individual differences from a perspective that emphasizes cognition and social learning. Surely it is not the only way to view major differences among people, as is evident from the many alternative personality approaches discussed throughout this volume.

The particular principles favored as the best explanations for the phenomena of personality are still controversial and sure to change. It would be surprising, however, if different basic laws were required ultimately to understand every possible trait or dimension of personality, such as dependency, aggression, self-control, altruism, and so on. For example, if reinforcement processes are important determinants of behavior, one would expect them to function in basically similar ways regardless of what is being reinforced. While the specific events that constitute reinforcers would differ, the principles of learning would be the same. Likewise, if observational learning is an important cause of behavior, one would expect modeling processes to be similar regardless of the particular behavior being modeled. Obviously the specific behaviors modeled by a "feminine" mother, for example, would differ from those shown by a less "feminine" parent, but the variables that control a child's adoption of the modeled behavior should be fundamentally similar. Moreover, if observational learning is an important determinant of behavior, one would expect the same principles to apply, regardless of whether the modeling occurs in school or in the home. And if such person variables as competencies, expectancies, and values help us understand individual differences in one type of behavior, they also should be relevant for understanding other types of behavior. As the principles of personality development become increasingly clear, they may permit us to elucidate the causes of socialized behavior regardless of its particular content.

SUMMARY

1. The basic mechanisms of social learning are important in understanding personality development. Two direct learning mechanisms are classical and operant conditioning. In *classical conditioning* contiguous association between a neutral and an arousing stimulus may change the value of the neutral stimulus. Such a mechanism may influence positive and negative attitudes and feelings in many con-

texts. In *operant conditioning* behavior patterns may be modified by changing the consequences (reinforcements) to which they lead.

2. Discrimination learning is a fundamental aspect of the socialization process. In almost every culture, growing up requires learning numerous behaviors that are acceptable and expected under some circumstances but prohibited or punished under others, producing many discriminations. When behavior yields similar consequences under many conditions, generalization occurs and the individual may display similar behavior patterns across diverse settings. Similarity in meaning as well as in physical characteristics results in increased generalization.

3. The patterning or sequencing of the outcomes produced by a particular behavior can be even more important than the type of outcome itself. While continuous reward or reinforcement for behavior may result in faster learning, irregular or intermittent reinforcement often produces more stable behavior that persists even when reinforcement is withdrawn. In life situations many potentially maladaptive behaviors are rewarded irregularly and may therefore become very resistant to change.

4. During socialization some of the child's behaviors may be encouraged or condoned in highly irregular ways. For example, one parent may approve of a certain type of behavior while the other disapproves. Likewise, peers may applaud behavior that adults discourage.

5. The influence of punishment on personality development is complex and depends on many conditions, such as its timing. Unlike conditions in laboratory studies of punishment, in the child's life punishment is often subtle and indirect. Punishment in socialization depends on many contingencies, such as the child's age and sex as well as the type of behavior and the setting.

6. Some of the most impressive features of a child's personality seem to develop independently of direct training by the parents. Many psychologists have invoked the theoretical mechanism of identification to explain the development of broad attributes and generalized behavior patterns similar to those of the parents and other significant social models.

7. Definitions of identification have three aspects: similarity in behavior (including feelings and attitudes) between a child and the model with whom he is identifying; the child's motive or desire to be like a model; and the process through which the child takes on the attributes of the model.

8. Studies of identification have investigated the effects of father-absence on personality development. Father-absent children generally tend to show less appropriate sex typing. However, children whose fathers are absent also may be less adequately socialized in various non-sex-typed behaviors. Father-absence thus may be one index of an inadequate home environment that has a debilitating influence on children of both sexes.

9. Some theorists suggest that identification is not a unitary process but rather that it involves observational learning and requires no special constructs. In their view, through observational processes children learn large and complex sequences of behavior. The developing child observes, synthesizes, and adopts components from many models. He or she acquires potential behaviors that may be utilized at appropriate times and in situations that require them. The process of observational learning includes four components: attention, retention, motor reproduction, and motivation.

10. Children are exposed to many models, and obviously they do not imitate all of them in similar degree. The characteristics of the model affect the observer's tendency to adopt his or her behavior. The model's nurturance, power, and similarity to the observer are especially important attributes that influence his impact on those who observe him. The effects of these model attributes depend on many conditions. For example, nurturance often enhances a child's tendency to emulate a parent or other social model, but nurturance may not be an essential prerequisite for the occurrence of imitation.

11. In addition to the model's attributes, the observer's characteristics influence the models to which she attends and the ways in which she may be affected by them. Sex is one important attribute determining the individual's susceptibility to influence from a social model.

12. Some psychologists postulated a unitary mechanism of identification through which the child internalizes a broad cluster of related traits and behaviors. This hypothesized cluster was believed to include appropriate sex roles, adult-like behavior, and conscience. To support this hypothesis, researchers have tried to show that people really develop the consistent, interrelated traits assumed to be the products of identification. Most of the findings, however, indicate that the personality dimensions included as effects of identification (such as masculinity-femininity, conscience, and impulse control) may be relatively specific and not closely related.

13. Person variables are the products within the individual of cognitive development and social learning history. They in turn regulate the

meaning of new experiences for the individual. The person variables described in this chapter are intended as tools in the conceptualization and study of the interaction between the individual and his or her environment. They are an attempted synthesis based on cognitive and social learning psychology.

14. Person variables include the individual's competencies, encoding strategies, and personal constructs, expectancies about probable outcomes, subjective values, and self-regulatory systems and plans.

CHAPTER 14

SEX-TYPING AND PERSONALITY DEVELOPMENT

In this chapter we will examine some of the socialization processes through which boys and girls gradually become psychological males or females. A study of these processes will illustrate more specifically many of the most important features of personality development and socialization. We will focus on the development of sex differences in social behavior rather than on the physiology and biology of sexual behavior itself. While we will deal mostly with the development of psychological sex differences, the discussion will also bring up many issues that are relevant to socialization in general.

This chapter thus is concerned with the nature of psychological sex differences in social behavior and also with how these personality differences develop. Instead of discussing many dimensions of personality superficially, it concentrates on one in depth. The development of psychological sex differences serves as an illustration of the development of personality differences in general, but it is also fascinating in its own right.

Sexual preferences and orientations (one's preferred sexual partners and activities) emerge as a result of many critical steps in development. Some important phases include the following (Cairns, 1979, p. 296):

1. Genes and hormones interact to form sexual structures before birth.
2. The child's gender at birth is recognized and permanently categorized by parents and society. The child acquires a gender self-concept,

a recognition of his or her permanent sex in the preschool years. Society's expectations about appropriate sexual behavior, and the pressures and examples of peers, are influences throughout childhood.

3. In adolescence and throughout adulthood social influences persist. The individual continues to interact with others and with the standards of society, and these interactions further influence his or her sexual preferences, values, and styles.

Almost universally an individual's gender is one of the most powerful determinants of how other people treat him or her. Gender also influences the views the individual develops about himself or herself. Established invariantly at birth, biological sex soon begins to direct much of one's psychological and social development, identity, and roles and values. Moreover, it continues to exert a dominant influence throughout life. Probably no other categorization is more important psychologically than the one that sorts people into male and female and their characteristics into masculine and feminine. And in recent years probably no other categorization has become more controversial. The controversy is based on many challenges to conventional, rigid sex roles and stereotypes about what it means to be a man or a woman.

Some of the issues raised by these challenges to traditional notions about sexual identity will be discussed later in this chapter. But first we will consider some of the personality differences found between the sexes. Then we will examine their causes and consequences. This analysis is intended to give the reader a deeper understanding of the complex processes through which social behavior and personality develop. Since "masculinity" and "femininity" are often defined in terms of such other traits as aggressiveness and dependency, the study of sex differences takes us into research on many other related domains.

Psychological Sex Differences

In some respects the differences between the sexes, not only biologically but psychologically, may seem self-evident. On closer examination, however, the nature of the psychological differences between the sexes is not nearly as simple as it may seem.

Perceived Sex Differences: Examples

Before examining formal studies on sex typing, it is informative to consider the subjective sex differences given by a young woman—call her "Amy Wilson"—when asked, during the course of her development, about sex differences and sex roles. Here are excerpts from Amy's comments at four ages.

At age 3½ Amy's concepts about sex differences were still vague and primarily limited to trying to distinguish the roles of mother and father:

Q. How are boys and girls different?

A. They're good (both boys and girls)—and they fight a little bit. They laugh sometimes.

Q. What do boys do that girls don't do? And what do girls do that boys don't?

A. They play outside with their daddies. They play outside with their selves and they swing around on the glider—they play outside with their mother.

Q. And when they grow up?

A. Boys be daddies. Girls be mommies, and have babies in their tummies. Mommies feed children and babies and daddies.

Q. And what do daddies do?

A. They wash the dishes.

Q. They do?

A. Well, sometimes.

When interviewed 18 months later at age 5, Amy made a more differentiated analysis, recognizing biological and role differences and focusing mainly on sex differences in aggressive behavior:

Q. How are boys and girls different?

A. Boys have penises and girls have vaginas.

Q. How else?

A. Boys make money to buy food. Girls want their children not to make too much noise. Boys work—sometimes help the mother, sometimes play with their children. Mothers—they try not to scream. Boys can grow up to be a gardener and girls want their children to be very, very quiet and good.

Q. What are the girl-things you do?

A. I play on swings and slides; I paint and make good art pictures. Boys play on slides and do the things girls do too; when they grow up they work and don't do the things girls do any more.

Q. Do you want to be a girl or boy?

A. A girl! I don't want to be a boy because they fight, hit girls, say I wanna kill you, fight their teachers, and get spanked—that's why I don't want to be a boy.

Q. Why do you do the girl-things you do?

A. Because I'm a girl—that's why I don't fight.

Q. Why don't you fight?

A. Because I don't want to—because it isn't nice—because then I would get punishment.

Q. Do boys get punished for fighting?

A. Yes, but they don't think they will—they're not so scared.

The analysis of role differentiation becomes increasingly sophisticated with age, as Amy's comments at age 7½ reveal:

Q. How are boys and girls different?

A. Men are much stronger than women. Boys grow up to be daddies, girls grow up to be mommies, and mothers have babies.

Q. How else?

A. Girls have more feelings. Boys have more strength.

Q. What are some of the girl-things you do?

A. Play handball—that's what girls and boys do, play two square, go on the slide. Sing, dance, spell. You mean what are the girl-things I do with no boys included? I don't play baseball, I don't play stick ball, I don't play hot box.

Q. Do you want to be a girl or boy?

A. A girl. Well, sometimes I wish I were a boy and sometimes I wish I weren't.

Q. Why?

A. Being a boy I could do scary things. For girls I would wear fancy dresses and be rich—live in a fancy mansion.

Q. Why do you do the girl-things you do?

A. Because I want to—I just do—I like the sport of it.

Q. What would happen if you did boy-things?

A. Oh I do boy-things sometimes, but there's nothing wrong with it.

Q. How come you don't like fighting?

A. Because girls don't fight—I guess they're too dainty. If you fight you can get in trouble. I guess boys are rougher, have more strength, don't tell on each other so much and so don't get into trouble so much.

As a mature woman, interviewed again at age 26, Amy Wilson now gave this subtle picture of sex roles and personality:

Q. How are men and women different psychologically?

A. Men are supposed to be more aggressive, stronger, more opinionated—more domineering—also have a stronger sex drive, I guess.

Q. What do men do that women don't do?

A. Things like car-racing, mountain-climbing—dangerous things—fight in wars, hunt, and kill—and make important decisions, like being president. They're also expected to provide for families. Women are supposed to create peace and harmony, care for children, be compliant, warm and giving—dependent.

Q. Do they have those qualities?

A. Not all of them. Some women are aggressive, wasteful, and self-aggrandizing.

Q. Would you rather be a man or woman?

A. I'd rather be a woman. I don't think I have the self-discipline to be a successful man—in terms of career—but I do have the qualities to be a successful, fulfilled, complete woman.

Q. How do you mean?
A. I'm attractive, competent, I love my children and am a good mother to them. I'm not selfish and I'm sexually responsive.
Q. What are some of the things you like most?
A. I like to dress nicely—I like pretty clothes.
Q. Why?
A. I like to dress nicely at home because it pleases my husband. When we go out it makes me feel good that he is proud of me—and I think it reflects well on him also. When I go shopping I like to look as elegant as possible because it makes the salespeople attend much better to me—they just get nicer then. My most feminine qualities? I am unassuming—I don't brag or boast.
Q. Why is that?
A. Because it's feminine.
Q. How would you be most different in personality if you were a man?
A. I'd put my work before my family. I would not allow myself to be so emotional—to react so strongly to things. I also wouldn't be able to get as much rest; I'd have to drive myself a lot harder.
Q. Why do you put your family before your work?
A. I put my family before my work because that's my responsibility—it's my job.

As Amy's comments indicate, from her viewpoint her feminine behavior reflects her subjective expectations about femininity, her cognitions about what it is to be female and the role responsibilities expected of an adequate woman. Her subjective viewpoint parallels to a large degree the objective conditions that have generated her feminine qualities and that serve to maintain them. Her expectations about the positive consequences of dressing attractively, for example, reflect her direct and vicarious reinforcement history in this regard; her cognitions about her role responsibilities presumably reflect the sanctions, rule system, and social structure of the environment in which she matured. The specifics of this socialization process will be discussed throughout this chapter. We will begin by surveying some of the main psychological sex differences revealed by research. The reader will note that these results support many of Amy's perceptions.

To discover personality differences between the sexes systematically, many researchers have tried to measure differences in the frequency or in the amount of particular behavior patterns typically displayed by males and females. In our culture the two behavior patterns with regard to which sex differences have received most research attention are behaviors aimed at inflicting injury on others (*aggression*) and at eliciting attention and help from others (*dependency*). Some of the main sex differences found for aggression and dependency respectively are reviewed briefly in the following sections and are summarized in Table 14-1.

	TABLE 14-1	
	SOME REPRESENTATIVE PSYCHOLOGICAL SEX DIFFERENCES	
Behavior	*Greater in*	*Source*
Physical and anti-social aggression (e.g., physical quarrels, fights, hyperaggressiveness, playful rough-housing)	Boys	Dawe, 1934; McCandless et al., 1961; Mischel & Mischel, 1971; Maccoby, 1980.
Rated Aggressiveness	Boys	Hattwick, 1937; Beller & Neubauer, 1963; Beller, 1962.
Self-rated Aggressiveness	Boys	Rothaus & Worchel, 1964; Wyer et al., 1965.
Dependency, Passivity	Girls (sometimes but not always: generally inconclusive)	Hovland & Janis, 1959; Kagan & Moss, 1962; Maccoby & Jacklin, 1974b; Mehrabian, 1970; Sears et al., 1953; Siegel et al., 1959.
Verbal Ability	Girls (beginning at age 11 years)	Maccoby & Jacklin, 1974a.

Aggression

Aggression is one of the key variables defining masculine and feminine behavior (Sears, 1963, 1965). Sex differences in aggression have been found as early as the age of three years. Boys are physically more aggressive and show more "negativistic" behavior; negative attention getting, antisocial aggression, and physical aggression are more characteristic of boys than of girls. Boys also participate in more physical quarrels in nursery school, have more aggressive contact with their peers, initiate more fights and conflicts, and tend to resist attack more often. These results (Table 14-1) appear to have considerable generality across cultures (Whiting & Whiting, 1962). Rating studies provide similar findings, judges rating boys as more negativistic and as generally more aggressive than girls.

The sexes also differ in their self-concepts with regard to aggression. Self-ratings indicate that boys see themselves as more directly and overtly aggressive, especially after their hostility has been aroused experimentally. Greater self-reported overt aggressiveness by males holds for a wide age range, having been found for people aged from 15 to 64 (Bennett & Cohen, 1959). Projective tests also indicate more direct aggression and hostility expressed by males (e.g., Gordon & Smith, 1965).

Dependency

Sex differences in dependency have also been studied thoroughly. In nursery school children, not many major differences have been found between the sexes on most dependency measures. At later ages (teens and college), however, girls sometimes seem to be more dependent, passive, and conforming than males (see Table 14-1), although the differences are often weak and inconclusive. Most of the findings are based on self-reports and trait ratings of dependency. Therefore it is difficult to separate the degree to which they reflect widely shared stereotypes that women are supposed to be more dependent from differences in the degree of actual dependency displayed by women versus men. Some evidence suggests that females may conform more than males, but certain factors may reverse this difference (e.g., Sampson & Hancock, 1967). For example, Iscoe and his colleagues (1964) report a significant race-by-sex interaction in conformity behavior. In this study, white females conformed more than white males, while black males were more conforming than black females. On the whole, girls are not more "suggestible" or susceptible to social pressure than boys (Maccoby & Jacklin, 1974a).

Although most research on sex differences has concentrated on aggression and dependency, other areas have not been ignored. In addition to studying differences on numerous personality variables, researchers have also explored sex differences in cognitive and intellectual functioning and in other domains (e.g., Maccoby & Jacklin, 1974b).

Intellectual-Cognitive Functions

Studies of American youngsters indicate, in general, that girls tend to do better than boys on tests of verbal ability. Girls, for example, tend to speak sooner and to be better in verbal articulation, word fluency, vocabulary, grammar, and spelling (e.g., Gesell et al., 1940; Irwin & Chen, 1946). Once one moves out of the American white middle-class group, however, the general superiority of girls to boys in verbal intellectual skills becomes more complex. Anastasi and D'Angelo (1952), for example, compared black and white preschool children in language development and found a significant sex-by-race interaction. That is, white girls were superior to white boys, while black boys were superior to black girls in length and maturity of verbal responses in a standard test situation. Still another study of children in Bristol, England, suggested that the verbal superiority often found in females may be culture-bound (Dunsdon & Frazier-Roberts, 1957). A random sample of all the schoolchildren showed boys to be superior on four oral vocabulary tests. But in spite of exceptions, females generally tend to be superior on tests of verbal ability, beginning at about age 11 years and extending at least through the high school years and perhaps beyond them (Maccoby & Jacklin, 1974a).

Sex differences are less clear on verbal reasoning tests, such as analogies. Sometimes boys do better on these tests (Klausmeier & Wiersma, 1964, 1965; McNemar, 1942), sometimes girls (Lee, 1965); and sometimes there is no difference (Bennett et al., 1959). Girls do learn to read sooner than boys (Balow, 1963; Anderson et al., 1957). Other studies show, however, that boys catch up by about the age of 10.

In general, the finding of some cultural variations indicated above limits conclusions, as does the fact that although girls may be superior to boys at an early age, boys may catch up or even excel later. Moreover, even though some sex differences in intellectual abilities have been found reliably, many of these differences tend to be small. This means that a child's sex may be a relatively minor factor in determining his or her mental ability in a particular area. In any classroom some boys probably will be superior to girls in vocabulary, and some girls will excel in spatial ability.

Sex differences have also been reported in a cognitive style described as "analytic" or field-independent as opposed to global or field-dependent (Witkin et al., 1962). The two measures most frequently employed in research on these styles are the Embedded Figures Test and the Rod and Frame Test. In the first, subjects have to find a simple hidden figure embedded in a more complex stimulus array. In the Rod and Frame Test a rod within a frame is projected on the wall of a darkened room, and the subject has to adjust the rod to the vertical as the frame is tilted. Boys and men tend to perform better and faster on these tasks than girls and women do, although sex differences are not found before the early school years (Maccoby, 1966). Witkin and his co-workers reported consistent sex differences only at age 17 and after, and once again the variations within each sex were greater than the consistent differences between the sexes.

In spite of some reported sex differences in cognitive styles, a close analysis of the total research on this topic indicates that the conclusions must be highly qualified. After an exhaustive review, Maccoby and Jacklin (1974a, p. 110) conclude that the belief that boys are more "analytic" than girls is one of many myths about sex differences. In fact, on cognitive style tests: "Boys are superior only on problems that require visual discrimination or manipulation of objects set in a larger context; this superiority seems to be accounted for by spatial ability . . . and does not imply a general analytic superiority (p. 110)." Thus, boys tend to excel in visual-spatial ability but not in more general analytic skills. This difference seems to begin in early adolescence.

In sum, a variety of sex differences have been found, especially on indices of physical aggression and on certain aspects of cognitive functioning. These average differences are important. However, within each of these domains there is considerable variability in the behavior of the same individual across situations. An individual's sex-typed behaviors may be relatively specific rather than highly generalized. A young boy may, for example, be good at baseball and still love painting, and he may like to tinker with tools and play with soldiers. The same child may also be extremely dependent on his mother's attention, may even like to dress his sister's dolls, may cry easily if he is hurt, but also may fight aggressively when peers provoke him.

Sex-Role Stereotypes and Identity

We all share global stereotypes about masculine and feminine traits based on average differences between the sexes. A "real" boy in the United States is supposed to do such things as climb trees, dirty his knees, and disdain girls, while a "real" girl plays with dolls, jumps rope, and loves hopscotch (Brown, 1965). These stereotypes serve as bases for judging others. Sex-role stereotypes may also function as standards by which people evaluate themselves.

Sex-role stereotypes are widely shared within a particular culture and to some extent across cultures (e.g., D'Andrade, 1966). Even within a relatively homogeneous subculture, however, individuals may vary in the degree to which they adopt sanctioned sex-role standards. For example, children, especially girls, from homes and schools that stressed individualized development departed more from conventional sex-role standards than did children from more traditional backgrounds (Minuchin, 1965).

Sex-role identity refers to the "degree to which an individual regards himself as masculine or feminine" (Kagan, 1964, p. 144). Kagan's formulation of sex-role identity stresses the person's global concept of his or her own overall masculinity or femininity. As he puts it (1964, p. 144):

> The degree of match or mismatch between the sex-role standards of the culture and the individual's assessment of his own overt and covert attributes provides him with a partial answer to the question. "How masculine (or feminine) am I?"

In the years since this simple conception of sex-role identity was proposed, it has become plain that the matter is more complex. An increasing number of people are unwilling to either ask or answer the traditional question "How masculine (or feminine) am I?" in the conventional ways. Some of the many controversies that surround the topic of sex-role identity are discussed later in this chapter.

The Development of Sex-Typing

In order to understand psychological sex differences properly one has to consider their development. Often the extensive investigations on the development of sex roles are grouped under the heading of "sex typing." *Sex typing* is the process whereby the individual comes to acquire, to value, and to practice (perform) sex-typed behavior patterns—that is, patterns that are considered appropriate for one sex but not for the opposite sex. What are the causes of sex-typed behavior?

Biological Determinants

The biological differences between the sexes are important in the development of psychological characteristics. For example, the fact that women bear children whereas men do not dictates many other differences in life roles. Beyond differences in the physical characteristics of the sexes, however, the biological or physiological approach has emphasized the possible effects of sex hormones on the development of psychological differences in nonsexual human behavior.

This biological emphasis is seen in the work of such researchers as Broverman and his associates (1968). These investigators suggest that sex differences in cognitive abilities reflect complex sex differences in biochemistry. They suggest that the relationships involved can be understood best by studying changes in people's cognitive processes induced by such organismic changes as variations in hormone levels and the administration of drugs. They speculate that "the sex differences in performances of simple perceptual-motor and inhibitory restructuring tasks are related, in part at least, to the differential effects of the 'sex' steroid hormones on activation and inhibition neural processes" (p. 42). The work of Broverman and his associates seems provocative, but for obvious ethical and practical reasons there has been little systematic experimentation with people on the possible role of sex hormones in the development of psychological sex differences.

Almost always the newborn's external sex organs match his or her internal biological sexuality, and sex is identified unambiguously at birth. In some rare cases that is not true. "Hermaphrodites" are those unusual newborns who have sexual organs of both sexes. For example, they may have external male genitalia but internal female sex organs, and in this case, genetically they are females (in chromosome tests). Because these persons have both male and female sex organs, it is sometimes not clear whether they should be considered male or female. Clinical studies have investigated some of these individuals whose assignment to one sex or the other on the basis of their external genitalia was either incorrect or ambiguous. Hampson (1965) studied 19 hermaphroditic patients who were assigned and reared in a sex contrary to their true biological or chromosomal sex (established by biochemical tests of the chromatin pattern, for example through a skin biopsy). "Without a single exception it was found that the gender role and orientation as man or woman, boy or girl, was in accordance with the assigned sex and rearing rather than in accord with the chromosomal sex" (p. 113).

Likewise, Money (1965a,b) reported that genetic males with internal male genitalia who had been reared as females in accord with their external genitalia maintained a feminine psychosexual and gender role throughout life. The implication is that a person with male hormones who has been raised as a girl will dress and behave like a girl and probably will marry a man. These studies vividly illustrate the importance of the psychological gender role assigned to the child early in its life (Money, 1975; Money & Ehrhardt, 1972).

Both Hampson and Money suggest that psychological variables are crucial in the establishment of sexual gender role. On the other hand, experimental research with lower animals suggests some possible interrelations between hormonal conditions, brain functions, and behavior (e.g., Hamburg & Lunde, 1966). The finding of greater aggression in males than in females (throughout human societies and among animal species closest to man) also strengthens the belief that sex differences in aggression have biological roots (Maccoby & Jacklin, 1974b). Diamond (1965, 1976) has challenged Money's environmental emphasis, arguing for inherent sexuality with a built-in bias beginning at birth. And indeed, Money himself has moved increasingly away from emphasizing only the environment, recognizing that constitution is also important for gender role (Money, 1970, 1976). It is premature to draw any final conclusions on this topic. However, even if hormonal and genetic variables prove to contribute significantly to psychological sex differences, the enormous importance of social learning in the development of sex roles seems evident. It seems most likely that a person's gender role involves the close interaction of both biological and psychological variables.

Some researchers have concentrated on sex differences in newborns in order to study possible innate sex differences before socialization practices exert their effects massively. Human neonatal behavior indicates some sex differences in activity level and in reactivity to a variety of stimuli. For example, sex differences occur in infants' responses to facial stimuli during the first year of life (Lewis, 1969). Girls vocalized and smiled more and showed greater differential expression to the facial stimuli, although boys looked longer. At age 2 to 3 months, girls are more sensitive to skin exposure than boys (Wolff, 1965). Newborn females seem to react more to the removal of a covering blanket, and show lower thresholds to air-jet stimulation of the abdomen (Bell & Costello, 1964). Newborn boys raise their heads higher than newborn girls do (Bell & Darling, 1965), and there are also sex differences in infant play behavior (Goldberg & Lewis, 1969).

The interpretation sometimes drawn from these early sex differences in response to stimulation is that they are innate. But as in other domains of personality, nature and nurture—heredity and environment—tend to be deeply and often inextricably entwined:

> the sex-typed attributes of personality and temperament . . . are the product of the interweaving of differential social demands with certain biological determinants that help produce or augment differential culture demands upon the two sexes. The biological underpinnings . . . set modal tendencies for cultural demands, and set limits to the range of variation of these demands from one cultural setting to another. Still within these

limits considerable variation does occur between families, between cultures, and in the nature of the behavior that a social group stereotypes as "feminine" or "masculine" (Maccoby, 1966, p. 50).

While biological limits and constraints have been recognized and acknowledged, most psychologists have emphasized socialization and cognitive processes as the causes of psychological sex-role characteristics.

Cognition and Learning

In the course of development young children soon recognize their sexual identity or gender. They rapidly develop a conception of their permanent sexual identity through the same observational and cognitive processes that permit them to understand the invariable identity of physical objects in the environment (Kohlberg, 1966). These concepts seem to occur early in development, generally before the age of five years. By the time children reach school age they clearly have learned the concepts "male" and "female" (Hartup & Zook, 1960; Kagan, Hosken, & Watson, 1961). Early during the course of socialization they also rapidly learn the stereotypes about masculinity and femininity prevalent in their subculture.

Sex-role concepts and stereotypes probably arise in part from children's observations of sex differences in bodily structure and capacities. When they reach the age of four or five years, children become distinctly aware of adult sex differences in size and strength. These perceived differences in turn may be associated with concepts about sex differences in power.

Some theorists emphasize the importance of cognitive strivings for consistency, and view consistency motivation as the crux of sex-role development. According to Lawrence Kohlberg, cognitive self-categorizations as "boy" or "girl" are made as reality judgments early in the child's development. Once formed, these judgments tend to be fairly irreversible, being maintained by the physical reality of one's sex: A person is male or female forever. Kohlberg's cognitive-developmental formulation gives this direct self-categorization of gender central importance as the fundamental organizer of sex-role attitudes and values:

> Basic self-categorizations determine basic valuings. Once the boy has stably categorized himself as male he then values positively those objects and acts consistent with his gender identity (1966, p. 89).

Kohlberg also says:

> The child's sexual identity is maintained by a motivated adaptation to physical social reality and by the need to preserve a stable and positive self-image (1966, p. 88).

Kohlberg's theorizing assumes that strong tendencies or strivings toward cognitive consistency lead the person to acquire values consistent with his cognitive judgments about himself (as discussed in Chapter 5). Granting the existence of such powerful strivings for cognitive consistency, just what are the processes through which the individual adopts his specific values and behaviors from among the many possibilities that could be consistent with his gender?

Kohlberg hypothesizes that after the child has categorized himself as male or female he then values positively whatever is consistent with his gender identity. That hypothesis is provocative. However, one has to explain how the boy learns and selects the particular sets of sex-typed behaviors that he adopts from the vast array that could be "consistent with his gender." There are many different appropriate ways of being a boy or a girl, and even more diverse ways of being a man or a woman, in any given culture. Boys and girls are exposed to a great variety of potentially appropriate sex-typed behaviors by same-sex models. From this diverse array of gender-consistent possibilities, they select and choose discriminatively. To understand sex typing fully we must account for individual differences in sex-typed behavior *within* each sex and not just for modal differences between the sexes. It is therefore necessary to go beyond cognitive self-categorization and consistency strivings to consider social learning.

Social learning theorists find it helpful to distinguish between the mechanisms through which the individual learns sex-typed behaviors and those that regulate her selection of particular sex-typed behaviors from the repertoire that is already available to her. As we have stressed before, people obviously do not perform all the behaviors that they have learned and could enact, and members of each sex know a great deal about the role behaviors of both sexes. In our culture both men and women know, for example, how to fight aggressively, and how to use cosmetics, although they differ in the frequency with which they perform these activities.

The acquisitional (learning) phases of sex typing involve cognitive and observational processes through which concepts and potential behaviors are learned. On the other hand, the individual's choice of selection of sex-typed behaviors from the available array that she already has mastered and knows how to execute depends on motivational and situational considerations. This distinction between acquisition and response selection is not limited to sex typing; it has also been made for all other aspects of social behavior by most current social learning theories. We are referring here to the previously discussed view that the acquisition of novel responses is regulated by sensory, attentional, and cognitive processes, but that direct and vicarious reinforcement is the important regulator of response selection in *performance*.

Boys and girls discover quickly that the consequences for many of the things that they try are affected by their sex. Indeed, that is exactly the meaning of "sex-typed" behaviors: Their appropriateness depends on the sex of the person who displays them. Sex-typed behaviors are those that are typically more expected and approved for one sex than for the other and that lead

The performance of sex-typed behavior depends on the expected consequences.

to different outcomes or consequences when performed by males as opposed to females in the particular community. Because they yield differential consequences for males and females, these sex-typed behaviors come to be performed with different frequency by the sexes and to have different value for them. Thus a person's sex influences the consequences she gets for many of the things she does and affects how people relate to her as well as how she reacts to herself.

Consider, for example, the sex-typed domain of dependency. Under many conditions dependency is an effective way for getting help when it is displayed by females but not by males. In an experiment with college students, women who were dependent received the most help, while dependent men were not helped more often than independent ones (Gruder & Cook, 1971). But the greater dependency that women may develop because it "works" for them in our culture also exerts a toll. For example, college women thinking about their distant future anticipated more dependency than men, and also expressed more concern and anxiety about it, probably realistically (Kalish, 1971).

Child-Rearing Practices and Sex-Typing

Parents, teachers, and other significant social agents tend to reward sex-appropriate behaviors and to punish or ignore sex-inappropriate responses. Even young children soon learn that their parents expect boys and girls to behave differently. For example, a group of five-year-olds were shown a series of paired pictures illustrating masculine and feminine activities (Fauls & Smith, 1956). The children were asked which activity Mother and Father would prefer for boys and girls (e.g., "Which does Mother want the boy to do?"). Children of both sexes indicated that parents wanted the child to perform sex-appropriate activities more often than sex-inappropriate activities.

Starting with different names, clothes, and color schemes for the nursery, parents seem to treat boys and girls differently, and children soon perceive important sex differences between their parents as well. In one study, seventh-grade boys and girls rated their mothers and fathers separately on a number of rearing variables (Droppleman & Schaefer, 1961). The results show that "girls as contrasted to boys report both mother and father to be more affectionate and as less rejecting, hostile and ignoring" (1961, p. 5). The authors conclude (1961, p. 5): "Females report that they received more affection as children than do males, and both sexes report that the female parent gives more affection than does the male parent."

In the strongly sex-typed behavior areas of aggression and dependency, we would expect the greatest differential treatment of boys and girls by their parents. Careful investigations of attitudes and training practices have been conducted for these two areas of special interest.

Parents tend to rear boys and girls most differently in the area of *aggression* (Sears, Maccoby, & Levin, 1957). Boys were given greater freedom in the expression of aggression toward the parents and toward other children. Girls were more often praised for "good" behavior and more often subjected to withdrawal of love for "bad" behavior. These reported differences are not strong, but they are consistent with the cultural sanction of physical aggression in males. "Prosocial" aggressions (verbalizations about the goodness or badness of behavior and verbal threats) are more acceptable for girls but are considered "sissyish" for boys. These results are consistent with the sex differences discussed earlier showing that boys are more frequently physically aggressive, while girls display more prosocial and verbal aggression.

Although parents tend to sanction physical aggression for boys more than for girls, they are not indiscriminate. They obviously do not condone aggression for boys regardless of circumstances and setting. This fact is illustrated in the finding that boys who were aggressive at school had parents who encouraged aggression toward peers; many of these boys, however, were nonaggressive at home, and their parents indeed punished aggression at home (Bandura, 1960).

Females probably are allowed to display greater *dependency* than males in our culture. Laboratory studies have demonstrated that permissiveness for dependency, and reward for dependency, increased children's dependency behavior. Heathers (1953), for example, found that children who accepted help from the experimenter in a difficult situation tended to have parents who encouraged them to depend on others rather than to be independent.

A positive relation between the demonstrativeness and warmth of parents and the dependency of their children has also been found. Mothers who are affectionately demonstrative respond positively to their children's dependent behavior and describe their children as high in dependency (Sears, Maccoby, & Levin, 1957). Similarly, a field study by Bandura (1960) indicated, among other results, that parents who reward dependency have children who tend to display a high degree of dependency behavior.

An experimental study by Goldberg and Lewis (1969) is especially important because it gives information on differentiation of sex-appropriate behavior in infancy. A free-play situation was used to observe sex differences in behavior toward the mother, toys, and a frustration situation at 13 months of age. Information on the children in the study at age 6 months was also available.

Boys and girls at 13 months showed clear differences in their behavior toward their mothers. Girls were more reluctant than boys to leave their mothers and returned to them more quickly and more often than did boys. The girls also touched their mothers more frequently and for a longer time period, and they played closer to their mothers than did boys. In the frustration situation, girls cried and motioned for help consistently more than boys.

When the children were 6 months old the mothers touched, talked to, and handled their daughters more than their sons. The mothers' greater attention to daughters at the early age may have been one of the causes of the finding that at age 13 months girls touched and talked to their mothers more than did boys.

In spite of these threads of evidence that boys and girls may be socialized differently by their parents, the degree to which parents treat the sexes differently is not clear. For example, overall evidence for different treatments is not strong, according to the review by Maccoby and Jacklin (1974b). In their view, although parents may react sharply when their children violate narrowly defined sex typing (as when boys want to play with dolls and dresses), evidence for clear differences in how parents react to sons and daughters in such areas as aggression and dependency is less clear. But other reviews point out that society shapes males and females in quite different ways with clear and often painful costs for both sexes (Block, 1973). In the present view, even when parents do not consistently respond differently to boys and girls, there are many other social forces that encourage sex differences in social behavior. These influences include the behaviors modeled by the child's peers, and the rules learned about what it means to be a boy or girl—rules that are learned cognitively and by observation without any direct "shaping" or reinforcement of the child.

Social Structure

Sex typing also is affected by influences outside the immediate family. To understand socialization and especially the development of psychological sex differences fully, we must recognize the role of the social system in which the individual lives. The emphasis on the person in psychology must not obscure the intimate dependence of personality on environment—and the vital role of social forces, institutions, and groups in molding that environment throughout the person's development.

Even within any one broad culture there are important differences among the component subcultures. For example, the extent to which children develop traditional sex-role concepts and sex typing depends on the degree to which they participate in a subculture that shares, models, and encourages those traditional attitudes and values (Minuchin, 1965).

On the other hand, some sex differences in socialization are found cross-culturally, as revealed in a survey of ethnographic reports (Barry, Bacon, & Child, 1957). Two competent judges rated the socialization data from 110 cultures, a majority of which were nonliterate. They judged sex differences in socialization on five variables: nurturance, obedience, responsibility, achievement, and self-reliance. The differences they found in childhood socialization pressures on these five variables are summarized in Table 14-2.

As Table 14-2 indicates, not only in our society but also in many other cultures, girls are socialized to become nurturant, obedient, and responsible, whereas boys are socialized toward greater self-reliance and achievement striving. These relations were not invariant, however, and there were exceptions. Since there were some reversals, and since many cultures showed no detectable sex differences on these dimensions, the evidence favors the role of socially learned rather than biologically established determinants. Nevertheless, it is likely that many of the sex differences in social behavior obtained cross-culturally partly reflect the widespread adaptation of cultures to universal bio-

TABLE 14-2
RATINGS OF CULTURES FOR SEX DIFFERENCES IN CHILDHOOD SOCIALIZATION PRESSURE ON FIVE VARIABLES

Variable	Number of Cultures	Both Judges Rate Socialization Pressure Higher for	
		Girls	Boys
Nurturance	33	17	0
Obedience	69	6	0
Responsibility	84	25	2
Achievement	31	0	17
Self-reliance	82	0	64

SOURCE: Adapted from Barry, Bacon and Child (1957).

logical variables such as child-bearing. The authors commented on the differences they obtained as follows:

> The observed differences in the socialization of boys and girls are consistent with certain universal tendencies in the differentiation of adult sex role. In the economic sphere, men are more frequently allotted tasks that involve leaving home and engaging in activities where a high level of skill yields important returns; hunting is a prime example. Emphasis on training in self-reliance and achievement for boys would function as preparation for such an economic role. Women, on the other hand, are more frequently allotted tasks at or near home that minister most immediately to the needs of others (such as cooking and water carrying); these activities have a nurturant character, and in their pursuit a responsible carrying out of established routines is likely to be more important than the development of an especially high order of skill. Thus training in nurturance, responsibility, and, less clearly, obedience, may contribute to preparation for this economic role. These consistencies with adult role go beyond the economic sphere, of course. Participation in warfare, as a male prerogative, calls for self-reliance and a high order of skill where survival or death is the immediate issue. The childbearing which is biologically assigned to women, and the child care which is socially assigned primarily to them, lead to nurturant behavior and often call for a more continuous responsibility than do the tasks carried out by men. Most of these distinctions in adult role are not inevitable, but the biological differences between the sexes strongly predispose the distinction of role, if made, to be in a uniform direction (Barry, Bacon, & Child, 1957, pp. 328–329).

Moderator Variables in Sex-Typing

Although the consequences produced by any behavior depend in part on the person's sex, they also hinge on numerous other considerations. The type of behavior, the situation in which it occurs, the individual's age, status, and other characteristics, are some of the many variables that interact with his or her sex to determine how people will react to him or her. The many variables that moderate the exact effects of the child's sex become evident from careful studies of child-rearing practices.

These practices depend not only on the sex of the child but also on the sex of the parent. For example, Rothbart and Maccoby (1966) found complex interactions between sex of parent and sex of child. Parents of preschool children listened to tape-recorded statements of a child's voice and indicated what they would say or do to their own sons or daughters in response to each statement. Mothers' reactions showed almost no overall average difference from fathers' reactions, but sex of parent did interact with sex of child. Mothers tended to be more permissive toward sons than toward daughters, whereas fathers tended to be more attentive and permissive toward their daughters than their sons. This interaction was most pronounced when the child expressed pain (complaining that the baby had stepped on its hand) but it did not affect many other behaviors strongly and it appeared for only one form of aggression (expression of direct anger at the parent).

Rothbart and Maccoby concluded that inconsistency between parents with regard to sex-typed behavior seems to be the rule and also that a parent's reactions could vary from one behavior area to another. The exact form of a behavior, the child's sex, and the sex of the parent reacting to it are all important variables in determining the consequences of the behavior. If parental reactions hinge on numerous situational variables, then global concepts like "permissiveness" (construed as primarily stimulus-free attributes of the parent) may be of only limited value in understanding the development of children's behavior.

An experiment by Taylor and Epstein (1967) illustrates how complexly sex roles influence behavior; at the same time it shows the discriminations people make as a function of moderating conditions. They exposed male and female college students to fictitious male and female opponents in a competitive situation. The aggressiveness of the students was assessed by having them set the amount of electric shock they wanted their opponent to receive after each trial. The fictitious opponent administered increasing amounts of shock to the students.

In accord with the cultural sanctions against physical aggressiveness toward women, both sexes administered less shock to the opponent believed to be a female, even when she herself administered increasingly higher shocks. When the highly aggressive opponent was thought to be male, however, it was the females who ultimately became most aggressive; now the females doubled the initial intensity of the electric shocks against their male antagonists. Thus even for a specific type of aggression, such as physical punishment, sex differences are moderated by such situational variables as the sex of the victim and the sex of the aggressor.

The behavior patterns that are appropriate for males as opposed to females also change as a function of the individual's age. Different forms of dependency, for example, may be broadly acceptable for both sexes when they are young but not in later phases of their development. When dependency is manifested by older boys it may be unacceptable, whereas similar dependent behaviors may be condoned for girls who are equally old.

Within any given society the particular clusters of behavior that are sex typed, the consequences for appropriate and inappropriate sex typing, the sex-role models that are valued and those that are disapproved, change significantly and repeatedly in the course of the individual's development. Most psychological studies of the development of personality in general and of sex typing in particular have been conducted with young children (usually under age seven) as the subjects. Yet some of the most important aspects of personality, and of distinctively male and female behavior, emerge at later ages—at and after puberty. It is at these later times that the individual practices adult sex-role behavior, not during the child's dress-up play in his parent's shoes, but in actuality and in his or her own right.

In early adulthood, rather than in childhood, sex-typed expectations become relevant for a host of new interpersonal and sexual behaviors. During adolescence, for example, sex differences in character, in the cultivation of skills, and in the expression of sexual feelings, become most apparent (Douvan & Kaye, 1957; Harris, 1959). It is also during adolescence that critical interactions between physical sexual maturation and psychological socialization may take place. For example, during adolescence boys whose physical development is retarded are more likely to develop personality difficulties, presumably because they cannot engage as successfully in many prestigious sex-typed activities, such as athletics (Mussen & Jones, 1957, 1958).

Some of the dramatic differences in sex-typed behaviors that commence in adolescence do not end there and continue to influence the individual for many years. Throughout their lives the role expectations and the role behaviors of the sexes differ in numerous critical respects. These patterns continue to change dynamically. They come under new influences as appropriate role demands and role models vary, and as the consequences for particular forms of sex-typed behavior shift, in accord with changes throughout the individual's life and in the larger culture.

In sum, sex-typed response patterns often are affected by the situation in which they are made and by such variables as the individual's age and the sex of the other persons in the situation. In research many interactions occur between the experimenter's sex and the sex of the subject. As the examples in this section indicate, the reinforcing consequences produced by behavior depend not only on the performer's sex and on the content of the behavior, but also on his or her age and the particular circumstances. Individuals learn to discriminate sharply in their behaviors, moderating their actions in the light of the probable consequences they may produce. Again we see that many conditions may combine to determine what the individual does. In addition, it is possible that these conditions may to some degree include innate differences between the sexes in their readiness to learn certain behaviors. In some readings of the state of research, this may be true in the case of aggression (Maccoby & Jacklin, 1974b), but that interpretation remains controversial.

The Correlates and Consistency of Sex-Typing

There are enormous individual differences in masculinity-femininity. As with most other dimensions of personality, research has revealed extensive correlations between masculinity-femininity indices and other personality measures.

Correlates

One set of investigations has studied the relations between indices of personality adjustment and sex typing. It was found that adolescent boys who had highly masculine interests (on the Strong Vocational Interest Test) when compared to those with highly feminine interests, had more positive self-concepts and more self-confidence on the TAT (Mussen, 1961). The children with more masculine interests were also rated by peers as more masculine.

The adolescents in Mussen's studies were reexamined to assess their adjustment when they reached their late thirties. Using many personality measures, Mussen compared the men who as adolescents had expressed more traditionally masculine interests with those who had reported more feminine interests.

> Comparison of the ratings assigned to the two groups showed that in adulthood, as during adolescence, those who had relatively feminine interest patterns manifested more of the "emotional-expressive" role characteristics—e.g., they were rated as more dependent but more social in orientation. In constrast, those with highly masculine adolescent interest patterns possessed, in their late teens and in their late thirties, more active, "instrumental" characteristics: greater self-sufficiency, less social orientation and, in adulthood, less introspectiveness. There was little congruence between the adolescent and adult statuses of the two groups with respect to several other characteristics, however. During adolescence, highly masculine subjects possessed more self-confidence and greater feelings of adequacy than the other group, but as adults, they were relatively lacking in qualities of leadership, dominance, self-confidence, and self-acceptance (Mussen, 1962, p. 440).

Thus sex-appropriate identification in adolescence is not a fixed sign of an overall enduring adjustment pattern. Adolescents who have stereotyped masculine interests may adjust more happily during adolescence and are rated more positively at that time. Middle-class adolescents who profess stereotypically masculine interests, attitudes, and values probably would fare better, especially with their peers, than would boys who express strongly feminine interests. These adolescent sex-typed preferences, however, do not guarantee a generalized pattern of adjustment for life. Indeed, Mussen (1962, p. 440) pointed out that:

> In general there seems to have been a shift in the self-concepts of the two groups in adulthood, the originally highly masculine boys apparently feeling less positive about themselves after adolescence, and, correlatively, the less masculine groups changing in a favorable direction.

The correlates of sex-typing have also been studied in experimental situations. For example, the relationships between sex-role preferences and the youngsters' susceptibility to verbal conditioning conducted by a male or female adult have been explored. In one experiment (Epstein & Liverant, 1963) boys between the ages of five and seven were divided according to whether they were very high or very low in masculinity (judged by their preferences on a scale). They were then exposed to a male or female adult who verbally approved whenever they answered "mother" (in one condition) or "father" (in another condition) to many questions. The masculine boys tended to be more readily conditioned by a male than by a female. This finding suggested that adult men had acquired greater reinforcement value for these youngsters. All the boys, regardless of masculinity scores, tended to condition more readily when the verbally approved response was "father" than when it was "mother."

The component of sex typing whose correlates have been studied most thoroughly is dependency. The findings indicate that dependency may have quite different meanings—and hence correlates—for girls than it has for boys. Sears (1963) found that for preschool girls dependency is correlated with indices of maternal permissiveness for dependency. The mother who approves of dependency and encourages intimacy with her daughter often has a daughter who engages in "positive attention seeking." For boys various forms of dependent behavior seem to be associated with "coldness in the mother, slackness of standards, and a rejection of intimacy by the father" (Sears, 1963, p. 60). The parents of these boys were described as "an inhibited and ineffectual mother—and to some extent father, too—who provides little freedom for the boy, and little incentive for maturing" (p. 62).

The different antecedents of dependency will seem more understandable if you consider the different consequences produced by dependency behaviors when displayed by boys and by girls. Dependency by girls more often gets approval from parents, teachers, and peers. It would be expected, therefore, that dependency in girls would be correlated with indices of parental warmth and satisfaction and with general adjustment and other signs of age-appropriate behavior. Dependency behavior in a boy, on the other hand, may reflect that he is not adequately performing sanctioned, age-appropriate, independent behavior. The dependent, clinging boy is more likely to be the one who shows poor adjustment on other indices and who is upsetting to adults.

Stability of Sex-Typed Behaviors

There are sex differences in the durability of various sex-typed behavior patterns. In the Fels Longitudinal Study, Kagan and Moss (1962) found some significant consistency between childhood and early adulthood ratings of achievement behavior, sex-typed activity and spontaneity for both sexes. Certain other variables, like dependency and aggression, were stable for one sex but not for the other. In particular, childhood dependency and passivity were related to adult dependency and passivity for women, but not for men. Conversely, "the developmental consistency for aggression was noticeably greater for males" (p. 95). They suggested that these sex-linked differences in the continuity of behaviors may reflect differences in their "congruence with traditional standards for sex-role characteristics" (p. 268).

Cross-Situational Consistency

Are children highly consistent across situations in their sex-role behaviors? *Dependency* and *aggression,* as we saw, are the two dimensions on which the sexes are often thought to differ most. Consequently these two dispositions were selected to serve as key referents for sex typing (Sears, Rau, & Alpert, 1965). That is, the appropriately sex-typed, "masculine" boy was defined as the one who is more aggressive and less dependent, whereas "femininity" was conceptualized as involving less aggression and more dependency. The Sears group looked for consistency on these dimensions of aggression and dependency to assess whether they are generalized traits. Their question here was, for example, is the child who is "feminine" (dependent, nonaggressive) in some situations also feminine in other settings in a consistent fashion?

To answer such questions, Sears (1963) studied five categories of dependency behavior. His categories were: negative attention seeking, for example, by disruption or aggressive activity; positive attention seeking, as in seeking praise; nonaggressive touching or holding; being near (for example, following a child or teacher); and seeking reassurance. The children were observed carefully at nursery school, and their behavior was sampled at different times and was scored reliably. Each child was observed in free play for many hours. Contrary to expectations, the children were not consistently dependent. The intercorrelations among the five dependency categories reached statistical significance in only one of the 20 consistency coefficients that were computed. A child's dependency in one setting thus was unrelated to his or her dependency in other settings. Reviewing their own data, Sears, Rau, and Alpert (1965) concluded that a unitary concept of dependency was not justified.

Other studies of dependency, summarized by Maccoby and Masters (1970), also indicate little consistency in observational studies when dependency is sampled in closely related situations. Mann (1959) obtained ratings of many two-minute observations of nursery children in free play on six kinds of dependency behavior. Only one of 15 intercorrelations among these components was significant. Likewise, observations of nursery school children revealed no relation between the frequencies of their "affection seeking" and "approval seeking" (Heathers, 1953).

Dependency seems to be much more consistent, however, when raters make broad, global judgments rather than observe specific behaviors. High correlations have been found among teachers' ratings of five dependency components in nursery school children (Beller, 1955). The correlations from such broad trait ratings often are impressively large. Unfortunately the presence of rating biases and stereotyped impressions in such trait judgments makes them hard to interpret (e.g., Mischel, 1968). If there is no consistency when boys and girls are measured on specific and objectively defined dependency behaviors, but there *is* consistency in broad, global ratings of their dependency, then the consistency may reside in the judges' biased concepts and not in the children's behavior.

Sears, Rau, and Alpert (1965) also investigated the consistency of aggression in their sample of nursery school children. Their results suggested some clustering of aggressive behaviors, especially in boys. But considering the large number of coefficients computed, and the generally modest magnitude of even those relations that reached statistical significance, there was no strong evidence for a broadly consistent aggressive trait.

The relations among other measures of sex role also were studied carefully by the Sears group. Their tests included several in which children chose among objects, toys, and activities that differed in their sex appropriateness. For example, the youngsters indicated whether they preferred a picture showing a child walking a doll in a buggy or a child playing cowboy. Other measures included the children's preferences for various real and symbolic play areas and activities. Adult observers then rated each child on a five-point scale of "sex typing," or the degree to which he or she behaved in accord with expectations for his or her sex. In addition, the children's doll play was scored for sex typing. Their willingness to adopt the opposite sex role in a game while interacting with their mother was also recorded. Agreement among raters was adequate and the scoring was done reliably.

Of main interest were the correlations among the sex-role measures themselves. There was some consistency among the measures for girls; for boys there was almost no consistency. The overall relations for both sexes were modest and complex. For example, while girls were somewhat consistent on certain sex-typed preference measures and boys were not, in their doll play these trends were reversed. In doll play the girls were not consistent in their tendencies to perform male or female adult work, while there was a trend toward such consistency for boys. Thus even within a fairly narrow subset of gender role measures, such as different aspects of doll play, the youngsters' behavior was far from consistent.

The relationships obtained by the Sears group are fairly representative of those found by other researchers on the same topic (e.g., Borstelmann, 1961; Hetherington, 1965; Mischel, 1966a, 1968). In sum, although substantial correlations may be found among masculinity-femininity self-reports and global ratings, consistency among indices of sex typing (such as dependency or aggression) tends to be limited when more direct and more diverse observational measures of behavior are used.

Changing Stereotypes and Sex-Role Bias

Although some aspects of an individual's sex-typed behaviors may be relatively stable, others may change, even in adulthood, especially when alterations occur in the social structures that support them. In recent years there have been some dramatic challenges to conventional sex roles in our culture, as exemplified in the Women's Movement. Some of these influences may be reflected in Amy Wilson's changing concepts of sex differences and sex roles when she was interviewed again four years later.

Amy Wilson revisited at age 30; a rising consciousness?

Q. How are men and women different psychologically?

A. The psychological differences are greatest in self-concept. Men feel dominant, important. Women are the "other." They are sort of what's left . . . unfortunately.

Q. What do men do that women don't do?

A. Men have more privileges in our society. They are better paid for the same work, have more legal rights, etc. They are seldom allowed to be passive, dependent, and nurturant—whereas these qualities are almost demanded of women.

Q. Would you rather be a man or a woman?

A. I'm proud and happy to be a woman—but I'll be a lot happier when society makes some of the fundamental changes necessary to ensure the maximum individual development of all individuals, men and women.

Q. What are some of the things you like most?

A. I like to feel I'm really stretching myself. That whatever I do, I'm using all my abilities to the fullest. I get no real satisfaction out of routine jobs just as much as I resent such tasks at home. I love being with my kids when we're exploring places or talking about ideas—I hate being forced into the role of chauffeur or—worse—nag.

Q. How would you be most different in personality if you were a man?

A. If I were a man I think I'd have a better self-concept without having to fight for it. I'd be less unassuming and as a consequence I'd probably do better in all my roles as well. I think in many ways I, as a female, have been brought up to be self-defeating. I too easily get distracted, too easily do the 'helpful' thing because I've been conditioned that way . . . and that's wrong.

At this juncture in her life, Amy seems to have a new consciousness of the role society has played in determining her behavior. She is far more aware now of the conditions which generated and serve to maintain the psychological differences she perceives and experiences between men and women. New in Amy's response is her conception of alternatives to the status quo and her desire to break down some of the existing inequalities and stereotypes. This reexamination and new consciousness reflect not only new information and a new emphasis on the nature of sex differences conveyed by the media and by the Women's Movement, but also Amy's personal experiences in her new career as a freelance writer.

Sex-Role Bias in Society

There has been a growing recognition in psychology, as well as in the Women's Movement, that psychologists, teachers, and parents should not unquestioningly perpetuate stereotyped sex roles (Bardwick, 1972). To automatically encourage boys and girls to accept the stereotyped roles society expects them to play may prevent each person from realizing his or her full potential. The sex role ideology, explicit or implicit, prevalent in the United States has been accused of producing an unfortunate "homogenization" of American women (Bem & Bem, 1972). It has been pointed out that there is widespread acceptance in America of an "unconscious ideology" about women. This ideology is reflected in the fact that the majority of American women end up in virtually the *same* role, that of homemaker, often combined with a dead-end job (e.g., sales clerk, secretary, factory worker). A woman often is consigned to her role on the basis of sex, without regard to her unique abilities and capacities. The American ideology regarding the female sex tends to close options to women and constrict ". . . the emerging self-image of the female child and the nature of her aspirations from the very beginning . . ." (Bem & Bem, 1972, p. 7). In contrast, a male is more likely to become whatever his talents and interests permit him to be, with great diversity in his occupational potential.

The same authors contend further that the American male also may be disadvantaged by the prevailing ideology; for example, he may be discouraged

Sex-role stereotypes should not prevent each person from realizing his or her full potential.

from developing such desirable traits as tenderness and sensitivity on the grounds that those qualities are "unmanly." Further, the relationship between males and females may suffer from the inequities in current sex-role stereotypes. Once we become conscious of this destructive ideology, changes may be necessary: (1) to prevent discrimination (at the legal and economic levels); (2) to avoid constrictive, personally debilitating sex-role socialization; and (3) to encourage institutions and ideologies that will nullify the presumed incompatibility of family and career for women in our society.

Many statements have been made about the constricted and inequitable nature of the traditional female sex roles and some of these assertions have been seen as unfounded propaganda by critics (e.g., Dechter, 1972). Although arguments have been abundant on all sides of this heated social issue, there has been some work on bias due to sex roles. For example, it has been asserted widely that clear sex-role stereotypes which prevent the full expression of individuality in interests and abilities are imparted early to children. A study of elementary school reading textbooks examined the treatment of males and females in the stories to which school children are routinely exposed (C. Jacklin and H. Mischel, 1973). The results were quite clear. Female characters in the children's reading texts were consistently underrepresented and were rarely main figures in the stories. Males were the heroes, carried the action, and experienced more positive consequences as a result of their own efforts and initiative. In contrast, females were passive, and whatever positive consequences they received came from the situation (e.g., from what others did for them, from luck) rather than from their own actions and initiative. These inequitable portraits of males and females became even stronger as the series of books progressed from kindergarten through third grade.

Sex-Role Stereotyping in Psychology

Sex-role stereotyping has been laid squarely at the door of psychology itself in a study by Broverman, et al. (1970). Clinically trained psychologists, psychiatrists, and social workers were asked to describe a healthy, mature, socially competent (a) man; (b) woman; (c) adult, sex unspecified. Judgments of what characterized mentally healthy males and females differed in a way congruent with stereotypic sex-role differences (see Table 14-3 for examples). The qualities used to define mental health for an ideal adult (of unspecified sex) closely resembled those attributes judged healthy for men but differed significantly from those considered to be healthy for women. For example, the healthy adult of unspecified sex was described as dominant, independent, adventurous, aggressive, and competitive. These adjectives were also used to describe the healthy adult male. In contrast, the healthy adult female was described as more submissive, less independent, less adventurous, less aggressive, less competitive, more easily influenced, more excitable in minor crises, and more conceited about her appearance. As the authors noted (p. 5), "this constellation seems a most unusual way of describing any mature, healthy individual."

TABLE 14-3 EXAMPLES OF TRAITS ATTRIBUTED BY CLINICIANS TO "HEALTHY" WOMEN COMPARED TO "HEALTHY" MEN	
"Healthy" Women Are Less	*"Healthy" Women Are More*
independent	submissive
adventurous	easily influenced
aggressive	excitable in minor crises
competitive	conceited about their appearance

SOURCE: Based on data from Broverman et al. (1970).

Moreover, this negative assessment of women was shared equally by the women professionals and by the men.

The implication is that a woman who is assertive and independent, or who is aggressive and adventurous, is likely to be judged maladjusted, while the same qualities in a male (or in a person of unspecified sex) are considered assets. In addition, stereotypic masculine traits (such as "very aggressive," "very worldly," "very logical") were seen twice as often as more desirable than were stereotypic feminine traits. Among the few feminine traits seen as desirable were "very talkative," "very tactful," and "very gentle." In sum, the overall results suggest that not only is "healthy male" synonymous with "healthy adult" and antithetical to "healthy female," but masculine traits are the ones that tend to be seen as desirable, while most feminine traits are seen as undesirable, even in the eyes of well-trained psychologists, psychiatrists, and social workers.

Consequences of Sex-Role Stereotypes

Sexual stereotypes have many painful effects. One of these negative consequences was pointed out by Matina Horner (1969, 1972) who suggested that in our culture women develop a "motive to avoid success." According to Horner, for men success is perceived as compatible with their sense of masculinity. But for women success often is a conflict-producing, mixed blessing, because professional success may imply failure in the personal sphere, and the qualities demanded for success at work may conflict with those required for success as a woman. Other researchers have disputed whether or not women really have a distinct motive to avoid success. But there tends to be agreement that in many instances in our culture success and failure have very different implications and consequences for men and women. For example, when a woman does succeed on a task considered "masculine," her performance is as likely to be attributed to her luck as to her skill (Deaux & Emswiller, 1974; see Figure 14-1).

Especially discouraging is the finding that when more women enter a high-status profession, its perceived prestige declines. Male and female college students were led to believe that certain high-status professions (e.g., college professor and physician) would have an influx of women. They rated the fields as less prestigeful and desirable than a control group informed that the proportions of women in these fields would remain stable and low. This devaluation was expressed equally by women and by men (Touhey, 1974).

Also unjust and frustrating is the fact that some professional work may be judged less favorably when it is done by women than by men, even when the work is identical (Goldberg, 1967). In this line of research, subjects were asked to judge a series of professional articles. The identical articles were shown as authored by either males or females simply by varying the name on them (e.g., John Simpson or Joan Simpson). Goldberg's results suggested that when U.S. college women were the judges they devalued the achievements of other women and they did so even in fields which are traditionally associated with women, such as dietetics and primary education.

A group of later studies, conducted in both the U.S. and Israel with both

FIGURE 14-1
What Is Skill for the Male May Be Luck for the Female

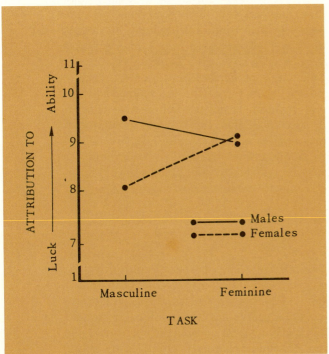

Graph showing that when females were able to find hidden pictures of such items as tire jacks and wrenches (masculine tasks) in a larger picture, their success was attributed partly to their luck, whereas the performance of males on this task was credited more to their skill. When the task was to discover hidden pictures of mops and double boilers (feminine tasks) the performance of both sexes was judged to be due to their ability to the same degree. (Adapted from Deaux & Emswiller, 1974, p. 82)

males and females, questions the existence of a generalized preference for male expertise (H. Mischel, 1974). Using the same method as Goldberg, this study found that professional sex bias in the U.S. depended on the particular field in which work was judged. Judges of both sexes preferred authors whose sex was the same as that normative for (or stereotypically associated with) the professional field in which the article was written. For example, bias was in favor of a female author in primary education but in favor of a male author in law. Israeli subjects subscribed to the same stereotypes as the U.S. subjects regarding the sex association of the diverse fields, but did not show the evaluative biases found in the U.S. These results highlight the complexity and specificity of existing sex biases, and show that they are double-edged, with discrimination against men (when they are in stereotypically female fields) as well as against women (when they venture into male-dominated fields).

Toward Androgyny?

Alert to the negative effects of rigid traditional sex-role stereotypes, Sandra Bem (1975) questioned the very notion of "masculinity" and "femininity" as two opposite ends of a single dimension. She reasoned that this bipolar dimension has obscured the possibility that individuals might be "androgynous," i.e., *both* masculine *and* feminine, as those terms are usually defined. Moreover, traditionally narrow sex-role concepts might inhibit persons from behaving flexibly across situations that threaten their stereotypes about sex-appropriate behavior. In this research, androgynous persons were defined as those who are not rigidly sex-typed but instead endorse masculine and feminine attributes equally. Specifically, an individual who endorses both types of attributes equally is defined as having an androgynous sex role (see Table 14-4). According to Bem, these individuals, whether male or female, may be more flexible (e.g., resisting social pressure to conform) than those who are more traditionally sex-typed. Although much more research is needed before firm conclusions can be reached, Bem (p. 643) speculates that the sex-role flexibility of androgynous people "enables them to engage in situationally effective behavior without regard for its stereotype as masculine or feminine. Accordingly, it may well be—as the Women's Liberation Movement has urged—that the androgynous individual will someday come to define a new and more human standard of psychological health."

Beyond Androgyny?

In spite of its appealing qualities, the concept of psychological androgyny has not escaped penetratingly sharp criticism, both of its measurement (Pedhazur & Tetenbaum, 1979) and of its rationale (Locksley & Colten, 1979). For example, consider the notion that androgynous people are better adjusted because they have greater flexibility in their behavior as a consequence of not being confined by sex stereotypes. A series of studies examined this idea by giving

TABLE 14-4
EXAMPLES OF ITEMS ON THE MASCULINITY AND FEMININITY SCALES OF BEM'S ANDROGYNY TEST

NOTE: On the test the items are mixed together. For each item the subject is asked to describe himself or herself by marking the appropriate number.

Masculine Items	Feminine Items
Acts as a leader	Affectionate
Analytical	Compassionate
Competitive	Feminine
Forceful	Gullible
Individualistic	Sensitive to the needs of others
Self-reliant	Sympathetic
Willing to take a stand	Warm

SOURCE: Based on Bem, 1974 (by permission).

1	2	3	4	5	6	7
Never or Almost Never True	Usually Not True	Sometimes but Infrequently True	Occasionally True	Often True	Usually True	Always or Almost Always True

subjects Bem's questionnaire for sex-role preferences and obtaining their scores for degree of androgyny versus traditional masculinity or femininity. The same subjects also were given many other measures, including those of self-esteem, helplessness, sexual maturity, and personal adjustment (Jones, Chernovetz, & Hansson, 1978). The hypothesis of better adjustment for the androgynous was not confirmed. On the contrary, for both sexes high masculinity scores (rather than androgyny) tended to predict better flexibility and overall adjustment. Such findings suggest that at least in our present society androgyny may not be the path toward optimal coping.

Even more serious are the conceptual criticisms of the androgyny concept itself. These critics note that in a society in which sex has such an extensive role in how everyday experience is structured, the concept of psychological androgyny is unjustified because it implies freedom from sex-related social and biological effects on personality and behavior. In reality such effects are everywhere because "sex is a structural feature of situations and of ongoing organizations of life experiences" (Locksley & Colten, 1979, p. 1017). In other words, these critics argue that our sex inevitably influences how people see us, what they expect, and what we ourselves perceive, expect, and do. If this is an unavoidable state of nature—there always will be males and females—then the "notion of psychological androgyny, with its implications of freedom from sex-related social effects on personality and behavior, is arbitrary at best" (Locksley & Colten, 1979, p. 1029).

Results of the type reviewed in this section should sensitize psychologists against inadvertently perpetuating traditional stereotypic conceptions of masculinity and femininity. Most psychologists would probably agree that concepts like "sex-appropriate behavior" (used throughout this chapter) merely describe the existing norms and practices of the culture and would insist that they do not necessarily endorse those norms. Yet we have seen that psychologists—just like most other people—may inadvertently perpetuate sex-role stereotypes. Fortunately, there appears to be a growing recognition that the conventional practices of society—which often may constrict human potentialities for both sexes—must not be confused with the ideals toward which its members should strive.

SUMMARY

1. Psychological sex differences and the sex-typing processes through which they develop are crucial aspects of personality. The subtlety and complexity of sex typing is illustrated by self-reports about perceived sex differences at different ages, from childhood to maturity, in the life of one person.

2. Aggressive behavior is one of the main dimensions on which sex differences have been consistently found. Boys show more physical aggression and antisocial aggression than girls as early as age three years. These differences appear cross-culturally and are found in rating studies, self-ratings, and projective tests.

3. Sex differences in dependency, another thoroughly studied variable, are not so clear-cut as those in aggression. At nursery school age few major differences in dependency are found. Later on, females are sometimes more conforming than males, but situational factors and socioeconomic demographic variables may reverse this difference.

4. Some sex differences have been found in intellectual functioning. Beginning early in adolescence boys tend to excel in visual-spatial ability; girls tend to have greater verbal ability.

5. Sex-role stereotypes are widely shared ideas about what is masculine and what is feminine, on the basis of average differences between the sexes within the culture. These stereotypes may serve as standards

for judging and evaluating one's own behavior as well as for judging others. There are great individual differences in the degree to which people adopt particular sex-role standards.

6. Sex typing is the development of patterns of behavior considered appropriate for one sex but not the other. The development of sex roles and sex typing involves biological determinants as well as learning and cognitive processes.

7. The biological or physiological approach emphasizes the possible effect of sex hormones on the development of differences even in non-sexual human behavior. Research with lower animals suggests interrelations between hormonal conditions, brain functions, and behavior. Studies with hermaphrodites dramatize the importance of the psychological gender role assigned to the child. Research with newborns suggests some sex differences in activity and sensitivity to a variety of stimuli.

8. Cognitive-developmental theory emphasizes the striving for cognitive consistency as a determinant of sex roles. According to this theory, once the cognitive self-categorization of "boy" or "girl" is made, then positive valuation of objects and behaviors consistent with this gender identity follows.

9. Social learning theories stress that children within every culture learn quite early about sex differences in behavior. Through observational learning children of both sexes know about, and are capable of performing, many role behaviors from both sexes. The sexes differ, however, in the frequency with which they perform these activities and in how they value them. Thus observational and cognitive processes, as well as direct experiences and motivational differences, are involved in the development of sex typing.

10. In the social learning view, because sex-typed behaviors yield different consequences when displayed by males and by females they rapidly become valued and practiced differentially by boys and by girls. Sex is an important determinant of how other people react to you and of how you react to yourself.

11. Parents and other significant social agents may encourage the child's sex-appropriate behavior and ignore or punish sex-inappropriate behaviors in the course of development. Aggression is the area in which boys and girls probably are reared most differently. Parents probably permit more physical aggression in boys than in girls. This sanction is not indiscriminate, however. Parents teach their children to discriminate in the expression of aggression with regard to circumstances and setting. The degree to which parents treat the sexes differently is not firmly established.

12. Social forces, institutions, and groups have a vital role in the development of psychological sex differences throughout the life cycle. Cultures differ in their sex-role standards, and even within a given culture there may be important subcultural differences. However, some cross-cultural differences in sex-role socialization have been found repeatedly. Many of the cross-culturally obtained sex differences in social behavior may partly reflect the widespread adaptation of cultures to universal sex differences in biological variables such as child-bearing.

13. Not only the child's sex, but also the sex of the people who react to her, can be important "moderators" determining some of the consequences she receives for her sex-typed behavior. There are many interactions, for example, between the sex of the parent and the sex of the child with respect to particular behaviors and situations. Thus in addition to the child's own sex, such other variables as her age, the sex of other people in the situation, and the type of behavior also interact to influence the consequences she gets for engaging in such sex-typed behaviors as aggression and dependency.

14. Within any society the role expectations and role behaviors of the sexes change significantly and repeatedly in the course of the individual's development. Some of the most important aspects of personality and of distinctively male and female behavior may emerge at and after puberty. Dramatic differences in sex-typed behaviors begin in adolescence and continue to influence the individual throughout her life. Sex-typed behavior changes as important role models change and new role demands are experienced. Changes in role standards in the larger culture also can influence sex-typed behavior substantially.

15. Many correlations exist between masculinity-femininity indices and other personality measures. For example, relations have been found between sex-typing and such indices of personality adjustment as positive self-concepts and self-confidence. Often these correlations are complex. Thus dependency in girls seems to be associated with different rearing patterns than dependency in boys. The durability of various sex-typed behaviors also differs for the two sexes.

16. Traditional sex-role stereotypes and sex-typing practices are being questioned and challenged increasingly. Sex-role biases are prevalent in society, including education and the mental health fields, and narrow sex-role stereotypes undoubtedly have negative, constrictive consequences that limit the human potentiality of both sexes. As part of the growing recognition of sex bias and the constriction produced by stereotypic sex-roles, there has been a move to measure—and perhaps encourage—increasing "androgyny" so that both sexes may achieve greater sex-role flexibility. But recently the androgyny concept itself has become the object of serious criticism.

CHAPTER 15

FRUSTRATION AND AGGRESSION

Personality psychologists tend to focus on frustration and aggression, on stress and anxiety, on painful experiences and defenses against them. Historically, this focus reflects, above all, the Freudian conception of personality dynamics, according to which, you will recall, man is engaged in a perpetual conflict between impulses seeking release and external frustrations and barriers that inhibit the expression of those impulses. For Freud and for many other theorists the experiences of frustration and anxiety, and the way in which the individual defends himself and deals with his frustrated motives and conflicts, is at the very core of personality. Frustration and aggression, anxiety, and defense are basic to the psychological coping process and to how people adapt. Therefore these topics will be the subject matter of this and the following two chapters. We will examine each of these topics and the concepts necessary to understand them.

Adaptive coping with the constant challenges and obstacles of life requires the ability to deal with frustration. This chapter examines how we react to frustration. The main questions here are: What happens when goal-directed behavior is thwarted? How do people cope with the problems that may arise when their ways of achieving satisfaction become blocked or interrupted?

What Is Frustration?

Frustrating Situations

Frustration occurs almost everywhere. Frustration results when there is an interruption in a sequence of organized or goal-directed behavior so that its completion and the goals or rewards associated with it are blocked or delayed (Figure 15-1). Frustration occurs, for example, when an infant's bottle is suddenly withdrawn, when the house key gets stuck in its lock, when the dog arrives for his feeding but finds his food bowl is empty, or when a friend fails to keep a date with you. A fundamental common denominator of these situations is that all involve an imposed interruption or delay of expected goal attainment.

Frustrations may be especially painful when they are caused by the person's own condition and when they are persistent. For example, the child with a new but enduring physical handicap—such as blindness after an accident—faces a world filled with frustration. Less obvious but also painful are the effects of the individual's own failures or incompetence—the flunked examination, the bungled job interview, the inept social encounter that leads to rejection.

Probably the most dramatic instances of prolonged frustration are those in which control over one's own life is interrupted and one is placed in enforced captivity (e.g., Biderman, 1967). The slave or the political prisoner, and even the involuntary military conscript, provide vivid examples of adaptation to total interruption of a life resulting in a massive disorganization of habitual behavior patterns.

Violations of Expectancy

In common-sense terms, frustration is most bitter when the person has built up high hopes and then is prevented from realizing them. The disgruntlement of severely disadvantaged minority groups, for example, seems to become most apparent and painful only after they have started to build hopes and expecta-

FIGURE 15-1

Frustration occurs when goal-directed behavior is blocked or interrupted before its completion. It is greatest when the blocked behavior pattern has often led to the expected outcome in the past.

tions for a better life. Frustration seems to be most keen when it involves the thwarting of a built-up hope or expectancy for important goal attainment. As was noted many years ago by de Tocqueville: "Patiently endured so long as it seemed beyond redress, a grievance comes to appear intolerable once the possibility of removing it crosses men's minds" (cited in Rubin, 1968). Indeed, as history attests, political dictators sometimes have shared de Tocqueville's insight and have proceeded to "treat" the disappointments of their people by systematically eliminating their hopes.

Thus the experience of frustration involves a thwarting of expected goal attainment. These expectations of gratification are the result of the individual's learning experiences. That is, the actions that we expect to execute smoothly and without interruption are those that have been "overlearned" or repeatedly practiced successfully on past occasions (Mandler, 1964). The more overlearned the sequence, the more arousing its disruption tends to be and the more aversive is the delay of expected gratification or goal attainment. Furthermore, the closer one gets to completion of the goal-directed activity, the more intense is the reaction to being interrupted and prevented from finishing (e.g., Haner & Brown, 1955).

Emotional Arousal

Intense frustration leads to a state of emotional arousal. Numerous bodily changes occur during high states of arousal and involve a variety of "autonomic" events (physiological changes mediated by the autonomic nervous system). These bodily changes may include an increase in heart rate and blood pressure, sweating, and vasoconstriction in the fingers (Elliott, 1974). We saw how some of these bodily changes may be measured in Chapter 9.

The emotional arousal produced by frustration is often manifested by an increase in the vigor or amplitude of behavior (Amsel & Roussel, 1952). Increased vigor produced by frustration has been found, for example, in the form of more energetic plunger-pulling or lever-pushing by children after frustration in experimental game situations (e.g., Haner & Brown, 1955; Holton, 1961). Similarly, frustrated rats have been shown to display dramatic increases in energetic behavior. It is not clear whether increased vigor of responses after thwarting is an intrinsic effect of frustration or a well-learned common reaction to it.

Persistence

Usually a first reaction to the interruption of behavior is to attempt to persist with the blocked sequence (Mandler, 1964). The cliché, "If at first you don't succeed, try again," fits the repetitive behavior typically found in first reactions to an imposed delay—as when one vainly repeats jiggling the stuck key in the lock, usually more and more vigorously, or when the toddler whose mother disappears behind the kitchen door starts pushing against it more and more forcefully, with increasing distress.

Does Frustration Have Unitary Effects?

Early theorizing speculated that frustration has unitary effects on behavior. One hypothesis, consistent with psychodynamic theory, was that extreme frustration (for example in psychosexual development) would lead the child to regress to earlier, more primitive forms of adaptation. This view suggests that frustration may adversely affect adaptation and may lead to more childish, regressive attempts that undermine the quality of the individual's behavior.

Frustration and Regression

How does frustration affect the quality of performance? To try to answer this question, one study observed the behavior of 30 nursery school children, first under normal free-play conditions and then after frustration (Barker, Dembo, & Lewin, 1941). In the free-play situation, each child was left alone to play with a set of standard play materials for a half-hour period. Observers recorded and scored the constructiveness of the child's play on a seven-point scale. Low scores were given for such unproductive behavior as superficially examining the toys, and high constructiveness scores were given for originality and creativity in play (for example, elaborate games and stories).

In the next phase of the study the frustration experience was induced. The child was again exposed to the standard toys, but now they were intermixed with some much more attractive ones. After the child became deeply engrossed in play the experimenter removed the attractive toys, placed them in a tantalizing play setting in another part of the room in the child's full view, and lowered and locked a wire screen wall to separate the child from the desirable toys. Thus the frustrated youngster and the standard materials were left on one side while the excitingly attractive toys were placed on the other side, in view but inaccessible to the child, for a period of 30 minutes.

Comparisons of the children's behavior in the free-play and frustration periods revealed dramatic differences. When frustrated and unhappy, children played much less creatively and tried in a variety of ways to overcome the barrier. Sometimes they pleaded with the experimenter, sometimes they aggressed against the experimenter or the barrier, and sometimes they became apathetic, talking about things outside the room and generally showing less interest and constructiveness in their play with the standard toys.

This experiment has been widely cited as showing that frustration leads to regression because the children's postfrustration play with the standard toys seemed less mature than their prefrustration play with the same toys. But it is not clear that this ingenious study really supports the psychoanalytic concept of regression as a response to frustration (e.g., Child & Waterhouse, 1952).

From the children's viewpoint the experimenter's behavior must have seemed deliberately cruel, irrational, and unjustified. It could be argued that the observed aggression against the experimenter and the barrier, and the accompanying decline of interest in the unattractive "standard" toys, may have been a more mature reaction than sheepish continuation of play with the standard toys. Obviously to the extent that a child was preoccupied with the barrier and trying to overcome it, he or she could not engage in creative play, and hence constructiveness scores declined.

Frustration sometimes may impair the quality of the interrupted performance (as it did in the above study), but under other conditions it may have different effects. In one study (Wright, 1942), for example, pairs of children were exposed to the frustration situation from the Barker, Dembo, and Lewin experiment just described. Some of the pairs were close friends while others were casual acquaintances. Pairs of close friends showed less decrement in the constructiveness of their play after frustration than did pairs of acquaintances. Thus the availability of a close peer helped to minimize the impact of frustration. Moreover, under some frustrating circumstances, there may even be an increase in the cooperativeness of play among close friends compared with casual friends (Wright, 1943); close friends became less hostile toward each other and more collectively aggressive against the frustrating experimenter. Observation of the children's reactions also revealed extensive differences in their modes of coping with frustration.

The Frustration-Aggression Hypothesis

A second hypothesis concerning the unitary effects of frustration suggests an association between frustration and aggression. A link between frustration as a stimulus and aggression as a response has been noted for years in many theoretical formulations. The strongest version of this idea was the classical "frustration-aggression hypothesis" (Dollard and associates, 1939). The essence of the original frustration-aggression hypothesis was that:

1. all frustrations increase the probability of an aggressive reaction and
2. all aggression presupposes the existence of prior frustration.

The hypothesis of an unlearned, invariable association between frustration and aggression is most compelling if aggression is conceptualized as an unlearned drive or instinct, and that indeed is how it was viewed by proponents of the frustration-aggression hypothesis.

If it is assumed that people (and other animals) have an instinct to inflict harm or injury on others, it seems plausible also to hypothesize that this instinct will function to enhance the organism's survival. The most adaptive function of aggression in the course of evolution might be as a way of coping with frustrations, especially those that threaten the organism's survival. In their evolutionary history perhaps organisms may have to develop "killer instincts" if they are to survive in their competition with others for the limited essential resources available to them. If nature supplies more organisms than resources for their maintenance, a struggle for survival readily develops and the aggressive animal may be more likely to win.

Aggression in Response to Frustration

It became clear some time ago that the frustration-aggression hypothesis, as originally formulated, was oversimplified and required modification (e.g., Bandura, 1973; Berkowitz, 1969). Changes have had to be made for two main reasons:

1. While aggression often may follow frustration, it is by no means the only possible response; there are vast differences among individuals and groups in their reactions to frustration. There also are major differences in any one individual's reaction to particular frustrations, depending on the situation.
2. It has been shown that aggressive reactions can occur without prior frustration. For example, unfrustrated preschool children observed an adult model physically aggress against a Bobo doll. Later these children readily imitated the model's aggressiveness and violently attacked the Bobo doll after the model had left the room (Bandura, 1965).

The modified frustration-aggression hypothesis recognizes that many conditions may affect the specific link between frustration and aggression. This

Does frustration always increase the probability of an aggressive reaction?

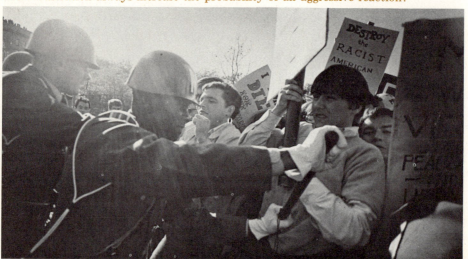

modified hypothesis takes special account of the learned inhibitions that people may acquire during socialization and that may block the direct expression of aggression. Nevertheless, the modified hypothesis still implies that aggression is the natural or prepotent, unlearned drive response to frustration.

Is Aggression an Instinct?

There is disagreement about the instinctual nature of aggression. The concept of aggressive instincts—of aggression as an innate drive or impulse—was seen most clearly in Freud's view that aggression and sex are fundamental instincts. A similar position is taken by some current observers of animal behavior in natural settings ("ethologists"). Most notably, the ethologist Konrad Lorenz (1966) believes aggression is a fighting instinct, in animals and humans, directed against members of the same species. Although Dollard and Miller (1950) emphasize the importance of learning in the socialization and channeling of aggressive impulses, they also see aggression as a basic drive that demands expression either directly or indirectly. Guided by this idea, many researchers have studied the conditions that may either enhance or inhibit the expression of aggression in response to frustration. Some of those conditions are discussed next.

Fear of Retaliation and Inhibition of Aggression

Aggression is inhibited when one expects counterattack or retaliation. The belief that the fear of retaliation is a deterrent to aggression is starkly evident in the "balance of terror" that characterizes the international nuclear arms race. Guided by the conviction that an aggressor will restrain himself if he faces a potentially destructive counterattack, military defense policies urge an awesome deterrent as an essential prerequisite for inhibiting the aggression of enemies.

In the interpersonal sphere, deterrents involve social punishments rather than atomic weapons, but the principles seem to be similar. Thus interpersonal cues suggesting that aggressiveness will be rewarded rather than punished tend to encourage observers to behave aggressively (Bandura & Walters, 1963). Children who watched models receiving rewards for aggressiveness tended to become more aggressive than did those who saw a model punished for aggression.

Human inhibitions about direct aggression also depend on subtler cues concerning the potential victim's power. For example, and not surprisingly, when military personnel are insulted by someone of higher rank they communicate little aggression, while a great deal of aggression is expressed when the insultor is of lower rank (Thibaut & Riecken, 1955).

When personal identity remains disguised and the individual can hide behind his bandit's mask, or Ku Klux Klan hood, or military uniform the likelihood of retaliation and punishment is less. When persons are thus "deindividuated" they may become more boldly aggressive, impulsive, and punitive (Zimbardo, 1969).

The aggressor's proximity to the victim and the nature of the pain cues that he can observe also affect his willingness to be physically aggressive. For example, bombardiers in wartime often report feeling immune about dropping their missiles on areas that are so far below them that they cannot really witness the damage they are inflicting. When the victim is closer and his or her pain is more evident, the aggressor may become more sensitized and hence more reluctant to administer severe punishments.

In some experiments on obedience, adults were hired to give electric shocks to another person ostensibly as part of a research project on human learning (Milgram, 1965, 1974). In fact the wires were disconnected, but the victim convincingly feigned the appearance of being hurt by the shocks. Many subjects "carried out their orders" and dutifully administered shocks at levels that they thought were torturous for the victim, supporting the notion that a surprisingly large number of people are capable of behaving like the Nazis who "simply did their job" and followed orders to murder their helpless victims (Fig. 15-2).

Of main interest to the present discussion was the finding that resistance to carrying out the punitive orders increased as the aggressor was placed nearer to the victim and observed his suffering more closely. Figure 15-3 summarizes the effects of the aggressor's proximity to the victim on the average amount of shock he or she administered.

While observing the victim's pain may inhibit aggression under some conditions, under other circumstances it may enhance and reinforce it. Thus, when a person is angered it may be reinforcing for him to see the individual who

FIGURE 15-2
Milgram's "Obedience" Situation
Subjects deliver "shock" to another person under various conditions of proximity. (From Milgram, 1974)

FIGURE 15-3
Severity of Shock Inflicted by Subjects as a Function of Their Proximity to the Victim

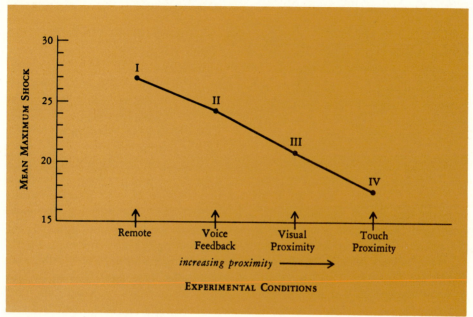

In condition I the subject neither sees nor hears his victim; in II he hears his victim's protests; in III he also sees his victim close up; in IV he must touch his victim, placing his hand on the shock apparatus. Adapted from Milgram (1965).

angered him being hurt (Feshbach, Stiles, & Bitter, 1967). That is, pain cues may serve as reinforcers under conditions of anger arousal. Since the aggressor often is angry he may find his victim's pain satisfying. On the other hand, if the aggressor is not experiencing anger, then seeing pain in the victim may inhibit him (as in the case of the bombardiers).

In sum, conditions that make aggression more rewarding for the aggressor tend to enhance aggressive behavior; conversely, aggression generally is less likely when it probably will be punished or nonrewarded. Some of the conditions that may enhance the probability of aggression are summarized in Table 15-1.

Inhibition and Anxiety

Dollard and Miller (1950), like Freud, believed many socialization practices really teach children to fear their own angry feelings. They say (1950, p. 148): "We assume . . . that anger responses are produced by the innumerable and unavoidable frustration situations of child life. . . . Society takes a special stand toward such anger responses, generally inhibiting them and allowing them reign only in a few circumstances (self-defense, war, etc.)."

TABLE 15-1	
EXAMPLES OF CONDITIONS THAT ENHANCE AGGRESSION	
Aggression Is Increased by	*Research Source*
Being attacked (insulted) by a non-powerful aggressor (rather than by a powerful one)	Thibaut & Riecken (1955)
Watching aggressive models rewarded	Bandura, Ross, & Ross (1963)
Anonymity	Zimbardo (1969)
Distance from victim	Milgram (1965, 1974)

Again like Freud, Dollard and Miller believed that problems in development to a large extent are caused by punishment for aggression, which leads the person to become anxious about angry feelings. They comment (1950, p. 148): "Parents intuitively resent and fear the anger and rage of a child, and they have the support of the culture in suppressing its anger." Guided by the psychodynamic belief that unacceptable angry feelings are repressed but may return in disguised form as symptoms, they wrote (1950, p. 148): "Lift the veil of repression covering the childhood mental life of a neurotic person and you come at once upon the smoking responses of anger."

Conflict and Indirect Aggression

What happens to aggression when its expression is prevented? The answer partly depends on whether aggression is conceptualized as a drive-like natural impulse provoked by frustration or as a learned but not inevitable response. First, consider aggression as a basic impulse or drive, as conceptualized both by psychodynamic theory and the behavioral version of that theory developed by Dollard and Miller.

Dollard and Miller hypothesized that frustration triggers the aggressive drive. They believed that aggression is the prepotent drive response to frustration. Often, however, the aggressive drive cannot be expressed directly against the perceived source of frustration. Blocking or inhibition may be caused either by objective danger (such as realistic fear of retaliation) or by anxiety about the expression of aggression (due to prior punishment for aggressiveness). As a result, the individual becomes conflicted. He or she experiences an approach-avoidance conflict between wanting to vent aggression and anxiety about the consequences of aggressiveness. To reduce this conflict, he or she may try to inhibit aggressive impulses.

Although the expression of aggressiveness may be inhibited, the impulse to aggress remains and presses for discharge in one form or another. According to

FIGURE 15-4
The Frustration-Aggression Hypothesis and Its Elaborations

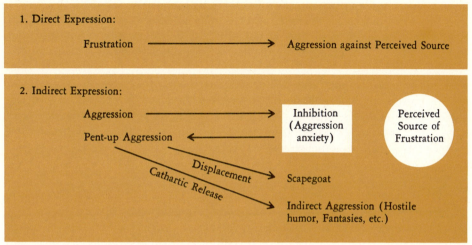

Frustration produces aggression: The aggressive impulse then is expressed directly or indirectly (e.g., through displacement). The form of expression depends on learned inhibitions and defenses.

psychodynamic theory, unexpressed impulses become "pent up" and must be released. Freud thought that impulses that are not discharged may gradually "build up" to the point where they lead to an explosive outburst. When direct expression and discharge are blocked, the drive may manifest itself indirectly in many forms.

Figure 15-4 shows some of these theoretical possibilities schematically. This scheme is suggested both by Freud's ideas on the nature of impulses and their transformation, and by Dollard and Miller's concepts concerning frustration-aggression. As the figure shows, aggressive impulses are triggered by frustration. When their direct discharge is blocked, they may be released indirectly through *displacement* to less threatening objects or by *catharsis*.

Displacement

Consider this example of displacement from Dollard and Miller (1950, pp. 432–433). George, a 14-year-old boy, had an arrangement with another boy for a Saturday outing to the country and planned the holiday carefully. On the morning of the trip the friend's mother called to say her son had a cold and could not go. Deeply disappointed, George pretended to his friend's mother that he accepted the circumstances and "he suppressed his anger since he had learned it was no use fighting the inevitable (p. 433)."

Later George started to play in his backyard where he happened to meet his 12-year-old sister. As usual, she teased him a little, but this time George flared up, struck her, and the two wound up in an intense quarrel that their mother had to terminate. Dollard and Miller interpret this case as an example of how anger and aggression are called forth as prepotent responses to frustration but are quickly suppressed because of prior inhibition learning. But, in their view, the aggressive drive is not eliminated but merely suppressed and rechanneled, and it emerges in displaced form in the boy's attack on his younger sister.

According to Dollard and Miller, displacement of aggression depends on several factors, including similarity between the cause of frustration and the available targets for aggression. Their drive theory of aggression suggests that aggression may be displaced from the real target to safer, less threatening "scapegoats" (such as subordinates at work).

Catharsis

To help release pent-up aggressive impulses in nondestructive ways, some theorists have encouraged therapeutic expression or "catharsis" of angry feelings by direct or vicarious participation in mildly aggressive enactments (e.g., violent plays). In its most extreme form, this position may suggest that frustrated people supposedly must cathart or vent their aggressive impulses gradually, or civilization faces the prospect of extreme violent outbursts of war and killing when the pent-up impulses burst forth uncontrollably. Critics attack this theory as a "drainage" or "pus" view of aggression. They suggest that catharsis, rather than draining off aggressiveness, much as pus is drained out of a festering wound, actually may lead to more aggressive behavior (Bandura, 1973; Berkowitz, 1970).

Does the expression of aggressiveness in a permissive setting indeed have the cathartic effect of reducing the person's subsequent level of aggression? The issue is still not fully settled. Several studies, however, suggest that the performance of aggressive responses in a permissive context maintains the original level of aggression or even enhances further aggression (Feshbach, 1956; Mallick & McCandless, 1966). For example, after play sessions with aggressive toys, children seemed to become more inappropriately aggressive than after play sessions with neutral toys (Feshbach, 1956). Rather than "draining" pent-up aggressive impulses, aggressive play and fantasy thus may actually increase the likelihood of open aggression.

These findings do not mean that aggressive fantasy must always increase violence. Under some conditions of high arousal fantasy might reduce violence, for example, by distracting the person long enough to help her inhibit herself effectively before acting (Berkowitz, 1969).

In a related vein, are there cathartic effects from observation of aggressive models and vicarious participation in aggression (such as watching filmed violence)? Some interpretations of Aristotle's ideas concerning vicarious participation in theatrical dramas predict a cathartic drainage or "emotional purge" after watching aggressiveness. While participation in emotional enactments may have many valuable effects, most research suggests that the probability of behaving aggressively generally increases after exposure to live, filmed, or televised violence (Bandura, 1973).

For example, Hartmann (1969) studied adolescent delinquents. In his experiment some of the delinquents were deliberately aroused to anger and some were not. Thereafter all the adolescents were exposed either to a film depicting aggressive behavior or to a film with nonaggresive content. The young delinquents became more aggressive after the aggressive film than after the nonaggressive film. Moreover, the aroused viewers generally were more aggressive after the aggressive film than were the nonangered ones. This finding contradicted the idea that catharsis might occur for angry subjects even if it did not happen for nonaroused viewers. Hartmann therefore concluded that instead of draining the aggressive impulses of the viewers, exposure to the filmed aggression increased their own likelihood of behaving aggressively, and did so especially if they had been aroused. Thus aggression seems to beget aggression.

Reducing Arousal

Physiological studies help to clarify the conditions that may reduce emotional arousal in response to frustration and aggression. In one set of investigations, the measures of arousal reduction were based on changes in vasoconstriction in the blood volume of the finger (measured by plethysmographic recording; Stone & Hokanson, 1969). The investigators wanted to see if a reduction in emotional arousal in response to frustration and attack really depended on an aggressive counterresponse or whether, instead, the victim could regain tranquility by nonaggressive means. That is, does the angered person have to "act out" angry feelings, or can he or she effectively handle and reduce emotional upset in other ways?

College students were frustrated by having a "fellow subject" (actually a confederate of the experimenter) aggress against them with painful electric shocks (Hokanson et al., 1968). This experiment was designed so that only friendly responses by the subject successfully reduced the attacks. The physiological measures revealed that under these circumstances reductions in emotional arousal gradually occurred only when subjects made *friendly* counterresponses to aggression.

In a similarly designed experiment, self-punitive behavior (self-administered shock) was made the response through which subjects could avoid receiving even more severe shocks from their aggressive frustrator. Under these conditions, reduction in emotional arousal was obtained by self-punitive behavior (Stone & Hokanson, 1969).

These studies most clearly indicate that cathartic-like emotional relief and tension reduction do not require an aggressive counterresponse against the source of frustration. Instead, given the appropriate conditions and history, virtually any response to frustration and pain can lead to reduction of the arousal state. Hokanson and his colleagues thus suggest that *any* response to frustration may have arousal-reducing effects *if* that response has previously been effective in terminating aversive or painful stimulation. Hence we must question the view that frustration produces a distinct form of emotional arousal and angry feelings that can only be reduced by direct or vicarious aggression.

Alternative Responses to Frustration

The previous sections have considered research and theory that conceptualize aggression as the natural, prepotent, drive-like reaction to frustration. These formulations recognize the importance of learning in the expression of aggression, but they view aggression as a basic drive that builds up and hence requires release either directly or indirectly. In contrast, several current learning theorists generally conceptualize aggression as learned response patterns and do not assume either instinctual or drive-like properties for them (Bandura, 1973; Berkowitz, 1970). They view frustration as potentially leading to many alternative responses, depending on the individual and the specific situation.

Social Learning View of Frustration and Aggression

A social learning view of aggression distinguishes between the acquisition of aggressive responses or capabilities and their performance. A repertoire of extensive aggressive skills may be acquired under emotionally neutral, nonfrustrating conditions:

> . . . military recruits acquire and perfect combat skills through many hours of target practice and simulated skirmishes; boxers develop hurtful pummeling abilities by using punching bags and sparring partners whom they do not necessarily intend to hurt; and huntsmen acquire the basic rudiments of hunting by shooting at inanimate targets before they go out in search of game. Indeed if aggressive repertoires were taught only while individuals were hostilely aroused and entertained injurious designs, many of the tutors and learners would probably be maimed during the acquisition phase (Bandura, 1969, p. 378).

During the course of socialization children are exposed to almost endless information relevant to the acquisition of elaborate aggressive skills. Through observation of filmed and televised violence at home, at school, and in the larger community, the child in our culture soon learns a set of potential aggressive behaviors. These potentially aggressive responses may range from angry verbal abuse and expressions of sarcastic annoyance and hostility to skills in the sophisticated use of knives, guns, karate blows and other murderous techniques for assaulting, hurting, and killing people.

FIGURE 15-5
Social Learning View of Frustration and Its Consequences

Frustration ⟶ Emotional arousal and disruption of overlearned response-reinforcement sequence

New Response $= f$ (Available alternatives and their probable reinforcement consequences)

Reaction to frustration is a function of the alternative responses available to the person and their probable reinforcement consequences in the situation. Whether or not the selected new response will be aggressive depends on prior learning history and current expectancies.

Although through observational and cognitive processes the person soon possesses an awesome repertoire for violence, the choice of aggressive or non-aggressive behaviors in any situation depends on numerous determinants. In the social learning view, a person may be more likely to react aggressively after frustration and emotional arousal because strong reactions are likely to work and thus to be reinforced under those circumstances. However, the relationship between frustration and aggression is not inevitable. Instead, aggressive behaviors are considered to be governed by the same principles as other socially learned response patterns: Their occurrence depends on the person's prior experiences in related situations and on current expectancies concerning the probable outcomes of the response alternatives available.

A close analysis of the family interactions in the homes of very aggressive children, for example, reveals that these youngsters grow up in a highly aggressive milieu (Patterson, 1976). Both the parents and the siblings in these families model aggression and stimulate and perpetuate it in each other and in the "problem" child. The aggressive child is thus both the "victim and architect of a coercive system," rather than an automatic responder to frustration. Fortunately, Patterson's systematic efforts to change the coercive system (by modeling and rewarding constructive alternatives to aggression) have proved highly effective in these families.

In sum, experiences that change the probable consequences of aggressive behavior, or that permit a reconceptualization of the meaning of the frustrating situation, affect the nature of the person's response to frustration and the likelihood of aggression. This social learning view is schematized in Figure 15-5.

Rewards for Aggressive Reactions to Frustration

The increased vigor or response amplitude so often seen in reactions to frustration may indicate that such strong reactions probably have helped the organism to cope with delay of gratification in the past. One of the most direct and effective ways of overcoming barriers and achieving blocked goals is to pursue them more forcefully. When a door that one needs to enter is stuck, a swift kick will often dislodge it; when a child's pursuit of a desired gratification is blocked by an interfering younger sibling, a hard punch will often successfully remove the competition.

Aggressive behavior often "gets results" most effectively. Assertive, forceful, dominating behavior is widely attended and often rewarded throughout our society. While passive protests may be politely acknowledged and then ignored, aggressiveness gets action and recognition. Through aggressiveness the ambitious executive pushes his way to the top, the lonely child gets attention, the social protestor achieves her confrontations, and the underprivileged ghetto resident instantaneously dramatizes his condition. Aggression demands attention. It often also removes barriers and achieves substantial redress of grievances. The prevalence throughout history of political dictators who achieved power through aggression attests to the potency of aggression as a route to personal gain. Given all these direct and vicarious rewards for aggression, the pervasiveness of violence as a response to frustration in our society should not be surprising. Too often in our culture, as one psychologist put it most simply, "aggression pays" (Buss, 1971).

Aggression without Frustration: The Case against TV Violence

It is important to note that aggression often may occur even when there has been no noticeable frustration to provoke it. Emotional arousal and anger are not necessary prerequisites for aggression. As Bandura (1973, p. 59) noted: "A culture can produce highly aggressive people, while keeping frustration at a low level, by valuing aggressive accomplishments, furnishing successful aggressive models, and ensuring that aggressive actions secure rewarding effects."

The occurrence and contagion of aggression, regardless of frustration, is evident in studies on the effects of viewing aggression on television (Geen, 1978). Although the television networks have taken pains to deny it, exposure to televised violence can have unmistakably negative effects even on viewers who are not especially aroused or frustrated (Liebert, 1972; Murray, 1973). For example, after watching aggressive film segments (from *The Untouchables*), children demonstrated a greater willingness to hurt others than they did after watching a neutral program that featured a track race (Liebert & Baron, 1972). And after watching violent cartoons for a specified time daily, children became more assaultive toward their peers (compared to other children who had watched nonviolent cartoons for the same amount of time; Steuer, Applefield, & Smith, 1971). Televised aggression also sensitizes the viewers so that they perceive greater violence around them, and become more favorable to aggression as a mode of resolving conflicts (Greenberg & Gordon, 1972).

The foregoing research indicates that observers may imitate aggressive models even if they have not been especially frustrated. But this tendency may be increased if the observer is in a frustrated state (Hanratty, O'Neal, &

Sulzer, 1972). Given the prevalence of frustrations in everyday life, the potential harm produced by filmed aggression becomes highly disturbing. The contagion of aggression is increased further when the models are shown reaping great rewards for their violence.

Dehumanization and Diffusion of Responsibility

Aggression may become especially intense when responsibility is diffused and the victim becomes dehumanized. Male college students in one study were asked to supervise a team of decision makers supposedly working in a nearby room. As supervisors, the subjects were instructed to deliver electric shocks to the decision makers whenever they proposed an inadequate solution to a bargaining problem (Bandura, Underwood, & Fromson, 1975). A light indicated the adequacy of the solution and the subjects were free to administer the shock in any of ten intensity levels from mild to painful. Actually there were no decision makers and no shocks were delivered.

Subjects were divided into two groups: individual responsibility and diffused responsibility. In the individual responsibility condition each subject was assigned to one person on the decision-making team and personally decided the shock level delivered. In the diffused responsibility condition, subjects were told that the levels of shock they selected were automatically averaged and that the average level was the one given to all the members of the decision-making team.

Subjects in each responsibility condition also overheard the decision makers characterized in one of three ways. In the humanized condition the victims were called "perceptive and understanding people"; in the dehumanized condition they were described as an "animalistic, rotten bunch"; and in the neutral condition nonevaluative references were made.

The findings revealed that dehumanization of the victims was the strongest determinant of aggression. Dehumanized victims—those who had been labeled as rotten animals—were punished more than twice as severely as humanized victims and considerably more severely than the neutral, unevaluated group. This pattern was found in both the diffused and individual responsibility conditions. Also as expected, more intense shock was delivered when responsibility was diffuse than when it was individual (see Figure 15-6).

At the end, after the experimental procedures, subjects answered questions about their reactions. When the victims had been dehumanized, subjects often made self-absolving justifications and generally did not condemn the punishment they had administered. They focused on the benefits of punishment, saying, "It gets more efficiency out of the group," and absolved themselves of personal guilt: "As an acting supervisor it was my job to punish poor performance. . . . If doing my job as a supervisor means I must be a son of a bitch, so be it" (p. 261). In contrast, when the victim was humanized and the subject had personal (individual) responsibility, she would tend to say such things as, "Morally and ethically, I couldn't give a painful punishment."

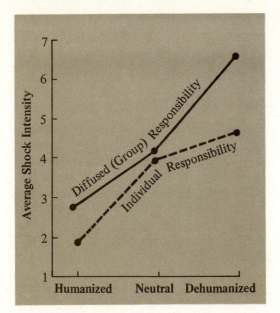

FIGURE 15-6
Average Intensity of Shocks Administered by Subjects as a Function of Diffusion of Their Responsibility and Dehumanization of the Victims.
From Bandura et al. (1975).

Stable Aggression: Enduring Individual Differences

While aggression is highly responsive to the specific situation, it can also become a quality that characterizes the person for long periods of time. For example, some boys become "bullies," others becoming "whipping boys," and these children may show relatively stable, distinct patterns of behavior over long periods of time (Olweus, 1974). Many studies now suggest that while the expression of aggression depends on the specific situation, there also are stable differences among people in their habitual level of aggression even over many years (Olweus, 1979). So the likelihood of an aggressive response depends not only on the nature of the situation but also on the individual's tendency to behave aggressively in certain classes of provoking situations.

Nonaggressive Reactions to Frustration

Although aggressiveness is often the response to frustration, nonaggressive reactions occur if the person has been appropriately rewarded for them in the past.

Constructive Reactions

Davitz (1952), working with 10 small groups of children, rewarded half the groups with praise and approval for making aggressive and competitive responses during a series of brief training sessions. The remaining groups were rewarded for cooperative and constructive behavior during the training periods. Thereafter all the children were frustrated by exposure to a film that was interrupted just as it approached its climax. At this point the children also were forced to return a candy that had been given to them earlier. Their reactions to these frustrations were recorded immediately on motion picture film in a free play situation. Analyses of the filmed behavior showed that children who had been rewarded previously for constructiveness responded more constructively to the frustration. On the other hand, children who had been rewarded for aggression in competitive games during training now reacted more aggressively to the frustrating experience.

As this study illustrates, responses to frustration depend on the person's social learning history. They also depend on modeling cues and other variables that affect expectancies about the probable consequences of behaviors and the meaning of the situation.

The social learning view recognizes that frustration is often followed by persistent emotional arousal. Such arousal, however, is not taken as a sign of pent-up aggressive impulses that press for release. Rather, as Bandura (1969) has suggested, the frustrated person may repeatedly revivify the upsetting event by thinking about it and thus rearouse intense emotions even after the frustrating incident has passed. If that is true, distracting oneself after frustration, or reinterpreting the event cognitively to render it less aversive, should reduce arousal. In contrast, thinking about the anger-inducing qualities of the frustration (e.g., the injustice of it) should enhance one's arousal.

Often a cognitive reinterpretation which is designed to excuse the frustration does seem to make it less anger-arousing. Frustrations and punishments are probably resented much less when they are not imposed arbitrarily but, instead, are explained reasonably (Pastore, 1952). For example, in one study children lost a cash prize because of another child's clumsiness (Mallick & McCandless, 1966). Children who heard the frustrating clumsiness reinterpreted (by explanations that the other child was "sleepy and upset") subsequently showed less aggression against their frustrator than did other children.

If a person's particular social learning history and cognitions critically affect aggressive reactions to frustration, then vast differences may be expected among individuals in how they deal with frustration—and indeed such differences are found.

Type A: Hurrying into a Coronary in Response to Frustration?

Responses to frustration depend on more than the situation: They also are affected by personal dispositions. One of the most relevant dispositions is a pattern called *"Type A"* that also seems to place individuals at higher risk of coronary heart disease. This coronary-prone behavior pattern (Glass, 1977; Friedman & Rosenman, 1974) is characterized by:

1. *Competitive achievement striving.* Type As tend to be involved in multiple activities, have many community and social commitments, and to participate in competitive athletics. They tend to be persistent and act as though they believe that with enough effort they can overcome any frustrations.
2. *Exaggerated sense of time urgency.* Type As tend to be impatient and irritated with delays (for example, on a waiting line, in a traffic snarl).
3. *Aggressiveness and hostility.* Type As may become especially aggressive in situations that threaten their sense of task mastery (for example, when personally criticized or under time pressure).

People who show these behaviors markedly are called Type As. Characterized by the opposite patterns of relaxation, serenity, and lack of time urgency are *Type Bs.* (Table 15-2 shows how the pattern is measured.) Compared to Type Bs, Type As have at least twice the likelihood of coronary heart disease, smoke more, and have higher blood levels of cholesterol. Type A individuals also tend to characterize themselves as more self-confident, impulsive, and higher in achievement and aggression. Most interesting for the present discussion, they also react differently to frustration. Specifically when confronted with a task (concept learning) whose challenge could not be met, Type As became more aggressive but Type Bs did not (Carver & Glass, 1978).

Helplessness and Apathy

Under certain circumstances when facing frustration, people may develop a sense of apathy and helplessness. Withdrawal, listlessness, and seeming emotional indifference are sometimes shown by prisoners and inmates of concen-

TABLE 15-2 MEASURING TYPE A		
	Type A Answer	*Type B Answer*
Has your spouse (close friend) ever told you that you eat too fast?	Yes, often.	Yes, once or twice. No, never.
How would your spouse (close friend) rate you?	Hard-driving, competitive.	Relaxed, easy going.

SOURCE: These selected examples are adapted from Jenkins Activity Survey (Glass, 1977).

tration camps. Presumably overwhelmed by their inability to do anything that will change their desperate lot, these victims seem to have given up.

This pattern of hopelessness has been illustrated clearly in experiments with animals. Consider a dog who first is placed in a situation where he can do nothing to end or escape an electric shock delivered to his feet through an electrified grid on the floor. Later the dog may sit passively and endure the shocks even though he can escape them now by jumping to a nearby compartment. Similar results are found when people are forced to endure uncontrollable negative events. For example, when college students in an experiment learned they could not stop a loud noise, they later listened to the noise passively and failed to escape it—even when the noise could have been terminated merely by moving a lever (Hiroto, 1974). Such states of *learned helplessness* may persist, generalize, and be very hard to overcome (Seligman, 1975, 1978); in turn they can produce apathy and depression.

Frustration Is Not a Unitary Phenomenon

When researchers first began to study frustration they thought it might be a homogeneous variable that leads to uniform effects, such as predominantly aggressive or regressive reactions. In fact, as happens with most other phenomena when they are examined closely, "frustration" turns out to be more complex than it at first seemed to be. Indeed "frustration" is not a unitary phenomenon (Lawson, 1965). As we have seen, frustration may be induced by diverse operations, and it can lead to many different behavioral consequences that depend both on the situation and on the person's dispositions.

SUMMARY

1. Frustrating situations involve an interruption or delay in the attainment of an expected goal. Learning experiences determine the particular behavior sequences that one expects will lead to gratification and also the strength of that expectation. The more successful a person has been in achieving a goal in the past, the more frustrating it is to have it blocked. Also, the closer one is to completion of the goal-directed activity, the more intense is the reaction to being thwarted.

2. Often the first reaction to interruption and delay of gratification is an attempt to persist with the behavior. Typically there is emotional arousal that may result in an increase in the strength of the behavior.

3. The hypothesis that frustration leads to regression to earlier more primitive forms of behavior is consistent with psychoanalytic theory.

While frustration may sometimes lower the quality of the behavior that was interrupted, it also may have other effects. There are vast individual differences in modes of coping with frustration.

4. The frustration-aggression hypothesis suggests that there is an unlearned and invariable association between frustration and aggression. This hypothesis is most compelling if aggression is conceptualized as an instinct or innate drive or impulse that seeks expression in direct release.

5. The direct expression of aggressive impulses in response to frustration is often blocked or punished. Hence the individual learns to fear retaliation and may become inhibited about expressing aggression directly.

6. Watching the suffering of the victim of an aggressive act may be a deterrent to physical aggression under some circumstances. However, under other circumstances (for example, when the aggressor is angry), the pain of the victim may actually enhance aggression.

7. Aggression is construed as a basic impulse or drive provoked by frustration in Dollard and Miller's behavioral version of psychodynamic theory. They posit that if inhibition of aggression occurs because of possible danger or anxiety, conflict results. The person seeks release of aggressive impulses but simultaneously becomes anxious about them. Attempts to inhibit the expression of aggressiveness do not remove the impulse, and the drive may manifest itself indirectly, as in "displacement" to a safer target.

8. Current social learning theories do not assume that aggression is an instinct or a drive, but rather view it as learned response patterns. These positions distinguish the acquisition of aggressive responses from the performance of aggression. Even in emotionally neutral, nonfrustrating conditions aggressive skills may be acquired. That is, through observational and cognitive processes during the course of socialization the child in our culture soon learns a set of potentially aggressive behaviors. He uses these behaviors when the motivational conditions are appropriate.

9. In the social learning view, the relation between frustration and aggression is not inevitable. Thus, while frustration and emotional arousal often are more likely to produce aggressive reactions, aggressive behaviors are believed to be governed by the same principles as other socially learned response patterns.

10. Aggressiveness is an effective attention-getter. A vigorous, aggressive response may remove a barrier, alleviate the frustration by satisfying the thwarted desire, and in other ways prove rewarding for the ag-

gressor. In our culture aggressiveness is often the most profitable response to frustration, and hence it may be a frequent one.

11. Aggression also may happen in the absence of any noticeable frustration if it is modeled, encouraged, and effective. An example of the routine transmission of aggression is televised violence; watching aggression may increase both the occurrence and the acceptance of violence. Dehumanizing the victim, and differing responsibility, also encourage aggression. Stable individual differences in habitual levels of aggression also have been found.

12. Nonaggressive reactions to frustration occur if they have proved effective in the individual's past. They are also more likely if nonaggressive reactions have been modeled by others and if the person believes that nonaggression will be the best course of action in the particular situation. Changes in cognitions and interpretations about the meaning of the frustration (e.g., its intentionality and arbitrariness) also may affect an individual's manner of coping with it.

13. Responses to frustration also depend on personal dispositions. For example, "Type A" individuals may tend to be more impatient with delays, and may be prone to coronary disease.

14. Other people may learn to respond to frustration with apathy and helplessness, believing there is nothing they can do effectively.

CHAPTER 16

ANXIETY AND STRESS

The emotion that has received the most attention in personality theory is anxiety. Indeed anxiety is a main concept in many of the theoretical orientations discussed in previous chapters.

The Meaning of Anxiety

Anxiety is most simply defined as an acquired (learned) fear; for the moment we will employ the terms *anxiety* and *fear* interchangeably, although they are often used in somewhat different ways. Examples of anxiety are all around us: the student who is anxious about taking examinations, the businessperson with anxiety about the financial future, the teen-age boy who is anxious about his appearance and sex appeal, and the child who wakes up anxious from a nightmare.

The Experience of Anxiety: An Example

Before we discuss anxiety abstractly, try to consider the experience of anxiety itself. Here is a description of the subjective feeling of anxiety, as reported by an adult male seeking psychological help:

That evening as we walked under the skyscrapers it seemed to me I could feel the giant buildings start to sway. Although I knew my fear was preposterous the imagined collapse of these huge giants was utterly terrifying. I was convinced that the towers would split and crash down on me and could already picture the people and traffic crushed under them. The strength sapped out of my legs and they became so weak I felt I could not take a step. It became hard to breathe, and so as not to choke I had to gasp for air with my mouth wide open. I felt my vision darkening and a splitting pressure filled my chest. I was afraid the buildings would really crash and at the same time I was afraid my son would notice my panic.

As this man's description indicates, the experience of anxiety involves an intense feeling of fear or dread of impending danger, accompanied by a state of autonomic physiological arousal. When the danger is objective, this kind of emotional reaction seems appropriate. In the example, if the buildings were really in danger of falling, as in an earthquake, the reaction would be understandable as reality-based fear. It is harder to comprehend when it seems objectively unjustified, or when the exact conditions causing the fear are difficult to identify. For example, anxiety may seem "irrational" when it is a response to dangers that are already past, or that are expected in the future but have not yet occurred, or that seem idiosyncratic or unusual. The distinction between an objectively justified fear and an irrational one is a matter of degree only and it depends on many considerations. For example, if the man who feared that the buildings would fall down had lost his wife and home in an earthquake two weeks earlier, his present anxiety would seem less irrational.

Characteristics of Anxiety

Although different individuals manifest intense anxiety reactions in different ways, the following three components often are found (Maher, 1966):

1. A conscious feeling of fear and anticipated danger, without the ability to identify immediate objective threats that could account for these feelings of apprehension.
2. A pattern of physiological arousal and bodily distress that may include miscellaneous physical changes and complaints. Common examples include *cardiovascular* symptoms (heart palpitations, faintness, increased blood pressure, pulse changes); *respiratory* complaints (breathlessness, feeling of suffocation); and *gastrointestinal* symptoms (diarrhea, nausea, vomiting). If the anxiety persists, the prolonged physical reactions to it may have chronic effects on each of these bodily systems. In addition the person's agitation may be reflected in sleeplessness, frequent urination, perspiration, muscular tensions, fatigue, and other signs of upset and distress.

3. A disruption or disorganization of effective problem-solving and cognitive control, including difficulty in thinking clearly and coping effectively with environmental demands.

From Trauma to Anxiety

Probably the clearest examples of anxiety reactions are found after the individual has experienced a life-threatening danger or trauma. A near-fatal automobile accident, an almost catastrophic combat experience, an airplane crash—these and similarly intense episodes of stress are often followed by a prolonged aftermath of anxiety. The emotional upset produced by actual dangers may be activated, after they have passed, by stimuli that remind the individual of those dangers, or by signs that lead him or her to expect new dangers. That is, stressful episodes generate anxiety that may persist or recur after the trauma is over.

After severe trauma, the victim is more likely to respond anxiously to other stress stimuli that occur later in life (Archibald & Tuddenham, 1965). Surviving victims of Nazi concentration camps, for example, sometimes continued for years to be hypersensitive to threat stimuli and to react to stress readily with anxiety and sleep disturbances (Chodoff, 1963). These observations support the idea that anxiety involves a learned fear reaction that is highly resistant to extinction and that may be evoked by diverse stimuli similar to those that originally were traumatic. That is, the fear evoked by the traumatic stimuli may be reactivated and also may *generalize* to stimuli associated with the traumatic episode. For example, after a child has been attacked and bitten by a dog, her fear reaction may generalize to other dogs, animals, fur, places similar to the one in which the attack occurred, and so on (Figure 16-1). Moreover, if the generalization stimuli are very remote from the original traumatic stimulus, the person may be unable to see the connection between the two and the anxiety may appear (even to her) particularly irrational. Suppose, for example, that the child becomes afraid of the room in which the dog bit her and of similar rooms. If the connection between her new fear of rooms and the dog's attack is not recognized, the fear of rooms now may seem especially bizarre.

From a learning point of view, anxieties after traumas, like other learned fears, may be interpreted in accord with conditioning principles. If neutral stimuli have been associated directly or vicariously with aversive events or outcomes (such as traumatic pain or danger), then they also may come to elicit anxiety in their own right. Such aversively conditioned emotional reactions may also generalize extensively to new stimuli (Figure 16-1). These generalizations may be based on dimensions of semantic as well as physical stimulus similarity, as was noted earlier. Clinical examples of aversive arousal and avoidance include many phobic and anxious reactions to objects, people, and social and interpersonal situations. Not only external events, but also their symbolic representations in the form of words or of thoughts and fantasies, may engender painful emotions. In our example of the child traumatized by

FIGURE 16-1
From Trauma to Anxiety

PHASE 1:   Traumatic episode

S₁ (e.g., attack by a dog) ⟶ traumatic reaction (pain, fear, etc.)

S₂ ⎫ stimuli
S₃ ⎬ closely associated
S₄ ⎭ with attack

PHASE 2:   Anxiety generated by stimuli associated with trauma (or similar to it)

S₂ ⎫
S₃ ⎬ ⟶ Anxiety
S₄ ⎭

the dog, even thinking about the incident, or the room in which it occurred, or similar rooms may terrify the youngster.

Stimuli closer or more relevant to those associated with emotional arousal tend to elicit stronger affective reactions. In one study, novice sports parachutists and control subjects were administered a specially constructed word association test (Epstein & Fenz, 1962; Fenz, 1964). The words contained four levels of relevance to parachuting. Throughout the word association tests, subjects' physiological reactions (GSR) were recorded to measure their emotional arousal in response to the various stimulus words. This procedure was followed on three days: One testing occurred two weeks before the scheduled jump, another testing was done the day before the jump, and a final test was administered on the day of the paracute jump.

The results showed more arousal in parachutists for parachute-relevant words. The effect was greatest for the words most relevant to parachuting, and the gradient of arousal was highest and steepest when the testing time was closer to the emotion-arousing parachute jump itself.

While traumas often may lead to anxiety, many other effects are also possible if the prevailing social conditions encourage them. One study examined differences between children in Israeli settlements subjected to frequent artillery shellings during Arab-Israeli conflicts and those from comparable settlements that were not shelled (Ziv, Kruglanski, & Shulman, 1974). The children in the shelled settlements appeared to cope actively with the stress and did so in ways that were supported by the social norms in their community. Specifically, they developed greater patriotism for the settlement in which they resided, showed more externally oriented aggressiveness, and became more appreciative of courage as a personality trait.

Theoretical Views of Anxiety

As was discussed in Part I of this book, each of the major theoretical orientations has conceptualized anxiety somewhat differently, in accord with its own views of what constitutes grave danger or threat for people. Thus Freudian formulations emphasize the breakthrough into consciousness of unacceptable impulses, learning theories focus on association with painful or aversive stimulation, and phenomenological-existential theories stress the perception of a basic threat to the self or to the individual's very existence as a personality (e.g., May, 1950). Still other formulations of anxiety construe it mainly as a state of distress and helplessness in which the organism has no alternatives (Mandler & Watson, 1966) or as a "disease of overarousal" (Malmo, 1957). Taken together these definitions provide a glimpse of the great variety of events that may constitute subjective danger for any particular individual and that may create anxiety.

There is no reason to restrict the meaning of anxiety to any single conception. Indeed it seems plausible that each individual has a somewhat different, personal set of threats that engender greatest anxiety for him or her. Because each person can conceptualize arousal states in somewhat different ways, the experiences that can be subsumed under the label "anxiety" may be almost endless, and they range from birth traumas to death fears. Therefore rather than seek a universally acceptable definition of anxiety, it may be more fruitful to examine how anxiety can be measured and to consider its antecedents, consequences, and correlates.

Trait Anxiety

A distinction has been made between *state* and *trait* anxiety (Spielberger, 1966). State anxiety is conceptualized as a person's momentary or situational anxiety and it varies in intensity over time and across settings. Trait anxiety, in contrast, refers to one's more stable, characteristic overall level of anxiety. Usually trait anxiety is measured by the person's self-report on questionnaires, as discussed next.

Self-Reported Anxiety

Anxiety inventories ask people to report the extent to which various anxiety responses generally characterize them. The MMPI is the forerunner and model for most anxiety questionnaires. For example, the most popular anxiety test, the Manifest Anxiety Scale or MAS (Taylor, 1953) borrowed from the pool of MMPI items. Construction of the scale started with selection of 200 items from the MMPI. These items were given to five clinical psychologists with instructions to identify those that seemed to tap manifest anxiety. To

TABLE 16-1
ITEMS SIMILAR TO THOSE ON THE MANIFEST ANXIETY SCALE

Item	High Anxiety Response
I rarely get really tired.	False
I am not a worrier.	False
I cannot keep my mind focused on anything.	True
I almost never blush.	False
Often I cannot keep from crying.	True
It's hard for me to attend to a job.	True
Often I think I am no good.	True

The subject must respond "true" or "false."

facilitate judgment, the clinicians were given a lengthy description of chronic anxiety reaction. Gradually the best items were selected and the meaning of the resulting scale was elaborated through extensive construct validity research. The items on anxiety scales like the MAS deal with various forms of anxiety such as feeling uneasy, worrying, perspiring, and experiencing unhappiness and discomfort (see Table 16-1).

Relations among Anxiety Measures

Are people who feel anxious in some situations likely to feel anxious in many other situations? For instance, are people who are anxious about taking tests also likely to worry more about their health or their family? The basic question is: Does "anxiety" constitute a broadly generalized trait? To study this question, investigators assess the correlations among people's anxiety responses on diverse measures (Sarason, 1978).

Substantial correlations are often found among different self-report anxiety questionnaires that deal with topics like "test anxiety" (anxiety about taking tests) or more "general anxiety" reactions (e.g., Sarason et al., 1960; Ruebush, 1963). For example, the correlation between scores on the Test Anxiety Scale for Children and the General Anxiety Scale for Children tends to be highly significant. The associations become low or negligible, however, when anxiety is measured by diverse methods, involving response modes and formats other than questionnaires—for example, measures of physiological (autonomic) arousal and actual avoidance behavior. The relations between self-reports of anxiety and physiological arousal are especially unreliable. Generally, physiological measures of anxiety tend to be unrelated to anxiety measured by self-report inventories (e.g., Katkin, 1965; Martin 1961).

Sometimes, however, significant correlations are found across response systems. For example, Geer (1965) administered a fear survey schedule to undergraduates in order to select a "high-fear" and a "low-fear" group for spider phobia. Equal numbers of high- and low-fear subjects were then assigned to an experimental and a control condition. In the experimental condition subjects were shown pictures of a spider; in the control condition they saw pictures of a snake. For all subjects, measures of autonomic arousal were taken physiologically (in the form of GSR responses through finger electrodes). When they were presented with pictures of spiders, people who had reported high spider fear on the inventory showed significantly greater arousal than did the other subjects. Moreover, this increased arousal was found only in response to directly relevant fear stimuli: When students with high fear of spiders were shown pictures of snakes, their arousal did not increase.

The relationships typically obtained between self-report measures of subjective arousal and physiological measures may be summarized this way:

> It is possible to obtain fairly reliable estimates as to what extent people notice or discriminate their internal visceral events. Such ratings show remarkable individual differences, varying from people who rarely if ever notice their guts acting up to others who report that their insides appear to be in a constant state of turmoil. When these reports about habitual perceptions of visceral events are compared with actual levels of physiological reaction in a stress situation, we find that at the extreme ends (that is, people who report very little or very much of such goings-on) there are rather striking differences in overall physiological activity. However, when the full range of individual differences is taken into account the relation between report and measured activity is positive but of rather small magnitude (Mandler, 1962, p. 317).

Interaction of Trait Anxiety and the Situation

Just as with most other personality traits, research has revealed that anxiety is not situation-free. Instead, anxiety reactions depend on the exact stimulus conditions and response mode as well as on the individual (Endler & Hunt, 1966, 1969). To make this point, Endler and Hunt devised a series of self-report anxiety inventories. On these questionnaires they varied both the type of threat situation and the mode of response to it.

The questionnaire sampled many situations, ranging from such innocuous events as "You are starting on a long automobile trip" and "You are undressing for bed" to more typically threatening situations, such as "You are on a ledge high upon a mountainside" (Endler & Hunt, 1969, p. 4). The response modes were systematically varied to include a wide range of possible reactions. They sampled the subjects' perceptions of their physiological reaction ("hands trembling," "fluttering feeling in stomach") as well as their self-reported feelings of anxiety (e.g., "can't concentrate").

The questionnaires were given to many different groups of students in many schools in order to sample a wide range of individual differences. The answers were submitted to sophisticated statistical analyses that provided separate estimates of the relative effects of hypothetical stimulus situations, response modes, and persons as determinants of test responses. The analyses consistently revealed that the most potent effects by far were the interactions of person, situation, and response mode. Taken alone, neither individual differences (persons) nor situations accounted for more than a trivial fraction of the test results. These findings suggest that anxiety is not a stimulus-free characteristic of the person, nor is it intrinsic to stimuli alone. Anxiety reactions depend jointly on stimulus, person, and response mode: That is, they depend on the individual, on the particular stimulus confronting him or her (e.g., "undressing for bed"), and on the specific mode of response measured (e.g., "hands trembling," "heart racing").

Anxiety and Performance

Many studies have examined how trait anxiety interacts with other variables to affect performance. Some researchers have conceptualized trait anxiety in motivational terms as an arousal state similar to a physiological drive and have studied its relation to performance. For example, people who differ in self-reported trait anxiety have been tested under various anxiety-arousing instructions to see who does best on different learning tasks. These tasks range from simple conditioning situations to measures of complex performance.

More than 70 years ago Yerkes and Dodson (1908) suggested that the relationship between arousal and performance could be depicted as an inverted U (Figure 16-2). Figure 16-2 shows that when arousal is low or absent, the individual is unmotivated and his performance is likely to be poor. When arousal is

FIGURE 16-2
The Hypothesized U Relation Between Arousal and Performance

extremely high, stimulation becomes excessive and performance deteriorates because the individual becomes overwhelmed and disorganized. Thus performance was believed to be of highest quality when anxiety or arousal was at a moderate level. Under these conditions the person is attentive and alert, but not swamped.

More recent research indicates that while the relationship between arousal level (or anxiety) and performance quality sometimes is curvilinear, the exact effects depend on many interacting variables, both in the person and in the specific situation. For instance, they depend on the person's self-reported "test anxiety" as well as on the difficulty of the task.

Interfering Self-Preoccupying Thoughts

Anxiety interferes most with effective performance when it arouses anxious, self-preoccupying thoughts (e.g., "I'm no good at this—I'll never be able to do it") in the stressed person. These thoughts compete and interfere with task-relevant thoughts (e.g., "Now I have to recheck my answers"). The result is that performance (as well as the subject) suffers (Sarason, 1979). The interference from self-preoccupying thoughts tends to be greatest when the task-to-

The possible impact of anxiety on performance depends both on the person and the situation.

be-done is complex and requires many competing responses. One just cannot be full of negative thoughts about oneself and simultaneously concentrate effectively on difficult work. Likewise, as the motivation to do well increases (as when success on the task is especially important), the highly anxious person may become particularly handicapped. That happens because under such highly motivating conditions test-anxious people tend to catastrophize and become even more negatively self-preoccupied, dwelling on how poorly they are doing. In contrast, the less anxious pay attention to the task and concentrate on how to master it effectively.

Anxiety and Achievement-Oriented Instructions

In our achievement-oriented society, great pressure is exerted on people to strive to compete and excel. Competition is actively encouraged, and children soon learn to make continuous comparisons between their accomplishments and those of others. This achievement-oriented and evaluative set is seen in grading throughout the school system and in the obvious competitiveness of sports and many activities of the business and professional worlds.

Does a competitive achievement orientation really improve the quality of human performance? Does a deliberate stress on "doing well" spur people to do better, to solve problems efficiently and to learn more effectively? Or, perhaps, might such an orientation have a boomerang effect on anxious individuals that interferes with effective problem-solving and creativity?

To study this problem researchers have examined the excellence of performance when students work under different orienting sets. Some subjects get threatening or achievement-oriented instructions that present the learning task as a "test" on which they will be evaluated; other students have to do the same tasks under neutral or relaxed instructions. Who does better?

FIGURE 16-3
The Interacting Effects of Trait (Test) Anxiety and Threat Instructions on Solution of a Difficult Task

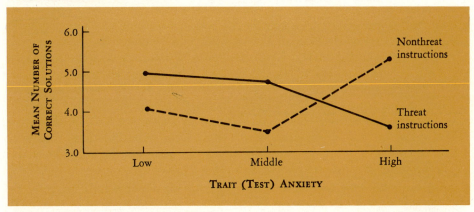

Drawn from data in Sarason (1961).

The effects of achievement orientation on performance may depend on the person's overall level of self-reported test anxiety. That is, individuals who differ greatly in test anxiety also may react quite differently to achievement-oriented instructions and to other anxiety-arousing cues. Specifically, when tasks are made more "test-like" and evaluative, people who are low in self-reported test anxiety often become more motivated and perform somewhat better than they do under neutral conditions. On the other hand, highly anxious persons tend to do less well when the motivating instructions emphasize the test-like, threatening features of the task (Sarason, 1966). An example of this interaction between threatening instructions and the subject's level of test anxiety is depicted in Figure 16-3. By now you will not be surprised by the reasons for this effect. High motivation and threat increase self-preoccupation and defeatism in test anxious people and hurt their performance. The same conditions may help less anxious people by motivating them to work harder (Sarason, 1978).

Reactions to Stress

Another approach to anxiety has examined it as part of the reaction to stress. "Stress" has been the label used to classify a host of potentially unpleasant or dangerous events that include unavoidable pain, excessive noise and fatigue under strenuous work conditions, and traumatic dangers, as well as more routine life changes. The main question here has been: What are the conditions that affect how stress impacts on people?

Impact of Degree of Stress

Obviously individuals differ in the events that they perceive as most stressful and anxiety-provoking. In general, however, the more objectively intense the stress, the greater and more upsetting the person's reaction to it. For example, during the bombing air raids of World War II in England the occurrence of traumatic aftermaths (in the form of intense or neurotic anxiety reactions) depended on the degree to which the individual had been victimized by the air raids. Among uninjured survivors of bombing attacks, for example, anxiety occurred much more often if the victim had suffered severe personal loss. Victims who had a relative killed in the air raid or whose homes were destroyed developed acute anxiety reactions much more often than did those who were less personally victimized or who were physically more remote from the center of the attack (Fraser, Leslie, & Phelps, 1943).

Similar conclusions emerge from studies of other traumatic episodes under combat conditions: The intensity of subsequent anxiety is directly related to the proximity of danger and to the objective probability of being killed or injured. Thus insomnia, gastrointestinal disturbance, feelings of nervousness, tremors, and similar signs of anxiety occur more often among front-line soldiers in active combat than among those in safer areas more distant from the main fighting zone (Star, 1949). Similarly, the incidence of anxiety in members of air crews depended partly on the number of combat missions they had participated in (Janis, 1949). Moreover, among combat pilots, "clinical neuroses" increase as their assignments become more dangerous (Tompkins, 1959).

In sum, while anxiety is a subjective experience it also is directly related to the severity and duration of external stress and danger.

Stress and Illness

Of course stress is not confined to the traumas of combat and war. Modern societies are stressful enough even in times of peace. In contemporary research, a stressful life event is defined as one that causes changes in, and requires or demands readjustment of, the average individual's normal life routine. Thus any life changes, including such potentially positive ones as marriage or such negative ones as the death of a child, may be considered stressful, but of course the events vary in degree of severity. Thousands of people have been asked to rate the severity of many life changes (from vacations through divorce and the terminal illness of a loved one), yielding scales of Social Readjustment (e.g., Holmes & Masuda, 1974; Holmes & Rahe, 1967).

Generally, a significant but modest association has been found between degree of stress and physical illness, with more stressful life events exerting a somewhat greater physical and emotional toll on most—but not all—people (e.g., Rabkin & Struening, 1976). Some people may be more psychologically hardy than others, resisting illness even when faced with highly stressful life events. For example, business executives who express attitudes of vigorousness about life, of being more oriented to challenge, also may experience less illness than do those who express opposite attitudes while encountering similarly high levels of stress (Kobasa, 1979). The people who face stress but remain healthy thus seem to perceive change not as a threat but as a challenge and an opportunity.

Cognitive Appraisal of Stress

A series of studies (e.g., Lazarus & Alfert, 1964) attempted to demonstrate that one's "cognitive appraisal" of a potential stressful event affects his or her emotional reactions to it. Subjects viewed a film that depicted some gruesome shop accidents. Not surprisingly, they reacted with arousal not just to the actual scenes but also to instructions that led them to anticipate the gory scenes before they saw them. Reactions thus depend on what people *believe* is happening or about to happen, regardless of the objective foundation of the belief. For example, if a man is told his children are in danger he will react with great arousal, even if he is being told a lie. One's specific cognitive appraisal of the total emotion-producing situation influences how one copes with it (Laza-rus & Averill, 1972). A variety of strategies can be used to help one cope with stress effectively, as will be discussed in the context of self-control (Chap-ter 18).

Effects of Warnings

Does it help to be forewarned of future stress and danger? Sometimes a person may be less likely to develop acute distress if she is given adequate warning and information about impending pain and stress than if she is uninformed and hence surprised by the traumatic event (Janis, 1958, 1971). That is, fore-warnings may help the person to brace herself psychologically for the trauma and to rehearse for it so that she can cope with it better when it occurs. This process, sometimes called "emotional inoculation," may involve either defen-sive self-desensitization or other forms of rehearsal that help to undermine the emotional upset of the trauma when it finally does occur. However, while some people may benefit from forewarnings, others may become debilitated by anticipatory anxiety. Moreover, many people may find it difficult to imagine traumatic experiences before they occur, especially if they have not had rele-vant past experiences with similar dangers.

In the military, for example, in spite of ample information and objective forewarnings, novices of combat missions reported that they felt only a sort of detached interest in flak bursts when they first encountered them. They did not feel the awesomeness of the situation personally until they actually saw a nearby plane hit or observed a friend injured or killed by shrapnel (Grinker & Spiegel, 1945). The same feeling of emotional detachment and subjective dis-belief was reported by many Jews in Nazi Germany before they personally saw or experienced persecution.

In many life situations forewarnings have great value because they permit the person to avoid the danger or somehow to guard or prepare against it. But what of situations in which the impending danger is inescapable or unavoida-ble and the person can do nothing to prevent the aversive situation?

To study an analogy to this type of stressful anticipatory situation some researchers have led adult volunteer subjects to believe that they might have to experience an unavoidable pain (usually in the form of an electric shock). While waiting, the subject is attached to equipment that monitors changes in emotional arousal (as evidenced by sweating or heart rate changes, for exam-ple). This arrangement permits study of how various conditions affect emo-tional activity during the waiting period as the person anticipates the una-voidable shock.

Effects of Predictability and Control

How does the ability to predict the nature and advent of an anticipated una-voidable stress affect reactions to it? Is anxiety greater when the person knows the details of the expected painful event, or when he or she is uncertain about what to expect and does not know what to predict?

In one study, college students were led to believe that an electric shock would be forthcoming. The experiment manipulated the information given to the students about the shock (Elliott, 1966). In one group the students were first given a "mild" shock as a sample of the forthcoming shock; subjects in a second group were given a sample shock of considerable strength and were led to believe that the forthcoming shock would be of similar intensity; in a third group the subjects waited for an unknown shock—they received no sample of the shock but were told that one would be forthcoming. Thereafter the students waited for the shock, and their reactions to it were measured. Self-reports indicated that anxiety was greatest for those in the group waiting for the unknown shock; these subjects, who had not sampled the shock, dreaded it most. This group also experienced the greatest rise in heart rate (relative to rest) while waiting, averaging an acceleration of about 20 beats per minute as compared with approximately 4 beats per minute in the other groups.

Even when persons cannot influence an aversive future outcome (for example, by escaping from it), they often prefer knowledge of it (Lanzetta & Driscoll, 1966) and will work to get such knowledge (Jones, Bentler, & Petry, 1966). People also tend to be less tense and aroused while waiting for a painful event when they know what to expect (Deane, 1961; Elliott, 1966). For example, subjects who had to submerge one of their hands in an ice bath reported less distress if they first received specific information about how the hand would feel (Leventhal and associates, 1979).

In another study, college females were exposed to stress in the form of aversive noise (Glass, Singer, & Friedman, 1969). The noise occurred either at predictable or at unpredictable times. The investigators assessed the effects of these stresses on subsequent tolerance for frustration (persistence at a difficult task) and performance efficiency.

When the noise was predictable it did not adversely affect later tolerance of frustration or performance, but when it was unpredictable it did produce adverse consequences. These adverse effects could be reduced substantially if, during the stress period, subjects believed that they could control the termination of the noise. Thus, it is most difficult to cope with unpredictable and seemingly uncontrollable aversive stimuli; people tend to be less upset and debilitated when they must cope with aversive events of the same magnitude if they think they can predict and control them (Staub, Tursky, & Schwartz, 1971). In general, people tend to prefer predictable aversive events, except when they can distract themselves from them (Miller & Grant, 1979).

It thus seems that the nature of anxiety reactions may partly depend on the alternatives available to the individual for coping effectively with the stress. Most people seem to react differently to stressful events that they think they can control and those that they believe are out of their control, although the specific relationships often are very complex and depend on the situation as well as on the person (Averill, 1973).

Anxiety, Avoidance, and Helplessness

Guided by Freud's theory, many personality psychologists have been most concerned with the effects of anxiety on avoidance behavior. The relationship between anxiety and avoidance is crucial for psychodynamic theory; it forms the basis for the Freudian conception of defense mechanisms.

Avoidance Behavior

Because anxiety is aversive we quickly try to reduce or avoid it. When the dangerous event is external—like an attacker—anxiety may be reduced by physical escape from the threatening situation or by other forms of problem-solving (such as calling for help). The reduction of the anxiety state in turn reinforces the behaviors that led to the relief. Consequently the person's successful escape or avoidance behaviors become strengthened.

The strengthening of successful escape behaviors may be adaptive to the extent that the organism can then more readily avoid similar future dangers. On the other hand, because the escape pattern was reinforced, the person may continue to avoid similar situations in the future when in fact they are no longer dangerous. That is, previously reinforced quick escape and avoidance maneuvers may prevent the person from learning that the danger feared is no longer there or that its aversive effects can be mastered. In that case the fearful person continues to defensively avoid similar or related situations instead of unlearning his or her fear of them. Hence avoidance reactions may be highly persistent (Seligman, 1975).

Reinforced escape and avoidance patterns, if widely generalized, may have debilitating consequences. As an example, consider the case of a little girl who has been sexually molested by an intruder at home. As a result of this traumatic experience the child may acquire a phobic reaction, not just to the painful encounter and the man who terrified her, but also to other men and to many aspects of sexual experience and intimacy. Her subsequent refusal of dates and her generalized avoidance of closeness with men would make it increasingly difficult for her to overcome her anxieties and to develop satisfying heterosexual relationships.

Conflict and Anxiety

Avoidance reactions may become most problematic when the threat stimuli are persistent and cannot be escaped by moving away from them physically. Often individuals cannot escape from the sources of possible anxiety around them by simply avoiding them. This is true when they are dependent upon and love the very people who threaten them.

In the course of socialization the same significant persons who nurture and care for the child and to whom the child becomes most deeply attached, are also the ones who discipline and punish him or her. For example, the same mother who reinforces the child with her attention and social approval may cause pain and anxiety. Thus the same social stimulus—the mother, in this example—that has been associated with positive rewards and gratification is also connected with pain because of the punishments she dispenses and the rewards that she withholds from the child. The phenomena of "ambivalence" and "conflict" may result whenever the same persons or objects who evoke positive feelings and approach tendencies are also the sources for negative emotions and avoidance reactions. This duality is common in life and it does not end with childhood. In an adult's life, for example, the same spouse who gives love may also be the source of many bitter frustrations. Hence, mixed feelings develop.

Just how the individual will feel and react in relation to these ambivalence-producing stimuli depends on many considerations. For example a child may be harshly punished by his father when he is physically aggressive to his baby sister, but may be warmly praised by his father when he is physically self-assertive with peers. If that happens consistently he soon may learn to expect positive gratification from his father in one context but punishment and aversive consequences in the other context. Thus in one situation he will expect praise and love from the same father who is the source of his anxiety in the second situation. These situations will be discriminated clearly, and anxiety associated with uncertainty and conflict therefore will probably be minimal.

Anxiety may be much higher, however, when the child is uncertain about the behaviors that will lead to punishment and those that will not, and when she does not feel that she can control the important aversive outcomes in her life. It may be especially difficult for a child to cope adequately if punishment from the parent (and other important people) is unpredictable and inconsistent so that she is unsure of what to expect. In that case the child may experience a more generalized dread, because threat and punishment are possible at almost any time and place.

Learned Helplessness

The natural response of organisms faced with threat of pain or punishment is to try to avoid or escape the aversive stimulation. What happens if animals—or people—are forced to experience uncontrollable events, as when electric shocks simply cannot be avoided, regardless of what one does? As noted earlier (Chapter 15), when we learn that negative or traumatic outcomes are uncontrollable a state of *learned helplessness* may develop. In that case, we may stop responding altogether and become apathetic, despondent, depressed.

Seligman (1975) and his associates first observed that after dogs had been given uncontrollable electric shocks they seemed to transfer their expectation

Learned helplessness may lead to depression and hopelessness

of helplessness to a new situation in which the shock was in fact avoidable. The behavior of these dogs who had "learned helplessness" sharply contrasted with dogs who had not been given the experience of uncontrollability (although they had received similar shocks). The helpless dogs easily became passive; they "wilted," became submissive, and gave up with relatively little effort in the new situation when shock again occurred but was controllable. The nonhelpless dogs, however, ran frantically around until they found the response that allowed them to escape the shock.

Learned helplessness has been observed not only in lower animals but also in people (Abramson, Seligman, & Teasdale, 1978; Hiroto, 1974; Seligman, 1975). The overall results suggest that after organisms experience uncontrollable negative events they may stop future efforts and exhibit helplessness even in new situations that objectively can be controlled. If uncontrollability is experienced repeatedly, people may develop depression and hopelessness, the very opposite of the sense of mastery and efficacy that we experience when we are confident that we can cope with the problems of our lives. As a result of learned helplessness, the person may stop responding and become apathetic.

While learned helplessness has been demonstrated convincingly in the laboratory, its tragic consequences are seen most compellingly in real life. Consider, for example, the children of America's migrant families whose fate was recorded by Coles (1970). Unlike typical middle-class children, these youngsters rapidly learn that their shouts and screams will not bring them relief:

Their pains and frustrations persist. A migrant mother described her own
helpless feelings this way:

Learned Helplessness

> My children, they suffer. I know. They hurts, and I can't stop it. I just
> have to pray that they'll stay alive, somehow. They gets the colic, and I
> don't know what to do. One of them, he can't breathe right and his
> chest, it's in trouble. I can hear the noise inside when he takes his
> breaths. The worst thing, if you ask me, is the bites they get. It makes
> them unhappy, real unhappy. They itches and scratches and bleeds, and
> oh, it's the worst. They must want to tear all their skin off, but you can't
> do that. There's still be mosquitoes and ants and rats and like that
> around, and they'd be after your insides then, if the skin was all gone.
> That's what would happen then. But I say to myself it's life, the way
> living is, and there's not much to do but accept what happens. Do you
> have a choice but to accept? That's what I'd like to ask you, yes sir.
> Once, when I was little, I seem to recall asking my uncle if there wasn't
> something you could do, but he said no, there wasn't, and to hush up. So
> I did. Now I have to tell my kids the same, that you don't go around
> complaining—you just don't (Coles, 1970, pp. 9–10).

The Importance of Perceived Control

Generally, it is good to believe that you *can* do something to control events.
Much human research now suggests that when individuals believe they cannot control events and outcomes they gradually develop a sense of helplessness and apathy (e.g., Wortman & Brehm, 1975). Conversely, when they are
led to think that they can influence and control events, that they can make
an impact on their environment, they become more alert, happier—they may
even live longer. In one dramatic illustration, a group of institutionalized el-
derly adults was given opportunities to make decisions actively and to be personally responsible for something outside of themselves (a plant). These people soon began to act more competently and to feel better, in comparison to
groups who were left in the usual passive institutional routine and for whom
all the decisions were made by the staff. Eighteen months later a follow-up
revealed that only half as many people had died in the active responsibility
group as in the comparison group (Rodin & Langer, 1977). Results like these
allow the general conclusion that:

> . . . Both people and animals are happier, healthier, more active, solve
> problems better, and feel less stress when they are given choice and con-
> trol. . . . [conversely] the lack of choice and control are detrimental and
> are generally bad. Depression, dysphoria, stress, passivity, illness, retar-
> dation of performance, and even death are among the deficits produced
> (Seligman & Miller, 1979, 367–368).

Coping with Tragedy: Making the Unchangeable Meaningful

So much of Western thought is oriented to active problem-solving and to achieving control and mastery over life that we rarely stop to consider the coping responses of the victims of life's many tragedies. Yet one of the most interesting aspects of the coping process is just how people manage to deal with such tragedies. For example, consider individuals who suffer serious accidents and become paralyzed. What types of interpretation can help them cope best with their lot? Researchers interviewed a group of such paralyzed accident victims, asking about their perceptions of the causes of their accidents (Bulman & Wortman, 1977). These accidents ranged from auto and diving accidents to gunshot wounds. A social worker and a nurse familiar with each case rated how well each person was coping.

Every accident victim raised the question "Why me?" In trying to cope with their misfortune they seemed desperately to seek meaning as they tried to "explain" the accident. Those who coped best felt that they could not have avoided the accident. They blamed no one else for it, saying such things as:

> "I really couldn't have avoided it; if I didn't dive, maybe—but I like to dive."
>
> "It just happened; we were engaged in a contact sport. We both were doing something we wanted to do. Really, I don't think I could have avoided it" (Bulman & Wortman, 1977, p. 361).

In sum, the best copers saw the accident as logical and inevitable, and somehow tried to give it meaning and even a purpose:

> . . . many of the reasons mentioned by the respondents in the informal questioning suggest a concern for order and meaning. This seems to be the case for those who attributed their accident to a reason of God (e.g., "He is trying to help me learn about Him"), to predetermination (e.g., "These things are always planned before your time by a Supreme Power"), or to probability (e.g., "Things had been going well, so the odds were that something bad would happen") (Bulman & Wortman, 1977, p. 362).

Finally, before leaving the topic of anxiety it should be noted that people may become anxious and upset not only about their lot in life and their actions but also about their thoughts. We can generate anxiety in ourselves with our ideas and memories. Thoughts about masturbation or infidelity, for example, as well as the sexual acts themselves, may evoke anxiety in a person for whom these events have become threatening. Similarly, a child may feel anxious if she thinks hostile thoughts about her mother, for example, or if she starts to experience prohibited sexual fantasies. When thoughts and feelings are dangerous, the individual may try to avoid them cognitively through various psychological maneuvers, as the next chapter discusses.

SUMMARY

1. Anxiety may be defined as an acquired (learned) fear. The experience of anxiety involves an intense feeling of fear or dread of impending danger accompanied by a state of autonomic physiological arousal. Often anxiety leads to difficulty in thinking clearly and coping effectively with environmental demands.

2. Each major personality theory has conceptualized anxiety in somewhat different ways. Thus Freudian formulations, for example, emphasize the breakthrough into consciousness of unacceptable impulses; learning theories focus on association with painful or aversive stimulation; and phenomenological-existential theories stress the perception of a basic threat to the self.

3. Life-threatening dangers or "traumas" result in the clearest examples of intense anxiety reactions. Moreover, a person's traumatic fear may generalize so that events and cognitions closely associated with the original traumatic experiences may later evoke anxiety reactions even after the objective danger is gone. If the anxiety spreads to stimuli remote from the traumatic stimulus, the connection may not be apparent and the anxiety may seem particularly irrational. Under some conditions, however, traumas may lead to active coping rather than to generalized anxiety.

4. Individual differences in trait anxiety usually are measured by a psychometric self-report inventory on which subjects indicate the extent to which various fears characterize them. Anxiety is not a situation-free personality trait. Anxiety reactions depend on the exact stimulus conditions and response mode measured, as well as on the individual. It is the interaction of all three of these sources that determines the anxiety reaction.

5. Anxiety affects the quality of performance. The exact effect of arousal level on performance depends on many variables, both in the person and in the specific situation. For example, anxiety hurts performance especially when it arouses negative, self-preoccupying thoughts.

6. Usually the intensity of anxiety reactions is directly related to the objective intensity and duration of the experienced stress. The particular events or stimuli that are stressful depend on the person's interpretation of them.

7. Uncertainty about the possibility of occurrence and the details of an expected painful event may cause greatest tension and arousal. Most normal adults also prefer an unavoidable painful event to occur

immediately rather than after a delay. People generally prefer to be able to predict and control inevitable stressful events. Adequate warning and information about impending stress may make the development of acute anxiety less likely. On the other hand, some people may become debilitated by anticipatory anxiety when they are forewarned. The value of warnings may depend on the individual's prior experience with similar danger.

8. Avoidance or escape behaviors performed in a state of anxiety become strengthened when they are successful in reducing the anxiety state. Ambivalence and conflict may result when the same persons (or events) are associated with both positive and aversive experience, as happens commonly in life. The very people the child loves and depends upon also may threaten and punish him or her.

9. When people repeatedly experience negative outcomes that they cannot avoid or control, they may get into a state of learned helplessness. In that state they may exhibit helplessness, depression, and "give up" even in new situations in which the outcomes actually could be controlled.

10. When people believe they cannot control outcomes, they may develop a sense of helplessness. In contrast, when they believe that they can influence and control the events in their lives, they tend to become happier and more effective. When tragic events do occur, we often attempt to cope with our misfortune by somehow giving it meaning.

CHAPTER 17

DEFENSE

An outstanding characteristic of human beings is that they can create great anxiety in themselves even when they are not in any immediate external danger. A man may be seated comfortably in front of his hearth, adequately fed and luxuriously sheltered, seemingly safe from outside threats, and yet torture himself with anxiety-provoking memories of old events, with terrifying thoughts, or with expectations of imagined dangers in years to come. He also can cognitively, within his own mind, eliminate such internally cued anxiety without altering his external environment, simply by avoiding or changing his painful thoughts or memories.

"Defense mechanisms" are attempts to cope cognitively with internal anxiety-arousing cues. Usually it has also been assumed, in accordance with Freudian theory, that these cognitive efforts are at least partly unconscious—that is, they occur without the person's awareness. Many defense mechanisms have been hypothesized, mainly in the framework of Freudian theory. These hypothesized defenses have been called "repression," "projection," "denial," "sublimation," "reaction formation," and so on, as previously discussed (Chapter 3). Each of these terms refers to a different way of reducing or eliminating anxiety.

Repression

Greatest attention has been devoted to repression, probably because of the theoretical importance of that concept in Freudian psychology and psychoanalysis. Because most theoretical issues and research studies have focused on repression, it will be the defense that this chapter will emphasize. Rather than dealing with many defenses superficially, we will concentrate on this important one in depth.

The Concept of Repression

Most people sometimes feel that they actively try to avoid painful memories and ideas and struggle to "put out of mind" thoughts that are aversive to them. Common examples are trying not to think about a forthcoming threatening surgical operation, and trying to shunt attention away from the unknown results of an important test. Psychologists often call such efforts to avoid painful thoughts "cognitive avoidance."

The existence of cognitive avoidance is widely recognized, and few psychologists doubt that thoughts may be inhibited. However, the mechanisms underlying cognitive avoidance have been controversial and have been interpreted in different ways. The basic controversy is whether or not cognitive avoidance includes an unconscious defense mechanism of "repression" that forces unacceptable material into an unconscious region without the person's awareness.

The psychoanalytic concept of repression as a defense mechanism is closely linked to the Freudian idea of an unconscious mind. The unconscious mind was seen by early Freudians as a supersensitive entity whose perceptual alertness and memory bank surpassed the same properties of the conscious mind (e.g., Blum, 1955). A chief function of the unconscious mind was to screen and monitor memories and perceptual inputs. This screening served to inhibit the breakthrough of anxiety-arousing stimuli from the unconscious mind to the conscious, or from the outside world to consciousness. Just as the conscious mind was believed capable of deliberately (consciously) inhibiting events by *suppression*, so the unconscious was considered capable of inhibition or cognitive avoidance at the unconscious level by *repression*.

Suppression occurs when one voluntarily and consciously withholds a response or turns attention away from it deliberately. Unconscious repression, in contrast, may function as an automatic guardian against anxiety, a safety mechanism that prevents threatening material from entering consciousness. Psychoanalysts offered clinical evidence for the existence of repression in the form of cases in which slips of the tongue ("parapraxes"), jokes, dreams, or free associations seemed to momentarily bypass the defenses and betray the person, revealing a brief glimpse of his repressed unconscious impulses.

Recall that Freud based his ideas concerning repression and defense on his clinical observations of hysterical women at the turn of this century. He noted that some of these patients seemed to develop physical symptoms that did not make sense neurologically, such as hysterical difficulties with vision, or cases of "glove anesthesia," in which the patient showed an inability to feel in the hands—a symptom that is impossible neurologically. In their 1895 studies of hysteria Freud and his associate Breuer hypnotized some of the patients and found, to their great surprise, that when the origins and meanings of hysterical symptoms were talked about under hypnosis, the symptoms tended to disappear. This finding proved beyond any doubt that the symptoms were not caused by organic damage or physical defects.

Partly to understand hysteria, Freud developed his theory of unconscious conflict and defense. In his view, such symptoms as hysterical blindness and hysterical anesthesias reflected defensive attempts to avoid painful thoughts and feelings by diversionary preoccupation with apparently physical symptoms. Freud thought that the key mechanism in this blocking was unconsciously motivated repression. Through repression the basic impulses that are unacceptable to the person are rendered unconscious and thereby less frightening. Because such diversionary measures are inherently ineffective ways of dealing with anxiety-provoking impulses, the impulses persist and press for release in disguised and distorted forms that are called "symptoms."

Studying Repression

Repression has remained a central concept for most psychoanalysts, and it has been the subject of a great deal of research for many years. In general, many of the early efforts to assess whether or not particular findings demonstrated the truth of Freud's concepts created more controversy than clarity. In more recent years it has been recognized that well-designed experiments on the topic of cognitive avoidance can provide useful information about cognitive processes and personality regardless of their direct relevance to the Freudian theory of repression.

Early experimental research on repression studied the differential recall of pleasant and unpleasant experiences (e.g., Jersild, 1931; Meltzer, 1930). These investigators seemed to assume that repression manifested itself in a tendency to selectively forget negative or unpleasant experiences rather than positive ones. It was soon pointed out, however, that the Freudian theory of repression does not imply that experiences associated with unpleasant affective tone are repressed (Rosenzweig & Mason, 1934; Sears, 1936). Freudian repression, instead, was believed to depend on the presence of an "ego threat" (for example, a basic threat to self-esteem) and not on mere unpleasantness.

Later it also was recognized that to study repression adequately one should be able to demonstrate that when the cause of the repression (the ego threat) is removed, the repressed material is restored to consciousness (Zeller, 1950a). This assumption was consistent with the psychoanalytic belief that when the cause of a repression is discovered by insight in psychotherapy the repressed material rapidly emerges into the patient's consciousness. In other words, if the threat is eliminated it becomes safe for the repressed material to return to awareness. Reports by psychoanalysts often have cited cases in which a sudden insight supposedly lifted a long-standing amnesia (memory loss).

In an empirical study, Zeller (1950b) tried to take these considerations into account. Experimental and control subjects first were administered a paired-associate learning task (i.e., associating nonsense syllables like ZIK and DEM). Three days later the subjects participated in a relearning task for the same material, and the two groups were shown to perform similarly. As soon as the relearning task was over, the subjects took a "block tapping" test that ostensibly measured their abilities. On this test the experimental subjects were "ego-threatened" by being led to believe that they had failed badly. Subjects in the control group were carefully convinced that they had done well. Immediately thereafter all the subjects were again presented with the paired-associate learning task. On measures of retention and relearning of this material, the ego-threatened (experimental) group now performed less well than the control group. This finding was interpreted as due to repression resulting from the ego threat that had been created in the experimental subjects.

After a delay of three days all the subjects were again administered the paired-associate learning task and, as expected, the experimental subjects still performed less well. Next, to undo the ego threat and thereby lift the repression, all subjects were readministered the block-tapping test, but now the people in the experimental group as well as those in the control group were led to believe that they had succeeded on it. When the paired-associate learning task was administered again, there were no retention or relearning differences between the groups. Seemingly, lifting the repression had caused recall to be restored.

Were Zeller's findings really due to repression? To answer this question, one must consider the possible effects of the failure experience. In other research severe failure experiences have been shown to impair performance, including speed of relearning (Weiner, 1966). Zeller's results therefore may not reflect repression, but only poorer learning under the conditions of emotional upset and disorganization experienced by the failure group. Moreover, whenever a measure of retention of material is inferred from the speed with which it is relearned, it becomes impossible to separate the role of original learning from that of remembering. Differential recall of material has been shown to stem from differences in initial learning and covert rehearsal of the material, at least under some conditions (e.g., Caron & Wallach, 1957). Thus Zeller's failure subjects, rather than repressing more, may simply have learned less after failure by becoming disorganized or unmotivated.

In view of these considerations, in the Zeller study how can we account for the improvement in relearning and recall found after the "repression" was lifted—that is, after the failure subjects experienced success? The simplest explanation might be that after the students were relieved of their distress they devoted themselves more efficiently to the recall and relearning task and hence performed better.

More than 10 years later D'Zurilla (1965) used a different strategy to study defensive changes in memory due to stress. In his experiment, control and experimental subjects (college students) first were shown 20 words and tested for recall of the words to establish that there were no preexperimental group differences. Next the subjects were exposed to a series of ten slides. Each slide contained one Holtzman inkblot (a modification of the Rorschach) and two of the words that had been shown to them previously. For each slide the subjects had to indicate the word that best described the inkblot. The experimental group was told that this was a test designed to detect latent homosexual tendencies. They were told that one of the two words on each slide was a response that homosexuals tend to give but the other word was given by normal people. The control group was told only that it was taking part in the development of a new psychological inkblot test.

After responding to all of the cards the students in both groups were given another recall test. Again there were no group differences. Now threat was induced in the experimental subjects. They were told that they had picked nine of the 10 "homosexual" words, whereas the control group subjects were told that they had done very well. After five minutes all the subjects took another recall test. The people in the control group improved from their prior recall performance, but, as expected, subjects in the experimental group did less well than they had before. The investigator then tried to remove the repression effect by revealing the deception to the subjects and explaining that the inkblot test did not measure homosexual tendencies. Finally, the last recall test was administered: On this test, as predicted, now that the threat had been removed, the two groups recalled equally well.

You might conclude that the concept of repression was supported by D'Zurilla's results. Some doubt is cast on this conclusion, however, by findings from interviews after the experiment in which the students were asked to describe what they had thought about during the poststress retention interval. Contrary to expectations from repression theory, most of the experimental subjects had thought about things related to the threatening task, while only a few control subjects had thought about the task at all. During the retention period the experimental subjects said they had thought about the inkblots, past memories, their "homosexual tendencies," and many other events. As the investigator noted, these cognitions could have reduced the efficiency of recall by competing with the responses to be recalled and interfering with them.

Holmes and Schallow (1969) recognized that the threatened subjects may have spent the poststress retention interval thinking about their problems and that these competing cognitions could have disrupted their efforts to recall the words. Therefore they decided to study the role of response competition and interference in the repression paradigm. In their study, Holmes and Schallow included an ego-threatened group and a control group. They also added a group that was not ego-threatened but that was distracted during the retention interval by exposure to irrelevant neutral stimuli.

After the threat, the ego-threatened group recalled less well than the control group, replicating the effect previously attributed to repression. However, recall in the interference group was below that of the control group and quite similar to that of the ego-threatened group. The investigators therefore concluded that response interference, rather than repression, may have caused the differential performance of the threatened and control groups. Their interpretation is plausible, but it does not completely rule out the possibility of a repression effect. A more recent laboratory study (using recall for successes versus failures) found no support whatsoever for repression effects (Tudor & Holmes, 1973). Likewise, an extensive review of experimental research on repression, after surveying many studies, led the reviewer to conclude that "there is no evidence to support the predictions generated by the theory of repression" (Holmes, 1974, p. 651).

Perceptual Defense and Cognitive Selectivity

The studies described in the last section tried to investigate repression as a defense that blocks the memory for material connected with an ego threat. If unconscious repression is a mechanism that guards against painful intrusions into consciousness, one might also expect it to screen and block threatening perceptual inputs to the eyes and to monitor auditory messages to the ears. Indeed, clinical reports from Freudian psychoanalysts suggest that in some cases of "hysteria" massive repression may prevent the individual from perceiving or consciously registering threatening stimuli such as sexual scenes or symbols.

One very severe instance of this hypothesized syndrome would be "hysterical blindness," in which the individual seems to lose his or her vision although no physical damage to the eyes or to the perceptual system can be detected. Case reports have suggested that such psychological failures to see might be linked to traumatic sexual experiences with resulting repression of stimuli that might unleash anxiety. Clinical case reports such as those on hysteria often may provide suggestive evidence, but they are never conclusive.

To go beyond clinical impressions, experimentally oriented researchers have tried to study repressive defenses by examining possible anxiety-reducing distortions in perception or in other forms of cognition. Since it was obviously both unfeasible and unethical to induce sexual traumas in human subjects, considerable ingenuity was needed to find even a rough experimental analog for perceptual defense and cognitive distortion.

Research Strategy

In the 1940s and 1950s a general research strategy was devised to explore perceptual defenses, guided by the then prevalent faith in projective devices as methods for revealing conflictful areas of personality. Specifically, proponents of projective methods believed that persons who did *not* give sexual or aggressive responses to ambiguous stimuli must be inhibiting or defending against this type of ideation, especially if the same stimuli generally elicited many such responses from most normal people. Consequently one could use the failure to identify potentially threatening percepts, such as anxiety-arousing sexual words or threatening scenes, as signs of perceptual inhibition or defense.

To accomplish this objective, one would have to present these threatening perceptual stimuli in decreasing degrees of ambiguity from a point at which subjects could reasonably interpret them in many ways to a point of definiteness that permitted only one clearly correct interpretation. A helpful device for this purpose was the tachistoscope, a machine through which potentially threatening words (e.g., "bitch," "penis," "whore") and neutral words (e.g., "house," "flowers") could be flashed at varying speeds. These stimulus words were presented on a screen very rapidly at first and then gradually exposed for increasingly long durations. The length of time required before each subject correctly recognized the stimulus served as his "defensiveness" score; the longer the time required to recognize threatening stimuli the greater the subject's defensive avoidance tendencies were assumed to be.

In one study college students viewed tachistoscopically presented words that were either emotional or neutral in meaning (McGinnies, 1949). Each student was requested to state what word she had seen after each exposure. If her answer was wrong the same word was presented again at a slightly longer exposure time, and the subject again tried to recognize it.

The emotional and neutral words used, and the mean recognition thresholds associated with them, are shown in Figure 17-1. It was predicted that such "taboo" words as "penis" or "raped" would be anxiety-laden and therefore more readily inhibited than neutral words such as "apple." As Figure 17-1 illustrates, the results confirmed this prediction, showing greater "perceptual defense" (longer recognition times) for taboo words than for neutral words.

FIGURE 17-1
Mean Thresholds of Recognition of Neutral and Emotion-Charged Words

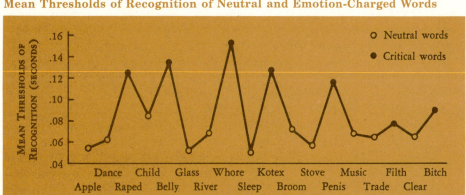

From McGinnies (1949).

Methodological Problems

An extremely serious methodological problem in perceptual defense research was pointed out by Howes and Solomon (1951), who called attention to the fact that the critical or "taboo" words used in perceptual defense experiments (e.g., McGinnies, 1949) were much less familiar to the subjects because they occurred much less frequently in the English language than did the "neutral" words. Hence it would not be surprising that people took longer to recognize them when they were ambiguously presented by the tachistoscope! Longer recognition time for taboo words could easily reflect unfamiliarity with the words rather than unconscious defense against their threatening meanings. Their data demonstrated a direct relation between infrequency of use and recognition time, so that a subject would show "defense" against such unusual words as "flume," "chaise," or "rapt."

Howes and Solomon also noted that the perceptual recognition situation placed the subject in an embarrasing pedicament. In the typical procedure, an undergraduate is brought to the laboratory by a professor or an assistant and is then exposed to brief and unclear stimulus presentations by the tachistoscope. The task is essentially a guessing game in which she tries to discern the correct word from fleeting fragments. On the first trial of a word she may, for example, see something like an "r" and a "p" and guess "rope." on the next trial she may say to herself "good grief, that looked like 'rape'!" But rather than make this guess to a professor or an assistant in the academic atmosphere of the scientific laboratory, she may deliberately suppress the response. Instead of saying what she thinks she sees, she offers "rope" again and withholds the "taboo" word until she is absolutely sure that this perception is correct.

Selective Perception

Under ambiguous conditions individuals may be somewhat more ready to interpret and construe unclear events in accord with their expectations and momentary states. Consequently if people have just failed they more readily perceive failure words (tachistoscopically presented); if they have just succeeded they may perceive success words at shorter exposures (Postman & Brown, 1952). Potentially need-satisfying stimuli also may be perceived somewhat more readily and may be made more salient. The observer may even endow these need-relevant valued stimuli with more striking characteristics, such as greater size and brightness (e.g., Bruner & Goodman, 1947).

The tendency to interpret ambiguities in the environment in accord with one's momentary drive state has been studied extensively. For example, moderately hungry subjects tend to produce somewhat more food-related responses than satiated subjects when they try to identify briefly exposed ambiguous stimuli (e.g., Levine, Chein, & Murphy, 1942; McClelland & Atkinson, 1948). This tendency, however, seems weak and is not correlated with the degree of hunger induced in the subjects. Indeed, under conditions of more intense deprivation people may become *less* likely to ideate about drive-related themes (Lazarus, Yousem, & Arenberg, 1953; Murray, 1959).

While there is no doubt that individuals interpret their environment subjectively, the intrusion of their subjective states and needs into their actual *perceptions* of the environment is a far more complex matter. The possible distortions of perception by unconscious needs have been of special interest to Freudian psychologists. If the unconscious system is as powerful as Freud's theory assumed, then it should produce distortions of perceptual and learning processes without the individual's awareness. One approach to this critically important topic has taken the form of experiments on "subception" (unconscious perception).

Subception and the Unconscious

Public interest in subception has been great because of its evident moral and social implications for subtly molding people's behavior without their awareness. What if stimuli—such as propaganda messages or advertisements presented below the threshold of perceptual awareness—could really shape people's beliefs and actions? During a movie, for example, if advertisements were secretly included and flashed too indistinctly for the victim's conscious awareness could his or her behavior be unconsciously influenced by the message? The potentialities—and the horrors—of "mind control" might be staggering; they are reminiscent of George Orwell's nightmarish *1984* and Huxley's *Brave New World*.

An experiment by Lazarus and McCleary (1951) attracted great attention because it seemed to demonstrate that subception does occur. In the first phase of their study, subjects watched as 10 nonsense syllables were projected on a screen supraliminally (above awareness thresholds) in random order. In the next phase the presentation of half the syllables was paired with electric shock to the subject, so that these "shock syllables" became the conditioned emotional stimuli eliciting the galvanic skin response (GSR). In the third phase of the study, the shock and nonshock syllables were again projected in random order, but now subliminally (at speeds too fast for clear awareness).

The two measures obtained from the subjects were their "conscious" recognition through verbal reports of the subliminal shock stimuli, and an "unconscious" index of recognition inferred from the emotional activity reflected in their GSR. It was assumed that if a subject does not report recognizing the shock-associated syllables, but the GSR measure shows that he is responding to them, then he must be recognizing them unconsciously. The investigators believed that they had found subception because when the self-report predicted the shock syllables poorly, the GSR predicted them relatively well. They interpreted these data as demonstrating that people can make unconscious discriminations of events that they cannot report recognizing consciously.

The foregoing conclusion of a subception effect is most exciting, but it has been seriously challenged. Some critics have interpreted the evidence for subception as reflecting nothing more than methodological problems (Eriksen, 1958, 1960).

They imply that when these problems are removed, subception disappears. Others have argued seriously that there is enough evidence to support the reality of subception, in spite of the difficulty of identifying the exact way it works (Dixon, 1971; Silverman, 1976).

Conscious Response Suppression or Unconscious Repression?

The conclusions that may be drawn from research on subception hence remain controversial and open to different interpretations. We are left with these fundamental questions: Do cognitive avoidance and selective perception merely involve suppression of responses so that they are less likely to become verbalized? Or are people driven by impulses whose meanings they unconsciously disguise beyond their own recognition? Can they thus be victimized unconsciously by their own psychic apparatus? Or can the phenomena of cognitive avoidance and "misperception" be understood as learned inhibitions without requiring a special concept of the unconscious as a psychic entity? Most critical, just what is the status of the unconscious as a force in psychic functioning? The problem is a complicated one that resists easy answers because it entails serious methodological difficulties in defining and determining whether another person is or is not consciously aware of a given event.

The term "consciousness" may be confusing because it has many meanings. "Awareness" is the most common definition for consciousness in psychological usage. Conversely, the "unconscious" tends to be equated with lack of awareness. But how do you know whether or not another person is aware or unaware of something? A means of judging awareness that has been favored by many clinicians involves highly indirect inferences about people's insight into their motivations, internal states, feelings, and dynamics. Such a clinical strategy depends most heavily on the clinical judge and her tools (for example, projective tests), and its limitations are serious, as we have seen (Chapter 8).

The more obvious and direct way to study awareness of an event is to ask people, and to get their own verbal reports of whether or not they have recognized its occurrence. In research on perceptual defense, for example, as we have seen, subjects are exposed to various stimuli (such as taboo words) and asked to report their perceptions. As was noted, however, such reports may not fully reflect private awareness.

There may be many reasons why a person's awareness and his verbalizations about it can be discrepant. One may not want to publicly acknowledge an event although aware of it (for example, because it is embarrassing or threatening). As pointed out before, students are unlikely to report seeing words like "penis" to their professor unless they are completely sure their perception is correct. Even when motivated to report accurately, words may not be capable of correctly describing subjective awareness. Consider, for instance, how difficult it would be to verbally describe the image of a face. Even a detailed verbal description of a stranger's face might still not permit one to recognize her in a crowd. The labels of language often are too gross to capture the nuances of the events to which they are applied, especially when the events keep changing rapidly.

The value of verbal self-reports about awareness depends on the adequacy of the interrogation method. Techniques to help the subject verbalize the experience have to be thorough and ingenious. Otherwise we might conclude that someone is unaware of an event when, instead, we merely have not asked the right questions.

Can people learn discriminations without awareness or consciousness? It would certainly be impressive evidence for the unconscious if important learning and discriminations were shown to occur in people without their awareness. Thus the role of awareness in the learning process is one of the most important theoretical issues. Eriksen (1960) undertook an extensive survey and analysis of research on human learning without awareness. The results led him to conclude that the existence of discrimination learning at levels not available to conscious awareness (equated with verbal report) has not been shown adequately. Although some simple human conditioned responses may be learned without awareness, in most forms of human learning awareness seems to play a major role (e.g., Dulany, 1962; Spielberger & De Nike, 1966) and facilitates the learning process dramatically.

These findings cast doubt on the unconscious as a powerful force in human discrimination and learning, and they have led some researchers to suggest abandoning the concept of the unconscious as a psychic entity:

> A science of personality is not furthered by the frequent tendency of psychologists to discuss the "unconscious" with all the ambiguity and reverence that religions accord to the soul. There is great need to spell out explicitly the assumed characteristics of the unconscious phenomena in terms of more commonplace psychological variables. To do so may destroy the titillating mystery that the unconscious seems to hold but then that is the business of science (Eriksen, 1960, p. 298).

Reviewing later developments, Eriksen (1966, p. 354) concluded that "the possibility must be seriously entertained that the concept of repression is only a very well-learned or overlearned response suppression."

Eriksen (1966) suggests that unpleasant or painful material may at first be consciously suppressed (rather than unconsciously repressed) and that response suppression, after sufficient rehearsal, becomes automatic. But it also seems possible that even without a deliberate suppression mechanism, painful thoughts and memories are less likely to be evoked and covertly rehearsed because they are aversive and less reinforcing than competing, potentially available cognitions. In the social learning view, just as the probability for the

occurrence of overt behaviors depends on their probable reinforcing consequences, so the presence of cognitions, images, and other covert events hinges
on the internal and external effects they produce for the person. In that view,
an individual will not make "unpleasant" covert responses unless they in fact
have become positively reinforcing (for example, by having stopped him in the
past from thinking about even more negative things).

The foregoing does not imply that people are aware of all the discriminations that they make. As personal experience attests, while during new learning we usually feel aware and even "self-conscious," once a behavior is mastered and over-learned it often seems to flow smoothly and automatically
without any subjective awareness whatsoever. We usually stay safely clear of
hot stoves, cross busy streets only when the traffic lights are appropriate, and
drive our cars for miles without self-conscious awareness of every step and discrimination made along the route. While learning to park a car may at first
require great awareness and self-conscious attention to subtle positional cues,
thousands of trials later one is likely to be unaware of the procedure (unless
startled by a sudden bump). And it is certainly true that without being aware
of it we very commonly bring our past knowledge to bear on how we act in
the world. Consider, for example, how "automatically" we know what to expect and do in familiar situations, like birthday parties or restaurants (Schank
& Abelson, 1977).

Understandably discouraged by experiments on unconscious processes, psychoanalytically oriented critics have been quite skeptical of the relevance of
many of these experimental studies for their theory (Erdelyi & Goldberg,
1979). They argue that it is confusing and misleading to study single processes
(such as repression) in isolation as lone variables outside the context of the
person's total psychic functioning. Such critics believe that these experimental
studies at best have value as independent and suggestive, but clinically irrelevant, analogs, and they doubt that long-term psychodynamic processes can be
studied under the artificial conditions of the typical laboratory experiment.
They attribute the discouraging findings to the artificiality of the measures
typically used in such research and to the hazards of generalizing from college
sophomores in a laboratory (or even from rats in a maze) to clinical populations and clinical problems. They assert that the mild anxiety induced by experimental threats to cognitively mature college students may have little relevance for understanding the traumas experienced by the young child trying to
cope with Oedipal fantasies, or the severely disturbed patient in the clinic.

For example, studies like the previously discussed experiment on repression
by Zeller (1950) provide only a remote analog of the motivational aspects of
clinical repression in Freud's theory (Madison, 1960), repression (or more
broadly speaking, any defense) involved motives that were associated with
traumatic childhood experiences for a particular individual. Suppose that failure on such tasks as Zeller's block-tapping was not preceded by similar childhood failures and hence did not arouse those residual childhood emotional
patterns. Then there would be no reason for the adult to repress rather than

to cope with Zeller's ego insults in other learned ways of dealing with threat. While studies like Zeller's provide interesting information about the effects of failure, they may not really inform us about the nature of repression.

Thus, many psychoanalytically oriented critics believe that evidence obtained from controlled experimental research conducted outside the clinical setting (such as the studies reviewed in the preceding sections) is largely irrelevant. On the other hand, as we have seen (Chapter 8), the clinician's judgments and intuitive procedures for inferring unconscious dynamics cannot be relied upon safely either. Consequently one has to seriously question not merely the methods of studying the unconscious but also the nature of the phenomenon itself, while remaining fully open to the possibility that better methods and studies will bring new understanding.

Subconscious Information Processing: Selective Cognition?

One promising but still unproven new direction is suggested by reformulating the issue of "perceptual defense" in information-processing terms. Such a reformulation treats "perceptual defense" as just one instance of the selectivity that occurs throughout cognition. Selectivity (or bias) occurs in our choice of the things to which we attend, the manner in which we organize and rehearse the flood of information that enters the sense receptors, and the response that we ultimately generate (Erdelyi, 1974). Hopefully, repression and perceptual defense can be studied more fruitfully when they are placed in the larger context of selective information processing (Broadbent, 1977; Erdelyi & Goldberg, 1979).

Consistent with this general cognitive reformulation, there have been new, vigorous efforts to demonstrate experimentally instances in which people seem to make systematic errors without awareness (Dixon, 1971). In one direction, investigators began by carefully defining "self-deception" (Gur & Sackeim, 1979). In their view, to be self-deceived a person must simultaneously hold two contradictory beliefs, one of which "is not subject to awareness; and the nonawareness of this belief is motivated" (p. 147). In two clever experiments the researchers tried to demonstrate that self-deception, as they defined it, really exists. They confronted college students with tape recordings of their own voices mixed in with the voices of others. Measures included the subjects' reports of whether the voice was theirs or not and also their GSR (to assess psychophysiological responding). For example, when subjects were incorrect in their reports of whether or not the voice was theirs, they had made correct identifications at another, nonverbal level of processing (inferred from their GSR measures). The patterns of discrepancy found between these measures led the investigators to conclude that genuine self-deception had occurred at least for some subjects.

In a somewhat related vein, Nisbett and Wilson (1977) attempted to demonstrate that circumstances can be arranged so that people are unaware of their cognitions and misidentify the causes of their own behavior. In one experiment, for instance, people were asked to evaluate articles of clothing. The results clearly revealed that the clothing article in the right-hand position was evaluated more favorably. But when asked whether position had any effect on their choice, people vehemently and consistently denied it. The researchers concluded from their study that sometimes we seem to have little insight into our own thought processes. Others, however, have challenged this interpretation of the results (Smith & Miller, 1978).

In a similar direction, some studies also suggest that sometimes our behavior is so overlearned that we act more or less automatically, mindlessly ignoring relevant information in repeatedly encountered situations (Langer, 1978). Likewise, we may develop more positive feelings toward objects that were previously encountered without consciously knowing that the object is familiar to us. That is, exposure to objects led to enhanced feelings for them, even when there was no recognition that the objects had been seen before (Wilson, 1979). Hypnosis also provides relevant evidence (Kihlstrom, 1980). Consider subjects who are hypnotized and instructed to forget what happened during the hypnotic state. Afterward they may be influenced by their hypnotic experience (e.g., instructions that they were given) even though those experiences are outside their awareness. Later, at a prearranged time, the experiences may be recovered. Clearly studies of this sort are reviving interest (and belief) in the possibility of subconscious information processing. The final verdict is not in, but it is plain that the issues will continue to receive the intense attention that they merit.

Patterns of Defense and the Coping Process

While some people react to anxiety-arousing cues by avoiding them cognitively, other people do not. Beginning with some of the earliest studies on the role of needs as determinants of perception, individual differences in "defensive" patterns have been found (e.g., Bruner & Postman, 1947).

Individual Differences in Cognitive Avoidance: Repression-Sensitization

The dimension on which these differences seemed to fall was a continuum of behaviors ranging from avoiding the anxiety-arousing stimuli to approaching them more readily and being extravigilant or supersensitized to them. The former end of the continuum included behaviors similar to the defensive mechanisms that psychoanalysts called denial and repression; the latter pattern—vigilance or sensitization to anxiety-provoking cues—seemed more like the intellectual ruminations subsumed under such mechanisms as intellectualization and obsessive worrying. This dimension now has become known as the *repression-sensitization* continuum. Repression-sensitization became the focus of much research both as a dynamic process and as a personality dimension on which individuals might show consistent patterns.

There is some individual consistency in defensive behavior across various learning, memory, and perceptual tasks (e.g., Eriksen, 1966). For example (Eriksen, 1952a), college students were given an ego-involving intellectual task on which they were led to feel that they were failing. As part of the procedure they were asked, under the guise of an intelligence test, to complete a series of sentences half of which actually could not be logically completed. Subsequently they took a memory test for recall of the sentences. On the basis of their test scores, subjects were categorized according to whether they remembered more of their successes relative to their failures (i.e., more completed sentences than incompleted sentences) or the reverse. The "repressing" reaction was attributed to the subjects who recalled more successes than failures; the "sensitizing" defense to the opposite pattern.

The 10 most extreme repressors and the 10 subjects with the strongest sensitizing pattern were then selected for a paired-associate learning task. On that task some of the word associates were highly affective (had long association times) and others were affectively neutral (had short association times) for the particular subject. It was found that the repressors (of the incompleted sentences) tended to learn and relearn the affective words more slowly than the neutral words. Thus individuals who displayed extreme cognitive avoidance in the recall of their failures also tended to require more time to learn affectively arousing words. In contrast, the sensitizers (subjects who previously recalled more failures than successes) showed no such tendency.

In general, individuals show some consistency in their cognitive avoidance of symbolic, anxiety-provoking cues such as threatening words (e.g., Eriksen, 1952b; Eriksen & Kuethe, 1956). Consistency evidence usually has been strongest when extreme groups are preselected. Reaction time and other measures of avoidance in the auditory recognition of poorly audible sentences with sexual and agressive content were significantly related to indicators of avoidance of sexual and aggressive sentence stems in a sentence completion test (Lazarus, Eriksen, & Fonda, 1951). People who more readily recalled stimuli associated with a painful shock also tended to recall their failures; those who forgot one were more likely to forget the other (Lazarus & Longo, 1953).

There also have been some failures to find consistency in cognitive avoidance patterns. Kurland (1954) reported a lack of generality in avoidance mechanisms. In his study psychiatric patients were judged as using either predominantly repressive or sensitizing ("obsessive-compulsive") defense mechanisms for handling anxiety. The judgments were made by psychiatrists who saw the patients in intensive psychotherapy three times weekly. The rated defense mechanisms obtained were unrelated to auditory recognition thresholds for emotional words.

In sum, sometimes there is some significant consistency in approach versus avoidance responses to threatening stimuli of various kinds, but generally the degree of consistency is not very strong. A tendency for some consistency in cognitive avoidance may exist at least when extremely high and low groups are selected (Eriksen, 1966). Correlations between cognitive avoidance on experimental tasks and various other measures of repression-sensitization also imply some consistency (e.g., Byrne, 1964; Mischel, Zeiss, & Zeiss, 1973). However, like most other dispositions, cognitive avoidance is not a stimulus-free trait: It depends on the situation as well as on the person's learning history.

Blunting versus Monitoring

People differ considerably in their disposition to distract themselves or to monitor for (be alert to) danger signals. One promising scale tries to identify information-avoiders and information-seekers as two distinct coping styles. The Miller Behavioral Style Scale (MBSS) consists of four hypothetical stress-evoking scenes of an uncontrollable nature (Miller, 1980, in press). On this measure, people are asked to imagine vividly scenes like "you are afraid of the dentist and have to get some dental work done"; or "you are being held hostage by a group of armed terrorists in a public building"; or "you are on an airplane, 30 minutes from your destination, when the plane unexpectedly goes into a deep dive and then suddenly levels off. After a short time, the pilot announces that nothing is wrong, although the rest of the ride may be rough. You, however, are not convinced that all is well."

Each scene is followed by statements that represent ways of coping with the situation, either by "monitoring" or by "blunting." Half of the statements

Some people cope with unpleasant events by mentally "blunting" (distracting themselves).

accompanying each scene are of a monitoring variety. (For example, in the hostage situation: "If there was a radio present, I would stay near it and listen to the bulletins about what the police were doing"; or, in the airplane situation: "I would listen carefully to the engines for unusual noises and would watch the crew to see if their behavior was out of the ordinary." The other half of the statements are of the blunting type. For example, in the dental situation: "I would do mental puzzles in my head"; or, in the airplane situation: "I would watch the end of the movie, even if I had seen it before." The subject simply marks all the statements following each scene that might apply to him.

To establish the scale's validity, college students were threatened with a low probability shock and allowed to choose whether they wanted to monitor for information or distract themselves with music. As expected, the amount of time spent on information rather than on music was predicted reasonably well by an individual's MBSS score. In particular, the more blunting items endorsed on the scale, the less time the person spent listening to the information and the more to the music. Thus individuals differ in the extent to which they choose to monitor or distract themselves when faced with aversive events; and these differences in coping style were related to their questionnaire scores.

In a related study the scale was given to gynecologic patients about to undergo colposcopy, a diagnostic procedure to check for the presence of abnormal (cancerous) cells in the uterus. Based on scale scores, patients were first divided into monitors or blunters. Half the women in each group were then given extensive information about the forthcoming procedure, and half were given (the usual) minimal information. Psychophysiological reactions, subjective reports, and observer ratings of arousal and discomfort were taken before, during, and after the procedures. The results revealed, again as expected, that monitors showed more arousal overall than blunters (for example, see Fig. 17-2 for the physician's rating of patient's tension during the exam). Most interesting, physiological arousal was reduced when the level of preparatory information was consistent with the patient's coping style. That is, physiological arousal was reduced for blunters who received minimal information and for monitors who received extensive information.

FIGURE 17-2
Doctor's report—tension during exam

From Miller, 1980, in press.

The total results clearly show strong individual differences in informational preferences during the coping process when people are faced with threats.

Subjective Control, Avoidance, and Monitoring

Whether you react to potentially painful stimuli by trying to avoid them cognitively or by becoming vigilantly alert and monitoring them may depend in part on what you can do to control the threat. Consider first the situation in which a person receives aversive stimulation but cannot control its occurrence. That is, the individual can do nothing to change the objective circumstances to render the aversive or negative stimuli less painful through his or her own problem-solving actions. Examples of this frustrating dilemma would include most experimentally induced stress experiments in which the researcher administers painful but unavoidable electric shocks to the subject, confronts him with embarrassing words or pictures, provides him with insoluble problems, or deprives him of food for long periods of time

Under all these conditions the aversive stimulation is essentially inescapable (unless the subject terminates the situation altogether by abandoning the experiment). If the subject can have no control over the painful stimuli by means of his own instrumental actions such as problem-solving, it may be most adaptive for him to avoid them cognitively and thus not think about them or attend to them. On the other hand, if escape from the noxious or distressing stimulation is possible and depends on the person's ability to find a solution (cognitively or physically), then "monitoring" vigilance or sensitization to the anxiety-arousing cues would be adaptive and often even essential for survival.

The foregoing speculations have received some experimental support. Reece (1954) tested subjects' recognition thresholds for various nonsense syllables in the first phase of his experiment. Thereafter, the subjects underwent a training period during which some of the syllables were paired with electric shock. In the final phase of the study the subjects' recognition thresholds after training were assessed again. Post-training recognition thresholds for the syllables were longer if during training the syllable-shock combinations were inescapable (i.e., subjects could do nothing to prevent them). In contrast, if subjects could escape shock during training by verbalizing the syllable as soon as it was presented then the syllables were later recognized as rapidly as in a control group that received no shock. Similar evidence comes from a study by Rosen (1954), who controlled for the effect of the electric shock itself.

Thus whether or not persons react to negative stimuli by avoiding them "defensively" in their cognitions and perceptions may depend on whether or not they believe that they can somehow cope with them by problem-solving and action. If adaptive action seems impossible, cognitive suppressive attempts may be more likely, but if the painful cues can be controlled by the person's actions then greater attention and vigilance to them may occur. This point is illustrated in a "blunting-monitoring" study that gave subjects a choice be-

	Information-Seeking	Distraction-Seeking
TABLE 17-1 **NUMBER OF SUBJECTS WHO SEEK INFORMATION** **(WARNING SIGNAL) OR DISTRACTION (LISTEN TO MUSIC)** **WHEN AVOIDANCE IS OR IS NOT POSSIBLE**		
Avoidance Possible	24	10
Avoidance Not Possible	11	23

SOURCE: Based on Miller, 1979.

tween stress-relevant information or distraction (Miller, 1979). The information was a warning signal for when an electric shock would come; the distraction was listening to music. Half the subjects were led to believe the shock was potentially avoidable; the rest believed it was unavoidable. As Table 17-1 shows, when subjects believed avoidance was possible, they preferred information; when they thought it was unavoidable, they preferred distraction.

The Meaning of Inconsistency

The belief in a special unconscious mechanism of repression is sometimes bolstered by the observation that people often seem to behave inconsistently. For example, in his self-reports a man may depict himself as well controlled, orderly, and unaggressive, but his stories on the TAT projective test may be full of murder and violence. Such discrepancies across response modes may seem intuitively to provide support for unconscious repressive mechanisms. These defensive mechanisms might inhibit the individual's motives in some contexts but permit repressed materials to slip through defenses under other, less guarded circumstances, such as in jokes or in fantasy expressions.

An alternative interpretation of the same phenomenon emphasizes the fact that the response mode in which behavior occurs influences the consequences to which the behavior leads. The consequences for similar content expressed in different response modes usually are drastically different. For example, an individual's thoughts, stories, self-reports, jokes, daydreams, and other responses all dealing with the same theme—such as aggressiveness—do not lead to similar consequences. A person whose projective test stories abound with violent themes might be diagnosed as having a healthy, active fantasy life. But the same individual probably would be institutionalized if he enacted similar content in interpersonal relations or if he expressed similar themes in his self-reports and self-descriptions. Because the consequences the individual receives for the same response pattern across different response modes are radically different he learns to discriminate sharply among them, and therefore his behavior across them becomes different (Mischel, 1968). For example, if sexual fantasies are gratifying and acceptable but sexual orgies are not, the individual may be expected to engage in the former rather than the latter.

But who does the punishing and the permitting when the "unacceptable" responses are primarily covert events such as thoughts and images? Obviously in the course of socialization persons somehow become regulators of their own behavior, punishing and rewarding themselves and judging their own actions, feelings, and ideas. The development of these self-regulatory mechanisms constitutes one of the most important topics in personality, and the details of this process are discussed in the next chapter.

SUMMARY

1. People can cognitively avoid internal anxiety-generating cues such as threatening thoughts. While the phenomenon of "cognitive avoidance" is widely recognized, a controversial issue is whether or not it involves a mechanism of unconscious repression.

2. The Freudian concept of defense mechanisms refers to attempts to cope cognitively with internal anxiety-arousing cues without awareness—that is, unconsciously. Freud thought that the key mechanism of defense entailed unconsciously motivated repression of unacceptable (anxiety-arousing) material. According to his theory, repressed impulses are not eliminated but are only camouflaged; hence, they may ultimately return in disguised and distorted forms, such as "slips" of the tongue or symptoms.

3. The concept of repression has been the subject of extensive research for many years. Although several empirical studies have been interpreted as supporting the concept of repression, alternative interpretations are possible (such as poorer learning under conditions of emotional upset and response interference due to stress).

4. Repressive "perceptual defenses" might produce anxiety-reducing distortions and avoidance in perception. Some researchers reasoned that if certain stimuli generally elicited many sexual or aggressive responses, then the *failure* to give such responses meant that the person must be inhibiting or defending against this type of ideation. Often a tachistoscope was used to present stimuli briefly, and the length of time required to recognize threatening stimuli (such as taboo words) was the measure of defensive avoidance.

5. Methodological problems left the conclusions uncertain. For example, the threatening words used in perceptual defense experiments

occur less frequently in the English language than the neutral words. Thus longer recognition time could result from unfamiliarity rather than from unconscious defense. Another difficulty lies in the problem of distinguishing between the subject's *report* and her *perception*. The subject in a perceptual recognition situation may see the taboo stimulus but may deliberately suppress her response because she is embarrassed about saying or admitting it. Other experiments on unconscious defense have been limited by many similar methodological dilemmas.

6. Evidence from controlled experimental research on unconscious defense and need-distorted perception is often negative. Many psychoanalytically oriented critics, however, maintain that most of this evidence is irrelevant. They point to the artificiality of the measures usually employed and to the hazards of generalizing from laboratory subjects to clinical populations and problems. Alternatively, the clinician's judgments and the intuitive procedures used for inferring the phenomena of unconscious dynamics have been questioned most seriously.

7. A major effort to assess the role of the unconscious has investigated learning and discrimination processes to see if they can occur without awareness or consciousness. In general, while some simple conditioned responses may be learned without awareness, awareness plays a major role in most forms of human learning. Yet, although most learning may require awareness, once behavior is mastered it often seems to proceed without subjective awareness. Similarly, painful or unpleasant material at first may be deliberately suppressed and this response suppression may gradually become automatic. Thus the phenomenon of "repression" may reduce to overlearned response suppression.

8. But it is also likely that selectivity and "bias" may occur in the ways people process information, sometimes without their awareness. For example, people may engage in motivated self-deception, and they sometimes seem to have little insight into their own thought processes.

9. Individual differences in coping with stress and anxiety-arousing cues seem to fall on a continuum from avoidance behaviors to supersensitive and vigilant ones. Repression-sensitization as well as blunting-monitoring are two concepts for studying such individual differences.

10. Whether one reacts to a painful stimulus by trying cognitively to avoid it or by becoming vigilantly alert to it may depend partly upon what one can do to control the threat. If adaptive action seems impossible, cognitive suppression may be more likely. If, however, the

potentially painful events can be controlled by the person's actions, then greater attention and vigilance to them may be found.

11. The inconsistent behavior of a person in different response modes (such as thoughts, self-reports, daydreams, and overt behavior) is often construed as evidence for unconscious repression. The defensive mechanisms are seen as inhibiting the individual's basic motives in some contexts but as permitting repressed materials to slip through in less guarded circumstances. The same phenomenon of inconsistency, however, may reflect the fact that consequences for expressing similar content in different response modes usually are drastically different. This difference leads a person to discriminate sharply among different response modes.

CHAPTER 18

SELF-CONTROL

Defensive reactions to frustration and anxiety are by no means the only forms of coping. This chapter examines some other important ways through which people solve problems and control their own behavior. These mechanisms have been called "ego controls," "internalization," and "processes of self-control." Regardless of the labels, in this chapter we will discuss some of the many ways in which individuals solve problems and evaluate and control their own behavior.

Frustration Tolerance and Voluntary Delay

The human ability to control events in the world has intrigued not only philosophers and psychologists but most laymen as well. This concern is reflected in such diverse concepts as "will power," "mastery," and "competence," and in their psychological opposites, such as "helplessness" and "hopelessness." All of these concepts involve the idea of volition ("will") and deal with the ability of individuals to affect their own outcomes and to influence their personal environments. Sometimes this influence is judged to be for the social good, and therefore prosocial or "moral"; often it is not. Always it entails the individual's efforts to modify conditions in the light of particular goals.

One especially striking characteristic of human "will" is that people frequently impose barriers on themselves, interrupting their own behavior and delaying available gratification. When a delay of gratification is imposed on an individual by external conditions or forces we talk about "frustration" (Chapter 15); when the delay is self-imposed we call it "self-control."

Delay of Gratification

The ability to voluntarily refuse immediate gratification, to tolerate self-imposed delays of reward, is at the core of most philosophical concepts of "will power" and their parallel psychological concept of "ego strength." It is hard to imagine socialization, or indeed civilization, without such self-imposed delays. Learning to wait for desired outcomes and to behave in the light of expected future consequences is essential for the successful achievement of long-term, distant goals. Even the simplest, most primitive steps in socialization require learning to defer one's impulses and to express them only under special conditions of time and place, as seen in toilet training. Similarly, enormously complex chains of deferred gratification are required for people to achieve the delayed rewards provided by our culture's social system and institutions.

Consider, for example, the self-imposed deferrals of pleasure required to achieve occupational objectives such as careers in medicine or science. The route leading to such a goal involves a continuous series of delays of gratification, as seen in the progression from one grade to the next, and from one temporal barrier to another in the long course from occupational choice to occupational success. In social relationships the culture also requires delays, as seen in the expectation that people should postpone sexual relations, marriage, and children until they are "ready for them." Although judgments of what constitutes such readiness differ greatly across cultures and among different people, some norms concerning appropriate timing are found in every society.

The importance of self-control patterns that require delay of gratification has been widely recognized by theorists from Freud to the present. The concept of voluntary postponement of gratifications for the sake of more distant, long-term gains is fundamental for many conceptualizations of complex human behavior.

Should Gratification Be Delayed?

The cultural norm of impulse delay is expressed most clearly in the so-called "Protestant Ethic," with its puritanical demands for self-restraint and its negative attitude toward pleasure. Understandably there are many strong reactions against such extremes of self-denial. Some thoughtful people question the wisdom of building a society on endless chains of deferred gratification. Others have experimented with more utopian communal societies, seeking simpler forms for the creation of a more satisfying community. The goals that people struggle toward in our society and the barriers that both they and the society impose need to be questioned. But although the particular goals and frustrations may change, it is difficult to conceive of organized life without some temporal delays and barriers. Even the simplest agricultural or folk community needs both delay and planning. The issue therefore is not delay of gratification in itself, but when, how, and for what one should delay.

Learning To Choose Delayed Gratification

The extreme self-imposed delay symbolized by the ethics of puritanism con-trasts sharply with the inadequate voluntary delay and the deficiencies in self-control that seem to characterize many people in our society. Inadequate delay patterns often are partial causes of antisocial and criminal behavior (in-cluding violence and physical aggression) and of failure to achieve reasonable work and interpersonal satisfactions (Mowrer & Ullmann, 1945). Thus while some personal and social problems stem from excessive frustration, others re-sult from the failure of individuals to learn and practice appropriate patterns of delay and restraint. Indeed, deficiencies in voluntary delay may become a prime source of frustration and may victimize the individual by guaranteeing him or her an endless chain of failure experiences in our culture. Consider, for example, the "high school dropout" who leaves school because he cannot tol-erate postponing pleasures and working for more distant goals. His school fail-ure in turn may sentence him to future vocational hardships and prevent him from achieving durable satisfactions. Given the magnitude of the social prob-lems associated with the inability to delay rewards, it becomes important to understand the causes of voluntary delay behavior in detail.

To explore the cognitive and social learning variables controlling self-imposed delay of reward, one research program has studied delay of reward and self-control with direct behavioral measures (Mischel, 1966b, 1974). In this research subjects usually have to choose among actual alternatives that vary in delay time and value (e.g., immediate smaller versus delayed larger re-wards) in realistic situations, as was discussed in Chapter 7. For example, pre-school children are given a choice between getting a less valuable but immedi-ate reward or a more attractive reward for which they must wait. This type of choice situation is depicted in Figure 18-1.

The figure shows the "clown box" with two windows displaying the two items in the choice (Mischel, 1970). The window in front of the smaller reward can be opened at once, whereas the window displaying the larger reward re-mains sealed for a predetermined time period. By depositing a token in the appropriate slot (in the clown's hands) the child may choose whether he or she wants to open the window in front of the smaller reward now or wait for the other window to spring open after a specified delay time. Basically similar choices involving age-appropriate outcomes have been presented to older chil-dren and adults by means of questionnaires that describe the choices verbally.

To a considerable degree a person's willingness to defer gratification de-

FIGURE 18-1
A Set of Paired Rewards in Place in the Magic Clown Surprise Box

From Mischel (1970).

pends on the outcomes that she expects from her choice (Mischel, 1966b, 1968). Of particular importance are the individual's expectations that future (delayed) rewards for which she would have to work and wait would actually materialize, and their relative value for her. Such expectations or feelings of trust depend, in turn, on the person's history of prior promise-keeping and on past reinforcement for waiting behavior and for other forms of planful, goal-directed self-control. When the attainment of delayed gratification requires the person to reach particular achievement levels, then her willingness to work and wait for these future outcomes also hinges on her expectations that she can adequately fulfill the necessary contingencies (Mischel & Staub, 1965). These expectations depend not only on her direct personal experiences, but also on her observation of the behavior of social models, such as peers, parents, and teachers.

Effects of Watching Impulsive versus Future-Oriented Models

Laboratory experiments have investigated most precisely the determinants of preferences for immediate, less valuable as opposed to more desirable but delayed outcomes and similar forms of self-control. To illustrate this type of experiment, here is one example in some detail.

The transmission of delay behavior through modeling without any direct reinforcement was studied by Bandura and Mischel (1965). They hypothesized that self-imposed delay of reward would be determined in part by the delay patterns displayed by social models. The study also compared the relative magnitude and stability of changes in delay-of-reward behavior as a function of exposure to real-life and symbolic (written) modeling cues.

In the initial phase of this experiment many children were administered a series of paired rewards. In each of these pairs they were asked to select either a small reward that could be obtained immediately, or a more valued item contingent on a delay period ranging from one to four weeks. For example, children chose between a smaller, immediately available candy bar and a larger one that required waiting. From the total pool of subjects those falling in the extreme upper and lower 25 percent of scores were selected for the succeeding phases of the experiment.

Children from each of these extreme groups (who exhibited predominantly either delayed-reward or immediate-reward patterns of behavior) were then assigned to treatment conditions. In one treatment children observed a live adult model who exhibited delay-of-reward responses counter to their own self-gratification pattern. For example, if the child was initially high in delay preferences, the adult model consistently chose immediate rewards. (He selected, for instance, a cheaper set of plastic chess figures immediately instead of a more attractive set available a week later.) The model also made explanatory statements about his choices. For example, he said: "Chess figures are chess figures. I can get much use out of the plastic ones right away." Or he commented: "You probably have noticed that I am a person who likes things now. One can spend so much time in life waiting that one never gets around to really living. . ." Conversely, children who initially displayed strong immediate reward preferences were exposed to models who chose delayed, costlier rewards. In other treatment groups children were similarly exposed to a model displaying delay-of-reward behavior opposite to their own, with the exception that the model's responses were presented only in written form rather than "live." In a final condition children had no exposure to any models.

Immediately following the experimental procedure the children's delay-of-reward responses were measured. In order to test the generality and stability of changes in delay behavior, they were reassessed by a different experimenter in a different social setting approximately one month later. The overall results revealed strong effects. Figure 18-2, for example, shows the mean percentage of immediate-reward responses produced by the high-delay children in each of the test periods as a function of treatment conditions. Children who had shown a predominantly delayed-reward pattern displayed an increased preference for immediate and less valuable rewards as a function of observing models favoring immediate gratification; conversely, those who had exhibited a marked preference for immediate rewards increased and maintained their willingness to wait for more valuable but delayed reinforcers following exposure to models displaying high-delay behavior. The effects of seeing the model's written responses were similar to those of watching live models, although less pronounced and less generalized.

Conclusions from this study were strengthened by the finding of similar effects when similar procedures were extended to a population of young prison inmates. Specifically, exposure to high-delay peer models substantially increased delay of gratification in 18- to 20-year-old inmates who initially had displayed an extreme preference for immediate rewards (Stumphauzer, 1972).

FIGURE 18-2
Effects of Modeling on Delay of Gratification

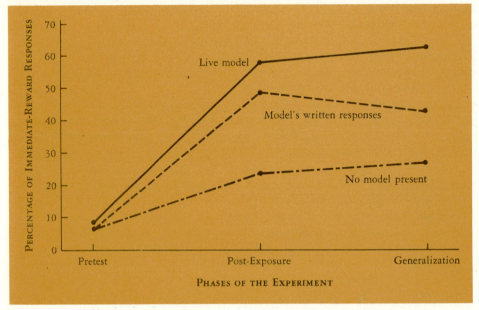

Mean percentage of immediate-reward responses by high-delay children on each of three test periods for each of three experimental conditions. (Adapted from Bandura & Mischel, 1965).

The effects showed some generalization and were maintained in a follow-up one month later.

Coping with Self-Imposed Delay of Gratification

Although choice preferences for immediate or delayed rewards are beginning to be understood, the psychological mechanisms during the delay period remain remarkably unstudied. Given that one has chosen to wait for a larger deferred gratification, how can the delay period be managed?

Theoretical Predictions

Freud (1911) provided one of the few theoretical treatments of how delay of gratification may be bridged. According to the psychoanalytic formulation, ideation arises initially when there is a block or delay in the process of direct gratification (Rapaport, 1967). During such externally imposed delay, according to Freud, the child constructs a "hallucinatory image" of the physically absent, need-satisfying object. This mental image provides fantasy satisfactions (e.g., Freud, 1911; Singer, 1955). But in spite of much psychoanalytic theorizing and speculation about the role of the mental representation of blocked gratifications in the development of delaying capacity, the exact process remains far from clear.

In their theoretical discussion of impulse control, Jones and Gerard (1967) hypothesized that "time-binding" (the capacity to bridge delay of gratification) probably hinges on self-instructional processes through which the individual increases the salience or dominance of the delayed consequences or outcomes of his or her action. In their view, any factors (situational or within the individual) that make delayed consequences more salient should enhance impulse control and voluntary delay. Their position also implies covert "self-reinforcement" processes through which the person may reinforce his or her own waiting behavior by vividly anticipating some of the positive consequences to which it will lead.

A cognitive-developmental view might lead one to expect that cognitively immature young children may more readily forget the delayed outcomes for which they are waiting, and hence cease to wait unless they are reminded of the relevant contingencies and rewards involved in the delay-of-gratification paradigm.

In line with the foregoing arguments, it seems most plausible that conditions that help individuals to attend mentally to the delayed reward for which they are waiting should sustain their ability to wait for it. In that case, any cues that make the delayed gratification more salient—that help persons to make deferred consequences psychologically more vivid or immediate (e.g., by letting them look at them, by visualizing them in imagination, or by reminding them of the object for which they are waiting)—should facilitate waiting behavior.

Such expectations seem congruent with the results of earlier work on choice of immediate, smaller versus delayed but larger rewards (Mahrer, 1956; Mischel & Staub, 1965; Mischel, 1966b, 1974). These earlier studies showed that an important determinant of preference for delayed rewards is the individual's expectation or "trust" that he or she will actually get the delayed (but more valuable) outcome. Consequently, conditions that increase the salience or visibility of the delayed gratification may enhance the person's willingness to wait by increasing subjective confidence that the delayed outcome will materialize and be available after the waiting time ends.

Therefore one might expect that voluntary delay behavior is easier when individuals convert, as it were, the deferred or delayed object into more tangible form by making it psychologically more immediate, as by providing themselves with symbolic representations or physical cues about it. The most direct way to focus attention on the deferred outcomes would be to have them physically present and facing the subjects so that they can attend to them readily and vividly. To investigate how attention to delayed and immediate outcomes influences waiting for them, one study manipulated the availability of those outcomes for attention during the delay time (Mischel & Ebbesen, 1970).

A Method for Observing Waiting Behavior

To study this problem a method was constructed in which very young (preschool) children would be willing to remain in an experimental room, waiting entirely alone for at least a short time without becoming upset and debilitatingly anxious. After the usual play periods for building rapport, each child was taught a "game" in which she could immediately summon the experimenter by a simple signal. This step was practiced repeatedly, until the child clearly understood that she could immediately terminate her waiting period in the room simply by signaling for the experimenter, who regularly returned from outside as soon as the child signaled. Next, the child was introduced to the relevant contingency.

She was shown two objects (e.g., food treats), one of which she clearly preferred (as determined by pretesting). To attain the preferred objects she had to wait for it until the experimenter returned "by himself." The child was, however, entirely free throughout the waiting period to signal at any time for the experimenter to return; if she signaled she could have the less preferred object at once but had to forego the more desirable one.

The Value of Not Thinking

To manipulate the extent to which children could attend to the reward objects while they were waiting, the rewards were removed from the experimental room in all combinations, creating four conditions with respect to the objects available for attention. Examples are shown in Figure 18-3. In one condition, the children waited with both the immediate (less preferred) and the delayed (more preferred) reward facing them in the experimental room so that they could attend to both outcomes. In another group neither reward was available for the subject's attention, both having been removed from sight. In the remaining two groups either the delayed reward only or the im-

FIGURE 18-3
Waiting for Delayed Gratification

From Mischel, Ebbesen, and Zeiss (1972).

FIGURE 18-4
Effects of Attention on Delay of Gratification

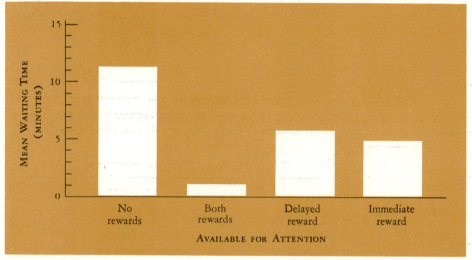

Based on data from Mischel and Ebbesen (1970).

mediate reward only was available for attention while the child waited. The measure was the length of time before each child voluntarily stopped waiting.

The initial theorizing about delay behavior led to predictions of results that were the direct opposite of the obtained findings (shown in Figure 18-4). It was predicted that attention to the outcomes available in the choice situation while waiting would enhance delay behavior; instead it sharply reduced delay of gratification. The children waited longest when no rewards were available for attention.

One of the most striking delay strategies used by some youngsters was exceedingly simple and effective. These children seemed to manage to wait for the preferred reward for long periods apparently by converting the aversive waiting situation into a more pleasant, nonwaiting one. They seemed to do this by elaborate self-distraction techniques through which they spent their time psychologically doing something (almost anything) other than waiting. Rather than focusing prolonged attention on the objects for which they were waiting, they avoided looking at them. Some of these children covered their eyes with their hands, rested their heads on their arms, or found other similar techniques for averting their eyes from the reward objects. Others seemed to try to reduce the frustration of delay of reward by generating their own diversions: They talked to themselves, sang, invented games with their hands and feet, and when all other distractions seemed exhausted, even tried to fall asleep during the waiting situation—as one child successfully did.

These observations suggest that diverting yourself from attention to the delayed reward stimulus (while maintaining behavior directed toward its ultimate attainment) may be a key step in bridging temporal delay of reward. That is, learning *not* to think about what you are awaiting may enhance effective delay of gratification much more than does ideating about the outcomes.

These observations seem consistent with theoretical considerations that focus on the aversiveness of frustration and delayed rewards. If wanting something but not being able to have it is actively aversive, it seems likely that cues that enhance the salience of the desired but still unavailable (delayed) reward should increase the aversiveness of the delay period. In that case, the greater and more vivid the anticipation of reward, the greater the frustration generated by its delay. When hungry, for example, it is easier to wait for supper if one is not confronted with the sight and smell of food.

This line of reasoning would suggest that conditions that decrease people's attention to the blocked reward—and that distract them by internal or overt activity from the frustrative delay of reward—would make it less aversive for them to continue their goal-directed waiting and hence permit them to wait longer for gratifications. In other words, just as cognitive avoidance and "blunting" through self-distraction may facilitate coping with anxiety (as noted in the last chapter) so may it help individuals to cope with other aversive stimuli, such as the frustration of waiting and wanting something that they cannot have yet.

Self-Distraction in Response to Frustration

If these ideas are correct then delay of gratification and frustration tolerance should be enhanced when the person can readily transform the aversive waiting period into a more pleasant, nonwaiting situation. He might do that by converting his attention and thoughts away from the frustrative components of delay of gratification and thinking instead about other things. Such distractions can be achieved if he can engage in activities, overtly or mentally, during the delay period that help him to suppress or decrease cognitively the aversiveness of waiting for the delayed but preferred outcome.

If that is true then voluntary delay of reward should be aided by any overt or covert activities that serve as distractors from the rewards and thus from the aversiveness of wanting them but not having them. Through such distraction the individual should be able to convert the frustrative delay-of-reward situation into a psychologically less aversive condition. Therefore motoric activities and internal cognitions and fantasy that can distract the individual from the rewards potentially available in the situation should increase the length of time that he will delay gratification for the sake of the more valuable reward.

Follow-up studies support this reasoning (Mischel, Ebbesen, & Zeiss, 1972). Children waited much longer for a preferred reward when they were distracted cognitively from the goal objects than when they directly attended to them. Another experiment demonstrated that only certain cognitive events (thinking "fun things") served as effective ideational distractors. Thinking "sad thoughts" produced short delay times similar to thinking about the rewards themselves. In a final experiment the delayed rewards were physically not available for direct attention during the delayed period. The children's attention to the absent rewards was manipulated cognitively by prior instructions.

It was found that cognitions directed toward the rewards while the children waited greatly reduced, rather than enhanced, the length of time that the children were able to delay gratification. Thus attentional and cognitive mechanisms that enhance the salience of the rewards substantially shortened the length of voluntary delay of gratification. In contrast, distractions from the rewards, overtly or cognitively, facilitated waiting for preferred but delayed reinforcement.

The data from these experiments seem to contradict the notion that "will power" requires one to bear up and force oneself to maintain directed attention to things that are aversive, difficult, or boring. Rather than trying to maintain aversive activities such as delay of reward through "acts of will" and focused attention, effective self-control may hinge on *transforming* the difficult into the easy, the aversive into the pleasant, the boring into the interesting, while still maintaining the task-required activity on which the ultimate reward depends.

You can create such transformations either by engaging in the appropriate overt distracting activity or changing your own mental content and ideation. A good way to master the difficult or aversive thus may be to think or do something pleasant while performing the necessary, task-relevant response (e.g., waiting, working). Rather than "willing" oneself to heroic bravery one needs to perform the necessary "difficult" response while engaging in another one cognitively.

Cognitive Transformations and Delay

If the young child is left during the waiting period with the actual reward objects (e.g., pretzels or marshmallows) in front of him, through instructions he can cognitively transform them in many ways that enable him to wait for long time periods (e.g., Mischel & Baker, 1975). If he cognitively transforms the reward stimulus, for example, by thinking about the pretzel sticks in front of him as little brown logs, or by thinking about the marshmallows as round white clouds or as cotton balls, he may wait long and patiently. Conversely, if the child has been instructed to focus cognitively on the arousing (consummatory) qualities of the reward objects, such as the pretzel's crunchy, salty taste or the chewy, sweet, soft taste of the marshmallows, he tends to be able to wait only a short time. Similarly, through instruction the children can easily transform the real objects (present in front of them) into a "color picture in your head," or they can transform the picture of the objects (presented on a slide projected on a screen in front of them) into the "real" objects by pretending in imagination that they are actually there on a plate in front of them (Moore, Mischel, & Zeiss, 1976).

Thus what is in the children's heads—not what is physically in front of them—determines their ability to delay. Regardless of the stimulus in their visual field, if they imagine the real objects as present they cannot wait long for them. But if they imagine pictures (abstract representations) of the objects they can wait for long time periods (and even longer than when they are simply distracting themselves with abstract representations of objects that are comparable but not relevant to the rewards for which they are waiting). Through instructions about what to imagine during the delay period, it is possible to completely alter (even to reverse) the effects of the physically present reward stimuli in the situation, and to cognitively control delay behavior (Mischel & Moore, 1980). But while in experiments the experimenter provides instructions (which the subject often obligingly follows) about how to construe the stimulus situation, in life the "subjects" supply their own instructions and may transform the situation in many alternative ways.

Summary

Taken collectively, research on delay-of-gratification and tolerance for self-imposed frustration suggests a two-part process. First consider the determinants of the *choice* to undergo frustrative delay for the sake of preferred delayed outcomes. This choice is influenced mainly by expectations concerning the probable consequences of the choice. These consequences include the relative subjective values of the immediate and delayed outcomes themselves as well as other probable reinforcing outcomes associated with each alternative. Expectancies about these outcomes depend on direct and vicarious past experiences and trust relationships, modeling cues, the specific contingencies in the choice, and so on (e.g., Mischel, 1966b). So if you really expect to get the delayed reward, and want it, you are more likely to wait for it.

Second, once the choice to self-impose delay of gratification has been made, effective delay depends on cognitive and overt self-distractions to reduce the aversiveness of the self-imposed frustration. For this purpose, the person needs to avoid the goal objects, generating his or her own distractions while maintaining the necessary behavior on which goal-attainment is contingent. An effective way of coping with the frustrations imposed by delay in many life situations is to transform the aversive delay period cognitively into a more positive or interesting experience. This can be achieved by doing something else, overtly or internally, while continuing to wait for the desired goal, or by cognitively transforming the desired goal objects to reduce their excessively arousing qualities. So if you can make the waiting easier for yourself, you are more likely to wait successfully.

The Growth of Self-Control Knowledge

We now know a good deal about what makes it harder or easier for young children to delay gratification. When and how do the children themselves acquire knowledge of the "delay rules" that make waiting less frustrating? For example, does the preschool child know that thinking about the arousing, desirable qualities of the rewards (the pretzel's crunchy taste, for instance) will make self-imposed delay more difficult? Questions of this sort have begun to be explored (e.g., Yates & Mischel, 1979) and the results suggest that children's understanding and knowledge of effective delay rules shows a clear progression in the course of development.

Most children below the age of about four years do not seem to generate clear or effective strategies of delay; indeed they sometimes even make waiting more difficult for themselves by focusing on what they want but cannot have (Mischel, 1981). By the age of five to six years they know that covering the rewards will help them wait for them while looking at the rewards or thinking about them will make it difficult. By third grade children spontaneously generate and reasonably justify a number of potentially viable strategies and clearly understand the basic principles of resistance to temptation. For example, avoid looking at the rewards because: "If I'm looking at them all the time, it will make me hungry. . . and I'd want to ring the bell." Often they also indicate the value of distraction from the rewards, or of negative ideation designed to make them less tempting ("Think about gum stuck all over them"). And by the time they reach sixth grade, children show considerable sophistication, utilizing ideal strategies that allow them to delay gratification with relative ease.

Cognitive Transformations and Stress Reduction

The discussion in this section has focused on voluntary delay of gratification, but the findings fit those from many other areas of self-control. For example, not surprisingly it helps to distract oneself when trying to endure various kinds of pain and stress (e.g., Kanfer & Seidner, 1973). A good deal of related research also leads to the conclusion that self-distraction, when possible, can be an excellent way to reduce unavoidable stresses like unpleasant medical examinations (Miller, 1979, 1980).

People also feel better if they use cognitive transformations to redefine stressful situations in more positive ways (Holmes & Houston, 1974). When stress and pain are inevitable (as in patients awaiting major surgery), the adage to look for the silver lining and to "accentuate the positive" may be wise. In one study, surgical patients were helped to reconstrue their threatening ordeal (Langer, Janis, & Wolfer, 1975). For example, they were encouraged to focus on the hospital experience as an escape from pressure and a "vacation" with a chance to relax, and were given other similar techniques for emphasizing the positive side. These patients tended to cope better with their traumas, seeming to experience less stress and requesting fewer pain relievers and sedatives.

Self-Reactions and Self-Regulation

People judge and evaluate their own behavior and reward and punish themselves. In the typical animal laboratory the organisms perform, and the experimenter or her apparatus reinforces them at predetermined points. Unlike the animals in the researcher's laboratory, people exert considerable control over the rewarding and punishing resources available to them. They congratulate themselves for their own characteristics and actions; they praise or abuse their own achievements; and they self-administer social and material rewards and punishments from the enormous array freely available to them.

A critical aspect of self-regulation thus stems from the fact that people assess and monitor themselves. Self-praise and censure, self-imposed treats and punishments, self-indulgence and self-laceration are manifestations of this pervasive human tendency to congratulate and condemn oneself. Learning research with animals generally was focused on the effects of environmentally or externally administered reinforcers. Much less is known about the processes through which persons learn to set their own performance standards and to make their own self-reward contingent upon their achieving these self-prescribed criteria. To adequately understand human social behavior, we must know how the person self-administers and regulates rewards and punishments that are in her own control (e.g., Masters & Mokros, 1974).

Studying Self-Reinforcement

To investigate self-reward and self-punishment, a method has been developed in which subjects (usually grade-school children) work on a performance task that seemingly requires skill (e.g., Bandura & Kupers, 1964). They have free access to a large supply of rewards (e.g., assorted candies, tokens exchangeable for prizes, small toys, and desirable trinkets). The experiments are designed so that the child's information about his level or quality of performance can be manipulated readily. For example, many of these studies use a realistic looking electronic bowling game on which the child bowls and receives feedback in the form of scores automatically illuminated on a display panel. The scores may be programmed by the experimenter so that the child gets fixed, predetermined feedback although he thinks the scores reflect his real performance.

Effects of Models

One study, for example, tested the hypothesis that patterns of self-reinforcement are acquired imitatively (Bandura & Kupers, 1964). Children in one group observed either peer or adult models who adopted a high criterion for self-reinforcement during a bowling game like the one described. In this condition the model praised and rewarded his performance (by helping himself to freely available treats) only when his bowling scores were high. When the model's scores were low he refrained from self-reward. In a second group children were exposed to models who exhibited a similar pattern of self-reward and self-disapproval except that these models adopted a relatively low criterion. Children in a control group observed no models. Tests of self-reward after exposure to the models revealed that the children's reinforcement patterns closely matched those of the model they had observed.

Figure 18-5 shows the children's self-reward when they achieved low, mod-

FIGURE 18-5
Self-Reinforcement at Each Performance Level by Control Children and Those Exposed to Adults Modeling High and Low Standards for Self-Reward

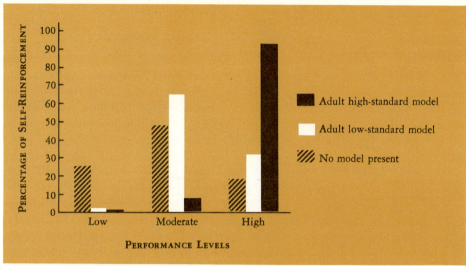

Adapted from Bandura and Kupers (1964).

erate, and high performance levels for bowling in each condition. Note that the children who initially were exposed to high-standard adults are the ones who later made their own self-reinforcement almost always contingent on high levels of performance. In contrast, children who had observed low-standard models, or no models, were relatively more casual and lenient in their self-reinforcement; they treated themselves generously even after moderate or mediocre achievements. Another part of the same study showed that adults generally served as more powerful models than peers in the transmission of self-reinforcing patterns.

In this and similar studies children's self-reward behavior was observed after exposure to the experimental treatments under conditions that led them to think they were all alone. In fact, the children were watched through a one-way mirror while they performed alone. The reason for providing the subjects with ostensible privacy is to assure that their performance does not merely reflect social pressure and "demands" from the experimenter. That is, the final testing conditions must be dissociated from the experimenter and their implicit demands if the person's behavior is to be taken as an index of his or her "internalized" standards (e.g., Aronfreed, 1968).

Under these conditions of privacy external constraints were minimal and the children could indulge themselves freely in self-gratification. However, they did not simply help themselves to all the rewards they could get; instead, they regulated their own behavior. The manner of self-regulation depended on numerous factors and especially on immediately prior observation of the standards employed by other people. It also has been shown that the modeled standards may persist and generalize: Children continue to set higher standards for themselves even in new situations several weeks after observing a high-standard model (Lepper, Sagotsky, & Mailer, 1975).

Do As I Say or Do As I Do?

How does the relationship between the standards that the socialization agent practices and those that he "preaches" to the child affect his impact on the child's subsequent self-control? Take, for example, the common case of the parent who tries to instill self-control in his child while he himself models self-indulgence. Consider the father who regularly urges his son to study hard while he himself lounges in front of the television set. When researchers refer to "consistency" in child-rearing practices they usually mean consistency in direct training techniques across different situations; almost no attention has been given to the effects of consistency or discrepancy between direct training and modeling procedures. When an adult model acts one way himself but imposes oppposite demands on the child, how will the child act afterwards when he is on his own: Will he do what the model did himself or what the model asked him to do? To investigate this question, Mischel and Liebert (1966) studied the effects of discrepancies in the stringency of the self-reward standards used by an adult and the criteria she imposed on a child.

In this study children participated with a female adult model in a task (the bowling game) that seemingly required skill but on which scores were experimentally controlled. Both the model and the subject had free access to a large supply of tokens that could be exchanged later for attractive rewards and prizes. In one condition, the model rewarded herself only for high performances but guided the subject to reward himself for lower achievements; in a second condition the model rewarded herself for low performances but led the subject to reward himself only for high achievements; in the third group the model rewarded herself only for high performances and guided the child to reward himself only for equally high achievements. After exposure to these experimental procedures the children's self-reward patterns displayed in the model's absence were observed and scored through a one-way mirror.

When the observed and imposed criteria were consistent they later were adopted and maintained readily by all children. The experiment illustrated that self-reactions are affected jointly by the criteria displayed by social models and the standards directly imposed on the child. The children's self-reward patterns were determined by a predictable interaction of both observational and direct training processes. As Figure 18-6 indicates, when the modeled and imposed standards were consistently high, the children adopted them uniformly. When they were inconsistent, the children who had been allowed to be lenient (although the model was stringent) all remained lenient. Those who had been trained to be stringent by a model who herself was lenient seemed conflicted, and about half of them remained stringent and half became lenient.

FIGURE 18-6
Self-Reward and Reward of Other Child, As a Function of the Initial Criteria Exhibited by the Model and Imposed on the Subject

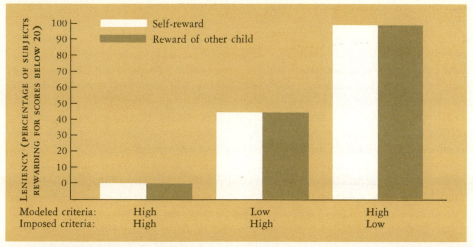

Adapted from Mischel and Leibert (1966).

Finally, in a posttest the children demonstrated the game to a younger child, still in the absence of external constraints and of the experimenter herself. It was found that the children consistently both demonstrated and imposed on their peers the same standards that they had adopted for themselves, hence transmitting their own learned self-reward criteria to others.

Compensation, Self-Congratulation, and Mood

Often self-reward seems to be a congratulatory reaction contingent on successful performance or attainment of adequate achievements, as in the previously discussed studies. Self-gratification also appears, however, under opposite circumstances, namely following painful failure or stress experiences. Not uncommonly, persons seem to become more generous with themselves after failure or other unhappy experiences, and indulge themselves with extra gratifications whose primary function may be to reduce the aversiveness of the prior unpleasant experiences. Such self-indulgence seems to have a therapeutic rather than a self-congratulatory effect.

When people think that they are doing well on a task they generally reward themselves more generously than when they believe that their performance is less meritorious (e.g., Kanfer & Phillips, 1970; Kanfer & Marston, 1963a,b). As expected, success on a task tends to increase self-reward on it and failure tends to lower self-reward for one's performance. But how do such success and failure experiences influence later, *noncontingent* self-gratification, that is, self-gratification in a domain that is objectively irrelevant to the initial success or failure?

If a person has experienced failure at work, for example, he might continue to recriminate himself later at home and self-punitively deprive himself of readily available pleasures. Or, instead, he might become more self-indulgent at home, engaging in self-therapeutic efforts to reduce the aversiveness of the earlier work failure. Similarly, after a successful achievement, the individual might feel more generally deserving and become more self-indulgent and generous to himself. Alternatively, some psychodynamically oriented theories might suggest that after success a person should have less need for gratification (and greater frustration tolerance) and would therefore become less self-indulgent.

To study the role of these emotional experiences in the self-regulation of gratification, one experiment investigated how success and failure experiences in an achievement activity affect subsequent self-gratification in a new non-achievement situation (Mischel, Coates, & Raskoff, 1968). In the new situation success was no issue; instead the child was able to indulge himself freely and noncontingently, as long as he wanted to do so and as generously as he wished. Specifically, grade-school children were led to believe that they had either succeeded or failed repeatedly in the bowling game. Just as in the earlier studies, the game seemed to require skill, but actually the scores were controlled electronically by the experimenter without the children's awareness. In one group children were led to believe that their bowling achievements were excellent while another group failed and a third (control) received no scores.

The main question was how these success and failure experiences would affect self-gratification in a new situation that permitted the children to indulge themselves freely and *noncontingently* with reinforcers. The new situation was an exceedingly simple activity structured to be so easy that all children could do it readily. The reinforcers were huge supplies of tokens that could be exchanged for attractive treats and that were available noncontingently so that the children could help themselves to as many as they wished. To minimize inhibitions each child was left entirely alone, although his behavior was observed through a one-way mirror.

After failure there was no significant self-therapeutic compensating or self-consolation through greater indulgence, nor was there self-deprivation of the available resources (Figure 18-7). The children who had a failure experience seemed to be able to separate it psychologically from the new and different maze task and were not statistically different from those who had received no scores at all for performance on the bowling game. The main effect, instead, was that children who had a successful experience later tended to become more generous and indulgent with themselves, gratifying themselves more than did subjects who had failed and those who had no performance feedback. Feeling strongly positive and "glowing with success" (Isen, 1970), the youngsters seem to have celebrated by helping themselves more generously to freely available, noncontingent gratifications.

Related research has shown the importance of the person's momentary emotional state not only for one's self-reactions but also for one's reactions to

FIGURE 18-7
Noncontingent Self-Gratification after Success and Failure

From sequential condition in Mischel, Coates, and Raskoff (1968).

others. Whether one feels good or bad, happy or sad, influences such diverse actions as generosity and charitability to other people as well as to oneself. Specifically, positive feelings tend to encourage greater generosity (e.g., Isen, Horn, & Rosenhan, 1973) and altruism (e.g., Rosenhan, Moore, & Underwood, 1976) as well as greater noncontingent self-gratification (e.g., Mischel, Coates, & Raskoff, 1968; Moore, Underwood, & Rosenhan, 1973). Such feelings also influence what we remember (Isen et al., 1978; Mischel, Ebbesen, & Zeiss, 1976). For example, when we are happy we are more likely to recall good (positive) information about ourselves.

The Variety of Self-Reactions

The work discussed so far in this chapter merely provided some selected examples from the large number of investigations that have dealt with the many aspects of self-reactions and self-control. Such researches are much too numerous to be even listed here comprehensively. They included, for example, experiments on the determinants of self-criticism (e.g., Aronfreed, 1968; Grusec, 1966), resistance to temptation (e.g., Burton, Maccoby, & Allinsmith, 1961; Mischel & Gilligan, 1964), and conscience and guilt after transgression (e.g., Grinder, 1964), as well as many other aspects of self-regulation (e.g., Kanfer, 1980; Meichenbaum, 1977; Thoresen & Mahoney, 1974).

Control of Visceral and Glandular Responses

Most work on personality and self-control has focused on the control of motoric and verbal behaviors—such as voluntary actions and choices. Through the application of reinforcement principles it also may be possible to achieve substantial control of autonomic responses, such as the "involuntary" glandular and visceral responses involved in emotion (Miller, 1969) and of the electrical waves that accompany brain activity (Stoyva & Kamiya, 1968).

Indeed, laboratory explorations with animals indicate that such supposedly involuntary bodily responses as salivation, kidney functions, stomach contractions, blood volume in the periphery of the body, heart rate, and brain waves all can be significantly affected by making reinforcement contingent upon increases or decreases in those responses. Some representative findings with animals are summarized in Figure 18-8.

As the figure shows, reward contingent on specific body changes affected those changes predictably. For example, reward for intestinal contractions increased the contractions, while reward for intestinal relaxation decreased them. The effects were highly specific, so that reward for intestinal contraction or relaxation did not affect heart rate. Conversely, heart rate was changed by rewarding increases or decreases in heart rate, but it was not influenced by rewarding changes in intestinal contractions. The implications of these findings are exciting for future forms of therapy directed at alleviating all sorts of emotional and psychosomatic problems. But as Miller (1969) has said, it is too early to promise any cures.

FIGURE 18-8
Modification of Intestinal Contraction and Heart Rate

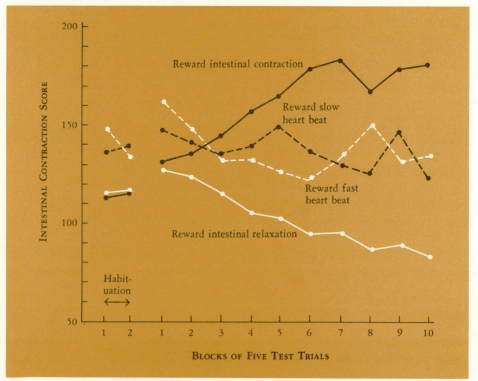

Graph showing that the intestinal contraction score is changed by rewarding either increases or decreases in intestinal contractions but is unaffected by rewarding changes in heart rate.

FIGURE 18-8 (*cont.*)

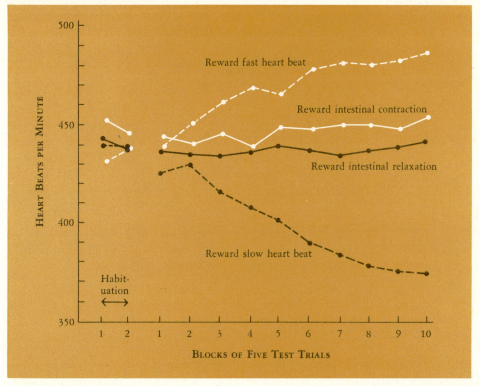

Graph showing that the heart rate is changed by rewarding either increases or decreases in heart rate but is unaffected by rewarding changes in intestinal contractions. (From Miller & Banuazizi, 1968.)

Biofeedback and Electric Zen?

In some human investigations of the same phenomenon, the individual is made aware of her own bodily responses (for example, by observing an ongoing recording of her brain waves). If she gets appropriate immediate feedback about changes in these responses she may learn to control them voluntarily (Kamiya, 1967), perhaps in a manner similar to that employed by Zen masters and mystics in their practice of self-control of bodily activities. Studies of this type suggest the possibility that people may be able to achieve far greater control over themselves and their own bodily states than usually has been believed. If individuals can learn and apply appropriate self-reinforcement and feedback principles to themselves they may be able to achieve mastery over many aspects of their being, including their physiological state.

The name adopted for human laboratory applications based on the foregoing operant conditioning research is "biofeedback." In the example illustrated in Figure 18-9, the subject receives biofeedback about her brain rhythms. A tone tells her when she achieves certain distinctive brain waves,

FIGURE 18-9
Example of Biofeedback

In this application, electrodes on the scalp monitor brain waves (EEG) shown on the polygraph console. The waves are filtered and converted into a tone. The subject receives continuous immediate feedback about her brain waves through the tones transmitted in the earphones.

such as those found in deep meditation. With increasing practice one may more easily achieve desired internal states, guided by feedback about one's physiological condition.

There are some fascinating parallels between the efforts to achieve control of internal bodily responses through biofeedback (and "operant conditioning") on the one hand and, on the other hand, the attempts of mystics (including those influenced by Zen, Yoga, and other "esoteric" traditions) to get into closer contact with their bodily states and internal "signals." Both strategies involve observing (monitoring) one's own inner states and changing them through some internal, and perhaps indescribable, effort. Ornstein (1972, pp. 195-196) compares the two strategies this way:

> There are, now, two major procedures available for contacting the weak signals within. In the esoteric traditions, one tries to turn off the competing activity, to turn day into night, so that the subtle signals are perceptible. In the newly developed feedback system, the "stars" are brought to consciousness by another method. The faint signals *themselves* are amplified, to make them perceptible even in the brilliance of the daylight. In the esoteric traditions, the "noise" is lessened; in biofeedback research, the "signal" is strengthened. In both cases, when these normally unconscious processes enter consciousness, we can receive this subtle information, and can learn to control what was previously an "unconscious" or "autonomic" process.

These parallels are intriguing. But it must be emphasized that although some popular reports "have given the impression that Electric Zen is just around the corner for all, this prophecy will be fulfilled only (if at all) after years of research" (Ornstein, 1972, p. 196). Similar cautions are being sounded by many other researchers who warn that the therapeutic benefit of biofeedback is still more of a promise than a fact (e.g., Blanchard & Young, 1973; Schwartz, 1973).

Controls as Traits

So far this chapter has examined experimental research on some of the conditions that determine self-control and self-reactions. In self-regulation, as in most other forms of behavior, great differences exist among individuals. As part of the long-standing tradition of examining individual differences on personality dimensions, many psychologists have studied self-regulatory behaviors as indices of traits. They have tried to relate these scores to other aspects of behavior (using the methods of construct validity discussed in Chapter 7).

Ego-Control and Ego-Resiliency

Two constructs are especially important for understanding individual differences in self-regulation, both as traits and as reflections of psychodynamics. These are the constructs of ego-control and ego-resiliency (Block & Block, 1980). *Ego-control* refers to the degree of impulse control in such functions as delay of gratification, inhibition of aggression, and planfulness. The second construct, *ego-resiliency,* refers to the individual's ability to adapt to environmental demands by appropriately modifying his or her habitual level of ego-control, thus functioning with some "elasticity." Together, these two constructs represent the core qualities of "ego" from a broadly psychodynamic perspective.

In studies with children, a number of experimental tasks have been developed to measure these two constructs. For example, to study individual differences in children's patterns of ego-control, the adequacy and type of ego-control were inferred from ratings of the children's tendency to inhibit impulses as well as from observations of their delay behavior in experimental situations (Block & Martin, 1955). The children also were exposed to a frustration similar to the one in the classic Barker, Dembo, and Lewin research (described in Chapter 15) in which a barrier separated the child from desired and expected toys. The "undercontrolling" children (those who had been rated as not inhibiting their impulses) reacted more violently to the frustrating barrier than did "overcontrolling," inhibited children. The undercontrolling youngsters also showed a greater decrement in their level of play constructiveness after being frustrated.

Individual differences in ego control also have been inferred from indirect measures such as responses to inkblots on the Rorschach test (e.g., Singer, 1955; Spivack, Levine, & Sprigle, 1959). Individuals who are high (rather than low) on such indices of ego control tend to be somewhat more able to control and inhibit their motoric activity; for example, they may be able to sit still longer or draw a line more slowly without lifting their pencil. These are only a few examples from much larger, meaningful networks of correlations that have been obtained to support the ego-control construct for many years (Block & Block, 1980).

In studies of the ego-resiliency construct, toddlers were evaluated for the degree to which they seemed secure and for their degree of competence (in a problem-solving task). The toddlers who were secure and competent also scored higher on measures of ego-resiliency when they reached the age of four to five years (Gove and associates, 1979; Matas, Arend, & Sroufe, 1978). As another example, ego-resilient children at age three years are also viewed as popular, interesting, and attractive a year later (Block & Block, 1980). A large network of associations like these, found with many measures over long periods of childhood, suggests that both the concepts of ego-control and ego-resiliency may offer useful characterizations of important individual differences.

Delay of Gratification

The beginning of this chapter discussed the determinants of delay of gratification found in experimental research. Delay of gratification has also been conceptualized as a personality trait (and part of the ego-control construct) on which individuals differ. The correlates of those differences have been studied (as was discussed in Chapter 7), yielding many relationships between preferences for immediate, smaller, or delayed, larger rewards and other theoretically relevant behaviors.

Two contrasting patterns of delay and impulsivity have been conceptualized as extreme poles (e.g., Mischel, 1974). On one end is the individual who predominantly chooses larger, delayed rewards or goals for which he must either wait or work. This person is more likely to be oriented toward the future (Klineberg, 1968) and to plan carefully for distant goals. He also is apt to have high scores on "ego control" measures, high achievement motivation, to be more trusting and socially responsible, to have a high level of aspiration, and to show less uncontrolled impulsivity. This extreme pattern resembles what has been called the "Puritan character structure." Socioculturally, this pattern tends to be found most often in middle and upper (in contrast to lower) socioeconomic classes, and in highly achievement-oriented ("Protestant Ethic") cultures. This pattern of high ego strength is also related to a relatively high level of competence, as revealed by higher intelligence, more mature cognitive development, and a greater capacity for sustained attention (Grim, Kohlberg, & White, 1968).

At the opposite extreme is the individual who predominantly prefers immediate gratification and declines the alternative of waiting or working for larger, delayed goals. Correlated with this is a greater concern with the immediate present than with the future, and greater impulsivity. Socioculturally, this pattern is correlated with membership in the lower socioeconomic classes, with membership in cultures in which the achievement orientation is low, and with indices of lesser social and cognitive competence.

In their extreme forms, both these patterns might be "maladaptive": the former might characterize an emotionally constricted person whose gratifications are perpetually postponed, and the latter, an impulsive person who does not behave in accord with long-term goals and who is not cognizant of the ultimate consequences of his present actions. Clinically, persons diagnosed as "delinquents" and "psychopaths" are often characterized by an immediate reward choice pattern (Shybut, 1968).

The foregoing polarity of gratification patterns has some descriptive value. It is limited, however, by the fact that self-control patterns tend to be highly discriminative. For example, Trinidadian lower-class subjects rarely chose to wait for promised delayed rewards. Instead they usually preferred immediately available, albeit smaller, gratifications (Mischel, 1958, 1961a). In their past experiences promises of future rewards had often been broken, and these people had participated in a culture in which immediate gratification was modeled and reward extensively (Mischel, 1961b,c). Nevertheless, the same people saved money, planned elaborately, and were willing to give up competing immediate gratifications in order to plan ahead for such future rewards as annual feasts, religious events, and carnival celebrations.

On the other hand, there also is a growing body of evidence that when self-control behaviors are studied comprehensively, with enough good measures, coherent, meaningful patterns tend to emerge (Block, 1977; Block & Block, 1980). These patterns suggest that there are significant threads of continuity in basic ego functions. The nature and meaning of these continuities is open to different interpretations (Epstein, 1980; Mischel, 1980). But it is increasingly evident that important individual differences in ego functions exist, and they are characterized both by stability and by change, both by coherences and by discriminativeness.

Perceived Locus of Control

People also differ in the degree to which they believe that they have self-control and feel personally responsible for what happens to them. According to Rotter (1966) such perceptions involve a dimension of "perceived locus of control" (also called "internal-external control of reinforcement"). *Internal control* refers to "the perception of positive and/or negative events as being a consequence of one's own actions and thereby under personal control" (Lefcourt, 1966, p. 207). Conversely, *external control* refers to the "perception of positive and/or negative events as being unrelated to one's own behaviors" (Lefcourt, 1966, p. 207) and hence beyond personal control. Individual differences on this

External control refers to the belief that events are unrelated to one's own behavior.

internal-external control dimension have been measured by a questionnaire that has yielded many correlates (e.g., Phares, 1978; Phares, Ritchie, & Davis, 1968; Rotter, 1966, 1975). For example, more intelligent people tend to perceive more outcomes as under their own control, presumably because they in fact can control their fate better than can less competent individuals.

People often react quite differently to situations in which the pay-offs or outcomes seem to involve luck or chance and those that, instead, appear to depend on their own skill. Many variables may affect whether or not an individual will attribute responsibility to herself for the outcomes that she encounters. For example, people attribute causality to internal sources more for success outcomes than for failure outcomes: They tend to credit success to themselves but to blame failure on external conditions (Fitch, 1970).

Internal-external control may not be a single dimension. For example, it is helpful to distinguish between perceived locus of control at the *personal* (self) and *ideological* (social system) levels (Lao, 1970). Thus among Black college students in the deep South, an "internal" belief in personal control (that is, attributing responsibility for personal outcomes to the self) was positively related to general competence. However, an "external" belief in social ideology (that is, blaming the "system" rather than the self for the Blacks' disadvantages in society) was related positively to creative, innovative behavior. As Lao noted, it is not always desirable and adaptive for the individual to believe in internal control and to blame himself. She reports that Black students who can focus on "system obstacles" (societal barriers and racial discrimination) seem to be more realistic in their assessment of the situation, and they are more likely to select innovative occupational roles and social action.

Perceived locus of control may be of special theoretical importance because it seems to influence how people may react to many situations (Lefcourt, 1972, 1980; Phares, 1973). We saw that reactions to stress seem to be affected by whether or not individuals believe they can control the stress stimuli (that is, prevent or terminate pain), as was discussed in Chapter 16. Perceived control over impending aversive stimuli appears to affect whether a person will react by cognitively avoiding them or by becoming vigilantly alert to them (Chapter 17).

Moral Behavior and the Superego

Another aspect of self-control whose consistency has been carefully studied is "moral behavior." A classic investigation more than 40 years ago exposed thousands of children to a host of situations in which they could cheat, lie, and steal in many settings, including the home, party games, and athletic contests (Hartshorne & May, 1928). The children were fairly consistent in their self-reported thoughts and opinions about moral issues when they were questioned in their classrooms. The correlations among various forms of these paper-and-pencil tests also tended to be relatively high. But when different forms of the tests were administered in diverse social settings (such as lying at home, cheating in Sunday school, stealing at club meetings, being dishonest in the classroom), the correlations were much lower. The more the situation was altered the more inconsistent the youngsters' moral behavior became.

Hartshorne and May did not suggest capriciousness in behavior. They recognized beyond-chance consistencies, but they stressed the relative specificity of responses and their dependence on the exact particulars fo the evoking situation.

> It may be contended of course that as a matter of fact we rarely reach a zero correlation, no matter how different may be our techniques, and that this implies some such common factor in the individual as might properly be called a trait. We would not wish to quarrel over the use of a term and are quite ready to recognize the existence of some common factors which tend to make individuals differ from one another on any one test or on any group of tests. Our contention, however, is that this common factor is not an inner entity operating independently of the situations in which the individuals are placed but is a function of the situation in the sense that an individual behaves similarly in different situations in proportion as these situations are alike, have been experienced as common occasions for honest or dishonest behavior, and are comprehended as opportunities for deception or honesty (Hartshorne & May, 1928, p. 385).

Burton (1963) reanalyzed some of the Hartshorne and May data from their most reliable tests of resistance to temptation. Often the resulting reanalysis has been cited as if it were evidence for the consistency of moral behavior. But Burton's reanalysis revealed no errors in the original work; it only reconstrued the same correlations in a way that emphasized the moderate (but statistically significant) consistencies that were found in the original study. Thus a person's moral behaviors across diverse situations are not totally unrelated (i.e., random), but they are far from consistent.

Hartshorne and May's finding of relative specificity in moral behavior fore-shadowed the results of later research. Since Hartshorne and May, most research on self-control and moral behavior has focused on three areas: moral judgment and verbal standards of right and wrong (e.g., Kohlberg, 1963); resistance to temptation in the absence of external constraints (e.g., Aronfreed, 1968); and feeling guilty after transgression (e.g., Allinsmith, 1960; Sears, Maccoby, & Levin, 1957). Behaviors across these three areas of morality are only minimally interrelated (e.g., Becker, 1964; Hoffman, 1963; Kohlberg, 1964). Moreover, within each subtype of morality, specificity again tends to be high, so that what a person does on one moral task is not necessarily related to what he or she does on another one (e.g., Aronfreed, 1968; Sears, Rau, & Alpert, 1965).

In sum, the data on self-control and moral behavior do not support the existence of a unitary, intrapsychic moral agency like the superego, not do they suggest a unitary trait of conscience or honesty. Rather than a homogeneous conscience that determines all aspects of self-control, people seem to develop subtler discriminations that depend on many conditions. Self-control patterns and moral actions as well as immoral ones are affected by the same discrimination learning that influences other forms of behavior (such as anxiety and cognitive avoidance) considered in earlier chapters.

People as Moral Philosophers

In addition to learning diverse forms of overt self-control, people also differ in their ideas and attitudes about justice, right and wrong, and the nature of conscience. Under the influence of Jean Piaget's studies of cognitive development in children, Kohlberg (1963) has studied these individual differences, focusing on the child as a "moral philosopher" who constructs theories about morality.

Influenced by Piaget's cognitive developmental stages, Kohlberg has hypothesized three levels of moral thinking (preconventional, conventional, and postconventional). He further suggests that each of the three levels contains two related stages. These six hypothesized stages of cognitive development are summarized in Table 18-1.

Kohlbeg believes that these six moral stages follow a developmental progression that is a function of increasing cognitive maturaton. While social experience may affect the rate of progress across stages, he believes that the nature of the sequence is fundamentally the same even in such widely different

TABLE 18-1
MORAL LEVELS AND DEVELOPMENTAL STAGES
ACCORDING TO KOHLBERG (1963, 1967)

Preconventional Level	STAGE 1: Orientation toward punishment. Deference to superior power. Goodness or badness is determined by the physical consequences of action.
	STAGE 2: Right actions are those that satisfy needs (mainly one's own needs). People share but in a pragmatic way, not out of a sense of justice or loyalty.
Conventional Level	STAGE 3: "Good boy–good girl orientation." Behavior that pleases or helps others and is approved by them is good behavior. Emphasis on conformity and on being "nice" to gain approval.
	STAGE 4: Focus on authority, fixed rules, and the social order. Right behavior consists of maintaining the given social order for its own sake. Respect is earned by performing dutifully.
Postconventional Level	STAGE 5: "Social contract orientation"—legalistic, utilitarian. Standards that have been agreed upon by the whole society define right action. Emphasis upon procedural (legal) rules for reaching consensus. Awareness of the relativism of personal values.
	STAGE 6: Emphasis on decisions of conscience and self-chosen, abstract ethical principles that are "logical, comprehensive, universal, and consistent." These abstract ethical principles are universal principles of justice, of reciprocity and equality of human rights, and of respect for the dignity of human beings as individuals.

cultures as the U.S., Taiwan, Mexico, Turkey, and Yucatan. A person's stage position is inferred from the kind of reasoning displayed on a moral judgment scale that presents a number of moral dilemmas.

Kohlberg (1968) argues for moral stages with many intriguing cases. For example, he cites the answers of a boy, Tommy, to the question, "Is it better to save the life of one important person or a lot of unimportant people?" At age 10, Tommy's answer seems to confuse the value of a human being with the value of the property that he owns. Thus he answers that he would save the many unimportant people because they might have more furniture and even more money collectively, although "it doesn't look it." At age 13, Tommy's answers start to show the characteristics of Stage 2, and gradually (at age 16) his orientation is closer to Stage 3.

A person's moral reasoning typically does not fit any one stage exclusively. As Kohlberg (1969, p. 387, Fig. 6.4) reports, on the average somewhat less than 50 percent of a subject's moral judgments fit a single stage, the remainder being distributed in the stages both above and below his most frequent one. Similarly, Bandura and McDonald (1963, p. 280) found that children from ages 5 to 11 years used different types of moral reasoning simultaneously. Among college students "not one of the subjects studied employed moral reasoning that was exclusively rated at any single level of development" (Fishkin and colleagues, 1973, p. 114).

Kohlberg's hypotheses will need much more research before final conclusions can be reached. Of special importance will be the relationship between a person's moral orientation and her moral behavior and other forms of self-control and social responsibility. Kohlberg suggests that people who "understand justice" act more justly. That point seems most reasonable in the abstract. However, the exact relations between moral thought and moral action merit much further empirical study and generally the associations that have been found are not high (Mischel & Mischel, 1976). A critical review of the total research within Kohlberg's approach and of his scale for assessing moral judgment concluded: ". . . There are *no* reported reliability estimates for the scale itself. . . . There is no clearly demonstrated connection between moral judgment, as measured by the Moral Judgment Scale, and moral action." (Kurtines & Greif, 1974, p. 468). One waits for future research to fill in some of the many gaps in our understanding of moral reasoning and its links to moral action.

How people reason about the solution of moral dilemmas is fascinating and age-related changes in this activity are especially informative. But an interest in moral reasoning does not reduce the need to understand the many other aspects and determinants of moral (and immoral) behavior. Alston (1971, p. 283), a philosopher, commenting on Kohlberg's position, puts it this way:

> . . . there is no reason to think that it [Kohlberg's moral stage assignments] will do the whole job. In fact, there is every reason to think that it will not. So long as there is any significant discrepancy between the moral judgment a person makes about a situation (or would make if the question arose) and what he actually does, there will be a need, in describing persons, for an account of what they are likely to do as well as what they are likely to think. And Kohlberg has given us no reason to suppose that there is no such significant discrepancy.

Generally, different measures of ideology, beliefs, and attitudes tend to be more closely related to each other than to what the person actually does in the same content area (Abelson, 1972; Mischel, 1968), although under some conditions clear connections may emerge (Zanna, 1981). This also seems to hold in the domain of morality, in which indices of moral ideology tend to relate well to other measures of social and political beliefs. For example, it is reassuring (but not particularly surprising) to find that a student responding to Kohlberg's moral dilemmas test with reasons involving principles of equality, the universality of all moral formulations, and concern with the issue of justice (thereby earning a Stage 6 score) would be unlikely to agree with a slogan such as "The best place for women in the [civil rights movement] is prone" (Fishkin et al., 1973). Similarly unsurprising, the same study found that individuals who dominantly justify their moral decisions in terms of law and order are less likely to endorse such slogans as "kill the pigs," "property is theft," and "turn on, tune in, and drop out." Such internal consistencies in belief statements were demonstrated by high correlations between moral reasoning that emphasizes law and order and a conservative opposition to radical violence on an ideology scale. These data provide further support for the well-established conclusion that answers to measures of political and social ideology tend to be consistent.

But while cognitive measures of beliefs and values may be both internally consistent and temporally enduring (E. L. Kelly, 1955), it is the link between them and behavior that remains tenuous (e.g., Abelson, 1972; Festinger, 1964; Kurtines & Greif, 1974). Sometimes the link is found, but often it is not. Therefore we should be alert to the fact that the same individual who espouses high moral principles also may engage in harmful, aggressive actions against others who violate his conceptions of justice. Pascal's comment, "evil is never done so thoroughly or so well as when it is done with a good conscience" is supported by the many historical and contemporary incidents in which the individuals who committed evil deeds seemed more deficient in compassion and empathy than in moral reasoning.

History is full of atrocities that were justified by invoking the highest principles and that were perpetrated upon victims who were equally convinced of their own moral principles. In the name of justice, of the common welfare, of universal ethics, and of God, millions of people have been killed and whole cultures destroyed. In recent history, concepts of universal right, equality, freedom, and national security have been used to justify every variety of crime including murder. Presidential assassinations, airplane hijackings, and massacres of Olympic athletes have been committed for allegedly selfless motives of highest morality and principle. The supreme moral self-sacrifices of the Japanese suicide pilots in World War II were perceived as moral outrages by others who did not share their perspective.

People may easily justify their own actions and commitments no matter how reprehensible they may seem to others. A wide variety of self-deceptive mechanisms may be used to facilitate and excuse the most horrendous acts.

Invocation of higher principles, dehumanization of victims, diffusion and displacement of responsibility, blame attribution, and the adoption of inhumane codes for self-reinforcement all may serve to maintain extraordinarily cruel aggressions (Bandura, 1973).

Hazards in Categorizing "Good" and "Bad" People

The extremely complex relations among diverse aspects of self-control within the same person, and the specific interactions between human conduct and the psychological conditions in which it occurs, prevent global generalizations about the "overall" nature and causes of moral—and immoral—actions. It is tempting but misleading to categorize people into the cross-situationally moral versus the broadly immoral. A world of good guys versus bad guys, as in the Western films in which the cowboys' white or black hats permit easy identification of the virtuous and the villainous, is seductive. More sophisticated social science versions of stratification systems that categorize people in terms of their overall level of morality, "ego strength," or "moral competence," unless carefully moderated, can lead to an elitism that is scientifically unjustified as well as socially hazardous (Mischel & Mischel, 1976). While it may be useful for some purposes to label and assess people's status on our dimensions of character and moral value, perhaps the greatest challenge to social science will be to discover the optimal conditions that can help people realize themselves in the ways they construe as best within the great range of capacities potentially open to them.

SUMMARY

1. People learn to evaluate and control their own behavior and act in the light of future-oriented considerations. There have been many approaches to these processes. Some studies on self-control have explored the determinants of the individual's willingness to delay immediate, smaller gratification for the sake of delayed but larger rewards and goals. The person's subjective expectations concerning the outcome of his choice influence his willingness to select delayed rather than immediate gratification. Will the delayed rewards for which one postpones immediate satisfaction actually materialize? Will they be worthwhile? Will one be able to earn them? A person's answers to these questions depend partly on his or her past history and on relevant social models. For example, after children were exposed to the patterns of delayed or immediate gratification displayed by social models, their own choices changed in accord with the preferences they had observed.

2. What are the psychological mechanisms through which persons can delay gratification for the sake of preferred but delayed outcomes? When young children attended to the available outcomes while waiting they were less able to wait for them. Thus under some conditions *not* thinking about the desired outcomes seems to enhance effective delay behavior. Delay of gratification may be helped by cognitive and overt self-distractions to reduce the aversiveness of waiting.

3. In the course of development, children acquire knowledge of effective rules for delay of gratification so that they can increasingly engage in the self-distractions and cognitive activities that make waiting less frustrating.

4. Another pervasive feature of human social behavior is the self-administration and regulation of rewards and punishments. Persons learn to set their own performance standards and to make their self-reward contingent upon achievement of the self-prescribed criteria. Children's patterns of self-reward are influenced by the models whom they have observed, as well as by standards imposed on them through direct training. Self-reward patterns are also affected by the individual's immediately prior experience. For example, achieving success in one setting may influence later self-gratification in a different situation.

5. Apart from self-reward, people show other diverse forms of self-control such as self-punishment, conscience, and guilt after transgression. Even in the area of visceral and glandular responses, which are generally thought of as "involuntary," some mastery and self-control may be achieved, since these responses can be sensitively influenced by appropriate rewards or feedback. Some parallels were noted between "biofeedback" research and esoteric techniques to achieve greater contact with one's own bodily states.

6. People differ greatly in the control patterns they use. For example, one approach to individual differences in self-control has related measures of "ego-control" and "ego-resiliency" to other relevant ratings and competencies throughout the course of development, establishing many meaningful patterns.

7. Individual differences in preference for delay of gratification also have been studied as a trait dimension and have been related to a variety of other behaviors.

8. There are great individual differences in perceived control over outcomes and perceived responsibility for the things that happen. Differences among people in perceived control have been conceptualized on a dimension of "internal-external" control of reinforcement. An

individual's status on this dimension is related to many other aspects of his personality and may affect his interpretation of different situations.

9. Individuals show some consistency in their control patterns across situations. However there also is much discrimination in control and self-reactions. Thus even people who often seem unable to wait for larger, delayed rewards may be able to delay gratification under the proper circumstances. Similarly, the associations found among measures of moral judgment, verbal standards of right and wrong, and resistance to temptation tend to be low. Hence there is little support for the existence of a unitary concept of morality or superego, or for a unitary trait of conscience or honesty.

10. There may be some developmental regularity in the formation of children's ideas and attitudes about justice and morality. Six moral stages, fundamentally the same regardless of social experience, have been hypothesized by cognitive-developmental theory. While there is some consistency in moral reasoning, the same individual tends to use moral reasoning both above and below his most "typical" stage level. The many hazards in trying to classify people into stable moral categories were noted.

CHAPTER 19

SOCIAL COGNITION AND THE SELF

"*Social cognition*" refers to how we perceive, know, and understand social stimuli, including ourselves and other people. A focus on social cognition, and on people as "knowers" and "perceivers" of behavior, including their own behavior, is of course central to the phenomenological, cognitive, and self theories discussed in Chapters 5 and 11. The ways we see the social world—our social cognitions—are the bases for how we relate to each other and to ourselves. Our perceptions and judgments of people, of their social behavior, and of ourselves, are the topics of this chapter.

Forming Impressions

To understand how enduring impressions about the self are formed, one may begin by seeing how impressions about other people are generated. Indeed the processes of forming self-impressions and of forming impressions of others may be identical (Bem, 1972; Kelley, 1973).

When you think about other people you do not describe their motoric acts objectively, nor do you analyze their specific responses in relation to particular stimuli. Instead, you form broad impressions about their characteristics as people, evaluate their intentions, and assess their worth. (What is Joe really like? What is Jane trying to do? Is she manipulating me?) To understand anyone's actions (including their own) perceivers try to find the reasons for them.

Heider (1958) has discussed many of the subjective or "common sense" features that people feel guide their perceptions of others and of themselves. These features include judgments about intentions, personal causation and causal responsibility, ability, effort, and motives. For example, in daily relations, our perceptions are affected dramatically by our assessments of whether or not an action was deliberate or accidental. Slamming a door, tossing a book, dropping a baby—the interpretation of these seemingly simple behaviors depends on inferences about the intentions and motives of the person who does them (Weiner, 1974). Similarly our judgments of ourselves and our behaviors presumably involve continuous self-assessments of our guilt or innocence, our responsibility or immunity, our effort or laziness.

The Perceived Causes of Behavior: Attribution

To understand other people and what happens to us we often ask ourselves why they acted as they did. Why did she not keep her promise? Why did he seem so cold and aloof at dinner? Why did the doctor seem so upset? All these questions seek to make *causal attributions* about behavior, to find the causes underlying actions (Kelley, 1980).

In making causal attributions people show some consistent biases toward certain kinds of attributions. One important bias is toward dispositional or internal causes (such as traits) rather than toward external (situational) causes when we try to explain behavior (Nisbett & Ross, 1980). In forming their impressions, people thus proceed like trait theorists. On the basis of behavioral cues they infer purposeful dispositions and motives in others and in themselves. Moreover, they tend to infer such dispositions even when they only have fragmentary and minimal cues.

Human observers tend to interpret even the simplest behaviors as signs of underlying traits and motives, and they easily attribute elaborate intentions to behavioral sequences, rapidly going from observed acts to hypothesized dispositions. They may even endow moving geometric shapes with purposes and emotions that range from anger through fear (Michotte, 1954).

For example, when people watch a disk, a large triangle, and a smaller triangle moving about, they tend to interpret the shapes as if they were human beings engaging in interpersonal conflicts and competitions: The larger triangle is seen as aggressive while the smaller one may be heroic and the disk timid (Heider & Simmel, 1944). From (1960) even suggests that what we think we see always depends on the intentions we ascribe to others. Not that people really believe that cartoons or moving shapes possess psychological qualities; the findings simply demonstrate how readily people can endow the agents of behavior with trait attributes, responsibilities, and intentions, especially under ambiguous conditions.

Organization of Impressions

The impressions we form of each other are not perceived as isolated bits of information, but rather as organized units. The nature of the organization depends on many variables, including the other cues in the situation, the sequence of observation, and the observer's concepts or categories.

Even the simplest impressions depend on the context. In one study subjects gave impressions of outline drawings of three faces—one "glum" one "frowning," and one "smiling"—presented in pairs (Cline, 1956). The judgments made about each face depended in part on the face with which it was paired. When paired with the glum face, for example, the smiling face tended to be seen as dominant, vicious, gloating, and bullyish; when paired with the frowning face, however, the smiling face was interpreted as peaceful and peace-making, and as wanting to help and to be friendly.

In our impressions we easily go beyond the information given to us and infer a whole cluster of related traits on the basis of a few "central" ones. If "warmth" is attributed to a person, he is more likely to be perceived as also being generous, good natured, happy, sociable, and wise (Asch, 1946; Wishner, 1960). But if "cold" rather than "warm" is part of the stimulus configuration, observers are more likely to see the person as ungenerous, unhappy, irritable,

Judgments about the meaning of behavior depend on the context and judge as well as on the behavior.

and humorless. Many factors may influence which traits in a given constellation will have "central" influence on the rest of the traits that will be attributed to the stimulus person (Wishner, 1960).

Implicit Personality Theories

People within a single culture often learn to make similar interpretations about the meaning of particular behaviors and attributes. "Tight" lips, "shifty" eyes, high foreheads, facial scars, are examples of the cues whose meanings as signs of personality may be identical for most members of a given culture. As a result of common learning experiences, observers may agree with each other about the meanings of such signs and may reach similar interpretations and labels from minimal cues. In our culture, people who wear glasses tend to be judged as more intelligent, industrious, and reliable than those who do not (Manz & Lueck, 1968); attractive children are seen as more intelligent, popular, and likely to go to college (Clifford & Walster, 1973); and if a woman makes eye contact with the perceiver, she will be judged more favorably than if her eyes are downcast (Tankard, 1970).

The perceiver's ideas about what traits go with or relate to other traits seem to form larger networks of relationships. These patterns of expected associations are called *implicit personality theories* (Schneider, 1973). Our implicit personality theories may lead us to overgeneralize from the behaviors we actually observe and infer that when a person seems to have one trait that other related traits will also be there, whether or not they really are (Berman & Kenny, 1976). On the basis of a few observations (watching a couple of friendly acts performed by an attractive woman with a warm smile, for example) we may begin to form an impression of a total consistent personality that goes far beyond the actual information we have. The resulting stereotypes may be extremely efficient for many forms of casual communication because they permit us to categorize experiences without much cognitive effort. They also may be tragic, as when ethnic cues become the bases for bitter discrimination and prejudice, or physical infirmities and handicaps become cues for ridicule and abuse among children.

Are our categories about other people just illusions in the minds of perceivers? Debates continue heatedly on this question (Block, Weiss & Thorne, 1979; Shweder & D'Andrade, 1979), but such pure illusions seem unlikely. Certain patterns of behavior probably tend to occur more often in reality; therefore, we also learn to expect them. For example, there may be a tendency for sociable behavior to co-occur with talkative and active behavior in certain types of persons (e.g., extraverts), just as sweet songs, feathers, and wings tend to co-occur in certain birds (e.g., canaries). The behavior of people is far from perfectly patterned, but it is also far from random. Ideas about people's traits arise from an interaction between the beliefs of observers and the characteristics of the observed (Cantor & Mischel, 1979; Mischel, 1979).

Constraints from First Impressions: The Costs of Categorizing

The total image or impression that emerges in person perception tends to depend on the *sequence* of observations. For example, if we learn first that a person is sociable and later that he or she is also introverted, our impression is quite different than if the sequence is reversed (e.g., Luchins, 1957). Much research has been devoted to the mechanisms through which new information may be added to the total impression. One model, for example, suggests a *weighting* process in which every piece of information is averaged into the total impression, but later information is given a smaller weight than data already processed (e.g., Anderson, 1965, 1974). The means through which impressions are formed of oneself and others are receiving increasing theoretical attention (e.g., Bem, 1972; Kelley, 1967). In general, first impressions are especially important and are given extra weight in the total image that is formed. The earliest information seems to serve as a conceptual anchor or base that influences the interpretation or weighting of later information. This biasing effect of initial information is the "primacy effect."

The first impression or category that an observer generates about events (including other people and himself) thus influences his further observations about those events. Both sophisticated scientists and naive subjects intuitively but often erroneously interpret small samples of observations as if they were highly representative (Kahneman & Tversky, 1973). Once an individual has categorized or grouped stimuli he may tend to retain the category he formed even when he gets contradictory evidence. Having formed his category or impression he may pay less attention to contradictory new information and may focus instead on information that confirms his hypothesis (Nisbett & Ross, 1980).

This constraining effect of a category has been shown in such diverse contexts as impression formation in person perception (e.g., Asch, 1946; Anderson, 1965; Wishner, 1960); hypothesis-testing in problem-solving (Davison, 1964; Wyatt & Campbell, 1951); and clinical diagnosis (e.g., Rubin & Shontz, 1960; Sines, 1959). In all these contexts people often generate impressions rapidly, even on the basis of little information, and then hold on to their hypotheses. For example, psychotherapists develop fairly stable images of their clients within the first four hours of psychotherapy. They tend to retain these categories more or less unchanged even after 24 therapy sessions (Meehl, 1960). In another study judges first formed their hypotheses about a subject by studying his biographical data and later observed him in nine role-playing situations. They employed the additional information mainly to confirm their initial conceptualizations (Soskin, 1959). Much other research also suggests that our hypotheses are not easily disconfirmed (Ross, 1977).

What we believe and expect about another person may affect not only how we feel and act, but also how the other person begins to act in turn. The perceiver's ideas thus may begin to shape the behaviors of the person who is perceived (Snyder, 1979). This process is illustrated in studies with college women. Some women volunteers served as interviewers, others were interviewed, and all conversations were recorded (Snyder & Swann, 1978). Some interviewers were led initially to believe that they were interviewing either an extravert or an introvert. In reality, they were assigned interviewees by chance alone.

When the interviewers thought that they were interviewing an extravert (or introvert in other conditions) they asked questions designed to confirm their expectations. In their eagerness to confirm their hypotheses, they seem to have unwittingly induced the interviewed person to act in ways that would confirm their expectations. Specifically, the women who were interviewed by interviewers who thought they were extraverts soon began to act more that way, displaying more poise, confidence, energy. Conversely, women who were interviewed by interviewers who thought them to be introverts, began to act more like introverts. Thus the interviewer's hypotheses seem to have led them to act in ways that forced confirmation from the other person, regardless of the other person's actual personality.

Self-Concepts

Just as we form impressions of other people so also do we generate concepts about ourselves. Each normal person experiences himself or herself as a distinct, continuous being or "object" with clear body boundaries. In the course of maturation, each individual develops attitudes toward that object and calls it names: "I" or "me" or "myself." To help make sense of ideas and feelings about oneself, psychologists and philosophers have created such terms as the "ego" or the "self." Each of these nouns represents a way of thinking and speaking about one's experience rather than a "thing" or a psychic entity.

The discussion so far of impression formation should make it plain that the individual's self-concepts are not a simple mirror-like reflection of some absolute reality. Rather, self-concepts, like impressions of other aspects of the world, involve an integration and organization of a tremendous amount of information. Although self-concepts are not a mirror of reality, they are correlated with the outcomes that the person has obtained throughout the past and expects to obtain in the future. The same basic social learning and cognitive variables that determine the social behaviors discussed in earlier chapters also presumably influence the development of self-concepts. The roots of our self-concepts are the impressions and evaluations that other people have of us in our interactions with them through the course of life.

While self-concept changes are related to the feedback that individuals get about themselves, the relationship may be influenced by many important variables. For example, people who are highly oriented to achievement and who are anxious to avoid failure may react quite differently to failure experiences than do people who are low in achievement striving (e.g., Atkinson & Feather, 1966; Heckhausen, 1969; Weiner, 1965, 1974). Depending on such moderating variables, the person may adopt many different strategies to cope with performance feedback. Hence self-concept changes are not a direct reflection of performance feedback; they are influenced by many other factors.

Self-concepts are related to other aspects of behavior, such as dependency, conformity, and susceptibility to influence. For example, Gelfand (1962) defined self-esteem in terms of the value individuals place on themselves and reasoned that this value depends upon past success and failure experiences. Presumably, then, high-esteem individuals have had a past history of chiefly positive reinforcement for their behavior, while low-esteem persons have failed in many situations.

Gelfand attempted to alter self-concept through administration of success or failure. Her results indicated that self-ratings changed significantly in the expected direction: Success increased self-esteem and failure decreased it, at least momentarily. Most interestingly, people low in initial self-esteem were more easily influenced to conform (by verbal conditioning) than were those high in rated self-esteem. This was interpreted as support for an earlier finding which had suggested that high self-esteem persons were generally less dependent upon situational pressures and hence less influenced by experimental manipulations.

Gelfand also found that, regardless of initial level of self-esteem, people who experienced failure became more susceptible to subsequent manipulations than those who experienced success. Finally, subjects exposed to experiences inconsistent with their customary self-evaluations (high-esteem persons who experienced failure and low-esteem persons who experienced success) were more influenced (on the verbal conditioning task) than were those whose experiences were congruent with their initial self-opinions.

In a more naturalistic investigation, Coopersmith (1967, 1968) studied a sample of normal, middle-class urban boys from preadolescence to early adulthood. He examined their family backgrounds through interviews and exposed the children to diverse personality and ability tests. For example, he assessed how high the children set their goals in situations such as the "bean bag" study illustrated in Figure 19-1. He then analyzed the patterns that emerged.

His results suggest that children with high self-esteem tend to be those who are more esteemed and more competent; they also tend to be those who are exposed to parental models who display high self-esteem (Coopersmith, 1967, 1968). Some of the specific child-rearing practices associated with self-esteem in the boys are summarized in Figure 19-2.

Coopersmith found that if he categorized the boys into three levels or degrees of self-esteem (low, medium, and high), certain traits seemed to best fit each level. Although there were many exceptions, and the relationships generally were of only modest strength, some consistent trends emerged (see Figure

FIGURE 19-1
Self-Esteem and Goal-Setting

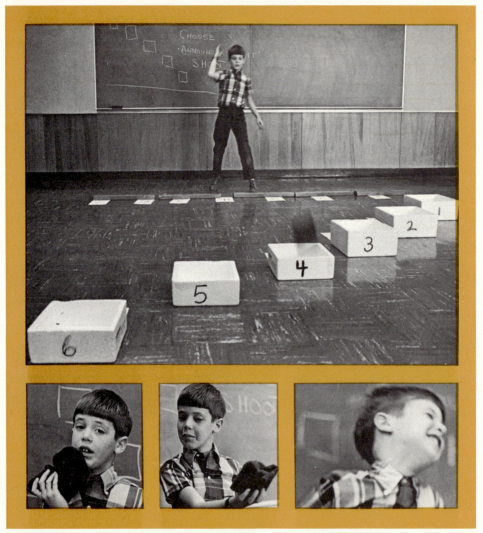

The more distant the target that the child selects in the "beanbag game" the higher the score that he could win but the greater the risk of failing. From Coopersmith (1968).

19-2). Coopersmith noted some of the trait terms that seem to best fit boys of different degrees of self-esteem; examples of these relationships are summarized in Table 19-1. As these examples suggest, the high-self-esteem youngsters seemed to be the ones who felt and behaved more competently. Presumably these qualities helped them to achieve more recognition and self-satisfaction and, in turn, their self-esteem was strengthened by their achievements.

FIGURE 19-2
Percentage of Children in Each Self-Esteem Group Rated Negatively by Their Mothers

Children with lower self-esteem were appraised more often by their mothers as having marked, frequent problems (black bars) rather than limited, infrequent ones, and also as being relatively destructive (white bars) rather than nondestructive. (Based on data from Coopersmith, 1967).

Self-Esteem and Selective Attention to the Self

Throughout this chapter we have assumed that the self may be viewed as an object about which information is available. Given this assumption, it becomes important to ask what determines the type of information about the self to which the individual attends. The potential information available about the self is almost boundless. Depending on where one looks and how one searches, it is possible to attend to widely diverse data about oneself. We can seek, and

TABLE 19-1
EXAMPLES OF TRAIT TERMS CHARACTERIZING BOYS OF HIGH AND LOW SELF-ESTEEM

Self-Esteem	Descriptive Trait Terms
High	Active, expressive, successful; little childhood destructiveness and not much anxiety; self-confident, optimistic.
Low	Discouraged, felt depressed, unlovable, fearful of angering others, isolated from others; shrank away from being noticed.

SOURCE: Based on Coopersmith (1968).

doubtless find, information to support our strengths or weaknesses, our successes or failures, almost endlessly. Since a person's experiences are neither completely successful nor totally negative, it is important to ask what determines selective attention to information about the self.

To explore this question one study attempted to experimentally alter the momentary self-esteem of college students with regard to mental abilities (Mischel, Ebbesen, & Zeiss, 1973). In a second phase the study assessed how the changes affected the students' selective attention to written information about their positive as opposed to negative personality traits. People who were led to feel more positive about their abilities, it was found, spent more time attending to other positive (relative to negative) information about their personalities. Thus, "feeling good" about oneself may produce further, chain-like effects on other aspects of the person's behavior: Persons who feel good about themselves may selectively channel their attention and cognitions to quite different experiences than do persons whose feelings toward themselves are more negative. The effects of success and failure depended both on individuals' expectancies in the situation and on their tendency to avoid threatening information. The latter tendency was inferred from scores on the Byrne (1964) "repression-sensitization" self-report scale. Thus alterations in self-esteem may produce changes in selective attention to other aspects of the self, but the effects are complex and depend both on momentary expectations and on more stable individual differences in information-seeking. Essentially similar conclusions come from much other research on the self (Gergen, 1971; Mischel, Ebbesen, & Zeiss, 1976).

People who differ on the dimension of perceived locus of control also may react differently to information about the self (Phares, 1978; Phares, Ritchie, & Davis, 1968). Groups of college students were selected who were either relatively "internal" or "external" on a self-report measure of perceived locus of control. As discussed in the last chapter, "internal" subjects are those who most often report that they control (cause and are responsible for) the reinforcements that occur in their lives; "externals," in contrast, say that these outcomes are due to luck or to other external conditions outside their control. These two groups then were administered a set of personality tests. Later they were provided reports that contained positive and negative information about their personalities. Externals recalled more of the negative material about themselves than did internals.

Self-Efficacy

Self-efficacy is a more specific concept than self-esteem. As discussed in earlier chapters, self-efficacy refers to the individual's belief that he or she can successfully execute the behaviors required by a particular situation. Such perceptions of one's own efficacy may importantly guide and direct one's behavior. The close connection between high self-efficacy expectations and effective performance is illustrated in studies of people who received various treatments to help reduce their fear of snakes. A consistently high association was found between the degree to which persons improved from treatment (becoming able to handle snakes fearlessly) and their perceived self-efficacy (Bandura, 1977). So if we assess perceived self-efficacy, (asking people to specifically predict their ability to do a given act successfully), we can predict the relevant behavior with impressive accuracy (Bandura & Adams, 1977). Results of this kind suggest strong and clear links between self-perceptions of one's competence and the ability to actually behave competently. Once again we see that when the right questions are asked people can be excellent predictors of their own behaviors.

The Self-Perception of Helplessness

As noted in earlier chapters, when people believe that there is nothing they can do to control negative or painful outcomes they may come to expect that they are *helpless* (Seligman, 1975). That is, they may learn to expect that aversive outcomes are uncontrollable, that there is nothing they can do. In that state, they also may become apathetic, despondent, and slow to learn that they actually *can* control the outcomes. Such states of helplessness may generalize, persist, and involve feelings of depression or sadness. The state of helplessness may have especially negative and persistent effects when the person believes that it reflects his or her own enduring, widespread internal qualities (e.g., "I'm incompetent") rather than that it is due to more momentary, external, or situational considerations (Abramson, Seligman, & Teasdale, 1978). Thus the person's attributions have an important part in determining how a state of helplessness affects that person.

Following frustration in the form of failure on a task, some individuals "fall apart" and their performance deteriorates. But other people actually improve. What causes these two different types of responses to the frustration of failure? One important cause may be how the person interprets the reasons for the experience. Children who believe their failure is due to lack of ability (called "helpless children") were found to perform more poorly after they experienced failure than did those who see their failure as due to lack of effort (called "mastery-oriented" children). Indeed, the "mastery-oriented" children often actually performed better after failure. Most encouraging, training the helpless children (those who attribute their failure to lack of ability) to view outcomes as the result of their own effort, results in their improved performance after a failure experience (Dweck, 1975).

When faced with failure, helpless children seem to have self-defeating thoughts that virtually guarantee further failure. This became clear when groups of helpless and mastery-oriented fifth-graders were instructed "to think out loud" while solving problems. When children in the two groups began to experience failure, they soon said very different things to themselves. The helpless children made statements reflecting their loss or lack of ability, such as "I'm getting confused" and "I never did have a good memory" (Diener &

<table>
<tr><td colspan="2">TABLE 19-2
EXAMPLES OF COPING STATEMENTS BY HELPLESS
AND MASTERY-ORIENTED CHILDREN</td></tr>
<tr><td>*Helpless*</td><td>*Mastery-Oriented*</td></tr>
<tr><td>"I'm getting confused"</td><td>"The harder it gets the harder
I need to try"</td></tr>
<tr><td>"There is a talent show this weekend, and
I am going to be Shirley Temple"</td><td>"I've almost got it now"</td></tr>
<tr><td>"This isn't fun anymore"
"I give up"</td><td>"I love a challenge"</td></tr>
<tr><td colspan="2">SOURCE: Based on Diener & Dweck, 1978.</td></tr>
</table>

Dweck, 1978, p. 458). In contrast, the mastery-oriented children never talked about their lack of ability. Instead, they seemed to search for a remedy for their failure, and gave themselves instructions to try to encourage themselves and improve their performance, such as "I should slow down and try to figure this out." Some examples of statements by the mastery-oriented children and by the helpless children are shown in Table 19-2. Note how the helpless children focus on irrelevant things that tend to be ineffective strategies for solving a problem.

Self-Awareness and Self-Perception

Much of what we do is "mindless" (Langer, 1978), guided by more-or-less automatic adherence to routines or "scripts" that are familiar and require little active attention (Abelson, 1976). Under such conditions, the self plays little role and we do not experience self-awareness; that is, we do not focus on ourselves. But one of the distinctive properties of the self is its capacity to be conscious of itself; its ability to take itself as the object of its own attention.

Self-Focus and Self-Monitoring

This idea of taking oneself as the object of one's attention is central to the theory of self-awareness (e.g., Duval & Wicklund, 1972). The theory holds that attention can be directed inward toward the self; that is, it can be "self-

TABLE 19-3
HIGH SELF-CONSCIOUSNESS ITEMS*

Private	*Public*
I'm generally attentive to my inner feelings.	I'm concerned about the way I present myself.
I'm always trying to figure myself out.	I'm concerned about what other people think of me.

* Examples from the private and public subscales of the Self-Consciousness Scale
SOURCE: Fenigstein, Scheier, & Buss, 1975.

focused." Or, alternatively, attention can be directed outward toward the environment. Self-focus has been created experimentally simply by confronting people with a mirror (or camera lens). The self-focused individual tends to be more likely to conform to salient, personal standards for behavior and to societal values than will the less self-aware person. And self-aware people tend to be more honest, helpful, and work harder. They also may be more aware of their dominant feelings or attributes in the situation, and generally show greater consistency and self-attention (Wicklund & Frey, 1980).

Self-focus or "self-consciousness" also has been measured as a personal disposition by questions like those shown in Table 19-3. People who are high in self-consciousness on this test do indeed seem to be more aware of themselves as objects (Carver & Scheier, 1978; Scheier & Carver, 1980), and tend to show many of the characteristics that can be induced when self-focus is created experimentally. But self-consciousness may not be a single dimension of individual differences. For some people self-consciousness is mostly a matter of how others view them, a concern with public reactions. For other individuals, however, self-consciousness is a private matter, and refers to awareness of one's own thoughts, feelings, and motives. Notice that different types of items are used to try to measure these two kinds of self-consciousness—a public type and a private type. (See Table 19-3.) These two aspects of self-consciousness may be related to *self-monitoring*, the tendency either to look toward the momentary situation to guide one's actions, or instead to look internally toward one's own standards (Snyder, 1979). A person who looks more to the situation for guidance might say to herself, for example, "This is a party at which sociable, friendly behavior is expected: That's how I should act now." In contrast, a person who looks inward might say "I feel depressed tonight and don't want to chit-chat."

How Do You Know What You Feel?

Another quality of the self is the subjective experience of emotions; we are aware of our own feelings and of our many different emotional states. This subjective impression—of fear, joy, anger, pride, shame—is a distinctive quality of self-perception. But how do such self-perceptions of emotion occur? One possibility is that the different emotions we feel might involve different physiological changes. Most of us surely feel that emotions like fear and anger seem to involve unmistakably distinct internal cues. In accord with the subjective conviction that clearly different emotions exist, psychologists and physiologists for many years tried to differentiate emotional states into specific types and to discover the particular patterns of bodily activity that might accompany each of these states. The general result of a good deal of investigation appears to be that, though there are sometimes subtle differences in the patterns of physiological responses associated with different emotions (e.g., Ax, 1953; Tourangeau & Ellsworth, 1978), what they have in common is far more striking. A diffuse state of general physiological arousal seems to characterize different emotional experiences.

Nevertheless, we all have the subjective impression of experiencing distinctly different feelings such as anger and euphoria. How can one account for these subjectively different experiences if the bodily arousal underlying them is the same? Discriminations among emotions are based mainly on situational cues rather than on distinctive visceral changes. On the basis of situational cues, the individual labels his or her state cognitively, assigning a name to the arousal. Thus emotions involve at least two components: a state of general physiological arousal and a cognitive appraisal of the situation (Schachter, 1964).

Often the source of emotional arousal is easy to identify. When faced by an attacking dangerous animal, or by an impending car crash, or by imminent of a loved person, the source of excitement is self-evident. The label attached to the experience in these cases depends on the source—the stimulus producing the arousal. Thus the emotional response to an attacking animal is probably *fear,* identified by the fact that a dangerous animal is approaching. Identification of the emotion also depends on the person's goal-directed response when confronted by the stimulus. For example, attempted escape from the animal also leads to calling the emotion fear. As another example, suppose that the arousal source is an insult. The resulting emotion is probably "anger," especially if the insulted person responds aggressively; but it might be "fear," if the insulted person views the insult as a prelude to greater attack. These examples illustrate that the label for the emotion depends in part on the *source* of arousal and in part on the *response* to it.

The emotional meaning attributed to arousing stimuli and response patterns depends on social learning and cognition. This point becomes most evident from anthropological reports of differences among cultures in the ways in which feelings are expressed. Visitors to a strange culture would make many mistakes if they tried to assess the meaning of emotional expressions in terms of their own social learning history. A Masai warrior honors a young man who looks promising by spitting in his face, an Andaman Islander greets a visitor by sitting down on his lap and sobbing his salutation tearfully, a scolded Chinese schoolboy takes a reprimand with cheerful grinning as a sign of his respect, and to show anger Navajo and Apache Indians lower the voice instead of raising it (Opler, 1967).

Within each culture people reach good agreement about the meaning of emotional cues. Sometimes, however, persons cannot correctly identify the source of their own arousal and are uncertain about their response to it. Under these ambiguous conditions cognitive and social variables play an especially dominant part in determining the experience. Depending on the cognitive label assigned, the context, and social cues from other people, the individual might experience the same physiological arousal pattern as anything from joy to hate.

Cognition and Physiological Arousal

Stanley Schachter (1964), whose experiments on the way we label emotions were crucial, has discussed his theory in relation to the controversial effects of smoking marihuana. He notes that, according to pharmacological reports, marihuana usually causes an increase in pulse rate, some rise in blood pressure, elevation in blood sugar and metabolic rate, and so on. Given these symptoms the smoker could consider himself either as "high" or as "sick." The smoker has to decide whether his feelings of dizziness, misjudgments of time and distance, and so on are "pleasant" or not, and his decision involves cognitive judgments that depend on social learning cues.

Schachter extended his provocative theorizing to the topic of obesity. He noted that hunger, although a primary motive, also may require cognitive identification. Attaching the label "hunger" to the physiological changes accompanying food deprivation is a learned cognitive act. The obese person, he speculated, may not have learned to attach the right label to her feelings and may not be discriminating properly between hunger and other intense emotional states.

Some support for Schachter's ideas concerning the effects of cognition on the experience of emotions comes from several experiments. For example, Schachter and Singer (1962) submitted college students to drug-induced autonomic arousal (through injections of epinephrine, a sympathetic stimulant). Some subjects were informed of the side effects of the drug while others were not, and subjects in a control group received a placebo injection (of saline solution). Thereafter all subjects were exposed to a confederate who was supposedly just another subject. The confederate modeled extensive verbal aggression and displayed anger toward the experimental procedure. The subjects who had been given the physiologically arousing drug without information about its effects were most susceptible to the angry model and became most angry themselves. Another part of the experiment established that subjects exposed to a euphoric confederate became most euphoric when they were physiologically aroused but not informed or misinformed concerning the side effects of the drug.

The total findings supported the hypothesis that if a person is in an aroused physiological state that he cannot explain, he will label his state in accord with the environmental cues determining his cognitions. On the other hand, if the person can explain her state rationally ("I'm experiencing these feelings because of the drug injection") then her evaluative self-labels will be less dependent on momentary situational cues. Momentary environmental cues were most influential when the subject was physiologically aroused by the epinephrine injection but misinformed about its effects and, secondly, when she was aroused but uninformed. The interacting effects of arousal and cognition are also shown in the cartoon in Figure 19-3. As the cartoon shows, physiologically aroused subjects interpreted their state in accord with the available modeling cues (the stooge's behavior) when they were misinformed about the nature of their arousal (lower portion of cartoon) but not when they had an appropriate explanation of the visceral arousal they felt (upper portion of cartoon).

In sum, an aroused individual's behavior may depend on her cognitive interpretation and labeling of the arousal. Her interpretation, in turn, depends on

The experienced emotion depends on how the aroused state is interpreted.

the cues available to her in the situation and on the meaning that these stimuli have acquired as a result of her prior learning and development. The subjective, phenomenal experience of emotion often seems to be labeled from contextual cues, and we know what we feel partly by seeing where we are and what is happening. To understand another person's emotional experiences fully we have to consider the person in her context and the complex relations between the contextual variations and subjective experience; to understand our own feelings, we may have to do the same.

The Schachter and Singer (1962) experiment has been challenged by new research that questions their conclusions (Maslach, 1979; Marshall & Zimbardo, 1979). Schachter and Singer (1979), however, continue to maintain their interpretation, and rebuke their sharp critics with equal vigor. What shall we conclude? A good deal of evidence indicates that we often do use external information to judge our inner states. But there also may be important exceptions. Indeed, many different types of information may influence how we experience, judge, and label our inner states (Schneider, Hastorf, & Ellsworth, 1979).

Causal Attributions and Emotions

The close links between cognition and emotion are also seen if we examine how "causal attributions" influence our emotional responses. Causal attributions refer to the perception of the causes of behavior (e.g., Kelley, 1973). For example, we may see the same event—say getting an A on an exam—as due to internal causes (such as high ability or hard work) or as due to external causes (such as the ease of the task or good luck). How we feel about the grade depends on whether we see it as due to internal or external causes. Generally, "pride and shame are maximized when achievement outcomes are ascribed internally, and minimized when success and failure are attributed to external causes" (Weiner, 1974, p. 11). In other words, a success that is perceived to be the result of one's ability or effort (internal causes) produces more positive feelings about oneself than does the same success when it is viewed as merely reflecting luck or an easy task (external causes). Conversely, we feel worse (e.g., experience "shame") when we perceive our failure as reflecting low ability or insufficient effort than when it is seen as due to bad luck or the difficulty of the particular task. For example, being fired from a job for one's incompetence has a different emotional impact than does being fired because the firm went bankrupt.

Not surprisingly, our perceptions of these causes may be biased in self-enhancing ways. For example, we are more likely to see ourselves as responsible for our actions when they have positive rather than negative outcomes. When we do well or succeed, it is to our personal credit; when we do badly or fail it is because we could not help it (e.g., Fitch, 1970; Schneider, Hastorf, & Ellsworth, 1979; Wortman et al., 1973).

FIGURE 19-3
The Schachter Experiments

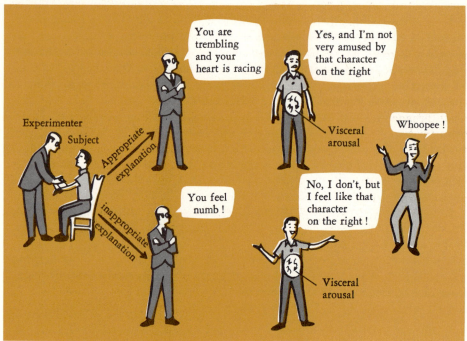

From Mandler (1962).

Self-Schemata

Self-concepts, also called "*self-schemata*" (Markus, 1977), include generalizations about oneself like "I am an independent person" or "I tend to lean on
people." Self-schemata are cognitions that arise from past experiences and,
once formed, guide how we deal with new information related to the self. To
illustrate, if you have strong self-schemata about being extremely dependent,
passive, and conforming, you would process and remember information relevant to those schemata more quickly and effectively than do people for whom
those schemata are not personally relevant (Markus, 1977). People have better
recall for information about traits that they believe describe them than
for traits that are not self-descriptive (Rogers, 1977; Rogers, Kuiper, &
Kirker, 1977). Thus we give things relevant to the self special cognitive treatment, for example by being more oriented and attentive toward them.

Self-Esteem

One of the most critical aspects of the self-concept is "self-esteem." Self-
esteem refers to the individual's personal judgment of his or her own worth
(e.g., Coopersmith, 1967). Self-esteem is such an important aspect of the self-
concept that the two terms are often used as if they were the same. Although
"self-esteem" is sometimes discussed as if it were a single entity, it may be

that persons evaluate their functioning in different areas of life discriminatively. These self-evaluations presumably reflect in part the feedback that they continuously get from the environment as they learn about themselves.

In one approach, self-concepts about one's adequacy may be thought of as consisting of both highly situation-specific, self-relevant performance expectancies and more generalized expectancies. According to Rotter (1954), "specific expectancies" refer to the individual's expectancies that a particular set of behaviors on her part will lead to particular outcomes (reinforcements) in the specific situation confronting her. "Generalized expectancies" refer to somewhat broader expectations regarding the probable outcomes of the person's behavior based on her past experiences and total history in similar situations. Both kinds of expectancies regarding future performance depend on information about past performance. The precise relationships between performance, performance feedback, and changes in the person's expectancies about herself have been studied extensively (e.g., Weiner, 1972).

Most studies on this topic are based on the "level-of-aspiration" situation devised by Kurt Lewin and extended by J. B. Rotter and others. In this situation, people typically are asked to verbalize their subjective expectations (sometimes their hopes or aspirations) with regard to how good their performance will be in a particular area. For example, students are requested to state their expectancies about the scores they are likely to obtain on tests of arithmetic reasoning, social competencies, interpersonal sensitivity, and so on. They are told to record their estimated scores for each of these tests on a scale (for example, 0 to 100) and are given information about norms and average scores obtained by other people who supposedly took the tests before.

Thereafter the students take parts of the tests and are given feedback about the quality of their performance. Depending on the experimental condition to which the individual is assigned, her score might be considerably above ("success") or below ("failure") her stated expectancy. All subjects are asked again to state their expectancies for the next series of performances. These new tests are described in ways designed to systematically vary their similarity to the tasks on which the person has already received feedback.

Studies of this type have shown that specific self-concepts about performance level generally tend to follow more or less directly the feedback people receive from their experiences. For example, after repeated failure on a task, a person usually expects to fail it again. Moreover, the expectancies formed in one situation also tend to generalize to other related situations to the degree that they are perceived as similar and as likely to lead to similar outcomes or reinforcements.

Cognitive Consistency

Perhaps the most compelling quality of the private or "phenomenological" self is its perceived continuity and consistency. The experience of subjective continuity in ourselves—of basic oneness and durability in the self—seems to be a fundamental feature of personality. Indeed the loss of a feeling of consistency and identity may be a chief characteristic of personality disorganization, as is seen in schizophrenic patients who sometimes report vividly experiencing two distinct selves, one of them disembodied (Laing, 1965).

Perceived Unity in the Face of Diversity

It seems remarkable how each of us normally manages to reconcile seemingly diverse behaviors into one self-consistent whole. A man may steal on one occasion, lie on another, donate generously to charity on a third, cheat on a fourth, and still readily construe himself as "basically honest and moral." People often seem to be able to transform their seemingly discrepant behaviors into a constructed continuity, making unified wholes out of almost anything (Mischel, 1969).

How can we reconcile our shared perception of continuity, our feeling of identity, with the equally impressive evidence, found throughout previous chapters, that on virtually all measures of personality substantial changes occur in the actual behaviors of the individual across even seemingly similar settings and situations? How can we understand the fact of the specificity of behavior in light of the equally compelling impression of basic consistency in ourselves and in people we know? Probably many complex factors are involved (Mischel, 1973a, 1979), but part of the answer to this question may be that people tend to reduce cognitive inconsistencies and, in general, to simplify information so that they can deal with it (Nisbett & Ross, 1980; Tversky & Kahneman, 1974). The overall evidence from many sources (clinical, experimental, developmental, correlational) suggests that the human mind may function like an extraordinarily effective reducing valve that creates and maintains the perception of continuity even in the face of perpetual, observed changes in actual behavior.

Cognitive Consistency Theory

Some conceptualizations of personality attach the greatest importance to cognitive strivings for consistency (e.g., Festinger, 1957; Kohlberg, 1966; Lecky, 1945). The most influential statement of this position is Festinger's "cognitive dissonance" theory.

Cognitive dissonance refers to relations between cognitions that, like the dictionary meaning of the word "dissonant," are harsh, grating, inharmonious, or contradictory (Festinger, 1957). According to Festinger, cognitive dissonance occurs if an individual knows two things that do not fit together. Consider, for example, a person who knows that he is extremely competent and intelligent, but simultaneously knows that he fails often. These two cognitions do not fit well together and hence are dissonant. Festinger further hypothesized that dissonance is an aversive, tension-producing state, and therefore that people are motivated to reduce or avoid it.

Festinger had the opportunity to observe a religious sect that was predicting a catastrophic flood. Knowledge of the flood was given to the people in the sect by direct communication from God. When the appointed day arrived, but the predicted catastrophe did not, considerable dissonance was generated in the group's members. Observation of their behavior revealed some of the ingenious ways in which people coped with dissonance. For example, at one point a message arrived from God announcing he had saved the world for the sake of the strength and light the sect had spread. After their prophecy had failed, many sect members became especially eager to hold press conferences "explaining" the reasons for the reprieve, presumably reducing their dissonance by trying to persuade others (and themselves) of the validity of their heavenly messages.

Festinger thus began his theory with the informal observation that people strive to reduce inconsistencies in their beliefs. He proposed that inconsistency among related beliefs generates cognitive dissonance and motivates the individual to do whatever is easiest to reduce dissonance and to regain cognitive consistency or consonance among beliefs.

Constructing Consistency

Consistency theories would predict that people should retain important cognitions about the self fairly stably. They may achieve consistency by distorting self-inconsistent cognitions regarding discrepant behaviors so as to make them seem more consonant with previous cognitions about the self.

Guided by dissonance theory, Aronson and Carlsmith (1962) reasoned that individuals are motivated to maintain consistent self-concepts. Extending this basic idea, they predicted that even if a person develops a *negative* self-relevant performance expectancy, he will seek to maintain it. That is, the person who has learned to expect poor performances from himself will experience discomfort when his performance turns out to be much better than he expected it to be. To reduce the discomfort or dissonance he feels, he will try to deny or minimize his superior performance.

In a laboratory study, false feedback was given to subjects on a series of tests to establish either excellent or poor performance expectancies (Aronson & Carlsmith, 1962). On a subsequent test the subjects performed again and were given false scores that either confirmed or disconfirmed their high or low performance expectancies. Under the guise of elaborate instructions the subjects were surreptitiously allowed to perform again and hence to alter their task responses on this retest. The conditions and results are summarized in Table 19-4.

As the table shows, people who had been given information inconsistent with their expectancies changed more of their responses than did those who had obtained consistent information. As predicted, subjects who had expected to do badly but who performed well seemed to exhibit more discomfort with their performance (as inferred from their changing more responses) than did

TABLE 19-4 NUMBER OF RESPONSES ALTERED ON RETEST		
	Obtained Performance on Test	
Expected Performance on Test	*High*	*Low*
High	3.9	11.1
Low	10.2	6.7

SOURCE: Adapted from Aronson and Carlsmith (1962).

those whose negative expectations had been confirmed by a poor performance.

study

In a similar vein, male college students were provided with plausible but false positive or negative information about their personalities to momentarily raise or lower their self-esteem (Bramel, 1962). Thereafter these subjects were led to discover a piece of negative information about themselves (specifically, that they had unconscious homosexual tendencies). Individuals with experimentally produced low self-esteem were more willing to accept the negative information than were those who experienced high self-esteem.

Similarly, experimentally induced increases in self-esteem may somewhat decrease an individual's tendency to cheat. This finding was interpreted as reflecting the unacceptable self-concept inconsistency that would be produced in high self-esteem subjects if they were to engage in dishonest behavior while experiencing high self-esteem (Aronson & Mettee, 1968). To avoid such dissonance they may have cheated somewhat less. It must be noted, however, that this finding was not strong.

The foregoing studies are just a few examples of many experiments on cognitive incongruity that have shown in general that persons tend to reduce inconsistencies between incompatible cognitions (e.g., Glass, 1968). People do minimize and avoid discrepant cognitions about themselves and others and reconstrue discrepant events to impose compatibility upon them.

Specific feedback about one's performance, such as arithmetic skill in the previously discussed level-of-aspiration design, is hard for most persons to deny and to distort. In life, however, most feedback about the self tends to be much more ambiguous and to involve vague qualitative appraisals of broad dispositions rather than concrete scores on specific performances. Under these more ambiguous conditions it is much easier to distort and to attend to information about the self selectively.

Some psychological constructs about ourselves have such broad and ambiguous semantic meanings that they are virtually impossible to disconfirm. For example, the construct that a particular woman is "very feminine," or that she is "basically hostile," may be potentially supported by almost any kind of evidence about her behavior. Since the construct about what constitutes "real" femininity, or "real" hostility, may be modified and progressively elaborated as new evidence becomes available, it can be stretched so that diverse behaviors are taken as confirmation of behavioral consistency. Almost any data can be made to fit such broad hypotheses about personality; hence the hypotheses may be stably retained.

An excessive "stretching" of constructs may produce difficulties, for example, in the form of hostile efforts to coerce the data of our observations into patterns that match our preconceived categories (Kelly, 1955). Sometimes such stretching violates the data so that the fit between observation and construct is poor.

Nevertheless we may try to squeeze our observations into the constructs available to us, even when the match is poor. According to George Kelly's personal construct theory, coercing round data into square categories often may produce serious problems for us, both as persons and as scientists.

On the other hand, the adaptiveness with which constructs may be extended helps us to encompass and unify the diverse and seemingly inconsistent components of our lives and of our own behavior. This conceptual breadth and flexibility of concepts helps us to achieve the sense of integration, of continuity and oneness, of wholeness that characterizes the normal subjective perception of oneself.

Stability of Trait Attributions

Consistency over time seems to be high for the self-concepts and for the attitudes and values that individuals attribute to themselves on trait-rating scales. E. L. Kelly (1955) compared trait self-descriptions obtained on questionnaires answered almost 20 years apart. During the years 1935 to 1938 several personality questionnaires were administered to 300 engaged couples. Most of these people were retested with the same measure in 1954. The questionnaires included the Allport-Vernon values test, the Bernreuter personality questionnaire, and the Strong Vocational Interest Blank, among others. Self-reports of attitudes about marriage were highly unstable. However, the consistency found for such self-concept ratings as self-confidence and sociability, and for self-descriptions of interests and of economic and political values, was remarkably high.

In general, the self-concepts reported on many personality questionnaires seem to show a good deal of stability (Byrne, 1966; Gough, 1957; Mischel, 1968). As previously discussed (Chapter 11), personal constructs as measured by Kelly's Role Construct Repertory Test (Reptest) also show much consistency over time (Bonarius, 1965). Thus there is a great deal of evidence that our cognitive constructions about ourselves and the world—our personal theories about ourselves and those around us—tend to be extremely stable and highly resistant to change (Nisbett & Ross, 1980). Data from many sources document this point. Studies of the self-concept, of impression formation in person perception and in clinical judgment, of attitudes, of cognitive sets guiding selective attention—all these phenomena and many more reveal the consistency and tenacious continuity of many human construction systems (Mischel, 1968, 1969). Often these construction systems are built quickly and on the basis of little information (e.g., Bruner, Olver, & Greenfield, 1966). But, once established, these systems, whether generated by "subjects" or by psychologists, become exceedingly difficult to disconfirm (Ross, 1977).

It may be that the dispositional labels people attribute to themselves and others and the self-concepts that they form are relatively permanent; they probably are more enduring than the behaviors to which they refer. Thus while what people *do* may be relatively situation-specific, they categorize and conceptualize themselves fairly stably with dispositional terms and motives that go far beyond the information directly available from observation of behavior.

Perceived consistency increases our feeling that we can predict other people and ourselves, and helps our world to seem more orderly and less chaotic. It might be distressing to believe that our most trusted friends are capable of disloyalty, or that those on whom we rely profoundly might be dishonest at times, or that those whom we love might change in unexpected ways that we really cannot predict. Thus consistency is often desired. But that is not always true: "surprise" and novelty also are valued under some conditions, at least within limits (Berlyne, 1966).

The over-attribution of consistency may be something people do unto others even more than to themselves. Jones and Nisbett (1971) note that when explaining *other* people's behavior we invoke their consistent personality dispositions: Steve is the sort of person who puts bumper stickers on his car; Jill tripped because she's clumsy. But when asked to explain our *own* behavior we are more likely to consider specific conditions: "AAA sent me this catchy bumper sticker in the mail" or "I tripped because it was dark." Thus Jones and Nisbett (1971, p. 58) theorize that "actors tend to attribute the causes of their behavior to stimuli inherent in the situation while observers tend to attribute behavior to stable dispositions of the actor." Jones and Nisbett analyze many possible reasons for this seemingly paradoxical state of affairs, including the tendency to treat every sample of behavior we observe from another person as if it were typical for him. It thus seems as if traits may be the consistent attributes that *other* people have. When describing other people, we seem to act more like trait theorists but when we attempt to understand ourselves we may function more like social behaviorists. If that is true it may be because we have more information about ourselves and the variety and complexity of the situations we encounter in our own lives, whereas we know others in only limited contexts and therefore tend to overgeneralize from their behavior in those instances.

SUMMARY

1. The processes through which we form our impressions of other people are similar to those through which we develop impressions about the self. Thus the study of how we perceive others may inform our understanding of self-perceptions. Impressions of the self, like impressions of other people and events, involve a complex synthesis and organization of a great deal of information. This information comes from observed behavior, but the perceiver goes beyond observation and seeks motives and dispositions to explain the behavior he or she sees.

2. During impression formation isolated bits of information are quickly organized into units. The organization depends on such things as context and sequence. Context is very important even in simple impressions. The same stimulus may be judged differently in different contexts. Moreover, any one attribute may lead us to infer a cluster of related traits.

3. The first impressions generated about others and about oneself may have a constraining effect by decreasing the attention paid to contradictory new information. Selective channeling or biasing of new information may be adaptive in coping with enormous informational inputs because it simplifies them.

4. The person's existing construct system influences his or her new impressions. Even when people know each other well, the impressions each forms of the other may depend more on his or her own categories than on the attributes of the other person. Regardless of what is being rated, the judgments we make tend to fall on a few dimensions of meaning, such as "good-bad."

5. Self-concepts (or "self-schemata") develop as a result of the outcomes a person has obtained in the past and expects to obtain in the future. Self-esteem is an important aspect of the self-concept. Concepts of adequacy or ability with regard to particular performance areas have been studied extensively. Specific self-concepts about performance level tend to depend on the feedback the person received from past performance. These expectancies may generalize to other situations to the degree that the situations are perceived as similar. Changes in self-esteem also may be mediated by factors other than performance feedback, for example, by the person's achievement orientation.

6. Self-esteem level has been related to other aspects of personality. Children with high self-esteem are those who are more esteemed by

others and more competent; and their parents also display high self-esteem.

7. Persons must attend selectively to the immense amount of information available about themselves. Determinants of selective attention include momentary self-esteem and more stable personality differences in information-seeking and perceived control.

8. Perceptions of self-efficacy and of helplessness are closely related to a person's behavior. For example, self-efficacy expectations predict improvement in treatment: People who expect to do well, really do well. Likewise, children who are helpless (believe failure is due to their lack of ability) do perform more poorly after a failure experience than do children who see their failure as due to a lack of effort.

9. Self-awareness can be created experimentally or studied as individual differences on such dimensions as self-consciousness and self-monitoring.

10. In the perception of feelings, although we may subjectively experience distinct emotions, corresponding distinct patterns of physiological responses generally have not been found. Instead, a diffuse state of general physiological arousal may characterize the various emotional experiences. The discriminations that we make among emotions are affected by cognitions and situational cues. The source of the arousal and the person's response to it affect the cognitive appraisal of that arousal and the label that the individual attaches to it. The meaning of arousal stimuli and response patterns depends on many considerations.

11. When you cannot easily identify the source of your own arousal and are uncertain about your response to it, cognitive and social variables may enter most strongly to determine your experience. If a person is in an aroused physiological state that he or she cannot explain plausibly, he or she may label this state in accord with the environmental cues and cognitions about them so as to explain the state reasonably.

12. Emotional reactions to an event also depend on its perceived causes. For example, a success that is seen as due to one's own ability or efforts (internal causes) produces more feelings of pride than does the same event when it is seen as due to luck or the easiness of the task (external causes).

13. We tend to perceive people as basically consistent even in the face of seemingly contradictory evidence from behavior. Consistency theories, such as Festinger's cognitive dissonance theory, view people as actively striving to reduce cognitive dissonance and to maintain cog-

nitive consistency, especially about important concepts like the self. People often minimize and avoid discrepant cognitions about themselves, and they may reconstrue events to render them compatible.

14. Self-concepts, attitudes, and values may show remarkable stability. Indeed the dispositional labels people apply to themselves and use in the formation of their self-concepts may be more enduring and situation-free than the actual behaviors to which they refer.

CHAPTER 20

THE INTERACTION OF PERSON AND SITUATION

As the end of this survey approaches, the reader may still be feeling somewhat uncertain about the view of the human being to which contemporary personality psychology leads, puzzled about the interplay of the individual's characteristics with the conditions of his or her life, and looking for a more complete perspective for understanding people. If so, this book has succeeded in giving a sense of the field as it exists; a deep concern with how to best conceptualize the person in personality psychology is widely shared within the discipline. The purpose of this final chapter is to examine more closely some of the bases of these concerns and to try to point, even if only tentatively and with no guarantee of success, toward hopefully promising future directions from the author's perspective (developed more fully in Mischel, 1973a, 1979). This perspective is offered not as the "final word" in the field; indeed, one of the few things that may be assumed with certainty is that the conceptualization favored (and required) in personality psychology will continue to evolve as the field grows and changes. The present perspective is intended only to offer one way of trying to construe and integrate some of the main current controversial issues in the field.

Some Basic Issues in Personality Psychology

One of the most challenging, persistent problems for the field of personality comes from the findings on the "specificity" of personality traits. The reader has encountered these findings throughout this volume and their implications produced a crisis in the area (e.g., Fiske, 1974). It is therefore not surprising that they are highly controversial and often debated vehemently (e.g., Epstein, 1980; Magnusson & Endler, 1977; Mischel, 1980).

Coherence and Continuity—with Discriminativeness

It is time to briefly review the meaning of the findings on "behavioral specificity." People often have been found to be consistent on measures of intelligence and on behavior patterns such as "cognitive styles" (problem-solving strategies) that are strongly correlated with intelligence (e.g., Witkin, 1965). Ratings of personality characteristics (by self and others) also show appreciable stability even over many years; moreover, self-ratings tend to agree with trait ratings by other judges (e.g., Block, 1977). And when one uses reliable and multiple measures it is possible to demonstrate meaningful, coherent patterns in people's lives, even over long periods of time. Stability over time has been found in such important areas as ego strength and flexibility (Block & Block, 1980), aggression (Olweus, 1979), and certain emotional states (Epstein, 1979). Each life has a coherence and continuity that is perceived both by the person and by those who know him or her.

Such continuity over time coexists with the fact that people also show great discriminativeness in their behavior as they cope with changing environmental demands. Hence, it is difficult to demonstrate impressive consistencies across situations when ongoing behavior is studied objectively as it occurs, rather than rated on broad trait dimensions (Block, 1977; Mischel, 1977). A given individual's actual behavior, while certainly not haphazard, often may be fairly specific to the situation. Relative specificity of behavior patterns was seen, for example, in the modest associations obtained among seemingly close indices of such sex-typed behaviors as dependency, and of sex-typing itself, as was discussed before (Chapter 13 and 14). Similar specificity was found for measures of self-control and moral behavior (Chapter 18), and for other personality dimensions, such as anxiety (Chapter 16) and cognitive avoidance (Chapter 17). While an individual may display some significant consistency on these traits, the degree of consistency found tends to be modest when behavior is measured objectively across situations, (rather than within similar situations over time).

There are many ways to interpret the findings of "behavioral specificity," but there is little doubt that personality organization is subtly differentiated across contexts while also coherent over time. Complex behavior is regulated by interactions that depend intimately on situational variables, as well as on dispositions. Humans are capable of extraordinary adaptiveness and discrimination as they cope with a continuously changing environment.

Seen from the vantage point of traditional trait theory, the specificity often found in behavior is a problem that tends to be attributed to defects in existing methods and measurements. Thus research evidence for the specificity of traits usually has been interpreted as due mainly to the inadequacies of the tests and the studies that used them (e.g., Alker, 1972; Block, 1977). As discussed before (Chapter 7), trait psychologists recognize the importance of the specific situation but believe that research has underestimated seriously the personal constancies in behavior. They correctly note that to test how well a trait can predict behavior requires that we sample adequately not only the trait but also the behavior that is to be predicted (Ajzen & Fishbein, 1977; Block, 1977; Epstein, 1979; Jaccard, 1974; Weigel & Newman, 1976). Unfortunately, past research often tried to predict single acts (for example, seeking help when failing) from a trait measure (e.g., self-rated dependency). While such efforts usually were unsuccessful, measures of traits may predict more effectively to a "multiple act criterion": a pooled combination of many acts or behaviors that are expected to relate to the trait.

While better measurements will surely improve the accuracy of prediction to some degree, the "specificity" so often found in studies of personality traits also may be viewed as accurately reflecting people's great discriminative facility and the inadequacy of global trait theories, not merely the biases of faulty measurement (Cantor & Mischel, 1979; Mischel, 1979). But the term "discriminative facility" (responsivity to changing conditions) seems preferable to "specificity" because it avoids the negative meanings implied by the "specificity" of behavior—the implications of inconsistency, fickleness, and unreliability in human nature.

Whereas discriminative facility is highly adaptive (Gibson, 1969), a reduced sensitivity to changing consequences (i.e., indiscriminate responding) may be characteristic of an organism adapting poorly. In fact, indiscriminate responding (i.e., extremely "consistent" behavior across situations) may be more characteristic of maladaptive severely disturbed or less mature persons than of well-functioning ones (Moos, 1968). While relatively more indiscriminate behavior tends to be found in more immature and/or disturbed individuals, its extent should not be exaggerated. Even extremely disturbed behavior, for example, may turn out to be highly discriminative when it is examined in detail (e.g., Lovaas et al., 1965), as we saw earlier (Chapters 9, 10).

Consistency in Some of the People Some of the Time

Bem and Allen (1974) recognized the discriminativeness so often displayed by most people on most of the personality dimensions studied, but proposed that consistency may characterize *some* people at least in *some* areas of behavior. They began by noting that traditional personality research on traits has assumed incorrectly that all traits would characterize all people. Bem and Allen suggested, instead, that while some people may be consistent on some traits, practically nobody is consistent on all traits; indeed, many traits that are studied by investigators may not even apply to many of the people who are studied. To get beyond this problem, Bem and Allen suggested looking only for those people who would be consistent on particular traits. Specifically, they tried to identify (preselect) those college students who would be consistent and those who would not be consistent on the trait of friendliness and conscientiousness. Their hypothesis was simply this: "Individuals who identify themselves as consistent on a particular trait dimension will in fact be more consistent cross-situationally than those who identify themselves as highly variable" (Bem & Allen, 1974, p. 512). The results, on the whole, supported the hypothesis; for example, students who described themselves as consistent in their level of friendliness tended to show a relatively consistent level of friendliness across a number of measures (such as ratings by their mothers, fathers, and peers, as well as direct observations of their friendliness in a small group discussion and in a waiting room). In contrast, those who described themselves as variable in their friendliness in fact tended to be less consistent.

The Bem and Allen study nicely demonstrated the point that individuals may (and do) display some consistency in some behavior patterns but not in others. For example, one person may show relatively consistent friendliness, another consistent dependency, and a third consistent honesty, but it is less likely that anyone will be consistent with regard to all of these dimensions. Consequently, when an investigator tries to compare many people on any given dimension, only some will be consistent but most people will be highly discriminative. Therefore, efforts to find cross-situational consistency in randomly selected samples of people are bound to yield poor results. It may be possible to demonstrate consistency, but, as Bem and Allen put it, only for "some of the people some of the time." Interestingly, it was the people themselves who predicted their own consistency, again providing support for the notion that each person knows his or her own behavior best (Chapter 11).

In a closely related direction many other researchers have also acknowledged the importance of situational variables for a large portion of people (Magnusson, 1980). But they also suggest that some people who are consistent may be identified. Hence these researchers treat "specificity-consistency" as a dimension of individual differences and attempt to discover those individuals who will be cross-situationally consistent (e.g., Campus, 1974). The degree to which this strategy will prove useful can only be determined by future research.

Finding the Appropriate Level

As noted earlier (Chapter 7), people can be categorized at different levels of abstraction. At the most molecular level, we may want to focus on relatively specific acts, like smiling or laughing or shaking hands. Categorizations at a relatively broad or "middle" level occur when we call someone a "comic joker type" or a "public relations type." And we form even more abstract categories when we use such broad trait terms as "extravert." Research suggests that categorizations at different levels of abstraction have different advantages and disadvantages, for example in the degree to which they provide richness of information, or vividness, or distinctiveness and differentiation (Cantor & Mischel, 1979). So whether we want to focus on relatively specific acts, or on broader, more abstract categories in our analyses of people depends importantly on our purpose (Mischel, 1979). For instance, a highly abstract level may be required for broad theories of personality about large categories of "people-in-general"; middle level categories may be more helpful for capturing the gist of how a particular person generally differs from others; and highly specific units may be needed to vividly and richly describe specific interactions between what the person does and the particular conditions in the environment.

Within each level of category it also may prove useful to search for the "best examples," the ideal or most typical instances: The members of everyday natural categories (categories like tables, chairs, and clothes) do not all have in common a set of single, essential features that are required for category membership. Instead of a single set of features shared by all members of a category, we may find a pattern of "family resemblance" (Chapter 2). Such patterns of family resemblance might characterize our everyday categories about people, and efforts to identify them may provide an interesting alternative to the traditional trait approach (Cantor & Mischel, 1979; Wiggins, 1980). It may be that when we form our everyday impressions of people we can agree easily about who is a more or less typical type of personality. If so, the study of the rules used to make such judgments will help reveal how we find consistency even when faced with endless variations in behavior. Clearly the discovery of how people find equivalences or basic similarities underlying diverse actions is one of the important challenges for the field.

The Study of Environments

While some psychologists have been searching for cross-situationally consistent people, others have been focusing more and more on the social and psychological environments in which people live and function. The dramatic increase of interest in the environment as it relates to humans is documented easily: From 1968 to 1972 more books appeared on the topic of human-environment relations from an ecological perspective than had been published in the prior three decades (Jordan, 1972). This new area still has not been given a final name; it is sometimes called environmental psychology and sometimes social or psychological ecology. Regardless of name, the field studies "the impact that physical and social environments have on human beings" (Moos & Insel, 1974, p. IX), and is concerned with "human problems in relation to an environment in which man is both victim and conqueror . . ." (Proshansky, et al., 1970, p. 4). The interest in the environment is a much

TABLE 20-1
SOME DIMENSIONS OF HUMAN ENVIRONMENTS

Dimensions	*Examples*
1. Ecological	Climate and geographical qualities; architectural and physical use of space and constraints (e.g., the walls of a prison)
2. Behavioral settings	School, drugstore, football game, church
3. Organizational	Size and type of staff in a hospital; student/teacher ratio in a school; population density
4. Characteristics of inhabitants	Age, sex, abilities, status of members
5. Perceived social climate (psychosocial characteristics)	Nature and intensity of personal relations
6. Functional properties	Reinforcement consequences for particular behaviors in that situation

SOURCE: Based on Moos (1973).

needed corrective for an area of psychology that historically has focused on the individual as a unit, often forgetting the intimate links between the person and the conditions of his or her life.

As is true in most new fields, a first concern in the study of environments has been to try to classify them, just as trait psychologists had tried to classify traits into a taxonomy (Chapters 2 and 7). Environments, like everything else, can be classified in many ways, depending mainly on the purposes and imagination of the classifiers. One typical effort to describe some of the almost infinite dimensions of environments was proposed by Moos and is summarized in Table 20-1. The classification in Table 20-1 calls attention to the complex nature of environments and to the many variables that can characterize them. These variables include the weather, the buildings and settings, the perceived social climates, and the reinforcements obtained for behaviors in that situation—to list just a few.

The classification alerts us to a fact that has been slighted by traditional trait oriented approaches to personality: Much human behavior depends on environmental considerations, such as the setting (e.g., Barker, 1968), and even on such specific physical and psychosocial variables as how hot and crowded the setting is, or how the room and furniture are arranged, or how the people in the setting are organized (e.g., Krasner & Ullmann, 1973; Moos & Insel, 1974). Many links between characteristics of the environment and behavior have been demonstrated. For example, measures of population density (such as the number of people in each room) may be related to certain forms of aggression (even when social class and ethnicity are controlled; Galle, Gove, & McPhersen, 1972). Likewise, interpersonal attraction and mood are negatively affected by extremely hot, crowded conditions (Griffitt & Veitch, 1971).

Some psychologists have tried to classify situations with characteristics ranging from gravity and the physical terrain to social norms (Sells, 1973). Focusing on the *perceptions* of observers, there also have been efforts to classify situations on the basis of their perceived similarity, emerging with such trait-like characterizations of situations as "positive," "negative," "passive," "social," and "active" (e.g., Magnusson & Ekehammer, 1973). Similarly, Moos and his associates have obtained ratings of the "perceived social climate" in such institutions as psychiatric wards, prisons, and schools (1973, 1974). These ratings are intended to measure such qualities as the perceived degree to which a given program or setting provides support (encouragement) for its members, fosters, spontaneity and involvement, and helps people have autonomy in decision-making.

Depending on one's purpose, many different classifications are possible and useful. To seek any single "basic" taxonomy of situations may be as futile as searching for a final or ultimate taxonomy of traits; we can label situations in at least as many different ways as we can label people. It will be important to avoid emerging simply with a trait psychology of situations, in which events and settings, rather than people, are merely given different labels. The task of naming situations cannot substitute for the job of analyzing *how* conditions and environments interact with the people in them (as discussed in later sections).

Searching for the Personality of Situations

One seemingly promising approach attempts to characterize the personality of situations (Bem & Funder, 1978). It tries to do so by creating a portrait of the personality traits of people who function particularly well in a given situation. Consider, for example, a situation in which children have a chance to delay taking an immediate, smaller reward in order to obtain a more preferred reward later. Bem and Funder exposed children to such a situation, measured how long they waited, and also asked the children's parents to rate their traits on a version of the Q-sort (a rating measure described in Chapter 11). The Q-sort ratings were used to make profiles of the personality of the ideal "delaying" child by simply seeing what traits had been used to characterize the children who waited longest in that situation.

The authors also proposed that the same method could be applied to create portraits of the ideal personality in other situations that should tap the same basic disposition—in this case, the tendency to delay gratification. For example, one can create another situation in which the child has somewhat different opportunities to defer instant pleasure for the sake of better but delayed gratifications and again get the Q-sort portraits of the youngsters who wait longest. To the degree that the portraits in the two situations overlap, one may conclude that the two situations are really psychologically similar. But to the degree that the two portraits are different, the two situations may really be tapping different personal qualities although both situations may appear to be similar. Hopefully a search for situations that yield similar personality portraits would yield situations that are basically similar (rather than situations that merely look alike in superficial ways). After such psychologically similar situations have been identified through their common Q-sort portraits, it should be possible to demonstrate consistency in the behavior that people will display in them. That is the gist of the Bem and Funder thesis, and it has aroused much interest by suggesting a way to uncover equivalencies among situations by finding the overlapping personality characteristics that they tap.

The logic of the Bem-Funder approach is appealing but it remains to be seen whether or not it will yield impressive cross-situational consistencies in behavior (across situations with similar Q-sort portraits). A first effort has been made to repeat the Bem-Funder study in the delay of gratification situation to see if similar results would be found again (Mischel & Peake, 1981). Although the same procedures were followed as closely as possible, the findings were quite different. That is, the distinctive Q-sort trait ratings that Bem and Funder found for children who showed the greatest delay were not found again when a new sample of children was exposed to the same situation in the same preschool. This failure to replicate the results raises questions about the stability and value of the Bem-Funder method for portraying the "personality" of situations, and suggests the need for more research before firm conclusions can be reached.

The Charge of "Situationism": Where Is the Person in Personality Psychology?

As noted earlier (Chapter 4), many critics feel that in recent years psychology has been overemphasizing the importance of the environment and the situation while underemphasizing—or even "losing"—the person (e.g., Bowers, 1973; Carlson, 1971). This is a serious charge; losing the person in personality psychology would be as bizarre as losing matter in physics or the elements in chemistry. The person is what personality psychology must be about; no one really disputes that. But there is disagreement about how to best study and conceptualize the person, as we saw throughout this book (especially in Parts I and II).

Bowers (1973, p. 307) attacks a "situationism" that emphasizes situations as the causes of behavior while "being inattentive to the importance of the person." Situationism is defined as an explanatory bias that tends "either to ignore organismic factors or to regard them as . . . subsidiary to the primary impact of the external stimulus" (Harré & Secord, 1972, p. 27).

Closely paralleling the charge of "situationism" is the humanistic protest to the behavioral approach in general. We have considered many aspects of the humanistic (phenomenological) position in Chapters 5 and 11. The essence of the humanistic protest is that behaviorally oriented psychologists (i.e., "situationists") treat and manipulate human beings as if they were externally controlled rather than free, self-determining beings who are responsible for their own actions and growth. Some of these criticisms and charges may seem justified objections against the pure environmentalism of B. F. Skinner's (1974) radical behaviorism. The characteristics of the environment interact with the attributes of the people in it, and it would be foolish to ignore either side of this interaction.

The recognition that the environment is important for human behavior is a welcome (even if tardy) insight for most personality psychologists. But a psychological approach requires that we move from descriptions of the environment—of the climate, buildings, social settings, etc., in which we live—to the psychological processes through which environmental conditions and people influence each other reciprocally. For this purpose, it is necessary to consider how the environment influences behavior and how people's behavior in turn shapes the environment in an endless interaction. To understand the interaction of person and environment we must consider *person variables* as well as environental variables, and we must analyze the nature of person-situation *interactions* psychologically. Later sections attempt to do just that.

The Prevalence and Meaning of Interaction

The new interest in environments (situations, psychological ecology) expressed by personality psychologists reflects in part increased dissatisfaction with traditional trait-oriented theories that tried to understand people without adequately considering the specific conditions of the individual's life from moment to moment. It also reflects a recognition that many important human behaviors not only fluctuate as the situation changes but also depend crucially on the mutual (reciprocal) influence of the person and the situation; that is, their "interaction." We noted repeatedly throughout this book that the effects of conditions depend on the individuals in them, and that the *interaction* of individual differences and specific conditions is usually crucial. For example, the impact of different types of classroom arrangements depends on the particular students in them; small group discussion that might be helpful for some students might be a bore or even a handicap for others.

Some researchers hoped that studies of persons, environments, and their interaction would answer the question "are persons or situations more important for predicting behavior?" But the question serves mostly to stimulate futile debates. The answer must always depend on the particular situations and the particular persons sampled. The question of whether individual differences or situations are more important is an empty one that has no general answer.

Moreover, in current debates on this topic, "situations" are often treated like entities that supposedly exert either major or only minor control over behavior, without specifying what, psychologically, they are or how they function. But while some situations may be powerful determinants of behavior, others are trivial. The relative importance of individual differences and situations will depend on the situation selected, the type of behavior assessed, the particular individual differences sampled, and the purpose of the assessment (Magnusson & Endler, 1977; Mischel, 1973a).

The Specificity of Situations (Treatments)

The other side of the coin of "behavioral specificity" is the realization that situations (or "treatments" in experimental and clinical contexts) also tend to produce specific rather than generalized effects, and that the effects are often weak (e.g., Sarason, Smith, & Diener, 1975). As one psychologist put it, "Although it is undoubtedly true that behavior is more situation specific than trait theory acknowledged . . . situations are more person specific than is commonly recognized" (Bowers, 1973, p. 307). That is, the impact of particular situations or treatments depends on the particular people in them. A particular "enrichment" course, or social influence effort, or creativity-training session, or therapy program might work well for some individuals but be ineffective (or even harmful) for others.

There is a growing belief throughout psychology and the social sciences that "treatments" may not have broad, highly generalized, stable effects. Specificity may occur because of the large range of different ways that different people may react to the "same" treatments and reinterpret them (e.g., Cronbach, 1975; Neisser, 1974), and because the impact of most situations usually can be changed easily by other "moderating" conditions (Mischel, 1974). Thus, even a relatively simple "stimulus" or "situation" may produce a variety of often unpredictable specific (and weak) effects depending on a large number of moderating variables and the many different ways in which the particular "subjects" may view them. (Recall, for example, the many variables that may determine whether or not one chooses to delay gratification, discussed in Chapter 18.)

The recognition that behavior is always determined by many variables and that a focus on any one of them will lead to limited predictions and generalizations is not confined to the area of personality psychology. This conclusion has been reached for "treatments" as diverse as interview styles in psychotherapy, teaching practices and classroom arrangements in education, and instructions to aid recall in memory experiments. For example, after a survey of research on memory we are cautioned that: ". . . What is remembered in a given situation depends on the physical and psychological context in which the event was experienced, the knowledge and skills that the subject brings to the context, the situation in which we ask for evidence for remembering, and the relation of what the subject remembers to what the experimenter demands" (Jenkins, 1974, p. 793). The same conclusions probably apply as well to the subject matter studied in any other sub-area of psychology.

As a consequence, it may become difficult to achieve broad, sweeping generalizations about human behavior; many qualifiers (moderators) must be appended to our "laws" about cause-and-effect relations—almost without exception and perhaps with no exceptions at all (Cronbach, 1975). On the other hand, while the need to qualify generalizations about human behavior complicates life for the social scientist, it does not prevent one from studying human affairs scientifically; it only dictates a respect for the complexity of the enterprise and alerts one to the dangers of oversimplifying the nature and causes of human behavior. That danger is equally great whether one is searching for generalized (global) person-free situational effects or for generalized (global) situation-free personality variables.

Conceptualizing Interaction

It has been easier to demonstrate the existence of extensive person-situation interactions than to explain them. It is now necessary to analyze the psychological bases for "interaction"; without such an analysis, an emphasis on interaction is in danger of being little more than the announcement of the obvious. Granted that both environments and individual differences are important and interact, how can the impact of situations be conceptualized in *psychological* terms?

In the author's view (Mischel, 1973a, 1979) the cognitive social learning variables described in Chapter 13 may provide one convenient step. Recall that these "person variables" are ways of thinking about individual differences from a perspective that blends contributions from personality and cognitive psychology. These variables refer to the products or residues within the person of his or her cognitive development, social learning history, and genetic endowment. These variables include the person's *competencies* to construct or enact behaviors under appropriate conditions. One also has to consider the person's *encoding* and categorization; how individuals construe themselves, other people, and situations. To analyze performance in given situations also requires us to consider the person's *expectancies* about outcomes, the *subjective values* of such outcomes, and *self-regulatory systems* and *plans*. These variables are not meant to exclude others, but only to give examples of the kinds of person qualities that seem clearly related to basic psychological processes and that demand a place in a comprehensive view of the individual. With these person variables as background, let us now consider more concretely how the interaction of persons and situations may work.

When Do Individual Differences Make a Difference?

The conditions or "situational variables" of the psychological environment may be conceptualized as providing the individual with information; this information influences person variables, thereby affecting how the individual thinks and acts under those conditions. "Situations" (environments) thus influence our behavior by affecting such person variables as how we encode the situation, the outcomes we expect, their subjective value for us, and our competencies.

Recognizing that the question "are persons or situations more important?" is misleading and unanswerable, one can now turn to the more interesting issue: *When* are situations most likely to exert powerful effects and, conversely, *when* are person variables likely to be most influential?

Psychological "situations" ("stimuli," "treatments") are powerful to the degree that they lead everyone to construe the particular events the same way, induce *uniform* expectancies regarding the most appropriate response pattern, provide adequate incentives for the performance of that response pattern, and require skills that everyone has to the same extent. A good example of a powerful stimulus is a red traffic light; it exerts powerful effects on the behavior of most motorists because they all know what it means, are motivated to obey it, and are capable of stopping when they see it. Therefore it would be easier to predict drivers' behavior at stop lights from knowing the color of the light than from making inferences about the "conformity," "cautiousness," or other traits of the drivers.

Conversely, situations are weak to the degree that they are not uniformly encoded, do not generate uniform expectancies concerning the desired behavior, do not offer sufficient incentives for its performance, or fail to provide the learning conditions required for sucessful genesis of the behavior. An extreme example of such a weak stimulus is the blank card on the TAT projective test (Chapter 8) with the instructions to create a story about what might be happening; clearly the answers will depend more on the story-tellers than on the card.

In sum, individual differences can determine behavior in a given situation most strongly when the situation is ambiguously structured (as in projective testing) so that each person is uncertain about how to categorize it, has to structure it in his or her own terms, and has no clear expectations about the behaviors most likely to be appropriate (normative, reinforced) in that situation. To the degree that the situation is "unstructured" and the person expects that virtually all responses from him or her are equally likely to be appropriate (i.e., will lead to similar consequences), the significance of individual differences will be greatest. Conversely, when everyone expects that only *one* response will be appropriate (e.g., only one "right" answer on an achievement test, only one correct response for the driver when the traffic light turns red) and that no other responses are equally good, and all people are motivated and capable of making the appropriate response, then individual differences become minimal and situational effects dominant. To the degree that people are exposed to powerful treatments, the role of the individual differences among them will be minimized. Conversely, when treatments are weak, ambiguous, or trivial, individual differences in person variables should have the most significant effects.

So far we have considered "treatments" like those in laboratory studies or therapy programs. But the complex social settings of everyday life also vary in the degree to which they prescribe and limit the range of expected and acceptable behavior for persons in particular roles and settings and hence permit the expression of individual differences (e.g., Barker, 1968; Price, 1974). In some settings the rules and prescriptions for enacting specific role behaviors greatly limit the range of possible behaviors (e.g., in church, at school, in a theater, at a conference), while in others the range of possible behaviors is broad and often the individual can select, structure, and reorganize situations with few external constraints. Because in particular settings certain response patterns are rewarded (effective) while others are not, different settings become the occasion for particular behaviors in different degrees.

Behavioral Appropriateness and Situational Constraints

Situations can be classified according to the range and type of behaviors considered appropriate within them. In one study, college students were asked to rate the appropriateness of 15 behaviors in 15 situations (Price & Bouffard, 1974). Examples of the behaviors are *run, belch, kiss, write, eat;* examples of the situations are *in class, on a date, on a bus, at a family dinner, in a restroom.* The average appropriateness ratings were calculated for each of the many combinations of behaviors and situations. These ratings could range from 0 ("the behavior is extremely inappropriate in this situation") to 9 ("the behavior is extremely appropriate in this situation"). To illustrate, Table 20-2 summarizes the average appropriateness ratings found for five behaviors in relation to five situations.

Analyses of this kind applied to a wide range of behaviors and situations can provide useful information. High values for a behavior indicate that it is considered appropriate in many situations, low values suggest that it is generally inappropriate. Likewise, the degree of *situational constraint* for a particular situation can be indexed simply by averaging the appropriateness ratings of the behaviors in that situation (e.g., the rows of Table 20-2). The results of follow-up research also indicated that situations that have high constraint tend to be seen as potentially embarrassing, as requiring more careful self-monitoring of one's behavior, and as demanding certain behaviors rather than others.

It would be especially interesting to examine the degree of *variation* among individuals (not just the average level) found for particular behaviors in particular situations. The most "powerful" situations would be those that usually

	Behaviors				
Situations	Run	Write	Mumble	Belch	Cry
Class	2.52	8.17	3.62	1.77	2.21
Family Dinner	2.56	2.58	2.54	2.50	3.21
Job Interview	1.94	4.85	1.31	1.21	1.37
Bar	1.96	5.38	6.21	5.04	3.44
Own Room	6.15	8.29	7.67	6.81	8.00

**TABLE 20-2
AVERAGE APPROPRIATENESS RATINGS FOR
5 BEHAVIORS IN 5 SITUATIONS**

Note: The higher the number the higher the rated appropriateness of the behavior in the situation.
SOURCE: Based on data from Price and Bouffard (1974).

allow little variation; the "weakest" situations would be those in which variation among people is typically high. Individual differences would be expected to exert the greatest influence in the weak (high variation) situations and to have the smallest effect in the powerful (low variation) ones.

Predicting from Situations and/or Persons

Person-condition interactions are never static, but environmental stabilities can be identified which help to account for continuities in behavior and permit useful predictions. While the psychology of personality cannot ignore the person, it is also true that behavior sometimes may be predicted and influenced simply from knowledge about relevant stimulus conditions, especially when those conditions are powerful. The potency of predictions based on knowledge of stimulus conditions is seen, for example, in studies that tried to predict the posthospital adjustment of mental patients. Accurate predictions of posthospital adjustment required knowledge of the environment in which the ex-patient would be living in the community—such as the availability of jobs and family support—rather than any measures of person variables or in-hospital behavior (e.g., Fairweather, 1967; Fairweather et al., 1969).

In another domain, to predict intellectual achievement it also helps to take account of the degree to which the child's environment supports (models and reinforces) intellectual development (Wolf, 1966). Finally, when powerful treatments are developed—such as modeling and desensitization therapies for phobias—predictions about outcomes may be best when based on knowing the treatment to which the individual is assigned (e.g., Bandura, Blanchard, & Ritter, 1969).

The significance of the psychological situation was vividly demonstrated in a simulated prison study conducted in the basement of a psychology department building (Haney, Banks, & Zimbardo, 1973). College student volunteers were selected carefully, on the basis of extensive interviewing and diagnostic testing, to have exemplary backgrounds and no antisocial tendencies. Nevertheless, less than one week after being exposed around the clock to what the authors refer to as the "inherently pathological characteristics of the realistically simulated prison situation itself," all subjects assigned to the role of "guards" were exhibiting extreme antisocial behavior—harassing and victimizing their "prisoners" brutally. The authors concluded that few of the "guards'" reactions could be attributed to individual differences on generalized dimensions (e.g., lack of empathy, excessively rigid adherence to conventional values) existing before they began to play their assigned roles. The potency of the situation undoubtedly left some lasting effects, particularly in beliefs, as evidenced by the subjects' postexperimental statements (e.g., "I learned that people can easily forget that others are human," p. 88). But it is also most likely that once the prison experiment was over, the "guards" gave up their newly characteristic aggressive and harassing behavior and all ex-subjects soon started to respond in terms of the current contexts of their lives.

While some situations can be extremely potent, often we need to know about person variables. Information about person variables becomes essential when relevant information about situations is absent or minimal, or when predictions are needed about how different individuals will respond to the same conditions, or when situational variables are weak. And as we saw in earlier sections, such predictions may be possible at least for "some of the people some of the time."

Mutual Influences between Persons and Conditions

Traditionally, trait-oriented personality research has studied individual differences in response to the "same" situation. But some of the most striking differences between persons may be found not by studying how they react to the same situation but by analyzing their *selection* and construction of stimulus conditions. In the conditions of life outside the laboratory the psychological "stimuli" that people encounter are neither questionnaire items, nor experimental instructions, nor inanimate events, but involve other people and reciprocal relationships (e.g., with spouse, with boss, with children). We continuously influence the "situations" of our lives as well as being affected by them in a mutual, organic interaction (e.g., Raush et al., 1974). Such interactions reflect not only our reactions to conditions but also our active selection and modification of conditions through our own choices, cognitions, and actions (Wachtel, 1973). Different people select different settings for themselves; conversely, the settings that people select to be in may provide clues about their personal qualities (Eddy & Sinnett, 1973).

The mutual interaction between person and conditions (so easily overlooked when one searches for generalized traits on paper-and-pencil tests) can-

Person variables also influence the "situations" one selects—including the people to whom one attends.

not be ignored when behavior is studied in the interpersonal contexts in which it is evoked, maintained, and modified. The analysis of complex social interactions (e.g., Patterson & Cobb, 1971) vividly illustrates how each of us continuously selects, changes, and generates conditions just as much as we are affected by them.

If you change your behavior toward another person he or she generally shows reciprocal changes in behavior toward you. In Raush's (1965, p. 492) studies of naturalistic interactions, for example, "the major determinant of an act was the immediately preceding act. Thus if you want to know what child B will do, the best single predictor is what child A did to B the moment before." Construed from the viewpoint of child A, this means that A's own behavior determines B's reactions to him; if A provokes B, B will reciprocate aggressively. In that sense, the person is generating his or her own conditions.

The other side of the interaction is the fact that B's behavior is always constrained by what A did the moment before. Studies of the interactions among husbands and wives illustrate this point (Raush et al., 1974). In these studies, husband-wife interactions were observed as the couples coped with such conflicts as how to celebrate their first wedding anniversary when each had made different plans. For example, Bob has arranged and paid in advance for dinner at a restaurant, but Sue has spent half the day preparing for a special dinner at home. As the couple realize their conflict and try to resolve it, their interactions continuously reveal that each antecedent act (what Sue has just said to Bob) constrains each consequent act (how Bob responds).

The meaning and impact of each act also depends on such additional considerations as the total context and situation in which it occurs as well as on the relationship and "style" that each couple develops. ". . . Situations thus 'inform' persons, selecting segments of personal experience; persons also inform situations, selecting segments to respond to" (Raush et al., 1974, p. 212). Such variables as the persons' constructs, expectancies, self-regulatory rules and plans presumably guide the situations that they select and generate, and how they interpret them; they influence the responses that they emit and that in turn shape their environment as much as they are shaped by them.

The conceptualization of behavior must be linked to the specific conditions in which it occurs. Rather than talk about "behavior," it may be more useful to tie specific patterns of behavior to the conditions in which they may be expected. Accurate descriptions require specifying as precisely as possible the response mode of the behavior as well as the conditions in which it is expected to be strong or weak. Thus rather than describe a person as "aggressive" it would be necessary to qualify the mode of aggressive behavior (e.g., verbal insults, but not physical attacks) and the specific circumstances (e.g., when criticized for poor athletic performance on the playground, but not in class). Such cumbersome, hyphenated descriptions would lack the "thumbnail sketch" appeal of global trait portraits. But they would remind us of the discriminativeness, complexity, and uniqueness of each individual's behavior, its dependence on conditions, and the risks of trying to abbreviate and oversimplify it.

In sum, an adequate approach to personality psychology must recognize the interdependence of behavior and conditions. It must recognize the human tendency to invent constructs and to adhere to them, as well as to generate subtly discriminative behaviors across settings and over time. It must be alert to the crucial role of situations (conditions) but can view them as informational inputs whose behavioral impact depends on how they are processed (interpreted) by the person. It also must consider how such information processing hinges, in turn, on person variables as well as on the prior conditions that the individual has experienced. And it has to recognize that the person selects and changes the situations of his or her life as well as being changed by them. "Personality psychology" does not have to be restricted to the study of differences between individuals in their consistent attributes; it must also help us understand each individual's cognitive and behavioral activities in interaction with the conditions of his or her life.

Toward a Unified Image of the Person?

Does a distinctive image of the person begin to emerge from the work discussed throughout this volume? Can one glimpse a more unified conception of the person in the study of personality? Some psychologists (e.g., Singer & Singer, 1972), including this author, think so. In the present view, this image seems to reflect a growing synthesis of several theoretical influences in current personality psychology. It is an image that seems compatible with many qualities of both the behavioral and the cognitive phenomenological approaches to personality and yet departs from each in some respects.

This image is one of the human being as an active, aware problem-solver, capable of profiting from an enormous range of experiences and cognitive capacities, possessed of great potential for good or ill, actively constructing his or her psychological world, interpreting and processing information in potentially creative ways, influencing the world but also being influenced by it lawfully—even if the laws are difficult to discover and hard to generalize. It views the person as so complex and multi-faceted as to defy easy classifications and comparisons on any single or simple common dimensions, as multiply influenced by a host of determinants, as uniquely organized on the basis of prior experiences and future expectations, and yet as studyable by the methods of science, and continuously responsive to stimulus conditions in meaningful ways. It is an image that has moved a long way from the instinctual drive-reduction models, the static global traits, and the automatic stimulus-response bonds of earlier times (discussed at many points in Part I). It is an image that highlights the shortcomings of all simplistic theories that view behavior as the exclusive result of any narrow set of determinants, whether these are habits, traits, drives, constructs, instincts, genes, or reinforcers. And yet it is an image that is sure to shift in still unpredictable directions as our understanding and knowledge increase.

pt of chpt. We influence situation and situation influence us.

SUMMARY

1. The sensitivity of behavior to the conditions in which it occurs may be interpreted as reflecting the adaptiveness and discrimination of which people are capable. Such discrimination facilitates the individual's attempts to cope with a continuously changing environment.

2. There are extensive individual differences in reactions to the same "stimulus" (situation, treatment) and some consistent differences in how a person behaves in particular classes of situations. For example, stability over time has been demonstrated for individual differences in ego strength and aggression.

3. To analyze and predict an individual's behavior adequately, individual differences generally must be linked to the conditions in which that behavior occurs. Prediction from trait measures may be improved by more adequately sampling the trait (e.g., multiple measures) and by pooling the behaviors that the trait is expected to predict (multiple act criterion).

4. Some of the consistency we see in behavior may be the result of abstract categorization. The advantages and disadvantages of categorizing behavior at various levels of abstraction depend upon one's purpose.

5. There has been growing interest in the environments in which the individual functions. Human environments can be classified according to many dimensions. Labeling and classifying situations, however, is only one aspect of the analysis of environments.

6. One attempt to characterize the "personality" of situations is based on the description of the personality traits of individuals who function especially well in a particular situation. The psychological similarity of two situations can then be evaluated in terms of the similarity of the trait portraits of individuals who function best in them.

7. As critics of "situationism" stress, an emphasis on the environment and on the conditions in which the person acts should not lead one to lose sight of the person. People can and do change and determine their environments through their own choices and actions. The relative importance of an individual's characteristics and of the situation in determining behavior depends on the particular individual differences, the type of situation, the behavior one is analyzing, and the purpose of the analysis.

8. Just as there is considerable "behavioral specificity," so also is there much specificity in the effects of most situations and treatments. While some conditions are powerful, others exert weak, specific, and ungeneralizable effects that require many qualifiers in efforts to find general laws about cause and effect relations.

9. Person variables help us to analyze the interaction of the individual and situations. Situations provide information that may affect each person variable—for example, the ability to generate behavior patterns, expectancies, the values placed on certain outcomes in the situation, the way the situation is construed. Powerful situations are those which everyone construes the same way, in which everyone agrees about the most appropriate behavior and has adequate competence and incentives to enact it. When situations are less powerful and more ambiguous, individual differences become more important. The expectancies, encoding strategies, values, and response capabilities that the person brings into the situation are especially important when the situation is unstructured and when there are few external restraints.

10. Behaviors and situations can be analyzed according to their range of appropriateness. Behaviors vary with regard to the range of situations in which they are appropriate; situations differ in the number and kinds of behaviors they allow. (Compare, for example, football games, church services, and family mealtimes.)

11. To predict behavior when situational variables are powerful, knowledge of the relevant situational variables is crucial. When situational variables are weak, when there is little known about them, or when the goal is the prediction of individual differences in response to the same situation, person variables become crucial.

12. Individual differences typically have been studied by holding the situation constant and observing the differences in the way people react to the same situation. Yet one of the most important differences between people is the way *they* select, influence, and change the situations of their lives. The interpersonal relations that comprise much of our daily lives are constantly selected and modified by us in accord with our competencies, constructs, expectancies, values, and plans. Each person generates many of the very conditions to which he or she then reacts in a series of continuous interactions between behavior and conditions.

REFERENCES

Abelson, R. Are attitudes necessary? In B. T. King & E. McGinnies (Eds.), *Attitudes, conflicts, and social change.* New York: Academic Press, 1972.

Abelson, R. P. A script theory of understanding, attitude, and behavior. In J. Carroll & T. Payne (Eds.), *Cognition and social behavior.* Hillsdale, N.J.: Erlbaum, 1976.

Abramson, L. Y., Seligman, M. E. P., & Teasdale, J. D. Learned helplessness in humans: Critique and reformation. *Journal of Abnormal Psychology,* 1978, *87,* 49–74.

Adinolfi, A. A. Relevance of person perception research to clinical psychology. *Journal of Consulting and Clinical Psychology,* 1971, *37,* 167–176.

Adorno, I. W., Frenkel-Brunswik, E., Levinson, D. J., & Sanford, R. N. *The authoritarian personality.* New York: Harper & Row, 1950.

Ainsworth, M. D. S., Bell, S. M., & Stayton, D. J. Individual differences in strange-situation behavior of one-year-olds. In H. R. Schaffer (Ed.), *The origins of human social relations.* New York: Academic Press, 1971.

Ajzen, I., & Fishbein, M. Attitude-behavior relations: A theoretical analysis and review of empirical research. *Psychological Bulletin,* 1977, *84,* 888–918.

Akamatsu, T. J., & Thelen, M. H. A review of the literature on observer characteristics and imitation. *Developmental Psychology,* 1974, *10,* 38–47.

Alexander, F., & French, T. M. *Psychoanalytic therapy.* New York: Ronald, 1946.

Alker, H. A. Is personality situationally specific or intrapsychically consistent? *Journal of Personality,* 1972, *40,* 1–16.

Allen, E. K., Hart, B. M., Buell, J. S., Harris, F. R., & Wolf, M. M. Effects of social reinforcement on isolate behavior of a nursery school child. *Child Development,* 1964, *35,* 511–518.

Allinsmith, W. The learning of moral standards. In D. R. Miller & G. E. Swanson (Eds.), *Inner conflict and defense.* New York: Holt, Rinehart and Winston, 1960, pp. 141–176.

Allport, G. W. *Personality: A psychological interpretation.* New York: Holt, Rinehart and Winston, 1937.

Allport, G. W. Motivation in personality: Reply to Mr. Bertocci. *Psychological Review,* 1940, *47,* 533–554.

Allport, G. W. Pattern and growth in personality. New York: Holt, Rinehart and Winston, 1961.

Allport, G. W. & Odbert, H. S. Trait-names: A psycho-lexical study. *Psychological Monographs: General and Applied,* 1936, *47* (1, Whole No. 211).

Alston, W. P. Comments on Kohlberg's "From is to ought." In T. Mischel (Ed.), *Cognitive Development and Epistemology.* New York: Academic Press, 1971.

American Psychological Association. *Standards for educational and psychological tests and manuals.* Washington, D.C.: APA, 1966.

Amsel, A., & Roussel, J. S. Motivational properties of frustration: I. Effect on a running response of the addition of frustration to the motivational complex. *Journal of Experimental Psychology,* 1952, *43,* 363–368.

Anastasi, A., & D'Angelo, R. A comparison of Negro and white preschool children in language development and Goodenough Draw-a-Man I.Q. *Journal of Genetic Psychology,* 1952, *81,* 147–165.

Anderson, H. H., & Anderson, G. L. (Eds.). *An introduction to projective techniques.* Englewood Cliffs, N.J.: Prentice-Hall, 1951.

Anderson, I. H., Hughes, B. O., & Dixon, W. R. The rate of reading development and its relation to age of learning to read, sex, and intelligence. *Journal of Educational Research,* 1957, *50,* 481–494.

Anderson, J. R., & Bower, G. H. *Human associative memory.* New York: Wiley, 1973.

Anderson, N. H. Primacy effects in personality impression formation using a generalized order effect paradigm. *Journal of Personality and Social Psychology,* 1965, *2,* 1–9.

Anderson, N. H. Information integration theory: A brief survey. In D. H. Krautz, R. C. Atkinson, R. D. Luce, & P. Suppes (Eds.), *Contemporary developments in mathematical psychology.* San Francisco: Freeman, 1974.

Archibald, H. C., & Tuddenham, R. D. Persistent stress reaction after combat. *Archives of General Psychiatry,* 1965, *12,* 475–481.

Arend, R., Gove, F. L., & Sroufe, L. A. Continuity of individual adaptation from infancy to kindergarten: A predictive study of ego-resiliency and curiosity in preschoolers. *Child Development,* 1979, *50,* 950–959.

Argyle, M., & Little, B. R. Do personality traits apply to social behavior? *Journal of Theory of Social Behavior,* 1972, *2,* 1–35 (Great Britain).

Aronfreed, J. The internalization of social control through punishment: Experimental studies of the role of conditioning and the second signal system in the development of conscience. *Proceedings of the XVIIIth International Congress of Psychology.* Moscow, USSR, August, 1966, *35,* 219–230.

Aronfreed, J. *Conduct and conscience: The socialization of internalized control over behavior.* New York: Academic Press, 1968.

Aronson, E. *The social animal.* San Francisco: Freeman, 1972.

Aronson, E., & Carlsmith, J. M. Performance expectancy as a determinant of actual performance. *Journal of Abnormal and Social Psychology,* 1962, *65,* 178–182.

Aronson, E., & Mettee, D. Dishonest behavior as a function of differential levels of induced self-esteem. *Journal of Personality and Social Psychology,* 1968, *9,* 121–127.

Asch, S. E. Forming impressions of personality. *Journal of Abnormal and Social Psychology,* 1946, *41,* 258–290.

Ash, P. The reliability of psychiatric diagnoses. *Journal of Abnormal and Social Psychology,* 1949, *44,* 272–276.

Atkinson, J. W. Motivational determinants of risk-taking behavior. *Psychological Review,* 1957, *64,* 359–372.

Atkinson, J. W. (Ed.). *Motives in fantasy, action and society.* Princeton, N.J.: Van Nostrand, 1958.

Atkinson, J. W., & Feather, N. T. *A theory of achievement motivation.* New York: Wiley, 1966.

Atthowe, J. M., Jr., & Krasner, L. A preliminary report on the application of contingent reinforcement procedures (token economy) on a "chronic" psychiatric ward. *Journal of Abnormal Psychology,* 1968, *73,* 37–43.

Averill, J. Personal control over aversive stimuli and its relationship to stress. *Psychological Bulletin,* 1973, *80,* 286–303.

Ax, A. F. The physiological differentiation between fear and anger in humans. *Psychosomatic Medicine,* 1953, *15,* 433–442.

Ayllon, T., & Azrin, N. H. The measurement and reinforcement of behavior of psychotics. *Journal of the Experimental Analysis of Behavior,* 1965, *8,* 357–383.

Ayllon, T., & Azrin, N. H. *The token economy.* New York: Appleton, 1968.

Ayllon, T., & Haughton, E. Modification of symptomatic verbal behaviour of mental patients. *Behaviour Research and Therapy,* 1964, *2,* 87–97.

Bach, G. R. Father-fantasies and father-typing in father-separated children. *Child Development,* 1946, *17,* 63–80.

Baldwin, A. L. A cognitive theory of socialization. In D. A. Goslin (Ed.), *Handbook of socialization theory and research.* Chicago: Rand McNally, 1969, 325–480.

Balow, I. H. Sex differences in first grade reading. *Elementary English,* 1963, *40,* 303–306.

Baltes, P. B. Life-span developmental psychology: Observations on history and theory. In P. B. Baltes & O. C. Brim, Jr. (Eds.), *Life-span development and behavior,* vol. 2. New York: Academic Press, 1979.

Bandura, A. Relationship of family patterns to child behavior disorders. Progress Report, U.S.P.H. Research Grant M-1734, Stanford University, 1960.

Bandura, A. Vicarious processes: A case of no-trial learning. In L. Berkowitz (Ed.), *Advances in experimental social psychology,* vol. II. New York: Academic Press, 1965, 1–55.

Bandura, A. *Principles of behavior modification.* New York: Holt, Rinehart and Winston, 1969.

Bandura, A. *Social learning theory.* Morristown, N.J.: General Learning Press, 1971.

Bandura, A. *Aggression: A social learning analysis.* Englewood Cliffs, N.J.: Prentice-Hall, 1973.

Bandura, A. *Social learning theory.* Englewood Cliffs, N.J.: Prentice-Hall, 1977.

Bandura, A. Self-efficacy: Toward a unifying theory of behavioral change. *Psychological Review,* 1977, *84,* 191–215.

Bandura, A. Reflections on self-efficacy. In S. Rachman (Ed.), *Advances in behaviour research and therapy,* vol. 1. Oxford: Pergamon Press, 1978.

Bandura, A., & Adams, N. E. Analysis of self-efficacy theory of behavioral change. *Cognitive Therapy and Research,* 1977, *1,* 287–310.

Bandura, A., Adams, N. E., & Beyer, J. Cognitive processes mediating behavioral change. *Journal of Personality and Social Psychology,* 1977, *35,* 125–139.

Bandura, A., Blanchard, E. B., & Ritter, B. Relative efficacy of desensitization and modeling approaches for inducing behavioral, affective, and attitudinal changes. *Journal of Personality and Social Psychology,* 1969, *13,* 173–199.

Bandura, A., Grusec, J. E., & Menlove, F. L. Observational learning as a function of symbolization and incentive set. *Child Development,* 1966, *37,* 499–506.

Bandura, A., Grusec, J. E., & Menlove, F. L. Vicarious extinction of avoidance behavior. *Journal of Personality and Social Psychology,* 1967, *5,* 16–23.

Bandura, A., & Jeffery, R. W. Role of symbolic coding and rehearsal processes in observational learning. *Journal of Personality and Social Psychology,* 1973, *26,* 122–130.

Bandura, A., & Kupers, C. J. Transmission of patterns of self-reinforcement through modeling. *Journal of Abnormal and Social Psychology,* 1964, *69,* 1–9.

Bandura, A., & McDonald, F. J. Influence of social reinforcement and the behavior of models in shaping children's moral judgments. *Journal of Abnormal Social Psychology,* 1963, *67,* 274–281.

Bandura, A., & Mischel, W. Modification of self-imposed delay of reward through exposure to live and symbolic models. *Journal of Personality and Social Psychology,* 1965, *2,* 698–705.

Bandura, A., & Reese, L. *Recovery from a heart attack as a self-efficacy restoration process.* Personal communication (August 1980).

Bandura, A., & Rosenthal, T. L. Vicarious classical conditioning as a function of arousal level. *Journal of Personality and Social Psychology,* 1966, *3,* 54–62.

Bandura, A., Ross, D., & Ross, S. A. Transmission of aggression through imitation of aggressive models. *Journal of Abnormal and Social Psychology,* 1961, *63,* 575–582.

Bandura, A., Ross, D., & Ross, S. A. Imitation of film-mediated aggressive models. *Journal of Abnormal and Social Psychology,* 1963, *66,* 3–11. (a)

Bandura, A., Ross, D., & Ross, S. A. A comparative test of the status envy, social power, and secondary reinforcement theories of identificatory learning. *Journal of Abnormal and Social Psychology,* 1963, *67,* 527–534. (b)

Bandura, A., Underwood, B., & Fromson, M. E. Disinhibition of aggression through diffusion of responsibility and dehumanization of victims. *Journal of Research in Personality,* 1975, *9,* 253–269.

Bandura, A., & Walters, R. *Social learning and personality development.* New York: Holt, Rinehart and Winston, 1963.

Bardwick, J. *Psychology of women: A study of biocultural conflicts.* New York: Harper & Row, 1972.

Barker, R. G. *Ecological psychology.* Stanford: Stanford University Press, 1968.

Barker, R. G., Dembo, T., & Lewin, K. Frustration and regression: An experiment with young children. *University of Iowa Studies in Child Welfare,* 1941, *18* (Whole No. 386).

Barker, R. G., & Wright, H. F. *One boy's day.* New York: Harper & Row, 1951.

Barry, H. B., III., Bacon, M. K., & Child, I. L. A cross-cultural survey of some sex differences in socialization. *Journal of Abnormal and Social Psychology,* 1957, *55,* 327–332.

Bass, B. M. Authoritarianism or acquiescence? *Journal of Abnormal and Social Psychology,* 1955, *51,* 616–623.

Bavelas, J. B. *Personality: Current theory and research.* Monterey, Calif.: Brooks-Cole, 1978.

Becker, W. C. Consequences of different kinds of parental discipline. In M. L. Hoffman and L. W. Hoffman (Eds.), *Review of Child Development Research.* Vol. I. New York: Russell Sage Foundation, 1964, pp. 169–208.

Bell, J. E. *Projective techniques.* New York: Longmans, Green, 1948.

Bell, R., & Costello, N. Three tests for sex differences in tactile sensitivity in the newborn. *Biologia Neonatorum,* 1964, *7,* 335–347.

Bell, R., & Darling, J. The prone head reaction in the human newborn: Relationship with sex and tactile sensitivity. *Child Development,* 1965, *36,* 943–949.

Bell, R., Weller, G., & Waldrop, M. Newborn and preschooler: Organization of behavior and relations between periods. *Monographs of the Society for Research in Child Development,* 1971, *36* (Nos. 1, 2).

Bell, R. Q. A reinterpretation of the direction of effects in studies of socialization. *Psychological Review,* 1968, *75,* 81–95.

Beller, E. K. Dependency and independence in young children. *Journal of Genetic Psychology,* 1955, *87,* 25–35.

Beller, E. K. Personality correlates of perceptual discrimination in children. Progress Report, 1962.

Beller, E. K., & Neubauer, P. B. Sex differences and symptom patterns in early childhood. *Journal of Child Psychiatry,* 1963, *2,* 414–433.

Bem, D. J. Constructing cross-situational consistencies in behavior: Some thoughts on Alker's critique of Mischel. *Journal of Personality,* 1972, *40,* 17–26.

Bem, D. J. Self-perception theory. In L. Berkowitz (Ed.), *Advances in experimental social psychology,* vol. 6. New York: Academic Press, 1972.

Bem, D. J., & Allen, A. On predicting some of the people some of the time: The search for cross-situational consistencies in behavior. *Psychological Review,* 1974, *81,* 506–520.

Bem, D. J., & Funder, D. C. Predicting more of the people more of the time: Assessing the personality of situations. *Psychological Review,* 1978, *85,* 485–501.

Bem, S. L. Sex-role adaptability: One consequence of psychological androgyny. *Journal of Personality and Social Psychology,* 1975, *31,* 634–643.

Bem, S. L., & Bem, D. J. Homogenizing the American woman: The power of an unconscious ideology. Unpublished manuscript. Stanford University, 1972.

Bennett, E. L., Diamond, M. C., Krech, D., & Rosenzweig, M. R. Chemical and anatomical plasticity of the brain. *Science,* 1964, *146,* 610–619.

Bennett, E. M., & Cohen, L. R. Men and women: Personality patterns and contrasts. *Genetic Psychology Monographs,* 1959, *59,* 101–155.

Bennett, G. K., et al. *Differential aptitudes tests manual,* 3rd ed. New York: Psychological Corporation, 1959.

Berger, S. M. Conditioning through vicarious instigation. *Psychological Review,* 1962, *69,* 450–466.

Bergin, A. E. Some implications of psychotherapy research for therapeutic practice. *Journal of Abnormal Psychology,* 1966, *71,* 235–246.

Bergin, A. E. The evaluation of therapeutic outcomes. In A. E. Bergin and S. I. Garfield (Eds.), *Handbook of psychotherapy and behavior change.* New York: Wiley, 1971, pp. 217–270.

Berkowitz, L. Control of aggression. In B. M. Caldwell & H. Ricciuti (Eds.), *Review of Child Development Research,* vol. 3, 1969.

Berkowitz, L. The contagion of violence: An S-R mediational analysis of some effects of observed aggression. In M. Page (Ed.), *Nebraska symposium on motivation.* Lincoln: University of Nebraska Press, 1970.

Berlyne, D. E. Conflict and arousal. *Scientific American,* 1966, *215* (2), 82–87.

Berman, J. S., & Kenny, D. A. Correlational bias in observer ratings. *Journal of Personality and Social Psychology,* 1976, *34,* 263–273.

Biderman, A. D. Life and death in extreme captivity situations. In M. H. Appley & R. Trumbull (Eds.), *Psychological stress.* New York: Appleton 1967, pp. 242–277.

Bieri, J., Atkins, A. L., Briar, S., Leaman, R. L., Miller, H., & Tripoldi, T. *Clinical and social judgment.* New York: Wiley, 1966.

Bijou, S. W. Experimental studies of child behavior, normal and deviant. In L. Krasner & L. P. Ullmann (Eds.), *Research in behavior modification.* New York: Holt, Rinehart and Winston, 1965, pp. 56–81.

Birnbrauer, J. S., Bijou, S. W., Wolf, M. M., & Kidder, J. D. Programmed instruction in the classroom. In L. Ullmann & L. Krasner (Eds.), *Case studies in behavior modification.* New York: Holt, Rinehart and Winston, 1965.

Blanchard, E. B., & Young, L. D. Self-control of cardiac function: A promise as yet unfulfilled. *Psychological Bulletin,* 1973, *79,* 145–163.

Blashfield, R. An evaluation of the DSM-II classification of schizophrenia as a nomenclature. *Journal of Abnormal Psychology,* 1973, *82,* 382–389.

Block, J. *The Q-sort method in personality assessment and psychiatric research.* Springfield, Ill.: Charles C Thomas, 1961.

Block, J. *The challenge of response sets.* New York: Appleton, 1965.

Block, J. *Lives through time.* Berkeley, Calif.: Bancroft, 1971.

Block, J. Advancing the psychology of personality: Paradigmatic shift or improving the quality of research. In D. Magnusson & N. S. Endler (Eds.), *Personality at the crossroads: Current issues in interactional psychology.* Hillsdale, N.J.: Erlbaum, 1977.

Block, J. Correlational bias in observer ratings: Another perspective on the Berman and Kenny study. *Journal of Personality and Social Psychology,* 1977, *35,* 873–880.

Block, J. An illusory interpretation of the first factor of the MMPI: A reply to Shweder. *Journal of Consulting and Clinical Psychology,* 1977, *45,* 930–935.

Block, J., & Block, J. The role of ego-control and ego resiliency in the organization of behavior. In W. A. Collins (Ed.), *The Minnesota symposium on child psychology,* (Vol. 13). Hillsdale, N.J.: Erlbaum (Wiley), 1980.

Block, J., & Martin, B. Predicting the behavior of children under frustration. *Journal of Abnormal and Social Psychology,* 1955, *51,* 281–285.

Block, J., Weiss, D. S., & Thorne, A. How relevant is a semantic similarity interpretation of personality ratings? *Journal of Personality and Social Psychology,* 1979, *37,* 1055–1074.

Block, J. H. Conceptions of sex role: Some cross-cultural and longitudinal perspectives. *American Psychologist,* 1973, *28,* 512–526.

Blum, G. S. *Psychoanalytic theories of personality.* New York: McGraw-Hill, 1953.

Blum, G. S. Perceptual defense revisited. *Journal of Abnormal and Social Psychology,* 1955, *51,* 24–29.

Bonarius, J. C. J. Research in the personal construct theory of George A. Kelly: Role construct repertory test and basic theory. In B. A. Maher (Ed.), *Progress in experimental personality research.* New York: Academic Press, 1965, pp. 1–46.

Borstelmann, L. J. Sex of experimenter and sex-typed behavior of young children. *Child Development,* 1961, *32,* 519–524.

Boudin, H. M. Contingency contracting as a therapeutic tool in the deceleration of amphetamine use. *Behavior Therapy,* 1972, *3,* 604–608.

Bowers, K. Situationism in psychology: An analysis and a critique. *Psychological Review,* 1973, *80,* 307–336.

Bowlby, J. *Attachment and loss,* vol. 1: Attachment. New York: Basic Books, 1969.

Braine, M. D. S. On learning the grammatical order of words. *Psychological Review,* 1963, *70,* 323–348.

Bramel, D. A. A dissonance theory approach to defensive projection. *Journal of Abnormal and Social Psychology,* 1962, *64,* 121–129.

Breger, L., & McGaugh, J. L. Critique and reformulation of "learning theory" approaches to psychotherapy and neurosis. *Psychological Bulletin,* 1965, *63,* 338–358.

Brehm, J. W. *A theory of psychological reactance.* New York: Academic Press, 1966.

Brill, A. A. *Basic principles of psychoanalysis.* Garden City, N.Y.: Doubleday, 1949.

Broadbent, D. E. The hidden preattentive processes. *American Psychologist,* 1977, *32,* 109–118.

Bronfenbrenner, U. Freudian theories of identification and their derivatives. *Child Development,* 1960, *31,* 15–40.

Broverman, D. M., Klaiber, E. L., Kobayashi, Y., & Vogel, W. Roles of activation and inhibition in sex differences in cognitive abilities. *Psychological Review,* 1968, *75,* 23–50.

Broverman, I. K., Broverman, D. M., Clarkson, F. E., Rosenkrantz, P. S., & Vogel, S. R. Sex-role stereotypes and clinical judgments of mental health. *Journal of Consulting and Clinical Psychology,* 1970, *34,* 1–7.

Brown, D. G. Masculinity-femininity development in children. *Journal of Consulting Psychology,* 1957, *21,* 197–202.

Brown, J. S. The generalization of approach responses as a function of stimulus intensity and strength of motivation. *Journal of Comparative Psychology,* 1942, *33,* 209–226.

Brown, J. S. Gradients of approach and avoidance responses and their relation to level of motivation. *Journal of Comparative and Physiological Psychology,* 1948, *41,* 450–465.

Brown, R. *Social psychology.* New York: Free Press, 1965.

Bruner, J. S. On perceptual readiness. *Psychological Review,* 1957, *64,* 123–152.

Bruner, J. S. Processes of cognitive growth in infancy. Heinz Werner Memorial Lectures, Clark University, December, 1967.

Bruner, J. S., & Goodman, C. C. Value and need as organizing factors in perception. *Journal of Abnormal and Social Psychology,* 1947, *42,* 33–44.

Bruner, J. S., Olver, R. R., & Greenfield, P. M. *Studies in cognitive growth.* New York: Wiley, 1966.

Bruner, J. S., & Postman, L. Emotional selectivity in perception and reaction. *Journal of Personality,* 1947, *16,* 69–77.

Bulman, R. J., & Wortman, C. B. Attributions of blame and coping in the "real world": Severe accident victims react to their lot. *Journal of Personality and Social Psychology,* 1977, *35,* 351–363.

Burton, R. V. Generality of honesty reconsidered. *Psychological Review,* 1963, *70,* 481–499.

Burton, R. V., Maccoby, E. E., & Allinsmith, W. Antecedents of resistance to temptation in four-year-old children. *Child Development,* 1961, *32,* 689–710.

Buss, A. H. Aggression pays. In J. L. Singer (Ed.), *The control of aggression and violence.* New York: Academic Press, 1971.

Butler, J. M., & Haigh, G. V. Changes in the relation between self-concepts and ideal concepts consequent upon client-centered counseling. In C. R. Rogers & R. F. Dymond (Eds.), *Psychotherapy and personality change: Co-ordinated studies in the client-centered approach.* Chicago: University of Chicago Press, 1954, pp. 55–76.

Byrne, D. Repression-sensitization as a dimension of personality. In B. A. Maher (Ed.), *Progress in experimental personality research,* vol. 1. New York: Academic Press, 1964.

Byrne, D. *An introduction to personality.* Englewood Cliffs, N.J.: Prentice-Hall, 1966.

Byrne, D. Attitudes and attraction. In L. Berkowitz (Ed.), *Advances in experimental social psychology,* vol. 4. New York: Academic Press, 1969.

Byrne, D., & Holcomb, J. The reliability of a response measure: Differential recognition-threshold scores. *Psychological Bulletin,* 1962, *59,* 70–73.

Cairns, R. B. The influence of dependency-anxiety on the effectiveness of social reinforcers. Unpublished doctoral dissertation, Stanford University, 1959.

Cairns, R. B. *Social development.* San Francisco: Freeman, 1979.

Campbell, D. T. Recommendations for APA Test Standards regarding construct, trait, or discriminant validity. *American Psychologist,* 1960, *15,* 546–553.

Campbell, D. T., & Fiske, D. Convergent and discriminant validation. *Psychological Bulletin,* 1959, *56,* 81–105.

Campbell, D., Sanderson, R. E., & Laverty, S. G. Characteristics of a conditioned response in human subjects during extinction trials following a single traumatic conditioning trial. *Journal of Abnormal and Social Psychology,* 1964, *68,* 627–639.

Campbell, J., & Dunnette, M. Effectiveness of T-group experiences in managerial training and development. *Psychological Bulletin,* 1968, *70,* 73–104.

Campus, N. Transituational consistency as a dimension of personality. *Journal of Personality and Social Psychology,* 1974, *29,* 593–600.

Cantor, N., & Mischel, W. Traits as prototypes: Effects on recognition memory. *Journal of Personality and Social Psychology,* 1977, *35,* 38–48.

Cantor, N., & Mischel, W. Prototypes in person perception. In L. Berkowitz (Ed.), *Advances in experimental social psychology,* vol. 12. New York: Academic Press, 1979.

Carlson, R. Where is the person in personality research? *Psychological Bulletin,* 1971, *75,* 203–219.

Caron, A. J., & Wallach, M. A. Recall of interrupted tasks under stress: A phenomenon of memory or of learning? *Journal of Abnormal and Social Psychology,* 1957, *55,* 372–381.

Cartwright, D. S. *Introduction to personality.* Chicago: Rand McNally, 1974.

Carver, C. S., & Glass, D. C. Coronary-prone behavior pattern and interpersonal aggression. *Journal of Personality and Social Psychology,* 1978, *36,* 361–366.

Carver, C. S., & Scheier, M. F. Self-focusing effects of dispositional self-consciousness, mirror presence, and audience presence. *Journal of Personality and Social Psychology,* 1978, *36,* 324–332.

Casler, L. Maternal deprivation: A critical review of the literature. *Monographs of the Society for Research in Child Development,* 1961, *26,* 1–64.

Cattell, R. B. Confirmation and clarification of primary personality factors. *Psychometrika,* 1947, *12,* 197–220.

Cattell, R. B. *Personality: A systematic theoretical and factual study.* New York: McGraw-Hill, 1950.

Cattell, R. B. *Personality and motivation structure and measurement.* Yonkers-on-Hudson: World Book, 1957.

Cattell, R. B. *The scientific analysis of personality.* Baltimore: Penguin Books, 1965.

Chapman, L. J., & Campbell, D. T. Response set in the F Scale. *Journal of Abnormal and Social Psychology,* 1957, *54,* 129–132.

Chapman, L. J., & Chapman, J. P. Illusory correlations as an obstacle to the use of valid psychodiagnostic signs. *Journal of Abnormal Psychology,* 1969, *74,* 271–280.

Child, I. L., & Waterhouse, I. K. Frustration and the quality of performance: I. A critique of the Barker, Dembo, and Lewin experiment. *Psychological Review,* 1952, *59,* 351–362.

Chodoff, P. Late effects of concentration camp syndrome. *Archives of General Psychiatry,* 1963, *8,* 323–333.

Chodorkoff, B. Self-perception, perceptual defense, and adjustment. *Journal of Abnormal and Social Psychology,* 1954, *49,* 508–512.

Chomsky, N. *Aspects of the theory of syntax.* Cambridge, Mass.: M.I.T. Press, 1965.

Clark, D. F. Fetishism treated by negative conditioning. *British Journal of Psychiatry,* 1963, *109,* 404–407.

Clifford, M., & Walster, E. The effect of physical attractiveness on teacher expectations. *Sociology of Education,* 1973, *46,* 248.

Cline, N. G. The influence of social context on the perception of faces. *Journal of Personality,* 1956, *25,* 142–158.

Cline, V. B. Interpersonal perception. In B. A. Maher (Ed.), *Progress in experimental personality research,* vol. 1. New York: Academic Press, 1964, pp. 221–284.

Colby, K. M. Things to come: Designing neurotic computers. In L. Krasner & L. P. Ullmann (Eds.), *Research in behavior modification.* New York: Holt, Rinehart and Winston, 1965, pp. 305–309.

Colby, K. M., & Hilf, F. D. *Multidimensional analysis in evaluating a simulation of paranoid thought.* Stanford Artificial Intelligence Laboratory Computer Science Department. Report No. CS-347, National Technical Information Service, Springfield, Va., 1973.

Coles, R. *Uprooted children.* New York: Harper & Row, 1970.

Coopersmith, S. *The antecedents of self-esteem.* San Francisco: Freeman, 1967.

Coopersmith, S. Studies in self-esteem. *Scientific American,* 1968, *218* (2), 96–106.

Cowen, E. L., Gardner, E. A., & Zax, M. *Emergent approaches to mental health problems.* New York: Appleton, 1967.

Crandall, V. J. Achievement. In H. W. Stevenson (Ed.), *Child psychology (Sixty-*

second Yearbook of the National Society for the Study of Education). Chicago: University of Chicago Press, 1963, pp. 416–459.

Crandall, V. J., Preston, A., & Rabson, A. Maternal reactions and the development of independence and achievement behavior in young children. *Child Development,* 1960, *31,* 243–251.

Cronbach, L. J. Statistical methods applied to Rorschach scores: A review. *Psychological Bulletin,* 1949, *46,* 393–429.

Cronbach, L. J. Beyond the two disciplines of scientific psychology. *American Psychologist,* 1975, *30,* 116–127.

Crow, W. J. The effect of training upon accuracy and variability in interpersonal perception. *Journal of Abnormal and Social Psychology,* 1957, *55,* 355–359.

Crow, W. J., & Hammond, K. R. The generality of accuracy and response sets in interpersonal perception. *Journal of Abnormal and Social Psychology,* 1957, *54,* 384–390.

Crowne, D. P., & Marlowe, D. *The approval motive: Studies in evaluative dependence.* New York: Wiley, 1964.

D'Andrade, R. G. Sex differences and cultural institutions. In E. E. Maccoby (Ed.), *The development of sex differences.* Stanford: Stanford University Press, 1966, pp. 174–204.

D'Andrade, R. G. Memory and the assessment of behavior. In H. Blalock (Ed.), *Measurement in the social sciences.* Chicago: Aldine, 1974.

Danet, B. N. Prediction of mental illness in college students on the basis of "nonpsychiatric" MMPI profiles. *Journal of Consulting Psychology,* 1965, *29,* 577–580.

Davison, G. C. The negative effects of early exposure to suboptimal visual stimuli. *Journal of Personality,* 1964, *32,* 278–295.

Davison, G. C. Systematic desensitization as a counterconditioning process. *Journal of Abnormal Psychology,* 1968, *73,* 91–99.

Davison, G. C., & Neale, N. M. *Abnormal psychology.* New York: Wiley, 1974.

Davitz, J. R. The effects of previous training on postfrustration behavior. *Journal of Abnormal and Social Psychology,* 1952, *47,* 309–315.

Dawe, H. C. An analysis of 200 quarrels of preschool children. *Child Development,* 1934, *5,* 139–157.

Deane, G. E. Human heart rate responses during experimentally induced anxiety. *Journal of Experimental Psychology,* 1961, *61,* 489–493.

Deaux, K., & Emswiller, T. Explanation of successful performance on sex linked tasks: What is skill for the male is luck for the female. *Journal of Personality and Social Psychology,* 1974, *29,* 80–85.

Dechter, M. *The new chastity and other arguments against women's liberation.* New York: Coward McCann, 1972.

DeNike, L. D. The temporal relationship between awareness and performance in verbal conditioning. *Journal of Experimental Psychology,* 1964, *68,* 521–529.

Dennenberg, V. H. Critical periods, stimulus input and emotional reactivity: A theory of infantile stimulation. *Psychological Review,* 1964, *71,* 335–351.

Diamond, M. A critical evaluation of the ontogeny of human sexual behavior. *Quarterly Review of Biology,* 1965, *40,* 147–175.

Diamond, M. Human sexual development: Biological foundations. In F. A. Beach (Ed.), *Human sexuality in four perspectives.* Baltimore, Md.: Johns Hopkins University Press, 1976, pp. 22–61.

Diamond, M. J., & Shapiro, J. L. Changes in locus of control as a function of encounter group experiences: A study and replication. *Journal of Abnormal Psychology,* 1973, *82,* 514–518.

Diener, C. I., & Dweck, C. S. An analysis of learned helplessness: Continuous changes in performance, strategy, and achievement cognitions following failure. *Journal of Personality and Social Psychology,* 1978, *36,* 451–462.

Diven, K. Certain determinants of conditioning of anxiety reactions. *Journal of Psychology,* 1937, *3,* 291–308.

Dixon, N. F. *Subliminal perception: The nature of a controversy.* London: McGraw-Hill, 1971.

Dollard, J., Doob, L. W., Miller, N. E., Mowrer, O. H., & Sears, R. R. *Frustration and aggression.* New Haven: Yale University Press, 1939.

Dollard, J., & Miller, N. E. *Personality and psychotherapy: An analysis in terms of learning, thinking, and culture.* New York: McGraw-Hill, 1950.

Douvan, E., & Kaye, C. *Adolescent girls.* Ann Arbor: Survey Research Center, University of Michigan, 1957.

Droppleman, L. F., & Schaefer, E. S. Boys' and girls' reports of maternal and paternal behavior. Paper read at American Psychological Association, August 31, 1961, New York City.

Dulany, D. E., Jr. The place of hypotheses and intentions: An analysis of verbal control in verbal conditioning. In C. W. Eriksen (Ed.), *Behavior and awareness.* Durham, N.C.: Duke University Press, 1962, pp. 102–129.

Duncker, K. Experimental modification of children's food preferences through social suggestion. *Journal of Abnormal Psychology,* 1938, *33,* 489–507.

Dunnette, M. D. People feeling: Joy, more joy, and the "slough of despond." *Journal of Applied Behavioral Science,* 1969, *5,* 25–44.

Dunsdon, M. I., & Fraser-Roberts, J. A. A study of the performance of 2,000 children on four vocabulary tests. *British Journal of Statistical Psychology,* 1957, *10,* 1–16.

Duval, S., & Wicklund, R. A. *A theory of objective self-awareness.* New York: Academic Press, 1972.

Dweck, C. S. The role of expectations and attributions in the alleviation of learned helplessness. *Journal of Personality and Social Psychology,* 1975, *31,* 674–685.

Dworkin, R. H. Genetic and environmental influences on person-situation interactions. *Journal of Research in Personality,* 1979, *13,* 279–293.

Dworkin, R. H., Burke, B. W., Maher, B. A., & Gottesman, I. I. Genetic influences on the organization and development of personality. *Developmental Psychology,* 1977, *13,* 164–165.

D'Zurilla, T. Recall efficiency and mediating cognitive events in "experimental repression." *Journal of Personality and Social Psychology,* 1965, *1,* 253–257.

Eddy, G. L., & Sinnett, R. E. Behavior setting utilization by emotionally disturbed college students. *Journal of Consulting and Clinical Psychology,* 1973, *40,* 210–216.

Edwards, A. L. *The social desirability variable in personality assessment and research.* New York: Dryden, 1957.

Edwards, A. L. Social desirability and the description of others. *Journal of Abnormal and Social Psychology,* 1959, *59,* 434–436.

Edwards, A. L. Social desirability or acquiescence in the MMPI? A case study with the SD scale. *Journal of Abnormal and Social Psychology,* 1961, *63,* 351–359.

Ekman, P., Friesen, W. V. & Ellsworth, P. *Emotion in the human face.* New York: Pergamon, 1972.

Elliott, R. Effects of uncertainty about the nature and advent of a noxious stimulus (shock) upon distress. *Journal of Personality and Social Psychology,* 1966, *3,* 353–356.

Elliott, R. The motivational significance of heart rate. In P. A. Obrist, A. H. Black, J. Brener, & L. V. D. Cara (Eds.), *Cardiovascular psychophysiology: Current issues in response mechanisms, biofeedback, and methodology.* Chicago: Aldine, 1974.

Ellis, A. *Reason and emotion in psychotherapy.* New York: Lyle Stuart, 1962.

Ellis, A. Rational-emotive therapy: Research data that support the clinical and personality hypothesis of RET and other modes of cognitive behavior therapy. *The Counseling Psychologist,* 1977, *7,* 2–42.

Ellsworth, P. C., & Carlsmith, M. J. Effects of eye contact and verbal content on affective response to a dyadic interaction. *Journal of Personality and Social Psychology,* 1968, *10,* 15–20.

Endler, N. S. The person versus the situation—A pseudo issue? *Journal of Personality,* 1973, *41,* 287–303.

Endler, N. S., & Hunt, J. McV. Sources of behavioral variance as measured by the S-R inventory of anxiousness. *Psychological Bulletin,* 1966, *65,* 336–346.

Endler, N. S., & Hunt, J. McV. Generalizability of contributions from sources of variance in the S-R inventories of anxiousness. *Journal of Personality,* 1969, *37,* 1–24.

Epstein, R., & Liverant, S. Verbal conditioning and sex-role identification in children. *Child Development,* 1963, *34,* 99–106.

Epstein, S. The measurement of drive and conflict in humans: Theory and experiment. In M. R. Jones (Ed.), *Nebraska symposium on motivation.* Lincoln: University of Nebraska Press, 1962, pp. 281–321.

Epstein, S. Toward a unified theory of anxiety. In B. A. Maher (Ed.), *Progress in experimental personality research,* vol. 4. New York: Academic Press, 1967, pp. 1–89.

Epstein, S. The stability of behavior: I. On predicting most of the people much of the time. *Journal of Personality and Social Psychology,* 1979, *37,* 1097–1126.

Epstein, S. *Behavioral consistency: Myth or reality?* Special debate presented at the meetings of the American Psychological Association, Montreal, September 1980.

Epstein, S., & Fenz, W. D. Theory and experiment on the measurement of approach-avoidance conflict. *Journal of Abnormal and Social Psychology,* 1962, *64,* 97–112.

Erdelyi, M. H. A new look at the new look: Perceptual defense and vigilance. *Psychological Review,* 1974, *81,* 1–25.

Erdelyi, M. H., & Goldberg, B. Let's not sweep repression under the rug: Towards a cognitive psychology of repression. In Kihlstrom, J. F., & Evans, F. J. (Eds.), *Functional disorders of memory.* Hillsdale, N.J.: Erlbaum, 1979.

Eriksen, B. A., & Eriksen, C. W. *Perception and personality.* Morristown, N.J.: General Learning Press, 1972.

Eriksen, C. W. Defense against ego-threat in memory and perception. *Journal of Abnormal and Social Psychology,* 1952, *47,* 230–235. (a)

Eriksen, C. W. Individual differences in defensive forgetting. *Journal of Experimental Psychology,* 1952, *44,* 442–446. (b)

Eriksen, C. W. Unconscious process. In M. R. Jones (Ed.), *Nebraska symposium on motivation.* Lincoln: University of Nebraska Press, 1958, pp. 169–227.

Eriksen, C. W. Discrimination and learning without awareness: A methodological survey and evaluation. *Psychological Review,* 1960, *67,* 279–300.

Eriksen, C. W. Cognitive responses to internally cued anxiety. In C. D. Spielberger (Ed.), *Anxiety and behavior.* New York: Academic Press, 1966, pp. 327–360.

Eriksen, C. W., & Kuethe, J. L. Avoidance conditioning of verbal behavior without awareness: A paradigm of repression. *Journal of Abnormal and Social Psychology,* 1956, *53,* 203–209.

Erikson, E. Growth and crises of the healthy personality: 1950. *Psychological Issues,* 1959, *1,* 50–100.

Erikson, E. *Childhood and society.* New York: Norton, 1963.

Erikson, E. *Identity: Youth and crisis.* New York: Norton, 1968.

Exline, R., & Winters, L. C. Affective relations and mutual glances in dyads. In S. Tomkins & C. Izard (Eds.), *Affect, cognition, and personality.* New York: Springer, 1965.

Eysenck, H. J. The effects of psychotherapy: An evaluation. *Journal of Consulting Psychology,* 1952, *16,* 319–324.

Eysenck, H. J. The effects of psychotherapy. In II. J. Eysenck (Ed.), *Handbook of abnormal psychology: An experimental approach.* New York: Basic Books, 1961, pp. 697–725.

Eysenck, H. J. *The biological basis of personality.* Springfield, Ill.: Charles C Thomas, 1967.

Eysenck, H. J., & Beech, R. Counterconditioning and related methods. In A. E. Bergin & S. L. Garfield (Eds.), *Handbook of psychotherapy and behavior change.* New York: Wiley, 1971.

Eysenck, H. J., & Rachman, S. *The causes and cures of neurosis: An introduction to modern behavior therapy based on learning theory and the principles of conditioning.* San Diego: Knapp, 1965.

Fairweather, G. W. *Social psychology in treating mental illness: An experimental approach.* New York: Wiley, 1964.

Fairweather, G. W. *Methods in experimental social innovation.* New York: Wiley, 1967.

Fairweather, G. W., Sanders, D. H., Cressler, D. L., & Maynard, H. *Community life for the mentally ill: An alternative to institutional care.* Chicago: Aldine, 1969.

Farina, A. *Schizophrenia.* Morristown, N.J.: General Learning Press, 1972.

Fauls, L. B., & Smith, W. D. Sex-role learning of five-year-olds. *Journal of Genetic Psychology,* 1956, *89,* 105–117.

Feather, B. W. Semantic generalization of classically conditioned responses. *Psychological Bulletin,* 1965, *63,* 425–441.

Feldman, R. B., & Werry, J. S. An unsuccessful attempt to treat a tiquer by massed practice. *Behaviour Research and Therapy,* 1966, *4,* 111–117.

Fenichel, O. *The psychoanalytic theory of neurosis.* New York: Norton, 1945.

Fenigstein, A., Scheier, M. F., & Buss, A. H. Public and private self-consciousness: Assessment and theory. *Journal of Consulting and Clinical Psychology,* 1975, *43,* 522–527.

Fenz, W. D. Conflict and stress as related to physiological activation and sensory, perceptual and cognitive functioning. *Psychological Monographs,* 1964, *78,* No. 8, (Whole No. 585).

Ferster, C. B., & DeMyer, M. K. The development of performances in autistic children in an automatically controlled environment. *Journal of Chronic Diseases,* 1961, *13,* 312–345.

Ferster, C. B., & Skinner, B. F. *Schedules of reinforcement.* New York: Appleton, 1957.

Feshbach, S. The catharsis hypothesis and some consequences of interaction with aggressive and neutral play objects. *Journal of Personality,* 1956, *24,* 449–462.

Feshbach, S., Stiles, W. B., & Bitter, E. The reinforcing effect of witnessing aggression. *Journal of Experimental Research in Personality,* 1967, *2,* 133–139.

Festinger, L. *A theory of cognitive dissonance.* Stanford: Stanford University Press, 1957.

Festinger, L. Behavioral support for opinion change. *Public Opinion Quarterly,* 1964, *28,* 404–417.

Fisher, J., Epstein, L. J., & Harris, M. R. Validity of the psychiatric interview: Predicting the effectiveness of the first Peace Corps volunteers in Ghana. *Archives of General Psychiatry,* 1967, *17,* 744–750.

Fishkin, J., Keniston, K., & MacKinnon, C. Moral reasoning and political ideology. *Journal of Personality and Social Psychology,* 1973, *27,* 109–119.

Fiske, D. W. The limits of the conventional science of personality. *Journal of Personality,* 1974, *42,* 1–11.

Fitch, G. Effects of self-esteem, perceived performance, and choice on causal attribution. *Journal of Personality and Social Psychology,* 1970, *16,* 311–315.

Frank, L. K. Projective methods for the study of personality. *Journal of Psychology,* 1939, *8,* 389–413.

Fraser, R., Leslie, I., & Phelps, D. Psychiatric effects of severe personal experiences during bombing. *Proceedings of the Royal Society of Medicine,* 1943, *36,* 119–123.

Freud, S. Psychopathology of everyday life. *Standard edition,* 1901, vol. 6. London: Hogarth, 1960.

Freud, S. Leonardo da Vinci: A study in psychosexuality. *Standard edition,* 1909, vol. II. London: Hogarth, 1957.

Freud, S. Formulations regarding the two principles of mental functioning, *Collected papers,* 1911, vol. IV. New York: Basic Books, 1959.

Freud, S. Instincts and their vicissitudes. *Standard edition,* 1915, vol. 14. London: Hogarth, 1957.

Freud, S. On transformations of instinct as exemplified in anal eroticism. *Standard edition,* 1917, vol. 18. London: Hogarth, 1955.

Freud, S. *A general introduction to psychoanalysis,* 1920. New York: Boni and Liveright, 1924.

Freud, S. *New introductory lectures on psychoanalysis,* W. J. H. Sproutt (transl.). New York: Norton, 1933.

Freud, S. *An outline of psychoanalysis,* J. Strachey (transl.), 1940. New York: Norton, 1949.

Freud, S. An outline of psychoanalysis. *International Journal of Psychoanalysis,* 1940, *21,* 27–84.

Freud, S. *Collected papers,* vols. I–V. New York: Basic Books, 1959.

Freund, K. Some problems in the treatment of homosexuality. In H. J. Eysenck (Ed.), *Behaviour therapy and the neuroses.* Elmsford, N.Y.: Pergamon, 1960, pp. 312–325.

Friedman, M., & Rosenman, R. H. *Type A behavior and your heart.* New York: Knopf, 1974.

From, E. Perception of human action. In H. P. David & J. C. Brengelmann (Eds.), *Perspectives in personality research.* New York: Springer, 1960, pp. 161–174.

Fromm, E. *Escape from freedom.* New York: Holt, Rinehart and Winston, 1941.

Fromm, E. *Man for himself.* New York: Holt, Rinehart and Winston, 1947.

Galle, O. R., Gove, W. R., & McPherson, J. M. Population density and pathology: What are the relations for man? *Science,* 1972, *176,* 23–30.

Gallimore, R., Weiss, L. B., & Finney, R. Cultural differences in delay of gratification: A problem of behavior classification. *Journal of Personality and Social Psychology,* 1974, *30,* 72–80.

Garcia, J., McGowan, B. K., & Green, K. F. Biological constraints on conditioning. In A. H. Black & W. F. Prokasy (Eds.), *Classical conditioning II: Current research and theory.* New York: Appleton-Century-Crofts, 1972.

Geen, R.G. Some effects of observing violence upon the behavior of the observer. In B. A. Maher (Ed.), *Progress in experimental personality research.* Vol. 8. New York: Academic Press, 1978.

Geer, J. H. The development of a scale to measure fear. *Behavior Research and Therapy,* 1965, *3,* 45–53.

Geer, J. H., Davison, G. C., & Gatchel, R. I. Reduction of stress in humans through nonveridical perceived control of aversive stimulation. *Journal of Personality and Social Psychology,* 1970, *16,* 731–738.

Gelder, M. G., & Marks, I. M. Aversion treatment in transvestism and transsexualism. In R. Green (Ed.), *Transsexualism and sex reassignment.* Baltimore: Johns Hopkins Press, 1969.

Gelfand, D. M. The influence of self-esteem on rate of verbal conditioning and social matching behavior. *Journal of Abnormal and Social Psychology,* 1962, *65,* 259–265.

Gelfand, D. M., Hartmann, D. P., Lamb, A. K., Smith, C. L., Mahan, M. A., & Paul, S. C. The effects of adult models and described alternatives on children's choice of behavior management techniques. *Child Development,* 1974, *45,* 585–593.

Gendlin, E. T. client-centered developments and work with schizophrenics. *Journal of Counseling Psychology,* 1962, *9,* 205–211.

Gergen, K. J. *The concept of self.* New York: Holt, Rinehart and Winston, 1971.

Gesell, A., et al. *The first five years of life.* New York: Harper & Row, 1940.

Getzels, J. W., & Jackson, P. W. *Creativity and intelligence.* New York: Wiley, 1962.

Gibson, E. J. *Principles of perceptual learning and development.* New York: Appleton, 1969.

Giberstadt, H., & Duker, J. *A handbook for clinical and actuarial MMPI interpretation.* Philadelphia: Saunders, 1965.

Glass, D. C. Theories of consistency and the study of personality. In E. F.

Borgatta & W. W. Lambert (Eds.), *Handbook of personality theory and research*. Chicago: Rand McNally, 1968, pp. 788–854.

Glass, D. C. *Behavior patterns, stress, and coronary disease*. Hillsdale, N.J.: Erlbaum, 1977.

Glass, D. C., Singer, J. E., & Friedman, L. N. Psychic costs of adaptation to an environmental stressor. *Journal of Personality and Social Psychology,* 1969, *12,* 200–210.

Goldberg, L. R. The effectiveness of clinicians' judgments: The diagnosis of organic brain damage from the Bender-Gestalt test. *Journal of Consulting Psychology,* 1959, *23,* 25–33.

Goldberg, L. R. Simple models or simple processes? Some research on clinical judgments. *American Psychologist,* 1968, *23,* 483–496.

Goldberg, L. R. The exploitation of the English Language for the development of a descriptive personality taxonomy. Paper delivered at the 81st Annual Convention of the American Psychological Association, Montreal, Canada, 1973.

Goldberg, L. R., & Werts, C. E. The reliability of clinician's judgments: A multitrait-multimethod approach. *Journal of Consulting Psychology,* 1966, *30,* 199–206.

Goldberg, P. A. Misogyny and the college girl. Paper presented at Eastern Psychological Association, Boston, Mass., April 1967.

Goldberg, S., & Lewis, M. Play behavior in the year-old infant: Early sex differences. *Child Development,* 1969, *40,* 21–31.

Golden, M. Some effects of combining psychological tests on clinical inferences. *Journal of Consulting Psychology,* 1964, *28,* 440–446.

Goldfried, M. R., & Goldfried, A. P. Cognitive change methods. In F. H. Kanfer & A. P. Goldstein (Eds.), *Helping people change: A textbook of methods* (2nd ed.). New York: Pergamon Press, 1980.

Goldfried, M. R., & Sobocinski, D. Effect of irrational beliefs on emotional arousal. *Journal of Consulting and Clinical Psychology,* 1975, *43,* 504–510.

Goldfried, M. R., & Sprafkin, J. N. *Behavioral personality assessment*. Morristown, N.J.: General Learning Press, 1974.

Gordon, J. E., & Smith, E. Children's aggression, parental attitudes, and the effects of an affiliation-arousing story. *Journal of Personality and Social Psychology,* 1965, *1,* 654–659.

Gormly, J., & Edelberg, W. Validation in personality trait attribution. *American Psychologist,* 1974, *29,* 189–193.

Gottesman, I. J. Heritability of personality. *Psychological Monographs,* 1963, *77,* 1–21.

Gottesman, I. J. Genetic variance in adaptive personality traits. *Journal of Child Psychology and Psychiatry,* 1966, *7,* 199–208.

Gottesman, I. J., & Shields, J. Schizophrenia in twins: Sixteen years consecutive admissions to a psychiatric clinic. In M. Manosevitz, G. Lindzey, & D. D. Thiessen (Eds.), *Behavioral genetics: Method and research,* 1969. New York: Appleton, pp. 677–691.

Gough, H. G. Identifying psychological femininity. *Educational and Psychological Measurement,* 1952, *12,* 427–439.

Gough, H. G. *Manual, California Psychological Inventory*. Palo Alto: Consulting Psychologists Press, 1957.

Gove, F., Arend, R., & Sroufe, A. *Competence in preschool and kindergarten predicted from infancy.* Paper presented at the Meeting of the Society for Research in Child Development, San Francisco, 1979.

Greenberg, B. S., & Gordon, T. F. Children's perceptions of television violence: A replication. In G. A. Comstock, E. A. Rubinstein, & J. P. Murray (Eds.), *Television and social behavior,* vol. 5. *Television's effects: Further explorations.* Washington, D.C.: GPO, 1972.

Greenstein, J. M. Father characteristics and sex typing. *Journal of Personality and Social Psychology,* 1966, *3,* 271–277.

Griffitt, W., & Guay, P. "Object" evaluation and conditioned affect. *Journal of Experimental Research in Personality,* 1969, *4,* 1–8.

Griffitt, W., & Veitch, R. Hot and crowded: Influences of population density and temperature on interpersonal affective behavior. *Journal of Personality and Social Psychology,* 1971, *17,* 92–98.

Grim, P. F., Kohlberg, L., & White, S. H. Some relationships between conscience and attentional processes. *Journal of Personality and Social Psychology,* 1968, *8,* 239–252.

Grinder, R. E. Relations between behavioral and cognitive dimensions of conscience in middle childhood. *Child Development,* 1964, *35,* 881–891.

Grinker, R. R., & Spiegel, J. P. *Men under stress.* Philadelphia: Blakiston, 1945.

Grossberg, J. M. Behavior therapy: A review. *Psychological Bulletin,* 1964, *62,* 73–88.

Gruder, C. L., & Cook, T. D. Sex, dependency, and helping. *Journal of Personality and Social Psychology,* 1971, *19,* 290–294.

Grusec, J. Some antecedents of self-criticism. *Journal of Personality and Social Psychology,* 1966, *4,* 244–252.

Guilford, J. P. *Personality.* New York: McGraw-Hill, 1959.

Gur, R. C., & Sackeim, H. A. Self-deception: A concept in search of a phenomenon. *Journal of Personality and Social Psychology,* 1979, *37,* 147–169.

Guthrie, E. R. *The psychology of learning.* New York: Harper & Row, 1935.

Halverson, C. Longitudinal relations between newborn tactile threshold, preschool barrier behaviors, and early school-age imagination and verbal development. *Newborn and preschooler: Organization of behavior and relations between period.* SRCD Monograph, vol. 36, 1971a.

Halverson, C. *Relation of preschool verbal communication to later verbal intelligence, social maturity, and distribution of play bouts.* Paper presented at the meeting of the American Psychological Association, 1971b.

Halverson, C. F., & Waldrop, M. R. Relations between preschool barrier behaviors and early school-age measures of coping, imagination, and verbal development. *Developmental Psychology,* 1974, *10,* 716–720.

Hamburg, D. A., & Lunde, D. T. Sex hormones in the development of sex differences in human behavior. In E. E. Maccoby (Ed.), *The development of sex differences.* Stanford: Stanford University Press, 1966, pp. 1–24.

Hampson, J. L. Determinants of psychosexual orientation. In F. A. Beach (Ed.), *Sex and behavior.* New York: Wiley, 1965.

Haner, C. F. & Brown, P. A. Clarification of the instigation to action concept in the frustration-aggression hypothesis. *Journal of Abnormal and Social Psychology,* 1955, *51,* 204–206.

Haney, C., Banks, C., & Zimbardo, P. Interpersonal dynamics in a simulated prison. *International Journal of Criminology and Penology,* 1973, *1,* 69–97.

Hanratty, M. A., O'Neal, E., & Sulzer, J. L. The effect of frustration upon imitation of aggression. *Journal of Personality and Social Psychology,* 1972, *21,* 30–34.

Harlow, H. F., & Harlow, M. H. Learning to love. *American Scientist,* 1966, *54,* 244–272.

Harlow, H. F., & Zimmermann, R. R. Affectional responses in the infant monkey. *Science,* 1959, *130,* 421–432.

Harré, R., & Secord, P. F. *The explanation of social behavior.* Oxford: Blackwell, 1972.

Harris, D. B. A scale for measuring attitudes of social responsibility in children. *Journal of Abnormal and Social Psychology,* 1957, *55,* 322–326.

Harris, D. B. Sex differences in the life problems and interests of adolescents, 1935 and 1957. *Child Development,* 1959, *30,* 453–459.

Harris, F. R., Johnston, M. K., Kelley, S. C., & Wolf, M. M. Effects of positive social reinforcement on regressed crawling of a nursery school child. *Journal of Educational Psychology,* 1964, *55,* 35–41.

Hartig, M., & Kanfer, F. H. The role of verbal self-instructions in children's resistance to temptation. *Journal of Personality and Social Psychology,* 1973, *25,* 259–267.

Hartmann, D. Influence of symbolically modeled instrumental aggression and pain cues on aggressive behavior. *Journal of Personality and Social Psychology,* 1969, *11,* 280–288.

Hartmann, H., Kris, E., & Loewenstein, R. M. Comments on the formation of psychic structure. In A. Freud et al. (Eds.), *The psychoanalytic study of the child,* vol. 2. New York: International Universities Press, 1947, pp. 11–38.

Hartshorne, H., & May, M. A. *Studies in deceit.* New York: Macmillan, 1928.

Hartup, W. W., & Zook, E. A. Sex role preferences in three- and four-year-old children. *Journal of Consulting Psychology,* 1960, *24,* 420–426.

Hase, H. D., & Goldberg, L. R. Comparative validity of different strategies of constructing personality inventory scales. *Psychological Bulletin,* 1967, *67,* 231–248.

Hathaway, S. R., & McKinley, J. C. A multiphasic personality schedule. (Minnesota): III. The measurement of symptomatic depression. *Journal of Psychology,* 1942, *14,* 73–84.

Hathaway, S. R., & McKinley, J. C. *MMPI Manual.* New York: Psychological Corporation, 1943.

Hattwick, L. A. Sex differences in behavior of nursery school children. *Child Development,* 1937, *8,* 343–355.

Hawkins, R. P., Peterson, R. F., Schweid, E., & Bijou, S. W. Behavior therapy in the home: Amelioration of problem parent-child relations with the parent in a therapeutic role. *Journal of Experimental Child Psychology,* 1966, *4,* 99–107.

Heathers, G. Emotional dependence and independence in a physical threat situation. *Child Development,* 1953, *24,* 169–179.

Heckhausen, H. Achievement motive research: Current problems and some contributions towards a general theory of motivation. In W. J. Arnold (Ed.), *Ne-*

braska Symposium on Motivation, 1968. Lincoln: Nebraska University Press, 1969, pp. 103–174.

Heider, F. *The psychology of interpersonal relations.* New York: Wiley, 1958.

Heider, F., & Simmel, M. An experimental study of apparent behavior. *American Journal of Psychology,* 1944, *57,* 243–259.

Hetherington, E. M. A developmental study of the effects of sex of the dominant parent on sex-role preference, identification, and imitation in children. *Journal of Personality and Social Psychology,* 1965, *2,* 188–194.

Hilgard, E. R. Experimental approaches to psychoanalysis. In E. Pumpean-Mindlin (Ed.), *Psychoanalysis as science.* Stanford: Stanford University Press, 1952, pp. 3–45.

Hiroto, D. S. Locus of control and learned helplessness. *Journal of Experimental Psychology,* 1974, *102,* 187–193.

Hobbs, N. Helping disturbed children: Psychological and ecological strategies. *American Psychologist,* 1966, *21,* 1105–1115.

Hoffman, M. L. Child rearing practices and moral development: Generalizations from empirical research. *Child Development,* 1963, *34,* 295–318.

Hokanson, J. E., Willers, K. R., & Koropsak, E. Modification of autonomic responses during aggressive interchange. *Journal of Personality,* 1968, *36,* 386–404.

Holmes, D. S. The conscious control of thematic projection. *Journal of Consulting and Clinical Psychology,* 1974, *42,* 323–329. (a)

Holmes, D. S. Investigations of repression: Differential recall of material experimentally or naturally associated with ego threat. *Psychological Bulletin,* 1974, *81,* 632–653. (b)

Holmes, D. S., & Houston, K. B. Effectiveness of situation redefinition and affective isolation in coping with stress. *Journal of Personality and Social Psychology,* 1974, *29,* 212–218.

Holmes, T. H., & Masuda, M. Life change and illness susceptibility. In B. S. Dohrenwend & B. P. Dohrenwend (Eds.), *Stressful life events: Their nature and effects.* New York: Wiley, 1974.

Holmes, T. H., & Rahe, R. H. The social readjustment rating scale. *Journal of Psychosomatic Research,* 1967, *11,* 213–218.

Holmes, D. S., & Schallow, J. R. Reduced recall after ego threat: Repression or response competition? *Journal of Personality and Social Psychology,* 1969, *13,* 145–152.

Holmes, D. S., & Tyler, J. D. Direct versus projective measurement of achievement motivation. *Journal of Consulting and Clinical Psychology,* 1968, *32,* 712–717.

Holton, R. B. Amplitude of an instrumental response following the withholding of reward. *Child Development,* 1961, *32,* 107–116.

Holtzman, W. H., et al. *Inkblot perception and personality: Holtzman Inkblot Technique.* Austin: University of Texas Press, 1961.

Holtzman, W. H., & Sells, S. B. Prediction of flying success by clinical analysis of test protocols. *Journal of Abnormal and Social Psychology,* 1954, *49,* 485–490.

Homme, L. Perspectives in psychology—XXIV. Control of coverants, the operants of the mind. *The Psychological Record,* 1965, *15,* 501–511.

Honigfeld, G. Temporal effects of LSD-25 and epinephrine on verbal behavior. *Journal of Abnormal Psychology,* 1965, *70,* 303–306.

Horner, M. S. Fail: Bright women. *Psychology Today,* November 1969.

Horner, M. S. Toward an understanding of achievement related conflicts in women. *Journal of Social Issues,* 1972, *28,* 157–176.

Hovland, C. I., Janis, I. J., et al. *Personality and persuasibility.* New Haven: Yale University Press, 1959.

Howard, K. I. The convergent and discriminant validation of ipsative ratings from three projective instruments. *Journal of Clinical Psychology,* 1962, *18,* 183–188.

Howes, D. H., & Solomon, R. L. Visual duration threshold as a function of word-probability. *Journal of Experimental Psychology,* 1951, *41,* 401–410.

Irwin, O. C., & Chen, H. P. Development of speech during infancy: Curve of phonemic types. *Journal of Experimental Psychology,* 1946, *36,* 431–436.

Iscoe, I., Williams, M., & Harvey, J. Age, intelligence, and sex as variables in the conformity behavior of Negro and white children. *Child Development,* 1964, *35,* 451–460.

Isen, A. M. Success, failure, and reactions to others: The warm glow of success. *Journal of Personality and Social Psychology,* 1970, 294–301.

Isen, A., Horn, N., & Rosenhan, D. Effects of success and failure on children's generosity. *Journal of Personality and Social Psychology,* 1973, *27,* 239–247.

Isen, A. M., Shalker, T. E., Clark, M., & Karp, L. Affect, accessibility of material in memory, and behavior: A cognitive loop? *Journal of Personality and Social Psychology,* 1978, *36,* 1–12.

Ittelson, W. H., Proshansky, H. M., Rivlin, L. G., & Winkel, G. H. *An introduction to environmental psychology.* New York: Holt, Rinehart and Winston, 1974.

Jaccard, J. J. Predicting social behavior from personality traits. *Journal of Research in Personality,* 1974, *7,* 358–367.

Jacklin, C. N., & Mischel, H. N. As the twig is bent: Sex role stereotyping in early readers. *The School Psychology Digest,* Summer 1973, pp. 30–38.

Jackson, D. N. *Jackson Personality Inventory Manual.* Port Huron, Mich.: Research Psychology Press, 1976.

Jackson, D. N. *Some preconditions for valid person perception.* Presented at 2nd Annual Ontario Conference on Personality and Social Psychology, Waterloo, Ontario, Canada, 1979.

Jackson, D. N., Chan, D. W., & Stricker, L. J. Implicit personality theory: Is it illusory? *Journal of Personality,* 1979, *47,* 1–10.

Jackson, D. N., & Messick, S. Content and style in personality assessment. *Psychological Bulletin,* 1958, *55,* 243–252.

Jackson, D. N., & Paunonen, S. V. Personality structure and assessment. In M. R. Rosenzweig & L. W. Porter (Eds.), *Annual Review of Psychology,* vol. 31. Palo Alto, CA.: Annual Reviews, Inc., 1980.

Janis, I. L. Objective factors related to morale attitudes in the aerial combat situation. In S. Stouffer, A. A. Lumsdaine, R. Williams, M. B. Smith, I. L. Janis, S. A. Stas, & L. Cottrell, Jr., *The American Soldier,* vol. 2: Combat and its aftermath. Princeton: Princeton University Press, 1949, pp. 362–410.

Janis, I. L. *Psychological stress.* New York: Wiley, 1958.

Janis, I. L. *Stress and frustration.* New York: Harcourt, 1971.

Jenkins, J. J. Remember that old theory of memory? Well, forget it! *American Psychologist,* 1974, *29,* 785–795.

Jersild, A. Memory for the pleasant as compared with the unpleasant. *Journal of Experimental Psychology,* 1931, *14,* 284–288.

Jones, A. Information deprivation in humans. In B. A. Maher (Ed.), *Progress in experimental personality research,* vol. 3. New York: Academic Press, 1966, pp. 241–307.

Jones, A., Bentler, P. M., & Petry, G. The reduction of uncertainty during future pain. *Journal of Abnormal Psychology,* 1966, *71,* 87–94.

Jones, E., & Gerard, H. B. *Foundations of social psychology.* New York: Wiley, 1967.

Jones, E. E., & Nisbett, R. E. The actor and the observer: Divergent perceptions of the causes of behavior. In E. E. Jones, et al. (Eds.), *Attribution: Perceiving the causes of behavior.* Morristown, N.J.: General Learning Press, 1971.

Jones, W., Chernovertz, M. E., & Hansson, R. O. The enigma of androgyny: Differential implications for males and females? *Journal of Consulting and Clinical Psychology,* 1978, *46,* 298–313.

Jordan, P. A real predicament. *Science,* 1972, *175,* 977–978.

Jourard, S. M. Experimenter-subject dialogue: A paradigm for a humanistic science of psychology. In J. Bugental (Ed.), *Challenges of humanistic psychology.* New York: McGraw-Hill, 1967, pp. 109–116.

Jourard, S. M. *Healthy personality: An approach from the viewpoint of humanistic psychology.* New York: Macmillan, 1974.

Jung, C. G. *Psychological types.* London: Routledge & Kegan Paul, 1923.

Jung, C. G. *Memories, dreams, reflections.* New York: Pantheon, 1963.

Jung, C. G. *Man and his symbols.* Garden City, N.Y.: Doubleday, 1964.

Kagan, J. The acquisition and significance of sex typing and sex role identity. In M. Hoffman & L. Hoffman (Eds.), *Review of child development research,* vol. 1. New York: Russell Sage, 1964.

Kagan, J. Continuity in development. Paper presented at the meeting of the Society for Research in Child Development, March 27, 1969, Santa Monica, Calif.

Kagan, J., Hosken, B., & Watson, S. The child's symbolic conceptualization of the parents. *Child Development,* 1961, *32,* 625–636.

Kagan, J., & Moss, H. A. *Birth to maturity: A study in psychological development.* New York: Wiley, 1962.

Kahneman, D., & Tversky, A. On the psychology of prediction. *Psychological Review,* 1973, *80,* 237–251.

Kalish, R. Sex and marital role differences in anticipation of age-produced dependency. *Journal of Genetic Psychology,* 1971, *119,* 53–62.

Kamiya, J. Conditioned introspection. Paper read at the Institute of Personality Assessment and Research, University of California, Berkeley, 1967.

Kanfer, F. H. Self-management methods. In F. H. Kanfer & A. P. Goldstein (Eds.), *Helping people change: A textbook of methods* (2nd ed.). Elmsford, New York: Pergamon Press, 1980.

Kanfer, F. H., & Marston, A. R. Determinants of self-reinforcement in human learning. *Journal of Experimental Psychology,* 1963, *66,* 245–254. (a)

Kanfer, F. H., & Marston, A. R. Conditioning of self-reinforcing responses: An analogue to self-confidence training. *Psychological Reports,* 1963, *13,* 63–70. (b)

Kanfer, F. H., & Phillips, J. S. *Learning foundations of behavior therapy*. New York: Wiley, 1970.

Kanfer, F. H., & Seidner, M. L. Self-control: Factors enhancing tolerance of noxious stimulation. *Journal of Personality and Social Psychology,* 1973, *25,* 381–389.

Kanfer, F. H., & Zich, J. Self-control training: The effects of external control on children's resistance to temptation. *Developmental Psychology,* 1974, *10,* 108–115.

Karoly, P. Operant methods. In F. H. Kanfer & A. P. Goldstein (Eds.), *Helping people change: A textbook of methods* (2nd ed.). New York: Pergamon Press, 1980.

Kazdin, A. E., & Wilson, G. T. *Evaluation of behavior therapy: Issues, evidence and research strategies*. Cambridge, Ma.: Ballinger, 1978.

Kelley, H. H. Attribution theory in social psychology. In D. Levine (Ed.), *Nebraska symposium on motivation*. Lincoln: University of Nebraska Press, 1967, pp. 192–238.

Kelley, H. H. The processes of causal attribution. *American Psychologist,* 1973, *28,* 107–128.

Kelley, H. H. The causes of behavior: their perception and regulation. In L. Festinger (Ed.), *Retrospectives on social psychology*. New York: Oxford University Press, 1980.

Kelley, E. L. Consistency of the adult personality. *American Psychologist,* 1955, *10,* 659–681.

Kelly, E. L., & Fiske, D. W. *The prediction of performance in clinical psychology*. Ann Arbor: University of Michigan Press, 1951.

Kelly, G. A. *The psychology of personal constructs,* vols. 1 & 2. New York: Norton, 1955.

Kelly, G. A. Man's construction of his alternatives. In G. Lindzey (Ed.), *Assessment of human motives*. New York: Holt, Rinehart and Winston, 1958, pp. 33–64.

Kelly, G. A. Training for professional obsolescence. Unpublished manuscript, Brandeis University, 1965.

Kety, S. S. Disorders of the human brain. *Scientific American,* 1979, *241,* 202–218.

Kety, S. S., Rosenthal, D., Wender, P. H., Schulsinger, F., & Jacobson, B. Mental illness in the biological and adoptive families of adopted individuals who have become schizophrenics. In R. R. Fieve, D. Rosenthal, & H. Brill (Eds.), *Genetic research in psychiatry*. Baltimore: Johns Hopkins University Press, 1975.

Kiesler, D. J. Some myths of psychotherapy research and the search for a paradigm. *Psychological Bulletin,* 1966, *65,* 110–136.

Kihlstrom, J. F. On personality and memory. In N. Cantor & J. F. Kihlstrom (Eds.), *Personality, cognition, and social interaction*. Hillsdale, N.J.: Erlbaum, 1980.

Klausmeier, H. J., & Wiersma, W. Relationship of sex, grade level, and locale to performance of high IQ students on divergent thinking tests. *Journal of Educational Psychology,* 1964, *55,* 114–119.

Klausmeier, H. J., & Wiersma, W. The effects of IQ level and sex on divergent thinking of seventh grade pupils of low, average, and high IQ. *Journal of Educational Research,* 1965, *58,* 300–302.

Klineberg, S. L. Future time perspective and the preference for delayed reward. *Journal of Personality and Social Psychology,* 1968, *8,* 253–257.

Kobasa, S. C. Stressful life events, personality, and health: An inquiry into hardiness. *Journal of Personality and Social Psychology,* 1979, *37,* 1–11.

Kogan, N., & Wallach, M. A. *Risk taking: A study in cognition and personality.* New York: Holt, Rinehart and Winston, 1964.

Kohlberg, L. The development of children's orientations toward a moral order: 1. Sequence in the development of moral thought. *Vita Humana,* 1963, *6,* 11–33.

Kohlberg, L. Development of moral character and moral ideology. In M. L. Hoffman & L. W. Hoffman (Eds.), *Review of child development,* vol. 1. New York: Russell Sage Foundation, 1964, pp. 383–431.

Kohlberg, L. A cognitive-developmental analysis of children's sex-role concepts and attitudes. In E. E. Maccoby (Ed.), *The development of sex differences.* Stanford: Stanford University Press, 1966, pp. 82–173.

Kohlberg, L. Moral and religious education and the public schools: A developmental view. In T. Sizer (Ed.), *Religion and public education.* Boston: Houghton Mifflin, 1967.

Kohlberg, L. The child as a moral philosopher. *Psychology Today,* 1968, 25–30.

Kohlberg, L. Stage and sequence: The cognitive-developmental approach to socialization. In D. A. Goslin (Ed.), *Handbook of socialization theory and research.* Chicago: Rand McNally, 1969, pp. 347–480.

Korner, A. F. Individual differences at birth: Implications for early experience and later development. *American Journal of Orthopsychiatry,* 1971, *41* (4).

Koss, M. P., & Butcher, J. N. A comparison of psychiatric patients' self-reports with other sources of clinical information. *Journal of Research in Personality,* 1973, *7,* 225–236.

Kostlan, A. A method for the empirical study of psychodiagnosis. *Journal of Consulting Psychology,* 1954, *18,* 83–88.

Krane, R. V., & Wagner, A. R. Taste aversion learning with a delayed shock US: Implications for the "generality of the laws of learning." *Journal of Comparative and Physiological Psychology,* 1975, *88,* 882–889.

Krasner, L., & Ullmann, L. P. *Behavior influence and personality: The social matrix of human action.* New York: Holt, Rinehart and Winston, 1973.

Krech, K., Crutchfield, R., & Ballachey, E. *Individual in society.* New York: McGraw-Hill, 1962.

Kremers, J. *Scientific psychology and naive psychology.* Groningen, Netherlands: Nordhoff, 1960.

Kurland, S. H. The lack of generality in defense mechanisms as indicated in auditory perception. *Journal of Abnormal and Social Psychology,* 1954, *49,* 173–177.

Kurtines, W., & Greif, E. B. The development of moral thought: Review and evaluation of Kohlberg's approach. *Psychological Bulletin,* 1974, *81,* 453–470.

Lacey, J. I., & Smith, R. L. Conditioning and generalization of unconscious anxiety. *Science,* 1954, *120,* 1045–1052.

Laing, R. D. *The divided self.* Middlesex, England: Penguin, 1965.

Lakin, M. *Experiential groups: The uses of interpersonal encounter, psychotherapy groups, and sensitivity training.* Morristown, N.J.: General Learning Press, 1972.

Landfield, A. W., Stern, M., & Fjeld, S. Social conceptual processes and change in students undergoing psychotherapy. *Psychological Reports,* 1961, *8,* 63–68.

Lang, P. J., Geer, J., & Hnatiow, M. Semantic generalization of conditioned autonomic responses. *Journal of Experimental Psychology,* 1963, *65,* 552–558.

Lang, P. J., & Lazovik, A. D. Experimental desensitization of a phobia. *Journal of Abnormal and Social Psychology,* 1963, *66,* 519–525.

Lang, P. J., Lazovik, A. D., & Reynolds, D. J. Desensitization, suggestibility, and pseudotherapy. *Journal of Abnormal Psychology,* 1965, *70,* 395–402.

Langer, E. J. Rethinking the role of thought in social interaction. In J. H. Harvey, W. J. Ickes, & R. F. Kidd (Eds.), *New directions in attribution research,* vol. 2. Hillsdale, N.J.: Erlbaum, 1978.

Langer, E. J., Janis, I. L., & Wolfer, J. A. Reduction of psychological stress in surgical patients. Unpublished manuscript, Yale University, 1975.

Lanzetta, J. T., & Driscoll, J. M. Preference for information about an uncertain but unavoidable outcome. *Journal of Personality and Social Psychology,* 1966, *3,* 96–102.

Lao, R. C. Internal-external control and competent and innovative behavior among Negro college students. *Journal of Personality and Social Psychology,* 1970, *14,* 263–270.

Lawrence, D. H. The nature of a stimulus: Some relationships between learning and perception. In S. Koch (Ed.), *Psychology: A study of a science.* New York: McGraw-Hill, 1959, pp. 179–212.

Lawson, R. *Frustration: The development of a scientific concept.* New York: Macmillan, 1965.

Lay, C. H., & Jackson, D. N. Analysis of the generality of trait-interferential relationships. *Journal of Personality and Social Psychology,* 1969, *12,* 12–21.

Lazarus, A. A. Group therapy of phobic disorders by systematic desensitization. *Journal of Abnormal and Social Psychology,* 1961, *63,* 504–510.

Lazarus, A. A. The treatment of chronic frigidity by systematic desensitization. *Journal of Nervous and Mental Diseases,* 1963, *136,* 272–278.

Lazarus, R. S., & Alfert, E. The short circuiting of threat by experimentally altering cognitive appraisal. *Journal of Abnormal and Social Psychology,* 1964, *69,* 195–205.

Lazarus, R. S., & Averill, J. R. Emotion and cognition: With special reference to anxiety. In C. D. Spielberger (Ed.), *Anxiety: Current trends in theory and research,* vol. II. New York: Academic Press, 1972.

Lazarus, R. S., Eriksen, C. W., & Fonda, C. P. Personality dynamics and auditory perceptual recognition. *Journal of Personality,* Sept. 1950/June 1951, *19,* 471–482.

Lazarus, R. S., & Longo, N. The consistency of psychological defense against threat. *Journal of Abnormal and Social Psychology,* 1953, *48,* 495–499.

Lazarus, R. S., & McCleary, R. A. Autonomic discrimination without awareness: A study of subception. *Psychological Review,* 1951, *58,* 113–122.

Lazarus, R. S., Yousem, H., & Arenberg, D. Hunger and perception. *Journal of Personality,* 1953, *21,* 312–328.

Leary, T. *Interpersonal diagnosis of personality.* New York: Ronald Press, 1957.

Leary, T., Litwin, G. H., & Metzner, R. Reactions to psilocybin administered in a supportive environment. *Journal of Nervous and Mental Diseases,* 1963, *137,* 561–573.

Lecky, P. *Self-consistency.* New York: Island Press, 1945.

Lee, L. C. Concept utilization in preschool children. *Child Development,* 1965, *36,* 221–227.

Lefcourt, H. M. Internal versus external control of reinforcement: A review. *Psychological Bulletin,* 1966, *65,* 206–220.

Lefcourt, H. M. Recent developments in the study of locus of control. In B. A. Maher (Ed.), *Progress in experimental personality research,* vol. 6. New York: Academic Press, 1972.

Lefcourt, H. M. The construction and development of the Multidimensional-Multiattributional Causality Scales. In H. M. Lefcourt (Ed.), *Advances and innovations in locus of control research.* New York: Academic Press, 1980.

Lemere, F., & Voegtlin, W. L. An evaluation of the aversion treatment of alcoholism. *Quarterly Journal of Studies on Alcohol,* 1950, *11,* 199–204.

Lepper, M., Greene, D., & Nisbett, R. E. Undermining children's intrinsic interest with extrinsic reward: A test of the "overjustification" hypothesis. *Journal of Personality and Social Psychology,* 1973, *28,* 129–137.

Lepper, M. R., Sagotsky, G., & Mailer, J. Generalization and persistence of effects of exposure to self-reinforcement models. *Child Development,* 1975, *46,* 618–630.

Leventhal, H., Brown, D., Shacham, S., & Engquist, G. Effects of preparatory information about sensations, threat of pain, and attention on cold pressor distress. *Journal of Personality and Social Psychology,* 1979, *37,* 688–714.

Leventhal, H., Jacobs, R. L., & Kudirka, N. Z. Authoritarianism, ideology, and political candidate choice. *Journal of Abnormal and Social Psychology,* 1964, *69,* 539–549.

Levine, R., Chein, I., & Murphy, G. The relation of the intensity of a need to the amount of perceptual distortion: A preliminary report. *Journal of Psychology,* 1942, *13,* 283–292.

Levine, S. J. Infantile experience and resistance to physiological stress. *Science,* 1957, *126,* 405.

Levine, S. J. Psychophysiological effects of infantile stimulation. In E. L. Bliss (Ed.), *Roots of behavior.* New York: Hoeber, 1962.

Lewin, K. *A dynamic theory of personality.* New York: McGraw-Hill, 1935.

Lewin, K. *Principles of topological psychology.* New York: McGraw-Hill, 1936.

Lewin, K. *Field theory in social science; selected theoretical papers,* D. Cartwright (Ed.), New York: Harper & Row, 1951.

Lewis, M. Infants' responses to facial stimuli during the first year of life. *Developmental Psychology,* 1969, *1,* 75–86.

Lieberman, M. A., Yalom, I. D., & Miles, M. B. *Encounter groups: First facts.* New York: Basic Books, 1973.

Liebert, R. M. Television and social learning: Some relationships between viewing violence and behaving aggressively. In J. P. Murray, E. A. Rubinstein, & G. A. Comstock (Eds.), *Television and social behavior,* vol. 2. *Television and social learning.* Washington, D.C.: GPO, 1972, pp. 1–34.

Liebert, R. M., & Allen, K. M. The effects of rule structure and reward magnitude on the acquisition and adoption of self-reward criteria. Unpublished manuscript, Vanderbilt University, 1967.

Liebert, R. M., & Baron, R. A. Some immediate effects of televised violence on children's behavior. *Developmental Psychology,* 1972, *6,* 469–475.

Lindzey, G., & Tejessy, C. Thematic Apperception Test: Indices of aggression in relation to measures of overt and covert behavior. *American Journal of Orthopsychiatry,* 1956, *26,* 567–576.

Little, K. B., & Shneidman, E. S. Congruencies among interpretations of psychological test and anamnestic data. *Psychological Monographs,* 1959, *73,* No. 6 (Whole No. 476).

Locksley, A., & Colten, M. E. Psychological androgyny: A case of mistaken identity? *Journal of Personality and Social Psychology,* 1979, *37,* 1017–1031.

Loehlin, J. C. *Computer models of personality.* New York: Random House, 1968.

Loevinger, J. Objective tests as instruments of psychological theory. *Psychological Reports Monographs,* No. 9. Southern University Press, 1957.

London, P. *Behavior control.* New York: Harper & Row, 1969.

LoPicolo, J., & Lobitz, W. C. The role of masturbation in the treatment of orgasmic dysfunction. *Archives of Sexual Behavior,* 1972, *2,* 163–171.

Lorenz, K. Z. *On aggression.* New York: Harcourt, 1966.

Lorr, M., Bishop, P. F., & McNair, D. M. Interpersonal types among psychiatric patients. *Journal of Abnormal Psychology,* 1965, *70,* 468–472.

Lott, A. J., & Lott, B. E. A learning theory approach to interpersonal attitudes. In A. G. Greenwald, T. C. Brock, and T. M. Ostrom (Eds.), *Psychological foundations of attitudes.* New York: Academic Press, 1968.

Lovaas, O. I. A behavior therapy approach to the treatment of childhood schizophrenia. In J. P. Hill (Ed.), *Minnesota symposia on child psychology,* vol. 1. Minneapolis: University of Minnesota Press, 1967, pp. 108–159.

Lovaas, O. I., Berberich, J. P., Perloff, B. F., & Schaeffer, B. Acquisition of imitative speech by schizophrenic children. *Science,* 1966, *151,* 705–707.

Lovaas, O. I., Freitag, G., Gold, V. J., & Kassorla, I. C. Experimental studies in childhood schizophrenia: I. Analysis of self-destructive behavior. *Journal of Experimental Child Psychology,* 1965, *2,* 67–84. (a)

Lovaas, O. I., Freitag, G., Gold, V. J., & Kassorla, I. C. Recording apparatus for observation of behaviors of children in free play settings. *Journal of Experimental Child Psychology,* 1965, *2,* 108–120. (b)

Lovaas, O. I., Freitag, L., Nelson, K., & Whalen, C. The establishment of imitation and its use for the development of complex behavior in schizophrenic children. *Behavior Research and Therapy,* 1967, *5,* 171–181.

Luborsky, L., & Spence, D. P. Quantitative research on psychoanalytic therapy. In A. Bergin and S. Garfield (Eds.), *Handbook of psychotherapy and behavior change.* New York: Wiley, 1971.

Luchins, A. S. Experimental attempts to minimize the impact of first impressions. In C. Hovland (Ed.), *The order of presentation in persuasion.* New Haven: Yale University Press, 1957, pp. 63–75.

Luft, J. Differences in prediction based on hearing versus reading verbatim clinical interviews. *Journal of Consulting Psychology,* 1951, *15,* 115–119.

Lynn, D. B., & Sawrey, W. L. The effects of father-absence on Norwegian boys and girls. *Journal of Abnormal and Social Psychology,* 1959, *59,* 258–262.

McCandless, B. R., Bilous, B., & Bennett, H. L. Peer popularity and dependence on adults in preschool age socialization. *Child Development,* 1961, *32,* 337–345.

McCardell, J., & Murray, E. J. Nonspecific factors in weekend encounter groups. *Journal of Consulting and Clinical Psychology,* 1974, *42,* 337–345.

McClelland, D. C. *Personality.* New York: Holt, Rinehart and Winston, 1951.

McClelland, D. C. *The achieving society.* New York: Van Nostrand, 1961.

McClelland, D. C. Longitudinal trends in the relation of thought to action. *Journal of Consulting Psychology,* 1966, *30,* 479–483.

McClelland, D. C., & Atkinson, J. W. The projective expression of needs: I. The effects of different intensities of the hunger drive on perception. *Journal of Psychology,* 1948, *25,* 205–222.

McClelland, D. C., Atkinson, J. W., Clark, R. A., & Lowell, E. L. *The achievement motive.* New York: Appleton, 1953.

McFall, R. M., & Twentyman, C. T. Four experiments on the relative contributions of rehearsal, modeling, and coaching on assertive training. *Journal of Abnormal Psychology,* 1973, *81,* 199–218.

McGinnies, E. Emotionality and perceptual defense. *Psychological Review,* 1949, *56,* 244–251.

McNemar, Q. *The revision of the Stanford-Binet Scale: An analysis of the standardization data.* Boston: Houghton Mifflin, 1942.

Maccoby, E. E. Sex differences in intellectual functioning. In E. E. Maccoby (Ed.), *The development of sex differences.* Stanford: Stanford University Press, 1966, pp. 25–55.

Maccoby, E. E. *Social development: Psychological growth and the parent-child relationship.* New York: Harcourt Brace Jovanovich, 1980.

Maccoby, E. E., & Jacklin, C. N. What we know and don't know about sex differences. *Psychology Today,* December 1974, 109–112. (a)

Maccoby, E. E., & Jacklin, C. N. *The psychology of sex differences.* Stanford: Stanford University Press, 1974. (b)

Maccoby, E. E., & Masters, J. C. Attachment. In P. H. Mussen (Ed.), *Carmichael's manual of child psychology,* rev. ed. New York: Wiley, 1970.

MacFarlane, J. W., & Tuddenham, R. D. Problems in the validation of projective techniques. In H. H. Anderson and G. L. Anderson (Eds.), *Projective techniques.* New York: Prentice-Hall, 1951, pp. 26–54.

Madison, P. *Freud's concept of repression and defense: Its theoretical and observational language.* Minneapolis: University of Minnesota Press, 1960.

Magnusson, D. (Ed.). *The situation: An interactional perspective.* Hillsdale, N. J.: Erlbaum, 1980, in press.

Magnusson, D., & Ekehammar, B. An analysis of situational dimensions: A replication. *Multivariate Behavioral Research,* 1973, *8,* 331–339.

Magnusson, D., & Endler, N. S. Interactional psychology: Present status and future prospects. In D. Magnusson & N. S. Endler (Eds.), *Personality at the crossroads: Current issues in interactional psychology.* Hillsdale, N.J.: Erlbaum, 1977.

Maher, B. A. *Principles of psychotherapy: An experimental approach.* New York: McGraw-Hill, 1966.

Mahoney, M. J. *Cognition and behavior modification.* Cambridge, Mass.: Ballinger, 1974.

Mahrer, A. R. The role of expectancy in delayed reinforcement. *Journal of Experimental Psychology,* 1956, *52,* 101–105.

Mallick, S. K., & McCandless, B. R. A study of catharsis of aggression. *Journal of Personality and Social Psychology,* 1966, *4,* 591–596.

Malmo, R. B. Anxiety and behavioral arousal. *Psychological Review,* 1957, *64,* 276–287.

Malmo, R. B. Activation: A neuropsychological dimension. *Psychological Review,* 1959, *66,* 367–386.

Mandler, G. Emotion. In E. Galanter (Ed.), *New directions in psychology I.* New York: Holt, Rinehart and Winston, 1962, pp. 267–343.

Mandler, G. The interruption of behavior. In D. Levin (Ed.), *Nebraska symposium on motivation.* Lincoln: University of Nebraska Press, 1964, pp. 163–219.

Mandler, G., & Watson, D. L. Anxiety and the interruption of behavior. In C. D. Spielberger (Ed.), *Anxiety and behavior.* New York: Academic Press, 1966, pp. 263–288.

Mann, R. D. A review of the relationships between personality and performance in small groups. *Psychological Bulletin,* 1959, *56,* 241–270.

Manz, W., & Lueck, H. Influence of wearing glasses on personality ratings: Cross-cultural validation of an old experiment. *Perceptual and Motor Skills,* 1968, *27,* 704.

Markowitz, A. Influence of the repression-sensitization dimension, affect value, and ego threat on incidental learning. *Journal of Personality and Social Psychology,* 1969, *11,* 374–380.

Marks, I. M., & Gelder, M. G. Transvestism and fetishism: Clinical and psychological changes during faradic aversion. *British Journal of Psychiatry,* 1967, *113,* 711–729.

Marks, J. Stauffacher, J. C., & Lyle, C. Predicting outcome in schizophrenia. *Journal of Abnormal and Social Psychology,* 1963, *66,* 117–127.

Marks, P. A., & Seeman, W. *Actuarial description of abnormal personality.* Baltimore: Williams & Wilkins, 1963.

Markus, H. Self-schemata and processing information about the self. *Journal of Personality and Social Psychology,* 1977, *35,* 63–78.

Marsden, G. Content analysis studies of psychotherapy: 1954 through 1968. In A. E. Bergin & S. L. Garfield (Eds.), *Handbook of psychotherapy and behavior change.* New York: Wiley, 1971.

Marshall, G. D., & Zimbardo, P. G. Affective consequences of inadequately explained physiological arousal. *Journal of Personality and Social Psychology,* 1979, *37,* 970–988.

Martin, D. G., Hawryluk, G. A., & Guse, L. L. Experimental study of unconscious influences: Ultrasound as a stimulus. *Journal of Abnormal Psychology,* 1974, *83,* 589–608.

Maslach, C. Negative emotional biasing of unexplained arousal. *Journal of Personality and Social Psychology,* 1979, *37,* 953–969.

Masling, J. M. The effects of warm and cold interaction on the administration and scoring of an intelligence test. *Journal of Consulting Psychology,* 1959, *23,* 336–341.

Masling, J. M. The influence of situational and interpersonal variables in projective testing. *Psychological Bulletin,* 1960, *57,* 65–85.

Maslow, A. H. Some basic propositions of a growth and self-actualization psychology. In G. Lindzey & C. Hall (Eds.), *Theories of personality: Primary sources and research.* New York: Wiley, 1965, pp. 307–316.

Maslow, A. H. *Toward a psychology of being,* 2nd edition. New York: Van Nostrand, 1968.

Maslow, A. H. *The farther reaches of human nature.* New York: Viking, 1971.

Masserman, J. H. Experimental approaches to psychoanalytic concepts. *Samiksa,* 1952, *6,* 243–261.

Masters, J. C., & Mokros, J. R. Self-reinforcement processes in children. In H. Reese (Ed.), *Advances in child development and behavior,* vol. 9. New York: Academic Press, 1974.

Masters, W. H., & Johnson, V. *Human sexual inadequacy.* Boston: Little, Brown, 1970.

Matas, L., Arend, R. A., & Sroufe, L. A. Continuity of adaptation in the second year: The relationship between quality of attachment and later competence. *Child Development,* 1978, *49,* 547–556.

May, R. *The meaning of anxiety.* New York: Ronald, 1950.

May, R. Existential psychology. In R. May (Ed.), *Existential psychology.* New York: Random House, 1961, pp. 11–51.

Meehl, P. E. The dynamics of "structured" personality tests. *Journal of Clinical Psychology,* 1945, *1,* 296–303.

Meehl, P. E. *Clinical versus statistical prediction.* Minneapolis: University of Minnesota Press, 1954.

Meehl, P. E. The cognitive activity of the clinician. *American Psychologist,* 1960, *15,* 19–27.

Mehrabian, A. The development and validation of measures of affiliative tendency and sensitivity to rejection. *Educational and Psychological Measurement,* 1970, *30,* 417–428.

Meichenbaum, D. *Cognitive-behavior modification.* New York: Plenum Press, 1977.

Meichenbaum, D. H., & Cameron, R. The clinical potential of modifying what clients say to themselves. In M. J. Mahoney & C. E. Thoresen (Eds.), *Self-control: Power to the person.* Monterey, Calif.: Brooks-Cole, 1974.

Meichenbaum, D. H., & Goodman, J. Training impulsive children to talk to themselves: A means of developing self-control. *Journal of Abnormal Psychology,* 1971, *77,* 115–126.

Melikian, L. Preference for delayed reinforcement: An experimental study among Palestinian Arab refugee children. *Journal of Social Psychology,* 1959, *50,* 81–86.

Meltzer, H. The present status of experimental studies of the relation of feeling to memory. *Psychological Review,* 1930, *37,* 124–139.

Merluzzi, T. V., Glass, C. R., & Genest, M. (Eds.). *Cognitive assessment.* New York: Guilford Press, in press.

Messick, S., & Jackson, D. N. Acquiescence and the factorial interpretation of the MMPI. *Psychological Bulletin,* 1961, *58,* 299–304.

Metcalfe, M. Demonstration of a psychosomatic relationship. *British Journal of Medical Psychology,* 1956, *29,* 63–66.

Michotte, A. *La perception de la causalite,* 2nd ed. Louvain: Publications universitaires de Louvain, 1954.

Milgram, S. Some conditions of obedience and disobedience to authority. *Human Relations,* 1965, *18,* 57–76.

Milgram, S. *Obedience to authority.* New York: Harper & Row, 1974.

Miller, G. A. The magical number seven, plus or minus two: Some limits on capacity for processing information. *Psychological Review,* 1956, *63,* 81–97.

Miller, G. A., Galanter, E., & Pribram, K. H. *Plans and the structure of behavior.* New York: Holt, Rinehart and Winston, 1960.

Miller, N. E. Theory and experiment relating psychoanalytic displacement to stimulus response generalization. *Journal of Abnormal and Social Psychology,* 1948, *43,* 155–178.

Miller, N. E. Liberalization of basic S-R concepts: Extensions to conflict behavior, motivation, and social learning. In S. Koch (Ed.), *Psychology: A study of a science,* vol. 2. New York: McGraw-Hill, 1959, pp. 196–292.

Miller, N. E. Some reflections on the law of effect produce a new alternative to drive reduction. In M. R. Jones (Ed.), *Nebraska symposium on motivation.* Lincoln: University of Nebraska, 1963.

Miller, N. E. Learning of visceral and glandular responses. *Science,* 1969, *163* (3866), 434–445.

Miller, N. E., & Banuazizi, A. Instrumental learning by curarized rats of a specific visceral response, intestinal or cardiac. *Journal of Comparative and Physiological Psychology,* 1968, *65,* 1–7.

Miller, N. E., & Dollard, J. *Social learning and imitation.* New Haven: Yale University Press, 1941.

Miller, S. M. Coping with impending stress: Physiological and cognitive correlates of choice. *Psychophysiology,* 1979, *16,* 572–581.

Miller, S. M. When is a little information a dangerous thing? Coping with stressful events by monitoring versus blunting. In S. Levine & H. Ursin (Eds.), *Coping and health: Proceedings of a NATO Conference.* New York: Plenum Press, 1980.

Miller, S. M., & Grant, R. P. The blunting hypothesis: A view of predictability and human stress. In P. Sjoden, S. Bates, & W. S. Dockens (Eds.), *Trends in behavior therapy.* New York: Academic Press, 1979.

Minuchin, P. Sex-role concepts and sex typing in childhood as a function of school and home environments. *Child Development,* 1965, *36,* 1033–1048.

Mirels, H. L. Implicit personality theory and inferential illusions. *Journal of Personality,* 1976, *44,* 467–487.

Mischel, H. Sex bias in the evaluation of professional achievements. *Journal of Educational Psychology,* 1974, *66,* 157–166.

Mischel, T. Personal constructs, rules, and the logic of clinical activity. *Psychological Review,* 1964, *71,* 180–192.

Mischel, W. Preference for delayed reinforcement: An experimental study of a cultural observation. *Journal of Abnormal and Social Psychology,* 1958, *56,* 57–61.

Mischel, W. Preference for delayed reinforcement and social responsibility. *Journal of Abnormal and Social Psychology,* 1961, *62,* 1–7.(a)

Mischel, W. Delay of gratification, need for achievement, and acquiescence in another culture. *Journal of Abnormal and Social Psychology,* 1961, *62,* 543–552.(b)

Mischel, W. Father absence and delay of gratification: Cross-cultural comparisons. *Journal of Abnormal and Social Psychology,* 1961, *63,* 116–124. (c)

Mischel, W. Predicting the success of Peace Corps Volunteers in Nigeria. *Journal of Personality and Social Psychology,* 1965, *1,* 510–517.

Mischel, W. A social learning view of sex differences in behavior. In E. E.

Maccoby (Ed.), *The development of sex differences.* Stanford: Stanford University Press, 1966, pp. 56–81. (a)

Mischel, W. Theory and research on the antecedents of self-imposed delay of reward. In B. A. Maher (Ed.), *Progress in experimental personality research,* vol. 3. New York: Academic Press, 1966, pp. 85–132. (b)

Mischel, W. *Personality and assessment.* New York: Wiley, 1968.

Mischel, W. Continuity and change in personality. *American Psychologist,* 1969, *24,* 1012–1018.

Mischel, W. Sex typing and socialization. In P. H. Mussen (Ed.), *Carmichael's manual of child psychology,* rev. ed. New York: Wiley, 1970.

Mischel, W. Direct versus indirect personality assessment: Evidence and implications. *Journal of Consulting and Clinical Psychology,* 1972, *38,* 319–324.

Mischel, W. Toward a cognitive social learning reconceptualization of personality. *Psychological Review,* 1973, *80,* 252–283.

Mischel, W. On the empirical dilemmas of psychodynamic approaches: Issues and alternatives. *Journal of Abnormal Psychology,* 1973, *82,* 335–344.

Mischel, W. Processes in delay of gratification. In L. Berkowitz (Ed.), *Advances in experimental social psychology,* vol. 7. New York: Academic Press, 1974.

Mischel, W. The interaction of person and situation. In D. Magnusson & N. S. Endler (Eds.), *Personality at the crossroads: Current issues in interactional psychology.* Hillsdale, N.J.: Erlbaum, 1977.

Mischel, W. On the interface of cognition and personality. *American Psychologist,* 1979, *34,* 740–754.

Mischel, W. Personality and cognition: Something borrowed, something new? In N. Cantor & J. Kihlstrom (Eds.), *Personality, cognition, and social interaction.* Hillsdale, N.J.: Erlbaum, 1980. (a)

Mischel, W. *Behavioral consistency: Myth or reality?* Special debate presented at the meetings of the American Psychological Association, Montreal, September 1980. (b)

Mischel, W. Metacognition and the rules of delay. In J. H. Flavell & L. Ross (Eds.), *Social cognitive development: Frontiers and possible futures.* New York: Cambridge University Press, in press.

Mischel, W. & Baker, N. Cognitive transformations of reward objects through instructions. *Journal of Personality and Social Psychology,* 1975, *31,* 254–261.

Mischel, W., Coates, B., & Raskoff, A. Effects of success and failure on self-gratification. *Journal of Personality and Social Psychology,* 1968, *10,* 381–390.

Mischel, W., & Ebbesen, E. Attention in delay of gratification. *Journal of Personality and Social Psychology,* 1970, *16,* 329–337.

Mischel, W., Ebbesen, E. B., & Zeiss, A. R. Cognitive and attentional mechanisms in delay of gratification. *Journal of Personality and Social Psychology,* 1972, *21,* 204–218.

Mischel, W., Ebbesen, E., & Zeiss, A. R. Selective attention to the self: Situational and dispositional determinants. *Journal of Personality and Social Psychology,* 1973, *27,* 129–142.

Mischel, W., Ebbesen, E. B., & Zeiss, A. Determinants of selective memory about the self. *Journal of Consulting and Clinical Psychology,* 1976, *44,* 92–103.

Mischel, W., & Gilligan, C. Delay of gratification, motivation for the prohibited gratification, and responses to temptation. *Journal of Abnormal and Social Psychology,* 1964, *69,* 411–417.

Mischel, W., & Grusec, J. Waiting for rewards and punishments: Effects of time and probability on choice. *Journal of Personality and Social Psychology,* 1967, *5,* 24–31.

Mischel, W., Jeffery, K. M., & Patterson, C. J. The layman's use of trait and behavioral information to predict behavior. *Journal of Research in Personality,* 1974, *8,* 231–242.

Mischel, W., & Liebert, R. M. Effects of discrepancies between observed and imposed reward criteria on their acquisition and transmission. *Journal of Personality and Social Psychology,* 1966, *3,* 45–53.

Mischel, W., & Masters, J. C. Effects of probability of reward attainment on responses to frustration. *Journal of Personality and Social Psychology,* 1966, *3,* 390–396.

Mischel, W., & Metzner, R. Preference for delayed reward as a function of age, intelligence, and length of delay interval. *Journal of Abnormal and Social Psychology,* 1962, *64,* 425–431.

Mischel, W., & Mischel, H. The nature and development of psychological sex differences. In G. Lesser (Ed.), *Psychology and educational practice.* Glenview, Ill.: Scott, Foresman, 1971.

Mischel, W., & Mischel, H. N. A cognitive social learning approach to morality and self-regulation. In T. Lickona (Ed.), *Moral development and behavior: Theory, research, and social issues.* New York: Holt, Rinehart and Winston, 1976.

Mischel, W., & Moore, B. The role of ideation in voluntary delay for symbolically presented rewards. *Cognitive Therapy and Research,* 1980, *4,* 211–221.

Mischel, W., & Peake, P. Failure of the Bem-Funder technique in the search for consistency. In M. P. Zanna, C. P. Herman, & E. T. Higgins (Eds.), *Variability and consistency of social behavior: The Ontario Symposium,* vol. 2. Hillsdale, N.J.: Erlbaum, in press.

Mischel, W., & Schopler, J. Authoritarianism and reactions to "sputniks." *Journal of Abnormal and Social Psychology,* 1959, *59,* 142–145.

Mischel, W., & Staub, E. Effects of expectancy on working and waiting for larger rewards. *Journal of Personality and Social Psychology,* 1965, *2,* 625–633.

Mischel, W., Zeiss, R., & Zeiss, A. R. Internal-external control and persistence: Validation and implications of the Stanford Preschool Internal-External Scale. *Journal of Personality and Social Psychology,* 1974, *29,* 265–278.

Money, J. Influence of hormones on sexual behavior. *Annual Review of Medicine,* 1965, *16,* 67–82. (a)

Money, J. Psychosexual differentiation. In J. Money (Ed.), *Sex research, new developments.* New York: Holt, Rinehart and Winston, 1965. (b)

Money, J. Response to paper by B. V. Zuger. *Psychosomatic Medicine,* 1970, *32,* 463–465.

Money, J. Ablatiopenis: Normal male infant-sex reassigned as a girl. *Archives of Sexual Behavior,* 1975, *4,* 65–72.

Money, J. Human hermaphroditism. In F. A. Beach (Ed.), *Human sexuality in four perspectives*. Baltimore, Md.: Johns Hopkins University Press, 1976, pp. 62–86.

Money, J., & Ehrhardt, A. *Man and woman: Boy and girl*. Baltimore: Johns Hopkins University Press, 1972.

Moore, B., Mischel, W., & Zeiss, A. Comparative effects of the reward stimulus and its cognitive representation in voluntary delay. *Journal of Personality and Social Psychology*, 1976, *34*, 419–424.

Moos, R. H. Situational analysis of a therapeutic community milieu. *Journal of Abnormal Psychology*, 1968, *73*, 49–61.

Moos, R. H. Conceptualizations of human environments. *American Psychologist*, 1973, *28*, 652–665.

Moos, R. H. Systems for the assessment and classification of human environments. In R. H. Moos, & P. M. Insel (Eds.), *Issues in social ecology*. Palo Alto, Calif.: National Press Books, 1974.

Moos, R. H., & Insel, P. M. (Eds.), *Issues in social ecology*. Palo Alto, Calif.: National Press Books, 1974.

Morse, W. H., & Kelleher, R. T. Schedules using noxious stimuli I. Multiple fixed-ratio and fixed-interval termination of schedule complexes. *Journal of the Experimental Analysis of Behavior,* 1966, *9,* 267–290.

Mosher, L. R., Feinsilver, D., Katz, M. M., & Wienckowski, L. A. *Special report on schizophrenia*. Bethesda, Md.: U.S. Department of Health, Education, and Welfare, National Institute of Mental Health, April 1970.

Moss, H. A., & Kagan, J. The stability of achievement and recognition seeking behavior from childhood to adulthood. *Journal of Abnormal and Social Psychology,* 1961, *62,* 543–552.

Mowrer, O. H., & Ullmann, A. D. Time as a determinant in integrative learning. *Psychological Review,* 1945, *52,* 61–90.

Mulaik, S. A. Are personality factors raters' conceptual factors? *Journal of Consulting Psychology,* 1964, *28,* 506–511.

Murphy, J. M. Psychiatric labeling in cross-cultural perspective. *Science,* 1976, *191,* 1019–1028.

Murray, E. J. Conflict and repression during sleep deprivation. *Journal of Abnormal and Social Psychology,* 1959, *59,* 95–101.

Murray, E. J., Auld, F., Jr., & White, A. M. A psychotherapy case showing progress but no decrease in the discomfort-relief quotient. *Journal of Consulting Psychology,* 1954, *18,* 349–353.

Murray, H. A. Foreword *An introduction to projective techniques,* H. H. Anderson & G. L. Anderson (Eds.), Englewood Cliffs, N.J.: Prentice-Hall, 1951, pp. XI–XIV.

Murray, H. A. (and collaborators). *Explorations in personality*. New York: Oxford, 1938.

Murray, J. Television and violence: Implications of the surgeon general's research program. *American Psychologist*, 1973, *28,* 472–478.

Murstein, B. I. *Theory and research in projective techniques*. New York: Wiley, 1963.

Mussen, P. H. Some antecedents and consequents of masculine sex-typing in adolescent boys. *Psychological Monographs*, 1961, *75,* No. 2 (Whole No. 506).

Mussen, P. H. Long-term consequents of masculinity of interests in adolescence. *Journal of Consulting Psychology,* 1962, *26,* 435–440.

Mussen, P. H., Conger, J. J., & Kagan, J. *Child development and personality.* New York: Harper & Row, 1979.

Mussen, P. H., & Jones, M. C. Self-conceptions, motivations, and interpersonal attitudes of late- and early-maturing boys. *Child Development,* 1957, *28,* 243–256.

Mussen, P. H., & Jones, M. C. The behavior-inferred motivations of late- and early-maturing boys. *Child Development,* 1958, *29,* 61-67.

Mussen, P. H., & Naylor, H. K. The relationship between overt and fantasy aggression. *Journal of Abnormal and Social Psychology,* 1954, *49,* 235–240.

Neisser, U. *Cognitive psychology.* New York: Appleton, 1967.

Neisser, U. Review of "Visual information processing." *Science,* 1974, *183,* 402–403.

Nisbett, R. E., & Ross, L. D. *Human inference: Strategies and shortcomings of social judgment.* Century Psychology Series. Englewood Cliffs, N.J.: Prentice-Hall, 1980.

Nisbett, R. E., & Wilson, T. D. Telling more than we can know: Verbal reports on mental processes. *Psychological Review,* 1977, *84,* 231–259.

Norman, W. T. Development of self-report tests to measure personality factors identified from peer nominations. *USAF ASK Technical Note,* 1961, No. 61–44.

Norman, W. T. Toward an adequate taxonomy of personality attributes: Replicated factor structure in peer nomination personality ratings. *Journal of Abnormal and Social Psychology,* 1963, *66,* 574–583.

Norman, W. T. Convergent and discriminant validation of personality factor measurements. Unpublished manuscript, University of Michigan, 1966.

Norman, W. T. To see ourselves as others see us!: Relations among self-perceptions, peer-perceptions, and expected peer-perceptions of personality attributes. *Multivariate Behavioral Research,* 1969, *4,* 417–443.

Nunnally, J. C., & Lemond, L. C. Exploratory behavior and human development. In H. W. Reese (Ed.), *Advances in child development and behavior,* vol. 8. New York: Academic Press, 1973.

Office of Strategic Services Assessment Staff. *Assessment of men.* New York: Holt, Rinehart and Winston, 1948.

Ohman, A., Erixon, G., & Löfberg, I. Phobias and preparedness: Phobic versus neutral pictures as conditioned stimuli for human autonomic responses. *Journal of Abnormal Psychology,* 1975, *84,* 41–45.

O'Leary, K. D., & Kent, R. N. Behavior modification for social action: Research tactics and problems. In L. Hamerlynck et al. (Eds.), *Critical issues in research and practice.* New York: Research Press, 1973.

Olweus, D. Personality factors and aggression: With special reference to violence within the peer group. In J. de Wit & W. W. Hartup (Eds.), *Determinants and origins of aggressive behavior.* The Hague, Netherlands: Mouton, 1974, pp. 1–36.

Olweus, D. Stability of aggressive reaction patterns in males: A review. *Psychological Bulletin,* 1979, *86,* 852–875.

Opler, M. K. Cultural induction of stress. In M. H. Appley & R. Trumbull (Eds.), *Psychological stress.* New York: Appleton, 1967, pp. 209–241.

Ornstein, R. E. *The psychology of consciousness.* San Francisco, Calif.: Freeman, 1972.

Ornstein, R. E., & Naranjo, C. *On the psychology of meditation.* New York: Viking, 1971.

Osgood, C. E., Suci, G. J., & Tannenbaum, P. H. *The measurement of meaning.* Urbana, Ill.: The University of Illinois Press, 1957.

Oskamp, S. Overconfidence in case-study judgments. *Journal of Consulting Psychology,* 1965, *29,* 261–265.

Palmer, R. D. Patterns of defensive response to threatening stimuli: Antecedents and consistency. *Journal of Abnormal Psychology,* 1968, *73,* 30–36.

Passini, F. T., & Norman, W. T. A universal conception of personality structure? *Journal of Personality and Social Psychology,* 1966, *4,* 44–49.

Pastore, N. The role of arbitrariness in the frustration-aggression hypothesis. *Journal of Abnormal and Social Psychology,* 1952, *47,* 728–731.

Patterson, G. R. Interventions for boys with conduct problems: Multiple settings, treatments, and criteria. *Journal of Consulting and Clinical Psychology,* 1974, *42,* 471–481.

Patterson, G. R. The aggressive child: Victim and architect of a coercive system. In L. A. Hamerlynck, L. C. Handy, & E. J. Mash (Eds.), *Behavior modification and families: 1. Theory and research.* New York: Brunner/Mazel, 1976.

Patterson, G. R., & Anderson, D. Peers as social reinforcers. *Child Development,* 1964, *35,* 951–960.

Patterson, G. R., & Cobb, J. A. Stimulus control for classes of noxious behaviors. In J. F. Knutson (Ed.), *The control of aggression: Implications from basic research.* Chicago: Aldine, 1971.

Paul, G. L. *Insight vs. desensitization in psychotherapy.* Stanford: Stanford University, 1966.

Paul, G. L. Insight versus desensitization in psychotherapy two years after termination. *Journal of Consulting Psychology,* 1967, *31,* 333–348.

Paul, G. L., & Shannon, D. T. Treatment of anxiety through systematic desensitization in therapy groups. *Journal of Abnormal Psychology,* 1966, *71,* 124–135.

Payne, F. D., & Wiggins, J. S. MMPI profile types and the self-report of psychiatric patients. *Journal of Abnormal Psychology,* 1972, *79,* 1–8.

Pederson, F. A. Consistency data on the role construct repertory test. Unpublished manuscript, Ohio State University, Columbus, 1958.

Pedhazur, E. J., & Tetenbaum, T. J. Bem Sex Role Inventory: A theoretical and methodological critique. *Journal of Personality and Social Psychology,* 1979, *37,* 996–1016.

Perlmuter, L. C., & Monty, R. A. (Eds.), *Choice and perceived control.* New York: Erlbaum, 1979.

Perls, F. S. *Gestalt therapy verbatim.* Lafayette, Calif.: Real People Press, 1969.

Peterson, D. R. Scope and generality of verbally defined personality factors. *Psychological Review,* 1965, *72,* 48–59.

Peterson, D. R. *The clinical study of social behavior.* New York: Appleton, 1968.

Phares, E. J. *Locus of control: A personality determinant of behavior.* Morristown, N.J.: General Learning Press, 1973.

Phares, E. J. Locus of control. In H. London & J. E. Exner, Jr. (Eds.), *Dimensions of personality.* New York: Wiley, 1978.

Phares, E. J., Ritchie, E. D., & Davis, W. L. Internal-external control and reaction to threat. *Journal of Personality and Social Psychology,* 1968, *10,* 402–405.

Phillips, J. S., & Kanfer, F. H. The viability and vicissitudes of behavior therapy. *International Psychiatry Clinics,* 1969, *6,* 75–131.

Phillips, L. Case-history data and prognosis in schizophrenia. *Journal of Nervous and Mental Diseases,* 1953, *117,* 515–525.

Phillips, L., & Rabinovitch, M. S. Social role and patterns of symptomatic behaviors. *Journal of Abnormal and Social Psychology,* 1958, *57,* 181–186.

Piaget, J. The general problems of the psychobiological development of the child. In J. M. Tanner & B. Inhelder (Eds.), *Discussions on child development: Proceedings of the World Health Organization study group on the psychobiological development of the child,* vol. IV. New York: International Universities Press, 1960, pp. 3–27.

Postman, L., & Brown, D. R. The perceptual consequences of success and failure. *Journal of Abnormal and Social Psychology,* 1952, *47,* 213–221.

Premack, D. Reinforcement theory. In D. Levine (Ed.), *Nebraska symposium on motivation.* Lincoln: University of Nebraska Press, 1965, pp. 123–180.

Price, R. H. The taxonomic classification of behaviors and situations and the problem of behavior-environment congruence. *Human Relations,* 1974.

Price, R. H., & Bouffard, D. L. Behavioral appropriateness and situational constraint as dimensions of social behavior. *Journal of Personality and Social Psychology,* 1974, *30,* 579–586.

Proshansky, H., Ittelson, W., & Rivlin, L. G. (Eds.), *Environmental psychology.* New York: Holt, Rinehart and Winston, 1970.

Rabkin, J. G., & Struening, E. L. Life events, stress, and illness. *Science,* 1976, *194,* 1013–1020.

Rachman, S. Systematic desensitization. *Psychological Bulletin,* 1967, *67,* 93–103.

Rachman, S., & Wilson, G. T. *Effects of psychotherapy.* Oxford: Pergamon Press, 1980.

Rapaport, D. The autonomy of the ego. *Bulletin of the Menninger Clinic,* 1951, *15,* 113–123.

Rapaport, D. On the psychoanalytic theory of thinking. In M. M. Gill (Ed.), *The collected papers of David Rapaport.* New York: Basic Books, 1967.

Raush, H. L. Interaction sequences. *Journal of Personality and Social Psychology,* 1965, *2,* 487–499.

Raush, H. L., Barry, W. A., Hertel, R. K., & Swain, M. A. *Communication conflict and marriage.* San Francisco: Jossey-Bass, 1974.

Raymond, M. S. Case of fetishism treated by aversion therapy. *British Medical Journal,* 1956, *2,* 854–857.

Reece, M. M. The effect of shock on recognition thresholds. *Journal of Abnormal and Social Psychology,* 1954, *49,* 165–172.

Rekers, G. A., & Lovaas, O. I. Behavioral treatment of deviant sex-role behaviors in a male child. *Journal of Applied Behavior Analysis,* 1974, *7,* 173–190.

Renner, K. E. Conflict resolution and the process of temporal integration. *Psychological Reports,* 1964, *15,* 423–438. Monograph Supplement 15-2.

Renner, K. E. Temporal integration: An incentive approach to conflict resolution. In B. A. Maher (Ed.), *Progress in experimental personality research,* vol. 4. New York: Academic Press, 1967.

Reynolds, G. S. Contrast, generalization, and the process of discrimination. *Journal of the Experimental Analysis of Behavior,* 1961, *4,* 289–294.

Rimm, D. C., & Masters, J. C. *Behavior therapy: Techniques and empirical findings.* New York: Academic Press, 1974.

Rodin, J., & Langer, E. Long-term effect of control-relevant intervention. *Journal of Personality and Social Psychology,* 1977, *35,* 897–902.

Rogers, C. R. *Counseling and psychotherapy: Newer concepts in practice.* Boston: Houghton Mifflin, 1942.

Rogers, C. R. Some observations on the organization of personality. *American Psychologist,* 1947, *2,* 358–368.

Rogers, C. R. *Client-centered therapy: Its current practice, implications and theory.* Boston: Houghton Mifflin, 1951.

Rogers, C. R. Persons or science? A philosophical question. *American Psychologist,* 1955, *10,* 267–278.

Rogers, C. R. A theory of therapy, personality and interpersonal relationships, as developed in the client-centered framework. In S. Koch (Ed.), *Psychology: A study of a science,* vol. 3. New York: McGraw-Hill, 1959, pp. 184–256.

Rogers, C. R. The actualizing tendency in relation to "motives" and to consciousness. In M. R. Jones (Ed.), *Nebraska symposium on motivation.* Lincoln: University of Nebraska Press, 1963, pp. 1–24.

Rogers, C. R. *Carl Rogers on encounter groups.* New York: Harper & Row, 1970.

Rogers, C. R. In retrospect: Forty-six years. *American Psychologist,* 1974, *29,* 115–123.

Rogers, C. R., & Dymond, R. F. (Eds.), *Psychotherapy and personality change; co-ordinated studies in the client-centered approach.* Chicago: University of Chicago Press, 1954.

Rogers, T. B. Self-reference in memory: Recognition of personality items. *Journal of Research in Personality,* 1977, *11,* 295–305.

Rogers, T. B., Kuiper, N. A., & Kirker, W. S. Self-reference and the encoding of personal information. *Journal of Personality and Social Psychology,* 1977, *35,* 677–688.

Rorer, L. G. The great response-style myth. *Psychological Bulletin,* 1965, *63,* 129–156.

Rosch, E. Cognitive reference points. *Cognitive Psychology,* 1975, *1,* 532–547.

Rosch, E., Mervis, C., Gray, W., Johnson, D., & Boyes-Braem, P. Basic objects in natural categories. *Cognitive Psychology,* 1976, *8,* 382–439.

Rosen, A. C. Change in perceptual threshold as a protective function of the organism. *Journal of Personality,* 1954, *23,* 182–195.

Rosenberg, B. G., & Sutton-Smith, B. Family interaction effects on masculinity-femininity. *Journal of Personality and Social Psychology,* 1968, *8,* 117–120.

Rosenblith, J. F. Imitative color choices in kindergarten children. *Child Development,* 1961, *32,* 211–223.

Rosenhan, D. L. On being sane in insane places. *Science,* 1973, *179,* 250–258.

Rosenhan, D. L., Moore, B., & Underwood, B. The social psychology of moral behavior. In T. Lickona (Ed.), *Moral development and behavior: Theory, research, and social issues.* New York: Holt, Rinehart and Winston, 1976.

Rosenthal, D. *Genetics of psychopathology.* New York: McGraw-Hill, 1971.

Rosenzweig, M. R., Krech, D., & Bennett, E. L. A search for relations between brain chemistry and behavior. *Psychological Bulletin,* 1960, *57,* 476–492.

Rosenzweig, S. A trans-valuation of psychotherapy: A reply to Hans Eysenck. *Journal of Abnormal and Social Psychology,* 1954, *49,* 298–304.

Rosenzweig, S., & Mason, G. An experimental study of memory in relation to the theory of repression. *British Journal of Psychology,* 1934, *24,* 247–265.

Ross, D. Relationship between dependency, intentional learning, and incidental learning in preschool children. *Journal of Personality and Social Psychology,* 1966, *4,* 374–381.

Ross, L. The intuitive psychologist and his shortcomings: Distortions in the attribution process. In L. Berkowitz (Ed.), *Advances in experimental social psychology,* vol. 10. New York: Academic Press, 1977.

Rothaus, P., & Worchel, P. Ego-support, communication, catharsis, and hostility. *Journal of Personality,* 1964, *32,* 296–312.

Rothbart, M. K., & Maccoby, E. E. Parents' differential reactions to sons and daughters. *Journal of Personality and Social Psychology,* 1966, *4,* 237–243.

Rotter, J. B. *Social learning and clinical psychology.* Englewood Cliffs, N.J.: Prentice-Hall, 1954.

Rotter, J. B. Generalized expectancies for internal versus external control of reinforcement. *Psychological Monographs,* 1966, *80* (Whole No. 609).

Rotter, J. B. Beliefs, social attitudes, and behavior: A social learning analysis. In J. B. Rotter, J. E. Chance, & E. J. Phares (Eds.), *Applications of a social learning theory of personality.* New York: Holt, Rinehart and Winston, 1972.

Rotter, J. B., Chance, J. E., & Phares, E. J. (Eds.). *Applications of a social learning theory of personality.* New York: Holt, Rinehart and Winston, 1972.

Royce, J. E. Does person or self imply dualism? *American Psychologist,* 1973, *28,* 833–866.

Rubin, I. The reduction of prejudice through laboratory training. *Journal of Applied Behavioral Science, 3,* 1967, 29–50.

Rubin, I. J. Analyzing Detroit's riot: The causes and responses. *The Reporter,* Feb. 22, 1968, 34–35.

Rubin, M., & Shontz, F. C. Diagnostic prototypes and diagnostic processes of clinical psychologists. *Journal of Consulting Psychology,* 1960, *24,* 234–239.

Ruebush, B. E. Anxiety. In H. A. Stevenson, et al. (Eds.), *Child psychology. The sixty-second yearbook of the National Society for the Study of Education.* Chicago: University of Chicago Press, 1963, pp. 460–516.

Russell, P. C., & Brandsma, J. M. A theoretical and empirical integration of the rational-emotive and classical conditioning theories. *Journal of Consulting and Clinical Psychology,* 1974, *42,* 389–397.

Rychlak, J. F. Is a concept of "self" necessary in psychological theory, and if so why? A humanistic perspective. In A. Wandersman, P. Poppen, & D. Ricks (Eds.), *Humanism and behaviorism: Dialogue and growth.* Oxford, England: Pergamon Press, 1976.

Sampson E. E., & Hancock, T. An examination of the relationship between ordinal position, personality, and conformity: An extension, replication, and partial verification. *Journal of Personality and Social Psychology,* 1967, *5,* 398–407.

Sandifer, M. G., Jr., Pettus, C., & Quade, D. A study of psychiatric diagnosis. *Journal of Nervous and Mental Diseases,* 1964, *139,* 350–356.

Sarason, I. G. The effects of anxiety and threat on the solution of a difficult task. *Journal of Abnormal and Social Psychology,* 1961, *62,* 165–168.

Sarason, I. G. *Personality: An objective approach.* New York: Wiley, 1966.

Sarason, I. G. Birth order, test anxiety, and learning. *Journal of Personality,* 1969, *37,* 171–177.

Sarason, I. G. The Test Anxiety Scale: Concept and research. In C. D. Spielberger & I. G. Sarason (Eds.), *Stress and anxiety,* vol. 5. Washington, D.C.: Hemisphere, 1978.

Sarason, I. G. *Life stress, self-preoccupation, and social supports.* Presidential address, Western Psychological Association, 1979.

Sarason, I. G., Smith, R. E., & Diener, E. Personality research: Components of variance attributable to the person and the situation. *Journal of Personality and Social Psychology,* 1975, *32,* 199–204.

Sarason, S. B., Davidson, K. S., Lighthall, F. F., Waite, R. R., & Ruebush, B. K. *Anxiety in elementary school children.* New York: Wiley, 1960.

Sartre, J. P. Existentialism. In W. Kaufmann (Ed.), *Existentialism from Dostoevsky to Sartre.* New York: Meridian, 1956, pp. 222–311.

Sartre, J. P. *Existentialism and humanism.* (tr. by Mairet.) London: Methuen, 1965.

Satir, V. *Conjoint family therapy.* Palo Alto, Calif.: Science and Behavior Books, 1967.

Savage, C., Savage, E., Fadiman, J., & Harman, W. LSD: Therapeutic effects of psychedelic experience. *Psychological Reports,* 1964, *14,* 111–120.

Schacht, T., & Nathan, P. E. But is it good for the psychologists? Appraisal and status of DSM-III. *American Psychologist,* 1977, *32,* 1017–1025.

Schachter, S. The interaction of cognitive and physiological determinants of emotional state. In L. Berkowitz (Ed.), *Advances in experimental social psychology,* vol. 1. New York: Academic Press, 1964, pp. 49–80.

Schachter, S., & Singer, J. E. Cognitive, social and physiological determinants of emotional state. *Psychological Review,* 1962, *69,* 379–399.

Schachter, S., & Singer, J. E. Comments on the Maslach and Marshall-Zimbardo experiments. *Journal of Personality and Social Psychology,* 1979, *37,* 989–995.

Schank, R., & Abelson, R. *Scripts, plans, goals, and understanding.* Hillsdale, N.J.: Erlbaum, 1977.

Scheier, M. F., & Carver, C. S. Individual differences in self-concept and self-process. In D. M. Wegner & R. R. Vallacher (Eds.), *The self in social psychology.* New York: Oxford University Press, 1980.

Schmidt, H. O., & Fonda, C. P. The reliability of psychiatric diagnosis: A new look. *Journal of Abnormal and Social Psychology,* 1956, *52,* 262–267.

Schneider, D. J. Implicit personality theory: A review. *Psychological Bulletin,* 1973, *73,* 294–309.

Schneider, D. J., Hastorf, A. H., & Ellsworth, P. C. *Person perception* (2nd ed.). Reading, Ma.: Addison-Wesley, 1979.

Schutz, W. C. *Joy: Expanding human awareness.* New York: Grove, 1967.

Schwartz, G. E. Biofeedback as therapy. *American Psychologist,* 1973, *28,* 666–673.

Scott, W. A., & Johnson, R. C. Comparative validities of direct and indirect personality tests. *Journal of Consulting and Clinical Psychology,* 1972, *38,* 301–318.

Sears, R. R. Functional abnormalities of memory with special reference to amnesia. *Psychological Bulletin,* 1936, *33,* 229–274.

Sears, R. R. Survey of objective studies of psychoanalytic concepts. *Social Science Research Council Bulletin,* 1943, No. 51.

Sears, R. R. Experimental analyses of psychoanalytic phenomena. In J. McV.

Hunt (Ed.), *Personality and the behavior disorders,* vol. 1. New York: Ronald, 1944, pp. 306–332.

Sears, R. R. Dependency motivation. In M. R. Jones (Ed.), *Nebraska symposium on motivation.* Lincoln: University of Nebraska Press, 1963, pp. 25–64.

Sears, R. R. Development of gender role. In F. A. Beach (Ed.), *Sex and behavior.* New York: Wiley, 1965, pp. 133–163.

Sears, R. R., Maccoby, E. E., & Levin, H. *Patterns of child rearing.* New York: Harper & Row, 1957.

Sears, R. R., Rau, L., & Alpert, R. *Identification and child rearing.* Stanford: Stanford University Press, 1965.

Sears, R. R., Whiting, J., Nowlis, V., & Sears, P. Some child rearing antecedents of aggression and dependency in young children. *Genetic Psychology Monographs,* 1953, *47,* 135–234.

Sechrest, L., Gallimore, R., & Hersch, P. D. Feedback and accuracy of clinical prediction. *Journal of Consulting Psychology,* 1967, *31,* 1–11.

Seligman, M. E. P. Phobias and preparedness. *Behavior Therapy,* 1971, *2,* 307–320.

Seligman, M. E. P. *Helplessness—On depression, development, and death.* San Francisco: Freeman, 1975.

Seligman, M. E. P. Comment and integration. *Journal of Abnormal Psychology,* 1978, *87,* 165–179.

Seligman, M. E. P., & Miller, S. M. The psychology of power: Concluding comments. In L. C. Perlmuter & R. A. Monty (Eds.), *Choice and perceived control.* Hillsdale, N.J.: Erlbaum, 1979.

Sells, S. B. A multivariate model of personality. In J. R. Royce (Ed.), *Contributions of multivariate analysis and psychological theory.* New York: Academic Press, 1973.

Shaffer, H. R., & Emerson, P. E. The development of social attachment in infancy. *Monograph of The Society for Research in Child Development,* 1964, *29,* No. 3.

Shure, G. H., & Rogers, M. S. Note of caution on the factor analysis of the MMPI. *Psychological Bulletin,* 1965, *63,* 14–18.

Shweder, R. A. How relevant is an individual difference theory of personality? *Journal of Personality,* 1975, *43,* 455–485.

Shweder, R. A., & D'Andrade, R. G. Accurate reflection or systematic distortion? A reply to Block, Weiss, and Thorne. *Journal of Personality and Social Psychology,* 1979, *37,* 1075–1084.

Shybut, J. Delay of gratification and severity of psychological disturbance among hospitalized psychiatric patients. *Journal of Consulting and Clinical Psychology,* 1968, *32,* 462–468.

Siegel, A. E., Stolz, L. M., Hitchcock, E. A., & Adamson, J. Children of working mothers and their controls. *Child Development,* 1959, *30,* 533–546.

Silverman, L. H. Psychoanalytic theory: The reports of my death are greatly exaggerated. *American Psychologist,* 1976, *31,* 621–637.

Sines, L. K. The relative contribution of four kinds of data to accuracy in personality assessment. *Journal of Consulting Psychology,* 1959, *23,* 483–492.

Singer, J. L. Delayed gratification and ego development: Implications for clinical and experimental research. *Journal of Consulting Psychology,* 1955, *19,* 259–266.

Singer, J. L., & Antrobus, J. S. Dimensions of day-dreaming: A factor analysis of imaginal processes and personality scales. In P. Sheehan (Ed.), *The adaptive function of imagery.* New York: Academic Press, 1972.

Singer, J. L., & Singer, D. G. Personality. In P. Mussen and M. Rosenzweig (Eds.), *Annual Review of Psychology,* vol. 23. Palo Alto, Calif.: Annual Reviews, Inc., 1972.

Skinner, B. F. *Science and human behavior.* New York: Macmillan, 1953.

Skinner, B. F. Behaviorism at fifty. In T. W. Wann (Ed.), *Behaviorism and phenomenology.* Chicago: University of Chicago Press, 1964, pp. 79–108.

Skinner, B. F. *About behaviorism.* New York: Knopf, 1974.

Skolnick, A. Motivational imagery and behavior over twenty years. *Journal of Consulting Psychology,* 1966, *30,* 463–478.

Smith, M. B. The phenomenological approach in personality theory: Some critical remarks. *Journal of Abnormal and Social Psychology,* 1950, *45,* 516–522.

Smith, E. R., & Miller, F. D. Limits on perception of cognitive processes: A reply to Nisbett and Wilson. *Psychological Review,* 1978, *85,* 355–362.

Snyder, M. Self-monitoring processes. In L. Berkowitz (Ed.), *Advances in experimental social psychology,* vol. 12. New York: Academic Press, 1979.

Snyder, M., & Swann, W. Behavioral confirmation in social interaction: From social perception to social reality. *Journal of Experimental Social Psychology,* 1978, *14,* 148–162.

Snyder, S. H., Banerjee, S. P., Yamomura, H. I., & Greenberg, D. Drugs, neurotransmitters, and schizophrenia. *Science,* 1974, *184,* 1243–1253.

Snygg, D., & Combs, C. W. *Individual behavior.* New York: Harper & Row, 1949.

Solomon, D. (Ed.) *LSD: The consciousness-expanding drug.* New York: Berkeley, 1967.

Soskin, W. F. Bias in postdiction from projective tests. *Journal of Abnormal and Social Psychology,* 1954, *49,* 69–74.

Soskin, W. F. Influence of four types of data on diagnostic conceptualization in psychological testing. *Journal of Abnormal and Social Psychology,* 1959, *58,* 69–78.

Spielberger, C. D. The effects of anxiety on complex learning and academic achievement. In C. D. Spielberger (Ed.), *Anxiety and behavior.* New York: Academic Press, 1966, pp. 361–398.

Spielberger, C. D., & DeNike, L. D. Descriptive behaviorism versus cognitive theory in verbal operant conditioning. *Psychological Review,* 1966, *73,* 306–326.

Spivack, G., Levine, M., & Sprigle, H. Intelligence test performance and the delay function of the ego. *Journal of Consulting Psychology,* 1959, *23,* 428–431.

Sroufe, L. A. *Knowing and enjoying your baby.* Englewood Cliffs, N.J.: Prentice-Hall, 1977.

Sroufe, L. A. The ontogenesis of the emotions. In J. Osofsky (Ed.), *Handbook of infant development.* New York: Wiley, 1978.

Star, S. A. Psychoneurotic symptoms in the Army. In S. Stouffer et al., *The American soldier,* vol. 2: *Combat and its aftermath.* Princeton: Princeton University Press, 1949, pp. 411–455.

Staub, E., Tursky, B., & Schwartz, G. E. Self-control and predictability: Their effects on reactions to aversive stimulation. *Journal of Personality and Social Psychology,* 1971, *18,* 157–162.

Stelmachers, Z. T., & McHugh, R. B. Contribution of stereotyped and individualized information to predictive accuracy. *Journal of Consulting Psychology,* 1964, *28,* 234–242.

Stephenson, W. *The study of behavior.* Chicago: University of Chicago Press, 1953.

Steuer, F. B., Applefield, J. M., & Smith, R. Televised aggression and the interpersonal aggression of preschool children. *Journal of Experimental Child Psychology,* 1971, *11,* 442–447.

Stone, L. J., & Hokanson, J. E. Arousal reduction via self-punitive behavior. *Journal of Personality and Social Psychology,* 1969, *12,* 72–79.

Stoyva, J., & Kamiya, J. Electro-physiological studies of dreaming as the prototype of a new strategy in the study of consciousness. *Psychological Review,* 1968, *75,* 192–205.

Stumphauzer, J. S. Increased delay of gratification in young prison inmates through imitation of high delay peer models, *Journal of Personality and Social Psychology,* 1972, *21,* 10–17.

Szasz, T. S. The myth of mental illness. *American Psychologist,* 1960, *15,* 113–118.

Taft, R. The ability to judge people. *Psychological Bulletin,* 1955, *52,* 1–28.

Tankard, J. Effects of eye position on person perception. *Perceptual and Motor Skills,* 1970, *31,* 883–893.

Tart, C. Increases in hypnotizability resulting from a prolonged program for enhancing personal growth. *Journal of Abnormal Psychology,* 1970, *75,* 260–266.

Taylor, J. A personality scale of manifest anxiety. *Journal of Abnormal and Social Psychology,* 1953, *48,* 285–290.

Taylor, S. P., & Epstein, S. Aggression as a function of the interaction of the sex of the aggressor and the sex of the victim. *Journal of Personality,* 1967, *35,* 474–486.

Terman, L. M., & Miles, C. C. *Sex and personality: Studies in masculinity and femininity.* New York: McGraw-Hill, 1936.

Thibaut, J., & Riecken, H. Authoritarianism, status, and the communication of aggression. *Human Relations,* 1955, *8,* 95–120.

Thoresen, C., & Mahoney, M. *Self-control.* New York: Holt, Rinehart and Winston, 1974.

Titus, H. E., & Hollander, E. P. The California F scale in psychological research: 1950–1955. *Psychological Bulletin,* 1957, *54,* 47–64.

Tompkins, V. H. Stress in aviation. In J. Hambling (Ed.), *The nature of stress disorder.* Springfield, Ill.: Charles C Thomas, 1959.

Touhey, J. Effects of additional women professionals on ratings of occupational prestige and desirability. *Journal of Personality and Social Psychology,* 1974, *29,* 86–89.

Tourangeau, R., & Ellsworth, P. C. *The role of facial response in the experience of emotion.* Unpublished manuscript, Yale University, 1978.

Truax, C. B., & Mitchell, K. M. Research on certain therapist interpersonal skills in relation to process and outcome. In A. E. Bergin & S. I. Garfield

(Eds.), *Handbook of psychotherapy and behavior change*. New York: Wiley, 1971, pp. 299–344.

Tudor, T. G., & Holmes, D. S. Differential recall of successes and failures: Its relationship to defensiveness, achievement motivation, and anxiety. *Journal of Research in Personality,* 1973, *7,* 208–224.

Tupes, E. C., & Christal, R. E. Stability of personality trait rating factors obtained under diverse conditions. *USAF WADC Technical Note,* 1958, no. 58–61.

Tupes, E. C., & Christal, R. E. Recurrent personality factors based on trait ratings. *USAF ASD Technical Report,* 1961, no. 61–67.

Tversky, A. Features of similarity. *Psychological Review,* 1977, *84,* 327–352.

Tversky, A., & Kahneman, D. Judgment under uncertainty: Heuristics and biases. *Science,* 1974, *185,* 1124–1131.

Tyler, L. E. *The psychology of human differences*. New York: Appleton, 1956.

Ullmann, L. F., & Krasner, L. *A psychological approach to abnormal behavior*. Englewood Cliffs, N.J.: Prentice-Hall, 1969.

Ulrich, R. E., Stachnik, T. J., & Stainton, N. R. Student acceptance of generalized personality interpretations. *Psychological Reports,* 1963, *13,* 831–834.

Vaillant, G. E. *Adaptation to life*. Boston: Little, Brown, 1977.

Vandenberg, S. G. What do we know today about the inheritance of intelligence and how do we know it? In R. Cancro (Ed.), *Intelligence: Genetic and environmental influences*. New York: Grune & Stratton, 1971, 182–218.

Vernon, P. E. *Personality assessment: A critical survey*. New York: Wiley, 1964.

Voegtlin, W. L., Lemere, F., Broz, W. R., & O'Hollaren, P. Conditioned reflex therapy of chronic alcoholism. IV. A preliminary report on the value of reinforcement. *Quarterly Journal of Studies on Alcohol,* 1942, *2,* 505–511.

Wachtel, P. Psychodynamics, behavior therapy, and the implacable experimenter: An inquiry into the consistency of personality. *Journal of Abnormal Psychology,* 1973, *82,* 323–334.

Wachtel, P. L. *Psychoanalysis and behavior therapy: Toward an integration*. New York: Basic Books, 1977.

Wade, T. C., & Baker, T. B. Opinions and use of psychological tests: A survey of clinical psychologists. *American Psychologist,* 1977, *32,* 874–882.

Wahler, R. G., Winkel, G. H., Peterson, R. F., & Morrison, D. C. Mothers as behavior therapists for their own children. *Behavior Research and Therapy,* 1965, *3,* 113–124.

Wallace, J., & Sechrest, L. Frequency hypothesis and content analysis of projective techniques. *Journal of Consulting Psychology,* 1963, *27,* 387–393.

Wallach, M. A. Commentary: Active-analytical vs. passive-global cognitive functioning. In S. Messick & J. Ross (Eds.), *Measurement in personality and cognition*. New York: Wiley, 1962, pp. 199–215.

Walters, G. C., & Grusec, J. E. *Punishment*. San Francisco: Freeman, 1977.

Walters, R. H., & Parke, R. D. The influence of punishment and related disciplinary techniques on the social behavior of children: Theory and empirical findings. In B. A. Maher (Ed.), *Progress in experimental personality research,* vol. 4. New York: Academic Press, 1967, pp. 179–228.

Wandersman, A., Poppen, P. J., & Ricks, D. F. (Eds.). *Humanism and behaviorism: Dialogue and growth*. Oxford, England: Pergamon Press, 1976.

Watson, D. L., & Tharp, R. G. *Self-directed behavior: Self-modification for personal adjustment.* Belmont, Calif.: Wadsworth, 1972.

Watson, J. B. *Behaviorism.* New York: Norton, 1925.

Watson, J. B., & Rayner, R. Conditioned emotional reactions. *Journal of Experimental Psychology,* 1920, *3,* 1–14.

Watson, R. I. Historical review of objective personality testing: The search for objectivity. In B. M. Bass & I. A. Berg (Eds.), *Objective approaches to personality assessment.* Princeton: Van Nostrand, 1959, pp. 1–23.

Wegner, D. M., & Vallacher, R. R. *The self in social psychology.* New York: Oxford University Press, 1980.

Weigel, R. H., & Newman, S. L. Increasing attitude-behavior correspondence by broadening the scope of the behavioral measure. *Journal of Personality and Social Psychology,* 1976, *33,* 793–802.

Weiner, B. Need achievement and the resumption of incompleted tasks. *Journal of Personality and Social Psychology,* 1965, *1,* 165–168.

Weiner, B. Effects of motivation on the availability and retrieval of memory traces. *Psychological Bulletin,* 1966, *65,* 24–37.

Weiner, B. *Theories of motivation: From mechanism to cognition.* Chicago: Markham, 1972.

Weiner, B. *An attributional interpretation of expectancy value theory.* Paper presented at the AAAS Meetings, February 1974, San Francisco, Calif.

Weir, M. W. Children's behavior in a two-choice task as a function of patterned reinforcement following forced-choice trials. *Journal of Experimental Child Psychology,* 1965, *2,* 85–91.

White, B. L. An experimental approach to the effects of experience on early human behavior. In J. P. Hill (Ed.), *Minnesota symposia on child psychology,* vol. 1. Minneapolis: University of Minnesota Press, 1967, pp. 201–226.

White, B. L. *Human infants: Experience and psychological development.* Englewood Cliffs, N.J.: Prentice-Hall, 1971.

White, B. L., & Held, R. Plasticity of sensorimotor development in the human infant. In J. F. Rosenblith & W. Allinsmith (Eds.), *The causes of behavior II.* Boston: Allyn & Bacon, 1966, pp. 60–70.

White, B. L., Kaban, B., Shapiro, B., & Attanucci, J. Competence and experience. In I. C. Uzgiris & F. Weizman (Eds.), *The structuring of experience.* New York: Plenum, 1976.

White, R. W. *Lives in progress.* New York: Dryden, 1952.

White, R. W. Motivation reconsidered: The concept of competence. *Psychological Review,* 1959, *66,* 297–333.

White, R. W. *The abnormal personality.* New York: Ronald, 1964.

Whiting, J. W. M., & Whiting, B. Personal communication on a current research project, 1962, Reported in Oetzel, R. Annotated bibliography in E. E. Maccoby (Ed.), *The development of sex differences.* Stanford: Stanford University Press, 1966.

Wicklund, R. A., & Frey, D. Self-awareness theory: When the self makes a difference. In D. M. Wegner & R. R. Vallacher (Eds.), *The self in social psychology.* New York: Oxford University Press, 1980.

Wiggins, J. S. *Personality and prediction: Principles of personality assessment.* Reading, Mass.: Addison-Wesley, 1973.

Wiggins, J. S. A psychological taxonomy of trait-descriptive terms: The interpersonal domain. *Journal of Personality and Social Psychology,* 1979, *37,* 395–412.

Wiggins, J. S. Circumplex models of interpersonal behavior in personality and social psychology. *The Review of Personality and Social Psychology,* 1980.

Wiley, R. C. *The self-concept,* vol. 1 (Rev. Ed.). Lincoln: University of Nebraska, 1974.

Willingham, W. W. Predicting success in graduate education. *Science,* 1974, *183,* 273–278.

Wilson, G. Introversion/extraversion. In T. Blass (Ed.), *Personality variables in social behavior.* Hillsdale, N.J.: Erlbaum, 1977.

Wilson, G. T., & O'Leary, K. D. *Principles of behavior therapy.* Englewood Cliffs, N.J.: Prentice-Hall, 1980.

Wilson, W. R. Feeling more than we can know: Exposure effects without learning. *Journal of Personality and Social Psychology,* 1979, *37,* 811–821.

Winder, C. L., & Wiggins, J. S. Social reputation and social behavior: A further validation of the peer nomination inventory. *Journal of Abnormal and Social Psychology,* 1964, *68,* 681–685.

Winterbottom, M. R. The relation of need for achievement to learning experiences in independence and mastery. In J. W. Atkinson (Ed.), *Motives in fantasy, action, and society.* Princeton, N.J.: Van Nostrand, 1958, pp. 453–478.

Wishner, J. Reanalysis of "impressions of personality." *Psychological Review,* 1960, *67,* 96–112.

Wissler, C. The correlation of mental and physical tests. *Psychological Review Monograph Supplement,* 1901, *3,* No. 16.

Witkin, H. A. Psychological differentiation and forms of pathology. *Journal of Abnormal Psychology,* 1965, *70,* 317–336.

Witkin, H. A., Dyk, R. B., Faterson, H. F., Goodenough, D. R., & Karp, S. A. *Psychological differentiation.* New York: Wiley, 1962.

Wittgenstein, L. *Philosophical investigations.* New York: Macmillan, 1953.

Wolf, R. The measurement of environments. In A. Anastasi (Ed.), *Testing problems in perspective.* Washington, D.C.: American Council on Education, 1966, pp. 491–503.

Wolff, P. Unpublished paper presented at the Tavistock Conference on Determinants of Infant Behavior, London, September, 1965. (Cited in Hamburg, D. A., & Lunde, D. T. Sex hormones in the development of sex differences in human behavior. In E. E. Maccoby (Ed.), *The development of sex differences.* Stanford: Stanford University Press, 1966, pp. 1–24.)

Wolpe, J. *Psychotherapy by reciprocal inhibition.* Stanford: Stanford University Press, 1958.

Wolpe, J. Behavior therapy in complex neurotic states. *British Journal of Psychiatry,* 1963, *110,* 28–34.

Wolpe, J., & Lang, P. J. A fear survey schedule for use in behavior therapy. *Behavior Research Therapy,* 1964, *2,* 27–30.

Wolpe, J., & Lazarus, A. A. *Behavior therapy techniques: A guide to the treatment of neuroses.* Oxford: Pergamon, 1966.

Wortman, C., & Brehm, J. Responses to uncontrollable outcomes. In L. Berkowitz (Ed.), *Advances in experimental social psychology,* vol. 8. New York: Academic Press, 1975, pp. 278–336.

Wortman, C. B., Costanzo, P. R., & Witt, T. R. Effect of anticipated perform-ance on the attributions of causality to self and others. *Journal of Personal-ity and Social Psychology,* 1973, *27,* 372–381.

Wright, M. E. Constructiveness of play as affected by group organization and frustration. *Character and Personality,* 1942, *11,* 40–49.

Wright, M. E. The influence of frustration upon the social relations of young children. *Character and Personality,* 1943, *12,* 111–122.

Wyatt, D. F., & Campbell, D. T. On the liability of stereotype or hypothesis. *Journal of Abnormal and Social Psychology,* 1951, *46,* 495–500.

Wyer, R. S., Weatherley, D. A., & Terrell, G. Social role, aggression, and aca-demic achievement. *Journal of Personality and Social Psychology,* 1965, *1,* 645–649.

Yarrow, L. J. Maternal deprivation: Toward an empirical and conceptual re-evaluation. *Psychological Bulletin,* 1961, *58,* 459–490.

Yates, B. T., & Mischel, W. Young children's preferred attentional strategies for delaying gratification. *Journal of Personality and Social Psychology,* 1979, *37,* 286–300.

Yerkes, R. M., & Dodson, J. D. The relation of strength of stimulus to rapidity of habit-formation. *Journal of Comparative Neurological Psychology,* 1908, *18,* 459–482.

Zanna, M. P., & Olson, J. M. Individual differences in attitude-behavior rela-tions. In M. P. Zanna, C. P. Herman, & E. T. Higgins (Eds.), *Variability and consistency of social behavior: The Ontario Symposium,* vol. 2. Hillsdale, N.J.: Erlbaum, in press.

Zeller, A. An experimental analogue of repression. I. Historical summary. *Psy-chological Bulletin,* 1950, *47,* 39–51. (a)

Zeller, A. An experimental analogue of repression. II. The effect of individual failure and success on memory measured by relearning. *Journal of Experi-mental Psychology,* 1950, *40,* 411–422. (b)

Zigler, E., & Phillips. L. Psychiatric diagnosis and symptomatology. *Journal of Abnormal and Social Psychology,* 1961, *63,* 69–75.

Zimbardo, P. The human choice: Individuation, reason, and order versus de-individuation, impulse, and chaos. In W. J. Arnold and D. Levine (Eds.), *Ne-braska symposium on motivation.* Lincoln: University of Nebraska Press, 1969, pp. 237–307.

Zimmerman, B. J., & Rosenthal, T. L. Observational learning of rule-governed behavior by children. *Psychological Bulletin,* 1974, *81,* 29–42.

Ziv, A., Kruglanski, A. W., & Shulman, S. Children's psychological reactions to war-time stress. *Journal of Personality and Social Psychology,* 1974, *30,* 24–30.

Zubin, J., Eron, L. D., & Schumer, F. *An experimental approach to projective techniques.* New York: Wiley, 1965.

GLOSSARY

Ability traits: Cattell's term for traits concerned with effectiveness in gaining a goal.

Aggression: Behavior motivated by the intent to hurt (which may or may not inflict harm).

Anaclitic identification: Hypothesized by Freud as the earliest form of identification based on the infant's intense dependency on the mother.

Anal stage: The second of Freud's psychosexual stages, it occurs during the child's second year. Pleasure is focused on the anus and on the retention and expulsion of feces. The events of toilet training may result in adult characteristics such as messiness or excessive orderliness.

Analytical psychology: Carl Jung's theory of personality. Humans are viewed as purposive and striving toward self-actualization. The unconscious includes a collective as well as a personal unconscious and is a healthy force.

Androgynous: A person or behavior neither stereotypically masculine nor feminine.

Anima: In Jung's theory, the feminine, passive element in the unconscious of every male.

Animus: In Jung's theory, the masculine, assertive element in the unconscious of every female.

Anxiety: A state of emotional arousal which may be experienced as a diffuse fear. In Freud's theory, the result of the struggle between an impulse and an inhibition.

Archetypes: Jung's term for the contents of the *collective unconscious*—images or symbols expressing the inherited patterns for the organization of experience (e.g., mother archetype).

Attitudes: Evaluative opinions or beliefs.

Aversion therapy: Procedures that pair attractive arousing, but problem-producing, stimuli with another stimulus that evokes extremely negative reactions. The positive stimulus comes to evoke some of the negative or aversive reactions or is at least neutralized. For example, alcohol may be paired with nausea-producing drugs.

Awareness: Most common synonym for consciousness in psychological usage.

Behavior: Includes emotions and covert mental activities, such as thoughts or "cognitions," as well as overt actions.

Behavioral assessment: The analysis of how an individual's behavior changes in response to changing stimulus conditions.

Behavior modification: Techniques used in behavior therapy which are derived from learning principles and experimentally validated.

Behavior sampling: Detailed information concerning the onset, magnitude, and duration of the behaviors of interest and the circumstances of their occurrence.

Behavior therapies: Therapies that try to change problem behaviors directly with techniques based on the concepts of learning theories.

Behavioral specificity: The dependence of a person's specific behavior on the particular situation in which it occurs.

Biofeedback: Use of equipment to provide immediate feedback about the activities of the autonomic and somatic systems; for example, giving information about heart rate or brainwaves to the person in whom they occur, at the time they occur.

Cardinal traits: Allport's term for a highly generalized disposition or characteristic that influences most aspects of an individual's behavior throughout life.

Castration anxiety: A male's fear of losing his penis. Freud believed this anxiety was central in the resolution of the Oedipus complex and in the boy's identification with his father.

Catharsis: The belief that the verbal or fantasy expression of an impulse leads to its reduction; a key concept in psychoanalytic theory.

Cathexes: Psychoanalytic term denoting the investment of instinctual impulses in objects.

Central traits: Allport's term for a trait that is less important and pervasive than a cardinal trait, but which still influences much of a person's behavior.

Classical conditioning (conditioned-response learning): A type of learning, emphasized by Pavlov, in which the response to an unconditioned stimulus (e.g., food) becomes conditioned to a neutral stimulus (e.g., a bell) by being paired or associated with it.

Client-centered (Rogerian) therapy: Approach to therapy developed by Carl Rogers. Emphasizes a nonevaluative, accepting atmosphere conducive to honesty and concentrates on present relationships and feelings rather than past roots of the client's difficulties.

Cognition: Refers to how we know the world through mental processes such as thinking, perceiving, and remembering.

Cognitive avoidance: Efforts to avoid painful thoughts, percepts, associations, or other cognitive events.

Cognitive consistency: Consonance among beliefs and perceptions. Research shows that in general people seek consistency, and tend to reduce inconsistency.

Cognitive dissonance: According to Festinger, an unpleasant state that occurs when a person knows two things that do not fit together. The theory of cognitive dissonance proposes that people try to reduce it by changing their cognitions or beliefs.

Cognitive restructuring: Therapeutic technique aimed at thinking about one's problems more constructively and less irrationally. Albert Ellis' Rational Emotive Therapy is a form of cognitive restructuring.

Cognitive social learning person variables: Person variables such as competencies, encoding strategies, personal constructs, expectancies, values, and plans that are the result of cognitive development and social learning history.

Cognitive styles: An individual's consistent ways of approaching and processing information, especially through perception, memory, and thought.

Collective unconscious: Inherited portion of the unconscious, as postulated by Jung. Consists of ancestral memories and archetypes.

Common traits: According to Allport, a trait that is shared in different degrees by many people.

Competence or "effectance" motivation: Desire to acquire mastery of a task for its own sake.

Competency: The individual's ability to transform and use information actively and to create thoughts and actions (as in problem solving), in contrast to a body of static cognitions and responses.

Compulsions: A ritualistic behavior that the individual feels compelled to perform.

Concept-formation: A type of thinking; requires the learning of categories and the rules for assigning instances to each category.

Conditioned aversion: Conditioning in which a positive stimulus is repeatedly paired with a negative stimulus, resulting in the negative reaction being made to the formerly positive stimulus.

Conditioned reinforcers (secondary reinforcers): A stimulus that has become reinforcing as a result of its association with an unconditioned stimulus or a primary reinforcer.

Conditioning: A basic form of learning (see also *classical conditioning; operant conditioning*).

Conflict: A state in which two or more opposing or mutually exclusive impulses, desires, or tendencies are present at the same time. In psychodynamic theory, continuous conflict within the personality arises from the struggle between the id, ego, and superego—between instinctual demands and the inhibitions that block them.

Consciousness: Total awareness; normal waking state.

Construct: In George Kelly's theory, a construct is a category that contains at least two individuals or events and excludes at least one other; it describes the way in which two things are seen as alike and as different from a third.

Constructive alternativism: Recategorization of individuals or events to facilitate problem solving; a concept in George Kelly's theory.

Contingency contracting (contracts): Contracts—made between an individual in treatment and his or her therapist—to achieve particular goals specifying the "contingencies" (conditions) under which positive or negative reinforcement may be given or withheld. For example, the person contracts to pay a disliked charity 50 dollars every time he or she smokes a cigarette, a dieter contracts to buy new clothes after losing a certain amount of weight.

Correlations: The relationship between two variables or sets of measures. May be either positive or negative, and expressed quantitatively in a coefficient of correlation.

Cue: Stimulus that directs behavior, determining when, where, and how the response (behavior) will occur.

Defense mechanisms: According to Freud, ways in which the ego unconsciously tries to cope with unacceptable id impulses, as in repression, projection, reaction formation, sublimation, rationalization.

Defensive identification: See *identification with the aggressor.*

Denial: In Freudian theory, a primitive defense mechanism in which a person denies a threatening impulse or event even though reality confirms it; the basis for development of repression.

Dependency: Behaviors aimed at eliciting attention and help from others.

Desensitization: Method of eliminating anxiety or fear responses to a stimulus in which the individual learns to make an incompatible response, such as relaxation, to a series of increasingly anxiety-evoking stimuli.

Discrimination: Differential response to two stimuli, for example, returning a found wallet, but not a loose five-dollar bill; crying in your room but not in class.

Discriminative facility: Responsivity to changing conditions.

Discriminative stimulus: Stimulus that indicates when a response will or will not have favorable consequences.

Displacement: Redirecting an impulse toward a less threatening target; a key concept in psychoanalytic theory.

Dispositions: Attitudes, traits, motives, which cause a person to respond in typical ways.

Drive: Any strong stimuli (internal or external) which impel action.

Drive-conflict theory: Posits the simultaneous existence of drive-like forces (approach tendencies) and of inhibitory forces (avoidance tendencies).

DSM III: The current diagnostic and statistical manual of the American Psychiatric Association.

Dynamic psychology: Theories, such as psychoanalysis, which emphasize concepts that imply movement (process, motives, and development) in contrast to more static approaches such as trait theory.

Dynamic traits: Cattell's term for traits that are relevant to the individual's being "set into action" with respect to some goal.

Ego: In Freudian theory, the conscious part of the personality which mediates between the demands of the id and of the world. Operates on the reality principle.

Ego-control: Degree of impulse control; important in delay of gratification, planfulness, and aggression inhibition (see also *ego-resiliency*).

Ego controls: Mechanisms through which people solve problems and control their own behavior.

Ego identity: According to Erikson, the individual's view of himself and of what others expect him to be; basic to the organization and development of personality.

Ego psychology: The variety of psychoanalytic theory that stresses ego functions and de-emphasizes instinctual drives.

Ego-resiliency: Refers to the individual's ability to adapt to environmental demands by appropriately modifying his or her habitual level of ego-control, thus functioning with some flexibility.

Electroencephalogram (EEG): Trace pattern recording the amplitude and frequency of brainwaves.

Electroencephalograph: Instrument that measures electrical activity within neural circuits of the brain.

Emotional inoculation: A process in which forewarnings or some form of rehearsal are used to help a person to prepare himself or herself psychologically for a trauma and to cope with it better when it occurs.

Emotional insight: A process in which a person "works through" his or her problems and comes to understand and accept his or her impulses fully, not merely in an abstract, detached, rational way.

Emotional stability: The opposite of neuroticism, according to Eysenck, who views emotional stability–neuroticism as an important trait dimension.

Existentialism: A theory that emphasizes freedom of choice and advocates taking full responsibility for one's own existence and the realization of one's full potential.

Expectancies: A person variable that includes behavior-outcome and stimulus-outcome expectancies and guides an individual's choices.

Extinction: The decrease in frequency of a response which follows the repetition of the response or, in classical conditioning, the repetition of the conditioned stimulus in the absence of the unconditioned stimulus.

Extravert: (1) In Jung's typology, the extravert is conventional, sociable, and outgoing and reacts to stress by trying to lose himself among people; (2) For Eysenck, extraversion-introversion is a dimension of personality along which all individuals can be placed at some point.

Extrinsic rewards: Rewards which are external to the behavior they are used to increase. For example, helping a disturbed child learn to speak by rewarding his or her efforts with food or hugs (see also *intrinsic rewards*).

Factor analysis: A mathematical procedure for sorting trait terms or test responses into clusters or factors; used in the development of tests designed to discover basic personality traits. It identifies items that are homogeneous or internally consistent and independent of others.

Fetishistic behavior: Behavior resulting from the production of emotional arousal by things or events that are neutral or even aversive for most individuals, e.g., becoming sexually aroused by baby-carriages or nasal mucus.

Field theories: Positions that construe behavior as determined by the person's psychological life space—by the events that exist in his or her total psychological situation at the moment—rather than by past events or by enduring, situation-free dispositions.

Fixation: A psychodynamic term referring to a process by which a person remains attached to a person or symbol appropriate to an earlier stage of development, and fails to progress satisfactorily through the stages of development.

Free association: A technique used in psychoanalytic therapy in which the patient is instructed to report whatever comes to mind, no matter how irrational it may seem.

Frustration: A state of arousal that may occur when a sequence of goal-directed behavior is interrupted and the desired goals are delayed or blocked.

Functional analysis: Behavioral analysis of the covariation between a particular behavior and the environmental conditions controlling it or covarying with it.

Functional autonomy (of motives): Gordon Allport's theory that most adult motives are independent of their instinctual roots. For example, a millionaire may continue to work for enjoyment and companionship though all his or her basic needs are met.

Galvanic skin response or GSR: Changes in the electrical activity of the skin due to sweating, as recorded by a galvanometer, and used as an index of emotional state; for example, in a lie detector test.

Gender self-concept: A recognition of one's sex as a permanent characteristic.

Generalization: Responding in the same way to similar stimuli. For example, when a child who has been bitten by a dog becomes afraid of all dogs (see also *discrimination*).

Generalized expectancies: J. B. Rotter's term for expectancies about outcomes that determine behavior and are assumed to be consistent across situations.

Gestalt psychotherapy: An approach developed by F. Perls that aims at expanding the awareness of self and putting the person in touch with his or her own feelings and creative potential. Often practiced in groups, use is made of body exercises and the venting of emotions.

Goal gradients: Gradients of changes in response strength as a function of distance from a positive or negative reinforcement or goal.

Hypochondriasis: Exaggerated attention to and anxiety about one's health.

Hysterical neurosis: A neurotic condition consisting of two subcategories: conversion reaction (physical symptoms such as paralysis or loss of sensation without organic cause) and dissociative reaction (disruption of a consistent unitary sense of self that may include amnesia, fugue, and/or multiple personality).

Id: In Freudian theory, the foundation of the personality, consisting of unconscious instincts and inherited biological drives; it operates on the pleasure principle.

Identification: (1) Similarity in behavior (including feelings and attitudes) between a child and the model with whom he or she identifies; (2) The child's motive or desire to be like the model; (3) The process through which the child takes on the attributes of the model.

Identification with the aggressor: According to Freud, the boy's castration anxiety and incestuous desires for his mother are resolved by identifying with his father (the "aggressor" or potential castrator) in the phallic stage of psychosexual development.

Identity crisis: According to Erikson, a point in psychosocial development when the adolescent or young adult defines his or her identity.

Implicit personality theories: Patterns of expected associations among personality traits.

Impulses: In psychoanalytic theory, instinctual impulses pass from the id to the ego where they are either discharged, inhibited, diverted by the operation of a defense mechanism, or sublimated.

Innate or primary biological needs: Inborn needs, such as the need for food, water, air, and warmth, which are essential for survival.

Insight: The intellectual and emotional understanding of one's motives and psychodynamics and the symbolic meaning of behavior.

Intellectualization: The tendency to deal with emotional conflicts in a detached, intellectual, and controlled manner.

Interscorer agreement: Degree of consistency among different judges scoring the same information. When scoring decisions are subjective, it becomes especially necessary to demonstrate interscorer agreement.

Intrinsic motives: Motives (e.g., curiosity, achievement, affiliation, identity, stimulation, and social approval) that do not depend on the reduction of primary drives (such as hunger and sex), and do not have specific physiological correlates.

Intrinsic rewards: Rewards based on the properties of a behavior as distinguished from extrinsic or external rewards. For example, playing the piano for the sounds produced rather than for praise from another person.

Introvert: According to Jung's typology, the introvert is shy, withdrawn, and prefers to be alone (see also *extravert*).

Learned helplessness: A condition in animals and humans which results from exposure to inescapable painful experiences in which passive endurance persists even when escape becomes possible.

Learned motivation: Dollard and Miller's concept for deriving human social behavior from its biological roots.

Libido: In Freudian theory, psychic energy that may be attached to different objects (e.g., to the mouth in the oral stage of psychosexual development).

Life space: Lewin's term for the determinants of an individual's behavior at a certain moment; it includes the person and his or her psychological environment.

Locus of control: The source or cause to which one attributes control over the consequences of one's behavior, either "internal" (caused by the actor) or "external" (caused by the situation or by chance).

Mandala: One of Jung's archetypes, a circle symbolizing the self and containing designs often divided into four parts.

Maturation: Development and growth with increasing age, primarily determined by genetic factors, and automatic when given the appropriate environment.

Moral anxiety: In Freud's theory, guilt about one's unacceptable feelings, thoughts, or deeds (see also *neurotic anxiety; reality anxiety*).

Motivational determinism: Freud's belief that everything a person does may be determined by his or her pervasive, but unconscious, motives.

Multiple act criterion: A combination of many acts or behaviors that are expected to relate to a trait.

Neo-analysts: Psychoanalysts, such as Adler, Erikson, Sullivan, Fromm, and Horney, who elaborated and modified Freud's views, placing more emphasis on ego processes and sociocultural forces than Freud did. Also called Neo-Freudians.

Neobehaviorists: Term applied to B. F. Skinner and others who experimentally analyze the observable conditions controlling behavior.

Neurotic anxiety: In Freud's theory, fear that one's own impulses will go out of control and lead to punishment (see also *moral anxiety; reality anxiety*).

Neuroticism: The opposite of emotional stability, according to Eysenck, who views neuroticism–emotional stability as an important trait dimension.

Nonverbal communication: Communication without words, for example by gestures, facial expression, and eye contact.

Objective measures: Procedures used in the gathering, scoring, and interpretation of data that are standardized, reproducible, and usually involve structured responses.

Observational learning: The process of learning through observation of a live or symbolic model. Requires no direct reinforcement.

Obsession: A thought that repeatedly occupies attention although the person prefers to be rid of it.

Oedipus complex: According to Freud, the love for the opposite-sex parent during the phallic stage of psychosexual development.

Operant conditioning: The increase in frequency of an operant response after it has been followed by a favorable outcome (reinforced).

Oral stage: First of Freud's psychosexual stages, when pleasure is focused on the mouth and on the satisfactions of sucking and eating, as during the first year of life.

Paranoia: Psychosis characterized by delusions of grandeur and persecution, often organized into a coherent, internally consistent system.

Peak experience: H. Maslow's term for a temporary experience of fulfillment and joy in which the person loses self-centeredness and (in varying degrees of intensity) feels a nonstriving happiness: a moment of perfection.

Penis envy: Envy of the male sex organ. Believed by Freud to be universal in women, to be responsible for women's castration complex, and to be central to the psychology of women.

Perceptual defense: Unconscious repressive mechanisms which screen and block threatening visual and auditory inputs.

Personal construct theory: G. Kelly's theory that behavior is determined by the way an individual categorizes his or her experiences; personal constructs. This position views humans as active, ever-changing creators of hypotheses and players of multiple roles.

Personality: Usually refers to the distinctive patterns of behavior (including thoughts and emotions) that characterize each individual's adaptation to the situations of his or her life.

Personality assessment: Efforts to measure and analyze an individual's behavior.

Personality coefficient: Phrase to describe the modest correlation (usually between .20 and .30) typically found in personality research linking responses on questionnaires to other behavior.

Personality structure: Allport's term for the individual's pattern of dispositions which he believed determined behavior.

Personality, study of: Seeks to generate theories about human nature and individuality and to understand the causes and meaning of important psychological differences among individuals.

Personologists: Those who study personality.

Person perception: The process through which people form impressions of each other and of themselves.

Phallic stage: Third of Freud's psychosexual stages (at about age five) when pleasure is focused on the genitals and both males and females experience the "Oedipus complex."

Phenomenological approach: Theory that emphasizes the person's experience as he or she perceives it.

Phenomenology: See *phenomenological approach*.

Pleasure principle: In Freud's theory, the basis for id functioning. Irrational, seeks immediate satisfaction of instinctual impulses.

Plethysmograph: Records changes in blood volume.

Polygraph: An instrument used to measure several physiological responses at the same time (e.g., heart rate, respiration rate, and muscle tension), recording them by deflecting a pen across a moving paper chart.

Primary drives: Inborn motives for behavior such as hunger, pain, sex.

Primary process thinking: Freud's term for the id's direct, reality-ignoring attempts to satisfy needs irrationally.

Projection: A defense mechanism by which one attributes one's own unacceptable aspects or impulses to someone else.

Projective tests: Tests (such as the Rorschach or TAT) that present the individual with materials open to a wide variety of interpretations based on the belief that responses reveal important aspects of the respondent's personality central in psychodynamic assessment.

Proprium: G. Allport's term for the region of personality that contains the root of the consistency that characterizes attitudes, goals, and values. Not innate, it develops in time.

Preparedness (biological preparedness): The capacity to acquire certain associations more easily than others (for example fear of snakes versus electrical outlets). Possibly innate.

Prosocial aggressions: Verbal threats and statements about the goodness or badness of behavior.

Prototype: The best or most typical example of a category; for example a robin is a prototypical bird, an ostrich is not.

Psychedelic or consciousness-altering drugs: Drugs that affect mental processes, such as LSD.

Psychodynamic approach: Theories that infer unconscious motives and conflicts and emphasize past experience, e.g., Freud's theory.

Psychodynamic behavior theory: Developed by John Dollard and Neal Miller in the late 1940s to integrate some of the fundamental ideas of psychoanalytic theory with the concepts and methods of experimental research on behavior and learning.

Psychogenic needs: Needs which are not physiological, such as achievement, affiliation, and competence.

Psychometric: Questionnaires, inventories, or rating scales that are objective and standardized.

Psychometric trait approach: Approach that emphasizes quantitative measurement of psychological qualities, comparing the responses of large groups of people under standard conditions, often by means of paper-and-pencil tests.

Psychosexual stages: According to Freudian theory, development occurs in a series of psychosexual stages. In each stage (oral, anal, phallic, and genital) pleasure is focused on a different part of the body.

Psychosocial stages: Erikson's eight stages of development; extending throughout life, each stage centers around a "crisis" or set of problems and the individual's attempts to solve it.

Psychotherapy: Professional attempts to effect change in thought, mood, and/or behavior through verbal and symbolic techniques. Psychotherapy may be conducted by a variety of trained persons in a variety of settings.

The Q-sort technique: A method of obtaining trait ratings; consists of many cards, on each of which is printed a trait description. The rater groups the cards in a series of piles ranging from those which are least characteristic to those which are most characteristic of the rated person.

Radical behaviorism: The view that the science of human behavior should focus on the prediction and control of the behavior of individual organisms by studying stimulus-response relationships without attention to any intervening psychological steps.

Rational emotive therapy: Albert Ellis' approach based on the idea that if people learn to think more rationally their behavior will become more rational and their emotional problems will be reduced.

Reaction formation: A defense mechanism that occurs when an anxiety-producing impulse is replaced in consciousness by its opposite.

Reality anxiety: In Freud's theory, the fear of real dangers in the external world (see also *moral anxiety; neurotic anxiety.*)

Reality principle: In Freud's theory, the basis for ego functioning. Rational; dictates delay in the discharge of tension until environmental conditions are appropriate.

Reality testing: In psychodynamic theory, the process by which the ego forms a plan for the satisfaction of a need and then tests this plan in order to see whether or not it will work.

Regression: In psychodynamic theory, reversion to an earlier stage; the return of the libido to its former halting places in development.

Reinforcement: Any consequence that increases the likelihood that a response will be repeated.

Reinforcement learning theory: Theory that reinforcement is necessary for learning to occur.

Reliability: Consistency or stability of a psychological test measured by a coefficient of correlation between scores on two halves of a test (*internal reliability*), alternate forms of the test, or retests with the same group of people being given the same test on two occasions (*temporal reliability*). *Interscorer agreement* is the degree to which different scorers arrive at the same judgments about the same test data.

Repression: According to psychoanalytic theory, an unconscious defense mechanism through which unacceptable (ego-threatening) material is kept from awareness. The repressed motives, ideas, conflicts, memories, etc., continue to influence behavior.

Repression-sensitization continuum: A dimension of differences in defensive patterns of perception ranging from avoiding the anxiety-arousing stimuli to approaching them more readily and being extravigilant or supersensitized to them.

Resistance: Difficulties in achieving progress in psychotherapy due to unconscious defenses as anxiety-producing material emerges during the treatment.

Response: Any observable, identifiable activity of an organism.

Response sets: Systematic ways of answering test or interview questions that are related to characteristics of the alternatives other than what the question is attempting to measure. Examples of response sets are *social desirability* (tendencies to endorse only socially desirable statements) and *yea-saying or acquiescence* (tendency to agree with items regardless of their content). Response sets hamper the interpretation of the test responses.

Role Play: A technique used in therapy by George Kelly and others in which an individual behaves as if he or she were another person (a parent, for example) in order to gain new perspectives.

Scapegoating: Directing aggression against a less powerful person or group than the one which is the source of the frustration or other antecedent of the aggression. Regarded by psychodynamic theory as a displacement of aggression, by social learning theory as the result of discrimination learning in which aggression against certain groups is modeled and highly rewarded.

Schema: Cognitive category that serves as a frame of reference for processing and evaluating experiences, for example *self-schema*.

Secondary or learned drives: In psychodynamic behavior theory (Miller and Dollard), drives such as fear, which are acquired on the basis of primary (unlearned, innate) drives and whose reduction is reinforcing.

Secondary process thinking: In Freud's theory, the type of thinking characteristic of conscious mental activity. It obeys the laws of grammar and formal logic, uses bound energy, and is governed by the reality principle, i.e., reduces instinctual tension by adaptive behavior.

Secondary traits: Allport's term for dispositions that are narrower, more specific, and influence fewer behaviors than do central traits.

Selective perception: The interpretation of unclear events in accord with the individual's expectations and momentary states.

Self: In the theory of Carl Rogers, the conscious perception of oneself and the values attached to these perceptions.

Self-efficacy: A. Bandura's term for the individual's beliefs about his or her own effectiveness; the expectation that one can successfully conduct the action required.

Self-efficacy expectations: The person's confidence that he or she *can* perform a particular behavior, like handling a snake or making a public speech.

Self-esteem: Refers to the individual's personal judgment of his or her own worth.

Self-focus: Process in which attention is directed inward toward the self. Also a personality trait similar to self-consciousness.

Self-realization: According to Jung, a basic goal of every individual, requiring reconciliation of complementary opposites in the personality (for example, conscious-unconscious, animus-anima).

Self-report: Refers to any statements a person makes about himself or herself: "structured" self-reports are statements in which the form of reactions to items is restricted.

Self-schemata (or self-schema): Cognitions about the self that arise from past experience and guide the processing of new information.

Self-system: Includes the standards and rules used in self-control and the expectations about what one can do successfully.

Semantic differential: Technique for studying the meanings of concepts or words; the subject rates each concept or word in a list that has opposite words at each extreme (e.g., warm-cold) and five points in between.

Sensory anaesthesia: Loss of sensory ability (e.g., blindness, deafness) or loss of feeling in a body part.

Sex-role identity: The degree to which an individual regards himself or herself as masculine or feminine.

Sex-typed behaviors: Behaviors that are considered appropriate for one sex but not for the opposite sex.

Sex-typing: The process whereby the individual comes to acquire, to value, and to practice (perform) sex-typed behaviors.

Situationism: The biased explanation of behavior in terms of external stimuli, ignoring or deemphasizing organismic factors.

Social learning theory: Approach to psychology that emphasizes social learning and cognitive processes and the active interaction between the individual and his or her environment; has been applied especially to the analysis and treatment of complex social and abnormal behavior in the fields of clinical and personality psychology.

Source traits: In R. B. Cattell's theory, the traits that constitute personality structure and determine surface traits and behavior.

Stage theories: Theories that hypothesize fundamental transformations in development that follow a fixed and invariant sequence.

Standardized tests: Tests which apply the same procedures, materials, scoring, and interpretation to all subjects.

State anxiety: State anxiety is conceptualized as a person's momentary or situational anxiety and it varies in intensity over time and across settings.

Stereotype: Overly simple generalization about a group that leads one to believe that every member of the group possesses certain characteristics (e.g., the belief that all women are dependent).

Stimulus: (1) Any observable, identifiable event or situation inside or outside the organism; (2) The occasion for a response; (3) A specific type of energy coming to the sense organ (e.g., a sound wave).

Stimulus-response (S-R) psychology: Approach to psychology that emphasizes stimuli, responses, and their relationships, while avoiding all inferences about possible mental steps that take place between a given stimulus (S) and the response (R).

Stress: A psychological and physiological state that results from a broad range of potentially unpleasant or dangerous events, which include unavoidable pain, excessive noise and fatigue, and traumatic dangers.

Subception: Unconscious perception, or perception without full awareness.

Sublimation: A process through which socially unacceptable impulses are expressed in socially acceptable ways.

Superego: In Freud's theory, the conscience, made up of the internalized values of the parents; strives for self-control and perfection, is both unconscious and conscious.

Suppression: Occurs when one voluntarily and consciously withholds a response or turns attention away from something (see also *repression*).

Surface traits: R. B. Cattell's term for clusters of observable trait elements (responses) that seem to go together, the manifestations of source traits.

Symptom substitution: The controversial psychoanalytic belief that new symptoms will automatically replace problematic behaviors that are removed directly (e.g., by behavior therapy) unless their underlying unconscious emotional causes also have been removed.

Systematic desensitization: A behavior therapy procedure designed to reduce incapacitating anxiety; an incompatible response (usually relaxation) is paired with progressively more anxiety-arousing situations until the individual is able to imagine or be in these situations without becoming anxious.

Telemetry: A procedure for studying physiological changes in real-life situations, for example, the physiological status of astronauts. The subject wears a miniature radio transmitter, which relays the signals picked up by the electrodes measuring bodily changes to a distant recording apparatus.

Temperament traits: R. B. Cattell's term for traits that determine emotional reactivity.

Testable: Term usually applied to a theory or hypothesis that means it is capable of being evaluated (confirmed or disproved) by empirical methods.

Time-binding: The capacity to delay gratification.

Trait: A persistent (enduring) characteristic or dimension of individual differences. Defined by Allport as a generalized "neuropsychic system," distinctive to each person, that serves to unify many different stimuli by leading the person to generate consistent responses to them.

Trait anxiety: A person's stable, characteristic overall level of anxiety (see also *state anxiety*).

Transference: In psychoanalysis, the patient's response to the therapist as though the therapist were a parent or some other important figure from childhood. Considered an essential aspect of psychoanalytic therapy.

Trauma (psychological): Events that have a lasting effect on mental life.

Type A: A type of person characterized by a behavior pattern of competitive achievement striving, time urgency, aggressiveness, and hostility. Individuals of this type are believed to be coronary-prone.

Typology: Ways of categorizing individuals into discrete categories or types (e.g., male, female; depressed, optimistic).

Unconscious: In psychoanalytic theory the part of the personality of which the ego is unaware.

Unconscious motives: Wishes or needs of which the individual is unaware but which influence both normal and abnormal behavior.

Unique traits: In Allport's theory, a trait that exists in only one individual and cannot be found in another in exactly the same form.

Validity: The degree to which a test measures what it is supposed to. Subcategories include (a) *content or face validity,* the extent to which the items on a test adequately represent a defined broader class of behavior; (b) *criterion validity,* the relationship between the obtained sample and other criterion data, either concurrently or predictively; (c) *construct validity,* the elaboration of the inferred traits determining test behavior.

Variable: An attribute, quality, or characteristic that may be given two or more values and measured or systematically varied.

INDEXES

AUTHOR INDEX

SUBJECT INDEX